# A treatise on the law of tender, and bringing money into court : not only in support of a plea of tender, but under the common rule : together with a chapter on offer of judgment.

Alva R. Hunt

*A treatise on the law of tender, and bringing money into court : not only in support of a plea of tender, but under the common rule : together with a chapter on offer of judgment.*
Hunt, Alva R. (Alva Roscoe)
collection ID CTRG96-B362
Reproduction from Harvard Law School Library
Includes index.
St. Paul : F.P. Dufresne, 1903.
lix, 720 p. ; 25 cm

*The Making of Modern Law* collection of legal archives constitutes a genuine revolution in historical legal research because it opens up a wealth of rare and previously inaccessible sources in legal, constitutional, administrative, political, cultural, intellectual, and social history. This unique collection consists of three extensive archives that provide insight into more than 300 years of American and British history. These collections include:

Legal Treatises, 1800-1926: over 20,000 legal treatises provide a comprehensive collection in legal history, business and economics, politics and government.

Trials, 1600-1926: nearly 10,000 titles reveal the drama of famous, infamous, and obscure courtroom cases in America and the British Empire across three centuries.

Primary Sources, 1620-1926: includes reports, statutes and regulations in American history, including early state codes, municipal ordinances, constitutional conventions and compilations, and law dictionaries.

These archives provide a unique research tool for tracking the development of our modern legal system and how it has affected our culture, government, business – nearly every aspect of our everyday life. For the first time, these high-quality digital scans of original works are available via print-on-demand, making them readily accessible to libraries, students, independent scholars, and readers of all ages.

**The BiblioLife Network**

This project was made possible in part by the BiblioLife Network (BLN), a project aimed at addressing some of the huge challenges facing book preservationists around the world. The BLN includes libraries, library networks, archives, subject matter experts, online communities and library service providers. We believe every book ever published should be available as a high-quality print reproduction; printed on-demand anywhere in the world. This insures the ongoing accessibility of the content and helps generate sustainable revenue for the libraries and organizations that work to preserve these important materials.

The following book is in the "public domain" and represents an authentic reproduction of the text as printed by the original publisher. While we have attempted to accurately maintain the integrity of the original work, there are sometimes problems with the original work or the micro-film from which the books were digitized. This can result in minor errors in reproduction. Possible imperfections include missing and blurred pages, poor pictures, markings and other reproduction issues beyond our control. Because this work is culturally important, we have made it available as part of our commitment to protecting, preserving, and promoting the world's literature.

**GUIDE TO FOLD-OUTS MAPS and OVERSIZED IMAGES**

The book you are reading was digitized from microfilm captured over the past thirty to forty years. Years after the creation of the original microfilm, the book was converted to digital files and made available in an online database.

In an online database, page images do not need to conform to the size restrictions found in a printed book. When converting these images back into a printed bound book, the page sizes are standardized in ways that maintain the detail of the original. For large images, such as fold-out maps, the original page image is split into two or more pages

Guidelines used to determine how to split the page image follows:

• Some images are split vertically; large images require vertical and horizontal splits.
• For horizontal splits, the content is split left to right.
• For vertical splits, the content is split from top to bottom.
• For both vertical and horizontal splits, the image is processed from top left to bottom right.

# A TREATISE

ON THE

# LAW OF TENDER,

AND

# BRINGING MONEY INTO COURT

NOT ONLY IN SUPPORT OF A PLEA OF TENDER,
BUT UNDER THE COMMON RULE,

TOGETHER WITH A CHAPTER ON
## OFFER OF JUDGMENT.

BY
ALVA R HUNT

ST PAUL
FRANK P DUFRESNE.
1903

HOUSEKEEPER PRESS,
Minneapolis Minn

# PREFACE.

It does not appear necessary to offer an apology, and none will be given, for submitting to the profession a text book which treats, in what has been the author's aim, of the Law of Tender and Bringing Money Into Court, in a logically arranged and comprehensive manner. How well this has been done remains for my professional brethren to decide. If the treatise meet with general commendation, the author will be amply compensated, in mind at least, for the labor expended, when not engaged in the practice of his profession, during a period of upwards of six years.

Being, it is believed, the pioneer treatise, perhaps it may be proper to say something as to the necessity for such a work, and the inducement or motive which led to its preparation. The trials and difficulties experienced by one lawyer in general practice, may be said to be a counterpart of the practice of every other lawyer. We had not long been engaged in practice before we had several cases in which the various questions relating to a tender were of importance. We could find no treatise comprehending the whole subject. The encyclopedists were so brief and general in their statements that they afforded no aid. Recourse, of necessity, was had to the decisions. We entered into a maze of perplexing and technically intricate questions. Scores of decisions bearing upon every point were read. For a period the subject seemed interminable and to defy logical arrangement, and, now, we are convinced, that at that time, we did not comprehend the subject in all its details as applicable to the particular cases under consideration. One case which continued in court upwards of five years, could have been disposed of within a year, appeals and all, and possibly within a month by motion, if we had had access to a comprehensive treatise. Sifting from a mass of several thousand decisions, all the various questions relating to the necessity for a tender, the manner of making, the time and place, to whom and by whom made, the amount, the kind and quality of the money or specific articles, etc., must be conceded to be a laborious and difficult task. We found, also, that those questions which follow the making of a tender, such as the consequences, keeping a tender good, abandonment, subsequent demand, and bringing money into court, were equally intricate and difficult to solve by such an examination of a mass of decisions as is the average practitioner able to give. These difficulties suggested the need for such a work as is the one between the covers of this book intended to be. The writer is not alone in his belief of the utility of such a work. During the years it has been in preparation, very naturally the subject has been the theme for discussion with many members of the profession, who, without exception, pronounced it a subject upon which a treatise was much needed.

The writer found that it was a distinct subject, apart from every other branch of the law. While it dovetails with other subjects (indeed what branch of the law does not?), he found that no writers upon contracts, mortgages, commercial paper, evidence, etc., who treated of it at all, did so in a comprehensive or in a topically arranged manner, and could not without a wide digression; a thing incompatible with the proper arrangement of their respective subjects. Of the truth of this the professional reader, to be convinced, has but to keep in mind the chapter titles of this treatise while making even the most cursory examination of the subject in the works referred to. That writers on other subjects were not able to give it the treatment the full subject demands, in no way detracts from the thoroughness of their labor or the quality of their work. One illustration will suffice. A writer on the law of mortgages may mention that a tender of the mortgage debt by the mortgagor before a foreclosure will discharge the lien, but can not, within the limits of that work, consider who, besides the mortgagor, may make a tender—as trustee, assignee, creditor, infants, etc, the consequences of making a tender or of a failure to make one before or after action brought at law or in equity, the consequences other than the effect upon the lien, to whom other than the original mortgagee a tender may be made, the sufficiency of a tender as to the manner of making, or as to the medium, amount or place, whether it should be kept good. Nor could he consider the questions raised by an abandonment of a tender, by a subsequent demand, or by bringing the money into court or a failure to do so, either at law or in equity. Moreover if the author should do so, the rules laid down would not be applicable in every particular to a tender made to a bailee, pledgee, vendor or vendee, or where made in rescission for fraud, nonperformance, infancy and the like; cases where the remedial powers of the court may be invoked either for equitable relief, or a legal

# PREFACE.

right, or for pecuniary remuneration. It seems unnecessary to mention that any legal writer upon such subjects as are here mentioned, could not be consistent with a logical arrangement of his subject, consider the question of a tender of specific articles upon all sorts of mercantile contracts, or enter into a consideration of money, or pleading and proof of a tender, or the practice governing a profert in curia, or bringing money into court upon the common rule.

Whoever examines this branch of the law for the first time or any number of times will agree with what has here been said. Moreover whoever acquaints himself with the table of contents herewith submitted, it is believed, will be convinced of the utility of a work of this character to the busy lawyer. A distinct subject, yet a part of nearly every branch of the law, makes of it a treatise which the lawyer in general practice with a knowledge of its scope, will have occasion to consult oftener than a work upon contracts, mortgages, judgments and other subjects

The method of treatment, the arrangement into chapters and sections, is his own, having been without any other treatise with which to aid his judgment. A Chapter on offer of judgment has been added for the reason that it appears to be akin to the main subject, although to discard it would in no way abridge the law of tender

A good book is sometimes worthless, owing to a poor table of contents and index. Particularly is this so of a law treatise The practicing lawyer cannot peruse a book from cover to cover in search of the law upon any question, when, perhaps within an hour he must make an argument or give an opinion The author, hoping to forestall any criticism upon this score, has not spared space, in his endeavor to make the table of contents, chapter headings and index, reflect, as it were, every question contained in the text

We have not accepted the opinions of ancient and modern jurists, unless convinced that they were founded in wisdom, and, therefore, have not hesitated when the occasion required it, to condemn a decision or doctrine as vicious in itself, or as tending to disturb the fixed rules of law

Doubtless many errors and imperfections will be found, but with perfection or imperfection, the author is conscious of having devoted to this creation what talent he has and industry without stint                                                                 ALVA R HUNT

Litchfield, Minnesota, November, 1903

# CHAPTERS.

---

# TABLE OF CONTENTS.

## CHAPTER I.

### DEFINITION AND WHEN A TENDER IS NECESSARY

## CHAPTER II

### THING TO BE TENDERED—MEDIUM

# CHAPTER III.

## THING TO BE TENDERED—SPECIFIC ARTICLES

# CHAPTER IV.

## AMOUNT TO BE TENDERED

## CHAPTER V.

### MANNER OF MAKING A TENDER

# CHAPTER VI

## TIME AND PLACE OF MAKING A TENDER

### I TIME

## II PLACE

# CHAPTER VII

## BY WHOM AND TO WHOM A TENDER MAY BE MADE

### I BY WHOM MADE

## CHAPTER VIII

### KEEPING A TENDER GOOD

# CHAPTER IX.

## THE CONSEQUENCES OF A TENDER AND REFUSAL

## CHAPTER X

### ACCEPTANCE OF A TENDER

## CHAPTER XI

### REFUSAL OF A TENDER

## CHAPTER XII

### SUBSEQUENT DEMAND

## CHAPTER XIII.

### ABANDONMENT OF A TENDER

## CHAPTER XIV.

### PLEADING AND PROVING A TENDER.

# CHAPTER XV.

## BRINGING MONEY INTO COURT.

## CHAPTER XVI.

### OFFER OF JUDGMENT

# TABLE OF CASES.

# THE LAW OF TENDER,

AND

# BRINGING MONEY INTO COURT.

# THE LAW OF TENDER,

## AND BRINGING MONEY INTO COURT.

---

### CHAPTER I.

#### DEFINITION AND WHEN A TENDER IS NECESSARY

**§ 1. Tender defined.—** A tender has been defined as being "an offer by a debtor to his creditor of the amount of the debt"[1] Again as "an offer to pay a debt or perform a duty"[2] So it has been said a "tender is an offer to perform a contract, or to pay money, coupled with a present ability to do the act"[3]

These definitions are indefinite Mr Justice BROWN enumerates, in a comprehensive and concise analysis, all the necessary elements which go to make a tender He said "A tender has a definite, legal signification It imports, not merely the readiness and the ability to pay the money, or to deliver over the deed, or the property, at the time and place mentioned in the contract, but also the actual production of the thing to be paid or delivered over, and an offer of it to the person to whom the tender is to be made"[4]

The offer in such case means not merely to present verbally, but also implies an actual proffer of the money or thing, and it must be distinguished from a mere proposal or proposition to do the thing.

[1] Rapalye & Lawrence Law Dic 1259

[2] 9 Bac Abr Title Tender

[3] Cockrell v Kirkpatrick, 9 Mo 688

[4] Holmes v Holmes, 12 Barb 137

**§ 2.  Distinction between a payment and a tender.**—The act of tender must be such that it needs only acceptance by the one to whom it is made to complete the transaction. A payment implies an acceptance and appropriation by one party of that which is offered by another in satisfaction, in whole or in part, of his obligation. It is the result of the harmonious acts of both the one who is to deliver and the one who is to receive. Whereas a tender is the act of one party in offering that which he admits to be due and owing, but which does not meet the approval of the other party, and therefore not accepted and appropriated by him in satisfaction of the demand.[1] The term therefore implies a refusal.

**§ 3.  A tender cannot be lawfully rejected.**—A tender cannot be lawfully rejected, yet the courts have frequently determined, in a given case, that the tender was rightfully rejected, but in such cases that which was rejected is something akin to a proposition, and the expression should be to the effect that the offer or proposition was rightfully rejected. The party offering may comply with all the formal requisites of a tender, yet, by reason of some defect in substance, it may amount merely to a proposition to pay,—now, as of a former date; or a less sum in satisfaction of a greater, etc. Or, if the offer lacks some of the formalities which go to make up a tender, as the actual production of the money, the offer amounts merely to a proposition to produce the sum and deliver if the other party is willing to receive.

**§ 4.  A waiver will not convert an offer of performance into a tender.**—In strictness, an offer to perform cannot be converted into a tender by a waiver. If an offer or proposition is accepted and the subject matter passed over, the law will not say that a person may not accept a defective or tardy performance in place of a perfect or full performance, if he so elects, and because it is accepted the offer is a tender. A payment or satisfaction of a demand may be made in other ways, the parties being willing, than by the acceptance of a technical tender. So, on the other hand, if a creditor, knowing that his debtor is seeking to satisfy a demand due him, rejects an offer, neglecting to direct the other party's atten

---

[1] Barker v. Brink, 5 Iowa 481

tion to defects in form or substance in his offer which then and there could have been remedied, such neglect is said to amount to a waiver, but such waiver does not make that which is not a tender one in fact. In practice, the law holds the creditor to the exercise of good faith towards his debtor, and merely takes from him the right to thereafter declare or insist upon a forfeiture or other right, by reason of such mistakes of the debtor. As the result in both cases is the same as that produced by a technical tender, the question is perhaps immaterial, further than to assist in fixing in the mind the difference between a mere offer or proposal and a tender.

§ 5. **When necessary—In general.**—At common law, wherever there is a debt or duty due and the thing due is either certain, or capable of being made so by mere computation, a tender of the debt or duty may be made[1] by the party who undertook to pay the money or perform the duty in the first instance, whose debt or obligation it is, or by one whose immediate property interest would be directly affected by a failure to pay the one or perform the other. In such cases, where the debtor or obligor has but to pay the money or perform the duty to discharge himself of the obligation, in order to stop the running of interest, or prevent the accruing of damages, or to save a forfeiture, or a penalty,[2] an actual tender is necessary.[3] The word *may*, when used in connection with such cases, means *must*.

It has been said that although a tender may be made in every case wherein the debt or duty is certain, it is not necessary to make one in every such case,[4] as where a bond is with condition to pay a rent charge which was before due, it was said no tender was necessary, as it is sufficient that the party be ready to pay when the rent is demanded upon the land. So, where an executor enters into a bond with condition to perform a will, it was held he was not bound to tender a legacy given by the will, but that the legacy remains as before, payable upon request.[5] But what is meant by this is,

[1] Green v Shurtliff, 19 Vt 592. 9 Bac Abr Title Tender (O).

State v Virginia Ry., 24 Nev. 88.

Wagenblast v McKean, 2 Grant's Cas 393.

[4] 9 Bac Abr Tit Tender (O).

[5] Fringe v Lewis, Leon 17; 9 Bac Abr Tit. Tender (O).

that where a sum of money is to be paid or a duty to be performed on request, the party whose duty it is to perform is not bound to take the initiative and seek the party who is to receive and make a tender to him. The execution of the bond, in either case mentioned, did not change the place of payment so as to compel the obligor to seek the obligee. If it had been holden in those cases, that no tender of the debt or duty was necessary before a demand, the rule would have been correctly stated. Where the debt or duty is certain or capable of being made so by mere computation, there is at this day no case where a tender is not necessary after the right to the immediate receipt of the debt or duty accrues if the party bound to perform desires to save a forfeiture, or stop the running of interest, etc. Where a debt or duty is to be paid or performed on demand, whether there be a privity of contract or the duty is imposed by law, on such demand the right to receive the thing accrues immediately, and the obligation to make a tender forthwith, or within a reasonable time thereafter as the nature of the case may require, is as imperative as in a case where the time and place for performance are fixed and known in advance.

§ 6. **When by vendor of chattels before recovering the purchase price—By vendee before recovering the chattels or bringing an action for damages.**—Where goods are to be delivered before the day appointed for the payment of the consideration, the promise to deliver is independent and a vendor cannot maintain an action for the price without averring and proving a tender of the goods to be delivered.[1] The goods can be recovered only when they have been selected, and in such case the vendee cannot bring an action to recover them when the time for payment arrives, without first tendering the purchase price, but he may bring such an action without making a tender, at any time after the default of the vendor and before the time for payment arrives, or he may at any time after the default of the vendor, whether the goods have been selected or not, bring an action to recover damages for the breach without tendering the purchase price.

[1] Dev v. Dox, 9 Wend 129. Thorp v. Thorp, 12 Mod 455 Bean v. Atwater, 4 Conn 3.

§ 7. **When unnecessary before recovering the purchase price—Partial payments—Amount bid at sheriff's sale.**—If it is the intention of the parties expressed in the contract, or implied from the nature of the contract, or of the thing sold, or situation of the parties, either in contracts concerning personal property or realty, that the payment of the purchase price shall precede the delivery of the chattels or conveyance, an action for the price may be maintained without first tendering the chattels or conveyance[1] The same rule is applicable to the recovery of partial payments, providing the action to recover the installments be brought before the time arrives for the delivery of the chattels or deed.[2] It has been held that the purchase money of land sold at sheriff's sale may be recovered without tendering a deed, that the delivery of the deed is an act to be performed subsequent to the payment of the money.[3] Payment is to precede a delivery of the property or a conveyance, when the time is fixed for the payment, but no time is fixed for the delivery of the thing, or doing of that which is the consideration for the payment[4]

In all such cases the price may be recovered without a tender of performance by the vendor, even though the latter has not title at the time fixed for payment, or the property is incumbered by a mortgage or other lien[5] Where payment precedes the delivery of the chattel or conveyance it is presumed the vendee relied upon his remedy against the vendor in case of a breach of the contract on his part

§ 8. **Where delivery and payment are concurrent acts.**—Where one agrees to sell and deliver personal property and another to receive and pay for it at the time of delivery, the delivery and payment are concurrent acts to be performed at the same time and place[1]

[1] Loud v Pomona L & W Co, 153 U S 564 s c 14 S Ct 928

[2] Eddy v Davis 116 N Y 247 s c 22 N E 362 Paine v Brown 37 N Y 228 Grant v Johnson 1 Seld 247, Harrington v Higgins, 17 Wend 376

[3] Negley v Stewart, 10 Serg & R 207

[4] Donovan v Judson 6 L R A 591, citing Morris v Sliter, 1 Denio 59, Mattock v Kinglake, 10 Ad & El 50 and note of Sargeant Williams to Pordage v Cole, 1 Wms Saund 320

[5] Hartley v James 50 N Y 38, Robb v Montgomery, 20 Johns 15, Sage v Ranney 2 Wend 532

[1] Crist v Armour, 34 Barb 378, Porter v Rose 12 John 209 Where the contract is silent both

The mere failure by one party to perform at the time and place specified in the contract releases the other party from his obligation; but before the latter (if the vendee) can recover the chattel, or any part of the purchase price already paid, or damages for the non performance, he must show not only that the vendor failed, but that he tendered the purchase price at the time and place agreed.[2] So in such cases, the vendor, before he can recover the purchase price or damages for a failure to take and pay for the articles, must show that he tendered the articles at the time and place agreed.[3] But where a vendee, who has reserved the right in the contract to designate the place of delivery, neglects to do so, a readiness and an offer to deliver the articles is sufficient to enable the vendor to recover the purchase price.[4] In such case, if the articles have not been selected, the vendor must set apart the articles he intends to apply upon the contract, otherwise he would have his money and the vendee would not know what articles were his. The rule requiring a tender by the party seeking to recover damages, or the price, etc,

as to the time and place of delivery the general rule is that the payment and delivery of the article are to be concurrent acts Newmark on Sales, § 225

[2] Anderson v Sherwood, 56 Barb 69, Crist v Armour, 34 Barb 378, Porter v Rose, 12 John 209, s c 7 Am. Dec 306, Dunham v Pettee, 4 Seld. 508 In every executory contract of sale of personal property, the articles are to be delivered somewhere, either at a place designated at the time of making the contract or to be thereafter designated, or at the place fixed by law, and there is no difference in the rule requiring a tender, in cases where the parties designate the place, and where the property is to be delivered at the place fixed by law, provided, however, that in the former case the parties do actually designate the place before the time for delivery arrives And in those cases, holding that in case of a failure to deliver the property at the place designated no tender is necessary, but that it is sufficient if the purchaser at the time and place fixed, is ready to pay the price (Woolner v Hill, 93 N Y 576, Vail v Rice, 5 N Y 155, Bronson v Wiman, 8 N Y 182, Coonley v Anderson, 1 Hill 519), the law is stated inaccurately, as in such cases, as well as in those cases where the law fixes the place, it is the readiness and willingness that constitutes the tender The idle ceremony of producing and counting down the money only being dispensed with

[3] Dunham v. Mann. 4 Seld 508 Dunham v Pettee, 1 E D Smith 500

[4] Hunter v Wetsell. 84 N Y 549

governs actions upon contracts for services [5] and actions upon any contract where the promises are mutual and dependent.

### § 9. Where goods are held for order for delivery.

Where it is the custom of manufacturers to hold goods in store for customers, after they are manufactured, to be delivered from time to time as ordered, and the time for payment arrives, it is unnecessary to tender the balance of the goods before bringing an action for the purchase price.[1] The goods belong to the party ordering them, and he cannot extend the time for payment by failing to order the delivery of all the goods.

### § 10 Where the subscription price of stock or the stock is sought to be recovered.

Where a note is given for subscription for stock in a corporation and the stock is to be delivered on payment of the note, a tender of the stock is a prerequisite to an action on the note.[1] So, on the other hand, the payor of the note must tender the money due on the note before he can maintain an action to recover the stock.[2]

The payment of the note given for the stock in such cases and a delivery of the stock are to be simultaneous acts, and neither party who has not abandoned the contract can put the other in complete default without a tender on his part.[3] And it has been held that a person who demands the right to subscribe for the capital stock of a corporation is not relieved from the necessity of making a tender, because the secretary of the corporation states to him that he has no stock for him.[4]

If the subscription is to be paid in installments, the obligation to issue and deliver the stock is regarded as mutual and concurrent with the obligation to make full payment, and an action to recover installments due may be maintained without tendering the stock, if there are other installments not due.[5] If stock is to be delivered to a trust company to be

[1] Nelson v. Plimpton F. E. C., 55 N. Y. 480

[1] Atkinson v. Truesdell, 127 N. Y. 230

[1] Holmes v. Morse, 53 Hun 58; Cooper v. McKee, 19 Iowa 286; St. Paul etc. Ry Co v. Robbins, 23 Minn 139; Courtright v. Deeds 37 Iowa 503

[2] Wescott v. Mulvane 58 Fed Rep 305 s c 7 C C A 242

[1] St Paul etc. Ry Co v. Robbins 23 Minn 139

[4] Ohio Ins Co v. Nunemacher, 10 Ind 234

[5] Minnesota Har Works v. Libby, 24 Minn 327

delivered to a purchaser upon payment, a delivery of the stock at the place, takes the place of an actual tender.[6] Where the stock or other thing is to be delivered to a third party on payment of a note, a tender of the stock or other thing is not necessary before enforcing payment of the note, for the reason, that, in such cases, it must be the intention of the parties that after payment of the note the thing will be delivered to the third party.[7]

It has been held, where a person subscribes for stock in a corporation and the amount subscribed is to be paid in installments under certain restrictions as the board of directors shall direct, that an action upon the contract for the subscription might be maintained without a tender of the stock, that it is sufficient to plead and prove that the plaintiff is ready and willing to deliver the stock on receiving payment.[8] Here the court distinguished between a subscription for stock and a sale of stock. So, it has been held in cases of subscription for stock, that as the certificate is not the stock but only a convenient representative of it, an action may be maintained for the amount of the subscription without a tender of the certificates before the action is brought.[9]

§ 11.  **On a conditional sale of chattels.**—On a conditional sale of personal property with possession delivered to the vendee, if the vendee wants to preserve his right to possession he must pay or tender the amount agreed upon at the time fixed for payment, even though the vendor has, before the time for payment, resumed possession.[1]

§ 12  **Where covenants are dependent—Recovery of damages or the purchase price**—Where covenants are concurrent and dependent, as where a deed is to be delivered and the purchase price is to be paid at the same time, neither party can put the other in default without performing or tendering performance on his part.[1] And in such cases a tender of a

[6] Reed v. Hayt, 17 N. E. Rep 418

[7] Holmes v Holmes, 53 Hun 52

[8] Seymour v Jefferson, 74 N W Rep (Minn) 119

[9] Columbia Elec Co v Dixon, 46 Minn 163, Marson v Deither 72 N W Rep (Minn) 38, New Albany, etc. R. R Co v McCormick, 10 Ind 499 s c 71 Am Dec 337 See note to the last citation

[1] Hunter v Warner, 1 Wis 126

[1] Cassell v Cooke 8 Serg & Raw 268 Wyvell v Jones, 37

deed is a prerequisite to bringing an action at law for the recovery of damages for a breach of the contract or to recover the purchase price.[2] The rule applies to a vendee of land by verbal contract within the statute of frauds.[3] So, the vendor, where the contract is within the statute, cannot enforce payment of the vendee's note given for the purchase price, without showing a tender of performance upon his part. As the costs in courts of law follow the judgment, the vendee must first be put in default before the vendor can subject him to the costs of litigation,[4] and vice versa.

If the purchase price is to be paid in installments and the deed is to be delivered on the payment of the whole consideration, the payment of the last installment and the delivery of the deed are concurrent acts, and if the vendor waits to bring his action for the purchase price until all the installments are due, he must make and aver an actual tender of the deed.[5]

Minn. 68; Grace v. Regal 11 S. & R. 351; Withers v. Atkinson, 1 Watts 236; Hill v. Grigsby 35 Cal. 656; Stokes v. Burrell 3 Grant's Cas. 211; Steveson v. Maxwell, 2 N. Y. 409; Atkinson v. Hudson, 44 Ark. 192; Robb v. Montgomery 20 Johns. 15; Freeson v. Bissell 63 N. Y. 168.

² Anderson v. Mills, 28 Ark. 175; Green v. Reynolds 2 Johns. 207; Jones v. Gardner 10 Johns. 266; Gazely v. Price 16 Johns. 267; Northrup v. Northrup, 6 Cow. 296; Slocum v. Despard 8 Wend. 615; Stewart v. Ludwick, 29 Ind. 230; Walling v. Kinnard, 10 Texas 508; Young v. Daniels, 2 Iowa 120 s. c. 63 Am. Dec. 477; Small v. Reeves, 14 Ind. 163; Mix v. Ellsworth 5 Ind. 517; Parker v. McAllister 14 Ind. 12; Goodwin v. Morey, 111 Ind. 68; Melton v. Coffelt 59 Ind. 310; Rudd v. Savelli, 44 Ark. 115; Laird v. Smith, 44 N. Y. 618; Goldman v. Willis 72 N. Y. Supp. 292. In England the difficulty surrounding the title being so great rendered it necessary to make an abstract of the numerous conveyances and instruments relative to title, and these being submitted to the purchaser's counsel it became usual for him to prepare the conveyance and the vendor afterwards presented himself to execute the deed. See Sugden on Vendors 217. Such a rule does not obtain in the United States, but the vendee to expedite matters may tender the deed. Camp v. Morse 5 Denio 161. See § 55.

³ Laffey v. Kaufman 66 Pac. Rep. (Cal.) 471. See Brown on St. of Frauds 122 as to the right of a vendee to recover the money or other consideration paid, and the correlative right of the vendor to enforce the vendee's note for the purchase money.

⁴ Anderson v. Mills 28 Ark. 175.

⁵ Beecher v. Conradt 13 N. Y. 108; Johnson v. Wygant 11 Wend. 48; Bean v. Atwater 4 Conn. 3; Eddy v. Davis 116 N. Y. 249 s. c. 22 N. E. 362.

and an averment that he was at the day ready and willing to convey is not sufficient.[6]

It has been held, where a vendee agreed to prepare a deed at his own expense, that the fact that he tendered a deed for execution which was not in accordance with the terms of the contract, did not excuse the vendor from performance, as it was his duty to prepare the deed.[7]

In an action at law to recover the purchase price it has been held that a tender of the deed or release, the covenants being dependent, was necessary even though the other party declares he will not accept it[8] or declares he cannot pay.[9] As long as both parties remain passive, the contract subsists until the rights thereunder are barred by the statute of limitations, and either party within the time may make a tender and on its refusal bring an action to recover damages for the breach, or to recover the portion of the price paid as upon a rescission,[10] as the case may be.

§ 13. **Same subject—Allowance by the probate court of claim for the purchase price—Action by guardian or personal representatives to recover the purchase price—Where a deed is to be delivered to third person.**—Where a tender of a deed is necessary before a vendor has an absolute right to the purchase money, a probate court may allow a claim for such money out of the estate of the vendee and direct it to be paid on condition that such deed be executed and tendered.[1]

Guardians and personal representatives cannot execute a deed without an order of the court having jurisdiction of the estate, and a suit may be maintained to recover the purchase price without a previous tender of the conveyance.[2] Where the owner of a life estate sells his estate to the owner of the fee, who goes into possession, the administrator of the vendor

[6] Parker v. Parmele, 20 Johns 130

[7] Klawebster v. Huber 22 N. Y. Sup. 815 s. c. 68 Hun 338

[8] Nelson v. Nelson 75 Iowa 710 s. c. 38 N. W. Rep 134, citing Courtright v. Deeds 37 Iowa 503 See Wyrell v. Jones, 37 Minn. 68

[9] Eddy v. Davis 22 N. E. 362, affirming 40 Hun 637

[10] See Lahd v. Smith 44 N. Y. 625

[1] Gale v. Best. 20 Wis. 48.

[2] Faulkner's Adm'r v. Williams 16 S. W. 352, see Grimnell v. Warner, 21 Iowa 11, Rutherford v. Haven, 11 Iowa 587; Barrett v. Dean 21 Iowa 423

can maintain an action for the purchase price without tendering a deed, as the estate by the death of the vendor is vested in the purchaser and he has received all he bargained for.[3]

If a deed is to be delivered to a third person who is to deliver it to the vendee on the latter paying the purchase price to the vendor, the latter, after delivering the deed, may collect the purchase price without tendering the deed to the vendee.[4]

§ 14. A tender unnecessary when, in cases where a mortgage is to be executed.—Where the covenants are concurrent and dependent the vendee, in absence of a waiver, cannot recover what he has already paid, or maintain an action for damages for a breach of the contract without tendering the full amount payable by him and demanding performance.[1] But where a vendee was to deliver a bond and mortgage on receiving a conveyance, it was held that it was not necessary before bringing an action upon the covenant for a refusal or neglect to execute the deed, to execute and tender the bond and mortgage. In that case the court observed that the decision is based upon the order of precedency in which the acts are to be done, and that an averment of a readiness to execute the bond and mortgage was sufficient because the mortgage would be inefficacious until the deed was given.[2]

§ 15. Effect of a failure of both parties to make a tender—Neglect by plaintiff after obtaining a decree.—Where, in contracts for the sale and conveyance of land, the acts to be performed by the respective parties are concurrent and the time for performance arrives and neither party has put the other in default, the contract is not annulled or abrogated. Slumbering upon their respective rights would terminate

[3] Reynolds v. Reynolds, 7 Mo. App. 622.

[4] Rollins v. Thornberg, 22 Iowa 389; Olmstead v. Smith, 87 Mo. 602.

[1] Tongue v. Newell, 16 App. Div. 500, s. c. 44 N. Y. Supp. 906; Ziehen v. Smith, 148 N. Y. 558, s. c. 42 N. E. 1080; Lawrence v. Mil-ler, 86 N. Y. 131; Newman v. Baker, 25 Wash. L. Rep. (D. C.) 170; Peckham v. Stewart, 31 Pac. 928; Rector v. Purdy, 1 Mo. 186; Green v. Green, 9 Cow. 46.

[2] West v. Emmons, 5 Johns. 191. See Leaird v. Smith, 44 N. Y. 618.

the contract only by such efflux of time as would create a bar
by the statute of limitation."[1]  So, it was held where a plaintiff had obtained a decree of specific performance and no time
was limited for performance, he would not be deprived of the
fruits of his litigation by tardiness in enforcing his rights
unless it was so great as to render the statute of limitation
available to the defendant; that his adversary has it in his
power to hasten the action of the plaintiff by tendering full
performance, and if he neglects or refuses to comply with the
decree, the court, on motion, may require him to do so within
a specified time on pain of having the decree set aside.[2]

§ 16. Tender of deed unnecessary before bringing ejectment
—Subsequent tender of purchase price.—The general rule is,
where the purchaser of land under an executory contract has
made default in payment, no notice to quit, or demand for the
amount due, or of the possession, or a tender of a deed is
necessary before bringing an action of ejectment.[1]  Bringing
the action is notice that the vendor will no longer acquiesce in
the delay, and it is the vendee's duty to act promptly by
tendering payment and asserting his right to specific performance of the contract.  If he suffers the vendor to recover,
his equity will be lost.[2]

It has been held that a vendee who has been let into possession of land under a contract of sale in which the vendor
covenants to deliver a deed after one installment has been
paid, must tender the second installment and demand a deed
or he will be in default and the vendor will be entitled to
bring ejectment to recover possession, though the first installment was properly paid and the vendor did not before bringing his action tender a deed.[3]  In such case, the vendor, being
in default in not tendering a deed, cannot maintain covenant for the purchase price.[4]

[1] Leaird v Smith, 44 N Y 618
[2] Redington v Chase 34 Cal
866
[3] Hotaling v Hotaling, 47 Barb
163, Wells v Smith, 7 Paige Ch
22, s c 31 Am Dec 274
[2] Tibbs v Morris 44 Barb 138

[1] Wright v Moore, 21 Wend
229
[4] Wright v Moore, 21 Wend
229, citing West v Emmons, 5
Johns 179 Frenchot v Leach, 5
Cow 506

**§ 17. Where the covenant to pay the price is independent.—**Where the vendee has ceased to make the payments on a contract to convey land and the vendor has resumed the possession, to warrant a recovery by the vendee of the amount paid, as for money had and received, a strict performance must be shown, unless the vendor expressly rescinded the contract. The covenant to pay is independent and the vendor cannot be put completely in default without a tender of performance by the vendee.[1]

**§ 18. When tender of price is necessary after debt is barred by the statute of limitation.—**A vendee in an executory contract for the purchase and sale of land, who has not paid the purchase price, is not relieved of his obligation to pay the price, though the statute of limitations has barred the right of action to recover the debt. The debt remains and the vendee, if in possession, cannot defeat an action for the recovery of the possession, or, if out of possession, he cannot recover the possession without paying or tendering the price.[1] The vendor's interest in the land continues until barred by the statute applicable to interests in realty.

**§ 19. Unilateral contracts.—**A person seeking to enforce a unilateral contract by which he is not bound and cannot himself be brought into court, must not only show that he was willing and ready at all times to perform all the requirements on his part, but also that he made a tender of performance before bringing the action.[1] Where there was further negotiation between the parties, occasioned by the vendor's inability to secure his wife's release of dower, a tender of the purchase price within the time for which the option was given to purchase was held to be excused.[2] A failure by the owner of property who has given another an option to purchase within thirty days, to furnish an abstract at once as agreed, was held no excuse for not making a tender of the purchase money within the time specified.[3]

[1] Green v. Green, 9 Cow. 46.

[1] McPherson v. Johnson, 69 Tex. 484.

[1] Miller v. Cameron, 45 N. J. Eq. 95, s. c. 1 L. R. A. 554; Ducie v. Ford, 8 Mont. 233; Keir v. Purdy, 51 N. Y. 629.

[2] Mansfield v. Hodgdon, 147 Mass. 304, s. c. 17 N. E. 544.

[3] Kelsey v. Crowther, 7 Utah 519.

§ 20. **Tender of note required when.**—Where the holder of a negotiable note demands payment, either of the maker, surety or indorser, he must have the note with him so that he can deliver it up after receiving payment. It is not necessary to have it in sight or offer to produce it. Such an offer is implied in the demand. The implied agreement is, that upon receiving payment the note will be surrendered. A demand for payment of a negotiable note or bill without having the instrument at hand to surrender to the maker or drawee is not sufficient to charge an indorser,[1] even though the payor did not know the instrument was not at hand and refused payment upon some other ground. As to an indorser, the holder must not be himself in default. The maker of a negotiable promissory note will be in default whether a demand be made or not, or, if a demand be made, whether the holder has the note at hand to deliver up or not, if he is not ready, willing and able to pay at place of payment on the day appointed. The rule is well settled that a failure to present a note for payment at maturity at the place designated for payment does not stop the accruing of interest unless a proper tender of payment is made by the maker.[2]

§ 21. **Tender of indemnity where note is destroyed.**—If a note has been lost or destroyed, the one entitled to the money must make a tender of indemnity to both the maker and indorser at the time of the demand and notice. As the maker is not bound to make payment on such demand without a surrender of the note, or a tender of indemnity in case it is lost, there is all the more reason that the indorser ought not to be required to make payment until the proper steps have been taken so as to enable him to take immediate action against the maker. Unless such indemnity be tendered both to the maker and indorser at the time of the demand and notice, the indorser will not be charged.[1] As to the maker however, a failure to tender such bond before action affects merely the question of costs, throwing them upon the plaintiff.[2]

[1] Eastman v Potter, 1 Vt 313

[2] Westcott v Patton, 51 Pac 1021

[1] Smith v Rockwell, 2 Hill 182, Strafford v Welch, 59 N. H. 46

[2] Randolph v Harris 28 Cal 562 See Hendon v North Car Ry, 37 S E Rep (S C) 156 where it is held that a tender of an indemnity bond, required by

Statutes authorizing a recovery upon a lost negotiable note or bill of exchange, upon giving a bond conditional to indemnify the maker, his heirs, etc., against all claims on account of the lost note, apply only to the remedy and in no way affect the rights or liabilities of the parties arising out of the proceedings to change a drawer or indorser. These are governed by the principles of the common law [3]

§ 22. Tender of note where demand is made for payment upon the original obligation—When an action has been commenced upon the original obligation.—If, after selling goods without any express agreement as to the time of payment, or they were sold on time and after the purchase price is due the seller takes the purchaser's negotiable time note for the amount without any agreement that the note shall constitute payment, the seller, if he demands payment upon the original obligation, must at the time of the demand return or tender to the purchaser his note. But the seller may commence an action to recover upon the original obligation (before or after the note matures) without first returning or making a tender of the note. It is sufficient if the note be tendered at or before the trial. In the first case the creditor cannot have his money and retain the note, and in the second case he cannot have a judgment and retain it [1]

The reason for the difference is that the negotiable note being in the nature of collateral, if the holder demands payment upon the original demand he must at the time of the demand surrender or tender whatever he holds that is collateral to the debt, and the debtor is not bound to pay the original obligation and trust to a subsequent return of the note, while in the latter case, the note not constituting payment and the original obligation being due, he may sue upon it at any time and the debtor is amply protected from the possibility of second payment or expense of a defense to an action upon the note by a tender of the note at or before trial

the statute before a corporation shall be required to reissue certificates of stock which have been lost, is excused if the right to reissue is denied

[3] Smith v Rockwell, 2 Hill. 482.

[1] O'Brien v. Jones, 38 Mo App 90. Moore v Fitz, 59 N H 572

**§ 23. A tender of funds received upon a wrongful sale of goods upon execution necessary when.**—After a levy and sale of goods upon execution, the judgment creditor cannot maintain an action or proceeding to obtain a new execution on the ground that the goods sold were not the property of the debtor, without first refunding the money or tendering it back [1]

**§ 24. Tender when necessary before recovering a statutory penalty.**—In order to recover damages or a penalty prescribed by statute, which without the statute could not be recovered, the aggrieved party must bring himself strictly within the provisions of the act. Thus where a statute provides that if a carrier refuse to deliver goods on a tender of the freight as shown by the bill of lading it shall be liable to damages in a certain sum, etc., a tender of a sum as freight, shown to be due by an expense account which was no part of the bill of lading was held insufficient to warrant a recovery of such penalty, and that a tender of the amount due as shown by the bill of lading was indispensable [1]

**§ 25. Before recovering collateral given to secure an usurious loan—By debtor to avail himself of a composition agreement—Recovery after an accord.**—In Tennessee it has been held that an action to recover collateral given to secure an usurious loan cannot be maintained without tendering the amount actually due before commencing the action, notwithstanding the court would not permit the lender as plaintiff to recover the amount actually due, if in stating his cause of action the usury was made to appear [1]

---

[1] Batchelder v Mason, 8 N H 121.

[1] Schloss v Atchison etc Ry Co, 22 S W Rep (Tex) 1014, citing Suth st Const 398 DeWitt v Dunn, 15 Tex 106, Garza v Booth, 28 Tex 478, Scogins v Perry, 46 Tex 110, Murry v Railroad Co, 63 Tex 407

[1] Causey v Yates 8 Hump 605 citing on the last point Isler v Brunson, 6 Hump 277 Exacting usury under the Tennessee statute being an inditable offence, it was held in these cases where the usury was made to appear in the complaint, that the plaintiff could not recover upon the well settled principle that the courts will not lend their aid for the enforcement of a contract made in violation of the law of the land But the contract not being void in o the borrower, as defendant, could not bring the usury forward to his own advantage except by paying what was actually due

In Minnesota an action to cancel a mortgage given to secure an usurious loan, or to recover anything paid upon an usurious contract, may be maintained without tendering or returning the thing received upon the contract.[2] To enable a debtor to avail himself of a composition agreement where all the creditors join in and agree to an extension of time and to accept notes, the debtor must tender the notes according to the agreement or the creditors will be remitted to their original rights.[3] A payment of a part of an undisputed claim furnishes no consideration for a promise by a creditor to discharge the debtor, and the creditor may bring an action to recover the unpaid part without returning or making a tender of the part paid.[4]

§ 26. **When necessary or unnecessary in equity—Setting aside a tax deed—Where amount due is uncertain—Surety entitled to subrogation—Costs.**—In equity the court has the power to award such judgment as the facts may show the plaintiff entitled to and to fully protect the rights of the other party by granting the relief conditionally upon the performance by plaintiff of that which he was by the contract bound to do,[1] and to save the party who was not put in default harmless from costs. Except in cases where the existence or preservation of the right depends solely upon a payment or tender, the rule is, although not universal, that in equity a tender is not necessary as a prerequisite to bringing suit for relief, and in such cases, a failure to make a tender before suit affects merely the right to interest and costs.[2] The plaintiff must make

[2] See Scott v Austin, 36 Minn 460

[3] Warbury v Wilcox, 2 Hilt 121

[4] See Martin v Bank 12 S E Rep (Mich) 72

[1] Lewis v Prendergast, 39 Minn 301, Rutherford v Hoven, 11 Iowa 587, s c 38 N W Rep 131, see Nelson v Nelson, 75 Iowa 710, s c 38 N W. Rep 135 citing Winton v Sherman, 20 Iowa 295

[2] Minneapolis etc. Ry Co, v Chisholm, 55 Minn 374, Ashurst v Peck 11 So (Ala) 511 Lewis v Prendergast, 39 Minn 301, Friceson v Bissell, 63 N Y 168, Stevenson v Maxwell 2 N Y. 409 Bruce v Tilson 25 N. Y 195; Brock v Jones 16 Tex 461, Downing v Plate 90 Ill 195 See Bundy v Summerlin, 142 Ind 92, Morrison v Jacoby, 114 Ind 84, See also Martin v Bank, 12 S W. Rep 558 when it is held that if the defendant in his answer denies plaintiff's claim, the objection that a tender is a condition precedent to the action, is waived

a tender if he desires to place the defendant in the wrong and subject him to a liability for costs.³ However, if the defendant subsequently denies plaintiff's right to the relief to which he is entitled, the question of a failure to make a tender, as bearing upon the right of the plaintiff to costs, becomes immaterial.⁴

A tender of the amount due is not necessary to enable a mortgagor to maintain a bill to prevent a foreclosure for more than is due.⁵ Nor is one necessary before bringing a suit to set aside a tax sale on the ground of fraud,⁶ or to redeem where the tax deed is made without authority of law,⁷ or to set aside a tax deed as a cloud on the title when land other than that sought to be charged is included in the assessment,⁸ or where the land is not subject to taxation,⁹ or where the assessment for any reason is wholly void.¹⁰ But where the tax is a valid claim, but some defect arising in course of the proceedings to enforce it renders it void, a decree removing a cloud on the title, or one to quiet title and cancel the tax deed, will be made conditional upon complainant paying the tax due.¹¹

A tender of the amount due before bringing a suit is not necessary if the amount due is uncertain, or is particularly within the knowledge of the other party, as where a person is entitled to an accounting,¹² or where one creditor is en-

³ Glos v. Goodrich, 175 Ill. 20; Glos v. McKeown, 111 Ill. 288, Gage v. Goudy, 141 Ill. 215, Cotes v. Rohrbeck, 139 Ill. 532, McCartney v. Morse, 137 Ill. 481, Gage v. Arndt, 121 Ill. 121.

⁴ See Martin v. Bank 42 S. E. Rep. (N. C.) 558.

⁵ Cole v. Savage 1 Clark (N. Y.) 361.

⁶ Dudly v. Little, 2 Ohio 504.

⁷ Adams v. Snow, 65 Iowa 435, s. c. 21 N. W. Rep. (Io.) 765, Hanscom v. Hinman 30 Mich. 419, Taylor v. Ormsby, 66 Iowa 109, s. c. 23 N. W. Rep. (Io.) 288, citing Binford v. Boardman, 44 Iowa 53, Crawford v. Liddle, 70 N. W. Rep. (Io.) 97, see Guidry v. Broussard, 32 La. Ann. 925 and

Beaux v. Negrotto 43 Id. 124.

⁸ Tit. Trust Co. v. Aylesworth 66 Pac. Rep. (Or.) 276.

⁹ See Morrison v. Jacoby 114 Ind. 81.

¹⁰ Sioux City Bridge Co. v. Dakota County, 81 N. W. Rep. (Neb.) 607, Powers v. Larabee, 2 N. Dak. 141, s. c. 49 N. W. Rep. 724.

¹¹ Hamilton v. Merrymar 45 N. W. Rep. (Mich.) 282, Hayes v. Douglas, 92 Wis. 129 s. c. 65 N. W. Rep. 482, Crawford v. Liddle 70 N. W. Rep. (Io.) 97.

¹² Zebley v. Farmer's L. & T. Co. 34 N. E. 1067, s. c. 139 N. Y. 461, Coolbaugh v. Roemer 32 Minn. 445.

titled to subrogation as to securities held by another creditor to protect the latter against loss on account of any dealing with the debtor.[13]

**§ 27. Same subject—Restraining water company from shutting off the water.**—One who seeks by injunction to restrain a water company from shutting off the water for nonpayment of the dues or tax, must first tender what is justly due[1]. So where one seeks to restrain by injunction any act for the collection of money, as where a tax in excess of the legal rate has been levied and is sought to be collected, a payment or tender of that part of the tax admitted to be legal is a condition precedent to the commencement of the action. In such a case the court said: An "averment of willingness to pay and willingness to bring the money into court without having made the tender, are insufficient and do not justify the court in exercising equitable jurisdiction while the plaintiffs themselves omit to do equity by paying or tendering payment to the defendant of that portion which by their own pleading appears to be due."[2]

**§ 28. Specific performance—Enforcing vendor's lien.**—In contracts for the purchase and sale of land, or of bargain and sale of personal property in cases where specific performance may be had where the promises or covenants are mutual and dependent, it is not necessary before bringing an action in equity to enforce specific performance of the contract for either the vendor or vendee to put the other party in default by performance or tender of performance of his part[1]. So,

[13] Koehler v Farmers' Bank, o N Y Supp. 745

[1] McDaniels v The Springfield Waterworks Co., 48 Mo App 273

[2] State Nat Bank v Carson, 50 Pac (Okla) 990; s p Watson v Major 50 Pac Rep (Colo App.) 741, Chicago etc v Commissioners 54 Kan 781, Overall v Puenzi 67 Mo 203, Bundy v Summerland, 142 Ind 92, People v Henderson, 12 Colo 399, Hagamin v Commissioners 19 Kan 394, Wilson v Longendyke, 32 Kan 270,

s c 4 Pac 361, Albany v. Auditor General 37 Mich 391

[1] Fall v Hazelrig, 45 Ind 576; Minneapolis etc Ry Co v Chisholm, 55 Minn 374; Stevenson v Maxwell, 2 N Y 109, Vaught v. Cain, 31 W. Va 424; Ashurst v. Peck, 11 So (Ala) 541, Brown v Eaton, 21 Minn 409, Nelson v Nelson, 75 Iowa 710, s c 38 N W. Rep 134, Winton v Sherman, 20 Iowa 295, Brook v. Hewit, 3 Ves 253, Hunter v Bales, 24 Ind 299, Irwin v. Gregory, 13 Gray

where the vendor of land has a lien for the purchase price, it is not necessary before bringing a suit to enforce the lien, to tender a deed. Where a vendee is entitled to a conveyance upon request, a suit in equity to enforce the contract may be maintained without a previous request or tender of the purchase price, unless the request, by the terms of the contract, is made essential to the right to enforce performance. In suits for specific performance the plaintiff need not aver a willingness or make an offer of performance in his complaint. The court can in its decree fully protect the rights of the defendant.

The question whether the plaintiff is in default on account of gross laches, or by reason of applying to the court for relief after a long lapse of time, go mainly to the existence or nonexistence of the contract at the time of bringing the suit, and the reader is referred to works on Specific Performance of Contracts and works on Equity Jurisprudence for a discussion of that question. Where the contract still subsists the decisions in most of the United States, and perhaps England, on the question of a tender before suit, or an offer in the complaint, support the rule as stated.

§ 29. **Same subject—Contrary rule—Waiver.**—There is a line of authorities which seem to support the contrary rule that a plaintiff must make an actual tender before bringing his suit. And there is another line of authorities holding

---

215, Lynch v Jennings, 43 Ind 276, Sons of Temperance v Brown 9 Minn 157, Lewis v Prendergast, 39 Minn 301 Sheplar v Green 96 Cal 218, s c 31 Pac 42, Wood v Rabe, 52 N Y Supr Ct 479, Brock v Jones 16 Tex 461, Gardner v Rundell 70 Tex 453, Luchetti v Frost 65 Pac Rep (Cal) 909, Rutherford v Hoven, 11 Iowa 587, Worch v Woodruff, 47 Atl Rep (N J Ch) 725, Banbury v Arnold, 91 Cal 606, s c. 27 Pac 934, citing Wilcoxson v Stitt, 65 Cal 596, s c 4 Pac 629, and Smith v Mohn, 87 Cal 489

2 Freeson v Bissell 63 N Y 168; Rutherford v Hoven, 11 Iowa 587; Grimmell v Warner 21 Iowa 11, Barrett v Dean, 21 Id 123

3 Bruce v Tilson 25 N Y 194

4 Vaught v Cain, 31 W Va 424, Brooks v Hewit, 3 Ves 253 Coolbough v Roemer, 32 Mit t 447. See Freeson v Bissell, 63 N Y 168, and Stevens v Maxwell 2 N. Y 168

5 See 3 Pomeroy's Eq. Jur 1408, Story's Eq § 771

1 Askew v Carr, 81 Ga 685, Sanford v Bartholomew, 33 Kan 38; Boyce v Frances, 56 Miss

that the making of a formal tender before commencing an action for specific performance is waived by some act or declaration of the other party, which would render a tender—as long as the position taken by the latter is maintained—a vain and idle ceremony, as where the vendor or vendee notifies the other party that he will not go on with the contract; [2] or, which is the same thing, denies its binding force,[3] or repudiates it,[4] either expressly, or impliedly as where a vendee without tendering a deed brings an action to quiet title,[5] or takes untenable grounds as to title, or claims interest where none is reserved, without receding or withdrawing his construction of the contract.[6] The decisions falling within the last group of authorities mentioned are found in the books of those states where prevails the equitable rule dispensing with the necessity of a tender before bringing suit—where the question of a waiver is immaterial—as well as in the books of those states adhering to the strict legal rule requiring a tender—where the question of a waiver is material—which tends to confuse the student or practitioner when making an examination of the subject.

---

See Klyce v. Broyles, 37 Id 524, Mhoon v. Wilkinson, 47 Id 633, Robinson v. Harbour, 42 Id 800, Kimbrough v. Curtis 50 Id 117 Greenup v. Strong 1 Bib 590, Bearden v. Wood 1 A K Marsh 450 Young v. Daniels, 2 Iowa 126. In the last case the court cited Story's Eq § 771, but at that place Judge Story is considering whether a contract is enforceable or not by reason of laches lapse of time, etc. See foot note to § 1107 Pomeroy's Eq Jur for a collection of cases upon this subject

[2] White v. Dobson, 17 Gratt. (Va) 262, Dulin v. Prince 124 Ill 76 McPherson v. Fargo, 74 N W Rep (N D) 1057 Brace v. Doble 52 N W. Rep 586; McKleroy v. Tulane, 34 Ala 78 Lyman v. Gedney 114 Ill 388, s c 29 N E 282, Smith v. Gibson 44 N W Rep (Neb.) 360, Long v. Miller 46 Minn 13 Brown v. Eaton 21 Minn 411, Veeder v. McMurray 70 Iowa 118; Crary v. Smith 2 N Y 60, Vanpell v. Woodward 2 Sand Ch 143; Pollock v. Brainard, 26 Fed Rep. 732, Tyler v. Ontzs 20 S W (Ky) 256

[3] Hopwood v. Corbin, 63 Iowa 218 s c 18 N. W Rep 911 Wright v. Young, 6 Wis 127, s c 70 Am Dec 153

[4] Gill v. Newell, 13 Minn 462. Lee v. Stone, 21 R I 123 See Deichmann v. Deichmann, 49 Mo 107, citing Brock v. Hidy. 13 O. St 303

[5] Sheplar v. Green. 96 Cal 218, s c 31 Pac 42

[6] Selleck v. Tallman, 87 N. Y. 106

**§ 30. Same subject—Barring right to specific performance.—**
It remains to be observed that a tender by one party is
necessary to put the other in default, or work a forfeiture, so
as to defeat the right of the latter to a specific performance
of the contract. In absence of a tender, the right to specific
performance continues until barred by the statute of limita
tions.[1]

**§ 31. Rescission on the ground of fraud—In equity.—**A person
who intends to rescind a contract on the ground of fraud
should do so as soon as he discovers the fraud. He ought to
return or tender back what he has received under the contract
so as to place the parties as near as possible in *statu quo*[1]
But a tender of the thing received is not a prerequisite to the
right to apply to a court of equity for relief, and a bill to
rescind may be maintained without a previous offer to restore
what has been received[2]

Ordinarily when the case is one coming within the jurisdic
tion of equity, such a rule is the only practical one, as the
amount to be returned will depend upon a variety of circum
stances, whether there has been a loss or deterioration of the
property through his fault, whether he should be charged
with the value of the use and occupation, etc[3] It is the
fraud that gives the right to relief in equity and all that is
necessary to justify a rescission by the court is, that the con
tract is one that a court of equity will cancel or rescind on
the ground alleged, that such grounds of rescission exist,

[1] Leard v Smith, 44 N Y 618

[1] Brady v Cole 164 Ill 116,
Cobb v Hatfield 46 N Y 533,
Sloan v Shiffer, 156 Pa St. 59;
Evans v Gale, 17 N H 373, Kim-
ball v Cunningham, 1 Mass 502,
Stevens v Hyde, 32 Barb 171
Tisdale v Buckmore, 33 Me. 461,
Thayer v Turner, 8 Met 550

[2] Kiefer v Rodgers, 19 Minn
32, Tarkington v Purvis, 25 N
E. Rep 879; McCorkell v. Kar-
hoff, 58 N W Rep (Io) 913; Garza v. Scott, 5 Tex Civ App 28C,
s. c 24 S W. Rep 89, Potter v

Taggart, 54 Wis 395, s c 11 N
W Rep 678, Perry v Boyd, 28
So Rep (Ala) 711 Ellison v
Beannahta, 16 Pac. (Okla) 177,
Maloy v Berkin, 11 Mont 138,
O'Dell v Burnham, 61 Wis 562,
Van Trott v Wiese, 36 Wis 139,
McGeary v Jenkins, 11 Atl Rep
(Pa) 315 In the last case which
was a suit for relief from a sher
iff's sale made in fraud of the
owner's right, the same rule was
applied

[3] Saxton v Seiberling, 48 O
St 554

and that the party seeking the relief has not lost the right by affirmance, laches or otherwise. [4]

Formerly under the old equity practice, a bill which did not contain a formal offer to return what had been received on a contract was demurrable, but this rule does not now obtain everywhere under that practice. [5] Under the code system, which merely requires a complaint to contain only a statement of the facts constituting the cause of action and the prayer for relief, no such averment is necessary. A willingness is sufficiently shown by a plaintiff by submitting his cause to the court which has the power to impose the proper terms of granting the relief [6] The rule in equity dispensing with a strict tender of the thing received upon the contract as a prerequisite to a suit to rescind upon the ground of fraud, seems to be applied alike to contracts of sale of realty and of personal property, and to the suit of the vendor or vendee. The same rules apply to the rescission of a contract executed under duress as apply to contracts voidable on the ground of fraud [7]

§ 32. Same subject—At law—Waiver.—At law the weight of authority seems to support a rule requiring a vendor or vendee, in rescinding a contract of sale of personal property on the ground of fraud to make an actual tender to the other party of the thing received upon the contract. Thus, if the vendee desires to recover what he has paid, he ought first to tender the property he received on the contract [1] Merely leaving a horse in the vendor's yard without any notice of his intention to rescind is no tender and does not amount to a rescission [2] If the vendor brings replevin he should, before bringing his action, return or tender the purchase price [3] If land has been conveyed in exchange for

[4] Nelson v Carlson, 55 N W Rep (Minn) 821. Knappen v Freeman, 50 N. W Rep (Minn) 533

[5] Jervis v Berridge, L R 8 Ch App 351, s. c 21 W. R 96

[6] Knappin v. Freeman, 50 N W Rep (Minn.) 533

[7] Morse v Woodworth, 29 N E Rep 525

[1] Perley v Balch 23 Pick. 283, s c 34 Am Rep 53, Thompson v Peck 115 Ind 512; Farwell v Hanchett, 19 Ill App 620, Moriarty v Steffeian, 89 Ill 528, Balme v Taylor, 36 N E Rep 269

[2] Thayer v Turner, 8 Met 553

[3] Conner v Henderson, 15 Mass 320, Thurston v Blanchard, 22 Pick 18, Deutzel v City Ry Co,

personal property and the grantee seeks to rescind on the ground of fraud, he must tender a reconveyance, and, when this is possible, an action to reclaim the goods without such tender is prematurely brought[1] An offer to trade back is not a rescission[5]

So, a tender of the amount received on a settlement with an insurance company or a railroad company, is necessary to a rescission on the ground of fraud,[6] unless the release given was made to cover matters not contemplated by the parties. Where a vendee goes to a vendor and announces his determination to rescind, and the latter refuses to assent to a rescission of the sale and repay the purchase price, it has been said that such refusal amounts to a waiver of the right to have a formal tender made[8] If a sum to be paid expressly as a compromise and not because so much is conceded to be due, the party receiving the payment cannot maintain an action to recover the balance claimed to be due and retain what he has received[9]

Where an insurance company elects to rescind its contract of insurance, under a clause declaring the policy null and void if any of the representations of the insured are untrue, it must as soon as it learns of the breach of the condition of the policy return or tender the premium received. The whole of the premium must be returned as the policy is avoided *in toto*, and from the beginning[10] The fact that a loss has oc-

45 Atl Rep (Md) 201. In the last case an agent without authority sold certain property See Sisson v Potter 21 L R A 206 which holds that no tender need be made

4 Wilbur v Flood 16 Mich 40 See Hendrickson v Hendrickson, 50 N W Rep (Io) 287 to the contrary.

5 Wilbur v Flood, 16 Mich 40, s c 93 Am Dec 203

6 Neiderhauser v. Detroit 91 N W Rep (Mich) 1028, Railway Co v Hayes, 10 S E Rep (Ga) 350 Brown v Insurance Co, 117 Mass 479, Pangborn v Insurance Co, 38 Mich 341, s c 35 N W Rep

814, and cases cited Contra O'-Brien v Chicago Ry, 57 N W Rep (Io) 425, Railway Co v Lewis, 109 Ill 120, Mullen v Railway Co, 127 Mass 86 Some of the code states seem to have adopted a more liberal rule

7 Louisville & N R Co v McEllory, 37 S W Rep 844 See Crippen v Hope, 38 Mich 344

8 Potter v Taggert, 54 Wis 395, s c 11 N W Rep 678

9 McMichael v Kilmer, 76 N Y 36, Bisbee v Ham, 47 Me 543

10 Schreiber v Insurance Co, 43 Minn 367, First National Bank v Assurance Co, 64 Minn 96, Harris v Assurance Society 64 N

curred and an action commenced to recover on the policy does not change the rule, as a party has a right to rescind a contract for fraud, at any time, on discovering the ground therefor  After action brought the money may be tendered, and, being one that must be kept good,[11] the tender must be pleaded, either in the answer or a supplemental answer, and the money brought into court.  But when a policy of insurance is not voidable from the beginning, but from the happening of a particular event, as placing an incumbrance upon the property, only so much of the premium as is unearned at the time of the happening of the event need be tendered, unless the policy contains a stipulation that the whole of the premium for the entire term shall be deemed earned, in which case no tender need be made  In the latter case the protection which the insured had to the happening of the event is the consideration for the premium paid.[12]  A policy of insurance containing a clause that it shall be null and void for any reason is not void absolutely, but voidable at the election of the insurer, and a failure upon discovering the fraud to take any steps to rescind the contract by returning or tendering what was received under the policy,[13] or giving notice of an intention to rescind where no tender need be made, is a waiver of the right to declare a forfeiture [14]  There must be no delay in rescinding [15]

§ 33.  **Same subject—Where a party is entitled to retain that which he received—Where judgment will give a defendant all he is entitled to**—One who attempts to rescind a contract on

[1] 196  Home Ins Co  v  Howard, 111 Ind 544, s c 13 N E Rep 103, Home Ins Co  v  Richards, 121 Ind 121  s c 22 N E Rep 875  Strong v  Strong 102 N Y. 69 s c 5 N E Rep 799 Geiss v Franklin Ins Co, 123 Ind  172, s c 24 N E Rep 99 and Weed v Insurance Co  116 N  Y  106, s c 22 N E Rep 229

[11] § 348

[12] See  Schreiber  v  Insurance Co, 43 Minn 367

[13] Schreiber  v  Insurance Co, 43 Minn 367. First National Bank

v  Assurance Co  64 Minn  96 Sweetman v  Prince 26 N Y 224

[14] Berry  v  Insurance Co, 30 N F Rep 254, Phoenix Ins Co v  Bover 1 Ind App 329, s c 27 N E Rep 628, Roby v  American Cent Ins Co 120 N Y 510, s c 24 N E Rep 808 Griffey v  New York Cent Ins  Co, 100 N Y 417, s c 3 N E Rep 309

[15] Strong v  Strong, 102 N Y 69, s c 5 N E Rep 799, Gould v  Cayuga Bank, 86 N Y 82

the ground of fraud, is not required to restore that which in any event he would be entitled to retain either by virtue of the contract sought to be set aside or of the original liability.[1] Thus, if a creditor is induced by fraudulent representations to accept in full satisfaction a per cent on a claim, the amount of which is not in dispute, it is not necessary as preliminary to right to recover the balance due that he repay or tender the per cent received.[2] Nor is a return necessary, either at law or in equity, if the judgment asked for will give the defendant all he is entitled to. Thus where a person was induced by the fraudulent representations of his partner to sell to him his interest in the partnership property for a sum paid in cash, and it was alleged in the complaint and made to appear that the defendant had received more than the amount paid, out of the avails of the property, and the complaint asked for an accounting, it was held not necessary to allege or prove an offer to return the money received on the sale[3]. It is not necessary to tender the consideration received as a prerequisite to an action to cancel a deed as being inconsistent with the power in a will, if the grantee has rents in his hand.[4] So, a tender of the amount received upon a compromise of a claim against an insurance company is not a condition precedent to a suit in equity to rescind the compromise upon the ground of fraud, if a recovery upon the policy is also sought. In equity full and complete relief can be given in the one action and the amount received by plaintiff may be credited upon the

[1] Kley v. Healy, 127 N. Y. 555, Garner v. Mangum, 93 N. Y. 642; Martin v. Ash, 20 Mich. 106

[2] Pierce v. Wood, 23 N. H. (3 Foster) 519

[3] Allerton v. Allerton, 50 N. Y. 670.

[4] Call v. Shewmaker, 69 S. W. Rep. (Ky.) 719. In Harris v. Assurance Society, 64 N. Y. 196, (citing Allerton v. Allerton) the court applied this rule to a defendant who asserts that the contract is fraudulent and void, and held that an offer of a judgment by the defendant company for the amount of the premium received was a compliance with the rule that no tender need be made where the judgment of the court will give the party all he is entitled to. But the decision is bad, as an offer of judgment by a defendant, who may or may not be good, certainly is not placing the parties in statu quo. Being sued did not take away the right to rescind and a tender should have been made.

amount due him under the policy.[5]  A tender by a plaintiff of
the amount received on a settlement with an agent or broker
is unnecessary to enable the plaintiff to recover the amount
of an overcharge or other item wrongfully included in the
account.[6]

§ 34.  **Same subject—Where the property received is destroyed
—Where goods are of no value.—**It is not necessary to make
a tender of the property received upon the contract in
advance of an action to recover the purchase price paid,
when the fraud is discovered too late to make a tender   As
where a horse bought at auction died before the purchaser
discovered that he had been induced to buy by the employment of puffers[1]  Nor, is it necessary to return or tender
the property to the vendor, where it was destroyed in making
the necessary chemical tests to determine that the article delivered is the one contracted for   A buyer is relieved from
the obligation  o return or tender the goods if they are of
no value to either the seller or buyer[2]  It is not enough to
allege and prove that the thing is of no value to the pur
chaser.  It must be entirely worthless to both parties.[1]

§ 35.  **Same subject — Where assignor had no title — Release
received—Promissory notes.—**Where a party is induced through
false representations to take an assignment of a lease
executed by one who had not title, a tender of the assign
ment or an offer of restitution is not necessary before
commencing an action based upon the deceit[1]  Nor, in such
cases is it necessary to tender a release received before com
mencing a suit to set aside a settlement, for upon a rescission the release becomes of no effect[2]  A promissory note, as
between the parties, is not property but a mere promise, and

[5] Reynolds v Westchester Fire
Ins Co, 8 App Div 193 s c 40
N Y Supp 336  See Hartford
Fire Ins Co v Kirkpatrick, 20
So (Ala) 651.

[6] Henderson v Brand, 31 S. E
Rep 551

[1] Staines v Shore 16 Pa St
200

[2] Pence v Langdon 99 U S
578, Thurston v Blanchard  22
Pick 18, Thayer v Turner  8
Mete 550

[1] Perley v Balch 23 Pick 283,
s c 34 Am Dec 56

[1] Cheney v Howell, 88 Ga 629
s c 15 S E 750

[2] Morse v Woodworth, 29 N E
Rep 525

upon a rescission for fraud, of the contract upon which it was given, it becomes of no effect and a tender of the note in advance of an action to recover the thing delivered is unnecessary. It is sufficient if it be delivered up at the trial.[3] Trover may be maintained in goods, against a third party who purchased them with knowledge of the fraud, without tendering the note received from the original purchaser, as it is a matter of no consequence to the former whether the note is restored or not.[4]

§ 36. Same subject — Reconveyance of stock — Receipt — Worthless stock.—In an action to recover money paid for shares in a proposed corporation on the ground that the plaintiff was induced to enter into the contract by false and fraudulent representations, a tender of a reconveyance is not necessary if the title to the stock did not pass.[1] Nor, in such case, is it necessary to return or tender a receipt or certificate acknowledging receipt of the money.[2] Nor is it prerequisite to an action to recover money paid for stock in a corporation to return or tender the stock when, at the time of discovering the fraud the stock was worthless.[1]

§ 37. Same subject—Unnecessary before bringing an action to recover damages—Money received from an insurance company on settlement effected by duress.—The rule is well settled that an aggrieved party may retain the property received through a fraudulent transaction and sue for damages sustained by the fraud perpetrated upon him, or if sued for the price recoup the damages sustained by him, but he cannot repudiate the contract and retain its benefits at the same time. If he retains the benefits no tender is necessary to enable him to recover damages.[1]

[3] Nichols v. Michael, 23 N. Y. 265; Royce v. Watrous 7 Daly, 87; Thurston v. Blanchard 22 Pick 18, Foss v. Hildreth, 10 Allen 76; Snow v. Alley, 144 Mass. 516, Berry v. Am Ins Co, 132 N. Y. 49, White v. Dodds, 42 Barb. 561, Gould v. Cayuga Bank 86 N. Y. 75. See Manning v. Albee, 11 Allen 520, Fraschieris v. Henriques, 36 Barb. 276

[4] Stevens v. Austin, 1 Met. 557
[1] Burns v. McCabe, 72 Pa. St 309
[2] Lewis v. Andrews, 6 N. Y. Supp 247
[1] Lewis v. Andrews, 127 N. Y. 673, Zang v. Adams, 48 Pac Rep (Colo) 509, Baldwin v. Marsh, 33 N. E. Rep. 975
[1] Wabash V P U v. James, 35 N. E. Rep (Ind) 919, citing Eng-

Where a compromise has been effected by fraud and duress, as by threats of criminal prosecution, the contract is without any legal efficacy either as a cause of action or as a defence to an action founded on or arising out of the agreement.[2] And where a person has been induced, in such manner, to compromise a claim against an insurance company a tender of the amount received by the insured is not a condition precedent to an action upon the policy.[3]

**§ 38. Rescission on the ground of breach of warranty—Where goods do not suit buyer.**—In those commonwealths where a person may either affirm a contract and recover damages, or rescind and recover what he has paid on account of the contract, and in those cases where the right to rescind is expressly given by the contract, when there is a breach of warranty, the party rescinding for such breach, before commencing an action to recover the purchase price already paid or whatever he has delivered thereon, must make a tender of the property to the seller.[1] Such tender ought to be made by delivering the property at the place where it was received,[2] and if the manner or place of the return is not such as to inform the seller of the rescission the pur

---

lish v Arbuckle 124 Ind 77, s. c 25 N E Rep 142 Insurance Co v Howard 13 N E Rep 103 Nysewander v Lowman, 124 Ind 258 s c 24 N E Rep 355 Michigan Ins Co v Naugle, 130 Ind. 79 s c 29 N E Rep 393 Johnson v Culver 116 Ind 276 s c 19 N. E. Rep 129 s p Jewett v Petit 4 Mich 508 citing Campbell v Fleming 1 A & E 40 3 N. & M 834 Masson v Boret 1 Denio 74 Galloway v Holmes, 1 Dougl 330, Smith v Hodson 2 Smith Lead Cas 124

[2] Insurance Co v Hull 25 L. R A 37, s c 37 N E Rep 1116 See Wieser v Welch 3 Det. L N 880, s c 70 N W Rep 438, where it is held that such a settlement will not abate a pending suit, and that a tender of the money received before the settlement was pleaded was in time But this was decided mainly upon the ground that no tender was necessary

[3] Hartford F Ins Co, v Kirkpatrick, 20 So (Ala) 651

[1] Ashley v Reeves 2 McCord 432 See Newmark on Sales, § 372 citing 2 Schuler on Personal Prop §578, Gates v Bliss, 43 Vt. 299, Butler v Northumberland, 50 N H 33; Osborne v Gantz, 60 N Y 540; Youghiogheny Iron Co v Smith, 66 Pa St 340; Dill v O'Ferrell, 45 Ind 268, Marsh v Low, 55 Ind 271 Ralph v Chicago etc Co, 32 Wis 177

[2] Paulson v Osborn, 35 Minn 90 s c 27 N W Rep 203 See Osborn v Rawson, 10 N W Rep 201

chaser should notify the seller that he has elected to rescind and that the goods had been returned.[3]

But a purchaser is relieved of the necessity to return the property if, on an offer to do so, he is told that the property would not be received.[4] He must, however, retain the articles or deposit them somewhere subject to the order of the seller. To support an action on the warranty it is not necessary that the property be tendered or returned.[5] Where a vendor is to furnish other articles in case those delivered do not suit, notice by the vendee that the articles delivered are not satisfactory is sufficient in the absence of an express agreement that the vendee is to return them, and in case other articles that are satisfactory are not delivered, the vendee may rescind without tendering the articles received[6]

§ 39. Rescission on the ground of mistake.—Where a person is entitled to rescind a contract on the ground of mistake, and he elects to rescind, he must return or make a tender of the property received or of the purchase price to the other party[1] There must be a complete restoration The rules as to the time and manner of rescinding a contract on the ground of a breach of warranty apply to a rescission upon the ground of mistake

§ 40. Returning goods after an inspection not a rescission.— A purchaser is not bound to receive what he has not bargained for, and the rule is universal, that the purchaser, on a tender of goods upon the contract, may take a reasonable time to examine and make tests for the purpose of determining whether the goods offered are of the requisite kind and quality. If the goods do not answer the description as to kind and quality, the purchaser should at once notify the seller of his objection to the articles and return or tender the goods to the vendor[1] by returning the goods to the place

[1] Paulson v. Osborn, 27 N. W. Rep (Minn) 903, citing on the necessity for notice, Smalley v. Hendrickson, 29 N J L 371, Dewey v Erie Borough, 14 Pa. St. 211, Moral School Tp v Harrison 74 Ind. 93

[4] The Champion Machine Co v Mann, 42 Kan. 372

[5] Ashley v. Reeves, 2 McCord 132.

[6] Housding v. Solomon, 87 N. W Rep. (Mich) 57, McCormick Hay Machine Co v Chesrown, 21 N W Rep 846.

[1] Lee v. Lancashire Ry Co., L R. 6 Ch. App 527.

[1] Reed v Randall, 29 N. Y 358, citing Fisher v Samuda, 1 Camp 190; Grimaldi v. White, 4 Esp R

where they were received. Returning articles under such circumstances is not a rescission, but merely a rejection of the articles tendered.

**§ 41. Rescission on the ground of a failure of consideration.**— Where there is a partial failure of consideration upon an entire contract, and the thing sold is personal property the purchaser, on a rescission, must return or tender to the seller the property received on the contract before commencing an action to recover the consideration paid [1] Where a contract of purchase and sale of chattels is severable and there has been a part performance and a default as to the residue, the authorities all agree that the vendee cannot rescind the contract in *toto*, by returning or tendering to the vendor the articles received; but he must keep and pay for the articles received and obtain his redress for the breach of the contract in some other way [2] If according to the terms of a

---

95; Millnor v Tucker, 1 Car & Payne 15; Sprague v. Blake, 20 Wend. 61; Hargrave v Stone, 1 Selden 73; Shields v Pettee, 2 Sand (N. Y) 262 And upon the question that the vendee can recover no damages unless he returns the goods Howard v. Hoey, 23 Wend 350; Hopkins v Appleby, 1 Stark 477; 2 Kent's Com 480, Parsons on Cont 175, Sedgwick on Damages 280 See also Haase v. Nonnemacher, 21 Minn 486

[1] Shields v Pettee, 2 Sand (N. Y) 262 See Colville v Besly, 2 Demo 139 This was a case of a bargain and sale of certain notes upon which there was a contract of endorsement The contract of endorsement was erased and the notes then sent to the purchaser It was held that this was not a part performance so as to cast upon plaintiff the necessity of returning or tendering the notes to the defendant, as upon a rescission, to entitle him to bring his action to recover the consideration which he had paid In New York, the rule appears to be that where the contract is entire and the articles are to be delivered in installments the vendee may use the articles as they are delivered, without waiting for the time for full performance to arrive, to find out if the vendor will fully perform; and that on default he may refuse to accept the residue and keep the articles received without payment Catlin v Tobias, 26 N Y 217

[2] The buyer, if he paid for the articles delivered may bring his action to recover damages for the failure to deliver the residue; or, if he did not pay for the articles received he may deduct the damages from the price of the articles received and offer to pay the difference or he may recoup the damages in an action for the price If he paid the entire consideration, his action may be for money had and received as upon

severable contract the articles are to be delivered in installments, or the value of each article is fixed, and the failure
of consideration consists in all or a portion of the goods in
one lot, or any article singly valued, proving to be not what
the vendee bargained for, or are found to be insufficient in
quantity, the contract being severable, the agreement to deliver each installment or each article singly valued is, as to
those articles, in the nature of an entire contract and the
vendee must return or tender the entire installment or the
article found deficient in quantity or quality, before he can
maintain an action for the price paid.

§ 42.  **Same subject—Where there is a total failure of consideration for a part of price paid—Entire failure—Forged notes—Counterfeit money.**—If part of a certain quantity of goods that have
been paid for is delivered and accepted by the purchaser, the
parties impliedly assent to a severance of the contract and
if the seller afterwards makes default in not delivering the
remainder, the buyer cannot rescind the contract in *toto* by
returning or tendering the part received, but he may rescind
as to the part not performed and recover that part of the
price covering the part not received   This has been said to
be in the nature of a total failure of consideration for part
of the price paid and not a partial failure of the whole.[1]
But if the part received is of no use to the purchaser without
the remainder, there would be no implied severance of the
contract, but a mere indulgence as to the manner and time
of delivery, and the purchaser on the seller making default
may rescind the contract in *toto* by returning or tendering
to the seller the part received

Where there is an entire failure of consideration, as where
the thing sold is entirely worthless to both the seller and
buyer (where the purchaser did not get what he really intended to buy), or the articles were taken from the buyer
by the true owner or voluntarily surrendered to such owner,

a rescission, or for damages for a
failure to deliver the residue  The
minimum amount of damages being the price paid, and more if
the value of the articles paid for
and not received is greater at the

time of the breach than the price
paid

[1] See 2 Kent's Benj on Sales
§ 500 citing Devine v  Edwards
101 Ill 138; Wright v Cook, 9 Up
Can Q B 605   Same 1 Corbin's
Benj on Sales  § 621

no return or tender of the articles need be made to enable
the vendee to recover the price paid, or defend against a re
covery upon the note given for the purchase price.[2] So, on
the other hand, if the consideration received by the seller en
tirely fail, as where forged notes or counterfeit money are
received in payment, on discovering the bogus character of
the consideration the seller may recover his property with
out returning or tendering the bogus paper or spurious
money.[1]

§ 43   Same subject—Recovery of price paid after eviction—
When land is encumbered.—If the subject matter of a con
tract be realty and the vendee has been dispossessed of the
entire property, by the owner of a paramount title, or he
voluntarily surrenders the possession to such owner, he may
bring an action to recover that part of the price already
paid without tendering unpaid installments (if any) or a re
conveyance.[1] So, where there has been a surrender or evic
tion as to a part of the land only, a tender of a release of the
contract, or a reconveyance, is not necessary before bringing
an action to set aside the sale or to recover the price paid.[2]
It is sufficient to make the tender at any time before trial.

So, where at the time of the delivery of the conveyance, the
land is subject to an incumbrance, not taken into account in
making up the purchase price, a tender of a release of the
contract or of the unpaid installments, if any, is not neces
sary to enable the vendee to maintain an action to recover
what he had paid   A vendee, however, if he has paid the
entire consideration, may remove the incumbrance and re
cover the amount paid on account of it from the vendor, or
if he has not paid the price he may tender the balance due,
less the incumbrance and enforce a conveyance

§ 44.  Same subject—Tendering a reconveyance or surrendering
possession before vendor acquires title —If the property has

[2] Taft v Myerscough 197 Ill
601
    It would seem that where the
forged notes or counterfeit money
are needed by the vendee, as evidence to enable him to recover
from the person of whom he re

ceived them they ought to be re
turned at some time before the
trial
    [1] Hawkins v Merritt 109 Ala
261 s c 9 So Rep 589
    [2] Robbins v Martin 9 So Rep
108 Rhorer v Bila 83 Cal 51

been conveyed, and at the time for the payment of the price the title fails, the grantee should be prompt in putting the other party in *statu quo* by a reconveyance of the land, or tender a deed; for if he retain the deed until the grantor actually acquires a title, it inures to his benefit by instantly vesting a good title in him.[1] So, if the vendee is in possession without a conveyance, and the title fails at the time fixed to convey, he should immediately surrender the possession, for, if the vendor acquire title before such surrender, he may tender a deed and defeat the right of rescission

§ 45.  **Rescission on the ground of non-performance.**—In Louisiana, a party to a synallagmatic contract cannot rescind it by reason of the non performance of the other party, unless he returns or tenders to the other party what was received from him, so as to put him in the same situation as he was before[1] A tender to the purchaser of the portion of the price received is prerequisite to maintaining an action to rescind the contract for the non-payment of the residue And a tender in such case is not dispensed with by reason of any liability of the vendee for rents and profits.[2] If a vendor desires to retain that portion of the price already received, he should bring a suit to enforce his lien; or, if the title has not passed, specific performance or ejectment, or, in case the possession has not been delivered to the vendee, he should put the vendee in default by a tender of performance and thereafter act upon the defensive When the covenants are concurrent and dependent a bare refusal to pay the balance of the purchase price on demand, in absence of a tender of a deed, is insufficient to put a vendee in default so as to defeat a recovery by the latter of what he has paid on the contract, where the vendor afterwards conveys the land to another.[3]

It is not perhaps within the scope of the subject of tender to consider all the cases where a rescission may be had on the ground of non-performance Unless something has passed

1 Deal v Dodge, 26 Ill 459  See Rhorer v Bila, 83 Cal 51
1 Grymes v Sanders 93 U S 55
2 Bryant v Stothart, 15 So (La ) 76
3 Wyvell v Jones, 37 Minn 68

under the contract to the party rescinding, the inquiry would be a digression. All the cases at law, when a tender of the thing received is, or is not, essential to a recovery of the consideration paid may be summarized, thus—if the contract be entire and the vendor has not impliedly consented to a severance, that part of the thing received must be returned, if the vendee desires to bring an action to recover the price paid as for money had and received. If the contract is entire and there has been a severance, by the vendee accepting a part without restrictions, or the contract is severable, no tender can be made of the articles received, for the reason that the contract cannot be rescinded in *toto* on the ground of the non delivery of the residue by the vendor, but the vendee, if he has paid the entire consideration, may rescind without any tender and recover that part of the price covering the articles not delivered.[4]

§ 46. **Same subject—In equity.**—There are cases of a failure to perform where equitable relief is necessary before a plaintiff can be placed in *statu quo*. In such cases a tender of the part received is not prerequisite to a suit for relief, as where a mortgagee refuses to pay over the full amount of the loan.[1] Or the heirs of a deceased son refuse to carry out an agreement for maintainence entered into between the deceased and his father.[2] In either case the court, as a condition to granting the relief cancelling the instruments,

---

[4] See Corbin's Benj. on Sales, § 621. n. 12 and § 1032 et seq n. 18 for a large collection of authorities upon this question.

An expression very common, and carelessly used, is, that when part of a contract has been performed and the vendor makes default the vendee may rescind the contract as to the residue and recover damages for the non performance. But this is a misapplication of the term rescission as damages cannot be recovered upon an express rescission, no matter upon what ground the rescission rests, and if there is nothing that can be recovered back the party rescinding is without remedy, for by an express rescission he acquiesces in the default, merely desiring to be placed in statu quo. An action for damages is based upon the default of the vendor without the consent and against the desires of the vendee. In which state of mind the latter is supposed to continue.

[1] Payne v. Loan & Guaranty Co 54 Minn 255

[2] Cree v Sherfy 37 N. E. Rep 787

can require the plaintiff to return whatever he ought in good faith to return.

§ 47. **Cancellation of insurance policy.**—Where an insurance company, in its policy, reserves a right to terminate the insurance at any time, upon notice to that effect, and refunding a ratable proportion of the premium for the unexpired term of the policy, it is necessary in order to effect a cancellation of the policy to seek the assured, on or before the day fixed for the cancellation, and pay or tender the unearned premium.[1] But where credit has been given for the premium, the company will not be required to make the insured a present of the amount of the premium in order to effect a cancellation.[2] Notice that the unearned premium will be returned and holding the amount subject to the order of, or until the insured calls for it, is not enough,[3] and the company will be held for a loss occurring subsequent to the date fixed in the notice for cancellation.

§ 48 **Suit to cancel contract tainted with usury**—A tender of the amount legally or justly due is not necessary before bringing a suit to have a contract delivered up and cancelled on the ground of usury,[1] or that the mortgage is a foreign corporation.[2] In these cases, as in other cases falling within the jurisdiction of equity courts, unless the contract is absolutely void and the right to a cancellation is given by statute without payment, the court will adjust the equities between

[1] Van Valkenburgh v The Lenox F Ins Co, 51 N Y. 465, Natch v American Cent Ins Co 152 N Y 635 s c 83 Hun 644, Griffen v New York Cent Ins Co, 100 N Y 417, see First National Bank v Assurance Co, 64 Minn 96.

[2] Stone v Franklin Ins Co, 105 N Y 543 s c 12 N E Rep 45 If a note had been given for the premium which had been negotiated the unearned premium must be tendered in money, if not negotiated and due it would be sufficient to tender the note conditionally on receiving the earned premium in money, if the note is not due it would be sufficient to endorse the unearned premium on the note; if several notes were given those representing the unearned premium only need be tendered

[3] Tisdell v New Hampshire Fire Ins Co, 155 N Y 163, s c 49 L R A 765, see Walthear v Penn F Ins Co, 2 App Div 328

[1] Spann v Sterns, 18 Tex 556
[2] Ross v New England &c Co 13 So Rep (Ala) 564

the parties by requiring the plaintiff to pay what is justly due

**§ 49.  Rescission on the ground of infancy.**—An infant may disaffirm a release of a claim,[1] or rescind a contract,[2] or an illegal sale of his real estate without making a tender of any property received by him by virtue of the contract or proceeding, except that portion of the property remaining under his control after he has attained his majority,[3] or that portion under his control at the time he seeks to rescind, if the contract be such as he may disaffirm before his majority.[4] Making a tender is not a condition precedent to the institution of a suit against a tutor or guardian to annul an account or settlement, made in error and while the infant was ignorant of his rights under undisclosed and concealed facts, or to set aside purchases of his property by an administrator or guardian. In such case there exists no contractual relations between the parties.[5] In annulling a final account it is sufficient for him to account for the property received which he would be entitled to have in any event or to offer to return the property if it is not something in specie belonging to the estate.

In Vermont, in some of the early cases, it was stated in general terms that an infant would not be permitted to rescind his contract and recover the articles parted with without first restoring the property or consideration received.[6] The same rule has been stated in the same general terms in New Hampshire.[7] But in Vermont in a later case it was held that the general rule was subject to an important qualification. The court in that case said: "A distinction is to be observed between the cases of an infant in possession

[1] Young v. West Virginia etc. Co. 42 W. Va. 112 s. c. 24 S. E. Rep. 615

[2] Haws v. Burlington etc. Ry. 64 Iowa 315 s. c. 20 N. W. Rep. 717 Jenkins v. Jenkins 12 Iowa, 195

[3] See Kane v. Kane 13 App. Div. 544 s. c. 43 N. Y. Supp. 662

[4] See Schouler Domestic Relations, § 416

[5] Rist v. Hartner, 44 La. Ann. 430, Wood v. Nicholls 33 La. Ann. 744 Heirs of Burney v. Ludeling 44 La. Ann. 632

[6] Price v. Sumner, 12 Vt. 28 s. c. 36 Am. Dec. 327 Taft v. Pike, 14 Vt. 405 s. c. 39 Am. Dec. 228

[7] Carr v. Clough 26 N. H. 280, s. c. 59 Am. Dec. 345

of such property after age, and when he has lost, sold, or de stroyed the property during his minority. * * * the property is to be restored if it be in his possession and con trol. If the property is not in his hand nor under his con trol, that obligation ceases."[8] This is undoubtedly the pre vailing rule almost, if not everywhere, and it is certainly supported by the policy of the law in protecting infants in their property rights until they have arrived at that age when the law declares them to be of sufficient discretion to manage their prudential affairs. No better reason for the rule exists than that given by the Vermont court. It said. "To say that an infant cannot recover back his property, which he has parted with under such circumstances, because by his indiscretion he has spent, consumed or injured that which he received, would be making his want of discretion the means of binding him to all his improvident contracts, and deprive him of that protection which the law designed to secure to him."[9]

[8] Price v Furman, 27 Vt. 268, s c. 65 Am. Dec. 194; citing Fitts v Hall, 9 N H 441; Robbins v Eaton, 10 N H 562, Moody v McKenny, 23 Me 517, 525, 526, Tucker v Moreland, 1 Am. Lead. Cas 260

[9] Price v. Furman, 27 Vt 268 As to the time when a contract may be disaffirmed on the ground of infancy, the rule generally accepted, in case of sales of land, is that it cannot be conclusively avoided till he is of age To protect the infant from loss that might occur by reason of the occupancy of the land by the purchaser during such minority, if the purchaser has not gone into possession, the minor or his guardian may resist an entry, or if the possession has been taken by the purchaser, the minor may enter and take and hold the profits Bool v Mix, 17 Wend 119, s c 31 Am Dec 285; Carr v Clough, 26 N H 280 s c 59 Am Dec 345, Stafford v Roof, 9 Cow

626, Price v. Furman, 27 Vt 268 s c 65 Am Dec 194, Zouch v Parsons, 3 Burr 1794; Lynde v Budd, 2 Paige's Ch 191, s. c 21 Am Dec 84; See Schouler's Domestic Relations § 109 But where personal property, chattels or money has passed to the possession of another under a contract of sale with an infant and the contract is not for necessaries the infant may disaffirm the contract before arriving of age, and that the infant may not be exposed to loss by the consumption or other disposition of the chattels by the purchaser, or loss of the money by reason of the subsequent insolvency of the seller, the infant, or his guardian for him may bring the appropriate action at once to recover that which the infant parted with under the contract Carr v Clough 26 N H 280, s c 65 Am Dec 345, Bool v Mix, 17 Wend 119 s c 31 Am Dec 285, Price v Furman, 27 Vt 268, s c 65 Am Dec 194

§ **50.** **Rescission on the ground of insanity.**—Insane persons receive substantially the same consideration under the law as do infants, with regard to the voidable character of their contracts, with the exception, however, that if a person deals fairly with a person of unsound mind, though apparently of sound mind, without knowledge of such unsoundness, he is entitled to be placed in *statu quo* upon the avoidance of the contract.[1] The supreme court of Indiana in considering such a contract, said "It has not, to our knowledge, been decided in this state or any other state that, where the contract has been entered into with knowledge of the insanity, and an unconscionable advantage has been taken of the insane person it is a necessary prerequisite to avoidance that a tender of that which has been received by such insane person shall be made. If the rule requiring the parties to be placed in *statu quo* includes, as a necessary element, the requirement that the party dealing with the *non compos* shall be ignorant of the incapacity, and shall not deal unfairly, it would seem to follow as an indispensable result that the presence of such knowledge and of an unfair advantage would discharge the rule, otherwise such elements of the rule are mere empty phrases. * * * If he may so deal with the possibility of retaining that so illy gotten, and with no possibility of losing that with which he parted, he is not restrained from attempting the advantage as opportunity offers."[2] As in the case of the avoidance of contracts by infants, whatever remains in the possession of the insane person in specie at the time of the rescission must be restored, but with the distinction that it need not be tendered as a prerequisite to a suit to rescind.

§ 51　**Tender in redemption of land sold on a statutory foreclosure—Before bringing suit to cancel mortgage—To set aside a foreclosure on the ground of fraud, etc.—To redeem where an accounting is necessary.**—A mortgagor who desires to bring a suit in equity to redeem land sold on a statutory foreclosure

---

[1] Boyer v. Berryman, 123 Ind. 451; Fay v. Burditt, 81 Ind. 433, Copenrath v. Kienly, 83 Ind. 18, Musselman v. Cravens, 47 Ind. 1

[2] Thrash v. Starbuck, 44 N. E. Rep. (Ind.) 543, citing Gibson v. Soper, 6 Gray, 288, Eaton v. Eaton, 37 N. J. L. 109, Crawford v. Scovelle, 94 Pa. St. 48, Halley v. Troester, 72 Mo. 73; see Meyer v. Fishburn, 91 N. W. Rep. (Neb.) 534

of a mortgage, must make a tender of the amount due before commencing the suit, and allege the tender and refusal and bring the money into court with the bill or complaint. Being purely a statutory right the tender is indispensable.[1]

Before a foreclosure the right to discharge the mortgage by payment of the mortgage debt or redeem as it is commonly called, is inherent in the mortgage and a tender of the amount due before bringing a suit in equity to redeem, or to declare a deed a mortgage and redeem,[2] is not absolutely necessary.[3] Nor is it necessary to make a formal offer to pay in the complaint.[4] Parties not bound by a foreclosure have not had their day in court and may maintain an action to set aside the foreclosure without making any tender.[5] So, where there has been a foreclosure, if the mortgagor has been guilty of fraud,[6] as where he obtains a decree for a much larger sum than the amount due,[7] or the sale for any reason is void,[8] or the redemptioner has been deprived of the privilege of redeeming by the wrongful act of the purchaser,[9] or it is necessary to take an account of the rent, taxes and repairs,[10] or the mortgagee has realized money from the use of the property or has unlawfully sold part of it,[11] or the mortgagor is entitled to damages on account of the removal

[1] Murphree v Summerlin 21 So (Ala) 470, Beebe v Buxton, 99 Ala 117, s c 12 So Rep 567, Beatty v Brown, 101 Ala 695, s. c 14 So Rep 368, Hoover v Johnson, 50 N W Rep (Minn) 475 Dunn v Hunt, 63 Minn 484, s c 65 N W Rep 948 Dickerson v Hayes, 26 Minn 100, Alley v Burnett, 134 Mo 320, s c 35 S W Rep 1137

[2] Hammett v White 29 So Rep (Ala) 547

[3] Dwen v Blake, 44 Ill 135, Thomas v Jones, 84 Ala 302, s c 4 So Rep 270, Nye v Swan, 49 Minn 431, s c 52 N W Rep 39, McCalley v Otey, 90 Ala 302 s c 8 So Rep 159 Beebe v Buxton, 12 So Rep 567, Webster v French, 11 Ill 254, Barnard v

Cushman, 35 Ill 451, Soell v Hadden, 85 Tex 182

[4] Ney v Swan, 49 Minn 431 s c 52 N W Rep 39, Quinn v Brittain, 1 Hoff Ch 353

[5] Amud v Scandinavian Am Bank, 27 Wash 16

[6] Cain v Gimon, 36 Ala 169

[7] Lockwood v Mitchell 19 Ohio 448 See Lane v Holmes, 55 Minn 379, where a larger sum than that due was by mistake included in the notice of foreclosure

[8] Thompson v The Commissioners, 79 N Y 54, Joplin v Walton, 40 S W Rep 99, Casserly v Witherbee, 119 N Y 522

[9] Kling v Childs 30 Minn 366

[10] Kline v Vogle 90 Mo 239

[11] Boyd v Beaudin, 54 Wis 193 s c 11 N W Rep 525.

and conversion of the fixtures,[12] and like cases, a tender before suit or even an offer in the complaint to pay what is due is not a prerequisite to the granting of relief. In all such cases the want of a tender before suit goes only to the question of interest and costs if taken into consideration at all.

In the case of a statutory foreclosure the statute fixes the terms of redemption, and except in the case of fraud the money must be paid or tendered within the time fixed and the statutory time cannot be extended to await the determination of a suit in equity for an accounting.[11] The plaintiff must tender some amount and take the risk of the sufficiency of his tender

§ 52. **Formal tender excused when.**—Where the payment of the price and the delivery of the property or conveyance are concurrent and dependent acts, a formal tender is unnecessary before bringing an action to recover damages for the non performance of the contract, or to recover what has been paid upon it, if at the time for performance the party to whom performance is due refuses to perform on his part on the ground that the time for performance is passed,[1] or declares positively that nothing is due him[2] or admits that a tender would be fruitless,[3] or refuses to execute a conveyance,[4] or refuses to deliver the property when demanded,[5] or a third party in whose possession the property was when sold refuses to surrender it,[6] or the party refuses to weigh up the goods or do anything to ascertain the quantity and declares the contract at an end,[7] or refuses to accept the notes representing the purchase price,[8] or refuses the

[12] Horn v Indianapolis 125 Ind 381 s c 25 N E Rep 558

[11] Hoover v Johnson, 50 N W Rep (Minn) 475

[1] Blewett v Baker, 58 N Y 611, Graham v Frazier, 68 N W Rep (Neb) 367

[2] Lacy v Wilson, 24 Mich 479

[3] Jackson v Jacob, 3 Bing N C 869, 5 Scott 79 3 Hodges 219

[4] Stone v Sprague, 20 Barb 509 Maxon v Yates, 88 N W Rep (Wis) 54

[5] Anderson v Sherwood 56 Barb 69

[6] Thompson v Warner, 31 Kan 533

[7] Post v Garrow 18 Neb 682 s c 26 N W Rep 580, Oelerich v Artz, 21 Md 524

[8] Ware v Berlin, 43 La Ann 534

money,[9] or stock,[10] or refuses to perform unless a request which he has no right to make is complied with,[11] or un qualifiedly refuses to accept the thing bargained for,[12] or in a threatening tone orders the plaintiff off the premises.[13] Nor is a formal tender necessary as a prerequisite to bring ing such an action, if the party to whom the performance is due be absent from the place of performance in those cases where his presence is necessary, or being present he in any way obstructs or prevents a tender.[14]

Where the acts to be done are concurrent, a formal tender need not be made by a vendee if at the time for performance, the vendor has not the title to the thing sold, or is unable to convey a merchantable title, as where the land to be con veyed is subject to dower, or subject to any incumbrance not taken into account in the contract, which renders perform ance on the vendor's part an impossibility.[15]  In any case,

[9] Bellinger v. Kitts, 6 Barb. 273. See Barker v. Parkerhorn, 2 Wash 112; Wesling v. Noonan, 31 Miss 599, Brewer v. Fleming, 51 Pa. St. 102, and Farnsworth v. Howard, 1 Coldw 215

[10] Curry v. White, 45 N. Y. 822

[11] Amsden v. Atwood, 68 Vt 322, s. c. 35 Alt. 311, Jones v. Tarlton, 9 M & W 675, Northern Colo Irrigation Co v. Richards 45 Pac Rep 423

[12] Howe v. Moore, 14 N. Y. Supp 236, MacDonald v. Wolff, 40 Mo App 302, Calhoun v. Vechio, 3 Wash 165, Blewett v. Baker 58 N Y 611, Cornwell v. Haight, 21 N Y 462

[13] Williams v. Patrick, 58 N E Rep (Mass) 583

[14] Co Litt 207a, n100, Indiana Bond Co v. Jameson, 56 N E Rep (Ind App) 37, Nelson v. Plimpton 55 N Y 480 citing Franchet v. Leach, 5 Cow 506, Traver v. Halsted 23 Wend 66, Colt v. Ambergrate 7 A & E N S 127, and Hochester v. De La Tour 2 E & B 678 In Butler v. Butler, 77 N Y 472 the contract was to furnish material and set up a gas machine which was to be paid for when completed. Af ter the material was delivered at the place, the vendee refused to allow the machine to be set up The vendor brought an ac tion to recover the price less $100, the cost of putting up the machine It was held that the title to the material remained in the vendor and that his remedy was for damages for a breach of the contract Where nothing more than a mere delivery of the arti cle is to be done, as where chat tles are to be delivered on board a vessel and the vessel is not furnished, a delivery of the arti cles on the beach or at the wharf where the vessel was to be, will enable the vendor to recover the price of the articles sold and the cost of putting the articles on board cannot be deducted Bolton v. Riddle, 35 Mich, 13

[15] Bennett v. Phelps, 12 Minn 326, Taylor v. Reed, 19 Minn 372, Morange v. Morris 3 Keyes, 48, Beier v. Spaulding 36 N Y Supp

before it can be said that a formal tender is waived, the party who is to receive must have placed himself in such a position as would make a tender to him an idle and unnecessary act.[16] A plaintiff, however, before he can recover damages for the breach, or what he had parted with under the contract, must show that he was able and willing, at the time fixed, to perform on his part.[17] It is his duty, in absence of notice or knowledge, prior to the day set for performance, that the other party will not or cannot perform when the day arrives, to be ready to perform his part of the agreement. In this class of cases (where the other party cannot or is unwilling to perform) not only is the formality of producing and offering the money or thing to be delivered dispensed with, but also such preliminary acts, as executing a deed, note, or mortgage, or separating and designating the articles intended to be applied on the contract and the like. It is sufficient if the party has at the time the title to the land and is willing to convey, or stands willing to execute the note and mortgage, or has property at the place of the kind required which he is willing to apply in satisfaction of the contract[18]

1056, citing Voorhees v Earl, 2 Hill 288, Baker v Robbins, 2 Denio 136, and Wheaton v Baker, 14 Barb 594, Karker v Haverly 50 Barb 79, Foote v West 1 Den 544 Hartley v James 50 N. Y. 38, Lawrence v Taylor, 5 Hill 107, Holmes v Holmes 9 N. Y. (5 Seld) 525, De Lavan v Duncan, 49 N. Y. 485 Marshall v Winninger, 46 N. Y. Supp 670 s c 20 Misc 527

[16] Jewett v Earl 21 J. & S. 349

[17] Nelson v Plimpton 55 N. Y. 480, citing Frenchot v Leach 5 Cow 506, Traver v Halstad, 23 Wend 66 Colt v Ambergate 7 A. & E N S 127 and Rochester v De La Tour 2 E. & B. 678 Robinson v Tyson, 46 Pa 286

[18] This rule does not apply where things indeterminate are to be delivered upon request. In such case the vendor after a request has a reasonable time to comply according to the custom and usage of the particular business, as in the case of manufacturer who must make the goods, or where a commission merchant must go upon the market to purchase them to fill the order Here, if the vendee after a reasonable time upon a request to order the goods, does not do so, the vendor may recover damages for the breach of the contract without having any articles on hand of the kind contracted to be delivered It is sufficient for the vendor to prove his ability to have manufactured the goods or to have purchased them as the case may be See Duryea v Bonnell 18 App Div 151, s c 45 N. Y. Supp 135

§ 53. **Same subject—Rule does not apply where a new contract is made.**—The rule as to a waiver of a tender does not apply to those cases where the minds of the parties meet in making a new contract, as where a creditor is induced to wait until a subsequent date for his pay by the debtor promising to pay in money instead of grain,[1] or the creditor stated that he has no use for the money and allows the debtor to retain it.[2] In such cases the contract is satisfied by substituting another.

§ 54 **Same subject—Where the creditor is absent from the state**—A formal technical tender is not necessary if the person to whom the thing or service is due be out of the state and has no place of residence therein   Lord Coke in his Commentaries, in stating the corollary of the rule as laid down by Littleton that—"it behooveth him that made the obligation to seek him to whom the obligation is made if he be in England," etc.—said "For if he be out of the realme of England he is not bound to seeke him, or to goe out of the realme unto him.  And for that the feofee is the cause that the feoffor cannot tender the money, the feoffor shall enter into the land as if he had duly tendered according to the condition"[1]  Where a statute provides that the sheriff shall before making a levy, tender a receipt to the person from whom a tax is due, if such person is a resident of and in the county a tender is excused if the party is a non resident of the county[2]  Where a tender is necessary before a person is entitled to the possession of any thing, or to enforce any right at law or in equity, where but for a tender the right would be lost, ignorance of the other person's residence is no excuse for not making a tender[3]

§ 55. **Where a tender is unnecessary—Actions by vendor or vendee—Obligor or obligee**—The general rule, that where the acts to be performed by the respective parties to a contract are concurrent, either party, before he can maintain an action

[1] Veazy v Harmony 7 Me 91
[2] Terrell v Walker 65 N C 91
[3] Co Litt § 310, Emlen v Lehigh 17 Pa St 76 s c 86 Am Dec 518

[2] Smith v Ryan, 11 S W 647
[3] See Sage v Ranney, 2 Wend 532

for a breach, either by way of damages or for the recovery of what has been paid upon it, must have tendered performance upon his part at the time fixed, applies, as elsewhere stated, to cases where there is merely a failure to perform by the other party. It does not apply to cases where the party who is to receive the thing or service, before the time for performance, makes any declaration which amounts to a repudiation or rescission of the contract, which would render a tender so long as the position taken by him is maintained a vain and idle ceremony. Thus, where prior to the time for performance one of the parties notifies the other that he can not perform,[1] or that his wife will not sign the deed and that he will have to give up the contract,[2] or that he will not go on with the contract, or will not execute a deed, or after a reasonable time has elapsed refuses or neglects, upon request, to order goods which are to be delivered upon request,[3] or denies that he made the contract,[4] or asserts that the contract is not binding upon him, or that he will not receive the deed and that he intends to abandon the contract,[5] or that the policy is forfeited,[6] or makes any like statement or declaration. The position taken by the unwilling party must be maintained until the time for performance. Mr. Parson, in his work on contracts, said: "If one bound to perform a future act, before the time for doing it, declares his intention not to do it, this is no breach of his contract, but if his declaration be not withdrawn when the time comes for the act to be done, it constitutes a sufficient excuse for the default of the other party."[7]

So, an action may be maintained to recover damages without a tender of the residue, where goods are to be shipped

[1] Bunge v. Koop 48 N. Y. 225, Dixon v. Oliver 5 Watts 509.

Lowe v. Harwood 139 Mass. 133, s. c. 29 N. E. Rep. 538.

[2] Bluntzer v. Dewees 79 Tex. 272, Lynch v. Postlethwaite, 7 Martin 69, s. c. 12 Am. Dec. 495.

[3] Vaughan v. McCarthy 59 Minn. 199, Morange v. Morris, 3 Keys 48, Maxon v. Gates 88 N. W. Rep. (Wis.) 55.

[4] Duryea v. Bonnell 18 App. Div. 151, s. c. 45 N. Y. Supp. 135.

[5] Hampton v. Speckenagle, 9 Su. & Raw. 212.

[6] Bank of Columbia v. Hagner 1 Pet. 455, Gill v. Newell 13 Minn. 462. McPherson v. Fargo, 74 N. W. Rep. (So. Dak.) 1057.

[7] Union Cent. Ins. Co. v. Caldwell 58 S. W. Rep. (Ark.) 355.

[8] 2 Parsons on Cont. 809. Crest v. Armour, 34 Barb. 378. Scribner v. Schenkel 60 Pac. Rep. (Cal.) 860.

in separate lots and the vendee refuses to accept the first consignment,[10] or where part of the goods bargained for have been delivered and the vendee refuses to accept any more.[11] Nor is a tender necessary to lay the foundation for such action, where the party to whom performance is due does or suffers any thing to be done with the thing to be delivered by him which renders certain a failure of performance on his part when the time for performance arrives; as where a payee disposes of securities which were to be delivered upon the payment of a certain sum,[12] or, after making a contract, the vendee puts it out of his power to convey the land or deliver the property by selling it to another,[13] or consumes the articles, or negligently allows them to become deteriorated or destroyed, or in any way places himself in that position relative to the thing to be done or delivered, that it is then certain that when the time arrives for performance it will be beyond his power to do so. In such cases the party not in default has an immediate right of action for his damages, or to recover what he has paid on the contract, and he need not wait for the time for performance to pass before bringing his action. So, in order to maintain an action to recover damages for non-performance or to recover what has been paid on account of the contract, a tender of performance by the aggrieved party is not necessary, if the other party has refused or neglected to perform that which was a condition precedent to performance on the part of the aggrieved party.[14]

Where a ship was taken under an agreement to repair it in consideration of a reasonable price, and to redeliver it when completed upon the payment of such price, and the shipwright demanded an exorbitant price and gave notice that he would not redeliver the ship until his price had been paid, it was held that a tender before commencing an action founded on the breach was unnecessary, as it was incumbent

10 Azema v Levy, 5 N Y Supp 418

11 McKnight v Watkins, 6 Mo App 118

12 Scott v. Patterson, 1 Pa Dist Ct 603

13 Lowe v Harwood, 29 N. E. Rep 538, s c 139 Mass 133;

Davis v Van Wyck, 18 N Y Supp 885, Bennett v Phelps, 12 Minn 326, Wyvell v Jones, 37 Minn 68, Auxier v. Taylor, 72 N W. Rep (Iowa) 291

14 See Chln v Bretches, 42 Kan 316, Allen v Pennell, 51 Iowa 537

upon the shipwright by the terms of the agreement to have delivered his bill of reasonable charges before payment.[15]

§ 56. Same subject—Act or omission dispensing with a tender must have occurred when—Proof of ability by plaintiff unnecessary.—The act or omission relied upon as dispensing with the necessity of a tender must have occurred prior to the time fixed for performance on the part of the party alleging the default.[1] Without any such declaration, act or omission by either party before the time arrives for performance, it is the duty of both to be ready at the time appointed and tender performance. The rule is well settled that one party to a contract cannot maintain an action at law for a breach when he himself is in default. Any thing said or done by one party after the other is in default will not relate back, mend the default and create a right of action where none existed

In all the foregoing cases where a tender of performance is rendered unnecessary by the declaration, act or omission of the other party, it is not necessary in order to recover damages for a breach, or what has been paid on the contract, for the plaintiff to show that he was able to perform on his part. Where, in a case of an agreement for the exchange of certain real estate, one of the parties before the time for performance arrived wrote to the other that he would give up the contract, etc. the court said: "It was suggested that it does not appear that plaintiff was able to pay the money which he was to pay. But he was personally bound for it, and the degree of his ability at any time before he was called on to pay was no concern of the defendant. The way for the defendant to test that was to tender performance on his side conditionally upon the plaintiff performing his part of the agreement."[2]

[15] Watson v Pearson 9 Jur N S 394 11 W R 702 8 L T N S 395

[1] Bank of Columbia v Hagner, 1 Pet 455; Newman v Baker, 25 Wash L Rep 170 See Union Cent Ins Co v Caldwell, 58 S W Rep (Ark) 355, which was an action to be relieved from a forfeiture of an insurance policy

[2] Lowe v Harwood 139 Mass 133, s c 29 N E Rep 538 citing Brown v Davis 138 Mass 458

See Crest v Armour, 34 Barb 378, citing Newcomb v Brackett, 16 Mass 161 Ford v Tley, 13

**§ 57. Same subject—Action to recover the thing paid upon the contract based upon what—Action for damages based upon what.**—An action to recover the thing paid upon the contract is based upon the rescission of the contract by the aggrieved party, and which in turn is based upon the express or implied rescission of the other party; while an action for damages proceeds upon the theory that the plaintiff has not rescinded but still considers the contract as subsisting, though broken. If a contract is expressly rescinded by one party because of the default of the other, damages cannot be recovered and the party rescinding, although excused from tendering performance on his part, cannot recover what he has paid upon the contract without returning or tendering what he has received upon it.[1]

**§ 58. Same subject—Before recovering commission by real estate agent when—Before recovering possession from mortgagee—Recovering on a life insurance policy—Cancellation of lease**

Eng. C. L. 188, Inhabitants of Taunton v. Caswell, 1 Pick. 275 Smith v. Lewis, 24 Conn. 629 Frost v. Clarkson, 7 Cow. 24 Lovelock v. Franklyn, 55 Eng. C. L. 371.

To this rule there is apparently an exception. In cases where the thing sold is specific and selected, the inability of the plaintiff to perform may be shown as a defence and is admissable upon the well established principal that one party cannot recover a money judgment at law if he is in default. Thus where in a contract to convey land the vendee prior to the day for performance repudiated the contract and the vendor brings his action for damages, it may be shown that at the time of the repudiation it was impossible for the vendor to have performed on the day fixed. His inability to carry out his agreement in the future existing at the time of the repudiation was a default on his part and perform-

ance by the plaintiff would be in no way hindered by the declaration of the defendant. It would be immaterial whether the defendant at the time he repudiated the agreement, knew of the inability of the plaintiff to perform. There cannot be a waiver of, or dispensation with anything that cannot take place.

Placing it beyond his power the property which by its terms cannot be paid until after the day for performance or conveying it away without a reservation for repurchasing within the time would be such a disabling as would place the vendor in default. Of course there is a possibility that the vendor might perform but it would depend upon the voluntary act of a third person in consenting to receive the mortgage debt before it was due or reselling etc. which cannot be considered.

[1] See Ashley v. Reeves, 2 McCord § 2

—If a principal notifies his agent who is authorized to sell land, that he will not execute a deed of the land sold, a tender of the purchase price is unnecessary, either by the purchaser or agent, to enable the latter to maintain an action to recover for his services in making the sale.[1] Where a mortgagee obtains possession of the mortgaged property and unlawfully retains it, the mortgagor may maintain an action to recover the possession without tendering the amount due on the mortgage. The mortgagee has his remedy by foreclosure if he desires to subject the property to the payment of his debt.[2] Where a life insurance policy is in force at the time of the death of the insured, the death creates the relation of debtor and creditor between the company and the beneficiaries, and a tender of unpaid premiums is not necessary before bringing an action to recover on the policy. The unpaid premium is a claim which may be deducted from the amount due on the policy.[3] So where a lodge denies that the policy holder is a member and refuses a tender of an assessment, the insured loses no rights by a failure to tender subsequent assessments.[4] Where a lessor covenants to repair and allows the premises to become untenantable the lessee may maintain an action to cancel the lease without a tender of the rent in arrears. An averment of a readiness to pay is sufficient.[5]

§ 59. **Same subject—Action for conversion.**—If a mortgagee of chattels in possession or a pledgee disposes of the property in denial of the mortgagor's or pledgor's rights, neither payment nor tender of payment of the debt is a prerequisite to an action for conversion.[1] A tender implies the right of the one to whom it is made to accept and retain the thing tendered, and when a mortgagee in possession or a bailee has put it out of his power to restore the property

---

[1] Vaughan v. McCarthy, 59 Minn. 199.

[2] Soell v. Hadden, 85 Tex. 182. Baxter v. B. L. Ins. Co., 119 N. Y. 450.

[4] Supreme Lodge K. of H. v. Davis 58 Pac. Rep. (Colo.) 595.

[5] Piper v. Fletcher 88 N. W. Rep. (Io.) 380

[1] Burton v. Randall, 46 Pac. (Kans. App.) 326. Kilpatrick v. Dean 5 N. Y. Supp. 956. Lucketts v. Townsend 3 Tex. 119, Saltus v. Everett, 20 Wend. 267, Wilson v. Little, 2 N. Y. 443. Hves v. Kenyon 7 R. I. 136. See Butts v. Burnett 6 Abb. Pr. N. S. 302

no right to have the whole debt also exists; and therefore
no tender in the nature of the case can be made. A tender
in its legal signification does not comprehend an offer of that
which a party is not bound to deliver.

A bailee who hires chattels for one purpose and uses
them for another, as where, according to the familiar illustration, he hires a horse to go to one place but goes with him
to another, or where a person secures promissory notes for
the purpose of discounting them for a certain purpose but
uses them in another way, a tender of the thing received
for the use of the thing is unnecessary before bringing an
action for conversion.[2] So, where a common carrier or other
bailee, without authority, sells the goods intrusted to his
care,[3] or unqualifiedly refuses to deliver them, claiming to
be the owner, or that the bailor has no right to them,[4] or
refuses to deliver them without the payment of a sum for
which he has no valid lien,[5] or refuse for other cause than
the non payment of his charges,[6] or transports them to a
different place to prevent their coming to the possession of
the consignee,[7] or takes the property for a temporary use in
disregard of the owner's right, no tender of the bailee's
charges and a demand for the property is necessary before
bringing trover for their value. So, where an agent disposes
of property as his own, no tender of the price agreed to be
paid by the principal need be made before commencing an
action to recover for loss of profits.[8]

§ 60.  **Same subject—Exception**—But where a bailor elects
to recover the articles, a claim on the part of the bailee
of a lien for a greater sum than is rightfully due him on

---

[2] Haynes v Patterson, 95 N Y 1.

In some of the books the rule is laid down, that if the hirer returns the article before trial the conversion would be temporary
and the damages would be small, perhaps nominal Cooley on Torts, p 457

[3] Saltus v Everett, 20 Wend 267; Staat v Evans, 35 Ill 455

[4] Long Island etc Co v Fitz

patrick, 18 Hun 390; Dows v. Morewood, 10 Baro 187

[5] Bowden v Dugan, 39 Alt Rep 467 See Rice v Indianapolis etc R R Co, 3 Mo App 27

[6] Adams v Clark 9 Cush 215, 57 Am. Dec 41.

[7] Baltimore etc R R Co v O'Donnell 49 Ohio St 489, s c. 21 L R A. 117

[8] Nading v Howe, 55 N E Rep (Ind App) 1032

account of the bailment does not dispense with the necessity of a tender of the amount of his lien.[1] So, a claim on the part of a pledgee, that the transaction was an out and out sale, will not divest him of his special interest in the property or relieve the pledgor from tendering the sum advanced.[2]

**§ 61. A tender by the United States, state, county, etc., is unnecessary.**—The United States, the several states and all political subdivisions and municipalities exercising original or delegated sovereign powers need not tender money due to their loan holders. "These debts are payable at a fixed and known place of payment and at a fixed period, at which time and place the loan holder is to present his evidence of debt and receive payment." Interest ceases to accrue on the day the debt is due whether the evidence of the debt be presented for payment or not. It is obvious that public disbursing officers cannot leave their post and go around the country searching for the individuals to whom the government owe money.[1] However, if a legal demand be presented

<hr />

[1] Loewenberg v. Railway Co. 56 Ark. 439, Hoyt v. Sprague, 61 Barb. 497. In Scarfe v. Morgan, 4 M. & W. 270, the bailee claimed a lien for a general balance besides a lien for the service. See Allen v. Corby, 69 N. Y. Supp. 7.

[2] Youngmann v. Briesmann, 4 Reporter 119, 67 L. T. 642, 41 Wkly. Rep. 148. Here the formality of producing the money may be dispensed with by some act or declaration of the party who is to receive but not a tender. There is a distinction between dispensing with the formalities of a tender and a waiver of a tender.

[1] Union v. Lehigh Coal Co. 47 Pa. St. 76, s. c. 86 Am. Dec. 518. In this case the rule above stated is applied to railroad companies, with the limitation that they must show that at and since the due date, they always had on hand a sum sufficient to pay the principal and interest due. The obli-

gation sued upon was a bond—which presumably was negotiable although it is not so stated in the opinion—in which case there must be a demand, as the company could not know in whose hand the bond would be when due. All that would be required of the company in such case would be to have on the day, a sum sufficient to pay the bond and keep it separate from their other funds. Here also the court overturned the well established rule that if the debtor desires to escape paying interest he must not, after the day for payment make use of the funds intended to be used in extinguishing the obligation, by holding that it was sufficient to have continually in its general funds a sum sufficient to pay the obligation. Citing Miller v. Bank of Orleans, 5 Wheat. 504, s. c. 34 Am. Dec. 741. No reason was advanced and none exists why large

and payment is refused a tender ought to be made thereafter to the holder, in order to bar interest and costs.[2] A state need not make a tender of money paid by a purchaser of public school lands before bringing a suit to rescind the sale, or an action to recover the possession, on the ground that the land was fraudulently purchased, for the reason, as has been said, that it is presumed that the state will in its own way make restitution to any of its citizens for any loss or damage which he may have sustained without wrong or fault on his part, through the illegal and unauthorized acts of its officers, when by such acts the state has received any thing of value. The state or any political subdivision is not required to make a tender of a sum as compensation before appropriating land under the power of eminent domain.[4]

§ 62. **Common-law rule as to tender of damages — Specific articles after a breach.**—At common law a tender is not allowed where the amount of the compensation is unliquidated, whether the right to the compensation is based upon a breach of a contract or is one arising out of a tort.[1] The right of the parties to have the amount due determined by a judicial inquiry is reciprocal, and neither party is allowed to determine in advance what the amount is, and have any advantage over the other by a demand, or a tender of the amount which he may consider sufficient compensation. It may not be, perhaps, profitable to note all the cases where the damages

corporations in respect to these two points should not be bound by the same rules of law as are smaller companies.

[2] See Alexander v. Oneida County, 76 Wis. 56, where a plea to the effect that there was ample money in the treasury to pay the demand and that it now brought the money into court, etc., but no money was brought in until later, was held not to be a tender.

[3] Cameron v. State 26 S. W. Rep 869, State v. Snyder, 66 Tex. 687, s. c. 18 S. E. Rep 106. In Louisiana a resident and tax payer may maintain an action to annul a sale of school land, without making a tender of the price paid. If the sale is annulled the purchaser must look to the authority which received the purchase money. Telle v. The School Board 44 La. Ann. 365.

[4] See § 301.

[1] Sewles v. Barrett, 4 N. & M. 260, 3 D. P. C. 13; Denver Ry. Co. v. Harp 6 Colo. 420, Green v. Shurtliff 19 Vt. 592, McDaniels v. Bank of Rutland 29 Vt. 230, s. c. 70 Am. Dec. 406, Cilley v. Hawkins, 48 Ill. 308, Roberts v. Beatty 2 Pen. & W. 63. Breen v. Texas R. Co., 50 Tex. 43.

accruing upon a breach of a contract are unliquidated. It is in general true, that uncertain damages accrue upon the breach of every contract, except contracts for the payment of a definite sum in money.

After a breach of a contract to deliver a given quantity of specific articles, unless the damages are capable of being reduced to a certainty by computation, a tender cannot be made, either of the articles or of money as damaged.[2] Specific articles are of fluctuating and uncertain value, and in case of a breach of a contract to deliver such articles, it becomes necessary to determine, by evidence, their value on the day fixed for delivery. A promissory note payable in "current bank notes" is not a contract to pay money, and after a breach, the amount due being indefinite a tender can not be made.[3] So, a tender cannot be made of a sum as compensation for the breach of a contract to lease land,[4] or for the sale of land, or to make repairs,[5] or for the breach of a contract of marriage, or of a bond or, to be brief, of any contract to do anything save the payment of a definite sum of money, where after the breach, the situation of the parties or the value of the thing or duty is uncertain, or has or is subject to change[6] A tender cannot be made where the right to compensation is founded upon a trespass committed on the person or property nor in cases of libel, slan-

[2] Day v Lafferty 4 Ark 450

[3] See McDowell v Kellar 4 Coldw (Tenn) 258 citing Lawrence v Dougherty 5 Yerg 435, Gamble v Halton Peck's Rep 130, Kirkpatrick v McCulloch 3 Hun 171 and Whiteman v Childress 6 Hun 303 Under the present Federal banking law National Bank Notes must be taken at par by other National banks and their redemption at par is secured by a deposit of bonds with the general government So now they being the only bank notes in circulation it can hardly be said that bank notes fluctuate, notwithstanding gold and silver money as bullion may go above or below par Gold coin and sil-

ver coin owing to the fiat as money are equal and National bank notes being convertible into gold or silver coin or the equivalent in any legal tender money at par must of necessity be equal to legal tender money, and being equal in this way it would seem that a promissory note to pay $1,000 in National Bank notes might after default be discharged by a tender and payment into Court of $1,000 of any legal tender money

[4] Cilley v Hawkins, 48 Ill 308

[5] Dearle v Barrett 2 A & L 82

[6] See Green v Shurtliff 19 Vt 592

der, malicious prosecution, false imprisonment, criminal conversation, debauching of daughter or servant, conversion, nor for an injury to the person or property occasioned through careless and wrongful acts.[7] In fine, all damages arising by reason of tortious acts are in general uncertain in character, and fit and proper for the investigation of a court or jury.[8]

**§ 63. A tender of damages for the commission of a tort allowed when.**—In England, a tender of a certain sum by way of amends, in cases where the damages are unliquidated, has been allowed under several statutes, particularly in cases of irregularity in the method of distraining,[1] of mistakes committed by justices of the peace[2] and in the case of negligent or involuntary trespass[3] In the United States similar statutes have been enacted in many, if not all, of the states[4] In Minnesota, and perhaps some other states, a tender of a sum of money as damages or compensation, may be made in all

[7] See The East Tenn Ry Co. v. Wright, 76 Ga 532, where it is held that if a part of the goods are lost or destroyed in transit, the carrier may tender the value of the goods so destroyed or lost. In Miami Powder Co v Port Royal, 38 S Car 78, s c 21 L. R. A. 123 certain goods had been damaged in transit The carrier offered, at the point of destination, to turn over the damaged goods upon the condition that the freight be paid Trover was brought for their value The question of whether the carrier had converted the goods turned upon the point whether, if the time the goods arrived at their destination in their damaged condition the carrier had a lien for the freight charges, and the question of the existence of the lien under the circumstances, was held to depend on whether the freight exceeded the damages The Court followed a former decision in that state, upon that point (Ewart v

Kerr, Rice L. 203, 2 McMull L 141), observing however that in that case the decision was by a divided court Under the principles applied in these cases, before the refusal to deliver goods amount to a conversion, the damages must equal or exceed the freight charges, and, it follows that the party damnified may make an estimate of the damages and tender the difference (if any) between the damages and the freight charges and on the other hand the carrier may estimate the damaged and tender the goods freight free or demand a balance is the case may be

[8] See Kaw Valley v Miller 12 Kan 20; Giles v Hart, 1 Ld Raym 250 s c 3 Salk 343

[1] 2 Geo II c 19

[2] 24 Geo II c 44, 11 & 12 Vic c 44

[3] 21 Jac I c 16, s 5

[4] Clark v Hallock, 16 Wend. 607 Slack v Brown, 13 Wend 390

cases of tort[5] In New York, conversion for the wrongful delivery of goods was held not to be one to recover "damages for a casual or involuntary injury to property," where a tender of a sum of money by way of amends may be made at any time before trial.[6] An early statute in Vermont, allowing a tender to be made in all civil actions at any time prior to three days before the term at which the writ is made returnable, was held to apply to cases only where a tender may be made at common law before action brought.[7] In Missouri, under a statute allowing a tender to be made at any time after action brought, it was held that the statute did not change the common law so as to allow a tender to be made where the action is in tort for unliquidated damages.[8]

§ 64. **Where the damages are liquidated** —Where, however, damages are liquidated or capable of liquidation by mere computation, as where a contract of carriage or other bailment provide for the payment of a certain sum in lieu of the article in case it is not delivered,[1] or where a given sum in money is to be paid in specific articles, or where payment is to be made in specific articles or services at a stipulated rate,[2] a tender of the damages as fixed by the contract may be made. So, a tender may be made where the damages have been liquidated by an award[3]

Under the old common law a tender could be made of the sum named in a penal bond for the performance of a collateral agreement[4] Then the sum named was the damages, but this was at an early date changed by an act of Parliament, so that now in England and also in the United States the obligor is liable upon the bond only for the actual damages, so that now a tender cannot be made of the damages. A tender of the sum named in a bond as a penalty, it being the

[5] 1894 G S Minn c 66 § 5406, see Leis v Hodgson, 1 Colo 393 Beach v Jeffrey 1 Ill App 283

[6] Clements v New York Cent Ry 9 N Y Supp 601

[7] Green v Shurtliff, 19 Vt 592; Hart v Skinner 16 Vt 138

[8] Joyner v Bentley, 21 Mo. App 26

[1] See 9 Bac Abr Tit Tender

[2] Ferguson v. Hogan, 25 Minn 135

See Taylor v Brooklyn Ry Co, 7 N Y Supp 625, where it is held that the statutes of New York make no distinction between a tender upon an award and a tender upon a contract

[4] See 3 Bl Com 334

(P)

full amount which the obligee could recover in any event, would undoubtedly be held good and save the obligor harmless from costs, unless there were other issues or equities to be adjusted. So upon the same principle, where the maximum amount of damages for wrongfully causing the death of person is fixed by statute, a tender of the maximum amount would be good, throwing the costs upon the party entitled to recover should he be so unwise as to refuse the tender.

Where the penalty for the doing of any act may be tendered by way of amends, as where a certain penalty is imposed upon a magistrate or minister for performing the marriage ceremony for a minor without the consent of the parent or guardian, it has been held that no sum of money short of the full penalty would be sufficient amends.[5]

§ 65. **Where the damages are nominal.**—Where the damages in case the plaintiff establishes a right to any damages would by merely nominal it would seem that as far as the damages were concerned a judicial inquiry would be entirely unnecessary, and that therefore the damages would be liquidated and that a tender of such damages might be made. In an action of trover where the property was returned and accepted pending the action, it was held that the defendant could protect himself against farther costs by tendering plaintiff nominal damages.[1]

§ 66. **Not allowed by reversioner, remainderman or life tenant to co-tenant of proportion of incumbrance.**—A tender cannot be made by a reversioner, remainderman or any life tenant to his co-tenant, of his part of an incumbrance for the payment of which he as such owner is bound to contribute, for the reason that the value of the estate of the respective co-tenants are unequal and uncertain in value depending upon the age, health and physical condition of the life tenant, which value must be determined by a judicial inquiry as of the date when the co-tenant was compelled to take up the incumbrance or as of the date of the trial, if the co-tenant holding the incumbrance holds it merely as an investment

# CHAPTER II.

## THING TO BE TENDERED—MEDIUM

§ 67. **Money defined**—Money as now recognized in every civilized community, is a common arbitrary standard of value, represented and recorded on metal or other substance, with and without regard to the value of the material, and made into convenient form, and designating denominate quantities, according to an established scale, which by common consent as a medium, serves the purpose of a common equivalent of all things of value; and, regard being had for quantities, passing from hand to hand in exchange for commodities, services and the like, and receivable in final discharge of all debts. According to Sir William Blackstone, "Money is an universal medium, or a common standard, by comparison with which the value of all merchandize may be ascertained; or it is a sign which represents the respective values of all commodities."[1] Money is a generic term, embracing every description of coin or notes recognized by common consent as a representative of value, in effecting exchange of property, or in payment of debts.

§ 68. **Legal tender — Lawful money — Specie — Currency.** — Money is said to be a legal tender when it cannot lawfully be refused by a creditor, when offered in payment of a debt due him. There is a wide distinction between the terms "lawful sum in money" and "legal tender."[1] Lawful money is any money which is recognized by law as a circulating medium. It may not have any legal tender character, or even expressly declared to be receivable in payment upon any obligation. Specie originally meant copper, gold and silver coin, hard money, cash; but it has now come by general usage in the United States, to denote gold and silver coin.[2] Currency is a broader term, including coin, bank-notes and other paper-money. "Currency" means "what passes among the people" as money.[3] Mr. Justice Field said, in considering a case where a note was made payable "in specie" that the term "currency" meant paper money.[4] But this does not seem to be in accord with the generally accepted meaning of the term. The treasury officials do not use the term currency alone, when referring to the paper money of the government, but use the term "paper currency."

§ 69. **Power to issue money.**—The power to issue money and declare the extent to which it shall be current is, from the necessity of having a stable and uniform standard, an attribute of sovereignty. A power assumed very early in the history of civilized governments. Sir William Blackstone

[1] 1 Bl Com 276

[2] Hopson v Fountain 5 Hump (Tenn) 140

[3] Martin v Bott, 46 N E Rep (Ind) 151

[2] See Webb v Moore 1 T B Mon (Ky) 483

Lockey v Miller, Phill (N C) 26. Webster's Dic, Repalje & Law Dic 329 see Ehle v Bank, 24 N Y 548

[4] Trebilcock v Wilson, 12 Wall 687

said—"as money is the medium of commerce, it is the King's prerogative, as the arbiter of domestic commerce, to give it authority or make it current."[1] The Supreme Court of Indiana has said, "it belongs to every independent state to declare by law what shall be deemed money, in the business transactions of its own citizens and to regulate the value thereof, and to determine its form and denomination. Such a medium of exchange is essential to the convenience and prosperity of any civilized and commercial people."[2] Money "as such medium, has no marketable value, but possesses such standard value as the law making power has assigned to it."[3]

The people of the United States in erecting the Federal Government with central and supreme authority, declared in their fundamental law that "The Congress shall have power * * * To borrow money on the credit of the United States; * * * To coin money, regulate the value thereof and of foreign coin,"[4] and further declared that the congress shall have power "To make all laws which shall be necessary and proper for carrying into execution the foregoing powers."[5] The power is expressly denied to the states, "no state shall * * * coin money; emit bills of credit; make anything but gold and silver coin a tender in payment of debts;"[6] The sovereign privilege is further protected and hedged about with stringent laws for the punishment of counterfeiting and the making and issuing of any token or other thing similar in form, color and size of any of the forms of money of the United States.

Where a power is given to do a particular thing it is not merely a power to declare an existing thing but with the power is delegated the authority to give effect to the thing itself. The express power to borrow money on the credit of the United States, includes the power to make the notes a legal tender, and this power is as broad as the like power over a metallic currency[7] If a metallic currency be made

[1] 1 Bl Com 276

[2] Brown v Welsh 26 Ind 116, S P Wood v Bullens 6 Allen, 516

[3] Henderson v McPike 35 Mo 255 S P Warnbold v Schlet

ing 16 Iowa 211; Brown v Welch 26 Ind 116

[4] Const U S art 1, § 8

[5] Id

[6] Const U S art 1 § 10

[7] (1883) Juillard v Greenman 110 U S 421 See Metropolitan

current by proclamation at a higher rate than its intrinsic value, a tender of such money, according to its current value, is good.[8] This power has been exercised by all governments.[9] So, a government may declare any form of money to be current at a lower rate than the rate at which it had theretofore circulated.[10]

It may be stated as axiomatic that an independent state in the exercise of its sovereign power may, with or without regard to the commercial or intrinsic value of the material, declare any thing a legal tender which the necessity and exigencies of the occasion may require.[11] The question whether the conditions warrant the exercise of such power, is one to be determined by the law making power when the question of exigency arises, and is not a judicial question to be afterwards determined by the courts.[12]

§ 70   **In what medium a tender should be made in payment of a debt.**—When a person creates a debt, or any other demand which may be carried into a money judgment and thus become a debt there is an implied understanding that it will be ultimately discharged in any form of money which the government has declared to be a legal tender in payment of debts, or with that which the government may thereafter, in the exercise of its sovereign power, make a legal tender. Upon this principle the "Legal Tender Acts," were held to be constitutional when applied to contracts, for the payment of money simply created before the passage of those acts as well as to those debts created subsequent. Mr. Justice Strong observed that "Every contract for the payment of money simply is necessarily subject to the constitutional power of the government over the currency, whatever that power may be, and the obligations of the parties is therefore assumed with reference to that power."[1] The same

Bank v Van Dyke 27 N Y 145 449

[8] Bac Abr Tender (B) 2

[9] Act of U S Congress June 28 1834 Proclamation of Queen Elizabeth Act U S Congress January 18 1837 Act U S Congress February 21 1853

[10] Burlington v Potter Dyer

[11] See Legal Tender Decision also McClarin v Nesbet 2 Nott & M (S C) 519

[12] Juillard v Greenman 110 U S 450

[1] Knox v Lee 12 Wall 549 S P Juillard v Greenman 110 U S 450 Buchegger v Schultz 14 Am Law Reg (Mich) 95

principle obtained in those cases where the courts have held that there was no implication raised, to pay a debt in coin, after the passage of the legal tender acts, merely from the fact that coin was the only legal tender at the time the contract was made.[2]

A tender in payment of a debt should always be made in lawful money,[3] but, as lawful money is not always a legal tender, if objection be taken at the time of the proffer to the form of money, on the ground that it is not a legal tender, other money acceptable to the creditor, or money possessing full legal tender qualities must be produced and offered in discharge of the obligation. The amount tendered in payment need not be composed of all of one form of legal tender, but may be made up of a part of each of the various forms of money having a legal tender character, provided the amount of each form of money included in the total amount tendered, does not exceed the amount for which each is a legal tender. If more is tendered of any one form of money than would be a lawful tender, if offered alone, the whole sum may be rejected. So, if any part of a sum of money offered in payment is not a legal tender, the tender is bad. If the law has declared a certain form of money a legal tender in payment of particular obligations, a tender of that form of money on those obligations has the same effect as if made in money possessing full legal tender qualities.[4]

§ 71. **Right of a creditor to designate the form of money—Money issued under an unconstitutional law—Relying upon judicial decisions.**—Where money which is not a legal tender is offered, the creditor, being under no obligation to receive it, may declare which of those forms not a legal tender he will receive in payment, and the debtor must produce the kind demanded or fall back upon his legal right and tender that which the law has made a legal tender. Only that medium is a legal tender which has been made so by a valid law. A tender made in money declared to be a legal tender

2 (1871) Maryland v. Baltimore & Ohio R. Co., 89 U. S. 105

3 Nelson v. McVey, 83 Ind. 108; Martin v. Bott, 16 N. E. 151

4 Thorndike v. United States, 2 Mason 1; see Longmette v. Shelton, 52 S. W. Rep. (Tenn.) 1078, where it is held that unless the tender be shown to be sufficient in amount, the court will not consider the question whether the medium is a good tender.

by an act which is unconstitutional is of no avail. The maxim, "*ignorantia juris non excusat*," applies A law that is unconstitutional, or invalid for any other reason, is of no effect and cannot be relied upon as authority for the doing of an act, nor as a protection for an act done. It is the same, with regard to its force, as if no enactment had ever been passed On the other hand, it has been held, that a tenderee has a right to rely upon the decisions of the highest tribunals in the land, and, that the lien of a mortgage given to secure the debt was not discharged by a refusal of a tender made in a certain form of money, after the act making that money a legal tender had been declared to be unconstitutional as applied to certain debts,[1] and before the decision was reversed [2] The tender being insufficient according to the law as then declared [3] In New Jersey, a tender under like circumstances was held not to be good The decision of the Supreme Court of the United States, holding the legal tender acts to be constitutional as to debts created prior to the passage of those acts, and reversing the former decision of that court, was handed down after the argument of the case before the Supreme Court of New Jersey, but before a decision was reached In that case, the court observed, that a change of the law by statute is only for the future, while a change by decision is retrospective and makes the law at the time of the first decision as it is declared in the last decision, as to all transactions that can be reached by it [4]

§ 72 *Discontinuing coinage—Demonetization—Tender where a prior issue is a legal tender and a subsequent issue is not.*— Discontinuing the coinage or issue of any particular form of money does not take from it the legal tender qualities it possesses. It must be demonetized by express statute Thus the coinage of the fractional silver money of the United States was discontinued by an act of Congress in 1853, and subsidiary silver coins of the same denomination authorized to be coined thereafter in the place of the fractional silver. The law fixing the fineness and weight of the subsidiary silver coin, and the extent of their legal tender character, in no way referred to the fractional silver money theretofore coined, and the latter continued in circulation without im-

---

[1] Hepburn v. Griswold 8 Wall 157

[2] Knox v. Lee, 12 Wall 457

[3] Harris v. Jex 55 N Y 121

[4] Stockton v. Dundee 22 N J Eq 56

5

pairment of its full legal tender character until the mint
laws of 1873 expressly limited the legal tender qualities of
all silver coins of the United States to payments not exceed
ing five dollars  Where a prior issue of any form of money
is a good tender upon a contract but a subsequent issue is
not at the time payment is sought to be made, it must be
shown that the money offered was of the first issue, or the
tender will be held bad.¹  As long as a coin is distinguishable
as such, and it has not been reduced in weight by any fraudu
lent practice, it continues a legal tender, at any distance of
time from its date of issue, though it may be somewhat rare
and differing in appearance from coin of like denomination,
but of later dates²  A fiat declaring money to be current at
a lower rate than the rate at which it formerly circulated
will not effect a tender which was theretofore made in such
money at the higher rate³  Where, after an obligation to
pay money is entered into, the money is appreciated or de
preciated by the government, a tender of such currency, of
the same nominal amount called for by the contract, is good.⁴

**§ 73.  Debt defined**—The general rule is, that all debts may
be discharged by a tender and a payment of any money which
the law has declared a legal tender for that purpose, what
ever may be the character or form of the promise to pay
Sir William Blackstone defined a debt, as a sum of money
due by certain and express agreement, as, by a bond for
determinate sum; a bill or note, a special bargain, or a rent
reserved on a lease, when the quantity is fixed and specific,
and does not depend upon any subsequent valuation to settle
it  So, money judgments are debts proved by matter of
record  and whether obtained in an action founded upon a
debt or upon some obligation not a debt, they are discharg
able in the same medium¹  It has been held, however, in
those cases where the courts have directed a money judg
ment to be entered in legal tender money of a particular
description, as for gold coin, that that part of the judgment
representing the costs, was payable in any legal tender
money²

¹ Shotwell v Denman, 1 N J.
L. (Cox) 174
² Atlanta Consol Street Ry Co
v Keeny 33 L R A 824
³ Barrington v Potter Dyer 81
⁴ The case of Mixed Money,
Davis's Rep 28  See Story on

Promissory Notes Sec 394, citing
Pothier De Vente N 416
¹ See Lane Co v Oregon, 7
Wall 79
² (1872) Phillips v Speyers 49
N Y 653, (1871) s p Phillips v
Dugan 21 O St 466 (1870) Chise

§ 74. **What is a legal tender in payments made by the United States.**—All appropriations and awards made by the government, for whatever purpose, are payable in whatever is a legal tender at the time of payment,[1] unless the act or resolution authorizing the payment provides that it be made in a particular kind of currency.[2] The non interest bearing obligations known as United States notes, and all interest bearing obligations of the United States (and the interest thereon), except in cases where the law authorizing the issue of such obligation has expressly provided that the same may be paid in lawful money, or other currency than gold and silver, shall be paid in coin.[3] All the various forms of money, excepting the gold certificates and silver certificates issued by the United States (including subsidiary silver and minor coins within the limit for which they are a legal tender), are available to the government in payment for all debts and demands owing by it, other than the coin obligations above referred to. National Bank Notes may be paid out by the government for all salaries, and other debts and demands owing by the United States to individuals, corporations and associations, excepting interest on the public debt, and in redemption of the national currency.

§ 75. **In payment of dues, debts and obligations due to the United States.**—Duties on imports are payable only in gold or

---

ler v. Renois, 43 N. Y. 209 (1871); Kellogg v. Sweeney 46 N. Y. 291, (1878) Hittson v. Davenport 4 Colo 169. See Butler v. Horwitz, 7 Wall 258. Sun Cheong Kee v. United States, 3 Wall 320, Carpenter v. Atherton 25 Cal 564, to the contrary. In Arkansas at one time the fees of court officers were payable in state script. But a tender of one entire sum in state script in satisfaction of a judgment which included the fees incurred in obtaining the judgment was held bad. White v. Prigmore 29 Ark 208. Undoubtedly such a statute would apply only to a tender of fees to an officer. After a successful party had paid the fees either in legal tender or script, and included them in the judgment the right to discharge the fees included in the judgment, in state script, would be gone. But an officer with an execution would be obliged to accept script in payment of his fees for enforcing the execution.

[1] See Latham v. United States 1 Ct. of Cl. 149.

[2] See Tvers v. United States, 5 Ct. of Cl. 509.

[3] Rev. St. 1873-4 § 3693; act January 14 1875.

silver coin, or in gold or silver certificates.[1] What is a good tender in payment of other obligations, debts and taxes due to the United States, is considered elsewhere, under the title, "Forms of money in the United States and their legal tender attributes."[2]

§ 76. **In payment of debts, obligations and taxes due a state—County—Town—School district.**—A state is prohibited by the constitution of the United States from making anything a tender in payment of debts, except gold and silver coin The object of the prohibitory clause, in connection with the express powers conferred by the constitution upon the Federal Government, is to secure, without any interference by the states, a fixed and uniform standard of value throughout the United States, by which the various money transactions of the citizens and of the government, might be regulated.[1] A state may provide by law, that taxes and other obligations and debts due it, may be paid in scrip, land warrants, bonds bank notes, or in anything it may see fit.[2]

A state, although it has power to create a private corporation, has no power to direct that any part of the debts

---

[1] Under Sec 3173 U S Rev St, demand treasury notes are receivable in payment of duties

[2] See § 108 et seq

"No gold or silver other than coin of standard fineness of the United States shall be receivable in payment of dues of the United States, except as provided in section twenty three hundred and sixty six, title 'Public Lands' and in section thirty five hundred and sixty seven, title 'Coinage Weights and Measures'" The section referred to are as follows Section 2366 "The gold coins of Great Britain and other foreign coins shall be received in all payments on account of public lands at the value estimated annually by the director of the mint and proclaimed by the secretary of the treasury, in accordance with the provisions of section thirty-

five hundred and sixty four, title 'The Coinage'" Section 3567 "The pieces commonly known as the quarter, eighth, and sixteenth of the Spanish pillar-dollar and of the Mexican dollar shall be receivable at the Treasury of the United States and its several offices and the several post offices and land offices at the rate of valuation following The fourth of a dollar or pieces of two reals at twenty cents the eighth of a dollar or pieces of one real at ten cents and the sixteenth of a dollar or half a real at five cents"

See Contra § 29 p 71 Postal Laws and Regulations (1893)

[1] See Story on the Const § 1372

[2] See Woodruff v Trapnall 10 How 358

due the corporation, shall be discharged with any thing but gold and silver coin. But the prohibition of the constitution does not apply to the authority which a state has over public corporation, and a state may, by law, provide that the taxes and other obligations due to a county, city, townships, or school districts, may be paid in bank bills or in any other thing.[j] Taxes due to a state, county, town or any public corporation, are payable in legal tender money only, except in cases provided by statute. It has been held that interest coupons on county bonds which contained the recital that they are receivable in payment of county taxes, were not a good tender in payment of such taxes, in absence of any statute.[4]

§ 77. Power of state to exclude any form of legal tender money in payments to it—After a personal judgment is obtained.—A state may not by law provide that debts due it shall not be discharged in legal tender money. Although a state may provide that taxes due it may be paid with something else than legal tender money, it is not so clear in principle, that it may by law exclude any or all of the various forms of legal tender money, in prescribing what it will receive in payment of taxes due it. However, the decisions seem to uphold the states in the exercise of such right. In an action by a state against a county to recover a sum in gold and silver coin claimed to be due for taxes, it was held that the legal tender acts making United States notes a legal tender for debts, did not apply to taxes imposed by a state; taxes not being debts within the meaning of those acts.[1] The Federal Supreme Court held it was bound by the decision of the state court, holding that the state taxes were required to be paid in gold and silver. In another case where land was sold for taxes, under a state law which required that the redemption money should be paid in specie, it was decided that a purchaser at a tax sale, while such law is in force, acquires a vested right to receive specie in payment; and that a law which provides for the redemption, in legal tender notes,

[j] Bush v Shipman, 5 Ill 186, see Wise v. Rogers, 24 Gratt (Va) 169.

[4] Morgan v Pueblo & Arkansas V R R, 6 Colo 478

[1] (1867) Lane County v Oregon, 7 Wall 71

from sales for taxes, made while such law was in force, was unconstitutional.[2] In the case last but one, above referred to, which arose in Oregon under state laws which required the sheriff to pay over to the county treasurer, the state and school taxes "in gold and silver coin;" and that the several county treasures shall pay over to the state treasure the state tax "in gold and silver coin," the Supreme Court of the United States, in considering the power of the states to levy taxes, was of the opinion that in respect to property, business, and persons, within their respective limits, their power of taxation remained the same as it was prior to the adoption of the constitution of the United States; that it was a concurrent power with that of the United States, and except in those cases of a tax on the same subject by both governments, where the supreme authority of the United States must be preferred, the power of the state was absolute; and, that if "the condition of any state, in the judgment of its legislature, requires the collection of taxes in kind, that is to say, by the delivery to the proper officers of a certain proportion of products, or in gold and silver bullion, or in gold and silver coin, it is not easy to see upon what principle the national legislature can interfere with the exercise, to that end, of this power, original in the states, and never yet surrendered."[1] But the decision turned upon the point that taxes were not "debts" within the meaning of the legal tender acts If a state goes into court and obtains a personal judgment, the judgment becomes a debt and it may be discharged in any legal tender money (including legal tender notes)[4]

§ 78. **What may be tendered by a state in payment of its debts.**—It is undisputed that in absence of express terms in a contract providing for payment in a particular form of money, that whatever the government has made a legal tender in payment of debts, must be received in payment of any debt owing by a state, county, town, or municipality But the question whether a state, or any of its political subdivisions or municipal corporations, may issue bonds or other

---

[2] (1870) Billings v. Riggs, 56 Ill 483

[3] Lane County v. Oregon, 7 Wall 71

[4] Rhodes v O'Farrell, 2 Nev 60

evidences of debts, which provide in terms, for payment in a particular form of money, such as gold coin, is unsettled. In Kentucky, under a statute authorizing a municipality to issue bonds, which is silent as to the mode of payment, it has been held that the municipality may make its bonds payable in gold coin.[1] But in Mississippi, under a law authorizing the issue of bonds by the levee board of that state, without any limitation as to the form of money in which the bonds were to be payable, it was held by the Supreme Court of that state, that bonds, which were in terms made payable in gold coin, were void.[2] The case was removed, by writ of error, to the Supreme Court of the United States, where it was decided that the bonds were solvable in the money of the United States, whatever its description, and not in any particular kind of money, and consequently were not void. The question, whether a state may by law provide that its bonds, or those issued by any of its political subdivisions, shall be paid in any particular form of money, was not decided. In California, under a statute authorizing the city to issue bonds payable "in gold coin or lawful money of the United States," a judgment of the lower court, affirming the validity of certain bonds alleged to be issued under authority of that statute, which were made payable "in gold coin of the United States of America of the present standard of weight and fineness," was reversed.[3] But the same court in a later case, where the same language—gold coin or lawful money of the United States—was used in the statute authorizing the issue of the bonds then in question, it was decided that the city authorized to issue the bonds had the option to make the bonds payable in gold coin or in lawful money.[4] Here the court in its reasoning, proceeded along the line, that as gold coin was lawful money, the statute really meant nothing, unless it was the legislative intent to give the city the option to name either mode of payment in the bond, as a bond payable in money, generally, could also be discharged in gold coin or lawful money

[1] Parson v. Board of Commissioners 97 Ky 119 s c 30 S W Rep 17, s p Judson v Bessemer 87 Ala 240 s c 4 L R A 742

[2] Woodruff v State, 66 Miss 298

[3] Skinner v Santa Rosa, 107 Cal 468, s. c 29 L R A 512

[4] Murphy v San Louis Obispo, 39 L R A 444

§ **79. Bank notes—When objected to—Refusal no ground for relief in equity—Offer to agent, clerk or officer.**—The bills or notes of a bank, or bank notes or bank-bills as they are commonly called, are generally treated as money in the various commercial transactions. They are not money in the strict sense of the term; they pass current as if they were money only by virtue of a general understanding or tacit agreement to that effect.[1] They have no legal tender qualities. The rule was early established in England, that a tender made in bank notes was good, if not objected to, at the time of the offer, that they were not money,[2] and the rule was applied both to the notes of the Bank of England[3] and the Bank of Bristol or "county bank-bills."[4] The same rule obtains in the United States, and there is no difference between the tender of national bank-notes[5] and those of state banks[6] A tender of bank bills, if objected to at the time, is bad, and such tender will not furnish ground to authorize a court of equity to decree a redemption, where, in consequence of such refusal, a redemptioner is not able to make a legal tender afterwards, before the right to redeem expires[7]

[1] See Woodruff v Mississippi, 162 U S 300; United States Bank v Bank of Georgia, 10 Wheat 333; Northampton Bank v Balliet, 8 W & S 311.

[2] (1790) Wright v Reed, 3 T R 554 See Donaldson v. Benton, 4 Dev & B 435

[3] Brown v. Soul 4 Esp 267, Gingley v Oakes 2 B & P 526

[4] Lockyer v Jones, Peak 180 N , Tiley v Courtier 2 C & J 16 N , Polglass v Oliver, 2 C & J 15, Owenson v Morse, 7 T R 64 Gillard v Wise 4 Barn & Cress 134

[5] Koehler v Buhl 94 Mich 196, s c 54 N W. Rep 157, Wood v Bangs, 48 Atl Rep (Del) 189, Lowry v McGhee, 8 Yerg (Tenn) 242

[6] Ball v Stanley, 5 Yerg (Tenn) 199, s c 26 Am Dec 263, Cooley v Weeks, 10 Yerg 112,

Fosdick v Van Hunson, 21 Mich 576; Lacy v Wilson, 24 Mich 479, Beebe v Knapp, 28 Mich 70, Mc Dowell v Keller, 4 Coldw 266, Corbit v Bank of Smyrna 2 Hari (Del) 235, s c 30 Am Dec 635, Welch v. Frost 1 Mich 30, s c 48 Am Dec 692, New Hope v Perry, 52 Am Dec 452 Bank of United States v Bank of Georgia, 10 Wheat 333 Jennings v Mendenhall 7 Oh St 257, Spann v Baltzell, 1 Flo 301, Wheeler v Knaggs, 8 Ohio 169, Seawell v Henry 6 Ala 226, William v Rorer 7 Mo 556, Noe v Hodges, 3 Hump 162, Snow v Parry, 9 Pick 539, Hallwell v Howard, 13 Mass 235, Keyes v Jasper, 5 Ill 305, Cummings v Putnam 19 N H 569 Contra Moody v Mahurin, 4 N H 296,

[7] (1835) Lowry v McGhee, 8 Yerg (Tenn) 242

The power of a collecting agent is limited to receiving for the debt of his principal that which the law declares to be a legal tender, or which is by common consent considered and treated as money, and passes as such at par,[8] and where such agent fails to object to current bank bills on the ground that they are not money, that objection is waived and the tender is good. So a clerk, being a person to whom a legal tender may be made, from the nature of his employ ment and the general powers he possesses as to the business entrusted to his care, has discretionary power to receive current bank bills in payment.[9] So, it has been held that a tender of current bank bills to a clerk of court, marshall, sheriff, constable, justice of the peace, or any officer author ized to receive money in redemption of property sold on judicial sales, or in satisfaction of judgment or on an execu tion, is good, and protects the defendant or party offering them, unless they were refused as not being a legal tender.[10]

---

[8] Ward v Smith, 7 Wall 656, see Wickliffe v. Davis, 2 J J Marsh 69.

[9] Hoyt v. Byrnes, 11 Me 175

[10] Welch v Frost, 1 Mich 30, People v Mayhew, 26 Cal 656, see Dougherty v Hughes, 3 Green 92, see also Griffin v Thompson, 2 How 244 McFarland v Gwin, 3 How 717 Prather v. State Bank, 3 Ind 756, Armsworth v Scotten, 29 Ind 195, see Chamblin v Blair, 58 Ill 385 Billing v Riggs, 56 Ill 483

*Note 1 No waiver by failing to object to uncurrent bills —* "The doctrine that bank bills are a good tender unless objected to at the time on the ground that they are not money, only applies to current bills, which are redeemed at the counter of the bank on presentation and pass at par value in business transactions at the place where offered Notes not thus current at their par value, nor redeemable on presen tation, are not a good tender to

principal or agent, whether they are objected to at the time or not." Ward v Smith 7 Wall. 417

If a tender is made in depreci ated bank notes the refusal to accept may be presumed to arise from the facts of such deprecia tion Cockerell v Kirkpatrick, 9 Mo 688

*Note 2 Loss by depreciation — When insolvency of bank is un known at the time of the tender —* Where bank bills are current and circulate at par and are redeem able at the time of the tender, and are sufficient to satisfy the debt at that time, the debtor is not to lose by any subsequent depreciation (Anonymous, Hayw. [N C] 184) unless, on its refusal the debtor mingles the bills with his other money, or uses them for his own benefit, and thereby abandons the tender Then he must pay that which is money Downman v. Downman, 1 Wash. 29

If a bank had actually failed, though unknown to both parties, the tender is not good, though the notes were current at the place of the payment at the time. This question was much discussed by Mr. Chancellor Walworth in a case where bank notes of a bank then insolvent were paid out by another bank upon a check. He said "The actual loss had been sustained by the failure of the bank while the plaintiffs in error were the holders and owners of the bill, and it is a maxim of the law that the loss is to him who was the owner at the time such loss happened, if both parties were ignorant of the loss at the time of making their contract. Hence, the one party intended to pay and the other supposed he was receiving the bill of a bank which was redeeming its bills at its counter. Supposing the inquiry had been made of the defendant 'Do you expect to sustain the loss if the bank should fail before you shall have parted with this bill?' The answer, according to the implied understanding of the parties, arising from the nature of the transaction and considering the bills of specie-paying banks as money would certainly have been in the affirmative. But, if he had been asked 'Do you understand that you are to bear the loss if it should hereafter be ascertained that the Franklin Bank has now actually failed and stopped payment?' he would unquestionably have answered 'No, in that event, as the loss will have happened while you was the owner of the bill, natural equity requires that you should bear it; and I shall expect you to take back the bill and give me one which is good.'"

Ontario Bank v. Lightbody, 13 Wend. 105; s. p. Harley v. Thornton, 2 Hill (S. C.) 509, Owenson v. Morse, 7 Term. R. 65, see Cambridge v. Allenby, 6 Barn. & Cressw. 373, Emily v. Lye, 15 East. 7; Ex parte Blackburn, 10 Ves. 204, Fogg v. Sawyer, 9 N. H. 365. Contra, Bayard v. Shunk, 1 Watts & Serg. 92, Young v. Adams, 6 Mass. 182, Scruggs v. Gass, 8 Yerg. 175, Lowrey v. Morrell, 2 Porter (Ala.) 282.

*Note 3. Loss falls upon whom when accepted by agent.— When used by agent.*— If bank bills are received by a collecting agent or other person authorized to receive payment for and on behalf of his principal, the loss occasioned by a subsequent depreciation falls upon the creditor the same as if the principal had received them in person, but, if the agent used the funds, so received, in his own business, as where a bank passes the funds so received to the credit of the principal and mingles the money with that of the bank, the agent must account to the principal for the full amount received in legal tender money. The agent having had the benefit of the principal's money at a time when it was at par will not be allowed to profit by the depreciation by substituting the same or the other uncurrent funds.

*Note 4. Tender of Bank—Notes in rescission.*— For the purpose of rescinding a contract, it is not necessary to tender back the identical bank-bills since in law one dollar is the equivalent of any other dollar. Michigan Cent. R. R. Co. v. Dunham, 30 Mich. 128. If after payment the particular bank bills become depreciated, the identical bills may be returned, if, at all times since the payment, they have been in the possession of the payee, but, if they have been paid away, then legal tender money or money not a legal tender to which no objection is taken must be tendered in return. To allow a party desiring to rescind a contract, to secure an equal amount of other notes of the same bank, after their depreciation, and tender them back, would, as was said in a case of a tender of Confederate notes under like circumstances, "afford plaintiff the opportunity to barter or make merchandise of those received by him, and afterwards substitute or replace them at small cost, and thus actually realize the amount claimed in addition to a recovery from defendant." Emerson v. Lee, 18 La. Am. 134.

*Note 5. Effect of an acceptance of bank notes on the liability of a surety.* — If bank bills are received upon an obligation for the payment of which some third person has assumed the obligation of a surety such person will be discharged regardless of whether the bank bills were received as absolute payment or conditionally, or whether the bank issuing the paper was insolvent at the time. Sureties are entitled to have the obligation on the due day immediately paid in cash, and the holder is not at liberty to accept anything which may or may not be paid at a future time at the risk of the surety. The same rule applies to a payment by check whether the check is good at the time or not, or is good at the time but before presentation the drawer fails unless, perhaps the worthlessness of the check be discovered on the day, and a new demand made for payment before it is too late.

*Note 6. Tender to bank of bills issued by it — After claim has been prosecuted to judgment.* — When a debt is due a bank, the debtor has a right to tender in payment of such debt the bills issued by the bank to which the debt is due. Commercial Bank v. Thompson, 15 Miss. 113, Bailey v. Bacon, 26 Miss. 155, Exchange Bank v. Knox, 19 Gratt. 739, Union Bank v. Ellicott, 6 Gill & J. 363, American Bank v. Wall, 56 Me. 167, Dunlap v. Smith, 12 Ill. 399, Niagara Bank v. Roosevelt 9 Cow. 409. And the bank is bound to receive them at par, as equivalent to gold and silver coin (Blount v. Windley 68 N. C. 1, Northampton Bank v. Balbet, 8 Watts & S. [Pa.] 311, or any legal tender. Banks issue their notes with the intent that they shall circulate as currency and when received back into the bank are reissued and kept in circulation as money and never being over due or subject to any equities the bank is bound to redeem them at their face or nominal value on presentation by any person at any distant of time from the issue thereof. Being thus endowed by the bankers themselves with this characteristic of money and put out by them as money it is but reasonable that they should be required to treat them as such, when tendered to them in payment of debts due them. But when a bank has prosecuted a claim to judgment the authorities are not agreed that the judgment debtor may discharge the judgment with the notes issued by the bank.

Where a judgment debtor, on motion, applied to the court to be allowed to bring into court the bills of the judgment creditor (a bank) and to have satisfaction entered, the court denied the motion, observing that the notes were not cash, and could not be brought into court as such. Coxe v. State Bank, 3 Halst. 172, s. c. 14 Am. Dec. 417. See Hallowell v. Howard, 13 Mass. 235. Contra Abbott v. Agricultural Bank, 19 Miss. 405. And, in another case, where the notes of a bank were tendered in payment of a judgment due it, the court said that a debt not in judgment could not be set off against a judgment, and, that when a judgment was ripe for execution, there can be but one answer, to wit, payment pure and simple. Thorp v. Wegefarth, 56 Pa. St. 82. Here however, the bank-bills had lost their character as a circulating medium, the bank having failed prior to the time of the tender. The court observed that there was no proof offered tending to show that the judgment debtor was the holder of the bills previous to the closing of the doors of the bank. As between the bank and the judgment debtor, in absence of all questions arising in case of insolvency of the bank, the rule that the debtor may pay the judgment in the bills of the bank would be in harmony with the rule applicable to payment to the bank of its own circulating notes prior to suit. See Northampton Bank v. Balliet, 8 W. & S. 311. In some states the right to discharge a debt due to or a judgment obtained by any bank, in the notes of such bank, has been expressly given by statute.

*Note 7. On obligations transferred to bank — Transfer by bank after maturity of debt — Payment to bank of legal tender money by surety — In depreciated currency — Transfer by bank before maturity.* The right to discharge a note held by a bank in the bills of the bank, is the same whether the note or other demand was given to the bank, or transferred to it by a third person, (Wright v. Taylor, 3 Gilm. 195) and it has been held that the right cannot be defeated by a transfer of the note by the bank after maturity. If, however, a surety or endorser has been compelled to take up a note or bill and he pays the bank legal tender money therefore, such right of the maker is gone. But if the surety or endorser at or after maturity, discharges the note in the depreciated paper of the bank, the maker thereby acquires the right to discharge the note in the same kind of funds. Wright v. Taylor, 3 Gilm. 195.

If the bank bills further depreciate after the payment by the surety or endorser, then sufficient bills, as will be equal in value to the nominal amount of the note must be tendered, or legal tender money must be produced and offered in payment.

The right before maturity to discharge a debt due a bank in the bills of such bank continues only so long as the bank is the owner of the debt or judgment. Where a claim had been assigned by a bank to the United States, Mr. Chief Justice Marshall said "A note given to pay money generally, is a note to pay in legal currency, and the right to discharge it with a particular paper, is an extrinsic circumstance depending upon its being due to the person or body corporate responsible for that paper, which right is terminated by a transfer of the debt." United States v Robertson, 5 Peters 660

*Note 8. Right to tender bank-bills after insolvency of bank—Bills acquired after insolvency—Bank may tender what.* — In case of the insolvency of a bank of issue as has been shown, the circulating notes of such bank immediately lose their character as money, and become merely a note for the payment of the money. Under such circumstances the insolvency must be taken into consideration, in determining whether they continue to be a good tender to the bank in payment of a debt due it. The general rule is, that in case of the insolvency of the bank its notes or bills are nevertheless a good tender to it provided the bank-bills came to the hand of the debtor before the insolvency. A bank cannot by an assignment of all its effects deprive the debtor of his right to pay in the notes of the bank. Blount v Windley 68 N C 1. Nor will the appointment of a receiver. Morse v Chapman 24 Ga 249, American Bank v Wall 56 Me 167

So it has been held that a tender of the bank-notes of an insolvent bank which would have been good if made upon the original instrument will be equally good upon a note given in renewal to the assignee of the bank Ewing v Anderson 3 Tenn Ch 364. But a tender to an assignee if kept good would only go to the extent of stopping the interest. After the insolvency a credi-

tor cannot buy up and tender to a bank or to the assignee or receiver, its bills in payment of his obligation to it. Diven v Phelps, 34 Barb 224, Dickson v. Evans, 6 T R 57; Clark v Hawkins, 5 R I 219; Exchange Bank v. Knox, 19 Gratt. 739, Finney v Bennett, 27 Gratt 365. The insolvency of a bank, fixes the status of its debts and the rights of its creditors, preventing them from getting a preference in payment, (Thorp v Wegefarth 56 Pa St 82) which could not be prevented if creditors were at liberty to buy up and treat that as money in paying their debts to the bank, which in contemplation of law ceased to be a circulating medium the instant the bank became insolvent. It "is not a question of set off, but a question as to the right of a bill holder to use the bills of the bank as a legal tender equivalent to gold and silver coin, in satisfaction of a debt due the bank." Blount v Windley 68 N C 1

However if a contract with a bank provided for payment in its notes these required after insolvency may be tendered at its maturity in satisfaction of the obligation for that is the thing in which payment is to be made. If not paid or tendered at maturity the obligation becomes a money demand and thereafter such notes could not be used in discharging the debt

A bank may tender in redemption of its bills any money which the law has made a legal tender. Where the law governing state banks required that it shall not at any time suspend or refuse to pay its bills in gold or silver coin a tender by a bank in redemption

of its bills, or the United States
legal tender notes was held good.
Reynolds v. Bank of State, 18
Ind. 467.

*Note 9. On obligations payable
in bank-bills — In current bank-
bills — Option to pay in bank-
bills — On contracts where value
of bank-bills is not stated — Contemporaneous parole agreement
to accept bank bills — Contemporaneous collateral agreement.
Tender of bank bills after default —* The authorities are almost
unanimous in holding that a note
or other obligation made payable
in bank bills, is not for the payment of money but is for the
delivery of specific articles. Lockey v. Miller, Phill. L. (N C) 26,
Patton v. Hunt, 61 N C 163,
Lange v. Kohne, 1 McCord, (S
C) 115; Morris v. Edwards 1
Ohio 189, Contra Spann v. Baltzell, 1 Fla 301. So, an obligation for the payment of a certain
number of dollars, with the
proviso that it may be discharged
in bank-notes, is a contract to
pay that sum in such paper.
Mitchell v. Waring, 1 J Marsh
233. Bank-notes are not money
in the strict sense, being treated
as money only by common consent, and a note payable in bills
of a particular bank, or in bank
bills generally is not negotiable.
Patton v. Hunt 61 N C 163.

Current bank notes are such as
are convertible into legal tender
money at the counter of the bank
where issued and pass at par in
the ordinary business transactions of the country. Pierson v.
Wallace, 7 Ark 282. If the obligation calls for payment in the
"current bank-money of the state
of Mississippi (Hopson v. Fountain, 5 Hump [Tenn] 140) or
current bank bills of any particu-

lar description, only those particular bills specified are a good
tender upon the obligation. If,
before the time for payment arrives the bills described cease to
be current a tender of them is
not good. If a note or other obligation is payable "in current
bank money," it may be discharged by a tender and payment of
the notes of any bank, which are
current and circulating at par.
Lockey v. Miller Phill L (N C)
26, s p McNulty v Bell, 1 Yerg
(Tenn) 502 s c 24 Am Dec 164.
In case of a breach of such contract the measure of damages is
the value of the bank-bills at the
time of the breach. (Lockey v
Miller, Phill L [N C] 26, Patton
v Hunt, 61 N C 163, Huston v
Noble 4 J J Marsh 130, Hopson
v Fountain, 5 Humph [Tenn]
140, Morris v Edwards, 1 Ohio,
189,) which is a matter of little difficulty, the damages being liquidated. Here, the value of the thing
in which payment is to be made
being fixed, that is bank-bill
circulating at par and worth one
hundred cents on the dollar,
legal tender money of the same
nominal amount as expressed in
the contract may be, on or after
the day fixed for payment, tendered in lieu of the bank bills.

Where a note for the payment
of a sum of money contains a
stipulation that it may be paid in
bank bills, the payor has the option of tendering legal tender
money or bank-bills and in such
case as well as those cases where
the contract is to pay an amount
of money in bank bills if nothing
is said as to the quality or character of the bank bills the payor
may tender bank notes that are
below par, taking care to tender
enough as will be equal in value

§ 80. **Tender of things other than money in payment of a debt—Goods—Gold dust—Bullion—City orders—County orders—Auditor's warrants—Post Office order—Script and warrants to political division issuing them.**—If a person produces and offers that which is not money in discharge of his debt, the offer does not constitute a tender even though the objection, that the thing offered is not money, be not taken at the time. An offer of "baled cotton" in payment of a debt is not good,[1] nor is an offer of goods, notwithstanding a surety stands by and offers to take the goods.[2] Gold dust has no

to the nominal amount of money expressed in the contract. Where a contract is to pay a certain amount of bank-bills, and nothing is said as to their value, the nominal amount in bank-bills of a going bank may be tendered, whether the bills are at or below par as compared with legal tender money. In the latter case, evidence being required to determine the value of the bills, the damages are unliquidated and a tender cannot be made either at maturity or after a breach in legal tender money. If the obligation is to pay in money, but before the day for the payment arrives the promisee agrees to receive bank bills in payment, a tender of the bank-bills at the day would be good by reason of the previous waiver. Warren v. Mains, 7 Johns 476.

But in such case the contract being payable in money, and bank-bills being receivable only by reason of a waiver as to the medium of payment, the bills tendered must be the equivalent of legal tender money, that is, bills that are current, redeemable and circulating at par. Evidence of a contemporaneous parole agreement between the maker and payee, that a note payable in

money generally may be paid in bank notes, or in any notes, is inadmissible to vary the legal effect of the note. Racine County Bank v. Keep, 13 Wis 233. But evidence is admissible of a contemporaneous collateral agreement, as between the maker and the payee or transferee, whereby it was agreed by the transferee (a bank) that it would redeem in gold, within a certain time, the notes of another bank which it had used in discounting the note. But the contract, and a tender of such notes, can only be shown as a defence by way of a counter claim in an action brought by the transferee. Racine County Bank v. Keep 13 Wis 209.

Where a note is payable in bank-bills a tender of such bank bills must be made on the day the note falls due. After the day a tender of such notes is insufficient. Huston v. Noble 4 J. Marsh 130. On such failure the obligation becomes a money demand. Morris v. Edwards 1 Ohio 189. The rules governing in such cases are no different from those applicable to notes made payable in any other specific articles.

[1] Lang v. Waters 47 Ala 624.
[2] Wilson v. McVey 83 Ind 108.

established value and is not a legal tender.[3]   Nor is bullion,
gold and silver bars, old spoons and rings.[4]

City orders are not good,[5] either between individuals, or between the city and its creditors.   This is so in the latter
case, even if it is the custom of a city to draw orders on its
treasurer in favor of each creditor, and a contractor at the
time of entering into a contract knew of the custom, and
rejects an order tendered, not on the ground that it is not
money, but on the ground that more is due.   Knowledge of
such a custom does not lay a creditor under any obligation
to comply with it   When he refuses an order "he thereby puts
the town on its guard, and those who have the management
of its prudential concerns, may then protect themselves from
damages by a suit, by a legal tender of the amount due."[6]

So, a tender of an order on a township treasurer is not
good![7]   Nor is a tender of county orders,[8] state auditor's warrants,[9] or post office orders.[10]   City scripts, warrants or other
evidence of a debt are not a good tender in payment of taxes,
assessments, or any obligation due a city or other political
division issuing them, unless there is a statute permitting
their use for that purpose[11]

§ 81.   Same subject—Creditor's overdue note—Bills of insolvent bank—Due bills—Receipt for account—Bills and notes of
third persons—Orders on third persons—Certificate of deposit—
Bonds to contractors, material men and laborers.— A tender of a
creditor's over due promissory note in payment of a debt due
him is not good[1]   In Massachusetts the same rule has been

---

[3] McCune v Erfort 43 Mo 131

[4] Hart v Flynn 8 Dana 191
In this case the note was payable
"In gold and silver"

[5] City of Helena v Turner, 36
Ark 577, Comstock v Gage 91
Ill 328

[6] Benson v Carmel 8 Me (8
Greenl) 110

[7] Lull v Cur 10 Mich 397

[8] Perry v Colquett, 63 Ga 311
See Howell v Hogins 37 Ark
110, where they are held a good
tender in payment of taxes

[9] Commonwealth of Kentucky

v Rhodes, 5 T B Mon 318

[10] Gordon v Strange 1 Exch
177, 11 Jur 1019

[11] Dubuque v Miller, 11 Iowa
583

[1] Baker v Walbridge 14 Minn
469, Cary v Bancroft 14 Pick
315 Bellows v Smith, 9 N H
285 Allen v Hartfield 76 Ill 358
Wilmarth v Mountford 4 Wash
C C 79 Bell v Ballance 1 Dev
L 391 Eiley v Mason, 6 Md
37, Thorp v Wegefarth 56 Pa
St 82 Dehon v Stetson 9 Met
341 William v Dooley 53 Ga 71

held to apply to a tender to a bank of its circulating notes,[2] but in New York the contrary has been held to be the law.[3] On this more is said elsewhere. Bank bills of a bank which has failed, although unknown to both parties, are not a good tender, as by the failure of the bank they have lost their character as money.

A due bill issued by the creditor is not a good tender to him, nor is a receipt for an account due from him, nor is the due bill or promissory note of a third person.[4] So an order on a third person,[5] or a draft accepted or unaccepted by the payee is not good.[6] A certificate of deposit issued by a bank is not a good tender.[7] However, such a tender has been held good in absence of an objection that the certificate was not lawful money,[8] but it is a questionable doctrine. The ordinary obligations of a bank to pay money, other than its circulating notes, ought not and in fact do not stand on any different principle than those of a private person. A certificate of deposit is not distinguishable, in legal effect, from a due bill payable in money, given by an individual. Where a contractor agrees to take his pay in bonds, notes, or anything other than money, a tender of the thing agreed to be paid, to the contractor or a subcontractor, is good. Material men and laborers however are not bound to accept a tender of anything except money, and the owner, to protect his property from liens, must tender money to them, and look to his contractor for his redress.

§ 82. Same subject—Exception to rule—Bank checks—Waiver —Refusal without specifying the objection not a waiver.— To the rule that a tender of that which is not money is not good, regardless of whether the objection be made at the time of the offer, that the thing offered in payment is not money or a legal tender, there is an exception in the case of a tender of a bank check. The general rule is, that an offer

2 Hallowell & Augusta Bank v. Howard, 13 Mass. 235.

3 Niagara Bank v. Roosevelt, 9 Cowen 409. Bruen v. Receiver etc. 9 Cowen 413 n.

4 Hull v. Pettit. 66 S. W. Rep. (Ky.) 188.

Hull v. Appel 67 Conn. 585 s. c. 35 Atl. 524.

6 Collier v. White 67 Miss. 133.

7 Dougherty v. Hughes, 3 Green 92.

8 Gradle v. Warner 29 N. E. (Ill.) 1118.

to pay in a bank check is not a sufficient tender[1]  Nor, is an offer of a certified check.[2]  But it has long been settled, both in England and America, that a tender of a bank check in payment is good, where it is refused, not on the ground that it is not lawful money, but upon some other ground which is not well taken.  Mr. Greenleaf said "If a tender is made in a bank check, which is refused because it is not drawn for so much as the creditor demands, it is a good tender."[3]  So, where the check was refused because the creditor had sold the property to some one else,[4] or, on the ground that he would not accept the award,[5] or that it is not made in time,[6] it is a good tender as far as the medium of payment is concerned.

It has been said "that mere silence is held to be a waiver of objections in the case of current bank notes, for the reason that they constitute the common currency of the country, and are, by all classes, paid out and received as money, which is a reason that does not fully apply to bank check,"[7] and, it would seem to be founded upon the better reason, to hold that a refusal to receive a check in payment without making a specific objection, does not constitute a waiver[8]  If a creditor undertakes to specify objections other than to the manner of making payment, it is reasonable to suppose that, but for those specified, the tender of the check would be acceptable.  While if he merely refuses it without giving his reasons, it is evident he does not want to receive the check at all  In the first case the debtor is met with some objection based on a reason which leads him to believe that tendering money would be thereafter an idle ceremony.  While, in the latter case, the creditor, whatever may have been his reason

[1] Collier v White, 67 Miss 133, s c 6 So Rep 618 Grussy v Schnider, 50 How Pr 134, Sloan v Petrie 16 Ill 262, Pogue v Greenlee's Adm'r 22 Gratt 724. Harding v Commercial Loan Co 84 Ill 251, DePoel v Shutt, 78 N W Rep (Neb) 288

[2] Larsen v Breene 12 Colo 180

[3] Greenl. on Ev. § 601; s p. Jones v Arthur, 8 D P. C 442, 4 Jur 859; Bonaparte v Thayer

52 Atl. (Md) 196, Pershing v Feinberg, 52 Atl Rep (Pa) 22

[4] McGrath v Gevner, 26 Atl Rep 502

[5] Walsh v St Louis Exposition, 101 Mo 534

[6] Duffy v O'Donovan 46 N Y 223

[7] Jennings v Mendenhall, 7 Ohio St 257

[8] See Jones v Arthur 8 Dowl P C 442

for refusing the tender of the check, does not say anything tending to mislead the debtor, who can immediately overcome the effect of a refusal of the check by producing and tendering that which cannot be legally refused

§ 83. **Stamped checks—Willingness to draw a check—Check of third parties—Necessary funds in hands of depositary—Funds subject to lien.**—If the revenue laws of the country require checks to bear a stamp, it must be so stamped and the stamp cancelled according to law, before it is tendered. A check must be fully executed ready for delivery, so that it may be legally used. Announcing a willingness to draw a check is not good. A tender of a bank check to be good in any case, must be that of the debtor. A check drawn by a third person will not do.

Where a debtor tenders his check, he must have, at the time of the tender, sufficient funds with the depositary to meet it. If there is a total absence of funds or the amount on deposit is less than the amount of the check the tender is not good, and it will not avail the debtor that he had funds elsewhere which he intended to deposit to meet the check, or, that the banker had promised to take care of it unless the latter had actually placed the required amount to the debtor's credit prior to the time of the offer of the check. Failing in this, the tenderee may show that a tender was not in fact made by proving that the tenderor was not ready at the time, regardless of all questions of waiver by failing to object to the check at the time it was offered to the tenderee. So if the debtor has funds on deposit but has put other checks out which cover in part, or the entire balance necessary to meet the check offered, the tender is not good. A creditor is not bound to enter into a race of diligence with other creditors holding checks. So if the funds on deposit are subject to a lien of the bank for a debt due it, the offer of the check would not be good. The question whether the bank would have waived its lien is immaterial. There must be no question as to the right of the tenderee to the funds on deposit.

§ 84. **Dishonored checks—Second presentation—Kind of funds on deposit.**—If a check be not immediately honored on presentation, the creditor may return it to the debtor. The

creditor is not bound to retain the check and present it a
second time, on the assurance by the debtor that the de
positary will then honor it.  If a second presentation could
be required, so could a third.  With the question whether the
depositary rightfully or wrongfully refused to pay the check,
the creditor has no concern.  If wrongfully refused the debt
or has his remedy against the depositary for damages, which
if it caused the loss of the property which the debtor was
seeking to redeem, might be considerable.

A party, drawing upon another, must provide for payment,
the kind of funds for which he draws.  A drawee is not bound
to pay other and different funds than those placed in his
hands by the drawer; unless the funds deposited were passed
to the credit of the depositor, at the current rate, making an
account payable simply in dollars and cents.  If the deposit
is in depreciated currency, and a check is drawn which does
not designate the character of the fund, but calls for a given
number of dollars and cents, the holder has a right to de
mand its payment in legal tender money,[1] and the fact th
there was reciated paper on deposit will not render the
ter     the check good

§ 85.  **Tender of check on depositary in payment of obligations
owned by it—Certificate of deposit—On obligations held for collection—Imposing conditions to acceptance.**—Where a person
has money on deposit with a bank, company or person, sub
ject to check, and such bank, company or person owns a note
or other debt due from the depositor, the depositor may ten
der his check drawn on the depositary, in payment of such
obligation[1]  The same rule has been applied to a tender to a
bank of its own certificate of deposit in payment of a note
held by it.[2]  But the certificate must be then due.  Such a
rule is just and equitable  The depositary being under obli
gation to instantly honor the check, certificate, or draft of
the depositor, ought not to require him to perform the idle
ceremony of withdrawing the money for the purpose of im
mediately handing it back  But a check or certificate of

[1] Lawrence v Schmidt, 35 Ill       [1] Shipp v Stacker 8 Mo 145
140, Galena Ins Co. v. Kupfer     [2] Lord v Favorite 29 Ill 149
28 Ill 332

deposit of a bank would not be a good tender to it, on a claim held by it for collection.[1]

If a bank check is tendered in payment, the creditor being under no obligation to receive it, may as a condition of his acceptance, require it to be certified,[4] or to be drawn payable to the order of himself, instead of the firm of which the tenderee is a member,[5] or to the order of any other person. If the parties cannot agree upon the form of the check the debtor should tender money.

§ 86. Tender of check in absence of creditor—To sheriff or other officer—Attorney—Agent.—By being at a place certain with a check drawn for the amount of the debt, in the absence of the creditor, is not a good tender. There can be no waiver unless the creditor is present and has an opportunity to object.[1] A sheriff or other officer to whom money may be paid in satisfaction of a judgment, or an execution, or in redemption of property sold on a mortgage sale, or on an execution sale, cannot receive in payment anything but legal tender money or its equivalent in other lawful money. A tender to a sheriff, of a certificate of deposit in redemption of a mortgage, was held bad, although he accepted it and issued a certificate of redemption.[3] In a case where a sheriff accepted a certified check in payment, the court said "We are met with the reply, that the sheriff accepted them as payment, and he was responsible upon his bond. But the parties were not to look to the sheriff's bonds for their security. It might so happen in some cases in different parts of the state that the sheriff's bond would not be sufficient security; his bondsmen might be irresponsible."[4]

So, a tender of a bank check by a mortgagor to an attorney authorized by the mortgagee to accept the mortgage money,

---

[1] See Whelan v. Reilley, 61 Mo. 565, where it is held that a bank as agent may receive in payment one of its own certificates of deposit.

[4] Duffy v. O'Donovan, 46 N. Y. 223.

[5] Murphy v. Gold, 3 N. Y. Supp. 804.

[1] Sloan v. Pertrie, 16 Ill. 262.

[2] See Lewis v. Larson, 45 Wis. 353 where a deposit of a check with a justice was held not to be a good tender either under the statute or at common law.

[3] Dougherty v. Hughes, 3 Green. 92.

[4] Thorn v. San Francisco, 4 Cal. 127. See Sandson v. Manage 41 Minn. 314, s. c. 43 N. W. Rep. 66 to the contrary.

is insufficient. In a case where this question was under consideration, the court observed, that it was going too far to say that an attorney has authority to accept a check because he has authority to accept a tender according to the law of the land; and, that the attorney did not go so far as to claim that he would have been at liberty to accept a bill or promissory note.[5] An agent has no implied authority to receive anything else than money in satisfaction of a debt due his principal. He cannot, therefore, take payment in a check.[6]

§ 87. **Tender of light-weight coins.**—The gold coins of the United States are a legal tender at their nominal or face value when not below the standard weight and limit of tolerance provided by law for the single piece, and, when reduced in weight below such standard and tolerance, they are a legal tender at a valuation in proportion to their actual weight.[1] The limit of tolerance at or above which they are a good tender at their nominal or face value in the various commercial transactions, and, when tendered to any of the United States Treasury officials, is one half of one per centum below the standard weight prescribed by law, after a circulation of twenty years, as shown by the date of coinage, and at a ratable proportion for any period less than twenty years.[2] There is below a note giving the standard weight and fineness of the various coins of the United States.[3]

[5] Blumberg v. Life Ins. R. S. Co. 1 Ch. 178. 66 L. J. Ch. N. S. 127. 75 Law T. 9 Rep. 627.

[6] Hall v. Storrs 7 Wis. 217. Buckwalter v. Craig 55 Mo. 71.

[1] U. S. Rev. St. 1874, § 3585. Act 12 Feb. 1873. 3 Mar. 1875.

[2] U. S. Rev. St. 1874, § 3505.

[3] *Coins of the United States, authority for coining and changes in weight and fineness.*

*Gold Coins — Double Eagle.*—Authorized to be coined act of March 3 1849. Weight, 516 grains fineness 900.

*Eagle*—Authorized to be coined act of April 2 1792. Weight 270 grains, fineness 916 2-3. Weight changed act of June 28 1834, to 258 grains. Fineness changed act of June 28 1834 to 899.225. Fineness changed act of January 18 1837 to 900.

*Half Eagle*—Authorized to be coined, act of April 2 1792. Weight 135 grains, fineness 916 2-3. Weight changed act of June 28 1834 to 129 grains. Fineness changed act of June 28 1834 to 899.225. Fineness changed act of January 18, 1837 to 900.

*Quarter Eagle.*—Authorized to be coined act of April 2 1792. Weight, 67.5 grains; fineness 916 2-3. Weight changed act of June 28 1834 to 64.5 grains. Fineness changed act of June 28

In adjusting the weights of gold coins under the coinage laws, a slight deviation from the standard weight is permissible; and coins of less heft than the standard weight, which have not been reduced by natural abrasion, may pass into circulation from the mint, and be a legal tender at their nominal or face value. But such deviation from the standard weight must not exceed in any single piece, one half of a grain in the double eagle and eagle, one fourth of a grain in the half eagle, the three dollar piece, the quarter eagle, and the one dollar piece. This limit of tolerance is not permitted in each piece, where a tender of a large quantity is made by

1834 to 899.225. Fineness changed, act of January 18, 1837, to 900.

*Three-Dollar Piece.*—Authorized to be coined, act of February 21, 1853. Weight 77.4 grains, fineness .900. Coinage discontinued, act of September 26, 1890.

*One Dollar.*—Authorized to be coined, act of March 3, 1849. Weight 25.8 grains, fineness .900. Coinage discontinued, act of September 26, 1890.

*Silver Coins—Dollar.*—Authorized to be coined, act of April 2, 1792. Weight 416 grains, fineness .892.4. Weight changed, act of January 18, 1837, to 412½ grains. Fineness changed, act of January 18, 1837, to .900. Coinage discontinued, act of February 12, 1873. Coinage reauthorized, act of February 28, 1878.

*Trade Dollar.*—Authorized to be coined, act of February 12, 1873. Weight 420 grains, fineness .900. Coinage discontinued, act of March 3, 1887.

*Half Dollar.*—Authorized to be coined, act of April 2, 1792. Weight 208 grains, fineness .892.4. Weight changed, act of January 18, 1837, to 206¼ grains. Fineness changed, act of January 18, 1837, to .900. Weight

changed, act of February 21, 1853, to 192 grains. Weight changed, act of February 12, 1873, to 12½ grams, or 192.9 grains.

*Columbian Half Dollar.*—Authorized to be coined, act of August 5, 1892. Weight, 192.9 grains, fineness, .900.

*Quarter Dollar.*—Authorized to be coined, act of April 2, 1792. Weight, 104 grains, fineness .892.4. Weight changed, act of January 18, 1837, to 103¼ grains. Fineness changed, act of January 18, 1837, to .900. Weight changed, act of February 21, 1853, to 96 grains. Weight changed, act of February 12, 1873, to 6¼ grams, or 96.45 grains.

*Columbian Quarter Dollar.*—Authorized to be coined, act of March 3, 1893. Weight, 96.45 grains; fineness .900.

*Twenty-Cent Piece.*—Authorized to be coined, act of March 3, 1875. Weight 5 grams, or 77.16 grains, fineness .900. Coinage discontinued, act of May 2, 1878.

*Dime.*—Authorized to be coined, act of April 2, 1792. Weight 41.6 grains, fineness .892.4. Weight changed, act of January 18, 1837, to 41¼ grains. Fineness changed, act of January 18, 1837, to .900. Weight changed, act of

the superintendent of the mint to a depositor; otherwise a depositor might be compelled to receive, for instance, any number of dollars, each weighing one fourth of a grain less than the standard weight. It is provided by law, that, in weighing a large number of pieces together, when delivered by the superintendent of the mint to a depositor, deviation from the standard weight shall not exceed one hundredth of an ounce in five thousand dollars in double eagles, eagles, half eagles, or quarter eagles, and the same deviation in one thousand three dollar pieces and one thousand one dollar pieces [4]

February 21, 1853, to 384 grains Weight changed, act of February 12, 1873 to 2½ grams or 38.58 grains

*Half Dime.*—Authorized to be coined, act of April 2 1792 Weight, 20.8 grains, fineness, 892.4 Weight changed, act of January 18, 1837, to 20⅝ grains Fineness changed, act of January 18 1837, to 900 Weight changed act of February 21 1853, to 19.2 grains. Coinage discontinued act of February 12, 1873

*Three - cent Piece*—Authorized to be coined, act of March 3 1851 Weight, 12¾ grains Fineness, 750 Weight changed act of March 3 1853, to 11.52 grains Fineness changed, act of March 3 1853, to 900 Coinage discontinued act of February 12, 1873

*Minor Coins—Five Cent (Nickel)*—Authorized to be coined act of May 16 1866 Weight, 77.16 grams; composed of 75 per cent copper and 25 per cent nickel

*Three Cent (Nickel)*—Authorized to be coined act of March 3 1865 Weight 30 grains; composed of 75 per cent copper and 25 per cent nickel Coinage discontinued, act of September 26, 1890

*Two Cent (Bronze)*—Authorized to be coined act of April 22

1864 Weight, 96 grains, composed of 95 per cent copper and 5 per cent tin and zinc Coinage discontinued, act of February 12, 1873

*Cent (Copper)*—Authorized to be coined act of April 2, 1792 Weight, 264 grains Weight changed, act of January 14, 1793 to 208 grains Weight changed by proclamation of the President January 26 1796, in conformity with act of March 3 1795, to 168 grains Coinage discontinued act of February 21 1857

*Cent (Nickel)*—Authorized to be coined, act of February 21 1857 Weight 72 grains composed of 88 per cent copper and 12 per cent nickel Coinage discontinued act of April 22 1864

*Cent (Bronze),*—Coinage authorized act of April 22 1864 Weight 48 grains, composed of 95 per cent copper and 5 per cent tin and zinc

*Half-Cent (Copper)*—Authorized to be coined, act of April 2 1792 Weight 132 grains Weight changed act of January 14, 1793 104 grains Weight changed by proclamation of the President January 26, 1796 in conformity with act of March 3 1795, to 84 grains Coinage discontinued act of February 21 1857

[4] U S Rev St. 1874 § 3535

In respect to the silver coins of the United States, a similar statutory provision exists as to the adjustment of weights, and any single piece (the one-dollar, the half and quarter dollar and dime) is not, if discovered, put into circulation from the mint, if its weight is below one and one-half grains less than the standard weight. And, as in the case of the gold coins, the same protection is by statute afforded a depositor at the mint, and when the superintendent of the mint tenders to a depositor a large quantity, he is not obliged to accept the money, if the deviation from the standard weight exceeds two hundredths of an ounce in one thousand one dollars, or in one thousand half dollars, or in one thousand quarter dollars; and one hundredth of an ounce in one thousand dimes.[5] The subsidiary silver coins, after being put into circulation through the mint under the foregoing restrictions, are a legal tender at their nominal or face value for an amount not exceeding ten dollars.[6]

In respect to the minor coins, in reference to the adjustment of weights at the mint, there must be no greater deviation from the standard weight, than three grains for the five cent piece, and two grains for the three and one cent pieces.[7] And they are a legal tender at their nominal or face value for all payments not exceeding twenty-five cents.[8]

§ 88.  **Gold coins reduced in weight by natural abrasion** — The reduction of weight of the gold coins of the United States, within the limit of tolerance heretofore mentioned, which does not affect their legal tender quality at their nominal or face value, when offered to the United States treasury or to any of its officials, must have been produced by natural abrasion, such as is occasioned by passing from hand to hand as part of the circulating medium of the country.[1] So, the reduction in weight below the limit of tolerance at which reduced weight they are a legal tender at a valuation in proportion to their standard weight, must have been occasioned by the same cause. The Secretary of the Treasury has authority to establish such rules and regulations, in the receipt of light-weight coin, as may to him seem

5 U. S. Rev. St. 1874 § 3536.  
6 Act of Congress June 9, 1879.  
7 U. S. Rev. St. 1874 § 3537.  
8 U. S. Rev. St. 1874 § 3587.  
1 U. S. Rev. St. 1874, § 3505.

to best afford protection to the government against fraudu
lent practices.  It is a reasonable inference from the fore
going, that when the gold coins are in circulation and passing
from hand to hand, the same rule applies as to their legal
tender quality as obtained when they are tendered to the
treasury officials.

§ 89.  **Silver coin reduced in weight by natural abrasion.**—
There is no limitation in reference to the legal tender char
acter of the silver coins of the United States, which have been
reduced in weight by natural abrasion.  There are surprising
ly few decisions involving this point.  In a case where a ten
cent piece was tendered as fare to a street car conductor,
but refused by him because it was worn smooth, the trial
court, in refusing to direct a verdict for the defendant (the
action was brought to recover damages for ejecting the pas
senger), said  The coin was not mutilated in the ordinary
sense of the term; that a portion of it was gone only by use,
by currency, that happens to any coin after it has passed
through numerous hands.  How long after use—such use as
the government intends  does a coin cease to be a coin?  And,
after adverting to the legal tender character of gold coin
diminished in value by natural abrasion, the court observed
that the limitation did not extend to silver coin   In its in
struction to the jury, the court, among other things, said
"If there has been no other abrasion, no other wearing away,
no other defacement of that coin except such as it has re
ceived in passing from hand to hand, then it is still, under the
laws of the country, a good ten cent piece, and was the fare
of the plaintiff"  And further, that if the government does
not choose to put any limitation upon the circulation it shall
receive, it continued to be a legal tender just as long as it is
circulating and receiving only such injury  as circulation
gives, that, every piece of money that passes through our
hands is to some extent abraded thereby, and the government
knows and expects that its coin will be abraded, will be
worn, and will be in that way defaced, and, that if the government does not withdraw coin that is only defaced in that
way, it is still a legal tender   On an appeal, the charge of

the court was sustained and the judgment for damages affirmed.[2] The same rule is applicable to the minor coins.[3]

§ 90. **Defaced and mutilated coins.**—A gold or silver coin, though defaced, remains of full value so long as it retains its original weight and fineness, and has the appearance of a coin, and its denomination can be determined on inspection. In the case hereafter referred to, where holes had been punched in a coin with a sharp instrument, leaving all the metal in the coin, the court was of the opinion, that, crowding the silver to one side did not have any effect to render them less valuable or a less lawful tender than before.[1]

§ 91. **Debased and counterfeit money.**—There is no positive statutory declaration, in reference to the legal tender character of gold or silver coin, diminished in weight, either within the limit of tolerance or below it, by fraudulent practices. The United States statutes, in reference to counterfeiting, make it a felony, for any person, fraudulently, by any art, way, or means, to deface, mutilate, impair, diminish, falsify, scale or lighten the gold or silver coin.[1] Although it is a crime to lighten such coin, the statute does not expressly make it a crime to pass such light coin. However, reading all the statutes in reference to counterfeiting together, it is at once apparent that the legislative intent was, and is to make the passing of light coin, diminished in weight by fraudulent practices, a crime.

In England, under a similar statute,[2] it was held that one who passed a sovereign, which had been filed so as to remove the milling, and upon which a new milling had been made, was guilty of passing counterfeit coin, a minority of the

---

[2] Jersey City & Bergen R. v. Morgan, 52 N. J. L. 60, s. c. 160 U. S. 288.

[3] Since writing the above, Judge Ryan of the Circuit Court at St. Louis, Missouri, in Ruth v. St. Louis Transit Company, according to a newspaper report in January 1902, held that "smooth" nickels must be accepted at their face value. The plaintiff had tendered a "smooth" five cent

piece in payment of his street car fare, but it was refused and he was ejected from the car, arrested and locked up over night. Plaintiff brought an action for damages and recovered a verdict for two thousand dollars.

[1] United States v. Lissner, 12 Fed. Rep. 840.

[1] U. S. Rev. St. 1874 § 5459.

[2] 24 & 25 Vict. Ch. 99 § 9.

judges dissented upon the ground, that while the statute made it a crime to lighten such coins, there was none making it an offence to pass light coin. But the majority of the court said that the removal of the milling and the making of a new milling, to restore the appearance of the coin, made it a counterfeit. Pollock, B., said: "It is like the case of a man taking part of the gold out of a sovereign, and filling up the hollow left with alloy and then passing it as genuine" Lord Coleridge, Ch J, said "If the word 'counterfeit' is to be taken in its ordinary or popular sense these coins seem to me to be counterfeit. In the ordinary sense of this word the idea of imitation is conveyed. These sovereigns have been filed and then a new milling added to make them imitate current gold coin." [3] A similar case has been before the United States courts. In that case the defendant was convicted in the district court of the crime of passing counterfeit coin The coins in question had had holes made in them, and the holes were filled with base metal. Some of the holes had been punched, crowding the metal to the side, but involving no loss of silver, while other holes were made by drilling out a part of the silver On an appeal, the appellate court in reference to the coins in which holes had been punched, said "We think it clear that a silver coin, duly issued from the mints, remains of full value as long as it retains all the appearance of a coin, and does besides contain all its original weight and fineness This being so, we cannot regard the addition of something to it as a criminal act of counterfeiting Passing such a coin works no injury to the person to whom it is passed" And as to the coins in which holes had been made by removing part of the silver and which were plugged with base metal, the court held, that they were counterfeit, and that such treatment of the coin constituted an act of counterfeiting, because it made the coin appear to be good for its face value which was not so before The verdict was set aside and a new trial ordered for the reason that the lower court did not distinguish between the holes which were made by taking away part of the silver and those made by crowding the silver out of place without removing any of it [4]

[3] Queen v Hermann L R 4 475 See 33 L R A 824 note Q B Div 284 18 L J M C 106, [4] United States v Lissner 12 40 L T N S 263 27 Week Rep Fed Rep 840

In the two cases referred to, the coins were first mutilated and then an attempt was made to restore their appearance; but coins reduced in weight by rubbing, or shaking in a bag, or by the use of acids, are also mutilated, although they may not be defaced, or need to be restored in appearance in order to be deceptive. To deliberately diminish the weight of a gold or silver coin in any way, without destroying its identity, with or without a fraudulent intent, makes it a counterfeit. If the fraudulent intent does not exist at the time the coin is diminished in weight, such act may not be a crime, but when any person tenders such coin to another with knowledge of such reduction in weight, he makes such act of diminishment in weight, his own, if he did not do it himself, and the crime of attempting to pass, or passing counterfeit coin, is complete. This is all that need be considered here in determining the legal tender status of such coin. In a case which arose in New Jersey, the trial court in its instruction to the jury, after considering the question of reduction in weight by natural abrasion, said, referring to the coin in question, that if it had been otherwise changed, wilfully changed, by being rubbed, or in any other way, why, it has ceased to be a lawful coin of the country, it has ceased to be a lawful tender.[1]

It seems that coin, made light by any means other than by natural abrasion, where their identity is not destroyed, even where they do not need to be restored in appearance, fall naturally in the category of counterfeit money. That which is the result of an unlawful act is not of itself always unlawful, but when the doing of an act is by law prohibited under pain of a penalty and the thing which is the result of any such unlawful act continues forever after a spurious thing, and the unlawful thing sought to be eliminated, that thing cannot be recognized as a lawful agency in performing the functions of those agencies that are lawful, and to protect which such prohibitory and penal laws were enacted. Hence it may be stated in conclusion, that counterfeit money, whether it is made by diminishing the weight, or otherwise debasing a genuine coin, as well as where the counterfeit is an entirely new article, made in the similitude of any of the forms of money, is not a good tender upon any obligation,

[1] See Jersey City & Bergen R. v. Morgan 52 N. J. L. 60

and, that there is no difference in principle, as to the sufficiency of such a tender, where the tenderor knew at the time of his offer that the money was spurious, and where he did not know it to be such. And the tenderee, to defeat the tender, may prove that any part of the money offered was spurious, even though he did not know it to be such at the time he refused it.

§ 92. **Accepting counterfeit money**.—As to the effect of accepting counterfeit money, it was decided in England, where a person to whom money was tendered accepted it and put it into his purse, but upon examining it before leaving the place, he discovered some counterfeit pieces, and for that reason he refused to carry it away, that, as he had not objected to the money before he accepted it, he could not do this afterwards.[1] When a state bank received, as genuine, forged notes purporting to be its own, and passed them to the credit of a depositor who acted in good faith, it was held that the bank receiving them was bound by the credit thus given, and the notes must be treated as cash. But in this case the court observed that there was a difference between the acceptance of the notes of another bank, and where it receives notes as its own genuine notes, that a bank is bound to know its own paper, and must be presumed to use all reasonable means, by private marks and otherwise to secure itself against forgeries. The court reviewed a line of analogous cases, where bills of exchange had been accepted and paid which afterwards were found to be forged; and cases where forged checks drawn on a bank were, on being deposited in that bank, carried to the creditor of the depositor. In each case the payor is bound to know the signature of persons drawing upon him.[2] Although this decision is undoubtedly sound in principle, the first case above referred to is not. A rule that would require a person to keep counterfeit money which he had inadvertently received is not supported by reason or justice. There is no similarity in principle, between the acceptance of what a person supposes to be good money, and the acceptance of goods where the rule *caveat emptor* applies. Counterfeit money has no value or quality whatever, besides it is an un-

---

[1] 5 Rep. 115. See Just 208, also Bac. Abr. Tit. Tender (B).

[2] United States v. Bank of Georgia. 10 Wheat 333.

lawful thing, while goods and chattels are not unlawful al
though they may be inferior in quality to that which the
party accepting them, at the time thought them to be. The
modern authorities seem to support the rule that payment
received in counterfeit money, or forged paper, is not good,
and in absence of negligence on the part of the person receiv
ing such money, or paper, he may recover back the consideration or recover upon the original demand.[1]

§ 93. **Tender on contracts providing for payment in a particular
kind of money—A question of law.**—Sometimes the bond or
note given as evidence of a debt contains words descriptive of
the money in which the obligation is to be discharged, and it
is sometimes difficult to determine whether the obligation
may be discharged with legal tender money solely, or is a
contract which may be also discharged in money not a legal
tender. The meaning of such restrictive or qualifying terms
has been held to depend upon the varying circumstances of
the country. But where the words have acquired a definite
and well defined meaning, parol evidence is inadmissible to
show that a particular kind of money was meant.[1] The ques
tion of the kind of money is one purely of law, and is not one
for a jury.[2]

§ 94. **Same subject—Specie—Lawful money—Current money —**
A note payable in specie has been held payable in legal tender
notes or any money made by law a legal tender in payment of
debts.[1] So, a contract to pay a sum in "lawful money," or
in lawful money of North Carolina, or in "lawful money of
the United States,"[4] may be satisfied by a tender and payment of legal tender notes, or any legal tender. Lawful
money of the United States is lawful money of any state. A

[1] See United States Bank v. Bank
of Georgia, 10 Wheat 333, Markle
v. Hatfield, 2 John 455, Young v.
Adams 6 Mass 182, Jones v.
Ryde, 5 Taunt 488 Fenn v. Harrison 3 T R 757 See § 113

[1] Lee v. Biddis 1 Dall 175

[2] Phelps v. Town 14 Mich 374

[3] Graham v. Marshall, 52 Pa
St 9 Jones v. Smith 18 Barb
752

[2] Davis v. Burton 52 Pa St 9
Shelby v. Boyd 3 Yates (Pa)
321

[4] Kroener v. Calhoun, 52 Pa
St 9 s c 5 Phil 468

[5] Cocke v. Kendall, Hempst
236

bond payable in "lawful current money of Pennsylvania," was held to be payable in money issued by the United States.[1] So, where a bond was payable in lawful money of North Carolina, money not a legal tender, was not allowed to be brought into court.[2] "Good current money"[3] and "current money" has been interpreted to mean constitutional money.[4] So, a note promising to pay $700.00 in "current money of Kentucky," was held to be a direct promise to pay the kind of money made current by an act of Congress, which was the only current money of Kentucky.[5] A check made payable in "current funds" is payable in gold or silver coin, or legal tender notes, or in anything that is made current by law as money.[6]

§ 95. **Same subject—Currency.**—Currency includes current money, but current money does not mean the same as currency.[1] Currency includes all forms of money which circulate as cash at par. So that a note, or other obligation made payable in currency, may be discharged in bank bills or other paper money, which pass as and for legal tender; or it may be paid in legal tender money; while such an obligation payable in current money, as has been shown, can only be discharged by a tender of legal tender money. In Missouri a note payable "in the currency of this state" was construed to be payable, either in gold or silver coin, or in the notes of the Bank of Missouri. The court observed, that if the note was "payable in current money of Missouri" then all necessity for construction is absolutely excluded, for the term explains itself and can only mean "tender money," gold and silver coin (then the only legal tender). So, a certificate of deposit payable "in currency" was held to be payable in

[1] Wharton v. Morris, 1 Dall. 124; Lee v. Biddis, 1 Dall. 170; Bond v. Pass, 2 Dall. 193.

[2] Shelby v. Boyd, 3 Yates (Pa.) 321.

[3] Moore v. Morris, 20 Ill. 258.

[4] Bainbridge v. Owen, 2 J. J. Marsh 463.

[5] McCord v. Ford, 3 T. B. Mon. 166. See 2 Cranch (U. S.) 10; 64 N. C. 381; Bainbridge v. Owen,

2 J. J. Marsh. 464; Bryan v. Masterson, 1 J. J. Marsh 225.

[6] Bull v. Bank of Kasson, 123 U. S. 105.

[1] McCord v. Ford, 3 T. B. Mon. (Ky.) 166.

[2] Cockrell v. Kirkpatrick, 9 Mo. 688; s. p. Ehle v. Chittenango Bank, 24 N. Y. 548. Contra Chambers v. George, 5 Litt 335.

money current by law or money equivalent in value circulating in the business community at par.[3]

Where an action was brought on a receipt "payable in currency" it was determined that "the court could assess damages because by 'currency' it understood bank bills or other paper money issued by authority, which pass as and for coin." that "a note payable in such money must be understood in coin [then the only legal tender money], or in such bank notes as were current with the coin requiring no proof of value *aliunde*, currency, or current bills, are deemed to be the value of cash, and exclude the idea of depreciated paper money."[4] A tender of "stump tail" or depreciated currency is not good, as such a contract as is here under consideration implies that payment is to be made in money which circulates at par. Currency was held not to mean money at a time, in Kentucky, when bank notes were the only money in circulation,[5] and "Kentucky Currency" was construed as meaning gold and silver at another time.[6] The reason for any local signification being attached to the term "currency," it is believed does not now exist.

§ 96. Contracts providing for the payment in a particular form of legal tender money—Discharged with what—Damages in what assessed—Form of judgment.—Where a government has by law declared several forms of money a legal tender in payment of all debts, can an individual, by contract, restrict his debtor to the use of one of those forms of money in payment of the debt, to the exclusion of all other forms of legal tender money? The power to issue money, to declare it current, and to fix the extent to which it shall be a legal tender, as we have seen, being an attribute of sovereignty, absolutely indispensable to the very existence of an independent government, it would seem to follow as a corollary that this power cannot be abridged or taken away, or the effect of the statutory enactment destroyed or annulled by the contract of individuals who may prefer one form of legal tender money

[3] Phelps v. Town 14 Mich 371, s p Webster v Pierce 35 Ill 158, Marine Ins Co v Thacher, 30 Ill 399

[4] Marine Bank v Rushmore, 28 Ill 463

[5] McCord v. Ford, 3 T. B. Mon 166

[6] Lampton v Haggard, 3 T. B. Mon 149

over another. A distinction between two forms of legal tender is not permitted in England, when used as money in payment of debts. In the United States few cases, if any, are to be found in the books, where, prior to the Rebellion, the right to discharge a debt with any legal tender, had been challenged. During the progress of that war and since, the courts have frequently considered the question, when called upon to determine what was a legal tender in payment upon contracts creating debts which provided, in terms, for payment in specie, gold coin, or silver coin, and the decisions prior to 1868 are unanimous in upholding the doctrine that individuals, by contract, cannot defeat or weaken the government's power over its currency, by stipulating for the exclusive payment of a debt in a particular form of money, or by prohibiting payment in a certain form of money, which the money-making power has deemed expedient to declare a legal tender.[1]

In 1866, in a case arising in New York, the foregoing doctrine was followed by the court of appeals, but on an appeal to the supreme court of the United States the doctrine was overturned. The latter decision was given in 1868, and was by a divided court, Mr. Chief Justice Chase writing the majority opinion, Mr. Justice Miller dissenting. The contract under consideration was a bond, executed in 1851 for the repayment in 1857, of the principal sum of $1,400.00, in gold and silver coin, lawful money of the United States, with interest, also in coin, at the rate of seven per cent. per annum. A mortgage on certain real estate was executed to secure the debt. After the passage of the legal tender acts, the purchaser of the property who had assumed the mortgage debt, tendered to the mortgagee $1,507 00 the nominal amount of the debt in dollars, in United States legal tender notes. The question was whether the tender of the United States notes was sufficient. The court held that a contract to pay a certain sum of money in gold or silver coin, is, in legal import, nothing else than an agreement to deliver a certain weight of standard gold, to be ascertained by a count of coins, each of which is certified to contain a definite proportion of that weight; that such a contract is not distinguishable in principle from a contract to deliver an equal weight of bullion of

[1] See notes 1, 2 3, 4 and 5, page 100 et seq

equal fineness; "that express contracts to pay coined dollars can only be satisfied by the payment of coined dollars. They are not *debts* which may be satisfied by the tender of the United States notes." The tender was held not sufficient in law, and the decree of the lower court, declaring the mortgage to be satisfied, was reversed. Having established this doctrine, it became necessary, in order that the doctrine might not be inoperative, to declare a rule applicable to such cases for measuring and assessing damages, and a mode of entering a judgment thereon and its execution. Therefore, it was decided that in such cases damages could be assessed in coined dollars and parts of dollars, equal in amount to the number agreed to be paid, and that the judgment thereon should be entered for the same kind of money.²

The same doctrine was followed by the same court in subsequent cases, where the contract was to pay a sum of money in gold and silver, lawful money of the United States,³ or in "gold,"⁴ or in "specie,"⁵ but still only by a divided court. The state courts constrained by the decisions of the United States Supreme Court, where cases involving similar contracts were before them for adjudication, have followed the doctrine promulgated by that court.⁶ It is an erroneous

---

² See notes 6 and 7, p. 111 et seq. (1868) Bronson v. Rodes, 7 Wall. 229. (1869) see Tyers v. United States, 5 Ct. of Cl. 509. As to the costs included in a judgment upon a coin contract the courts have almost uniformly held that they were payable in money generally, and, to effect this result the judgment has been entered, so that the demand is payable in coin and the costs in currency. Chrysler v. Renois 43 N. Y. 207, Kellogg v. Sweeney, 46 N. Y. 291, Phillips v. Dugan 21 Oh. St. 466, Hittson v. Davenport, 4 Colo. 169. The Federal court, in one case at least did not split up the judgment. Butler v. Horwitz, 7 Wall. 258.

³ (1869) Bronson v. Kimpton 8 Wall. 444.

⁴ (1873) The Emily Souder, 17 Wall. 666.

⁵ (1871) Trebilcock v. Wilson 12 Wall. 687.

⁶ See note 8, page 115 et seq. (1869) Rankin v. Demott, 61 Pa. St. 263, (1869) Bobo v. Goss, 1 S. C. 262; (1870) Warren v. Franklin Ins. Co. 104 Mass. 521, (1870) Stark v. Coffin, 105 Mass. 328, (1870) Chrysler v. Renois, 43 N. Y. 209, (1871) Walkup v. Houston, 65 N. C. 501, (1871) Phillips v. Dugan 21 O. St. 466, Foster v. Atlantic & Pacific Ry. Co., 1 Mo. App. 390, Hittson v. Davenport, 4 Colo. 169. The Chespeake Bank v. Swain 29 Md. 183, (1870) McGoon v. Shirk, 54 Ill. 408, (1872) Brown v. Darby, 14 Fla. 202, Calhoun v. Pace, 37 Tex. 451, (1872) Smith v. Wood, 37 Tex. 616, (1876) Churchman v. Martin 54 Ind. 380; (1870) McCalla v. Ely, 64 Pa. St. 254. Watson v. San Francisco,

doctrine but until it is overthrown by the same court, or changed by statute, it must be considered to be the law of the land. The same rule in reference to assessing damages, and the form of the judgment, has since been applied to contracts to deliver coin as a commodity, and to cases of conversion of coin where there is no express contract to pay in coin.[7]

50 Cal 523, Chamberlin v Vauer, 51 Cal. 75. See Murphy v San Luis Obispo, 39 L. R. A. (Cal) 444; Belford v. Woodward, 158 Ill. 122, Contra. (1871) Wills v Allison, 4 Heisk. 385. In Illinois, it was held where a mortgage, given to secure the payment of a note payable in lawful money, was foreclosed and the premises sold for $537 00, the purchaser having paid gold that although there was no express contract to pay gold, it was a debt payable in gold by operation of law, and that a tender of the amount necessary to redeem in United States Treasury notes was insufficient (1871) Morrow v Rainey, 58 Ill 357 In a subsequent case, the same court went a step further and declared that the legal tender acts did not operate to authorize a tender of greenbacks in redemption from a deed of trust, which had matured prior to the passing of those acts The foreclosure was more than three years after the passage of those acts, and there was no express agreement to pay gold and no one paid gold at the sale A payment of "greenbacks" to the master in chancery was held insufficient (1871) Chamberlain v Blair, 58 Ill 385

Opposed to this is a decision of the Supreme Court of California holding that a judgment of foreclosure is a debt within the meaning of the act of Congress which provides that the United States

Treasury notes shall be a legal tender in payment of debts (1864) People v Mayhew, 26 Cal. 656

[7] See notes 8 and 9, page 115, et seq.

Note 1 The passage of the acts of Congress, known as the "Legal Tender Acts," gave rise to much litigation concerning this question One among the first cases involving this point, after the passage of those acts, came before the district court in the city of Philadelphia The defendant had executed a bond with warrant of attorney, for twenty eight thousand dollars payable "in specie, current gold and silver money of the United States in which it was stipulated "that no existing law or laws and no law or laws which may be hereafter enacted shall operate or be construed as operating to allow payment to be made in any other money, than that above designated" and further that "the said obligors expressly waiving the benefits derived or to be derived from such law or laws" A judgment was entered on the bond and a fi fa issued, in which the sheriff was required to levy the debt and interest "in specie, current gold and silver money" The court, on motion, set aside the fi fa on the ground that it was irregular, as a final judgment is necessarily for lawful money and payable in any money which the law has made a legal tender and said (Hare, J)

"There is nothing in which the public at large have a greater interest than in the currency, which is to the social system what the circulation of the blood is to the natural body, which brings to the labor the reward of toil, to the merchant the returns of commerce, to the agriculturist facilities for exchanging his production, which is literally and without overstatement, the means of luxury, of comfort and of daily bread to each and all in their several stations. It feeds and supplies the community in peace, it arms and maintains the soldier who is the defence of the state in war, it is next to light and air and beyond all secondary and artificial agents the most general, the most pervading and powerful influence and that on which most depends. Its uniformity, its stability, its security, and still more the confidence felt in its security are in their turn the spring on which it rests and by which alone it can perform its vast and delicate functions. Hence the power of saying what shall be money, at what rate money shall be taken and what it shall be worth has in all civilized countries and almost from the outset of civilization been deemed one of the badges and attributes of sovereignty and assigned to the central and supreme authority of the state. Is that which may indeed be perverted or abused but which, yet abused or not must be exercised uniformly and according to some common rule in order to be of utility at all. This being the object and design for which the coining and money-making power was given to the government of the United States in common with all other governments, we may well doubt whether, when that government has exercised its high prerogative, by deciding that certain modes or forms of values shall all be money, and all be money equally, that the same nominal quantity of each shall be worth as much as any of the others, it can be competent for the citizen to discriminate in a matter where the law of the land has refused to distinguish, to make a bargain excluding those with whom he contracts from a means of payment which the law has decided shall be open to and available for all and encumber them with a debt of a new and special nature not capable of being discharged in the way in which ordinary debts are by law payable. Congress, in the exercise of its supreme authority, declares that silver and Treasury notes shall be legal tender for the payment of all debts, that a debtor who comes with these or any of them in his hand and proffers them to his creditor shall be freed from all further obligation that all liability on his part either in person or property shall forthwith cease. Not so says the creditor, by the magic of a few words on this paper I will create a debt and impose an obligation to which the enabling and beneficial provision of the statute shall not be applicable, which gold which silver or which government paper shall not be capable of extinguishing which must be paid in a particular way of my own choosing that will as I think be more beneficial to me whatever may be its effect in depriving my debtor of the right of choice given him by congress. Surely, this is to run counter, not only to the spirit, but to the very letter of an act which applies in terms to all debts, without excepting any, or in any way providing or implying that there may or can be a right to create debts to which it shall not apply. These considerations certainly have much weight, and may well induce a doubt, whether a contract, by which a debt must be paid only in one form or mode to the exclusion of others, which in the eye of the law, are of equal validity, and in which it has declared, that all debts shall be payable is consistent with public policy and valid." (1864) Shollenberger v. Watts, 10 Am. L. Rep. 553. See 52 Pa. St. 9 (1866).

The same views were no less clearly expressed by Mr. Chief Justice Wright of the Supreme Court of Iowa. The question under consideration was, can a person to whom was loaned $700.00 in United States gold coin, pay the loan in United States Treasury notes, though he promised to pay the loan in coin? The courts after considering these powers of a government to make money said: "Anything thus made a legal tender must be received in payment of a debt and the party cannot by inserting an obligation to pay in one rather than another of these legally equivalent values, compel payment in the coin or currency so named. Any other rule it seems to us, would defeat the whole purpose and policy of the law and render nugatory the provisions of the statute. How more completely could a discontented and law resisting constituency defeat the letter and spirit of an act which applies without excep

tion, to all debts and contracts? If one man can do this, so can another. And if two, so a thousand, and all persons in every department of life. The consequences would necessarily be, that a law passed because of a peculiar public exigency—an exigency demanding the prompt exercise of all the vital functions of the Government—passed even for the very preservation of the national life, would become inoperative in the individual or general transactions, and it would be left to the citizen to discriminate in a matter where the law of the land refused to discriminate'." (1864) Warmbold v. Schlicting, 16 Iowa 244.

The Supreme Court of Louisiana, in considering a case where a plaintiff insisted on payment being made in gold, said, referring to the legal tender act: "The act in question was based exclusively upon reasons of a public character, which, in the opinion of the law-making power imperatively demanded that Treasury notes should be made equal in legal value to coin; and parties have no more right to stipulate that their contracts shall not be governed by it, than those of a particular locality have of agreeing among themselves that this or any other law passed by competent authority shall not be in force in such locality.' (1866) Gallaino v. Pietro 18 La. Am. 10.

In another case, where a charter party made in Calutta provided that the freight should be paid if the cargo was discharged in the United States in silver or gold dollars, the court (Monell J) said, "The main question is can a contract to pay in silver or gold dollars be satisfied by payment in any other kind of money? * * * * Gold and silver coin at their established value for all legal purposes do not change, they are never depreciated or appreciated. It is erroneous to say that the market for gold fluctuates, except when it is trafficed in as a commodity. As coin, or as medium of currency, its value, as fixed by law, does not change with the mutations of trade and commerce. All other things rise or fall, in the fluctuations of business, by comparison merely Congress having created paper money, and rendered it, nominally, for all legal purposes, equal to gold, there no longer remains, in legal contemplation, any difference between them The practical or actual depreciation of the former below the value of gold, is not produced by any law, but is occasioned by the laws of trade of supply and demand, and other causes for which the law is not accountable * * * As a circulating medium, gold or silver are not subject to any of the rules or principles, which regulate contracts It is used only to purchase property to discharge obligation and to pay debts A paper dollar having been made equal to a gold dollar it must be accepted as such in satisfaction of any contract for the payment of money and no form or force of words can be used by contracting parties to give to a gold dollar a legal value as money above a paper dollar A dollar is 100 cents, no more no less whether it is silver gold or paper And when congress declared that a paper dollar shall be current and pass for and represent and be of the same value of one hundred cents for

all purposes of traffic and paying debts, it becomes equivalent of one hundred cents, in any other substance and form " (1866) Wilson v. Morgan, 4 Robt. (N. Y.) 53, s. c. 30 Hun. 86. 2 Abb. Pr. (N. S.) 14.

The same rule was held to apply to a contract made in Havana, to be performed in New Orleans. (1866) Gallaino v. Pierto, 18 La. Am 10. So a tender of United States legal tender Treasury notes was held sufficient on a contract which provided that the principal and interest 'shall be paid in the current coin of the United States in full tale or count, without regard to any legal tender that may be established or declared by any law of Congress " In this case the court observed ' Had the contract called for payment in United States Treasury notes, can there be any doubt as to the right of the debt or to discharge it by paying gold' Surely not, because gold is a legal tender, made so by law If then, a contract stipulating for the payment of Treasury notes can be satisfied by the tender and payment of gold, will not the converse of the proposition equally hold true, and permit a contract payable in gold to be discharged and satisfied by legal tender notes " (1866) Apple v Walman, 38 Mo 194 So, where a contract requiring payment of interest in gold was under consideration, the Supreme Court of Illinois observed, "Neither the Supreme Court of the United States, nor this court recognizes two legal standard of value A dollar is a dollar whether payable in gold or in national currency, and ten per cent payable in gold may be lawfully paid, dollar for dollar, in any currency which the general government has declared to be a legal tender in payment of a debt." (1875) Reinback v. Crabtree, 77 Ill 182, s p. Black v. Lusk, 69 Ill 70

Legal tender notes were held to be a good tender in payment of rent reserved in a lease, which provided for payment in "lawful silver money of the United States of America." (1864) Schallenberger v. Brinton, 12 Am L Reg (Pa) 591  Also where $500 borrowed money was to be repaid in gold  Buchegger v. Schultz, 11 Am L. Reg 95 (Mich)  So, the value of gold over legal tender notes was held not a subject for consideration,  in  an  action brought on a note payable in express terms "in gold" the court holding that the notes was payable in dollars generally  (1865) Whetstone v. Colley, 36 Ill 328

Where a contract stipulated for payment of a specific sum of money in gold, or if paid in paper money, the amount thereof necessary to purchase the gold at the place of payment it was held, that on a failure to pay gold, the same nominal sum in legal tender notes  would discharge the obligation  Here the court said the contract contemplated gold coin, and not that metal in any form not constituting money  If that is not so, then the stipulation to pay paper money enough to buy the specific sum in gold, means nothing for such a sum in paper money as would purchase ingots worth five hundred dollars would simply be that sum in paper money, and there would be no premium possible The parties having by contract fixed the amount of the debt in gold, it results that the same sum

in "greenbacks" will discharge it. It has been said by the Supreme Court of California, that, "If it were admissible in judicial proceedings to open the door to evidence to show, for instance, that at a particular date a hundred dollars in United States notes were worth only forty dollars in gold coin, not only would the laws of Congress making these notes lawful money and a legal tender be annulled and held for nought, but consequences of a most preposterous and disastrous character would be likely to follow  (1865) Higgins v. Bear River Co, 27 Cal 153

So are many decisions to the effect that the law does not recognize any distinction between one hundred cents in gold coin and one hundred cents in paper or in any  other  form  of  currency (1867) Bank of the State v. Burton 27 Ind 426; (1868) Chambers v. Walker, 42 Ala 444, (1865 Wood v  Bullens, 6 Allen 516, (1865) Bush v  Bradley, 11 Allen 367, (1865) Burling v  Goodman, 1 Nev 314, (1866) Graham v Marshall, 52 Pa St 9 (1867) Murray v  Harrison 47 Barb 484, s c 30 How Pr 90, (1868) Murray v  Gale, 52 Barb 427, 5 Abb Pr (N S) 246, (1866) Rodes v  Bronson, 34 N Y 649 (1866) Laughlins v  Harvey, 52 Pa 9, (1867) Shaw v  Trunesler 30 Tex 390, (1867) Jones v  Smith, 48 Barb 552 (1866) See Riley v  Sharp 1 Bush 348

In a case arising long prior to the passage of the so called legal tender acts, where a due bill was given for $895 payable in dimes, the court refused to recognize a difference between the various kinds of legal tender money then in circulation (dimes being at that time a fractional part of a dollar and a legal tender in payment of debts in any amount, and held that the contract may be discharged in eagles or in silver dollars or in dimes. (1843) Atchafalaya etc. Comrs. v. Benn, 3 Rob. (La.) 414.

*Note 2. The measure of damages for a breach of a contract to pay a debt in gold coin, etc.—In what assessed.* — A strictly logical rule deducible from the foregoing principles is that on a failure to pay a debt which was in terms to be paid in specie, or gold, or silver coin, or any legal tender currency, as in any case of failure to pay a debt the damages are the same number of dollars as sessed in money generally as is expressed in the contract. In a case to which we already have had occasion to refer, the court referring to gold coin and legal tender notes said "It is only by virtue of law that either is a legal tender and as such, the law has made them exactly equivalent for the purpose of payment and a failure to pay a given sum in gold cannot possibly beget an obligation to pay a greater sum in legal tender notes, whatever premium men may voluntarily choose to give for gold when forced to obtain it for a specific purpose or when impelled by a spirit of speculation or by a weak distrust in the government." (1866) Brown v Welch, 26 Ind. 116.

Mr. Justice Cooley, where the lower court had permitted evidence to be introduced to show that gold was worth a premium of fifty percent in United States legal tender treasury notes, said "The legal damages for a failure to pay $500 in gold cannot possibly exceed $500 in any lawful currency, and when a court renders judgment for any greater damages upon such a contract, it sets aside and disregards the legal tender acts altogether." Buchegger v Schultz, 13 Mich 420, s c 11 Am. L Reg 95.

In Kentucky, the court, apparently not recognizing United States treasury notes as a legal tender, by holding that a person who had received them without prejudice might return them and take judgment for his debt, nevertheless said "Under the laws of this state a note to pay $431.43 13 in gold is simply an undertaking to pay that sum in money, and that no recovery can be had in damages for the failure to pay the debt in gold on account of its supposed enhanced value over money which was not a legal tender." (1866) Riley v Sharp, 1 Bush 318.

So, in Missouri where the action was to recover $480 on a promissory note, which provided in terms for payment in gold and on account of the bullion value of gold being then at a premium of 40 per cent over "greenback" the trial court had awarded judgment for 40 per cent more than the face value of the note, the supreme court said "The error consists in attributing to money a marketable or commercial value and a liability to fluctuation in price to which other property by the accident of trade is subject, and in supposing that instead of the value of money being a thing fixed and established by law, it was a question to be determined by the court in every case on the testimony of witnesses. The judgment was reduced to the face value of the note and entered for money generally. The court observed that if "greenbacks" were not a legal tender, they could be refused when tendered in payment of the judgment Henderson v. McPike, 35 Mo. 255.

*Note 3. The measure of damages for the breach of a contract to deliver specific quantity of gold or silver coin as a commodity — In what assessed —* It may be prudent here to advert briefly to another question which is not clearly within the scope of the immediate inquiries but which is closely connected with the same subject of inquiry, What is the measure of damages resulting from a breach of a contract to deliver a specific quantity of gold or silver bullion or of gold or silver coin as a commercial commodity and in what are the damages to be assessed?

It has ever been the settled law that the damages for a breach of a contract to deliver unselected specific articles or articles selected at the time of entering into the contract of sale where the vendee elects to sue upon a breach is the market value of the thing to be delivered at the time of the breach. Gold and silver either in coin or bullion, is a legitimate article of commerce. It is not unlawful to deal with it as a commodity. Brokers and others may agree to deliver coin of a particular description for what they deem a sufficient consideration as they may agree to deliver any other thing in which it is not unlawful to deal. But a contract to deliver an article of commerce is entirely different from a contract creating a debt. Money dealers may for their own convenience treat money as

merchandise, and speak of gold or silver as being above or below par, but when it is spoken of in this manner it is with reference to the dollar as a standard of value. If the gold or silver dollar is regarded as money, it is itself the standard of value, and the statement that it is above or below par is a statement that 100 cents is worth more or less than 100 cents. When used as a commodity it is estimated according to its intrinsic or commercial value. Wright v. Jacobs, 61 Mo 19; (1868) Frank v. Calhoun, 59 Pa St 381. See Thompson v. Riggs, 5 Wall 663, and (1867) Bank of Commonwealth v. Van Vleck, 49 Barb 503. When used as money, according to the declared value. All the foregoing decisions in reference to debts made payable in terms in gold or silver coin distinguish such contracts from those contracts for the delivery of gold or silver coin as a commodity and recognize the general principles applicable to the latter. Monell J. said "As an article for traffic gold either in coin or bullion is regulated by the same rules that govern other commodities. Contracts for its purchase or sale are valid and are regarded like contracts for the purchase or sale of merchandise. There is a wide difference however between gold and silver as merchandise and as money. A contract to buy or sell gold cannot be specially enforced an action for damages being entirely adequate: the rule of damages being in such case probably the market value of the gold." And, further "a contract to deliver one thousand dollars of gold is a very different contract from the one to pay such sum in gold." Wilson

\ Morgan, 1 Robt. 58, s c. 30
How, 386, 1 Abb Pr. (N. S) 174.
The latter may be satisfied by a
tender and payment of gold coin
or its equivalent in any legal tender, while the former, like all contracts for the delivery of specific
articles, may be discharged by a
tender of the required amount in
kind and quality of the thing
agreed to be delivered

Where a lease reserved "the
yearly rate of four ounces, two
pennyweights and twelve of pure
gold, in coined money," it was
held that the contract was for
gold as a commodity, and that
damages for the failure to make
a payment was the market value
of the gold estimated in treasury
notes of the United States (1867)
Sears \ Dewing, 14 Allen 413
(The error in this decision is in
assuming that the value of treas
..y notes as compared with the
bullion value of gold dollars is
the standard for assessing damages, but as treasury notes as
dollars, are worth 100 cents the
same as the gold dollar the judgment may be discharged in the
legal tender gold dollars of 100
cents so that the error does not
effect the result) It was held
that where specie was advanced
during the Revolutionary War,
when specie was a commodity in
the market and did not circulate
as currency its value should be
calculated in money at the time
it was advanced McConnice "
Curzen 2 Call (Va ) 358

The courts in attempting to
give effect to the intent of the
parties, without doing violence to
the language of the contract or
the legal tender laws have created some considerable confusion in
determining whether the contract
under consideration was for the
delivery of the commodity or
merely for the payment of the
money. Thus, where a promissory note was for the payment of
"$500 in gold," the court was of
the opinion that gold in ingots, or
dust from the mines, would have
satisfied the contract. (1864)
Thayer \ Hedges, 23 Ind 111.
While in another case where the
same number of dollars was to
be paid in gold, the court held
the contract to be for the payment of money, which could be
discharged by the tender and
payment of any legal tender
money. (1865) Buchegger v.
Schultz, 13 Mich 420, s c 14 Am
L Reg 95, s p. Whetstone v.
Cooley, 36 Ill 328 But the difference is immaterial in such
cases, as in the former case the
damages are liquidated, $500 in
gold, as a commodity, would be
100 gold dollars, if gold bullion
was at 125, and the damages
would be $500 in money which
would purchase the $100 in gold
coin as a commodity and $500 is
the amount of damages in the
latter case So where the contract stipulated for payment in
"$3 000 in gold coin of the United
States aforesaid, of the present
standard weight and fineness,
notwithstanding any law which
now may or hereafter shall make
anything else a tender in payment of debts " the court said:
"The reference to the govern
ment standard was only a convenient mode of fixing the agreed
fineness of the coin and the selection of American coin instead
of Spanish was a circumstance of
no importance and it was held
to be a contract for specific chattles and that the damages was
the bullion value of that much gold
coin At that time the bullion

value of a gold coin was worth 44 per cent above its money value (1866) Dutton v. Pailaret, 52 Pa. St. 109; s. p. (1867) Myers v. Kaufman, 37 Ga 609. See Bank of Prince Edward Island v. Trumbull, 53 Barb 159 The construction of the contract is for the court; after that is determined the law, not the court, fixes the mode of determining the measure of damages and in what assessed. The same rule of damages apply to contracts stipulating for payment of a given number of ounces of silver or gold (Essex Co v Pacific Mills, 14 Allen 389) and to contracts providing in terms for payment of a given quantity of foreign coin. (1804) See Faw v Marsteller, 2 Cranch 10

*Note 4  Same subject—Conversion of coin* — The same principles which we have been considering apply in an action for conversion of coin  If a bailee on a demand fails to deliver specific coin deposited with him, he is answerable in damages for the conversion to the amount realized by him by his wrongful act (Bank of the State v Burton, 27 Ind 426), or if he has not disposed of it or has disposed of it at a sacrifice, then the market value at the time of the demand  (1868) Cushing v Wells F & Co 98 Mass 550; (1868) Gibson v Groner, 63 N C 10  (1875) Greentree v Rosenstock, 61 N Y 583 (1869) Mitchell v Henderson, 63 N C 643 (1864) Frothingham v Morse, 45 N H 545, see Thompson v Riggs 5 Wall 663

Where the bailee has disposed of the coin the bailor has his election and may sue for money had and received, or in trover  There may be some conflict of the authorities as to whether, in trover

the damages should be computed on the basis of the value as of the date of the conversion, or as of the date of the demand, or whether the damages should be computed on the basis of the highest market price between the time of the conversion and the time of bringing the action.  But in connection with the subject under consideration, the measure of damages in actions founded upon a breach of a contract to deliver gold or silver bullion or coin as a commodity, is important only in determining in what they are assessed  It is an ancient rule of law that damages are assessable in money only  Courts have no power to assess damages in anything else nor to give judgment for the delivery of the possession of the article agreed to be delivered, except where the article was identified and the title to the thing had passed and then only when the appropriate action is brought to determine the right to possession  and even in that action the plaintiff is entitled to an alternative judgment for money damages in case possession cannot be had  It is well settled that courts of equity will not decree the specific performance of contracts concerning chattels, except where they are incapable of being reproduced by money damages as where they have a special value to the purchaser over any pecuniary estimate as rare or unique articles, or where the damages would be uncertain, as in the case of the assignment of things in action  Pomeroy s Eq Sec 1402

But where the money value of articles, recovered in damages, will ordinarily enable the vendee to go upon the market and purchase others of like kind and quality, the law has wisely confined the remedy on a breach, to a recovery of those damages in money generally A different rule would be in conflict with one of the most cogent reasons for the creation of a legal tender, namely, that of having a common equivalent which will enable a person to discharge an obligation when he has found that he cannot carry it out in terms, thus relieving him of what might be otherwise a perpetual obligation If a vendor fails to deliver one hundred gold dollars on a certain day, the vendee is at liberty on that day to take sufficient money and go upon the market and buy that number of gold dollars Clearly his damages would be the sum expended, together with legal interest up to the time the vendor paid the judgment for damages If the vendee did not have the money on that day and lost valuable opportunities to use or dispose of the gold at a profit, or had the money but could not find the gold, losing the same opportunities it is something over which the law has no control To attempt to furnish a rule of damages for loss of opportunities would lead to endless speculation into so remote a field that they could not be estimated approximately, even after the close of a business career So if the vendor did not have the money with which to buy gold to fulfil his contract or had the money to buy but like the vendee above referred to, could not find it any number of decree of the court thundered at him would be in vain, and the litigation a fruitless ceremony. It is a maxim of law, as well as of equity, that courts will not attempt to give

judgment and decrees requiring things to be done, when circumstances over which the litigant has no control, may render performance impossible Replevin would not be appropriate to the enforcement of such contracts. No particular coin or bullion having been set apart and designated at the time of making the contract as that to be delivered, the title to any specific thing would not have passed It is apparent that an action for damages is the only remedy for the breach of such contract, and that the measure of damages is the market value of the gold or silver coin, as bullion, assessed in money

*Note 5 Form of the judgment and in what payable* —Since the damages resulting from a breach of a contract either to pay a certain sum of money in gold or silver coin, or to deliver a specific quantity of such coin as a commodity is to be assessed in money, it follows that the form of the judgment must be for the recovery of money generally At common law all money judgments are required to be entered for money generally expressed in the units of the monetary standard or scale of the realm The statutes of the United States require that "the money of account of the United States shall be expressed in dollars or units dimes or tenths, cents or hundredths, and mills or thousands. * * * and all accounts in the public offices, and all proceedings in the courts shall be kept and had in conformity to this regulation" Act April 2. 1792. U S Rev St. 1874, § 3563

The supreme court of Iowa, in considering a case where $700, with interest, was to be paid in gold observed "It could make no difference that the parties had stipulated for one kind of currency, rather than another, for, in legal estimation or to the mind of the court, when a recovery was sought, there could be no difference recognized between those things which the law treated as equivalent. Or, to speak more plainly, the judgment would not be for $700, with interest, payable in 'gold' or 'silver,' any more than it would be for horses, if payable in horses, or for treasury notes if such was the contract. A judgment in such a proceeding is necessarily for so much, not gold, not silver, not treasury notes not any kind of money by name, but such a sum, payable of course, in whatever the law esteems lawful, and has made a legal tender." (1864) Warmbold v. Schlichting, 16 Iowa, 211 citing Wood v. Bullens 6 Allen 516 The court referred to the Massachusetts case, where a note for $500 with interest, was in terms payable in specie. The court in that case declared that "a judgment in a suit upon a note must be rendered for a certain sum in money, expressed in dollars and cents." (1863) Wood v. Bullens, 6 Allen 516, s p Howe v Nickerson, 11 Allen 400 Tuft v Plymouth Gold Mnfg Co, 14 Allen 407. In Michigan, Cooley, J declared the same rule to be the law in a case where $500 in gold was to be paid on a note. Buchegger v Schultz 13 Mich 420

The same rule was recognized in New York, where the contract was in terms to be discharged by payment of "silver or gold" dollars (1866) Wilson v Morgan, 4 Rob 58 s c 30 How Pr 386 1 Abb P (N. S) 174 At nisi prius (Pa) Harr, J in an action where

judgment had been entered requiring payment "in specie current gold or silver moneys, said 'A final judgment in debt, covenant of assumpsit, or indeed in any proceeding instituted for the recovery of money or damages, is necessarily a judgment for so much lawful money, payable in any money which the law esteems lawful and has made it a legal tender." And a fi fa issued on such a judgment which required such money to be made thereon was held irregular Shollenberger v Watts, 10 Am L Reg (Pa) 553 So, in Louisiana where the action was brought to recover gold the court said "The courts have no power to render a judgment payable in one species of money only, and, therefore, a judgment rendered upon a note payable in gold, cannot be made payable in gold only, but must be for the payment of so many dollars, without specifying the kind (1866) Gallamo v Pierro, 18 La Ann 10

So, in Missouri, the court, in considering a gold note said 'Now suppose the creditor here had sued on his note and come into court to enforce its collection the court would not have entered judgment payable in gold, but simply for so many dollars found due him." (1866) Appel v Woltmann 38 Mo 194 The same rule was recognized in Indiana, (1865) Brown v Welch, 26 Ind 116, and in Texas, (1867) Shaw v Trunesler 30 Tex 390; (1869) Flournoy v Healy 31 Tex 590 In Illinois the same principle was announced Whetstone v Colleg 36 Ill 328 And in Alabama, it was held that where a verdict assessing plaintiff's damages was for a given number of dollars "in gold," that

the words "in gold" were super-
fluous, and in making up the judgment entry they need not be regarded   (1868) Chambers v. Walker, 12 Ala. 415; (1869) s p Flournoy v Healy, 31 Tex. 590  So, in
North Carolina, where the note
sued upon was to be paid  in
gold  or its equivalent in the currency of the country, the Supreme Court said that there was
no authority to warrant a judgment for coin, in an action for a
money demand  and in another
action of the same kind, a judgment for treasury notes, or in the
same kind of action an alternative
judgment for coin or treasury
notes  (1869) Mitchell v Henderson, 63 N. C 643

The foregoing principles have
ever been, from the earliest time,
both in English and in American
jurisprudence  the common doctrine unchallenged by the courts
until in 1868 when the Supreme
Court of the United States, by its
decision, unsettled the doctrine on
every point  The principles sought
to be established by that decision
and those following it and the
soundness of the rule will be considered in succeeding notes

*Note 6  Form of judgment*—
In ordering a judgment to be entered for coined dollars, the Supreme Court of the United States
clearly transcended its power and
ursurped that of the law-making
power  A court sitting for the
trial of causes at law, or an appellate court or a court of equity,
when awarding money judgments
simply, have absolutely no control
over the form of the judgment
The books abound in cases where
applications were made to the
trial court to correct an error in
the form of the judgment entered
by the clerk  or where the trial

court refused to order the proper
judgment to be entered  In such
cases the question is never, What
latitude of discretion has a trial
court? nor what was the intention
of the court? but is on the facts
found, What judgment does the
law authorize? If the form of
judgment, or the kind, depends
upon the views of the judge, the
questions are at once suggested
Why does the statute, with such
minuteness, provide the several
forms in replevin  the form in
trover, and in the various other
kinds of actions? And, Why is
the clerk of court, in performing
the ministerial duty of entering
a judgment, left to follow the
statutes and the common law?

Sir William Blackstone said
'The judgment though pronounced or awarded by the judges, is
not their determination or sentence, but the determination and
sentence of *the law*  It is the
conclusion that naturally and regularly follows from the premises
of law and fact  *  *  *  which
judgment or conclusion depends
not therefore on the arbitrary
caprice of the judge, but on the
settled and invariable principles
of justice  The judgment, in
short is the remedy prescribed by
law for the redress of injuries,
and the suit or action is the
vehicle or means of administrat-
ing it  What that remedy may be
is indeed the result of deliberation
and study to point out, and therefore the style of the judgment is,
not that it is decreed or resolved
by the court, for then the judgment might appear to be their
own  but, 'it is considered,' *con-
sideratum est per curiam*, that the
plaintiff do recover his damages,
his debt, his possession, and the
like  which implies that the judg-

ment is none of their own; but the act of law, pronounced and declared by the court, after due deliberation and inquiry " 3 Blackstone Com. 396 And this exposition by that eminent commentator has ever been prior to the decision in question adopted and approved. See Kramer v. Rehman, 9 Iowa 111; Ætna Ins. Co. v. Swift, 12 Minn. 437; Truett v. Legg, 32 Md 147, Freeman on Judg See 2 and 3. "Judgment is the conclusion of law, upon facts found or admitted by the parties, or upon their default, in course of the suit " Tidd's Pr 962. That a court has no power to direct a judgment to be entered for gold coin, or any particular form of money, had been prior to this decision of the United States Supreme Court, decided by the Supreme Courts of no less than ten or a dozen states See Ante Note 5 same section. The decision is in direct conflict with the only Federal statute upon that point That statute provides that "The money of account of the United States shall be expressed in dollars or units, dimes or tenths and mills or thousandths, and all accounts in the public offices and all proceedings in the courts shall be kept and had in conformity to these regulations " Act April 2 1792, U S Rev St 1874, § 3563 Mr Chief Justice Chase, speaking for the court, admitted that the statute was a general regulation, and related to all accounts and to all judicial proceedings, but his reasons for overriding the law are neither logical or well connected He says, "When, therefore, two descriptions of money are sanctioned by law, both expressed in dollars and both made current in payments it is necessary in order

to avoid ambiguity and present a failure of justice, to regard this regulation as applicable to both alike," and then follows by declaring that when coin contracts are sued upon, the judgment may be entered for coined dollars

Prior to the controversy occasioned by the passage of the legal tender acts, there were a few cases, in which judgments were entered for something other than money The cases referred to arose in Maryland and Virginia, during the Colonial days. In one of the cases referred to, the court of appeals affirmed a judgment of the trial court, awarding a judgment for 8030 Wt tobacco and 441 Wt tobacco costs (1728) Skirvan v. Willis, 4 Har & M (Md) 183 But the court, in principle, was not so far off, as tobacco was at that time a staple article and practically the only legal tender in the country

The law of the land should be uniformly applied No good reason can be advanced why, when a person desires gold or silver coin as bullion, to use in the arts, or for export, the purpose matters not the vendee in such a contract is entitled to a judgment payable in that commodity only, while the law denies the right to have such a judgment to a vendee in a contract for pigs of lead, or or iron, or for any other commodity.

*Note 7 Conflicting points —* Other points are suggested to us, wherein the decision in Bronson v Rodes, does not harmonize with other branches of the law It is in conflict with the legal definition of a debt and of obligations to deliver specific articles. A contract providing for the payment of a certain number of dollars in gold or silver coin, is either a contract creating a debt, or an obligation for the delivery of that number of coined dollars as a commodity. The contract cannot be both. A debt is a sum of money due by a certain and express agreement. Where a debt is created, nothing remains to be done but to pay a fixed and specific amount. The consideration is always executed. But with an obligation to deliver a specific article, the contract is not to pay money, but to deliver something. The consideration may not be executed in advance of the delivery of the article, or paid at the time of the delivery, but may be paid long afterwards. All debts mean money due. Obligations to deliver specific articles, may comprehend whatever the parties may choose to name. The laws pertaining to each of these contracts are essentially different. Is the contract that was under consideration in Bronson v Rodes one creating a debt or an obligation to deliver a specific article? The court said Bronson was an executor and Metz (Rodes grantor) a borrower of the estate. The amount borrowed was $1,400.00. It bore interest. The definite and specific amount of money to be repaid was $1,400.00. Both the principal and interest were to be paid in gold and silver coin *lawful money of the United States*. It has all the ear marks of a debt. The court said *it was a loan of money*. After reviewing, to some extent, the history of state bank notes and the apprehension felt, at that time (1857) as to their convertibility into coin it observed. "It is not to be doubted then that it

was to guard against the possibility of loss to the estate, through an attempt to force the acceptance of a fluctuating and perhaps irredeemable currency in payment, that the express stipulation for the payment in gold and silver coin was put into the bond. There was no necessity in law for such a stipulation, for at that time [1857] no money, except of gold or silver, had been made a legal tender. The bond without any stipulation to that effect would have been legally payable only in coin. The terms of the contract must have been selected, therefore, to fix definitely the contract between the parties, and to guard against any possible claim that payment, in the ordinary currency, ought to be accepted." (p. 246). After thus admitting that it was a debt and, that at the time the bond was executed, with or without the stipulation, it could only have been discharged by that which the government had declared a legal tender for the payment of debts and that the terms of the contract must have been selected to guard against any possible claim that payment in the ordinary currency (referring to bank-bills) ought to be accepted the court speaking through the Chief Justice, by an illogical course of reasoning, arrived at the conclusion that the creditor through his superabundance of caution in guarding against the possibility of a claim of right on the part of the debtor to discharge debt in bank-bills, must intended also to guard again g compelled to receive any form of money which the government might thereafter make a legal tender in payment of debts, and, therefore, held that such contracts were not "debts" within the meaning of the legal tender acts, and were not distinguishable in principle from contracts to deliver specific articles. Here, we have a case of a debt that is not a debt. If the contract created a debt, the decision is in direct conflict with the fundamental principles of law, that the sovereign power has sole and supreme control over its currency, the power from which the authorities to pass the legal tender acts is derived, and, consequently, it is in conflict with those laws. If it were a contract to pay money, the decision violates the principles of law, recognized and declared several times by the same court, that such contracts are necessarily subject to the constitutional power of the government over the currency, and that the obligations of the parties is necessarily assumed in reference to it. Whether the contract created a debt, or was for the delivery of specific articles, the form of judgment entered does not harmonize with the form authorized by the law in either case. If the contract was to deliver specific articles, it violates the rules of law, in reference to the mode of assessing damages, and the rule fixing the measure of damages. The law pertaining to each of the foregoing points is considered elsewhere. The court assumes that money has a commercial value; that 100 cents is worth more or less than 100 cents, and that its value is regulated by the market value of the gold or silver bullion in a dollar, as it is

forced above or below 100 cents by the legitimate demand of commerce, or by gamblers and speculators; that the fiat of a sovereign power has nothing to do with the rate at which its currency shall circulate, that United States legal tender notes is a fluctuating currency, and that the value of the notes go above or below par, and that too, without deciding whether legal tender notes or gold coin or silver coin is the standard.

The court in its argument, by which it arrived at its conclusions made its comparison between the wrong things. It compared the declared or nominal value of legal tender notes with the market value of the bullion in a coined dollar. The declared value the government controls, while the value of bullion is controlled by the law of supply and demand. If declared values had been compared (and it seems absurd to compare equals) it would have found that they were equal and that $1,400.00 in 1857 was equivalent to $1,400.00 in 1868. The decision was by a divided court, and it has not since been approved by an unanimous decision. It was contrary to the decisions of the courts of last resort in no less than fifteen states of the union and had none to support it. A decision in conflict with so many branches of the law must of necessity need constant defending, and, whenever that court gave a decision upon some other question which in the slightest tended to weaken it, some of the judges responsible for that decision have found it necessary to reiterate their views in separate opinion. See Juilliard v. Greenman 110 U

S. 424, Woodruff v. Mississippi, 162 U. S. 300. It is apparent that that court has gone too far.

Judicial decisions, like all rules of conduct, to be effective and permanent must be founded upon right reason. If founded upon error, they do not settle a rule of conduct, but tend the more to unsettle it. They will never be entirely approved and accepted. Succeeding generations do not readily subscribe to opinions handed down to them, that cannot be maintained with reason and justice. So this question has come and will come again, until settled so as to uphold the government in the free exercise of its powers and the people in their inalienable right to discharge their debts, untrammelled by the exactions of lenders in anything the government may make a legal tender for that purpose.

*Note 8. Coin as a commodity —* One among the first, if not the first case where the doctrine was applied by the Federal court to contracts for the delivery of coin as a commodity, was where the particular contract was a lease reserving rent in the following words "yielding and paying 'therefor, * * * the yearly rent or sum of £15 current money of Maryland, payable in English golden guineas weighing five pennyweights and six grains at thirty-five shillings each, and other gold and silver at their present [1791] established weight and rate according to the act of assembly." Here a judgment of the lower court awarding the plaintiff damages assessed in currency according to the bullion value of gold,

was reversed, and a judgment was directed to be entered for coin. (1868) Butler v. Horwitz, 7 Wall 258, (1869) Tyes v. United States, 5 Ct of Cl. 509. The same rule was followed, where an action was brought to recover freight, on a bill of lading executed in Whampoa, for the transportation of a cargo to New York, which provided for payment in sterling money. (1869) Forbes v. Murray, 3 Ben 497. So where a note was to pay "one thousand pounds sterling lawful money of Great Britain, at the Merchants' National Bank in the city of New York, with interest at 7 per cent" a judgment for coin was directed to be entered. (1871) The Surplus, etc of the Edith 5 Ben 444. So, the same rule was applied in an action to recover on a lease, where the yearly rent of "four ounces, two pennyweights, and twelve grains of pure gold in coined money," was reserved (1870) Dewing v. Sears, 11 Wall 379.

The foregoing decisions where the contracts were for the payment of a certain sum in foreign coin, are in conflict with the general doctrine, that foreign money not being current or a legal tender, contracts providing for payment in such money are contracts for the payment of a certain quantity of gold or silver as a commodity and the damages resulting from a breach of the contract is the value of such foreign coin at the time of the breach assessed in money generally. The Supreme Court of the United States in a later case, where the action was to recover damages for the wrongful taking of mortgaged property, where the mortgage debt was to be paid in gold, observed, Mr Chief Justice Waite delivering the opinion, that while it had been decided that a judgment upon a contract payable in gold *may* be entered for payment in coined dollars that the court had never held that in all cases it *must* be so. And, in making this admission, although leaving it optional with the debtor to ask for a judgment for coin or paper currency, nevertheless recognized the rule, that the measure of damages (in that case the plaintiff did not ask for a coin judgment) for the breach of a contract to deliver a specific quantity of coin as bullion, is the value of the coin as bullion at the time of the breach assessed in dollars and cents generally. (1878) Gregory v Morris 96 U S 619. The court, however adhered to the former ruling that there was no difference in legal effect between contracts to pay a sum of money in coin of a particular description and contracts to deliver coin as a specific article and that such contracts can only be discharged by a tender and payment of the particular coin or thing agreed to be delivered and in nothing else unless the creditor or vendee waives his right by agreeing to accept something else.

*Note 9    Where there is no express contract to pay in coin—Conversion.*—In those cases holding the doctrine that contracts to pay or deliver gold as money or as a commodity can only be discharged by a tender and payment of the identical thing agreed to be paid either before or after judgment, considerable stress was laid upon the fact that it was an express agreement to pay or deliver coin of a certain description. Notwithstanding this emphasis given to the term "express contract," the authorities have fallen into some confusion as to the rule for assessing damages and entering judgment, in cases of conversion of coin, where there was no express agreement whatever. We have already had occasion, in a preceding note, to refer to those cases in conversion and those actions against bailees for failing to deliver specific coin where the well settled rule applicable to all cases of conversion of specific chattles namely that the damages are the market value of the thing to be delivered (the time is here immaterial), assessed in money generally followed by a judgment expressed in dollars and cents was applied and we will not repeat what was there said.

On the other hand it has been held that the measure of damages for a conversion of $500 of gold was $500 and interest in gold and the judgment should be entered for gold. (1872) Phillips v Speyers 49 N Y 653. The same rule was applied previously by the same court in an action against a hotel keeper to recover for a loss of gold coin which had been delivered to the clerk of the hotel for safe keeping. (1871) Kellogg v Sweeney 46 N Y 291. So where an insurance agent had collected certain premiums in gold a judgment was rendered against him for gold coin. (1870) Independent Ins Co v Thomas 104 Mass 192. The last case at least was upon the authority of the leading decisions of the Supreme Court of the United States.

§ 97. **What does not raise an implication to pay in coin.—**
It has been held that a contract must expressly provide for
payment in coin.[1] The fact that gold or silver money is the
only legal tender money of the country where a contract is
entered into, does not raise an implication where the contract
is to be completed in another country, that in the latter
country it is to be paid in coin.[2] So, it was decided that a bill
of exchange for £100, drawn in England and payable in this
country, was not necessarily payable in coin. In that case
the court said, that, neither the fact that the bill was drawn
in London, nor that its amount is expressed in pounds, can
be construed as an expression that it is to be paid in coin
rather than treasury notes. Where the charter of a state
bank required that it should not, at any time, refuse payment
of any of its notes in gold or silver, it was held, nevertheless,
that a tender by the bank of United States treasury notes, in
redemption of its bank bills, was good.[3] So, the same rule
was applied where the general law required bank bills to be
redeemed "in the lawful money of the United States."[4] So,
the fact that coin was the only legal tender at the time a contract was made, does not raise an implication that payment is
to be in coin.[5]

There can be no implication arising from surrounding facts
and circumstances. It has never been decided squarely that
an implied promise to pay a debt in gold may be gathered
from the instrument evidencing the debt. Although the Supreme Court of the United States has said: "Conceding that
such an undertaking may be implied, where there is no
express promise to pay in gold, still the implication must be
found in the language of the contract. It is not to be gath-

---

[1] Fox v. Minor, 32 Cal. 130.

[2] (1865) Trecottin v. The Ro-
chambeau, 2 Cliff. 465. (1866)
Swanson v. Cooke, 30 How. Pr.
385. In Nova Scotia the contrary
was held to be the law where the
contract, made before the passage
of the legal tender acts in the
United States, provided for payment in "dollars and cents of the
United States currency," Nova

Scotia Teleg. Co. v. American
Teleg. Co., 4 Am. L. Reg. (U. S.)
365.

[3] (1866) Curry v. Courtenay, 103
Mass. 316.

[4] (1862) Reynolds v. Bank of
State, 18 Ind. 467.

[5] (1863) Metropolitan Bank v.
Van Dyck, 27 N. Y. 400.

[6] (1874) Maryland v. Baltimore
& O. R. Co., 89 U. S. 105.

ered from the presumed or real expectation of the parties,"[7] and in a similar case said: "That there is a well recognized distinction between the expectation of the parties to a contract and the duty imposed by it. Were it not so, the expectation of results would always be equivalent to a binding engagement that they should follow."[8]

An award upon a claim against the government was held to be payable in any currency which is a legal tender at the time of payment; the fact that the appropriation was passed in former years when gold and silver were the only legal tender, did not entitle the claimant to receive payment exclusively in specie.[9] A promise to pay dividends or profits in gold was held not implied, merely from the fact that the contract of insurance provided for the payment of premiums and losses in gold.[10] So, where the consideration of a promissory note, was a loan of gold and silver money, it was held that the note was not necessarily payable in gold.[11] And the same rule was applied where the words "American gold" followed the words "value received" in a promissory note.[12] But a contract to deliver "$10,000 current funds of the United States, at 15 cents on the dollar," to be delivered ten months from this date, was construed to be an agreement to pay $1,500 in gold for $10,000 in legal tender notes, and on a default, an action for damages was sustained.[13]

A general deposit of gold coin in a bank, although the banker designates each deposit on the pass book of the customer, as "coin" (or as "currency" if treasury notes are deposited) is not payable exclusively in gold. In such a case where coin was refused and a tender made of legal tender notes, the court said "The clear inference from the whole testimony is that the deposits of the defendants were made without condition or special agreement of any kind, and in such case the law is well settled that the depositor parts with the title to his money and loans it to the bank," that "the

[7] Maryland v. Railroad Co., 22 Wall. 105.

[8] Knox v. Lee, 12 Wall. 457.

[9] (1866) Latham v. United States 1 Ct. of Cl. 149.

[10] Luling v. Atlantic Mut. Ins. Co. 50 Barb. 520, (1872) Affirmed in 51 N. Y. 207.

[11] (1866) Currie v. Abadie 25 Cal. 502, s. p. Maryland v. Railroad Co. 22 Wall. 105.

[12] (1866) Hart v. Kohlsaat 36 Ill. 130.

[13] (1873) Cook v. Davis 53 N. Y. 320.

transaction was unaffected by the character of the money in which the deposit was made, and the bank becomes liable for the amount as a debt, which can only be discharged by such money as is by law a legal tender." [14] So, to the same effect are other decisions [15] In Illinois, a result contrary to the foregoing principles was arrived at, by the court deciding that the legal tender acts did not operate to authorize a redemption from a trust deed which matured before the passage of those acts, with such funds. There was no express agreement to pay gold, and the mortgagor paid the nominal amount necessary to redeem in "greenback" to the master in chancery. Which payment was held insufficient. [16] So, where there was no express agreement to pay gold, but a purchaser at a mortgage sale having paid that kind of money to the master in chancery, it was decided that the debt became payable in gold by operation of the law [17]

§ 98. **Specific contract acts** —In California, soon after the passage of the legal tender acts, a statute was enacted providing that "In an action on a contract or obligation in writing, for the direct payment of money, made payable in a specific kind of money or currency, judgment for the plaintiff, whether the same be by default or after verdict, may follow the contract or obligation, and be made payable in the kind of money or currency specified therein," and it is upon this act known as the "Specific Contract Act" that the decisions of the courts in California upon the question of the manner of discharging contracts to pay a sum of money in coin and the mode of enforcing them, given prior to 1868, as well as some of the decisions of a later date, are based Under this act, only that kind of money specified in the contract is a legal tender in payment thereof, and in an action on such a contract judgment may be recovered, which can only be discharged in the same kind of money. The act has been held applicable to contracts created prior to, as well as to

14 (1867) Thompson v Riggs, 5 Wall 663

15 (1869) Davis v Mason, 3 Or 154, (1868) Chesapeak Bank v Swain, 29 Md 483, (1868) Gumbel v Abrams, 20 La Ann 368

16 (1871) Chamblin v Blau 58 Ill 385

17 (1871) Morrow v Rainey, 58 Ill 357

1 Act of April 27, 1863, Cal Code Civ Proc Sec 667

those made subsequent to its passage.[2] And the courts of that state have gone so far as to hold, that a tender of United States legal tender notes, made prior to the passage of the Specific Contract Act, upon a note payable in gold, was not a defence in an action to recover on such note brought after the passage of that act.[3] In an early case arising under that law, it was decided that the act was not in conflict with the acts of Congress making United States notes a legal tender in payment of debts.[4] But in Nevada, a similar act was held to be in conflict with the legal tender acts, and unconstitutional,[5] but that decision was afterward overruled and the act upheld.[6] In Massachusetts, the court refused to enforce in kind a contract made in California, payable specifically in gold coin, although it might be so enforced in the latter state under the Specific Contract Act[7]

[2] (1864) Carpentier v Atherton, 25 Cal 564, (1864) Galland v Lewis, 26 Cal 46 Otis v Hazeltine 27 Cal 81, (1865) Myer v Kohn 29 Cal 278, (1867) Bennett v Stearns 33 Cal 468, (1894) Sheehy v Chalmers 36 Pac Rep 511

[3] Galland v Lewis 26 Cal 46

[4] Carpentier v Atherton, 25 Cal. 564

[5] (1865) Milliken v Sloat 1 Nev 481

[6] (1869) Linn v Minor 4 Nev 462

[7] Tufts v Plymouth Mining Co, 14 Allen 407 These acts are in direct conflict with the legal tender acts The Supreme Court of the United States in the legal tender cases Mr Justice Strong delivering the opinion, said in answering the various arguments advanced by the counsels against the validity of the legal tender acts that there is a wide distinction between a tender of quantities or of specific articles, and a tender of legal values That the enforcement of contracts for the delivery of specific articles belongs exclusively to the domain of the state legislation while contracts for the payment of money are subject to the authority of Congress at least so far as it relates to the means of payment See Knox v Lee 12 Wall 549

The specific contract acts of California and Nevada in express and unequivocal terms deal directly with contracts for the direct payment of money No reference is made to coin as bullion or as a commodity, and in their application they have been applied to money demands and the means of payment Although Congress has supreme control over the currency, and the states have no power to issue money or to declare it current yet if such acts are valid a state may nullify any act of Congress relative to the national currency by permitting its citizens to contract with reference to discharging their debts exclusively in one form of

§ 99.  **Tender** upon contracts with option to pay in different forms of money.—Where an agreement for the payment of money contains an alternative provision permitting payment to be made in either of two forms of legal tender money, as where a note is payable in gold or silver, the debtor may, either before or after default, tender in payment either kind of money he may choose. So he may do so upon a judgment, recovered upon such a contract. The question whether he may tender any other form of money, other than those kinds mentioned, is considered elsewhere.

§ 100.  **What may be tendered upon a contract payable in gold or the equivalent.**—There is a lack of harmony of the authorities, where the agreement is to pay in one kind of money or its equivalent in another kind, or is to pay a certain sum in a specific kind of money or its equivalent, without specifying definitely the equivalent. Where the contract was to pay gold "or the equivalent of such gold coin if paid in legal

money to the exclusion of all other money made available by law for that purpose and lending the aid of its courts to enforce payment in kind. The acts are of course, in conflict with the provisions of the constitution vesting in Congress the power to establish a uniform standard of value from which the authority was derived to pass the legal tender acts. If a state may use the same power, it may defeat the uniformity of the standard and consequently the standard itself. Story on Const § 1372.

The fact that the privilege is open to all citizens to make contracts with reference to receiving payment in any of the various forms of money, or even if confined to those forms endowed with a legal tender character by the government does not make the acts less obnoxious. If a state may give a choice between ten forms of money, it may restrict the choice to two, or even give no choice at all, and provide that a certain kind of money only shall be a legal tender in payment of debts and of the judgment entered thereon. Thus not only overriding the general provisions of the constitution, but also disregarding the express provisions prohibiting a state from making anything but gold and silver a legal tender. This is the very thing a creditor and debtor may do under the acts in question, as the acts do not mention gold or silver but "any money or currency." Passing judgment on these acts in the light of history, the inevitable conclusion is that they were passed for the express purpose of avoiding the effect of the enforcement of the legal tender acts. A more direct and wilful denial of and subversion of the power of the Federal Government over its currency could not well be imagined.

currency" it was held that it was payable in any legal tender money.[1] So, where the contract provided for payment of a specific sum in gold, or if paid in paper, an amount thereof necessary to purchase the gold, the court held that the debtor could not be compelled to pay any greater sum than that mentioned in the contract, in legal tender notes.[2] So, it was decided, in Texas, that a promissory note made "payable in gold coin, or the equivalent thereof in the United States legal tender notes," was a contract to pay the number of dollars mentioned in any legal tender.[3]

The court, in each case above referred to, declared, that since the law had made a paper dollar the equivalent of a gold dollar, and a legal tender for all debts, it was the equivalent for the purpose of discharging money demands. The authorities upholding the contrary rule, hold that the amount of gold or silver coin called for by the contract must be tendered, or sufficient of the equivalent as will purchase the amount of coin required[4]

---

[1] (1865) Reese v Stearns, 29 Cal 273

[2] (1866) Brown v Welch, 26 Ind 116

[3] (1870) Killough v Alford, 32 Tex 457, (1867) S P Jones v Smith, 18 Barb 552

[4] (1870) Wells, Fargo & Co, v Van Sickle 6 Nev 45, (1869) Mitchell v Henderson 63 N. C 643 (1882) Atkinson v Lanier, 69 Ga 460, (1871) Bond v Greenwald, 4 Heisk 153 These decisions, with possibly one exception, were based upon the rule laid down by the Supreme Court of the United States that contracts for the payment of a certain sum of money in specie or in gold coin, or in silver coin are in legal effect, contracts for the delivery of that amount of coin as a commodity, and can only be discharged by a tender and payment of the kind of money specified, and that in case of a default and an action thereon, the creditor may have

judgment payable specifically in the kind of money called for by the contract. The difficulty encountered by the courts in determining the measure of damages to be estimated in the equivalent illustrate how, when the wrong premises are laid down and followed, as many different results as minds may be obtained If such contracts are in fact contracts for the payment of coin is a specific article, then the measure of damages should be computed, as in other cases of a breach of a contract to deliver specific articles according to the market value of the coin at the time of the breach of the contract This was the rule adopted in Tennessee ([1871] Bond v Greenwald 4 Heisk 153) and in North Carolina (1869) Mitchell v Henderson, 63 N C 643

In Nevada (Wells, Fargo & Co v Van Sickle 6 Nev 45) and Georgia (Atkinson v Lanier 69

§ 101. **What is a good tender upon a contract entered into in a state in rebellion with reference to payment in its currency.** —Where a contract for the payment of a certain sum of Ga 100) the damages were computed as of the time and place of trial. In the case arising in the latter state gold was at a premium at the maturity of the note, but subsequently became at par with currency. Judgment was given for the value of the gold at the time of trial, estimated in currency, with interest from the maturity of the note. The court based its rule for the measure of damages upon the reason that where the two kinds of money became equal in value, a judgment for the value of coin estimated at its bullion value, when it was at a premium, would require payment of a larger sum than the note called for. While the decision is an attempt to do justice to the debtor, and is as equitable a rule (the contract being in fact a money demand or debt) as could be adopted by a co't considering itself constrained by the rules laid down by the Federal court, yet it is not in harmony with any rule of law. If agreements to pay a sum of money in coin are in effect contracts to pay that amount in kind and quality, as a commodity then the creditor was equitably entitled to the value of his gold at the time of the breach of the contract, for that would have been what he would have received if the debtor had not defaulted. So, if it was a money demand, as the court seemed to think by refusing to give a judgment that would require payment of more money than the note called for, the damages would not be measured by the bullion value of a gold dollar at any time since each dollar of whatever kind as money is worth exactly 100 cents, and the damages would be the number of dollars agreed to be paid, assessed in money generally. The rule adopted by the court in assessing damages according to the currency value of gold, does not take into consideration the value of silver money, or other kind of money made current by law, for they are also the equivalent of gold coin in some amount. The difficulty lies in applying rules applicable only to contracts for the delivery of specific articles to money demands and vice versa, and applying to both kind of contracts remedies foreign to both. Where a note providing for the payment of a certain sum in gold of a certain standard value or of gold and silver coin, contains a stipulation that in default thereof to pay an additional sum as damages equal to the difference between the value of such coin and United States treasury notes. It was held that the alternative provision for damages in case of a default, did not defeat the specific agreement to pay coin. (1865) Lane v Gluckauf 28 Cal 288 (1867) s p. Burnett v Stearns 33 Cal 468. In California, where contracts with such alternative provisions have been considered, it was held that they came within the Specific Contract Act of that state. In Indiana, however where there was no such statute, the same rule was adopted and a judgment was given which could only be discharged "in gold coin of the United States." (1876) Churchman v Martin 54 Ind 380

money is entered into within the borders of a country, the inhabitants of which are in rebellion against lawful author ity, and the contract is between persons thus in rebellion, or is between any other persons, but is made with reference to the money issued by such insurrectionary government, a tender of the nominal amount due, in such money, of course, would be held good by the courts erected by such rebellious people, either before or after their independence had been acknowledged. This was so, in the "Thirteen Colonies" during the War of Independence, and after its successful termination. But where a rebellion is not successful, and the courts acknowledging the lawful authority, are called upon to adjust the contracts entered into by those who were in rebellion, or by those who recognized the insurrectionary government by contracting with reference to payment being made in money issued by that government, the most the courts have done, in reference to such obligations where such money constituted the sole or chief circulating medium, was to hold that such contracts were payable in money, and were not contracts for the delivery of specific articles [1]

In Virginia, after the "War of the Rebellion," a majority of the supreme court, in the first case which came before it involving this question, regarded contracts payable in Con federate money as contracts payable in specific articles, and held that the damages for a breach was the value of the money at the time of delivery [2] This doctrine, followed con sistently, would mean that after a rebellion had been sup pressed, and the value of the money so issued was entirely destroyed, and the debtor had retained the notes which he had tendered previous to the collapse of the insurrectionary government, he might then deliver the worthless paper, though he had received value. This doctrine was not there consistently followed, if followed at all, each succeeding case being distinguished,[3] until the decisions were practically in harmony with those of other commonwealths [4] A note pay

[1] Wooten v Sherrard 68 N C 331 See Coco v Calligan, 21 La Ann 421

[2] Dearing v Rucker, 18 Grat 434

[3] See Lohman v Crouch 19 Gratt 331, Magill v Monson 20 Gratt 527

[4] See Stoves v Hamilton 21 Gratt 273, Parish v Dyce, 21 Gratt 303

able on its face in bank-bills, is a contract for the delivery
of specific articles, but they have never been the sole cur
rency of a country as were the treasury notes of the Con
federacy. The latter were issued by that government with
the intent that they should circulate as money, and were
deemed and treated as such in all ordinary transactions.[5]

§ 102. **Same subject.**—A tender of money issued by an in
surgent government upon such contracts, after that govern
ment had collapsed, would, of course, not be good. So, it has
been held repeatedly, by the courts of the lawfully constitut
ed authority, when called upon to consider the effect of a
tender of such money made during the progress of the re
bellion, upon a contract made in reference to payment in
such currency,[1] or upon a contract made previous to such in
surrection,[2] that the tender was not good. Such a tender is
not good, whether made upon a contract which in terms
specifies that payment is to be made in such currency, or
is drawn payable in money generally. The contract is payable in the amount of lawful money, which the number of
dollars mentioned in it may be proved to have been worth
at the time the contract as made; and, if the contract is
drawn payable in money generally, oral testimony may be
resorted to for the purpose of showing that the contract
was made with reference to such money, as a basis of value
for the purpose of determining the actual amount in legal
tender money to be paid[3]

Although such contracts are held to be payable in actual
money, yet, evidence being required to determine the amount
to be paid, the damages are unliquidated, and a tender in
legal money cannot be made unless provision is made by

[1] Wooten v Sherrard 68 N C
334

[1] Lynch v Hancock 14 S C 66
Wooten v Sherrard 68 N C 334
Graves v Hardesty 19 La Ann
186

[2] Love v Johnston, 72 N C 415

[3] Lynch v Hancock 14 S C 66
Wooten v Sherrard, 68 N C 334

In such cases the money issued
by an insurgent government be

ing the standard or measure of
value within the sphere in which
it circulated, it could not be said
that it was above or below its
nominal or face value Hence, in
determining the amount to be
paid in legal money, evidence
must be had of its purchasing
power at the time of making the
contract as compared with that
of legal money

statute for the tender of a certain amount of legal money for each dollar mentioned in such contracts.[4]

A general, who has with an army of the constitutional authority retaken territory and reestablished lawful authority over the people of such territory, has no power, by proclamation or otherwise, to make legal currency out of the money issued and put into circulation by such community attempting to overthrow the lawful authority.[5]

§ 103. **Contracts made in ceded or conquered territory.**— Where foreign territory is acquired by purchase or by conquest, the debts created in such territory before such acquisition, with reference to payment being made in the money of that country, are payable in the money of the country taking over such territory. In either case, whether the debt fell due prior to annexation and remained unpaid until after, or the contract does not fall due until after annexation, the purchasing power of the money theretofore current in the acquired territory, is ascertained by comparison with the purchasing power of the money of the purchasing or conquering nation at the time the debt is due, and an equal amount of money in purchasing power of the latter country will discharge the contract. In this way the creditor will receive the equivalent in purchasing power, of that for which he bargained. But if the conquering nation takes over the entire territory of the conquered country, thereby destroying its monetary system, in such case contracts, falling due after the annexation, would have to be discharged in an amount of money of the conquering nation as would be equivalent to the purchasing power of the nominal amount of the foreign money mentioned in the contract, at the time the contract was entered into. The same equitable consideration would obtain in this, as in the case of contracts payable in money of an insurgent government.

In either case, whether the value of the foreign money is to be ascertained as of the date of payment, or as of the date of the contract, evidence is required aliunde to determine the amount to be paid, and a tender of domestic money could not be made in the first instance. It may be observed,

---

4 Compton v. Major, 30 Gratt. 180, Wooten v. Sherrard, 68 N. C. 334

5 Parker v. Bloas 20 La. Ann. 167; Order of General Butler May, 1862

however, that where a contract fell due prior to annexation, and a court of the suzerain power is called upon to consider the effect of a tender made at maturity, and maintained in the money in which the contract was made payable, they would undoubtedly hold, that payment having been offered in money then a legal tender upon such contracts, the tender was good and produced all the legal consequences of a valid tender.

If a treaty was entered into, or a law enacted by the country acquiring such territory, providing for the adjustment of all debts contracted in the ceded or conquered territory prior to annexation, in the money of the suzerain power, according to a certain scale, then a tender may be made in the money of the latter country, as no evidence would then be required to determine the amount to be paid. It is also to be observed that, where a people in rebellion have secured their independence, the same rules as above set forth as applicable to cases where the monetary system of a country ceding territory is not destroyed, would apply to contracts entered into in the territory over which the new government is erected prior to or during the rebellion, which were made payable in the money of the mother country.

§ 104.  **Contracts payable in foreign money.**—A contract for the payment of a sum designated in foreign money in such money may be discharged anywhere by a tender and payment of the required amount of such foreign money  In any case, whether it is a domestic contract to pay a sum designated in foreign money, or, is a contract made abroad but payable here, or there, in any foreign money, it is regarded by the courts, other than those where such money is current, as a contract for the delivery of specific articles, and consequently domestic money is not a good tender upon such obligation  Foreign money, not being current, the damages for a breach of such contract would be the commercial value of the foreign money at the date of the breach  This is the rule for assessing damages, adopted in all cases where a contract is made with reference to payment of a sum desig nated in foreign money in such foreign money, whenever it is sought to be enforced in the courts of another country.[1]

So, the same rule as to damages apply where the contract is sued upon in the country where made, although payable abroad in domestic money. Thus, where a bill is drawn and endorsed in one country and is payable in another, on its dishonor by the acceptor, the holder is entitled to recover of the drawer the value of the sum expressed on the face of the bill, in the currency of the place where it is payable, assessed in domestic money.[2] Although the bill is drawn for a certain sum in domestic money, a tender in the home country of domestic money cannot be made, as evidence of the amount of the re exchange is necessary to determine the amount to be paid

§ 105. **Where a sum in foreign money is to be paid in domestic money—Alternative provision.**—Where a stated sum in foreign money is payable in domestic money, as where the yearly rent of six pence sterling per acre is payable "in current money of the state of New York, equal in value to the money of Great Britain," although not a contract to pay money generally, the value of the domestic money being fixed by the contract, to be equal to that of Great Britain, sufficient domestic money, gold, silver, greenbacks, or any legal tender money as will equal the amount in value of the foreign money, may be tendered upon the obligation[1] Care must be taken to tender enough

Foreign money not being a legal tender and the contract not being payable in it but in domestic money, the former is not a good tender upon such contract The terms referring to foreign money are used merely to denote the amount of domestic money to be paid A tender of such foreign money would not be good upon such contract, should the debtor follow the creditor beyond the seas, where the money men

[1] Forbes v. Murray, 3 Ben (U S Dist Ct) 197; The Mary J Vaughan, 2 Bm 47. Olanyer v Blanchard, 18 La Ann. 616; Cary v Courtenay, 103 Mass 316, Hill v Trustees, 7 Phila (Pa) 28, Christ Church v Fueshel 4 P F Smith, 71, s c 54 Pa St 71

Hogue v Williamson 20 L R A 481

[2] Suse v Pompe 8 C B N S 138

[1] Stranaghan v Youmans, 65 Barb 392 Olanyer v Blanchard 18 La Ann 616

tioned is current, and offer it there in payment  There the contract would be one payable in foreign money.  Where a contract contains a proviso that a certain sum expressed in foreign money may also be discharged in domestic money, as where the ground rent, reserved in a deed was "the yearly sum of 21 Spanish coined fine silver pieces of eight and one third part of a piece of eight, each piece of eight weighing 17 pennyweight and six grains, or so much lawful money of the province of Pennsylvania as shall be sufficient from time to time to purchase said coin," the contract may be discharged by a tender and payment of the foreign coin mentioned, or in whatever money is a legal tender of the home country.[2]  If in the currency of the latter country, care must be taken to tender enough.

§ 106.  **Where a sum in domestic money is payable in foreign money—Foreign money made current.**—Where a stated sum in domestic money is payable in foreign money, a tender of that sum in domestic money is good[1]  In such case the damages are liquidated.  One hundred dollars in Spanish or English money would always be worth just one hundred dollars, although the quantity of foreign money might vary at different times.  A tender of the latter would be good, care need only be taken to tender enough  If foreign money is made current by law, a tender in such money is good[2]  This has been done in England on several occasions, and in the United States, under the authority vested in Congress by the constitution Spanish milled dollars were at one time made current[3]  But now, in the United States, it is declared by positive statute, that no foreign gold or silver coins shall be a legal tender in payment of debts[4]

§ 107.  **Contracts payable in script or warrants**—A note or other obligation for the payment of a certain sum in city or state script, or for a certain sum of money, with the proviso that it may be paid in such script, must be paid in script on the day it is due, otherwise it becomes payable in constitu

2 Mather v  Kinike, 51 Pa  St  125
1 Ward v  Bidgwin, Lat  84
2 Wade's Case  5 Rep  114

1 See Act June 28  1834
4 U. S  G  S  1874  § 3584  Act, 21 Feb  1857; see §§ 2366, 3567, G  S  1874

tional money.[1]  If the fees of a sheriff are by law payable
in script, a tender of one entire sum in script, in payment
of a money judgment and the fees, is bad.[2]

After a judgment, and the fees of the various officers have
been included in the judgment, the fees cannot be separated
from the demand, and script tendered in payment of the
fees and money on the demand, but money must be tendered
in payment of the whole judgment.  The reasons are, that
the judgment creditor may have discharged the fees in
money, and, by incorporation in the judgment the fees be
come a part of the debt.  It is only when the fees are due
the officer and are due from the plaintiff or defendant inde
pendent of the judgment, that they may be, under the stat
utes, discharged in script   Where an assessment may be
paid in warrants, and the warrants are required to be sur
rendered for cancellation, a tender of a warrant for a larger
sum than the amount due, with the request that the amount
of the assessment be endorsed upon the warrant, is not
good.[3]

§ 108.  Forms of money in the United States and their legal
attributes.—There are in circulation in the United States,
ten different forms of money, each constituting a legal cir
culating medium, but with different legal qualities   The
term, "forms of money," as here used, does not signify the
shape into which the material is wrought, but refers both
to the material and its legal attributes as money

§ 109.  Gold coin.—Gold coin is now issued in denomina
tions of two and a half, five, ten, and twenty dollar pieces,
called respectively quarter eagles, half eagles, eagles and
double eagles[1]  These coins, with the three dollar,[2] and the
dollar pieces[3] and other gold coins heretofore issued by the
Federal Government, are a legal tender in all payments, at
their nominal or face value, when not reduced below the
standard weight and limit of tolerance provided by law for

[1] Hoys v  Tuttle, 8 Ark  124·
White v  Prigmore, 29 Ark  208
[2] White v  Prigmore, 29 Ark.
208
[3] Swamp Land Dist. v  Gwynn,
70 Cal  566

[1] Authorized by Act of April 2,
1792.
[2] Authorized by Act of February 21, 1853.
[3] Authorized by Act of March
13, 1849

the single piece, and when reduced below such standard and tolerance, they are a legal tender at valuations in proportion to their actual weight.[4]

§ 110. **Standard silver dollar.**—The standard silver dollar as issued under the act of Congress, February 28 1878, together with all silver dollars theretofore issued of like weight and fineness,[1] are a legal tender, at their nominal or face value, for all debts and dues, public and private,[2] except when otherwise expressly stipulated in the contract.[3] Under the law as it now stands, a vendor or lender, has the right to stipulate with the vendee or borrower, at the time of making the contract, that the purchase money or loan shall not be paid in standard silver dollars. This provision, giving a right to exclude by contract the silver dollar as a medium of payment, cannot be construed as giving a right to name any other form of money in which payment shall be made. If the contract, when made, did not exclude the standard silver dollar, the vendor or lender cannot insist that such a clause be inserted as a condition of his performing. If such a stipulation is made after making the agreement, and before the time for payment arrives, it would be without consideration and void, and such money would be, nevertheless, a legal tender in payment of such obligation, unless a new contract was entered into based upon some additional consideration.

A stipulation under this law excluding the standard silver dollar as a medium of payment, would not render a tender bad, of an amount of subsidiary silver coin within the limit as to amount, for which it is a legal tender. There is no law permitting any discrimination by individuals, against the subsidiary silver coins or any form of money excepting the standard silver dollars and Treasury Notes.[4] The trade dollar is not now a legal tender.[5]

4 Act of February 12 1873, U S Rev Stat. § 3585; Standard of tolerance, see § 87

1 Authorized by Act of April 2 1792, Coinage discontinued, Act of February 12 1873

2 Baldwin v Baker, 121 Mich 259 s c 80 N W Rep 36

3 20 U S Stat L c 20

4 Authorized by Act of Congress, July 14, 1890

5 Joint resolution of Congress, No 17, July 22, 1876

§ 111. **Subsidiary silver.**—The silver coins of smaller denominations than one dollar are the half dollar,[1] Columbian half dollar,[2] quarter dollar,[3] Columbian quarter dollar,[4] twenty-cent piece,[5] the dime,[6] the half dime,[7] and the three cent piece,[8] and they are all legal tender in a sum not exceeding ten dollars in one payment, upon all dues, public and private.[9] The fractional silver coins issued prior to 1853, now come within the law limiting the legal tender qualities of silver coins of smaller denomination than one dollar, to payments not exceeding ten dollars.

The amount tendered in payment, providing it does not exceed ten dollars, may be wholly of half dollars, or wholly of any one of the other denominations, or it may be made up of a portion of each. A tender of twenty dollars in payment of any obligation, made up of ten dollars in half dollars, five dollars in quarter dollars, and five dollars in dimes, would not be good. The object of the law is to limit the whole amount of the lesser silver coins, which a creditor is obliged to receive on any one payment, to ten dollars, without regard to the denomination of the coins making up the total. Where a contract provides for partial payments, an amount of subsidiary silver, within the limit for which it is a legal tender, may be tendered on each payment. But if two or more payments are in arrears, and the various payments are not evidenced by separate instruments, such as promissory notes, (with the possible exception of interest coupons in the hand of the holder of the principal note), then the payment in arrears being part of one and the same debt, are due and demandable as one debt, and only one sum of subsidiary silver, within the limit prescribed by law, is a lawful tender in payment on such obligation. If a creditor consents to receive a part of his demand and it is paid to him in subsidiary

---

[1] Authorized by Act of April 2, 1792.

[2] Authorized by Act of August 5, 1892.

[3] Authorized by Act of April 2, 1792.

[4] Authorized by Act of March 3, 1893.

[5] Authorized by Act of March 3, 1875.

[6] Authorized by Act of April 2, 1792.

[7] Authorized by Act of April 2, 1792.

[8] Authorized by Act of March 3, 1851, Coinage discontinued February 12, 1873.

[9] 21 U. S. Stat. 7, c. 17, Act of June 9, 1879.

silver, he cannot refuse subsidary silver up to the limit, in payment of the balance due, though he would receive twenty dollars in such silver on the entire demand. The limitation applies to any one payment.

Where a creditor, holding two or more obligations, presents them for payment at one time, the debtor may tender an amount of subsidary silver coin allowed by law as a legal tender, upon each and every obligation, and the residue of each obligation in whatever other form of money the law declares a legal tender. Thus, where notes of the denomination of tens, twenties and fifty dollars, amounting to $53,650 00, were presented to the Bank of Missouri for redemption, a tender of five dollars in subsidiary silver (then the limit)[10] upon each note, and the residue of each note in gold coin, was held good.[11] The reason upon which the rule is founded, is, and it was so held in that case, that each note constituted a single debt, and that the concentration of all the notes in the hand of one person did not consolidate the debts. In another case arising in Michigan, where thirty bills of the denomination of five dollars were presented at one time by one person, to a bank for redemption, and the bank tendered to the holder three hundred half dollars, issued under Act of Congress of February 21, 1853, the tender was held good.[12] A debtor has the right, not only to prefer one creditor over another, but also to provide for one debt to the exclusion of another owing to the same person, and may, in the exercise of that right, provide for the payment separately of two or more debts due to the same person.[1] And, it is his privilege to pay his debts separately in such medium of payment as the law makes applicable, and of which he cannot be deprived at the mere option of the creditor.

Where money is issued by the government, and endowed with a certain legal tender character, it retains such character until it is expressly taken away by statute. Thus, the Act of Congress, January 18, 1837, declaring that half dollars, quarter dollars, dimes, and half dimes shall be a legal tender for all debts in any amount, was not affected by the

---

[10] Act of Congress, February 21, 1853.

[11] Boatman etc Inst v Bank of Missouri, 13 Mo 197.

[12] Strong v Farmers' Bank, 4 Mich 350.

[1] 9 Bac Abr tit Tender (B) 2.

Act of February 21, 1853, regulating the weight of such coins and declaring that coins issued under the provisions of that act should be a legal tender "in payment of debts for all sums not exceeding five dollars." After the passage of the latter act, up to the codification of the mint laws in 1873, the half dollar, quarter dollar, dimes, and half dimes, issued prior to 1853, were a legal tender in any amount, while those issued after that date were a legal tender for sums not exceeding five dollars.[14]

§ 112. **Minor coins.**—The minor coins are, the five cent (nickel),[1] three cent (nickel),[2] two cent (bronze),[3] one cent (copper),[4] one cent (nickle),[5] one cent (bronze),[6] and the half cent piece (copper)[7] And they, severally or together, are a legal tender at their nominal or face value for any amount not exceeding twenty five cents in any one payment.[8]

§ 113. **Gold certificates**—Gold certificates are issued by the government in denominations of not less than twenty dollars, in exchange for gold coin and bullion,[1] and are receivable in payment of customs, and all public dues.[2] They are not a legal tender, but when offered in discharge of any obligation, other than those for which they are expressly made receivable, to a person who can waive the objection that they are not a legal tender, and the objection is not made to them on that ground, the offer of payment in such medium is good.

[14] Bank of State v Lockwood, 16 Ind 306

[1] Authorized by Act of Congress May 16, 1866

[2] Authorized by Act of Congress, March 3, 1865; Coinage discontinued, Act of September 26, 1890.

[3] Authorized by Act of Congress, April 22, 1864; Coinage discontinued, Act of February 12, 1873

[4] Authorized by Act of Congress, April 2, 1792; Coinage discontinued, Act of February 21, 1857

[5] Authorized by Act of Congress, February 21, 1857; Coinage discontinued, Act of April 22, 1864

[6] Authorized by Act of Congress April 22, 1864

[7] Authorized by Act of Congress April 2, 1792; Coinage discontinued, Act of February 21, 1857.

[8] Act of February 12, 1873, G St U S § 3587

[1] Authorized by Act of March 3 1863, and Act of July 12, 1882

[2] Act of July 12 1882

**§ 114. Silver certificates.**—Silver certificates are issued in denominations of one, two, five,[1] and ten dollars, and upwards, in exchange for the standard silver dollar, deposited with the Treasurer in sums of not less than ten dollars,[2] and are receivable in payment of customs, taxes, and all public dues. Like gold certificates, they are not a legal tender, but the objection to them on that ground may be waived when offered in payment of debts, by not taking the objection at the time. The National Banking Association are prohibited from being members of any clearing house association, in which silver certificates, as well as gold certificates, are not receivable in settlement of clearing house balances.[1]

**§ 115. Treasury notes.**—There was issued under an act of Congress, July 14, 1890, in payment of silver bullion, notes of the government called "Treasury Notes." These notes are a legal tender for all debts, public and private, except where otherwise expressly stipulated in the contract. What has been said in reference to the standard silver dollar, applies with equal force to the treasury notes. The laws giving to both, respectively, their legal tender character are the same.

Demand treasury notes, authorized by Act of July 17, 1861, and Act of February 12 1862, are a legal tender to the same extent as United States notes;[1] but Act of February 25, 1862, provided for the substitution of United States notes in place of demand notes, and the latter are cancelled when received by the government, and few if any of these notes are now in circulation. The interest bearing Treasury notes, issued under authority of the Act of March 3, 1863, and June 30, 1864, are a legal tender to the same extent as United States notes for their face value, excluding interest: Provided, That Treasury notes, issued under the act last mentioned, shall not be a legal tender in payment or redemption of any notes issued by any bank, banking association, or banker, calculated and intended to circulate as money.[2]

---

[1] Authorized by Act of March 3, 1887

[2] Authorized by Act of February 28, 1878

[3] Act of Congress, July 12, 1882

[1] These notes were receivable in payment of duties. See U S Rev St § 3173

[2] U. S. Rev St §§ 3589, 3590

**§ 116.  United States notes.**—The United States notes, now well known as "Greenbacks" and "Legal Tenders,"[1] are a legal tender for debts, both public and private, except duties on imports and interest on the public debt.  The passage of the various acts of Congress, familiarly known as the "Legal Tender Acts," gave rise to much controversy relative to the power of Congress to declare any form of money a legal tender, other than gold and silver coin.  But repeated judicial decisions, in which all phases of the questions of the functions of sovereignty, its implied powers, the express powers granted by the states to the United States, and those reserved to the state, were minutely and carefully considered, and the acts held to be constitutional[2]  Under such a power, money declared to be a legal tender for all debts, may be tendered in discharge of debts created before the enactment of the law as well as those created after its passage.[3]  As to debts created prior to the passage of a law, no distinction is made between those falling due after the law is enacted and those due prior to its enactment[4]

---

[1] Authorized by Act of Congress, February 25, 1862, July 11, 1862, and March 3, 1863

[2] People v Naylem, 26 Cal 656 Higgins v Bear River Co , 27 Cal 153 Carpenter v Northfield Bank 39 Vt 16, Belloc v Davis, 38 Cal 242, Shollenberger v Brinton, 52 Pa St 9, Verges v Giboney, 38 Mo 458, Brown v Welch, 26 Ind 116 Latham v United States, 1 Ct of Cl 149, Lick v Faulkner 25 Cal 404, Curiac v. Abadie, 25 Cal 502, Van Husan v Kanouse, 13 Mich 303, Wilson v Tidlecock, 23 Iowa, 331, Roosevelt v Bull's Head Bank, 45 Barb 579 Metropolitan Bank v Van Dyke 27 N Y 400 Murray v Gale 52 Barb 427, Hintrager v Bates 18 Iowa, 175, George v Concord, 45 N H 434 Maynard v Newman, 1 Nev 227, Jones v Harker, 37 Ga 503, Thayer v Hedges, 23 Ind 141 Milliken v Sloat 1 Nev 573, Reynolds v Bank of the State, 18 Ind 467, Breitenbach v Turner, 18 Wis 118, Johnson v Ivey 4 Coldw (Tenn ) 608, Borie v Trott 5 Phil (Pa ) 366; Knox v Lee 12 Wall 457, overruling Hepburn v Griswold, 8 Wall 603

(1873) Black v Lush, 69 Ill 70  (1869) O Neil v McKewn 1 S C 147, (1870) Knox v Lee, 12 Wall 457, partially overrulin Hepburn v Griswold 8 Wall 603 (1871) Barrington v Fisher 45 Miss 200, (1875) Longworth v Mitchell, 26 Oh St 331, (1810) Verges v Giboney 38 Mo 458 (1871) Bowen v Clark, 46 Mo 405, (1864) People v Naylem 26 Cal 656 (1872) People v Cook 44 Cal 638, Lovejoy v Stewart 23 Minn 94

[4] Higgins v Baer River Co 27 Cal 153

It was maintained by those attacking the monetary system of the United States, particularly that part of its policy relating to its paper currency, that the exercise of the foregoing power could only be justified as a war measure, but Mr. Justice Gray, in a comprehensive and able opinion, in a case where the right of the United States in time of peace, to make Treasury notes a legal tender in payment of private debts, was denied, said: "Under the power to borrow money on the credit of the United States, and to issue circulating notes for the money borrowed, its power to define the quality and force of those notes as currency is as broad as the like power over a metallic currency under the power to coin money and regulate the value thereof. Under the two powers, taken together, Congress is authorized to establish a national currency, either in coin or in paper, and to make that currency lawful money for all purposes, as regards the national government or private individuals" [5] So that the question of the power of the United States government to make any form of money a legal tender in payment of debts, both public and private, which it may see fit in the exercise of its inherent sovereign power, either in time of war or in time of peace, and in discharge of debts contracted prior to or subsequent to the passage of the law, may now be considered as firmly established. And such is the power of all independent governments

§ 117. National bank notes —The National bank notes are not a legal tender, but they are receivable at par in all parts of the United States in payment of taxes, excises, public lands, and all other dues owing to the United States, except duties on imports. They are also receivable in payment of all salaries and other debts and demands owing by the United States to individuals, corporations and associations within the United States, except interest on the public debt, and redemption of the national currency [1] A national bank is required to take and receive at par for any debt or liability due it, any and all notes or bills issued by any lawfully organized national bank [2]

[5] (1883) Juilliard v Greenman 110 U S 421
[1] U S Rev St 1873–4, § 5182 See §§ 3473, 3475.
[2] U S Rev St 1873–4, § 5196 Associations organized for the purpose of issuing notes payable in gold are excepted

**§ 118.  Tender for redemption — Paper currency. —** United States notes, fractional currency notes, gold certificates, silver certificates, and Treasury notes of 1890, are redeemable by the Treasurer, and when not mutilated so that less than three fifths of the original proportion remains, by the several assistant treasurers, at their face value. United States notes are redeemable in coin, in sums not less than fifty dollars, by the assistant treasurers in New York and San Francisco. Treasury notes of 1890 are redeemable in coin, in sums not less than fifty dollars, by the Treasurer and all Assistant Treasurers.¹ Silver certificates are redeemable in standard silver dollars only, or exchangeable for other silver certificates. Gold certificates are redeemable in gold coin. National bank notes are redeemable in United States notes ² by the Treasurer but not by the Assistant Treasurers. They are also redeemable by the bank issuing them,³ and, in legal tender money only if demanded.

The paper currency above specified, when mutilated so that less than three-fifths, but clearly more than two-fifths of the original proportion remains, are redeemable by the Treasurer only, at one half the face value of the whole note or certificate. Fragments not clearly more than two fifths are not redeemed, unless accompanied by the affidavit mentioned below. Fragments less than three fifths are redeemed at the face value of the whole note, when accompanied by an affidavit of the owner or other person having knowledge of the facts that the missing portions have been totally destroyed. The affidavit must state the cause and manner of the mutilation, and must be sworn and subscribed to before an officer qualified to administer oaths, who must affix his official seal thereto, and the character of the affiant must be certified to be good by such officer or some other having an

---

¹ The Treasury officials have adopted the practice of permitting persons presenting coin obligations for redemption to elect whether they will take gold coin or silver coin. A practice wholly unwarranted by law.

² Act of Congress, Jun 20 1874; Compilation of Comptroller, House Document No 612, 1900. See Act July 14, 1890, and Circular, Treasury Department, No 123, 1896. There seems to be some discrepancy between these various circulars and the statutes as to kind of funds to be used by the Government in redeeming bank notes.

³ See U S Rev St 1874 §§ 5172, 5226, 5227, 5234.

official seal. Signatures marked (X) must be witnessed by two persons who can write, and who must give their place of residence. The Treasurer may exercise such discretion under this regulation as may to him seem needful to protect the Government from fraud. Fragments not redeemable are returned.

§ 119. **Same subject—Fractional silver and minor coins.**—Fractional silver coins, and coins of copper, bronze, or nickel may be presented in sums or multiples of twenty dollars, assorted by denominations in separate packages, to the Treasurer or any Assistant Treasurer for redemption or exchange into lawful money. No foreign, mutilated, or defaced silver coins, or coins to which paper or other substance has been attached as an advertisement or for any other purpose, will be received. Reduction by natural abrasion is not considered mutilation  Minor coin that is so defaced as not to be readily identified, that is punched or clipped, will not be redeemed or exchanged  Pieces that are stamped, bent, or twisted out of shape, or otherwise imperfect, but showing no material loss of metal, will be redeemed [1]

§ 120. **Gold coins and standard silver dollars**—Gold coins and standard silver dollars being standard coins of the United States are not redeemable

[1] See Circular, Treasury Department, No 66, 1897

# CHAPTER III.

## THING TO BE TENDERED—SPECIFIC ARTICLES.

**§ 121. Kind of specific articles—In general.**—Where a contract is an executory agreement for the sale and delivery of specific articles, or is a note payable in such articles, the articles not being selected, it becomes necessary for the payor or vendor to inquire into and determine the kind of property he is bound to deliver. A term applicable to more than one kind of property may become, by custom and usage, applicable to a particular species A note payable in cattle can be satisfied only by a tender and payment of the required

number of animals of the bovine genus, although it is said
that the term sometimes includes sheep, goats, horses, etc
Any of the domestic animals, such as horned cattle, horses,
mules, asses, sheep and swine can be tendered in payment of
a note payable in stock, or live stock; and in those countries
where goats are kept for domestic purposes, they come under
the same head. Turkeys, chickens, geese, ducks, guineas and
peafowl are the common barn yard fowl, and the required
number of any species, or the number made up of a portion
of each species, would be a lawful tender on a note payable
in fowl. So, the required quantity in weight or measure of
any of the cereals, such as wheat, rye, barley, buckwheat and
Indian corn can be tendered in payment of a note made pay
able in grain[1] If the parties intend to confine the contract
to a particular kind of property, or species or genus of
animals, the kind intended should be specifically named.

§ 122. **Wares of a particular trade.**—Where the promise is
to pay a certain sum in wares of a particular trade, the con
tract or note can only be discharged by the delivery or tender
of such wares as are entire, and of the kind and fashion in
use at the time specified for payment.[1] Articles of mer
chandise out of fashion are practically unsaleable, and for
that reason they would not be a lawful tender It is pre
sumed that the contract is made with reference to the kind
of property that, at the time for payment, would be then
in ordinary use and marketable. A note payable in "wagon
work" does not mean that it can be discharged in labor such
as hauling, nor simply work to be performed by the maker
of the note in the construction of wagons, but means both
labor and material bestowed upon wagons or parts of wagons
either complete or incomplete[2] In determining the meaning
of the term used, descriptive of the thing in which a note
may be discharged, the court, where the meaning of the term
is not obvious, will take into consideration the occupation
of the payor, the custom and usage of the particular business
Thus, a blacksmith who has given his note payable in "black-
smithing" could not tender performance by presenting himself and offering to do work on any material which the payee

---

1 Chipman on Cont 31        2 Johnson v Seymour 19 Ind
1 Dennett v Short, 7 Greenl. 150    24

might furnish. He must furnish material when requested, such as new horse shoes, and put them on, as well as reset old shoes.

**§ 123. Articles wanted for a particular purpose.**—Where the article to be delivered is stated to be for a particular purpose, as where a horse is wanted for the dray, or cattle for beef, a cow for milch, or a machine to do a certain work, the thing tendered must reasonably answer the purpose. If the purpose for which the article is wanted is known to the seller, but it is described by the buyer independently of the object for which he wants it, he cannot reject the tender on the ground that it will not answer the purpose, if it answers the description as to kind and quality.[1]

**§ 124. Merchandise of a particular description—Part answering description.**—If the contract calls for an article of a certain description, or a certain brand of merchandise, the thing tendered must answer the description in kind and quality or it may be rejected. The vendee is not bound to accept an article different in kind from that bargained for.[1] Where a sale is made of a particular brand of tobacco, as "Parkins's Crooked Brand," a delivery of any tobacco not so branded, no matter what its quality might be, would not be a compliance with the terms of the sale.[2] So, if the contract is for the delivery of blue paint, the kind tendered must be of that color.[3] When the contract calls for cattle of a certain age, a tender of cattle older than the specified age, though of more value, will not do.[4] If only a part of the goods tendered answer the description, the vendee may reject the

[1] Chanter v Hopkins, 4 M & W 399, et seq. See Heyworth v Hutchinson, L. R. 2 Q B 447; Behn v Burness, 3 Best & S 751; Wieler v Schelizzi 17 C B 619; Krenger v Blanck, L R 5 Ex 179; Mason v Chappell, 15 Gratt 572; Hamilton v Ganyard, 3 Keys 45; Pacific Iron v Newhall, 34 Conn 67; Brown v Murphee, 31 Miss 91; Pease v Sabin, 38 Vt 432; Deming v Foster 42 N H 165; Rogers v Niles, 11 Oh St 48; Hargous v Stone 5 N Y 73.

[1] Azemar v Cassella, L R 2 C P 431, s c 36 L J, C P 124.

[2] Hyatt v Boyle 5 Gill & Johnson, 110, s c 25 Am Dec 276.

[3] Borrekins v Bevan 3 Rawle 23 s c 23 Am Dec 83.

[4] Vassau v Campbell, 79 Minn 167.

whole, and it has been held that he must do so, or he will be held to accept the whole as a substituted performance.[5]

**§ 125. Same rule applies to all contracts for the future delivery of specific articles.**—In reference to the kind of articles to be tendered, the same rule applies to all executory agreements for the sale and delivery of specific articles, as govern in the case of a note made payable in specific articles, and it does not matter whether the consideration is to be paid on delivery or the vendee is to have credit or the consideration is executed.

**§ 126. Note payable in either of two kinds of property—In two kinds.**—Where a note is payable in either of two kinds of specific articles, the tender must be wholly of one kind or of the other. The contract is in the alternative, and for the convenience of the payor, and it cannot be construed that the payor has the privilege of paying a portion in one kind and the remainder in the other.[1] Where a note for eighty dollars was made payable within eight days after date, in good West India rum, sugar, or molasses, at the election of the payee, it was held, that in the absence of any election on the part of the payee within the time, the payor was bound to tender the amount of the note in one of the articles mentioned.[2] But "if a note is made payable in cattle and grain, the debtor may pay such part of each as shall suit his convenience,"[3] but he cannot tender the full amount of the debt in one kind. Where a note is payable one half in specific articles and the other half in money, or the whole is payable in specified quantities of two or more specific articles at the same time and place, a tender of one kind of property without the other will be invalid, as it is one entire debt and the creditor is not bound to receive a part without the whole.[4]

---

[5] Reuter v Sala, L R 4 C P D 239; Tailing v O Riordin 2 Ir L R 82; See Brandt v Lawrence, 1 Q B D 344

[1] Chipman on Cont 32, Pothier on Ob No 217

[2] Townsend v Wells 3 Day R 327

[3] Chipman on Cont 32

[4] Chipman on Cont 40, Pothier on Ob No 199

§ 127.  **Right of selection by payee—Due bill—Note—Waiver of right of selection—Duty of payor.**—There are agreements for the payment of specific articles where the creditor has the right of election as to the kind of goods he will receive in payment of the debt.  If a merchant give a due bill payable in goods, or a mechanic such a bill payable in work, it is implied that the merchant will deliver such goods to the holder of the bill as he shall select out of the goods on hand unselected by any other customer, or not made or previously designated by the merchant for some one else.[1]  They must be tendered in such quantities, from time to time, as the creditor may elect,[2] and at the merchant's regular selling price.  The creditor has no right to insist on a reduction in the price merely on the ground that he can purchase the same goods cheaper elsewhere; nor can the merchant compel the creditor to accept the goods at an advance over the prevailing or his regular selling price.  So, in the case of the mechanic, he must deliver any article in his shop kept for sale, which the creditor may, from time to time, select, and if the article desired is not on hand, he must make, within a reasonable time, any such article as is usually made at such shop, or perform such labor as may be desired, as is within the line of the mechanic's business.

In all such cases the merchant or mechanic must treat the creditor with that consideration, as to fair dealing, with which all honest mechanics and merchants treat their customers.[3]  The consideration being paid in advance, the temptation is great to advance the price of the goods or slight the work, and in such cases the debtor is held to a strict performance and absolutely fair dealing.  Any refusal to deliver articles selected, or perform the work requested, or any unfair dealing as to fixing the price of the articles selected will entitle the creditor to recover the amount of the debt in money.

If, instead of a due bill, the merchant or mechanic gives a note for a certain sum to be discharged in goods, and no time for payment is fixed, the rights and duties of the parties

---

[1] Vance v Bloomer, 20 Wend 196

[2] Buck v Burk, 18 N. Y 337, Vance v Bloomer, 20 Wend. 196

[3] Chipman on Cont 29

are the same as in the case of a due bill, "but if a time of payment be fixed, the payment is not demandable at different times, nor has the holder of the note a right to select the articles; but the maker of the note may, at the time of payment, tender such articles as he shall choose, and the rights and duties of the parties are the same, as though the note were given for cattle or grain."[1] If the payee or holder of a note has the right of designating what particular kind of property he will receive in payment of the note, and he does not make a selection up to the time fixed for payment, it is a waiver of his right, and the right of such designation vests in the payor, whose duty it is to exercise the right and tender property at the time fixed for payment.[5]

§ 128. **Election to pay in money instead of property.**—Mr Chipman, in his essay on contracts for the payment of specific articles, said "All agreements to pay in specific articles are presumed to be made in favor of the debtor and he may, in all cases, pay the amount of the debt in money in lieu of the articles, which, by the terms of the contract, the creditor had agreed to receive, instead of money."[1] Where a note for one hundred dollars is made payable in wheat at a future day, the payor has his election of tendering sufficient wheat at the market price as will amount to one hundred dollars, or he may pay or tender one hundred dollars in money The same is true where the price per bushel is fixed by the note. In the latter case if the price falls below that fixed, it is reasonable to suppose that payment would be made in wheat, and in money, if wheat becomes dearer.

There are cases in which the value of the articles were stipulated, where the rule of damages adopted where there was a breach of the contract, would seem to indicate in such cases that the creditor has no option but to tender the amount of the debt in the articles specified. Thus, where a contract was to pay nineteen hundred dollars in specific payments of money, and a given sum in specific quantity of whiskey, the court held

---

[4] Chipman on Cont 30

[5] Johnson v Seymour, 19 Ind 21, Townsend v Wells, 3 Day R 327

[1] Chipman on Cont 35, Pothier on Ob No 197 Pinney v Glea-

son, 5 Wend 393 Roberts v Beatty, 2 Penn & Watts, 63 Butcher v Carlile 12 Gratt 520, Campbell v. Clark, 1 Hemp 67, Plowman v Riddle 7 Ala 775 that the damages for a failure to deliver the whiskey, were unliquidated, being measured by the value of the property at the time of the breach.- So where a stipulated rent was payable in grain, at a specified price per bushel, it was decided that the damages for a breach of the contract must be ascertained by valuing the grain at the current market price at the time when the rent was payable.[1] But the weight of authority seems to support the rule as before stated. Pothier puts a case, like that of the rent payable in grain, where a lease of a vineyard at a fixed rent, expressed in the usual terms of commercial currency, is payable in wine. In such case the lessee is not obliged to deliver the wine, but may pay the rent in money.[4] Mr. Chipman, in speaking of a note for one hundred dollars payable in wheat at seventy-five cents per bushel, said: "This case falls within the same principle and the debtor may pay the money instead of wheat, for the nature of the contract is this: the creditor agreed to receive wheat instead of money and as the parties concluded the price of wheat would, at the time of payment, be seventy-five cents per bushel, to avoid any dispute in relation to the price, fixed it in the contract, at seventy-five cents per bushel, and if wheat at the time of payment be at fifty cents per bushel, still the debtor may pay in wheat at seventy-five cents. If the parties had intended that the risk in the rise and fall of the price of wheat, should be equal with both, the contract should have been for the payment of a certain number of bushels."[5]

In all such cases the promisor having an election, the creditor cannot, before default, require payment to be made in property, and, after default the right of electing to pay in property having been lost, the creditor cannot require payment in anything that the debtor is not at liberty to pay. "If he tenders the article on the day fixed by the agreement, he may plead it, and continue his right to pay the property instead of the money."[6]

[2] Edgar v. Boies 11 Serg & Raw 445
[3] Meason v. Phillips Addis' Rep 346
[4] Pothier, 347 No 197
[5] Chip on Cont 35, Pinney v Gleason, 5 Wend 394 Brooks v Hubbard, 3 Conn 58
[6] Roberts v. Beatty, 2 Penn & Watts, 63

**§ 129.  Tend of a part in property and the balance in money.—**
Although an agreement to pay a debt in specific property
instead of money is presumed to be made in favor of the
debtor, does the privilege accorded by law to the debtor,
to pay the debt in money instead of property, allow him to
pay a part of the debt in the specific articles and the balance
in money? Mr. Chipman in his essay on contracts for the
payment of specific articles, was of the opinion, in the ab
sence of all authority, that where the property was described
in kind, as where a note for one hundred dollars is made
payable in cattle, a principle which would allow a tender to
be made of eighty dollars in cattle and twenty dollars in
money, "should be adopted as convenient in practice and
having a tendency to prevent litigation."[1]   In absence of
such a rule the creditor could refuse a tender of ninety nine
dollars in cattle and one dollar in money, and, thus convert
the whole debt into a money demand, and, it must be ad
mitted that in a great many cases, a rule that would allow
the debtor to make change in money, would be as much of
a benefit to the creditor as to compel him to accept the
entire debt in the articles specified in the note   And the
debtor would not be required to make any sacrifices in ten
dering property of a greater value than the face of the note.
On the other hand it may be asserted, and with much more
reason to uphold the argument, that the debtor having as
sumed to pay in cattle at his option, he must at his peril,
tender cattle of the fair cash value of one hundred dollars,
or cattle above that price which he is willing to relinquish
in satisfaction of the debt, or take advantage of the option
given him by law, and pay the whole debt in money   Again,
the creditor may have reasons for wanting the number of
cattle which the amount of the note would purchase, or none
at all, in which case a less number would not supply the
want.  It must be admitted that the rule which would allow
a creditor to tender a sum of money as change, could not be
construed so as to definitely fix the limit, so that one animal
valued at ten or twenty dollars, which the creditor might
not have any use for, could not with as much reason be
tendered with eighty or ninety dollars in money as the re
verse.

[1] Chip on Cont 59

**§ 130. Same subject—Property described by value.**—When a note is made payable in specific articles which are not described in kind, but by value, as in the case of a note payable in a horse worth one hundred dollars, in must be understood that the creditor wants to procure a horse for a particular purpose, and a horse of the value fixed must be tendered, or the debtor will be liable for the full amount of the debt in money. The creditor may want a good strong plow horse or dray horse, and to compel him to accept a pony or an old horse worth thirty five dollars and the balance in money would be manifestly a violation of the terms and spirit of the contract.[1] In a case where a note for thirty dollars could be discharged in a horse, mule, or colt at a valuation, and a horse valued at fifteen dollars, another at twelve and a half dollars, and two and one half dollars in money, was offered in payment of the note, the court said that it was obvious that the payee might find it to his interest to have a horse, mule, or colt worth thirty dollars, and very much to his injury to have two or three of either, worth ten or fifteen dollars each.[2]

The rule that the debtor must tender property of the full value of the face of the note, whether the property is described in kind or by value, is undoubtedly the correct rule, having common sense and justice to support it, while a rule that a tender of part of the debt in property and the balance in money, although a case can be conceived where it might be a benefit, would be subject to abuse and therefore dangerous to adopt as a general rule.

**§ 131. When the payor may make an election—When by payee —Waiver—Duty of payor.**—If a note can be discharged on a day certain either in work or money, the payor has until the day fixed to make his election.[1] Unless the note is drawn payable on or before, the payor cannot elect to pay the note in property before the day fixed. The holder of such a note is not bound to receive the goods in payment at a place or on a day different from that appointed in the note.[2] Where the payee of a note has an election as to the kind

---

[1] Chapman on Cont 39
[2] Wales v Erwin, 2 Dev (N C)
[2] Orr v Williams, 5 Hump 423     183
[1] Deel v Berry, 21 Tex 463

of property he will receive in payment, he must make the election in such season as will enable the payor to deliver the articles selected within the time limited for payment. The payor, having engaged himself to perform on that day, has a right to insist on performing. To make payment at a subsequent time would be, perhaps, to incur additional expense, take additional time, and possibly interfere with other engagements. Should the payee neglect to designate the property up to the time the note becomes due, it is a waiver of his right, and the right of such designation devolves upon the payor, whose duty it is to exercise the right and make a tender of the property at the time and place of payment, otherwise he becomes liable to pay the amount in money[1]

If a merchant gives a due bill to be paid in goods without specifying any time for payment, the merchant may, after the lapse of a reasonable time, by notice, require the payee to select goods in payment, a right which arises from the unreasonableness of holding a person to a perpetual responsibility. After such notice the payee would have a reasonable time in which to make his selection. The length of time would be governed by the situation of the parties, the kind and use to which the goods were to be put, the manner and custom of dealing between merchants and their customers in that particular business and the length of time the merchant intends to remain in business, if made known to the holder of the due bill

§ 132  **Right of election when lost—Consequences—Election irrevocable**—Notwithstanding the option given to the debtor to pay his debt in specific articles instead of money, yet in order to secure the benefit of such an agreement, he must act upon the option at the time specified for performance, by paying or tendering the specific articles. After that time the note not being discharged, his right of election is lost, and he becomes liable for a demand in money[1]  The same is true

[1] Johnson v Seymour, 19 Ind 24  Townsend v Wells, 3 Day R 327

[1] Chipman on Cont 37· Deel v Berry, 21 Tex 463, Roberts v Beatty 2 Penn & Watt 63, Townsend v Wells, 3 Days R 327  Pinney v Gleason 5 Wend 293  Brooke v Hubbard 3 Conn 58, Schmier v Fay, 12 Kan 184, Grant v Burleson, 38 Tex 214 Perry v Smith 22 Vt 306 Read v Sturtevant 40 Vt 521  Morey v Enke 5 Minn 392  Plowman v

where the note or contract may be discharged on the day of payment in depreciated bank notes.[2] In an action to recover the amount of a note which could have been discharged in specific articles on a certain day, in default of a valid plea, the clerk may assess the damages the same as upon any note payable in money.[3] Where a person is under obligation to deliver, within a time stated, a certain land warrant, a breach of the contract changes the claim into a money demand, and such liability cannot be defeated afterwards by a tender of the warrant.[4]

If no time for payment is designated in a chattel note, or it is made payable on demand, there can be no default until after a demand has been made.[5] After a demand, the payor must forthwith make his election to pay in property, and make a tender of the articles at the place of payment. So, where a note for three hundred dollars was made payable in painting on demand, with twenty days' notice when to begin work, it was held that the payor having failed to commence the work within the twenty days, he became liable for the amount of the note in money.[6] An election once made is irrevocable[7]

§ 133. When the payor must make an election on neglect of payee.—Where a note can be discharged on or before a day certain, in one of two or more kind of articles at the election of the payee, it has been held, that if the payee did not signify his election but delayed beyond the time, a tender

Riddle 7 Ala 775, McRae v Raser 9 Port 122 Wales v Erwin 2 Dev (N C) 183 Stewart v Donelly 1 Yerg 176, Millar v McClain 10 Yerg 245 Games v Manning 2 Green (Iowa) 251, Wiley v Shoemak 2 Green (Iowa) 205 Phillips v Cooley, 2 Green (Iowa) 456 Church v Feterow 2 Penn 301, Johnson v Seymour 19 Ind 24 Cockrell v Warner 14 Ark 345 Fleming v Potter 7 Watt 380 Barnes v Graham 4 Cow 452, Newton v Galbraith 5 Johns 119 McKee v Beall 3 Lit 191; Campbell v Clark, 1 Hemp 67, Van Hooser v

Logan, 3 Scam (Ill) 389 Borah v Curr, 12 Ill 66 Bilderbeck v Burlingame, 27 Ill 338, Trantor v Hibbard 56 S W Rep (Ky) 169 Contra Beede v Proehl, 34 Minn 407

 - Saunder v Richardson 2 Sm & M 90

3 Van Hooser v Logan, 3 Scam (Ill) 389

4 Bolster v Post 57 Iowa 698, s c 11 N W Rep 637

5 Morey v Enke 5 Minn 392; Campbell v Clark, 1 Hemp 67

6 Baker v Muer 12 Mass 121

7 Gloe v Chicago Ry 91 N W Rep (Neb) 547

must be made forthwith by the payor in one of the kinds of property specified, selected by him, or the demand becomes payable in money.[1] So, where a payee had neglected for a period of three years to make a selection, the payor was said to be in default for not having made the selection himself.[2] In an early English case, where the condition of a bond required the obligor, at a day and place, to pay twenty pounds or deliver ten kine, at the choice of the obligee, held, a tender must be made both of the money and kine.[3]

§ 134. **Demand by payee unnecessary—Rule with respect to demand, and recovering the amount of note in money where no place of payment is specified.**—Where a note is payable in specific property on or before, or on a day certain, a demand is not necessary to enable the holder on a default, to maintain an action for the money.[1] Nor is a demand necessary where payment is to be made on the happening of a particular event, when the knowledge of the event is equally within the knowledge of both parties.[2]

There is no difference in the rule in regard to a demand, or in the rule in reference to the right of the payee on default, to recover the amount of the note in money, in those cases where no place of payment is stipulated in the note It is well settled that where no place is expressly appointed for the delivery of specific articles on a chattel note, and the articles are portable, such as grain, salt, cattle or furniture and the like, the debtor must deliver them at the mill,

[1] Townsend v Wells, 3 Day R 327, Johnson v Seymour, 19 Ind 24

[2] Gilbert v Danforth 6 N Y 585 Here the payee, previous to the time for performance, notified the payor not to deliver the articles util requested, and the payor having failed to deliver articles of his own selection within a reasonable time after the day for performance, it was held that the payee was not deprived of the right of selection, at least not until a failure upon his part, within a reasonable time after

a request to make a selection A demand having been made for the articles before the payor took the initiative, a failure to comply rendered the payor liable for the amount in money

[3] Fordley's Case, 1 Leon 88

[1] Elkins v Parkhurst, 17 Vt 105, Games v Manning, 2 Green (Io) 251, Wiley v Shoemak, 2 Green (Io) 205, Cockrell v Warner, 14 Ark 345, Fleming v Potter, 7 Watt 380, Thomas v Roosa, 7 Johns 461 McKee v Beall, 3 Lit 191 Campbell v Clark, 1 Hemp 67

[2] McKee v Beall 3 Lit 191

warehouse, or residence of the creditor, as would be suitable
under the circumstances of each case; but if the articles to be
delivered are cumbrous, or the thing to be done is the performance of labor, the debtor must before the day for payment, ascertain from the creditor where he will receive the
goods, or have the work done, and if a reasonable place be
designated, he must tender performance at the place on the
day fixed.[3]

§ 135.  **Waiver of the right to recover the amount in money.**—
If, after a payor of a chattel note becomes in default, the
payee demands payment in goods, the demand is a waiver of
the previous breach, and the payor has a second opportunity
to deliver or tender the articles in payment of such obligation   But a failure to deliver the articles on such demand
gives the holder of the note an immediate right of action.[1]

§ 136   **No waiver by agent—Negotiability of note after default**—An agent has authority to receive payment on a
promissory note only according to its terms, and payment in
any other mode is not good   If a promissory note, payable
in specific articles, becomes a cash note by reason of the default of the payor, a delivery of property to an agent not
specifically authorized to receive the articles after the time
limited, not being in pursuance of his authority, is not obligatory on the principal and consequently not a payment on
the note[1]   It has been said that a chattel note after it is due,
becomes to the holder the same as a cash note, possessing
like negotiable qualities, and subject to like liabilities and
remedies[2]

§ 137.    **Where no right of election is given.**—There are notes
made payable in specific articles, where the language used
clearly points out the thing to be paid, leaving no option on
the part of the debtor to discharge the obligation in money.
Thus, in the case of a note for the payment of "eighty nine
dollars, to be discharged in good merchantable brick, common

[3] Phillips v  Cooley, 2 Green
(Io) 156, Morey v  Enke, 2 Minn
392

[1] Games v  Manning, 2 Green.
Io  251

[1] Stewart v  Donelly, 1 Yerg
176

[2] Wiley v  Shoemak  2 Green
(Io ) 205

brick at four dollars per thousand, and sand brick at five dollars per thousand," it was held that the intent was clear that the note was for the payment of brick alone, and not for the payment of eighty nine dollars in money.[1] So, a contract for the payment of a given sum, "payable in good merchantable pig metal," points out by direct and positive language, the thing which is to be paid. The court said, that the language used was not of the same import as the expression, "may be paid in pig metal," which, if used, would have implied an election to pay in the thing named or not, as it might suit the convenience of the obligor, and that the price, twenty-nine dollars per ton, mentioned in the contract, was merely the medium by which the quality of the thing contracted for was to be ascertained.[2] So, where a contract for the future conveyance of land, requires that the vendee shall labor for a specific period for the vendor, it was held that the vendor could not entitle himself to a conveyance by tendering a sum of money as an equivalent for the non performance of the labor,[3] unless, perhaps, the performance of the work was prevented by the vendor. In those cases where the note is made payable in a given quantity of any specific articles, as a note for one hundred bushels of wheat, or ten sheep and the like, the debtor has no option, but must tender payment in kind. The price not having been fixed by the parties, either by the unit or in the aggregate the value is uncertain and the damages in case of default unliquidated.

In all cases, whether the obligation be in the form of a note, or an executory agreement for the sale and delivery of specific articles, where it is the manifest and determinate meaning of the contract, and apparent, that, but for a desire on the part of the creditor or vendee to have the specific property described at the time fixed for delivery, the contract would not have been entered into, or the note drawn in that way, the property called for by the agreement and not money must be tendered at the time and place agreed. To allow, in such cases, a tender of money in place of the property would be to render contracts for the future delivery of specific articles very uncertain of fulfillment. A vendor then could take advantage of a rising market or a more advan-

---

[1] Mattox v. Craig 2 Bibb 584.  
[2] Cole v. Ross 9 B. Mon. 393.  
[3] Brewer v. Thorp 3 Ind. 262.

tageous offer by merely tendering back the purchase price. The doctrine is well settled, that the damages for the breach of a contract for the delivery of specific articles, where the price has not been fixed, is not the price of the articles at the date of the contract but their value at the time of the breach

§ 138. **Duty to deliver the whole.**—In all contracts for the delivery of specific articles, the promisor is bound to tender at one time, the whole amount agreed to be delivered, for the contract is entire, and the creditor is not bound to receive a part. As where a party is to deliver a horse and a note, a tender of the horse alone would not be good, the note must also be tendered [1] But the parties may sever the contract, by tendering and receiving a part, when it becomes but a contract for the residue,[2] which may be tendered in kind   On a contract where the payor has an option to pay in property or money, if a part of the debt is tendered in property, the creditor may accept the property, and insist that the balance be paid in money, and if the balance of the debt, at the time for delivery be not forthcoming in property, the residue becomes a money demand

§ 139. **Value of the article**—As has been said   if a note for one hundred dollars is made payable at a future date in wheat, the payor may tender sufficient wheat at the market price to pay the note   But in cases where the price of the article to be delivered is not fixed by market quotations, or it has no fixed standard of value, the payor of a note, in order to exonerate himself must tender the article at its fair cash value, otherwise the tender will be unavailing [1] The thing to be delivered must not only be tendered at a fair cash value, but must be of the value stipulated   Thus, a horse worth thirty seven dollars and fifty cents is not a legal tender on a note for sixty dollars payable in a horse worth from forty to fifty five dollars and the balance in cash notes; [2] even though the difference should be tendered in the other articles specified   Where the articles to be delivered are measured in the aggregate in money, the goods tendered

1 Streeter v Henley 1 Ind 401
2 Vance v Bloomer 20 Wend 196 Robert v Beatty, 2 Penn 69

1 Dewes v Lockhart, 1 Tex 535
2 Henley v Streeter 5 Ind 207

must be at the market price, or current value;[3] or if they be such that they have no standard market price, then at the fair cash value, at the place of delivery, measured in the legal units, dollars, dimes, and cents, and not upon a valuation computed according to the bullion value of coin, gold or silver. If the amount due is expressed in foreign coin, then the goods tendered must equal in value the bullion value of the foreign coin designated, at the place of delivery of the goods. So, if the amount to be delivered is expressed in foreign money generally, the goods tendered must equal the exchange value of such foreign money in the country where the goods are to be delivered. In both cases the goods must be offered at their fair cash value, or market value, at the place of delivery, measured in the legal tender money of the country where the contract is to be performed

If a due bill be given payable in merchandise at not above twenty-five per centum over cost price, the goods are to be delivered at twenty five per cent over the price paid by the merchant, and not the market price at the time of delivery[4] It has been held that where a note is made payable in merchandise "at a fair wholesale factory price" or at the wholesale factory price, and a particular scale was meant, the goods could be tendered according to the scale intended; and that evidence of the custom and usage of manufactures and dealers was admissible to show that by those terms a certain scale of prices was meant[5] If the agreement is to accept a certain number of shares of stock in payment of a note, shares of the corporation named, of the value at the time of the agreement, must be tendered and not shares after they had been inflated[6]

§ 140. Appraisal—If the property to be delivered is to be appraised, the appraisal must be made in the manner, and by the persons designated in the note. Where a party promised to pay fifty dollars and interest, one year after date, in a horse at the appraisal of two persons named, a tender of a horse appraised by one of the parties only, was held in-

3 Hall v. Williams, 2 Bav. (S C) 433

4 Buck v Burk, 18 N Y 337

5 Barrett v Allen, 10 Ohio, 126; Avery v Stewart, 2 Conn 69

6 Tranter v Hibberd, 56 S W Rep (Ky) 169

sufficient. The fact that the other person was absent from the state was held not to be a valid excuse The payee having relied upon the judgment of the two persons named, and the payor having undertaken to procure their appraisal, and having failed, he must pay the amount in money.[1]

Where a vendor secures the attendance of partial appraisers who rate the property at an extravagant price, a tender of such property is not good [2] Where the law requires lumber to be surveyed, leather to be sealed, or any property to be inspected, the property tendered must be surveyed, sealed, or inspected, as the case may be, so that the same may be lawfully used for sale.[3] A contract or act done in contravention of a statute is void, although the statute in flicts a penalty only, for the reason than such penalty implies a prohibition.

§ 141. **In the absence of the vendee or creditor** —If a tender is attempted to be made in the absence of the vendee or creditor, by designating and setting apart, at the time and place fixed for delivery, the articles intended to be applied in satisfaction of the obligation, the vendor or debtor must see to it that they are of the kind and quality described. The vendee or creditor, although he ought to be present to receive the articles, is not legally bound to be present, and nothing is waived by him unless he is present and has an opportunity to object. And in an action to recover damages for a breach of the contract for a failure to deliver the articles contracted for, or to recover on the note, the plaintiff will prevail unless the defendant pleads a tender, and proves that the articles answered the description as to kind, and were of the quality expressed or implied by the agreement.[1]

§ 142. **Selling from stock without replenishing—Selection by holder of due bill** —Where a due bill is given payable in goods to be selected from the stock of a merchant, and the time for payment is not limited, he may continue selling goods without replenishing his stock. As long as he retains suffi

---

[1] Lamb v Lathrop. 13 Wend. 95 See Bohannons v Lewis, 3 T B Mon (Ky) 376

[2] See Price v Cockran, 1 Bibb (Ky) 570

[3] Jones v. Knowles, 30 Me 402, Elkins v Parkhurst, 17 Vt 105

[1] Jones v Knowles, 30 Me 402

cient goods to meet the due bill the other party cannot complain that he is left to select from an interior assortment of goods less marketable than those on hand on the date of the contract.'

## § 143. Opportunity for inspection—Returning goods—Breach of original contract and not of warranty.—Specific articles must be tendered in such a manner that the vendee may have an opportunity to examine and determine whether they are those for which he bargained. If they do not answer the description as to kind and quality, he is not bound to return them, but may reject them at the place of delivery, or wherever it is the express or implied understanding that he shall examine them.[1] Where articles are tendered that do not answer the description, it is a breach of the principal contract, and not a breach of any warranty of quality.[2]

## § 144. Quality of the article to be delivered—In general.— In all cases where the goods have not been selected by the purchaser, but are described in kind, after determining the thing in kind that may be delivered, there still remains to be determined the grade or quality of the article which will comply with the express or implied agreement of the parties. The question of the quality of the article to be delivered in compliance with the express or implied warranty, collateral to and founded upon contracts of bargain and sale, and agreements for the sale and delivery of the various species of personal property, constitute a complex and intricate subject; and will only be considered here, in reference solely to executory agreements for the sale and delivery of specific articles, and the delivery of property upon due bills and notes payable in specific articles. The object being to confine the discussion to the consideration of the things necessary to make a valid tender, which implies the act of compliance with a prior agreement to deliver something.

A tender, in reference to specific articles, refers solely to the act of the vendor or debtor in making an offer, and such a disposition of the property to be delivered on an executory

² Buck v Burk, 18 N Y 337.
¹ Grimoldby v Wells 10 L R
C P C 391 Heilbutt v Hickson
7 L R C P C 438 Couston v

Chapman, 22 L R H L 250
² Hawkins v Pemberton, 51 N
Y 198, White v Miller, 71 N Y
118

agreement, at the time and place agreed, that the title will pass to the vendee or creditor, together with the actual or constructive possession. As the title to specific articles cannot be vested in a person without his consent, either previously given or given at the time of the offer, a tender necessarily includes, besides the manner of doing the thing, a strict performance of the contract as to kind and quality, otherwise the vendee or creditor might be vested with the title to property which he had not agreed to receive. The act of delivering property may remain to be done in compliance with a contract, but such delivery may not involve any questions relating to a tender. Thus, on a contract of bargain and sale, the property is selected, and a subsequent delivery of it does not constitute a tender in any sense. Where the property is selected and the price agreed, the title passes to the vendee and the sale is complete.[1]

At the time the article is selected certain duties and obligations rest both upon the vendor and vendee, the one to disclose latent defects known to him, to make no fraudulent representations, to practice no deceit and the like, the other to use his faculties in attending to those qualities of the article he buys which are reasonably within his observation. All of these questions are not necessarily involved in the making of a tender. So, it may be observed, that to discuss the duties, rights and remedies of the parties to a sale of chattels (where the articles are selected and the title passes) would be to digress, and follow one of the many branches of the law which merely dovetail laterally with the subject in hand. Whenever there is an implied warranty of quality founded on a sale of selected articles, the same warranty is implied in the case of an executory agreement for the sale and delivery of articles of the same description. The only difference being that, in the latter case, the warranty is construed with greater strictness. So, also, in the latter case, a warranty is more readily inferred in a given case, than it would be in an executed sale of like articles where the rule *caveat emptor* is invoked. Indeed, in such case, a warranty might not be implied at all, while in the case of an executory

[1] Rail v. Little Falls Lumber Co., 47 Minn. 422; Terry v. Wheeler, 25 N. Y. 520; McNamara v. Edmister, 11 Hun 597.

agreement to supply chattels, a warranty of quality is almost universally implied.

**§ 145. Same subject**—Where the contract is executory, to supply a particular kind of goods or manufactured articles, not defined or selected and set apart at the time of making the contract, the implied warranty is that the articles shall be of medium quality [1] or goodness, merchantable or fit for the purpose intended, and that they will bring the average market price [2] In making a tender of goods on an executory contract, the vendor makes the selection, and under such circumstances he is called upon to exercise greater diligence and care against defects than in other cases   If purchased for a declared purpose, the implied warranty is that it is reasonably fit for that purpose.[4]

Where the contract is for the delivery of animals for a particular purpose, and their adaptability depends upon their disposition and training, the animals tendered must be fit for the purposes intended   Thus, where the contract is for a carriage horse, or one for a woman to drive, a tender of a horse that is vicious or habitually runs away, could be rejected. So, if a horse is wanted for teaming or any driving purpose, a balky horse would not be a lawful tender Whether the purpose be declared or not, or known to the vendor or debtor, a balky horse, or one that is a stump puller, or one that has any bad or vicious habits, or is unsound in body in any particular, is not a good tender on any agreement to furnish a horse   If the agreement is to furnish a retriever, or a dog for a herd, an untrained dog, even though it was the kind usually trained for the purpose intended would not be a good tender

[1] 9 Bac Abr Tit Tender (B) 2
[2] 2 Kent's Com 479, Elkins v Parkhurst, 17 Vt 105 Gray v Cox, 4 D. & R 108, Jones v Bright 3 M & P. 155 5 Bing 533, Howard v. Hoey, 23 Wend 350, Jones v Just, L R 3 Q B 197, Mody v Gregson, L R 4 Ex 49, Morley v Attenborough, 3 Ex 500, Merriam v Field, 24 Wis 640, McClung v Kelly, 21 Iowa, 508, Hamilton v Gauvard 3 Keys (N Y) 45

[3] Dounce v Dow, 64 N Y 411 Van Wyck v Allen, 69 N Y 61 Robertson v Amazon, 7 Q B D 598, Walker v Pue, 57 Md 155, Randall v Newson, 2 Q B D 102

[4] Gray v Cox, 4 C B 108, Bluett v Osborn, 1 Stark. 384.

§ 146.  **Same subject—Provisions for consumption or for resale.**—In the case of the sale of provisions for immediate domestic use, the implied warranty is that they are wholesome.[1] But if the provisions are sold as articles of merchandise for resale, and not for consumption by the vendee, a warranty of quality is not implied.[2] But in the case of executory agreements for the sale and delivery of uninspected provisions, a warranty that they are wholesome and fit for the use for which they are intended, is implied in both cases. Otherwise the vendee could be compelled to accept articles which he would not have selected, either for consumption or resale, had he an opportunity to inspect them at the time of negotiating for the purchase of articles of that description.

§ 147.  **Same subject—Sale by sample.**—In a sale by sample there is an implied warranty that the commodity sold and to be delivered, shall be of the same quality and condition as the sample. A delivery of the whole, if it be like the sample, is a compliance with the contract  The undertaking of the vendor is to furnish articles of the same quality and like character as the sample, and the vendee buys on his own judgment and at his own risk as to everything else.[1]

Defects in the quality of the articles delivered, if they extend equally through the bulk, and were fully exhibited in the sample, does not give the vendee a right to reject the goods tendered. In sales by sample, the same rule obtains, as applies to a sale where the vendee had an opportunity to inspect the whole bulk  The fact that the vendor is entrusted with selection and separation of the required number or quantity, as is usual in executory agreements to furnish specific articles, does not vary the rule, further than to require the vendor to see to it that the bulk corresponds with the sample in kind and quality.

§ 148.  **Same subject—Property having grades.**—Some species of property has well known grades, and from the highest to the lowest grade has a market price. A note for one hundred dollars made payable in wheat, lumber and the like, or

[1] Hart v Wright, 17 Wend 260    Rep (Minn) 163, Niedman v.
[2] Hanson v Hartse, 73 N W    Keller, 49 N. E. Rep. (Ill.) 210.
[1] 2 Kent's Com. 481.

a contract to deliver one hundred dollars' worth of any such commodity, can be discharged by a tender of one hundred dollars' worth of any grade, from the highest to the lowest, providing the particular grade is of such quality that it is marketable.[1] But where the note is made payable in a specific quantity, as a note for one hundred bushels of wheat, "it is presumed that the parties had in view wheat of an average quality, which would bring the average market price, neither wheat of the first, nor most inferior quality. Therefore, that wheat only, which would bring the average market price, at least, is a valid tender on such note." [2]

§ 149. **Same subject—Property having no grades.**—Where property to be delivered has no established grades, but is of the kind where the price in each case is a matter of mutual agreement, and no price is agreed, the article tendered must be of the kind called for by the agreement, and free from any material defects. Pothier said "In regard to things which the debtor of a thing certain may validly offer in order to discharge himself from his obligation, observe, that it is necessary that they should be good and merchantable; which is to say, that they have no material defects. He who owes a horse indeterminately, is not admitted to offer a horse that is blind in an eye, lame, or short winded, nor one that is very old. Yet if the thing have no material defects, and the debtor can transfer the irrevocable property in it to the creditor, he may give such a thing of the kind as he pleases." [1]

§ 150. **Same subject—Uniform quality—Average quality.**—In any case the articles tendered must be of uniform quality. Thus, where a promissory note was payable in "half blooded merino wool" it was held that a tender of wool, of which a portion was of less degree of fineness than the half blooded merino, and an equal portion of a greater degree of fineness than the standard, so that the whole quantity, taken together, was of the average degree of fineness, was not sufficient. That all the wool must be at least of the degree of fineness required by the contract.[1] The rule is the same whether the

---

[1] See Jones v. Knowles, 30 Me. 402

[2] Chip on Cont 33

[1] Pothier on Ob No 284   Chip on Cont 32

[1] Perry v Smith, 22 Vt 301

quality of the article was expressed or implied. It has been held, where a contract provided for the delivery of a bunch of cattle of average quality between a maximum and minimum condition, that at least one-fourth of the cattle tendered should be above the minimum grade.[2] But the true construction of such a contract is that all the cattle should be above the minimum quality and all together range in quality from the minimum to the maximum grade.

§ **151. Same subject—Conditions attached to contracts for the delivery of unselected articles—Caveat venditor.**—It has been said that there are two conditions attaching to a contract for the delivery of unselected articles at a future day. A condition precedent whereby the vendor is permitted to reject the articles if they fall short of the required quality; and a condition subsequent giving him a right to return them for the same reason, after the inspection.[1] If below the average quality and unmarketable, they may be rejected at the time the vendor or debtor offers them in satisfaction of the agreement. Or, if the articles are set apart and designated at the time and place fixed for delivery, in the absence of the vendee or creditor, and he comes later to the place and makes an examination, and finds that they do not comply with the express or implied warranty as to quality, he may reject them at that time. The title does not pass at the time of designating and setting apart the articles intended to be delivered, unless they are the articles contracted for. The creditor or vendee in such cases is not bound to return them, but may notify the vendor or debtor that he rejects them. If it is impossible to examine the articles at the time of the tender, he may return them after taking a reasonable time for inspection, or they may be returned at the time the contract of the parties impliedly or expressly provides that the purchaser shall examine them. In all cases of executory agreements for the sale and delivery of unselected specific articles, the rule *caveat venditor*, and not *caveat emptor*, governs.

2 Vassau v. Campbell, 70 Minn. 167

1 Grimoldby v. Wells, 10 L. R. C P. 391. Here there appears to be a distinction without a difference In either case the goods are rejected before the title passes

§ 152. Same subject—Implied warranty founded upon what.—
It is said that the implied warranty of quality is founded
upon the usage of trade; that it is the mutual understanding
and intent of the parties that manufactured goods shall be
merchantable, and that a thing sold for a particular purpose
shall be reasonably fit for that purpose; and, by the civil law,
which has been followed in South Carolina and Louisiana, a
sound price implies a warranty of soundness against all
faults and defects. But a better, or at least an additional
reason for the warranty, it would seem, in contracts for the
sale and delivery at a future day, of unselected articles, is,
that the vendee does not have an opportunity to examine the
articles in advance, but they are prepared, or selected, and
brought forward at the appointed time and place by the ven
dor, solely upon his judgment as to quality and fitness, and the
vendee has no alternative but to accept or reject the articles
brought forward. A tender, in such cases, implies the bring
ing forward and offering the required number of specific ar
ticles selected by the vendor to discharge his contract, and not
a large quantity from which the vendee may choose a sufficient
number of the quality desired  It may be observed, in pass
ing, that in the case of manufactured articles contracted to
be delivered by the manufacturer, the implied warranty that
they are of good quality and fit for the purposes intended,
is all the stronger by reason of the manufacturer's superior
knowledge of the manufactured article

§ 153. Same subject—Express warranty does not exclude implied warranty.—If there is an express warranty as to quality,
the thing tendered must be of the quality warranted  An
express warranty does not exclude the natural implied war
ranty of quality founded upon every executory agreement
for the sale and delivery of unselected articles.

§ 154. Same subject — Inspection and acceptance — Caveat
emptor—Burden of proving the quality when rejected goods are
destroyed.—If, on an agreement for the sale and delivery of
specific articles, the articles are brought foward and an opportunity given the vendee to inspect them, and he thereupon
accepts them, the executory agreement becomes an executed
contract, and the rule *caveat emptor* applies; and the duties,

rights and remedies of the parties, founded upon deceit, concealment and fraudulent representations, are the same as apply to any other executed contract of sale. If the goods are rejected, or they were set apart and designated for the vendee in his absence, and were lost or destroyed without the fault of the tenderee, in any subsequent controversy respecting them, the burden of proving the quality and condition of the articles is upon the tenderor.[1]

§ 155. **Promissory notes—In general.**—If a contract of sale provides that the vendee is to give his note for the purchase price, it is presumed that the parties had in mind a negotiable promissory note for the amount due, bearing interest at the legal rate, if the rate is not expressly agreed, payable to the vendor or bearer, or to the order of the vendor; at the residence of the vendee if he lives within the state, or generally without mentioning any place of payment. If drawn payable at a place different from the residence of the payee, or that specified in the contract, a tender thereof will not be held insufficient, if the creditor has an opportunity to examine the notes, and makes no objection to their form, but rejects them upon another ground.[1]

If no time for payment is fixed by the agreement, the note tendered must be payable within a reasonable time. What would constitute a reasonable time, in a given case, is to be determined by the custom and usage, as to giving credit, in the particular line of business of the vendor, or the time usually granted in giving credit on sales of articles like the particular thing sold. Wholesalers and manufacturers have different rules as to the time of payment for various classes of goods, ranging from ten days to a year. On sales of merchandise to a consumer by a retailer, the time in most places does not exceed thirty days. In some portions of the country a custom prevails of making advances, both of money and goods, to farmers and planters on the strength of the incoming crop; in which case a tender of a note for such advances made payable at or about the time such crop is usually thrown upon the market, would be good. Where the thing sold is real estate, a short time note is not presumed to have

[1] Jones v Knowles, 30 Me. 402    Rep. (Mich) 128, s. c 3 Det. L N.
[1] Slesinger v Bresler, 68 N W    347.

been intended, as it is not the custom to give thirty, sixty
or ninety day notes in payment of farms, etc. Such payments
are usually annual, and in the absence of an express agreement as to the time, a note drawn payable in one year, would
be the shortest time that could be required. The number of
notes to be given would aid in determining the time in case
the parties were so careless as not to include the time specifically in their contract, and a dispute arose. If two, three,
or five notes were to be given, it is reasonable to suppose
that two, three, or five annual payments were intended.

If the agreement is silent as to how many notes the vendee
shall give, and more than one time of payment is not fixed,
the sale being one transaction the vendor is bound to receive
one note. If the consideration could be split up, and more
than one note could be required, there would be no limit, and
in case of default in payment, and the notes had been trans
ferred to different persons, or even in the hand of the vendor,
the vendee would be liable to several actions, and separate
costs in each action.

§ 156. In what payable—Days of grace.—If the kind of note,
the amount, rate of interest, and time and place of payment
are fixed by the agreement, the note tendered must comply
with the terms of the agreement or it may be rejected.
Where a contract for the delivery of a note for eight hundred
dollars to be "payable in cigars, at their real cost value in
Baltimore," it was held that a tender of a note, in which the
price of the cigars was fixed at thirty dollars per thousand,
was bad [1] In absence of an agreement to the contrary, the
note must be only for the payment of money, payable in
dollars generally. The creditor or vendor could not, without
a previous stipulation, require the note to be drawn payable
in a particular kind of money. If the contract so provides.
certain kind of money may be excluded as a medium of payment,[2] and the bill or note will be negotiable; yet in absence
of any such contract, the rule as to the kind of money a note
is payable in, is the same as may be tendered in payment of
any debt, and it needs no description.

A creditor or vendor, in absence of an agreement to that

---

[1] Sharp v. Jones, 18 Ind 314     Act of Congress, February 28,
[2] Standard silver dollars  See       1878

effect, cannot require a note to be drawn so as to waive the days of grace.

**§ 157. Agreement by contractors to receive notes—What sub-contractors must receive—Material-men and laborers.—**Where a contractor agrees to receive bonds, or note and mortgage in payment, a sub contractor is bound to receive payment from the owner as provided in the principal's contract, should he fail to secure his pay from the contractor, and there remain anything due from the owner. Sub-contractors are bound to take notice of the mode under which the contractor has a right to require the owner to discharge his liability; and he cannot require payment from the owner to be made in anything else.[1] Otherwise he could insist on receiving cash, and place a lien on the property, when the mode of payment was inconsistent with the right to have a lien. If the proper tender is not made to him of the article in which he is to be paid, he may maintain an action for a money judgment.[2]

Material men and laborers, however, are not bound to accept anything in payment except money, whatever may be the contract between the owner and the contractor,[3] and the owner to protect himself from mechanic's liens must tender money to them.

**§ 158  Refusing notes when the insolvency of maker was concealed—Insolvency of vendee before delivery of the goods—After the delivery of the goods and before the tender of the note.—**If goods are sold to be paid for with the note of the vendee, or by a bill accepted by him, and the vendee was in fact insolvent at the time of making the contract of sale, and that fact was concealed from the vendor, he may refuse a tender of such note or bill and keep the goods, if they have not been delivered. If on the route in possession of a carrier, he may

1 Jones v Murphy, 61 Iowa 165, s c 19 N W Rep 598, Stout v Golden, 9 W Va 231, McKeugh v Washington, 8 W Va 666, Bowen v Aubrey, 22 Cal 566, Henley v Wadsworth, 38 Cal 356; Reeve v. Elmendorf, 38 N J L 125

2 Farmers Loan & Trust Co, v Canada & St L R R Co., 127

Ind 250, S C 26 N E Rep 786

3 Farmers Loan & Trust Co. v. Canada & St L R R Co., 127 Ind 250, s. c 26 N E Rep. 786. Barker v Buell, 35 Ind. 297; Colter v. Frese, 45 Ind 96, Duncan v Bateman, 23 Ark 327, Huck v Gaylord, 50 Tex, 578; Pitts v. Bomar, 33 Ga. 96.

exercise the right of *stoppage in transitu*, and, even if they
have passed into the possession of the vendee, if distinguish
able, and the rights of other creditors have not intervened,
he may replevy them.  He has a right to rescind the contract
on the ground of fraud.  If the goods are sold upon a certain
credit, that is to be paid for by a note or bill payable at a
future time, and before the paper is delivered the vendee be
comes insolvent, the vendor may reject a tender of the note
or bill, and if the goods have not been delivered, he may re
tain them, or stop them in transit, but beyond this he cannot
pursue the goods.

If the goods have been delivered, and they were sold upon
a certain credit, the subsequent insolvency of the vendee will
not give the vendor a right to reject a tender of the note or
bill.  In a case where goods were sold to be paid for by a bill
to be drawn at a future day, payable at a certain time from
date, it was held that the vendor must draw the bill and
tender it for acceptance.  The vendee having previously dishonored several bills, did not excuse the vendor from drawing
a bill and tendering it for acceptance.[1]  Credit having been
extended to a vendee, any subsequent change in his financial
condition does not enable the vendor to refuse to accept the
vendee's bill, and require him to tender a bill accepted by a
person satisfactory to the vendor.[2]

§ 159.  **Substituting the note of the assignee for that of the
vendee.**—Where a contract for the sale of land provides that a
note shall be given for the deferred payments, the assignee
of such a contract cannot substitute his note for that of the
vendee and compel a conveyance upon a tender of his note.[1]
In such cases, it is a necessary inference that the character
and solvency of the vendee was an inducement to the contract.
So, the same rule applies, where the contract provides for
the giving of a mortgage securing the deferred paymen..  The
vendor cannot be deprived of his right to rely upon the
covenants of the vendee.  It is a general rule that rights
arising out of a contract cannot be transferred if they are
coupled with a liability.  In all such cases, an assignee must

---

[1] See 2 Comyn on Cont. 229,
Reed v Mestaer.

[2] See 2 Comyn on Cont 229.

[1] Rice v Gibbs, 58 N. W Rep
(Neb) 724.

either tender the whole purchase price in cash, or the note of the original vendee, in case the vendor will not receive the cash.

Where the vendor has the notes of the vendee for the purchase price, and under the agreement is to give a deed and accept a mortgage back when a certain number of the notes are paid, an assignee of the contract, the required payments having been made, may tender a mortgage upon the land securing the payment of the remaining notes and demand a deed [2] Here, the personal liability of the vendee upon which the vendor has a right to rely, is not lost to him.

§ 160. **Notes of third persons — Short-time notes — Demand notes.**—Where a vendee or debtor is to pay the consideration or debt in notes of third parties, and no particular notes are specified, the notes tendered must be negotiable and not overdue so that there cannot arise any question of equities existing between the maker and the payee. They may be notes in which the vendee or debtor is named as payee; or notes payable to any third person, provided they have been transferred so as to preserve their negotiability. So, notes drawn payable to the creditor or vendor, may be tendered, but in this case, however, if the agreement is that the debtor or vendee shall endorse the notes delivered, they must be so endorsed before the tender.

Where the purchase price is to be paid in notes, the vendor's note would not be a good tender on such an agreement, as there is no presumption that a creditor will take up his note before it matures. And, if past due, or in any case, it is reasonable to suppose that if the creditor or vendor had had in mind his note, specific mention would have been made of it, and an agreement arrived at. A vendee will not be permitted to trick the vendor out of his property by leading him to expect something in payment which he can realize upon, and then tender in payment the vendor's obligation. If the sale was for cash, or credit was extended, the vendor's note, bill, or account would not be a legal tender.

If the contract does not specify the time when the notes are to be payable, they must be short time notes, or notes falling due within a reasonable time after the date stipulated

---

[2] Wagner v. Cheney, 16 Neb 202, S C 20 N. W Rep 222.

for delivery. Sixty, ninety days, six months, or even one year, would not be an unreasonable time, as notes falling due within a year are such as are the most readily negotiated. Long time notes with two, three, or five years to run, whether secured or unsecured, are not easily negotiated, being desirable only to investors. It is presumed, in absence of a stipulation as to the time, that the parties had in mind short time notes. A tender of demand notes would of course be good.

§ 161. Same subject—Notes in payment or as collateral.—
The question frequently arises, where a note or bill of a third person is taken for or on account of a debt, or on account of the purchase price, whether the acceptance of such note or bill constitutes payment  Where there is an express stipulation that the note or bill is to be received in full discharge of the contract, there is of course no occasion for a controversy.  There is in this case, as well as where such an agreement is implied, a complete substitution of the debt represented by the bill or note for the obligation of the debtor or vendee, and consequently payment of it.  Any loss on account of the insolvency of the maker of the note falls upon the transferee.

Where no express agreement appears, the intent is to be deduced from the facts and circumstances of each case.  If a debtor holding the note or bill of a third person, payable to his order, endorses it without qualification and passes it to his creditor for and on account of a pre-existing debt, he is liable upon the endorsement in the event of its dishonor, on receiving proper notice; and in such case it is a matter of little moment whether it was accepted as payment or merely as collateral, excepting as to the right of the creditor to sue upon the original obligation before the maturity of the note  Or, if such a note so endorsed, is passed to a contractor or vendor, the question whether it was received as payment or merely as collateral might be material in determining whether the latter was entitled to a lien  An antecedent parole agreement, as well as any written agreement is admissible as between the transferor and transferee, or as between the former and subsequent purchasers with notice, to prove that the note or bill was to be taken in sole reliance upon the maker, and was endorsed in order to transfer the title in pursuance of that agreement.[1]

If a note or bill is payable to bearer, and it is passed to a creditor by delivery, on account of an antecedent debt, the rule appears to be, that in absence of an express agreement that it shall constitute payment, in case of its dishonor the creditor may tender the note back, and sue upon the original obligation. But where a debtor or vendee transfers such a note or bill, for a contemporaneous debt, without endorsement, a presumption arises in absence of an express agreement to the contrary, that the instrument constitutes the consideration; that it was a sale of the note or bill at the risk of the creditor; from his having taken it without endorsement. But this presumption may be overthrown by proof that it was taken as collateral merely. Whether the note or bill of a third person be payable to bearer or to payee named or order, and whether it is delivered for and on account of a pre-existing debt or upon a contemporaneous debt, if it be endorsed by the debtor or vendee, the personal liability, evidenced by the endorsement, raises the presumption that the bill or note constitutes conditional payment only.

§ 162. Same subject — "Good obligations" — Insolvency of maker.—It has been held that where the vendee is to pay the purchase price, not in his own note or in any particular notes, but in "good obligations," the vendor has a right to refuse a tender of notes that do not answer that description, but if notes are tendered and accepted, the use of the word "good" does not expressly or impliedly guarantee that the makers are solvent; the notes having been received as good[1] Where the vendee agrees to take the notes back if not good, on the maker becoming insolvent, the vendor or creditor may tender the notes back and recover upon the original obligation.[2] Such a tender is good even though the vendee or creditor had parted with the notes, and got possession of them again solely for the purpose of making the tender

Where the agreement is to accept certain notes in payment of goods sold, and before the delivery of the goods the

[1] First National Bank v. National Marine Bank, 20 Minn. 63, Downer v. Chesebrough, 36 Conn 89

[1] Corbet v Evans, 25 Pa St. 310.

[2] Bell v Ballance, 1 Dev. (N. C) 391

notes prove not to be good, a tender of such notes is not good, unless there was an express agreement to accept them and take the chances of the notes being paid.[3] An offer to pay in the notes of a bankrupt is not a good offer of payment on any executory agreement, unless there is an agreement to take them upon the sole responsibility of the maker. So, after the goods are delivered, or the consideration has passed, if the maker of the note is discovered to be a bankrupt, or financially irresponsible, a tender of such note does not constitute a good tender, in absence of an express agreement that the note shall constitute payment, and that the vendor or creditor shall assume the risk of collecting it. An agreement that the vendee or debtor shall endorse the note without recourse, would be some evidence that the note was to be taken on the sole responsibility of the maker. The same rule applies, whether the notes of certain persons named were to be received, or the notes of persons not named. When a person parts with his property in consideration of a promise that he shall be paid for it in notes, obligations, or other evidence of debts against third persons, he is not bound to accept the obligation of one who is insolvent, in absence of an agreement that he shall take the note and rely upon the responsibility of the maker. This is true even when he has not expressly bargained for good paper

§ 163.   Same subject—False representations as to the solvency of the maker.—Fraud always vitiates a contract, and whatever may be the agreement as to who shall assume the risk of collecting a note or bill, if the vendee or debtor makes any false representations as to the solvency of the maker of a note or the acceptor of a bill, upon which the vendor or creditor relied, a tender of such instrument may be rejected.

§ 164.   Same subject—General rules.—From the foregoing the general rule may be deduced, that, in the absence of fraud, if there is an express agreement to take a certain note in payment at the risk of the transferee, and the maker was insolvent at the time of making the agreement, or became insolvent before the time for the delivery of the note, such note is nevertheless a good tender on the contract, it being

[3] Roget v Merret, 2 Cai. (N. Y.) 117.

presumed, it being his duty, that the vendor satisfied himself as to the solvency of the maker at the time of making the agreement, or chose to risk it in any event. If no particular note or notes were mentioned, only such notes as are good at the time of the tender, will be a good tender whether there is an express agreement for good paper or not.

§ 165. **Same subject—Endorsement and assignment.**—Where a contract provides that payment is to be made in notes of third parties, the notes intended to be delivered in compliance with the contract, if they are payable to the payee or order, must be endorsed by such payee. The effect of a tender correctly made is to vest the creditor with the legal title to the property tendered; and without an endorsement, the legal title to the notes could not be transferred.[1] An assignment or endorsement (without recourse at least) is necessary, as a delivery of a note payable to order, without an assignment or endorsement on it transfers only the equitable title and puts upon the transferee the burden of satisfying the maker as best he can, that the note is his; and if an action is commenced to enforce payment, the holder is put to the trouble of proving an assignment by evidence de hors the instrument. If the notes are payable to third parties and by them endorsed to the debtor or vendee, the creditor or vendor must be satisfied with any endorsement which the third parties may have made upon the notes  An assignment, or an endorsement without recourse, is sufficient

If a note or bill is payable to bearer or holder, or to order and it has been endorsed in blank, the title to the note or bill passes by delivery and a tender of such note unendorsed by the vendee or debtor is a compliance with a contract to pay in negotiable instruments, even though the instrument was not to be received in full discharge of the obligation of the vendee or debtor; or though the vendee or debtor in his agreement to pay in notes guaranteed the note or bill to be good  An agreement to endorse a third person's note is not implied from a warranty of the solvency of the maker  In the first case, if the note or bill turns out to be bad, the creditor may tender it back and recover upon the original

[1] Henley v Streeter, 5 Ind 207,   Eichholtz v Taylor, 88 Ind 38   Streeter v Henley, 1 Ind. 401,

contract, and in the other case he may recover upon the guaranty, or upon the original contract if the instrument was not accepted in absolute payment.

If the note or bill is drawn payable to the order of the vendee or debtor, or has been endorsed to him or order, and there is no specific agreement that the note or bill is to be taken at the risk of the creditor, the instrument tendered must nevertheless be endorsed unqualifiedly, by the payee or endorsee, as the case may be. If assigned, or endorsed without recourse, it would militate against a recovery upon the original contract by raising the presumption that the instrument was taken in payment, in sole reliance upon the responsibility of the maker. A delivery of a negotiable instrument payable to bearer or holder unendorsed, would not raise any such presumption.

If there is an express agreement that a note or bill is to be endorsed by the vendee or debtor, he must endorse the instrument whether it be such as pass by endorsement or by delivery merely. In such case the endorsement means not merely writing the name on the instrument so as to pass the title, but such an endorsement as will amount to a separate collateral undertaking to pay the instrument, conditional upon default of the maker and on receiving due notice of its dishonor. A note of a third party to which the vendee or debtor has only an equitable title will not be a good tender upon a contract to pay in negotiable instruments, even though the vendee or debtor endorses it.

§ 166. **Same subject—Endorsement or assignment where placed —Guaranty.**—The assignment, or endorsement of whatever kind, must be upon the instrument or an allonge. Negotiable instruments payable to order may be transferred by an assignment written on a separate paper, but such an assignment separates the evidence of ownership from the instrument, and renders a note non-negotiable, according to the strict rule of the law merchant, in the hand of the transferee. Where a person agrees to pay in obligations of third persons, the inference is that negotiable notes or bills are intended; and a tender of negotiable instruments in such a way that they, in the hand of the transferee, at once become non-negotiable, would not be a compliance with the agreement.

Where an agreement provides that a note shall be guaranteed, the guaranty intended is the ordinary guaranty of payment, written upon the instrument. If the note is non negotiable, a tender of such note with the blank endorsement of the party who is to guarantee the payment, is insufficient. There must be a special guaranty written thereon.[1]

§ 167. **Responsibility of surety, guarantor, or endorser.**—If a surety, guarantor, or endorser is to be furnished, the contract must be unqualified. If the agreement does not specify who the surety, guarantor, or endorser shall be, and is silent as to the financial ability of the person who is to be secured, or provides for a good, or a good and sufficient surety, etc., the person signing in such a capacity must be solvent, and from whom the amount of the note could be collected. The intent of the parties is, and the term implies, as between the debtor and creditor, besides the undertaking to pay in a certain event, that the surety, guarantor, or endorser is able and will pay the debt if called upon.

§ 168. **Bills of exchange.**—If bills of exchange are tendered on a contract to pay in negotiable instruments of third parties, whether drawn by the vendor or creditor or by another, the bills must have been accepted by the drawee before they are tendered. The drawee, as a debtor for goods sold or for funds deposited with him belonging to the drawer, is under no legal obligation to accept a bill, any more than a debtor, upon request, is bound to execute a promissory note for the amount due or to become due to his creditor. The drawee may not become a party to the bill. Only such a bill, where all the persons contemplated as parties when the bill is drawn, have assumed the liability intended, can be tendered in satisfaction of such a contract. Until accepted it only amounts at most to an equitable assignment of the funds. If the drawee has been supplied with funds for the purpose of meeting the bill; or if there is an implied contract to honor drafts, as in the case of a banker with whom a cash account is kept by the drawer, it is incumbent on the drawee to honor the bill if the balance on deposit is sufficient. But in case payment or acceptance is refused, the drawee is answerable,

[1] Sharp v Jones, 18 Ind 314; Corbet v Evans, 25 Pa. St 310

not as a party to the bill, but to the depositor, in tort for
not honoring it.[1]  A tender of a blank acceptance, accompanied by a letter authorizing the draft to be filled out with
the proper sum, has been held a sufficient offer of performance.[2]

§ 169.  **Notes how executed.**—Where the agreement is to pay
in promissory notes, whether those of the vendee or debtor,
or those of third persons, the paper tendered, to constitute a
compliance with the agreement, must be written in the language of the country where the agreement is made; but the
signature of the maker may be written in the maker's native
language.  If notes of third parties are offered, the signature
must be written by the maker.  The signature of the maker
of a note, in case of a dispute or death of the maker, can be
proven to be genuine by the testimony of persons familiar
with his handwriting, or by comparing it with other writings
proven to have been written by him, while in the case of a
note signed by the maker's mark, it is more difficult to prove
that it is the note of the one it purports to be, as the holder
is limited in his proof, in almost every case, to the testimony
of the subscribing witnesses who, when wanted, may be dead,
blind, insane, or in foreign parts, in which event he would
be required to prove the signatures of the subscribing witnesses.  So, if the maker's name is signed by a third person,
in case of a dispute the burden of proving the authority of
such third person to sign the maker's name is upon the holder,
which could not be put upon a person agreeing to receive
payment in notes of third persons.  A printed signature does
not prove itself, but requires proof that it was adopted and
used by the maker,[1] and notes of third persons so signed, for
that reason, may be rejected   Notes signed in any way so
as to indicate who the payor is, are negotiable, provided they
conform in other particulars to the requirements of negotiable instruments   But in the case of an agreement to receive
payment in negotiable instruments of third parties, the vendor or creditor cannot be required to accept any paper, where
the burden of proving its execution is in any way increased by
reason of the signature being different from a written signa-

---

[1] Daniels  on  Neg.  Inst.  Ch.
XVIII, Sec. 1.

[2] Dana v  Fiedler, 1 E  D. Smith,
463

[1] 1 Daniels on Neg. Inst. Ch. II

ture in full, in the maker's handwriting. It is reasonable to presume that if such notes were submitted to the creditor or vendor before the agreement was made, he would not have agreed to receive them. If a vendee or creditor is to give his note, and he cannot write, a note signed with his mark, or signed in his name by a third person, properly witnessed, is a good tender upon such an agreement. The whole instrument must be expressed in writing and it may be upon any material.[1] Where the agreement is to pay in notes of third parties, the tenderee is entitled to a reasonable time to ascertain if the signatures are genuine.

§ 170. **Instruments of doubtful negotiability.**—It is often very difficult to determine, in a given case, whether or not the instrument offered in payment is negotiable  If ambiguous in terms and its negotiability doubtful it may be refused   A person who has contracted to receive payment in negotiable paper cannot be required to take any chances on paper which is not readily recognizable by the average business man as negotiable.  He ought not to be compelled to establish its negotiability in a court of law, in an endeavor to shut out equities existing between the original parties.  The rule by which written promises to pay are determined to be negotiable or not, is well settled   A negotiable promissory note as defined in the books, is an unsealed written instrument in which the engagement to pay by the maker, to a person therein named or order, or to bearer, is certain, not dependent upon any conditions, certain as to the time of payment or capable of being made certain at the election of the holder, definite as to the amount to be paid, and payable in legal tender money.[1]

§ 171. **Deed—Where contract is silent as to quality.**—Where a deed is to be delivered in pursuance of an agreement to convey land, the instrument tendered must comply with the contract as to kind, and contain the warranties and personal covenants specified. If the contract is silent as to the quality of the deed to be delivered, whether there is an express or implied undertaking to convey a good title, a tender of any

---

¹ 1 Daniels on Neg Inst Ch II    ¹ 1 Daniels on Neg Inst Ch I

Story on Notes and Bills, § 1

instrument containing apt words of conveyance will be a sufficient compliance with the agreement if the vendor in fact has a good title. No particular form is necessary to constitute a deed. "An estate in fee may be created by the usual and solemn forms of conveyance,"[1] and "a deed does not, *ex vi termini*, mean a deed with covenants of warranty, but only an instrument with apt terms conveying the property sold."[2] Where there was an implied agreement to make a good title, and the covenant was "to execute a deed to the premises," it was held that "by covenanting to execute a deed, no greater duty or obligation can be intended than to execute a conveyance or assurance of the property, which may be good and perfect, without warranty, or personal covenants."[3]

In Kentucky, in an early case, where a bond provided for a "good and sufficient deed" the court held, that a bond to make a good and sufficient deed to land, requires a deed with general warranty.[4] And in a later case, where the bond required the vendor "to make or cause to be made a sure and indefeasible right and title, such as the state makes, * * * in fee simple," a decree of the trial court in an action for specific performance, requiring the vendor to convey the land by a deed of special warranty, was reversed; the appellate court holding that the bond called for a deed of general warranty and not a deed with a special warranty.[5] In Pennsylvania, a covenant to convey in fee simple was held satisfied by a deed with special warranty, that a deed with general warranty was not required[6]. But it was not decided that a deed without any covenants, if tendered, would not have been good. In Arkansas, it was held that a bond for "a deed of conveyance in fee of the legal title," means a "good and sufficient" conveyance with the usual covenants[7]

[1] Frost v Raymond, 2 Camp Rep 191

[2] Ketchum v Evertson, 13 Johns 359

[3] Van Esp v Schenectady, 12 Johns 436 See Nixon v Hyserott, 5 Johns 58; Kyle v Kavanaugh, 103 Mass. 359

[4] Fleming v Harrison, 2 Bibb 171, S C 4 Am Dec. 601

[5] Kelly v Bradford, 3 Bibb 317, S C 6 Am Dec 656, citing Cowan v White, Smead 177; Sug. Vend. 117

[6] Espy v. Anderson, 14 Pa. St 308

[7] Rudd v Savelli, 44 Ark 115, citing Watkins v Rogers, 21 Ark 298.

**§ 172. Deeds of "warranty"—With the "usual covenants"—Quit claim.**—Where a contract is to convey by a deed of "warranty" or by a deed with the "usual covenants," the deed tendered must contain the covenants ordinarily used in the place where the agreement is made. The usage is not uniform. Mr. Washburn said, "The three covenants ordinarily found in deeds of conveyance in the Eastern States are * : * namely, of seisin, and right to convey, against incumbrances and of warranty. In English deeds there is a covenant for further assurances, which is also found in deeds in use in some of the Middle States, and a covenant of quiet enjoyment. It is said that the covenant of seisin is not in use now in England, being embraced in the right to convey, while in the Western States, Pennsylvania, and the Southern States, the covenant of warranty is not infrequently the only covenant inserted. In Iowa, a covenant of warranty is held to embrace the whole three above mentioned. It is said that covenants for further assurances are not in general use in this country. In Ohio, the usual covenants are of seisin and warranty."[1]

In absence of a stipulation as to the kind of a deed a vendor is to furnish, but he is to make a good title, a tender of an ordinary deed of quit claim would not be good. A party who relies upon a mere quit claim does so at his peril, and is put to the trouble of first seeing that there is an estate to be conveyed. Such a conveyance passes only whatever title the grantor has.[2] Although the authorities hold that an agreement to execute a deed of land which does not provide for a deed with general or special warranties and personal covenants, is satisfied by a deed with any apt words of conveyance, yet the vendee could not be required to accept a deed which in terms would estop him from relying upon the implied warranty of title, or covenants running with the land. Where the contract is to convey only such an estate or interest as the vendor has, a tender of a quit claim deed is a

[1] 3 Wash. Real Prop. 447 (4th ed.) citing Wms Real Prop 69, Caldwell v. Kirkpatrick, 6 Ala. 60, Van Wagner v Van Nostrand, 19 Iowa, 426. Foote v Burnett, 10 Ohio, 317, Armstrong v Darby, 26 Mo. 517, Colby v. Osgood, 29 Barb 339, Funk v Cresswell, 5 Iowa, 62, and Walk Am Law, 382

[2] Marshall v. Roberts, 18 Minn 405, May v Le Claire, 11 Wallace 232.

performance of the agreement.[3]   Nor need the wife join in the deed.[4]

## § 173.  Deed executed by guardian—Personal representatives—Assignee—Trustee.

Where a contract of sale of land is made with a guardian or personal representative, or an assignee or receiver, or any person holding land in trust, the contract is satisfied by a tender of a deed in the usual form, in which no warranties or personal covenants are made.  Guardians, personal representatives, assignees and receivers have no power to bind the trust estate by personal covenants and warranties.[1]

Nor has the trustee of an express trust such power   The bare legal title being in the trustee, the deed is his and not that of the cestui que trust.   The trustee in accepting what was conveyed to him under the trust, is not obliged to assume any responsibility as to title when called upon to convey   Where a person covenants to convey by a warranty deed, and dies before the time arrives to convey, a tender is good of a deed in the usual form, without containing any personal covenants or warranties, executed by the executor or administrator, pursuant to the license of the probate court   The purchaser, in such case, must rely upon the contract to convey a good title, if a breach subsequently occurs  and pursue his remedy against the estate or the proceeds in the hands of the heirs, as the case may be

## § 174.  Deed without the personal covenants of the wife.

If a contract of sale is made with the husband alone, and he covenants to execute a warranty deed, a tender of a warranty deed in which the wife has joined  but in which she has not made any personal covenants, is good.  If any one other than the vendor has the title  the vendor, if he has contracted to give a deed of warranty, must first secure the title to be conveyed to him, so that the covenants will be his   A deed direct from the owner to the vendee will not do   If a husband agrees to give a mortgage deed to secure his debt, and nothing is said as to the wife assuming the obligation, the mortgage

1 Kerney v Gardner 27 Ill 162       1 Bishop v O Connor  69 Ill
4 Ketcham   v   Evertson   13      131 Hall v Marquette, 69 Iowa
Johns 358                         376 S C 28 N W Rep 647

deed should contain the ordinary personal covenants on the part of the husband, but none on the part of the wife. So, in any case where there is no personal liability to pay a debt, as where the mortgage is given by a third party to secure the debt of another, a tender of a mortgage deed without any personal covenants on the part of the mortgagor, is good.

§ 175. **Deed—By whom executed—Under a power of attorney.**—If a vendor is to give a deed of warranty, the vendee is not bound to accept a deed executed under a power of attorney, although the deed tendered may have in it the covenants ordinarily in use. In the first place under such an agreement, or under any agreement where it is not specifically provided for, the vendee is not bound to accept a deed executed under a power at all, as such a conveyance multiplies the proof of title; and in the second place, as to the warranties and personal covenants at least, the authorities are not agreed that an attorney in fact has the power to execute a deed of warranty. It was held in a case where the power authorized the attorney to "execute, seal, and deliver in their names, such conveyances and assurances in the law of the premises, unto the purchaser, * * * as should or might be needful or necessary according to the judgment of the said attorney," that "The attorney was authorized to sell and to execute conveyances, and assurances in the law, of the land sold, but had no authority to bind his principal by covenants."[1] The contrary has been held to be the rule.[2]

The weight of authority is that a mere naked power to convey, does not authorize the attorney to execute a deed with covenants of warranty. An exception to such a rule might well be made in the case of a tender of a deed authorized by a power, where the prospective purchaser is informed by the agent that he has a power of attorney authorizing him to sell and convey the land, and he afterwards enters into a contract of purchase and sale of such land with such agent, wherein the consideration is to be paid in cash and the contract is silent as to who shall execute the deed and the kind

[1] Nixon v. Hyserott 5 Johns 58. See Gibson v. Colt 7 Johns 390. Heath v. Nutter 50 Me 378, and Howe v. Harrington, 18 N. J Eq 495

[2] Vance v. Hopkins 1 H J Marsh 275 S C 19 Am Dec 92, Peters v. Farnsworth 17 Vt 155, S C 40 Am Dec 671

of deed to be delivered. If an agent having a power to sell and convey land, enters into an agreement in behalf of his principal to exchange lands, the agent, in absence of express authority in the power to effect an exchange, must produce and deliver the kind of deed agreed to be delivered, executed by the principal. A power of attorney in general terms to sell and convey land, does not authorize an exchange of land; nor the giving of credit. Such a power imports a sale for cash.

Powers of attorney receive a strict construction, and the authority is never extended by intendment or construction beyond that which is given in terms. This rule is applied to the limitations and restrictions as well as to the scope of the power. A power to sell at a particular time, as on a designated person arriving at a certain age, or on the death of a particular person, or upon any other contingency, must be strictly complied with, and a deed executed by an attorney in fact, which does not come clearly within the limitations, may be rejected.

A power executed by two persons, constituting and appointing an agent to convey their lands, does not authorize the agent to convey the land owned by one.[3] The deed to the individual holdings must be executed by the owner. A principal may always tender a deed of the kind to be delivered, instead of one executed by his attorney in fact. But if the power is coupled with an interest he may not be permitted to take the purchase money. A power to sell and convey land cannot be delegated to another by the trustee, whether it is a mere naked power or a power coupled with an interest. The same rule applies to guardians, personal representatives, assignees and receivers. One of two executors cannot delegate his authority, by giving a power of attorney to convey land to his co-executor.

§ 176   Same subject—Where the title is not in the vendor — Where a vendor contracts to give a warranty deed, he must tender such a deed executed by himself. If the legal title is not in the vendor he must first take a conveyance running to himself. A deed from the person having the title, direct

---

3 Gilbert v How, 45 Minn 121

to the vendee, will not do.[1] The presumption is that where
a vendee insists upon having a stipulation in the contract of
sale calling for a deed with warranties and personal covenants, he does so relying upon the solvency and character of
the vendor. The same rule applies where the vendee must
rely upon the implied warranty as to title, having neglected
to stipulate for a deed of warranty

If a quit claim deed is to be delivered, all the vendee need
do when the time to convey arrives is to tender his deed.
That the title is in some one else does not matter, except
where he has agreed to secure deeds to outstanding interests.
Where the vendor is to convey by deed of quit claim, he must
not, through his acts, suffer the title to pass from him, or to
become encumbered after the date of the contract of sale.
The question of what title the vendor must have at the time
of tendering a deed, is considered elsewhere.[2]

§ 177.  Same subject—Partnership lands.—Where the agreement is to convey land belonging to a partnership, the deed
offered must be signed individually by all the partners; and
their wives must join in the deed, otherwise the purchaser
would be forced to go into equity to establish that the wives
had no dower in such land   A husband or wife, as the case
may be, must always join in a deed executed by the other,
unless the contract is for the purchase and sale of the interest of one.  But where the land is held by the husband in
trust, the wife need not join; nor need the husband when the
wife is the trustee   If a mortgage deed is to be given, the
husband or the wife, as the case may be, must join in the
mortgage

§ 178.  Phraseology—Description of the land —As has been
said, in considering the quality of a deed where the contract
is silent as to the quality, any instrument containing apt
words of conveyance is sufficient  So, the same may be said,
generally, of the language to be used, where, by contract,
land is to be conveyed by deed or by a good and sufficient

---

[1] See Rudd v Savelli, 44 Ark
145  See also O Keefe v Dyer, 52
Pac Rep (Mont) 196 where it
was held that a tender of a quit
claim deed by the vendor, executed by an assignee was good,
where it was not shown that the
vendee could suffer any damages.
[2] § 229 et seq

deed. The vendor is obliged "to execute a deed so drafted
and executed as to leave no reasonable doubt of its legal sufficiency to convey the land."[1] It has been said the language
should be sufficient in point of law, intelligible without
punctuation, and clear without the aid of stops or parenthe-
ses. The description of the land must be sufficient to enable
the purchaser to identify it; and sufficient to authorize a register of deeds to enter the instrument on the index as conveying the land intended. A party may convey his estate by will
or deed, describing it merely as "all my estate" without any
other description, and the instrument will be good and operative;[2] but such description requires evidence to locate the
premises, and will not be tolerated in a deed offered in compliance with a contract to convey.

§ 179. **Description of the estate—Reservations.**—The particular estate to be conveyed must be described with certainty,
and a vendee may demand a deed which correctly describes
and defines the estate to be taken. So, if there are any
reservations specified in the contract, the deed offered must
explicitly recite them sufficiently at least so as not to reserve
more than was intended. A deed offered by a grantor containing the words "excepting and reserving" to the grantor
"all gas, oil, coals, ores, and other minerals or mineral deposits in, under, or on said premises," was held not to comply
with the contract of sale which contained the exception; the
grantor "hereby reserves * * * all oil and gas in or under the said land, with free mining privileges of all kind."
The term, "with free mining privileges of all kind," following
the reservation as to oil and gas, being construed not to be
a reservation of other minerals not mentioned in the contract.[1] The vendor cannot reserve anything not specifically
mentioned in the contract. It appears, however, by a West
Virginia case that where land was sold for a certain price,
a portion of which was to be paid at a future time for which
notes were to be given, and where nothing was said as to a
purchase money lien, that, when the deed was executed the

[1] Shouse v. Doane, 20 So. Rep.
(Fla.) 807.

[2] Richards v. Edick, 17 Barb.

265, citing Fish v. Hubbard Admrs., 21 Wend. 652.

[1] Moody v. Alexander, 145 Pa.
St. 571.

vendor had a right to insert in it a clause, reserving a lien for the unpaid purchase money.[2] But this would not be a limitation or reservation affecting the estate to be conveyed.

§ 180. **Naming the grantee.**—A deed tendered in compliance with a covenant to convey must name the grantee, but it need not give him any other name than that used by him in the contract of sale. The question is not what name or description will be held sufficient after a deed has been accepted, but how must the vendee be designated in a deed, so that he would be legally bound to accept it. Where land is purchased by a firm, or a mortgage is to be given to the firm, the deed must run to the partners in their individual names, and not in their firm name.[1] A tender, on coming of age by one in rescission of a purchase of land made during his minority, of a deed to the property purchased executed in blank, was held to be good. The court observed, the seller in such case has authority to insert the grantee's name.[2]

§ 181. **Naming grantor in body of deed.**—The grantor must be named in a conveyance, and if the land is to be conveyed free and clear of all incumbrances, the wife's name must also appear in the body of the deed as one of the grantors. The weight of authority seems to support the rule, that unless all those persons whose interests are to be conveyed are described as grantors their interest does not pass by a conveyance which they have merely signed and acknowledged. A contrary rule seems to have been adopted in New Hampshire.

§ 182. **Signature of the grantor.**—A deed must be signed by the persons whose interests are to be conveyed by affixing their legal name. As the law recognizes only one Christian name, the middle name or initial need not be used. If the title was taken by the grantor in a particular name, in conveying the property he should use the same name, so that the grantee will not be compelled to furnish evidence that the next preceding grantee and his grantor are one and the same person. Where a grantor cannot write he may make

[2] Findley v. Armstrong, 22 W. Va. 113.

[1] Todd v. Rines, 26 Minn. 204.

[2] Kane v. Kane, 13 App. Div. 544, S. C. 43 N. Y. Supp. 662.

his mark, which should be properly witnessed. If the grantor cannot write in the language of the country where the instrument is to be recorded, he may write his name in any language in which he can write. Although there is some difference of opinion as to how an attorney in fact should sign a deed, the better way, it seems, would be for the attorney to sign the principal's name, it being his deed, followed by the attorney's name, with appropriate words of description, showing that he signed the name of the principal under proper authority. The instrument then, on its face, purports to be that of the principal, executed in his name under proper authority. A vendee may reject a deed executed by an attorney in fact, unless the power authorizing the conveyance be first placed upon record, otherwise the power might be lost, destroyed or withheld from record, and the vendee put to great trouble and expense in establishing his title in equity.

§ 183. **Executed on what material—In what language—Legibility—Acknowledgment.**—A deed may be written or printed, or partly written and partly printed. It may be on paper vellum or parchment A deed written in any language is good, but a vendee is not bound to accept a deed written in a foreign language, as that would necessitate a translation However, if the deed is to be executed by a person living in a foreign country, it would be presumed that the parties had in mind a deed written in the language of the country where it is to be executed It must be legible and "free from all such interlineations and erasures as are reasonably calculated to throw suspicion or cast doubt upon the paper, as a valid, bona fide conveyance." [1]

A deed which is tendered in compliance with a contract of sale must be signed, sealed, acknowledged and witnessed according to the law of the place where the land is situated, so that it will be entitled to be placed on record A grantee is not bound to accept a deed which has never been acknowledged, though purporting to be; and, in an action by the grantor against his grantee to recover the price, parole evidence is admissible to show that the deed tendered was not

---

[1] Shouse v Dane, 20 So Rep (Fla) 807

so acknowledged at the time he refused to accept it.[2]  If the revenue laws require it to be stamped, stamps in the proper amount must be affixed and properly cancelled before it is offered to the vendee.

§ 184.  **Taking advice of counsel—Certificate that taxes are paid.**—Where a deed is tendered, the tenderee must be given a reasonable time to look it over and take advice of counsel, to satisfy himself that the deed complies in all respects with the kind he contracted to receive   If the law of the place where a deed is to be recorded, require it to be endorsed by the proper officer to the effect that all the taxes upon the land are paid, before it is entitled to record, it need not be so endorsed before delivery, but if the vendee has not expressly assumed any unpaid taxes, he may take a reasonable time to ascertain if the taxes are in fact paid, and if they are not paid he may refuse to accept the deed.

§ 185.  **Number of deeds —**Where lots are sold at auction separately, and a certificate given for each lot, and several lots are purchased by one person, the seller must, if required, execute and tender separate deeds for each lot.[1]  But if several tracts are included in one sale, one deed conveying all the land is all that the vendor can be required to execute.

---

- Tatum  v   Goforth, 9 Iowa,　　1 Van Lep v  Schenectady, 12
247　　　　　　　　　　　　　　Johns  435

# CHAPTER IV.

## AMOUNT TO BE TENDERED.

§ 186. Entire amount—Naming the sum—Difference between debt and recoupment or set-off—Difference between purchase price and an incumbrance.—A debtor must tender the entire sum due, and nothing short of an offer to fully perform by a tender of every thing the creditor is entitled to receive is sufficient. A party to whom a sum of money is due may properly refuse to receive the same in parcels; he has the right to the whole, and the party bound to pay cannot require him to accept a part.[1] A party making a tender must name the sum which he wishes to tender; unless a sum is named, the tenderee cannot determine as to the sufficiency of the sum.[2] An agreement by a creditor to apply money in his possession belonging to a third person, in part payment of the debt, is without consideration, and not binding; and a tender of the difference between such sum and the amount otherwise due is insufficient.[3] A legal tender cannot be made of the difference between the amount of a note or other obligation for the payment of money and a set off.[4]

If by the terms of a contract of sale, the vendee is to assume a mortgage and pay the balance of the purchase price in cash, and a larger sum than is taken into account in the contract is afterwards found to be due on the mortgage, a tender in cash of the difference between the amount actually due on the mortgage and the contract price of the land is sufficient.[5] The same rule applies where it is afterwards found that the land is encumbered by liens, which were not taken into account in making up the total purchase price.[6] If the vendor reserves a right to repurchase, on exercising the right he need not tender the amount of such lien to the vendee unless the vendee has been compelled to pay it in order to protect himself. On an agreement to recovery when the vendor is to

[1] Brandt v. Chicago R. Co., 26 Iowa 114; Baker v. Gasque, 3 Strobh. 25; Spoon v. Frambach, 83 Minn. 301

[2] Knight v. Abbott, 30 Vt. 577. See Chase v. Welch, 7 N. W. Rep. (Mich.) 895

[3] Fisher v. Willard, 20 N. H. 421

[4] Phillpotts v. Clifton, 10 W. R. 135; Eastman v. Longshorn, 1 N. & M. (N. Car.) 194; Searls v. Sadgrove, 5 E. & B. 639; Pershing v. Feinberg, 52 Atl. Rep. (Pa.) 22; Greenhill v. Hunton, 69 S. W.

Rep. (Tex. Civ. App.) 440. See Smith v. Curtiss, 38 Mich. 393 to the contrary. See also, Young v. Borzone, 66 Pac. Rep. (Wash.) 135. And see Rand v. Harris, 83 N. C. 486, when it is held that a tender may be made of the difference between the amount of a note or other obligation for the payment of money and a recoupment

[5] Klawelter v. Hubrer, 68 Hun 338, S. C. 22 N. Y. Supp. 815; Walling v. Kinnard, 10 Tex. 508

[6] See Rhorer v. Bila, 83 Cal. 51

pay for improvements, a tender of the purchase price without the costs of the improvements is bad. If the costs of the improvements have not been determined, it is not necessary to offer a specific sum, but he must offer to pay the reasonable value of such improvement.[7]

§ 187. **Where the quantity of land sold falls short—Where a vendor receives insurance money.**—On a contract of sale of land, if the quantity of land falls short of the amount represented, the vendee is entitled to have what the vendor can convey with an abatement out of the purchase money for so much as the quantity falls short, and if the amount to be deducted is capable of liquidation, as where unimproved land is sold for a certain sum per acre, or for a gross sum, and each acre is of equal value, the vendee may make a tender of the difference between the whole purchase price and the value of the land which the vendor is unable to convey, and, on the other hand, where the demand is liquidated and the vendee does not abandon the contract, the vendor may return or tender the amount for the number of acres the tract falls short, and save himself from costs[1] But such rule would apply only where the shortage is small and unimportant  Where a purchaser of real property, at the request of the seller, took out a policy of insurance in the name of the seller, and the latter thereafter collected for a loss, it was held that, on a tender of the purchase price less the amount of the insurance received, the purchaser was entitled to a conveyance.[2]

§ 188. **After mortgagee declares whole sum due.**—Where a mortgage or deed of trust provides that, in case of a default in the payment of interest, the whole debt shall become due and payable, at the option of the creditor, and such a default occurs and the creditor exercises his option, a tender thereafter of less than the whole debt is insufficient.[1] If the mortgagor has, from mere neglect, failed to perform his contract according to the strict terms, and the whole debt thereby becomes due and payable, a court will not interfere to relieve

[7] Wylie v Matthews, 60 Iowa 187, S C 11 N. W Rep 232

[1] Walling v Kinnard, 10 Tex 508.

[2] Brikhage v Tracy, 83 N W Rep (S D) 363

[1] Detweiler v Breckenkamp, 83 Mo 45

him without a tender of the whole debt.[2] A mortgagor having once exercised the option [3] cannot recall it, and legally refuse a tender of the whole debt. In such cases,[1] and in those cases where the mortgagor has an option to pay the mortgage at any time,[5] he may tender the amount of the principal and the interest then due, without tendering the amount of the inter est coupons not due.

§ 189. **A tender where part is furnished by agent at his risk— Tender to agent of less than the sum claimed—Same to an attorney.**—Where an agent was sent to tender a certain sum to a creditor, who demanded a larger sum, and the agent thereupon offered the balance at his own risk, the tender was held good.[1] If an agent is sent to demand a certain sum, a tender of a less sum to the agent is not good, where the agent has no authority to compromise the claim.[2] So, where a claim is lodged with an attorney for collection, a tender to the attorney of a less sum than the amount of the claim in his hands is not good, although the less sum is the sum actually due. If there is a dispute as to the amount, the debtor should seek the creditor and make a tender of the sum due to him personally. An attorney, unless instructed to accept a less sum, has no authority to compromise his client's claim.

§ 190 **Railroad fare—Ticket fare—Train fare.**—A railroad company may make a reasonable regulation as to the payment of fares by passengers, and in the exercise of such power may require passengers who go aboard their trains without purchasing a ticket to pay a reasonable sum in excess of the ticket fare. But the order to justify a refusal of a tender made by a passenger on board the train of the regular ticket

[2] Glassy v Schneider 50 How Pr 131

[3] Commencing an action is sufficient notice that the holder of the mortgage elects to treat the whole sum due Hunt v Keech, 3 Abb 204

[4] Magnusson v Williams, 111 Ill 159

[5] Bailey v The County of Buchanan 115 N Y 297

[1] Reed v. Golding 2 M & S 86 See Wylie v Matthews, 11 N W Rep (Iowa) 232, where an agent offered to pay the reasonable value of improvements although instructed to pay no more than twenty five dollars Held not good as it was made without authority

[2] Chipman v Bates 5 Vt 143

fare, the railroad company must have afforded the passenger a reasonable and proper opportunity to procure a ticket. In New York, it has been held that it is the duty of a railroad company to keep its ticket office open until the departure of the train [1] The amount of fare to be tendered, therefore, in such case, depends upon the reasonableness of the opportunity afforded the passenger to procure a ticket.[2]

§ 191.   **On contracts with penalty.**—It is well settled, says Mr. Sedgwick, that no damages for the mere non payment of money can ever be so liquidated between the parties as to evade the provision of law fixing the rate of the interest. Where a bond was given conditioned that if certain bills were not accepted, the obligor should pay the amount of them, with ten per cent by way of a penalty, it was insisted that the damages were liquidated   But Lord Loughborough said, "In cases like the present, the law having by positive rules fixed the rate of interest, has bonded the measures of damages" [1] In a case arising in New York, the court said, "Liquidated damages are not applicable to such a case   If they were, they might afford a secure protection for usury, and countenance oppression, under form of law."[2]   In such cases it is sufficient to tender the amount of the principal debt and interest at the legal rate   So, a tender of the sum justly due by the conditions of a bond, after a breach, though less than the penalty, is sufficient [3]

§ 192.   **In redemption for tax sale—By joint tenants or tenants in common—Proceedings to ascertain the proportionate amount due.**—To effect a redemption from a tax sale, the redemptioner must pay or tender in addition to the amount of the purchase money, all premiums and penalties allowed by law [1]   Where the redemption money is offered to the officer

[1] Porter v The N. Y. Cent R R Co, 31 Barb 353

[2] See on the subject, Du Laurans v The First Division of the St P & P Ry, 15 Minn 49, State v Hungerford 39 Minn 6, Chicago B & Q R R Co v Park, 18 Ill 464, St Louis A & C R. Co v Dalby, 19 Ill 364, The Jeffersonville R Co v Rogers, 28 Ind 3, also Crocker v The

New London W. & P R R Co, 24 Conn 249, Phettiplace v Northern Pac R, 54 N W Rep (Wis) 1092

[1] Orr v Churchill 1 H Black 232

[2] Gray v Crosby 18 John R 219.

[3] Tracy v Strong, 2 Conn 659

[1] Lamar v Sheppard, 84 Ga. 561, S C 10 S E Rep. 1084

authorized to receive it, it is the duty of the redemptioner to tender the full amount demanded by law, though it is not demanded by the officer.[2] And the sum legally due must be tendered even though the collector makes excessive charges for the costs of sale.[3] A tender of the amount due for taxes, where steps have been taken to enforce payment, need not include any fees not earned.[4]

If a joint tenant or tenant in common buys at a tax sale his co tenant need tender to the purchaser only his pro rata of the entire tax.[5] In some of the states, if not all, any person, owning or claiming an interest in or lien upon land, may pay or tender to the proper officer his proportionate part of the entire tax for which the land was sold, but if the interest is undivided, application must first be made to the courts to determine the proportionate part to be paid by such part owner.[6] Where a part of the land is transferred after the tax is levied and assessed, the purchaser is entitled to an appointment of the tax and is not obliged to pay the entire amount of tax on the whole tract as a condition of freeing his own part from the lien of the tax.[7]

**§ 193. Interest—Days of grace—Where no interest is reserved—After default—After a demand—Subsequent change of rate by statute—Rate to be paid to surety—Rate where no interest is reserved in a foreign contract—By an acceptor of a foreign bill—By drawer—Usury.**—The amount tendered must be sufficient to cover both principal and interest.[1] Such sum must include interest up to, and including the last day of grace.[2] If a contract for the payment of money at a certain time does not mention interest, a tender on the day of the principal without interest is good.[3] Where a watch was pledged for $82, to be

[2] Harmon v. Steed, 19 Fed. 779.

[3] Eustis v. Henrietta, 11 S. W. Rep. 720.

[4] Converse v. Jennings, 13 Gray 77.

[5] Winter v. Atkinson, 28 La. Am. 650.

[6] 1891 G. S. Minn., § 1604.

[7] Rochford v. Fleming, 71 N. W. Rep. (S. D.) 317. In Minnesota the parties may agree upon the division of the taxes either in writing or by appearing in person before the auditor but the division, if thought to be unreasonable may be rejected by that officer. Where the parties do not agree the auditor may make the division. 1894 G. S. Minn. § 1625.

[1] Woodworth v. Morris, 56 Barb. 97. See Hamar v. Dimmick, 11 Ind. 105.

[2] Smith v. Merchants Bank, 11 Ohio C. C. 199.

[3] Connell v. Mulligan, 21 Miss. 388. Hines v. Strong, 46 How. Pr. 97, S. C. 56 N. Y. 670.

returned in thirty days on the payment of $87, a tender of the latter sum was held sufficient, the five dollars bonus being regarded in lieu of interest.[4] If no interest is bargained for where the amount is to be paid at a certain time, after default a tender is not good unless the sum offered includes interest, at the legal rate, from date fixed for payment. So where a sum of money is payable on demand, interest at the legal rate accrues after a demand and refusal. If no time is specified for the payment of a sum of money, it is payable immediately and interest begins to run from the date of the contract.[5] Where an order for the amount on deposit in a savings bank was presented to the bank, and payment was refused, a tender by the bank fifteen days later of the exact amount due on the day of the demand was held bad.[6]

If subsequent to the creation of a debt on which no interest was reserved, but interest afterwards accrues by way of damages, or subsequent to the creation of any obligation such as a judgment and the like, on which interest accrues at the legal rate by virtue of the statute, the legal rate is changed, either to a higher or lower rate it is sufficient to tender interest at the then prevailing rate. A principal whose debt has been paid by his surety, must tender to the surety the amount paid by him together with interest on that sum from the day of payment at the legal rate, even though the principal contract bore interest at a lower rate. So, on the other hand, if the principal contract bears interest at a higher rate than the legal rate, the principal need tender only the sum paid by the surety, and interest from the day of payment at the legal rate. A principal does not agree to pay his surety the same rate as is stipulated for in the principal contract

Where a foreign contract to pay money does not bear interest, after a default in the payment the sum due bears interest at the legal rate of such foreign country. If the rate of interest reserved in a foreign contract is legal where made it is the rate to be paid everywhere, even though such a rate of interest would be usurious, if the contract was entered into in the country where it was sought to be enforced. An acceptor of a foreign bill, where no rate of

[4] Hines v Strong 46 How Pr
97 S C 56 N Y 670
[5] Horn v Hansen 56 Minn 43
Purdy v Philips 11 N Y 406

[6] Weld v Elliot 33 N E Rep
(Mass ) 519

interest is expressed in the bill, where he has allowed interest to accrue thereon by way of damages, must pay or tender the amount of the bill and interest at the legal rate of the country where the bill is payable, but the drawer who binds himself to pay in case the acceptor does not, must pay or tender the amount of the bill and interest thereon after default, at the legal rate of the country where the bill is drawn, wherever it is sought to be enforced against him.[7]

Where the statute works a forfeiture of all the interest on an usurious contract, or prohibits the recovery of interest in excess of a certain rate, a tender of the amount legally due is sufficient.[8] In such a case, a bill to foreclose the mortgage given to secure the debt, which claimed such usurious interest, was dismissed at the complainant's costs on the mortgagor's payment into court of the amount legally due.[9] Although a debtor does not in his estimate of the amount due include any interest, yet, if, as a matter of fact, he tenders enough money to cover the actual debt and interest, the tender is good.[10]

§ 194.  On an accord.—As stated elsewhere,[1] the authorities are not in harmony on the question of a tender of performance upon an accord. In those jurisdictions where a new agreement, which imposes a new duty upon the debtor that is or may be burdensome to him or beneficial to the creditor, is held to create a new consideration, such new agreement is the satisfaction of the old claim[2] and a tender of the amount specified in the accord will be sufficient to bar an action upon the old claim or obligation[3] But in those jurisdictions where the contrary rule prevails, nothing short of a tender of the full amount due on the original obligation will be of any avail.

§ 195.  Tender of a less sum—Mistake—Amount of deficiency—Where the amount is exclusively within the knowledge of creditor—Wrongfully depriving debtor of means of ascertaining the

[7] Gibbs v Fremont, 9 Exch 25 See Suse v Pompe, 8 C B N S 138

[8] Shivor v Johnston, 62 Ala 37

[9] Blythe v Small, 67 Ill App 319

[10] Rudolph v Wigner, 36 Ala 698

[1] § 367

[2] See Massilon Engine Co v Prouty, 91 N W Rep (Neb) 384.

[3] See Stewart v Langston 30 S E Rep (Ga) 35

amount—Waiver of objection to amount—Extent of waiver—Effect of acceptance.—A tender of a sum less than the amount due will not stop the running of interest[1] or discharge the lien of a mortgage,[2] or annul a foreclosure sale,[3] or entitle a vendee to a decree of specific performance of a contract for the conveyance of land, when the payment of the purchase price is a condition precedent.[4] If refused it does not amount to a payment *pro tanto*.[5] It has been decided, repeatedly, that "where a man does not know exactly what is due, he must at his peril take care to tender enough."[6] A mistake in tendering an amount less than the sum due is the misfortune of the tenderor and cannot have the same legal effect as a tender of the full amount due. The general rule is that the amount of the deficiency does not make any difference. Where the amount tendered was forty one cents short of the amount due, the tender was held bad.[7] So where the amount due was $649.11 and the deficiency was seventy cents the tender was held not good.[8]

Where the amount due is exclusively within the knowledge of the creditor, as where the debtor is entitled to an accounting, and the creditor on demand neglects or refuses to indicate the correct amount that is due, the debtor may tender so much as he thinks is justly due, and if less than the true amount, the tender nevertheless will be good. Here the duty rests upon the creditor to furnish the information and if he refused to do so he will not be permitted to take advantage

[1] Henry v Sansom, 36 S W Rep (Tex) 122. See Smith v Anders 21 Ala 782, Dixon v Clark, 5 C B 365. See also Metropolitan Bank v Commercial Bank 71 N W Rep (Io) 26 where the sum tendered as part payment was by an agent who had collected that sum upon the obligation intrusted to it. The tender having been kept good it was held that there was no liability for interest

[2] Graham v Linden 50 N Y 547

[3] Dickerson v Hayes 26 Minn 100

[4] Sanford v Bartholomew, 33 Kan 38

Pulyer v State 3 Gill & J 10

[5] Astley v Reynolds Str 916 See on s p Baker v Gasque 3 Strobh 25, Shotwell v Dennin, 1 N J L 174, Patnote v Sanders, 41 Vt 66 Brandt v Chicago & R R Co 26 Iowa 114, Shuck v Chicago & C R R Co, 73 Iowa 333 S C 35 N W Rep 429 Helphrey v Chicago & C R R Co 29 Iowa 480

[7] Boyden v Moore 5 Mass 370
[8] Wright v Behrens 39 N J L 413

of his own wrong. So, if the tenderee, by any act, deprives the tenderor of his means of ascertaining the exact amount due, a tender of a less sum than is actually due will be as effectual in preserving the tenderor's rights as a tender of the full sum. Thus where a vendor obtained possession of a contract of sale upon which the payments made by the vendee had been indorsed, and wrongfully destroyed it, a tender of a less sum than that actually due was held sufficient to support an action for specific performance[9]

When the sum tendered to a creditor is less than the sum due, and is refused on the ground that he is not bound to receive the money,[10] or on any collateral ground, and not on the other ground that the amount is too small,[11] the tenderee waives the objection to the insufficiency of the amount[12] A waiver of the objection that the amount tendered is too small, does not preclude the tenderee from recovering the whole amount due. So, the acceptance of a less sum than the amount due does not effect the creditor's right to recover the balance,[13] where the amount due is not in dispute.

§ 196. Tender of a larger sum—As the sum due—In payment of a less sum—Requesting change—Where a debtor offers in payment as the sum due, a larger sum than is actually due, or offers such larger sum in payment of a less sum, and he does not impliedly or expressly request any change to be returned, the tender is not objectionable,[1] for a tender of a

[9] Downing v Plate, 90 Ill 268
[10] Flanders v Chamberlain, 21 Mich 305
[11] See Brewer v Fleming, 51 Pa St 102
[12] In Bender v Bean 12 S W Rep 241, the court said that 'If the sum offered is inadequate, the inadequacy should be objected to and the correct amount indicated It will not do to maintain silence as to objections which if expressed might be met, and afterwards assert them to the owner's prejudice" As to indicating the exact amount due the foregoing is not correct as applied to the facts of the case under consideration, which was in attempted redemption from a tax sale when the amount due could be readily ascertained by computation or by an application to the proper officer In no case is the creditor bound to indicate the amount due, excepting where it is peculiarly within his knowledge

[13] Patnote v Sanders 41 Vt 66 Carpenter v Welch 40 Vt 251

[1] Patterson v Cox 25 Ind 261 Houston D & W T R Co v Campbell 40 S W Rep 131 See Pinney v Jorgenson, 27 Minn 26

greater sum includes the less sum.[2]   A tender of £20 9s. 6d. in bank notes and silver was held to support a plea of tender of £20.[3]  It is a general rule that if a debtor goes to his creditor with a sum of money larger than is actually due, and lays it down with a request that the creditor take what is due him, the tender is good, "for *omne majus continet in se minus*; and the other ought to accept as much of it as is due to him."[4]

But in such case the tender is not really of a larger sum, but of the sum actually due; for it is not the intention of the debtor that the creditor shall take more than is due.  This rule is subject to the qualifications that the money must be of the kind and denominations capable of the proper division  In a case where a debtor tendered a £5 bank note and desired the creditor to take £3 10s. out of it, it was held not to be a good tender of the fractional sum  Le Blanc, J., said "The case in Lord Coke refers to monies numbered.  If I tender a man twenty guineas in the current coin of the realm, this may be a very good tender of fifteen, for he has only to select so much, and restore me the residue  But a tender in bank notes is quite different  In that case, the tender may be made in such a way that it is physically impossible for the creditor to take what is due and return the difference.  If £3 10s. could be tendered by a note for £5, so it might by a note for £50,000."[5]  There is no difference in principle, between a tender of a bank bill of the denomination of twenty dollars and a tender of twenty dollars gold piece, where the amount due is a fractional part of that sum

§ 197.  Same subject—Waiver of objection that change must be furnished—What does not constitute a waiver.—Where a larger sum than the amount actually due is offered in such a way that the tenderee cannot take from the sum proffered the amount actually due, the tender is, if the sum the tenderor concedes to be due is the sum actually due, neverthe-

2 Douglas v Patrick 3 T R 683

3 Dean v James 4 B & Ad 517 N M 392

4 Wade's case 5 Co 115 S P Dean v James 4 B & Ad 518 1 N & M 393 Hubbard v Chen

ango Bank, 8 Cow 88, Bevins v Rees 5 M & W 306 7 D C P 510 3 Jur 608

Patterbee v Davis 3 Camp 70  s p Robinson v Cook, 6 Taunt 336  See Hubbard v Chening Bank, 8 Cow 88

less sufficient, if the tenderee bases his refusal entirely upon some collateral ground as where he demands a larger sum,[1] or that the tender is too late. So, the tender is good if the tenderee refuses to receive the money unless a condition is complied with, as where a certain amount be fixed upon as due on a separate account.[2] It being the duty of the debtor to tender the exact amount due, a bare refusal by the creditor to receive the money is not a waiver of the objection that he was required to furnish change. In the case hereinbefore referred to, where a £5 bank note was tendered with the request that the creditor take £3 10s out of it, the creditor merely said, "I will see you another time," and walked away, it is held that such a tender was not good. So, where the creditor, on being tendered seven sovereigns in payment of a claim amounting to £6 17s 6d merely said, "You must go to any attorney," the tender was held to be bad.[3]

§ 198. **Same subject—Debtor not bound by the sum tendered —Pleading a tender of a less sum and proving a tender of a greater—Pleading a tender of a greater sum and proving a tender of a less sum where the less sum is all that is due.**—Where a party was entitled to an accounting with a mortgagee and tendered a larger amount than was necessary to redeem, which was refused and the mortgagor was compelled to bring a bill in equity to redeem and put to the necessity of proving the balance due it was held that there was no reason why the plaintiff should be bound by the sum tendered, if by mistake and ignorance of the facts he tendered a larger sum than was actually due.[1]

So, at law a debtor is not bound by the tender of a larger sum, even though such larger sum was tendered as the sum which the creditor was to receive and not as the sum of which he was to take the amount actually due. And, if sued, he may plead a tender of a less sum, and support it by proof of a tender of the larger sum.[2] But a plea of tender of a cer-

[1] Cudman v Lubbock 5 D & R 289 Sanders v Graham, Cow 111 Peoples Fur Co v Crosby 77 N W Rep (Neb) 658

[2] Berans v Rees, 5 M & W 306

Batterbee v Ouds 3 Camp

70, s p Block v Smith, Peakes N P C 89

[3] Brady v Jones 2 D & R 305
[1] Tucker v Buffum 16 Pick 46
[2] Dean v James 4 B & A, s
c 1 N & M 392

tain sum will not be supported by proof of a tender of a less sum, even though no more was due than the sum proved to have been tendered.[3]

§ 199.  Same subject—Street car fares—Railway fares.—Mod ern decisions, in reference to the tender of fares to common carriers of passengers, have established an exception to the general rule that a tender of a larger amount than is due with the request for change is not good.  Common carriers operating street cars stop their cars at least at every street cross ing along the line, at the beck of those desiring to ride.  The passenger is not expected to procure a ticket, and is taken on board and the contract for carriage is thus entered into with the expectation that the passenger will tender cash.  In such case a passenger is not bound to tender the exact fare but the conductor is bound to furnish change for a reasonable sum.  The obligation to furnish a reasonable amount of change must be considered as one which the law imposes from the nature of the business.  The authorities, however, are not agreed as to the limit of the sum that may be offered to the conductor of a street car for the purpose of having him deduct the fare and return the residue.  In California, a tender of a five dollar gold piece in payment of a five cent fare was held to be reasonable.  The court said further, that it does not follow that a passenger may tender any sum, however large.  "If he should tender a hundred dollar bill, for example it would be clear that the carrier would not be bound to furnish change."[1]  In New York, a tender of a five dollar bill in payment of a five cent fare, was held, as a matter of law, to be unreasonable and that a rule of the company limiting the amount of change to two dollars, which a conductor is required to furnish, was a reasonable provision for the convenience of the public, and that notice of such a rule need not be brought home to a passenger.[2]

Considering the immense volume of passenger business done by common carriers within the past half century, both

John v. Jenkins, 1 C. & M. 227; 3 Tyr. 170

[1] Barrett v. Market Street Ry. Co., 81 Cal. 296.  See Hibbell v. Central Park, R. R. Co., 34 Cal. 616.

[2] Barker v. Central Park N. & C. R. R. Co., 151 N. Y. 237; 35 L. R. A. 489, 55 Abb. L. J. 45; 45 N. E. Rep. 550.

by water and by rail, and the number of cash fares collected, there is surprisingly little to be found in the books on this question. In a case where the sum offered was in payment of passage on a steam railway, and a twenty-dollar gold piece was offered to the conductor in order that one dollar and twenty-five cents might be taken out of it, the court said: "The plaintiff tendering at last a twenty-dollar gold coin in payment, either when he was about being put off or after he had been put off, makes no difference, I think in the case, for that was not reasonable offer to pay which required more than $18, to be paid back in change."[1]

## § 200. On several demands—Not a tender on one demand—Paying debts separately—Tender on different demands held by

[1] Fulton v. Grand Trunk R. R. 17 U. C. Q. B. 428. Here a piece of money sixteen times as great as the sum due was held to be unreasonable while in the California case one hundred times the amount was declared to be reasonable. In none of the cases is the exact limit fixed excepting in the New York case where a rule of the carrier providing for change to be given by its conductors for a sum forty times as large as the fare was held to be reasonable. There is an irreconcilable difference. Conductors on steam trains do collect cash fares running into dollars and the mere fact that conductors on steam trains expect to receive tickets, does not warrant the discrepancy between the reasonableness of the amount tendered to them in payment of a fare and the amount tendered to street car conductors as is indicated by these decisions. The court, in each case, laid emphasis on the amount of the fare to be paid. But the amount of the fare, except to a very limited extent, ought not have any bearing upon

the question, but rather the rule should be based upon the denomination of the pieces of money that a common carrier ought to expect to have offered occasionally. Although pieces of money of smaller denomination than five and ten dollar pieces are more plentiful in circulation than those of larger denomination, yet the demand for their use is greater, and the experience of the average person is that they are soon paid away, and that the number of times they find on boarding a street car, that they have a coin under five dollars in their pocket and the times when they found they have only a five or ten dollar-piece is not disproportionate to the demands in general circulation upon the respective pieces. A common carrier operating a street car ought to be prepared to change a ten dollar piece if necessary and carrier operating steam trams a twenty dollar bill. That several pieces of large denomination might be tendered on the same trip designedly should not effect the rules

**several persons separately.**—Where a person is indebted upon two or more demands and they are held by the same creditor, he may make a tender of one entire sum upon all the demands.[1] But if the tender is refused on the ground that the amount offered is not sufficient to pay all the claim, and the amount offered is insufficient in fact, the tender will not be good as to any of the separate demands. Thus a tender of an amount which is insufficient to pay fifty bonds of $1,000 each, but which is enough to pay forty nine of the bonds, will not stop interest on all except $1,000.[2]

A debtor may pay his debts separately, and may therefore designate upon what debts the money tendered is to apply. If he is indebted to the same person upon three demands, he

[1] Johnson v. Grange, 45 Mich. 14; Thetford v. Hubbard, 22 Vt. 440. Where a boom company was entitled to charge 20 cents a thousand for tolls and 50 cents a thousand feet for the running and delivery of logs, a tender of a sum sufficient to cover both charges was held sufficient, without separating the sums and making a distinct tender as to each. Johnson v. Grange, 45 Mich. 14. See Strong v. Farmers' & C. Bank, 4 Mich. 360, where a bank tendered three hundred half dollars to the holder of thirty of its bills of the denomination of five dollars each. The tender was held good, but the decision turned on the point whether three hundred half dollars issued under the act of Congress of February 21, 1853, were a legal tender. If the thirty bills constituted one demand the money was not; if each bill in the hands of the same person was a separate demand each could be paid with five dollars in half dollars. See also Fletcher v. Daugherty, 13 Neb. 224, where an action had been commenced before a justice to recover on a note given for the interest on a mortgage debt and the defendant in open court tendered to the justice the amount due on the mortgage and the note sued upon, with costs to date, the tender was held bad. The justice was in no sense the agent of the plaintiff and had no authority to receive any money for him in excess of the amount involved in the suit. But where a mortgage debt is due, either by the efflux of time or where a mortgagee on default, has exercised his option and declared the whole debt to be due, a tender may of course be made to the mortgagee of the entire principal and interest. Bailey v. County of Buchanan, 115 N. Y. 297.

[2] People's Sav. Bank v. Borough of Norwalk, 56 Conn. 547. See Hardingham v. Allen, 5 C. B. 793; 12 Jur. 584; 17 L. J. C. P. 198. In Shuck v. Chicago etc. Ry. Co., 35 N. W. Rep. 429, $175 was tendered to cover the damages for the killing of two animals. The jury found the value of one to be $70 and the other of the value of $125. The tender was held insufficient as to the liability for the killing of either animals.

may tender one sum upon two, leaving the third unprovided for. So, if there is a statute permitting a tender to be made after a suit is commenced, and several distinct claims have been included in the complaint, a tender of the whole amount of one of the claims with costs of the action, is a good tender *pro tanto* under the statute.[3] It has been held that where a person has separate demands against several persons, an offer of one sum for the debts of all would not support a plea stating that a certain portion of the sum offered was tendered for the debt of one.[4] Where a person was indebted on different demands to several persons separately, and when they were together, he tendered them one sum sufficient to satisfy all their demands, which they refused to receive on the ground that more was due, it was held to be a good tender.[5]

In a case where a tender was made to one creditor, in gross, of the amount due him and the amount due on a claim held by a third person, it was held to be a good tender of the sum due the creditor to whom the tender was made, he having refused without objecting to the form of tender on account of being entitled only to the one demand.[6] A tender cannot be made by one debtor of an amount due upon several claims only one of which is due from him.[7]

§ 201. **Same subject—Laying down a sum and requesting each to take what is due him—Tender where a number of articles are separately pledged—Principal note and interest coupons—** If a tender is made by laying down a sufficient amount to cover all demands, and each creditor present is invited to

---

[3] Carleton v Whitcher, 5 N H 289

[4] Strong v Harvey, 3 Bing 304

[5] Black v Smith Peak, N. P 88. See Thetford v Hubbard, 22 Vt 440

[6] Douglas v Patrick, 3 T R 683. This case is apparently, in conflict with the general rule that a mere objection to a tender without assigning any reason, is not a waiver of the objection that a larger sum was offered than was due where the tender was made in such a way that it was

impossible for the creditor to take what was actually due him without furnishing change. One demand was due to A B & C jointly, and one to C separately. The debtor tendered to A the sum due on both demands and it does not appear that the money was of such denomination that A could have taken the amount of the joint demand and restored the residue to the debtor.

[7] Hall v Norwalk Ins Co 57 Conn 105

take what is due him, and the money is capable of the proper division, the tender would be good, as it would be in effect a separate tender to each creditor, and no different from the cases where a debtor lays down a sum more than is sufficient to pay a single demand and invites his creditor to take what is due him. Where separate and distinct articles or lots are deposited as collateral security for separate advances, the debtor may tender an amount sufficient to cover the advances on any number of articles or lots[1]. Interest coupons, though negotiable when detached from the bond, and are for that purpose considered independent instruments, are not, however, a distinct debt in the hands of the holder of the bond and not negotiated, and a tender to the holder of the bond of the entire amount of principal and interest is not a tender of two demands[2]

§ 202   **Costs—What costs—Nonsuit—Attorney fees**.— A tender, made after the suit has been commenced, in order to bar a recovery of subsequent interest and costs, must be of such sum as will cover the amount due, with the interest to the day of the tender, and such costs as have accrued in the suit up to that time[1] The costs to be included in a sum tendered, comprehend everything accrued at the time of the tender, or which must of necessity be expended by the plaintiff in disposing of the matter of record, which the plaintiff under the statute would be entitled to include in a money judgment, and also all expenses incurred by a plaintiff or defendant in

---

[1] Nelson v. Robson, 17 Minn 284

[2] Bailey v. County of Buchanan, 115 N. Y. 297

[1] Freemans v. Fleming 5 Iowa 160, Barnes v. Green, 30 Iowa, 114 Young v. McWaid, 57 Iowa 101, Burt v. Dodge, 13 Ohio 131, Lichtenfels v. The Enos B Phillips 53 Fed Rep 153 Walsh v. Southworth, 2 L. M. & P 91, 20 L. J. M. C. 165 6 Exch 150, State Bank v. Holcomb 7 N. J. L 193, McDaniel v. Upton 45 Ill App 187, Martin v. Whistler, 62 Iowa 416, Globe Soap Co v. Liss, 73 N. Y. Supp 153, Bernstein v. Levy, 68 N. Y. Supp 833, Keith v. Smith, 1 Swan (Tenn) 92 Smith v. Anders, 21 Ala 782, Rockefeller v. Weiderwax 3 How Pr 383, Litton v. Wells 22 Hun 123 Seeger v. Smith, 74 Minn 279, Louisiana Co v. Le Sassier, 28 So Rep (La) 217 Parr v. Smith, 24 Am Dec 162 A tender by a surety after an action has been commenced against the principal must include costs The Hampshire Mufgrs' Bank v. Billings, 17 Pick 87 See Samuels v. Simmons, 60 S. W. Rep (Ky) 937

caring for the property where the possession is not wrongfully withheld.[2] When a statute allows an attachment before
the maturity of a debt and a writ is issued and sustained, a
tender when the debt falls due must include the costs of the
attachment.[3]

After a foreclosure by advertisement is commenced, a tender which does not include the attorney fees stipulated for in
the mortgage, and printers' fees incurred, is insufficient and
will not stop the foreclosure.[4] But where there is an attempt
to foreclose by advertisement, and the notice is withdrawn
because it is imperfect, the mortgagee is not entitled to demand the attorney fee.[5] So, if for any reason the foreclosure
proceedings are not binding upon the mortgagor or a subsequent encumbrance, such person not bound need not tender
the attorney fee or the costs of the foreclosure.[6]

Where a plaintiff, in good faith, has subpoenaed his witnesses in the usual mode, and has placed himself under a legal
liability to pay them if they attend, he is entitled to a tender
of their fees, and it makes no difference whether he has
actually paid or tendered the witnesses their fees or not.[7]
But if the witness has not been paid and there is sufficient
time by the use of ordinary diligence, to notify the witness
not to attend, the fees need not be tendered. The plaintiff, in
any event, would be entitled to the cost of the subpoena and
the officers' fees for serving it. The sum tendered must cover
all the costs. Where $617.27 was tendered, which sum was
$1.47 in excess of the debt, but the costs then accrued were
$2.17, it was held that the maxim *de minimis non curat lex*
did not apply, and that the tender did not prevent the recovery of subsequent costs.[8]

The sum tendered must include, not only the costs accrued
but the costs of a nonsuit,[9] otherwise the plaintiff would be

[2] See Coffman v. Hampton, 2
W. & Ser. 377.

[3] Anderried v. Hull, 45 Mo.
App. 202.

[4] Miones v. Yellow Medicine
County Bank, 45 Minn. 335,
Sheetes v. Woodard, 57 Mich. 213,
s. c. 23 N. W. Rep. 775.

[5] Collar v. Harrison, 30 Mich.
66.

[6] Gage v. Brewster, 31 N. Y.
218, Cotterlin v. Armstrong, 101
Ind. 265, Benedict v. Gilman, 4
Paige 58, Vroom v. Ditmin, 4
Paige 526.

[7] Smith v. Wilbur, 35 Vt. 133.

[8] Wright v. Beherns, 39 N. J.
L. 413.

[9] Strusguth v. Pollard, 62 Vt.
157.

left to make some disposition of the case of record at his expense. If the party making a tender after action brought is entitled to a nonsuit on paying the amount of his tender into court, he must include in the sum tendered the taxable attorney's fees provided in such cases. The rule, undoubtedly, in actions at law is, that the attorney fee to which plaintiff would be entitled should he prevail in absence of a tender, must be tendered with the other fees and disbursements. But a different rule would apply in equity where the amount of the attorney fee is discretionary with the court.[10] Where, on an appeal, the appellant is entitled to certain attorney fees in case he prevails, a tender made after an appeal has been taken must include the attorney fees taxable in the appellate court. In all such cases, except when the trial is *de novo* and execution issues out of the appellate court, the appellant is entitled to have some disposition made of the case in the lower court, and for that purpose must take a judgment of affirmance, or of reversal, as the case may be, which judgment carries the taxable attorney fees.

§ 203. **Same subject—Furnishing information as to costs incurred—Waiver of claim for costs.—**Where the costs are fixed by statute, or they may be determined by the officer under restrictions, a plaintiff is under no obligation to provide a taxation or to state the amount, and a failure to state the amount on request will not relieve the defendant from the consequences of a tender of an insufficient amount.[1] But where the costs incurred are peculiarly within the knowledge of the plaintiff, he is bound to furnish information as to the amount when requested. Where no inquiry was made by a defendant who knew a suit had been commenced, it was held that the plaintiff was under no ob'      n to inform the tenderee that he had summoned wit        Knowing that suit had been commenced, the defenda      ld have inquired.[2] If, at the time of making a tender of the amount of a debt the debtor does not know that a suit has been commenced and the creditor does not inform him of that fact, nor make any claim for costs, but refuses to accept the amount tendered solely on

10 See Merrill v Jones 39 Neb        1 Willey v Laraway 64 Vt 566
763                                  2 Smith v Wilbur 35 Vt 133

the ground that it is insufficient to pay the debt, it is waiver of all claims for costs.[1]

§ 204.  Same subject—Time when an action is commenced.— The general rule is, that an action is not commenced until the defendant is served, or the writ or summons is placed in the hands of the sheriff for service.  Guided by this rule, the Supreme Court of Massachusetts approved a ruling of the trial court, "that for the purposes of the tender, the commencement of the action was the time when the writ was delivered to the sheriff to be served," and held that the tender of the amount of the debt without the costs, was sufficient when made after the writ had been sent out to the sheriff, but before it had been received by him[2]  The writ or summons must be delivered to the officer with the intent that it shall be served forthwith.  Where it is placed in the hands of the officer with instructions to hold it, a tender need not include the cost  In such case the writ is under the control of the plaintiff, he may keep it indefinitely, or may never use it.[2]  It has been said that the purchaser of a writ is not to be regarded, under all circumstances, as the commencement of a suit, that it may be purchased to be used on a contingency[3]  Where the action is commenced by the delivery of the writ or summons to the officer, the plaintiff is entitled to all costs incurred by him so far, but placing the writ in the hands of the officer for service, or sending it away for that purpose, does not, however, entitle the plaintiff to the fees of the officer for serving it, if the plaintiff has it in his power, by the use of ordinary diligence, to recall the writ[4]

The strict rule, that the action must be actually commenced, either by the actual service on the defendant or by the delivery of the writ or summons to an officer for service, before the plaintiff is entitled to costs, is not universal  In New York it has been held that, although an action for every purpose may not be commenced until a copy of the declaration is served, yet if the plaintiff, in good faith, has incurred

[1] Haskell v Brewer, 11 Me 258 See Vreeland v Waddell, 67 N W. Rep (Wis.) 51

[1] Emerson v White, 10 Gray 351

[2] See Holdridge v Wells, 4 Conn 151

[3] Haskell v Brewer, 11 Me 258

[4] See Call v Lathrop 39 Me 134

costs which the defendant would have to pay if the action should proceed to judgment against him, the amount tendered must include such costs. Thus, when a creditor has employed an attorney to bring suit, a declaration is prepared and filed, and a rule entered to plead, and the plaintiff is proceeding with all diligence to serve the defendant with a copy of the declaration and notice of the rule, the costs incurred in filing the declaration, etc., must be tendered although service has not been effected at the time of the tender.[5] So, in the justice court, where the summons has been issued for the purpose of having it served, the defendant, in making a tender, must include the amount of the justice's fees for issuing the summons, but he need not tender costs of entering suit, for the justice ought not to enter an action on his docket until the summons has been served and returned.

§ 205. Amount required to discharge a mortgage lien—To redeem—Must include taxes paid by the mortgagee when—Where a mortgage contains a covenant that in default of the mortgagor paying the taxes and assessments on the land, or in keeping the premises insured, the mortgagee may do so, and the amount so paid, together with the necessary expense attending to the same, shall be a lien upon the land, the mortgagor in seeking to discharge the mortgage must pay or tender, in addition to the amount of the mortgage debt, the sum so paid by the mortgagee.[1] mortgagor, in seeking to discharge a mortgage debt, where it is stipulated in the mortgage, or the statute provides that in case the taxes, assessments, etc., are not paid, the mortgagee may pay the same together with all costs and penalties, and have a lien therefor, need not tender to the mortgagee the amount of any tax or assessment paid by him before the same became delinquent. Nor, where the mortgage has been foreclosed, need a mortgagor or any person entitled to redeem, tender to the purchaser the amount of taxes paid by the mortgagee before they had become delinquent, though included in the amount bid at the sale. A tax payer has until the last day given by law in which to pay his taxes, and until he is in default, any payment of taxes for him is a voluntary payment.

5 Retan v. Drew. 19 Wend 304.　　1 Equitable Life etc. v. Von Glahn. 107 N. Y. 63.

A purchaser at a mortgage foreclosure sale is bound to know the extent of the power given by the mortgage, and whether the taxes, assessments, etc., included the amount claimed to be due, were paid at a time when the mortgagee was legally authorized to do so. So, a person entitled to redeem land sold on a mortgage foreclosure sale, need not tender to the purchaser the amount of taxes and assessments paid by him subsequent to the sale, even though they were then delinquent.[2]

§ 206. Same subject—Unsecured claims—What liens need not be paid by mortgagor—Purchaser in possession under a mortgage.—A mortgagor in redeeming from mortgage or execution sale is not bound to pay a claim not secured[1] nor a claim constituting an independent lien, held by the holder of the certificate of sale[2] even though the holder of the certificate has put himself in line for redemption from the senior lien, by complying with a statutory provision, requiring a notice of his intention of redeeming to be filed. A redemption by the owner annuls the sale, and does not affect the second lien except by advancing it and improving the security. But if the holder of the certificate is in possession rightfully and claims to hold possession under a mortgage, he could not be disturbed in his possession unless the mortgage be also paid.

§ 207. Same subject — Acceptance by sheriff of less than amount bid.—If a redemptioner applies to the sheriff or other officer authorized to receive the money, to redeem lands sold on a mortgage or execution sale, he must pay or tender to the officer, in addition to the amount bid at the sale and interest, the fees of such officer for receiving the money and executing his certificate. If he tenders a gross sum which is accepted by the officer as sufficient, and the sum is sufficient to satisfy the purchaser's claim, the redemption is good, and any short-

---

[2] Nopson v Horton, 20 Minn 268, Wyatt v Quimby, 65 Minn 537, s c 68 N W Rep 109, Spencer v Levering, 8 Minn 461 (Gil. 410), Gorham v Ins Co, 64 N W Rep 906

[1] Bacon v Cotterell, 13 Minn 194

[2] Warren v Fish, 7 Minn 347, Nopson v Horton, 20 Minn 268

age must be deducted from the fees of the officer.[1] If a redemptioner deposits too little to pay the mortgage debt he must bear the consequences, the officer acts merely in an official capacity, and it is the business of a redemptioner to see that he deposits the proper amount.[2]

§ 208. **Same subject—Rate of interest—Change of rate by statute.**—If the rate of interest is not specified in the mortgage or note, the redemptioner must pay or tender, in addition to the sum bid at the sale, interest at the legal rate from the date of the sale. If the rate of interest specified is less than the legal rate, interest at the legal rate must be paid or tendered. By the foreclosure the conventional agreement is wiped out, and the obligation becomes one in the nature of a judgment, on which interest at the legal rate commences to run. If between the date of sale and day on which a redemption is sought to be made, the legal rate is changed to a higher or lower rate, interest must be computed at the legal rate on the day of the tender. In some of the states if the rate of interest provided for in the mortgage note is higher than the legal rate, interest must be paid on the sum bid at the sale at the rate specified in the mortgage, however, not to exceed ten per centum.[1] If a mortgagee is in possession, or is receiving the rents and profits, he is entitled only to receive interest at the legal rate on taxes paid by him, and the mortgagor is entitled to redeem on paying that rate.[2] In redeeming land from an execution sale, interest at the legal rate only need to be paid or tendered.[3]

§ 209. **Same subject — Joint tenants — Tenants in common — Owners of distinct part—Lienor—Tenant for life and remainderman—Parcels sold separately.**—Joint tenants, tenants in common, persons who have purchased a part of the mortgaged premises, or acquired such an interest in a part of the premises as will entitle them to redeem, and lien holders who have a lien upon any portion of the lands covered by the mortgage, must pay the whole amount bid at the sale, or the

[1] Bovey De Laittre Lumber Co v Tucker, 50 N W Rep (Minn) 1058

[2] Horton v Maffitt, 14 Minn 289

[1] Gen St Minn, § 6040

[2] Martin v Lennon, 19 Minn 67

[3] See Steele v Hanna, 91 Ala. 190

entire mortgage debt if he is not bound by the foreclosure.[1] If the purchaser is a joint tenant or tenant in common, the redemptioner, if a cotenant, need tender only his equitable proportion of the encumbrance. But this rule does not apply to life tenants and remaindermen, as a judicial investigation is necessary to determine the amount due. Where a mortgage embraces two parcels of land, and upon a foreclosure by advertisement such parcels are separately sold, at a separate price for each parcel, a junior mortgagee of one of the parcels may redeem from the sale that parcel only which is embraced in his mortgage. And the rule is the same whether the two parcels are sold to different purchasers or both to the mortgagee or any other person. As long as they are sold for a distinct price for each, the rights and interest in each parcel are separate and distinct.[2]

§ 210. **Same subject—Foreclosure for more than is due.**— The only right of redemption from an execution or a mortgage sale on a foreclosure by advertisement is that given by statute, and can be exercised only as prescribed by statute, and such a redemption cannot be made by a tender of less than the amount bid at the sale, even where the foreclosure was for a larger sum than was actually due.[1] Before the time for redemption has expired, a court of equity may allow a redemption to be made by paying the amount that is actually due, upon a sufficient excuse being shown for not applying to the court before the sale, to prevent a sale for more than was due. A subsequent encumbrancer, who, in order to redeem from a prior mortgage sale by advertisement, is obliged to pay a sum greater than the amount actually due on the prior mortgage, may recover back the excess.[2]

§ 211. **Same subject—Mortgagee in possession—Request for information as to amount due.**—A mortgagee in possession is bound to account not only to the mortgagor, but to the subsequent encumbrancers for the rents and profits, or for the

---

[1] Knowles v. Robinson, 20 Iowa 101, Street v. Beals, 16 Io. 68, Massie v. Wilson, 16 Io 390, Raynor v. Raynor, 21 Hun 36
[2] Tinkcom v. Lewis, 21 Minn 132

[1] Dickenson v. Hayes, 26 Minn 100
[2] Bennett v. Healey 6 Minn 240 See Seiler v. Wilbur 29 Minn 307

value of the use and occupation of the land. If a mortgagee is in constructive possession he is chargeable only with the amount of the rents actually received by him.[1] If the annual rents or occupation value exceed the interest and expenses, the mortgagee is chargeable with legal interest on the net annual surplus. He is entitled to deduct for all necessary repairs; for reasonable disbursements and expenses necessary for the protection of the estate and for taxes paid while in possession.[2]

The right to an accounting, however, does not extend the time in which to redeem, nor will the bringing of an action to redeem extend the time; and a mortgagor or subsequent encumbrancer must, before the time allowed him to redeem has expired, demand to be informed of the balance due, and if informed tender that sum. It is the duty of a mortgagee in possession, on an application being made to him, to inform the redemptioner (or the mortgagor if the application is before a foreclosure) of the balance due him. If he neglects to do so, or the redemptioner thinks the sum stated is too large, he must tender so much as he thinks is due. If the mortgagee makes known to him the amount due, he tenders a less sum at his peril. So, if he does not demand to know the amount due, any sum less than that bid at the sale is tendered at his peril.[3] If he tenders a less sum than is actually due, where, on making a request he is not informed of the balance due, the tender will be good, although thereafter in the decree allowing him to redeem he is required to pay a larger sum.

### § 212. Same subject—Junior encumbrancer not bound by a foreclosure—Subsequent lien holder who is bound—Failure to produce affidavit as to the amount due—Not bound to pay costs when

[1] Pough v. Davis 113 U. S. 542.
[2] 3 Pomeroy's Eq. § 1215 et seq.
[3] Bender v. Bean, 52 Ark. 132, to the contrary, holding that if the sum offered is inadequate, the inadequacy should be objected to and the correct amount indicated. The court observed, "It will not do to maintain silence as to objections which if expressed might be met and afterwards assert them to the owner's prejudice." The decision does not seem to be sound in principle. A tenderor who is the first actor should inform himself so that he will know how much to offer. The fact that he must get his information from the mortgagee instead of a third person does not relieve him of the duty of making an inquiry.

—**Statutory foreclosure.**—A person holding a junior encumb rance on land, who is not bound by a foreclosure, cannot redeem from the sale, but he must redeem, if at all, from the entire mortgage by paying the whole amount of it "The party offering to redeem proceeds upon the hypothesis that, as to him, the mortgage has never been foreclosed, but is still in existence, therefore, he can only lift it by paying it"[1] The same rule applies where the mortgagee purchases at the sale, and where some third person acquires the rights under the foreclosure by purchase or by a redemption A third person who has purchased at a mortgage sale or taken a deed from a purchaser or an encumbrancer who has redeemed from a sale, where the foreclosure is void as to the mort gagor, or inoperative as to a subsequent encumbrancer, stands as an assignee of the mortgage as to the mortgagor or such subsequent encumbrancer not bound by the fore closure[2]

A subsequent lien holder who is not bound by a fore closure of a senior mortgage, must pay or tender to the pur chaser or to his immediate preceding redemptioner the full amount of the senior mortgage regardless of the amount bid at the sale He need not tender the amount of any lien which the purchaser or the immediate redemptioner was compelled to discharge, unless, perhaps, the purchaser is in a position to claim the rights of a mortgagee in possession The party taking up such liens is merely subrogated to the rights of the original holder Where the redemption is sought to be made through a lien holder who by reason of not being bound was compelled to lift the mortgage, it is not necessary to pay to the party not bound by the foreclosure the amount of his lien, unless he is in a position to claim the benefits of a mortgagee in possession, and the subsequent redemptioner desires to secure the possession. A subsequent lien holder, who is not bound by a foreclosure of a senior mortgage, may

1 Collins v Riggs. 14 Wall 491, Martin v Fridley, 23 Minn. 13, Vanderkemp v Shelton 11 Paige 28, Bradley v. Snyder 14 Ill 263, Johnson v Harmon. 19 Iowa, 56, Knowles v Roblin 21 Iowa 101

See Brainard v Cooper. 10 N Y 356

2 Robinson v Ryan 25 N Y 320, Martin v Fridley 23 Minn 13

redeem without paying the costs of such foreclosure,[3] as it was an action in which he was in no way concerned. Since, by the foreclosure and the afflux of the time limited in a decree or by statute, the legal title is vested in the senior mortgagee or purchaser at the sale, a junior encumbrancer, who is not bound by the foreclosure, who redeems by lifting the senior mortgage, acquires the legal estate and all the benefits of the foreclosure without paying any of the expenses[4] But the loss of the costs and disbursements to the senior mortgagor may be justified on the ground of his carelessness in not making the junior lien holder a party to the action

A subsequent lien holder who is bound by the foreclosure, must pay or tender to the immediate prior redemptioner the full amount for which the property was sold, together with the amount of the claim under which he redeemed,[5] and the amount of each prior encumbrance which he was compelled to discharge  The senior redemptioner cannot tack an unsecured claim to his lien and make the payment of such debt a condition of allowing a redemption, nor will the party offering to redeem be required to pay a lien held by the senior redemptioner, unless the senior redemptioner has placed himself in lien for redemption by complying with the statute as to that particular lien[6] and not then unless such lien is senior to the one held by the party seeking to redeem  It has been said that if a person redeems from the purchaser without complying with the statute requiring the production and filing of an affidavit showing the amount actually due on his lien, and afterwards another lien holder attempts to redeem, the want of the affidavit may be fatal, and that it would probably be sufficient for him to tender a nominal sum beyond the original purchase money and interest[7]

Where a statutory foreclosure is not binding as to a subsequent encumbrancer in making a redemption such encumbrancer must pay the amount of the mortgage and not the

3 Gage v Brewster 31 N Y 218 reversing, 30 Barb 387, s p Cotterlin v Armstrong 101 Ind 25

4 See Gage v Brewster, 31 N Y 218, dissenting opinion of Mullin J

Where a lien is valid upon its face a subsequent redemptioner is not bound to contest the right of a prior redemptioner to redeem See Todd v Johnson 57 N W Rep 320

6 Buchanan v Reed, 13 Minn 172

7 The Bank of Vergennes v Warren, 7 Hill 91

amount bid at the sale. Nor is he bound to pay the costs of the statutory foreclosure.[8]

§ 213. **Same subject—Usurious mortgage—Waiver of defense —Where mortgage is void — Void as to interest only — Foreclosure for default in the payment of interest — Of principal** —In those commonwealths where interest in excess of the limit fixed by the statute cannot be recovered, a mortgagor who has failed to interpose the defence of usury, or who has neglected to invoke the aid of a court of equity to restrain a statutory foreclosure for such illegal excess, is deemed to have waived his rights, and in redeeming the land from the foreclosure sale he must tender the full amount bid at the sale.[1] But where a statute declares that an usurious mortgage is absolutely void, and the mortgagor may recover from the mortgagee whatever sum he may be compelled to pay third persons on account of the usurious obligation, the purchaser at a sale on a foreclosure by advertisement, with notice of the usury, acquires no estate or interest in the land,[2] and a mortgagor need not tender anything whatever. So, the same rule is applied where the statute works only a forfeiture of the entire interest where the foreclosure is for a failure to pay such illegal interest. There being no binding obligation to pay such interest there can be no default in failing to pay it.[3]

But where the foreclosure is for a default in the payment of the principle, and the amount bid at the sale includes the principle and the illegal interest, the mortgagor would in any event have to tender the amount of the principal due at the date of the sale, and the interest on that sum sub

[8] Benedict v Gilman 4 Paige 58; Vroom v Ditmas, 4 Paige 526 In such cases a purchaser at the sale stands as an assignee of the mortgage as to a subsequent encumbrancer who is not bound by the foreclosure, and although he may have paid at the sale only half as much as the mortgage debt, yet he is, nevertheless on a redemption by such subsequent encumbrance, entitled to the whole amount of the mortgage debt On the other hand if he paid the full amount of the debt and the costs he looses the latter

[1] Taylor v Burgess, 26 Minn 547 See Woolfolk v Bird 22 Minn 341, Connell v Smith, 27 Minn 133 The statute in reference to usury on which these decisions were based, was afterwards changed so as to work a forfeiture of the principal and interest

[2] Scott v Austin, 36 Minn 460, Exley v Berryhill, 37 Minn 182 See Jordan v Humphrey 31 Minn 495

[3] Chase v Whitten 53 N W Rep (Minn) 767

sequent to the sale of the legal rate. Here, a foreclosure being based on a default in the payment of a sum that is a legal claim against the mortgagor, and usury being an affirmative defence which must be pleaded in order to be availed of, it would seem that a mortgagor who had neglected to set up that defence, if the foreclosure was by action, or to apply to a court of equity for the purpose of restraining the mortgagee from foreclosing for such illegal interest, if the foreclosure is by advertisement, would waive the defence and be deemed to have acquiesced in the claim, and that in redeeming, he must tender the full amount bid at the sale. But where the default consists in failing to pay the principal, and the sum stated to be due in the notice of foreclosure included the illegal interest, and the property at the sale only sold for so much as would discharge the principal, the question is free from doubt. The mortgagor would be bound to tender the full amount bid at the sale, and he would be left to contest the questions of waiver should the mortgagee seek to secure a deficiency judgment.[1]

§ 214    Same subject—Who may take advantage of defence usury—The most common rule is, that the debtor only can plead usury as a defence or make it the basis for affirmative relief,[1] and that the debtor by failing to avail himself of the defence or remedy granted him by the statute acquiesces[2] in any proceedings instituted by the creditor for the collection of the debt, and that one who purchases the land subject to a mortgage securing an usurious loan,[3] or purchases the equity of redemption[4] or takes a junior mortgage on the land,[5] or acquires a judgment,[6] or any other lien upon the land, is bound by such acquiescence of the debtor and he cannot at-

[1] See First National Bank v. Turner (Kan) 42 Pac 926, and Same v. McInturff, 43 Pac Rep (Kan) 839. When it is held that a payment on a note is a payment on the principal debt and not on the interest which is forfeited.

[1] Phillips v. Ogle 21 D C 199, Hull v. Taylor 28 S W Rep 590, Peoples Bank v. Jackson 43 S C 89, Chapins v. Mathot 91 Hun 565 s c 36 N Y 835

[2] See Tillotson v. Ney, 88 Hun 101 s c 34 N Y Supp 606

[3] Dickerson v. Bankers' L & Ins Co 93 Va 198 s c 25 S E Rep 518 Parker v. Hotel Co 96 Tenn 252 Vaughn v. Mutual Bldg Assn 36 S W Rep 1013

[4] Hull v. Alliance Bldg Co (S P) 60 N W 752

[5] Stickney v. Moore 108 Ala 590 s c 19 So 76

[6] Chapins v. Mathot 91 Hun 565 s c 36 N Y 835

tack the mortgage on the ground that it is tainted with usury.[7] In redeeming, such a purchaser or junior lien holder must pay or tender the full amount bid at the sale.[8]

§ 215. Same subject—Where mortgage debt bears interest at a greater rate after maturity than before.—Under some statutes a stipulation in a note that it shall bear interest after maturity at a greater rate than it bears before maturity, being in the nature of a penalty,[1] is voidable at the option of the debtor. In absence of a statute such agreements are no more void

---

[7] See American Rubber Co. v. Wilson, 55 Mo. App. 656, Voorhies v. Stead, 63 Mo. App. 370. These cases, however, seem to be based on a statute.

[8] It is held in Minnesota, where the law works a forfeiture of the principal and interest and declares an usurious contract absolutely void, that a failure on the part of the mortgagor to have a foreclosure by advertisement of an usurious mortgage, enjoined, does not estop him from avoiding the sale and the mortgage, by an action for that purpose where the mortgagee or an assignee of the mortgage with notice of the usury before foreclosure purchase at the sale Scott v. Austin 36 Minn. 460, Exley v. Berryhill, 37 Minn. 182.

As to innocent purchasers, "The general rule is that where the debtor suffers property pledged or mortgaged to be regularly sold to an innocent purchaser, he will not be permitted to question the validity of the sale on the ground that the original security is infected with the usury." Jordan v. Humphrey 31 Minn. 197. And when a subsequent encumbrancer, without knowledge that the prior encumbrance is tainted with usury, redeems from the

sale under it, the same principle of equitable estoppel would protect him in such case as it would had he purchased at the sale without such knowledge. But where a subsequent encumbrancer has knowledge of the claim that the first mortgage is usurious, but the mortgagor has not commenced his action and avoided the sale and mortgage can he redeem by paying the amount bid at the sale? In absence of authorities (there may be some we have not found) it would seem that a rule permitting such encumbrancer to redeem would be just and equitable, and would be founded upon the laches of the mortgagor. A mortgagor ought to be diligent in applying to a court of equity to have the foreclosure enjoined, or in bringing his action for the purpose of avoiding the sale and mortgage, and having it determined prior to the expiration of the time allowed him to redeem. A subsequent encumbrancer has no assurance that the action will ever be commenced or if commenced, that it will result in favor of the mortgagor.

[1] See Omaha & Co. v. Hanson, 46 Neb. 870 s. c. 65 N. W. Rep. 1058 to the contrary.

than is the penal clause in a bond.[2]  A party consenting to the insertion of such a stipulation, cannot give himself no further concern about it, and expect to treat it as void at all places and at all times, expecting the courts to interpose his defence to prevent a judgment being taken against him for more than the amount to which a court, on a proper showing, would reduce the claim.  Therefore, if a mortgage securing a note or other obligation, with a stipulation for the payment of a greater rate of interest after maturity than it bears before, is foreclosed, and the mortgagor, if the foreclosure is in equity, fails to interpose his defence, or if the foreclosure is by advertisement, fails to have enjoined a sale for any more than the principal and interest at the legal rate, he waives his defence, and in redeeming he must tender the full amount bid at the sale.[3]  The same rule has been held to apply where a party waives his defence in advance of suit by giving new notes including such excessive rate of interest.[4]  So also, it has been held that such a waiver binds subsequent encumbrancers.[5]

Where a statute declares the taking of a greater rate of interest after maturity, than that contracted to be paid before, to be illegal and to work a forfeiture of the entire interest, the same rule applies as obtained in those cases where the statute works a forfeiture of the entire interest where the contract is usurious.[6]

§ 216  Specific articles—Tender of more than is contracted for—Failure to object no waiver when—Where the amount offered is included in a greater mass.—In reference to the quantity of specific articles to be delivered in payment of a note or in compliance with a contract of sale, the rule is that the payee or buyer is entitled to refuse the whole of the goods tendered, if they exceed the quantity agreed upon, and the payor or seller has no right to insist upon the payee or buyer accepting all, or upon the payee or buyer selecting out of a larger quantity delivered the amount necessary to satisfy the con

[2] See Ward's Admrs v Cornett, 22 S E Rep (Va) 494, where it is held that a bond is not void for usury where it provides for usurious interests only after maturity

[3] Bidwell v Whitney 4 Minn 76

[4] Martin v Lemon, 19 Minn 67

[5] Mills v Kellogg, 7 Minn 469

[6] Chase v Whitten, (Minn) 53 N W Rep 767

tract.[1] Thus a tender of fifty-three tons of scrap iron from which the purchaser could select forty tons, was held bad.[2] So was a tender of forty-eight gallons of rum in a cask containing seventy-two gallons.[3]

In a case where a vendor had delivered to a carrier in one crate and with one invoice, the goods ordered by the defendant, together with other goods not ordered, the court said "If there is any danger or trouble attending the severance of the two, or any risk that the vendee might be held to have accepted the whole if he accepted his own, he is at liberty, as this defendant was, to refuse to accept at all." The court further observed, that the defendant could hardly understand the plaintiff to say in effect: "Take out of the crate what you ordered; if you do not like to have the rest let them lie where you please or remove them to some convenient distance." And it was held that he was not under any obligation to undertake the obligation and trouble imposed upon him by the latter course, and that he was at liberty to refuse to accept.[4] So, where a contract called for a certain quantity of washed wool, and the tender was of both washed and unwashed wool, it was held that, "A tender of a larger bulk from which plaintiff might with great labor have selected the quantity, and of the quality they had purchased, was an insufficient tender."[5]

The objection to a tender of a specific article, that more is offered than was contracted for, is not waived by a failure to object to it at the time.[6] The contract must be strictly and literally fulfilled[7] by making such a separation and designation of the exact amount of the property to be delivered, that the title thereto will vest in the party who is to receive it, whenever the tenderor as payor of the note wishes to insist on the defence that the note is paid in an action by the payee to recover the amount of the note in

[1] Cunliffe v. Harrison 6 Ex. 903, Reuter v. Sala 4 C P D 239, Hart v. Mills, 15 M & W 85

[2] Perry v. Mount Hope Iron Co, 16 R I 318

[3] Gallup v. Cott. (Conn) Rix v. Strong 1 Root 55 Nichols v. Whitney 1 Root 443

[4] Levy v. Green 1 E & E 969

[5] Stevenson v. Burgin 49 Pa St 36

[6] Perry v. Mount Hope Iron Co. 16 R I 318; Levy v. Green 1 E & E 969

[7] Brownfield v. Johnson, 128 Pa St 254

money; or a vendor desires to recover the purchase price. A refusal to receive the articles upon some ground other than the objection to the quantity, would be a waiver of the latter objection to the tender only where there was some concurrent act to be performed by the other party. Such waiver would be available only in resisting some claim on the part of the vendee. There are decisions holding that, where there is sold a given quantity of property lying in mass, its separation from a mass indistinguishable in quality, in which it is included, is not necessary to pass the title, where the intention to pass the title to the property without such separation is clearly manifested. This was so held where the owner of wheat lying in a mass in his warehouse sold a portion of it, and executed a receipt acknowledging himself to hold the wheat subject to the purchaser's order. The court in reviewing the authorities said "None of them go to the extent of holding that a man cannot, if he wishes and intends to do so, make a perfect sale of a quantity, without actual separation, where the mass is ascertained by the contract and all parts of the same value and indistinguishable from each other."[8] The seller retains possession of the wheat as bailee. As to third persons the parties are tenants in common of the entire mass. Such a case does not really involve any questions relating to a tender, being merely a bargain and sale of a definite portion of an designated undivided whole

§ 217. **Tender of a less quantity—Delivery of part before the time for performance—Consequences of an acceptance of part of on the day for performance** — A tender of a less quantity of specific articles than is bargained for is not good[1]. An acceptance of part does not render the vendee liable for the whole amount to be delivered. If a part of the goods are delivered before the time for performance arrives, the vendor may return the part so received on a failure of

[8] Kimberly v. Patchin, 19 N. Y. 330, and cases cited

[1] Robert v. Beatty, 2 Penn. 63, Oxendale v. Wetherell 9 B. & C. 386. See Drown v. Smith, 3 N. H. 299. See also Hayden v. Demets. 53 N. Y. 426 where the sale was of 50,000 pounds of copper, and warehouse receipts for 49,066 were tendered the vendor having other copper sufficient to make up the difference. A refusal to receive the copper solely on the ground that they could not pay for it was held to be a waiver of the objection to the amount

the other party to complete the contract, or he may retain
and pay for so much as he had received. If, on the day
fixed for delivery, a tender of a portion of the whole amount
contracted to be delivered, is accepted, a strict performance
is waived, and the other party has a reasonable time to tender the balance, unless the acceptance of a portion is qualified
by the declaration that no more will be received. Where
the vendee does not declare that he will not receive any
more of the goods and the vendor intends to go on and com
plete the contract, an acceptance of a part does not render
the vendee liable to pay for the part so received before the
balance of the goods is delivered. If the portion received
is applied on a note payable in specific articles, and the payor
does not tender the residue within a reasonable time, the
payor may recover the balance due in money.

§ 218.  Contract to deliver by installments—Consequences of
retaining part after default -- Note payable in installments —
When unpaid installments become a money demand.—If a con
tract of sale provides for a delivery in parcels at different
times, and the whole is not delivered according to agreement,
the buyer may return the part already received. The almost
universal rule is, that the purchaser, if he retains the part
delivered, disaffirms the entirety of the contract and must
pay for the portion so retained, less damages for the failure
to deliver the residue[1] The contrary rule obtains in New
York, and some other states  There the vender may retain
the goods delivered, and the vendor cannot recover anything
for them, unless the delivery of the balance was waived[2] If
a note payable in specific articles is payable in installments,
and a part of the installments are paid at the time and
place fixed, a failure to meet subsequent installments will
not entitle the payee to return the parts already received
A failure to pay any installments at the time and place
agreed, converts the unpaid installment into money demand

[1] Pixler v Nicholas 8 Iowa 106,
s c 74 Am Dec 298, Britton v
Turner, 6 N H, 481, s c 26 Am
Dec, 713, Bast v Byrnes, 51 Wis
531, s c 37 Am Dec 841, Wolf
v Gerr, 13 Iowa 339  See Roberts
v Beatty 2 Penn 63

[2] Catlen v Tobias, 26 N Y 217,
Haslack v Mayers, 26 N J L
284  Witherow v Witherow, 16
Ohio 238  See Jennings v Lyons,
39 Wis 553

**§ 219. Contracts for the delivery of a given quantity "more or less" or 'about" or for an amount as shall be determined by the purchaser.**—The Supreme Court of the United States, Mr. Justice Bradley delivering the opinion of the court, in considering a case where the contract was for eight hundred cords of wood, "more or less, as shall be determined to be necessary by the post commander for the regular supply," and the post commander determined that forty cords of wood would be required which was in fact all that was necessary, laid down the general rules governing such cases, thus: (1) Where a contract is to sell or furnish certain goods identified by independent circumstances, such as an entire lot deposited in a certain warehouse, or all that may be manufactured by the vendor in a certain establishment, or that may be shipped by his agent or correspondent in certain vessels, and the quantity is named with the qualification of "about" or "more or less" or words of like import, the contract applies to the specific lot, and the naming of the quantity is not regarded as in the nature of a warranty, but only as an estimate of the probable amount, in reference of which good faith is all that is required of the party making it.[1]  (2) But where no independent circumstances are referred to, and the engagement is to furnish goods of a certain quality or character to a certain amount, the quantity specified is material and governs the contract. The addition of the qualifying words, "about" "more or less" and the like in such cases, is only for the purpose of providing against accidental variations arising from slight and unimportant excesses or deficiencies in number, measure, or weight.[2]  (3) If, however, the qualifying words are supplemented by other stipulations or conditions which give them a broader scope or more extensive significancy, then the contract is to be governed by

---

[1] Where a sale was of all the spars manufactured by a certain person, say about 600 averaging 16 inches, it was held that a tender of 196 spars, which were all of the specified lot that averaged 16 inches, was a substantial performance of the contract. McConnell v Murphy, L R 5 P C C 203  So where 44 tons of scrap iron was delivered, being all of a heap estimated to be about 150 tons, the tender was held good  McLay v Perry, 44 L T N S 152

[2] A contract calling for 25,000 feet of lumber, was held not to be satisfied by a delivery of 16,000 feet  Creighton v Comstock, 27 Oh St 548

the added stipulation or condition. In the case under con
sideration the qualifying stipulation, "as shall be determined
to be necessary by the post commander," left the matter of
the amount to be delivered to that officer, and the law required of him only good faith[3]

§ 220.   Construction of contracts for the court—Performance
a question of fact for the jury.—The construction of a contract
is for the court. What would be a reasonable or substantial
performance of a contract is, ordinarily, a question for a
jury. But there may be such a variance between the amount
named in the contract and the amount tendered, that the
tender as a matter of law, would not constitute performance.

§ 221.   Tender by receiptor (or bailee) where a value is affixed
to each article—When the value is fixed at a gross sum.—When
specific articles have been delivered by an officer, to a
receiptor, and a value is affixed to each article named in
the receipt, a tender of a part of such property is good, and
if such tender is refused by the officer, he cannot recover
of the bailee the value of the part tendered[1] The value of
each article is inserted in order to fix the extent of the receiptor's liability if he fails to return any part of the goods[2]
Where the value of all the goods is fixed at a gross sum, a
tender of part will not do[3]

---

[1] Brawley v United States 96
U S 168   See Benj on Sales 3rd
Ed § 9, et seq, and cases cited

[1] Remick v Atkinson, 11 N H
256 s c 35 Am Dec. 193

[2] Drown v Smith 3 N H 299
Wakefield v Stedman, 12 Pick
562

[3] Drown v Smith, 3 N H 299

# CHAPTER V.

## MANNER OF MAKING A TENDER

15

§ 222.  **Actual offer — A proposition — Declaring intention — Request to present a note—Interrogating the creditor as to his willingness to accept—Announcing a readiness or willingness—Declaring upon what account the tender is made —** In making a tender there must be an actual offer on the part of the tenderor to pay a certain sum, or to deliver the article, or perform the duty which he is under obligation to do.  A bare proposition to pay a certain sum is not a tender[1]  A proposition to pay a mortgage debt if the mortgagee will strike out the usurious interest, without producing and offering the money legally due, is not a tender.[2]  A mere announcement of an intention of making a tender,[3] or a request to present a note for payment,[4] or a simple inquiry as to whether a party would accept the money[5] does not constitute a tender  So, laying money down on a table and asking for an extension of time which was granted, was held not to amount to a tender[6]  Where a claim is in litigation, preparing a receipt in blank and offering to pay whatever might be ascertained to be the proper sum due, is not a tender of payment[7]  Nor is an offer of the amount due to the plaintiff by defendant's attorney, while making his argument in the case[8]  So, merely

[1] Eastman v District Township, 21 Iowa, 590 Liebbrant v Marron Lodge 61 Ill 81, Rogers v Peoples Sav Assn 55 S W Rep (Tex Civ App) 383, Shendine v Gaul, 2 Dall 190 Augier v Equitable B & L Assn 35 S E Rep (Ga) 64 Deering v Hamilton, 83 N W Rep (Minn) 44  See Bowen v Holley 38 Vt 574

[2] Harmon v Magee, 57 Miss 410

[3] Stone v Billing 107 Ill 170, affirmed 63 Ill App 37 s c 47 N E 372

[4] Butts v Burnett, 6 Abb Pr (N S) 308

[5] Steele v Biggs 22 Ill 643, Ladd v Patten 1 Cranch, C Ct 263.

[6] McInerney v Lindsay 56 N W Rep (Mich) 603

[7] Chase v Welch 45 Mich 345, s c 7 N W Rep 895

[8] Keyes v Roder, 1 Head 19.

asking "Have you a receipt?" is not good, even though the money is produced.[9]

A mere announcement of a readiness to pay a note, does not constitute a tender.[10] Nor the statement by a debtor to his creditor, "here, I am ready."[11] So, a statement by a mortgagor to the mortgagee that he was ready to pay the amount due upon the mortgage, when he kept the money which was in a bag under his arm, was held insufficient.[12] A statement by a party that he was not aware of the exact amount due, but that if anything was due he was ready to pay it, is not a tender of the balance due.[13] Sending a written communication demanding the cancellation of a contract, and expressing a willingness to return the money theretofore paid on the contract, where an antecedent tender is necessary, is not a substitute for a tender, and when not actually declined, is not even an excuse for not making it.[14] A declaration of a willingness to pay the value of certain labor bestowed upon an article, when it should be delivered, is an offer to close with any tender which might come from the other party, and is not equivalent to an actual tender, and will not support an action in replevin to recover the article.[15] So, a subsequent encumbrancer must tender the principal, interest, and costs to the mortgagee. Merely stating what he will do, and paying the money into court, is not sufficient to stop interest or stop proceedings on the mortgage.[16] Bringing money into court for the use of the plaintiff without first offering it him is no tender.[17] In no case does a mere readiness and willingness to pay a debt amount to a tender without an actual offer by one party and a refusal by the other.[18] A person in making a tender must declare upon what account it is made.

[9] Ryder v. Townsend 7 D. & R. 119

[10] Bacon v. Smith, 2 La. Am. 411

[11] North v. Mallett, 2 Haywood (N. C.) 151

[12] Suckling v. Coney, Nov. 74

[13] Scott v. Franklin, 15 East 428

[14] Adams v. Friedlander, 37 La. Am. 350

[15] McIntyre v. Carver, 2 W. & Ser. 392

[16] Hornby v. Cramer, 12 How. Pr. 490

[17] Phoenix Ins. Co. v. Overman 52 N. E. Rep. (Ind. App.) 773

[18] Smith v. Foster, 5 Or. 44, Sheridine v. Gaul, 2 Dall. 190

§ 223.   **Readiness and ability—Tenderor's ability to borrow—Having the money at a distance—Refusal does not dispense with ability.**—It is essentially requisite that a person who intends to make a tender not only actually offers to pay the money or perform the duty to be by him paid or performed, but that he has it in his power, at the time of his offer, to pay the one to perform the other. "In order that an offer to perform should operate as performance itself and extinguish a lien, it should be unequivocal, and reasonably capable of being understood by the other party as a *bona fide* tender of the requisite thing, act, or service; and the verbal elements should be accompanied by circumstances fairly implying control of the necessary means and possessing the necessary ability."[1]   A mere willingness is not sufficient, nor is the fact that a party is able to pay on the day fixed for payment.[2] The money or thing must be in his immediate control ready for delivery.[3]

It is not sufficient that a third person is present from whom the money might be borrowed, unless the third person has the money at hand and actually consents to loan it for the purpose of a tender. Mere ability to borrow is not sufficient for any purpose.[4]   If a third person is present with the money and joined in the offer, it can make no difference to the tenderee from whose custody the money comes, the material thing is the ability, readiness, and willingness of the tenderor to vest the title in the tenderee.[5]   It has been held in an English case, that an offer by a third person to go upstairs and fetch a certain sum which the debtor had offered to pay his creditor, when the offer was refused, constituted a tender, but it is very questionable authority.[6]

---

[1] Selby v. Hurd, 46 N. W. Rep (Mich.) 180

[2] Myers v. Byington, 34 Iowa, 205

[3] Niederhauser v. Detroit, 91 N. W. Rep (Mich.) 1028

[4] Sargent v. Graham, 5 N. H. 440, s. c. 22 Am. Dec. 469  See Carrington v. Payne

[5] Martis v. Thomas, 101 Ind. 119.

[6] Harding v. Davis, 2 C. & P. 77 Smith v. Old Dominion B. & L. Assn., 119 N. C. 257, s. c. 26 S. E. Rep. 40, is equally questionable There a refusal to receive the amount of a debt, on a statement by the debtor that he had the money in a bank in the same building was held to dispense with the actual production of the money  So Steckel v. Standley, 47 N. W. Rep (Iowa) 489, where

Best, C. J., in the same case, said: "I agree that it would not do if a man said, 'I have got the money, but must go a mile to fetch it.'" A statement by a debtor that he can get the money in five minutes,[7] or that he can get it the next morning, does not constitute a tender.[8] Nor is an offer to pay a certain sum if the creditor would go to a certain bank.[9]

A count of the money is not necessary where a party absolutely refuses to receive it; but a refusal to have anything to do with the debtor or his money does "not dispense with existing ability to make the payment, that is, the actual possession of the money, or having it within convenient reach."[10] The refusal of the creditor amounts to nothing if it be made to appear that the money or thing was not at the time at the immediate command of the debtor.[11] Where the debtor stated that he had the money ready to pay, it was held error to exclude evidence that he then had the money with him ready to pay.[12]

§ 224. **Same subject—Check must be drawn—Deed or other instrument must be executed**—If the debtor intends to give a check on his banker for the amount due, he must have it drawn at the time of offering to pay, and that fact made known to the creditor. An offer to draw a check is not a tender,[1] and the creditor will waive nothing if the check be not actually drawn. So, where a person intends to make an offer of performance, if he is required by the contract to furnish a deed, mortgage, note, or other instrument, he must execute the kind of instrument called for by the contract and have it ready, capable of immediate delivery at the time

---

the tenderor had money in another bank in the same town and could have produced it is still more questionable authority. See West v. Averill, 80 N. W. Rep. (Iowa) 555.

[7] Breed v. Hurd, 6 Pick. 356.

[8] Blair v. Hamilton, 48 Ind. 32.

[9] Stakke v. Chapman, 83 N. W. Rep. (So. Dak.) 261. In Shöp v. Todd, 38 N. J. Eq. 324, it was held where a mortgagee, after commencing foreclosure proceedings, demanded payment of the mort-

gage debt, that a promise to pay as soon as the money could be obtained from a bank a few miles distant was a valid tender.

[10] Wynkoop v. Cowing, 21 Ill. 570.

[11] Steele v. Briggs, 22 Ill. 643. See Wyllie v. Mathews, 11 N. W. Rep. (Iowa) 232. See also West v. Averill, 80 N. W. Rep. (Io.) 555.

[12] Pinney v. Jorgenson, 27 Minn. 26.

[1] Durham v. Jackson, 6 Wend. 22.

of his offer. The rule is not different in this respect, whether the delivery of the instrument is a condition precedent or subsequent, or is to be met with a concurrent act on the part of the other party. If he desires to discharge himself of the obligation, or to lay the foundation for an action for affirmative relief, and makes an offer for that purpose, he must be ready and able to make an immediate delivery on his part.[2] But where the vendor has rendered a strict performance unnecessary by incapacitating himself to convey,

[2] The declarations of the other party amounting to a refusal to go on with his part of the contract, made at the time of an offer of performance, has been held to dispense with the readiness. Thus, in cases where a party was to execute a bond for the hire and safe-keeping of certain slaves, it was held that demanding the slaves and notifying the owner that he was ready to execute the bond was sufficient tender where the owner refused to deliver the slaves, declaring he intended to work them himself. Abrams v. Suttles, Bush (N. C.) L. 99. In this case the court does not distinguish between ability in the sense of being ready then and there to deliver the thing and ability as used in the sense that the party can or might execute such a bond. The courts err in applying to such cases the rule that any act or declaration of the opposite party which hinders or prevents an actual tender dispenses with the actual production of the thing to be delivered. Such rule applies to cases where a party is about to produce and tender something and is told not to do so, or otherwise hindered; but such hindrance does not dispense with readiness and the ability to then and there deliver the thing. Where a party is notified by the other party in advance of the time of performance that he will not perform, it will excuse not only an actual tender of performance but any preliminary preparation such as the execution of an instrument for such a notification, if not withdrawn, is a repudiation of the contract, and the willing party may sue to recover damages for such a breach. But even where the party has such previous notice, if he wishes to discharge himself of the obligation in cases where he is the first actor or to bring an action for specific performance, he must at the time of his offer be actually ready. In cases such as the slave cases, where a party is willing to perform, and present himself at the time for performance, expecting then and there to complete the transaction, but before he can make himself ready the other party repudiates the contract, not on the ground that the first party is not ready, but because he does not intend to perform himself, the repudiation of the contract amounts to a waiver of the want of preparation on the part of the willing party, and in an action for damages he is bound to show only as evidence of good faith that he could have performed and intended to do so. In such cases a tender is unnecessary.

as where he sells the land to another, the deed need not be executed and tendered.[3] The English rule is, it seems, in contracts to convey land, that the vendee must prepare the conveyance and tender it for the execution.[4] In the United States the rule is that the vendor must furnish the conveyance.[5] The vendor should be allowed a reasonable time to prepare the conveyance, after a tender or payment of the purchase money. And it has been held that the vendee should not be allowed to retire immediately and bring an action, but should, after waiting a reasonable time present himself to receive the deed.[6] But the rule requiring the vendee to present himself a second time to receive the deed does not now obtain.

§ 225. **Same subject—Where concurrent acts are to be performed—Where services are to be rendered—Notice that services will not be needed.**—When the act to be done requires the concurrence of both parties, a refusal to perform by one party will ordinarily discharge the other from the actual performance, but before he will be entitled to claim the benefit of an actual performance he must show an actual ability, at the time of the refusal, to perform on his part, for otherwise the performance by him was not prevented by the declaration of the other party.[1] If the thing to be done is the performance of certain services, the employe must be ready at the appointed time and place to enter upon his duty, and offer to do so.[2] If the services to be performed require implements, or tools or material, and the employe is to furnish them, he must have the tools or material there ready. In such cases by presenting himself empty handed, he would not be ready

3 Knight v. Crockford, 1 Esp. N. P. 190.

4 Baxter v. Lewis, Forest's Exch. 61. See Byers v. Aiken, 5 Pick (Ark.) 119.

5 Gray v. Dougherty, 25 Cal. 278; Tinney v. Ashley 15 Pick. 546; Hill v. Hobart, 16 Me. 164; Fairbank v. Dow, 6 N. H. 164; Walling v. Kinnaird, 10 Tex. 508.

6 Fuller v. Hubbard, 6 Cow. 13; Hackett v. Huson, 3 Wend. 250; Fuller v. Williams, 7 Cow. 53.

1 Mills v. Huggins 3 Dev. 58. Where a party previous to the time of performance conveys away land over which he had agreed to maintain a right of way a refusal to pay money was held not to put the vendee in default so as to support an action for the unpaid installments. Eddy v. Davis, 22 N. E. Rep. 362, S. C. 40 Hun 637.

2 Griffin v. Brooklyn Ball Club, 73 N. Y. Supp. 864.

or able to perform and his proffer would amount to nothing. However, a person who had been previously notified that his services would not be needed or accepted at the appointed time, would not be required to take the time or the trouble, or to incur the expense necessary to transport himself, or his tools, or material, to the appointed place to perform the idle ceremony of offering his services.[1]

§ 226. **Ability must be made to appear.**—Actual ability, accompanied by the immediate physical possibility of reaching out and laying hold of the money or thing to be delivered and making a manual proffer of it, or placing it in a position so that the tenderee if he choose may lay hold of it, must not only exist as a fact, but it must be made to appear at the time that the party has the money or thing ready for delivery.[1] Merely stating, "I will pay you the money I offered you yesterday," even when the money is in the desk near by, is not sufficient, if "it does not appear where the money was, whether it was in the desk or not, so that the witness by opening could immediately get it  *  *  *  It ought to appear that the money was there, capable of immediate delivery."[2]  So, when certain goods sold were to be paid for in good promissory notes, an offer to pay the price in notes, even though the vendor demanded a part in cash, was held bad, where it was not made to appear that

---

[1] If the party bound to render services, before the time for performance is notified that the services will not be needed he has the election to consider such act as a breach of the contract and bring an action immediately, or wait till the appointed time arrives and then be in readiness to render the services. Howard v Daly 61 N Y 362, s c 19 Am Rep 285

The election will be evidenced by the acts of the party. The action will be for damages for not being permitted to work and may be brought at once to recover damages for a breach of the whole contract, or he may wait until the expiration of the time limited for the completion of the services. The measure of damages in any case is prima facie the entire amount of the wages agreed to be paid but the employer may show in mitigation of damages that the party has found employment elsewhere, or that similar employment has been offered and declined, or that he might have found employment by use of reasonable diligence

[1] Fuller v Little, 7 N H 535, Pinney v Jorgenson, 27 Minn 26

[2] Glasscott v Day, 5 Esp 48.

the debtor had the notes in his possession and was willing and ready to deliver them.[3]

That the money or thing is present ready for delivery, may be made to appear by exhibiting the article itself, or by the declaration of the tenderor,[4] but it must be carried and had at the place in such a manner that the tenderee may lay hold of it, examine or count it, and reduce it to possession if he desires to do so. There must be no obstacles in the way of the tenderee exercising immediate dominion over the property, as some further act to be performed by the tenderor. Thus a tender would not be good if the money was retained in a pocket or concealed about the person.[5] It would seem not to be sufficient if the money is retained in an envelope, although the debtor show the envelope to his creditor and shake it at him.[6]

§ 227. Tenderor must have title—Question of title not material.—The tenderor is not only required to have the thing ready for immediate delivery, but he must have the title. A tender of money or property known to be in the wrongful possession of the tenderor, or if in the rightful possession the payment or delivery of it would be a misappropriation or embezzlement, may be rejected by the tenderee.[1] For if accepted under such circumstances, the property could not be retained as against the real owner. If the tender is refused upon some other ground, and it is afterwards proven that the tenderor did not have the title, the offer to pay the money or deliver the article would not amount to a tender, even though the real owner afterwards might say that he would not have objected to such use of his property. In no sense is that a tender which the party at the time has not the right to perform. A tenderee does not waive any defect in a tender which is concealed from him. It is presumed that he would have rejected the tender on the further ground that the tenderor did not have the title, if that fact had been made known to him at the time of the offer. In contemplation of law, a party to an obligation, or a creditor, will not

[3] Mills v. Huggins, 3 Dev 58
[4] Pinney v. Jorgenson, 27 Minn 26
[5] Bakeman v. Pooler 15 Wend 637

Leatherdale v. Sweepstone 3 P & C 342
[6] Strong v. Blake 46 Barb 227
[1] Reed v. Bank of Newburg, 6 Page 337

knowingly become the receiver of stolen goods, or a party to
an embezzlement of money, or misappropriation or conversion of goods. If the property had been stolen the tenderee
would be legally as well as morally bound to restore it.
The question of a tenderor's title to, or method of obtaining
the thing tendered, is material only as far as it affects his
ability to make an actual valid transfer so as to vest the
title in the other party if the offer is accepted.[2] Thus, where
a purchaser of shares of capital stock, desiring to rescind
the sale, borrowed for that purpose a like number of shares
and tendered them to the broker, it was held to be a good
tender.[3] So, where a party who had sold certain notes, borrowed them for the purpose of tendering them back to his
transferor, a tender of them was held good.[4]

§ 228. The article tendered must be unencumbered—Returning
property subject to a lien—A tender of specific articles will
not be good if mortgaged or subject to any lien not taken
into account in the contract of the parties.[1] And the defect in
the tender will not be cured by making it appear that the
party holding the lien would have waived it.[2] If the article
has been accepted without knowledge of the lien, and such
transfer does not *ipso facto* destroy the lien, the tenderee
may return the property.

§ 229. Title necessary where the contract is to give a deed
with covenant of seisin—Against encumbrances—Where vendor
is to furnish a "good and sufficient deed"—"A lawful deed of
conveyance"—Common-law rule—Sale of several tracts separately
to one person.—Where, in a contract for the sale of land, the
vendor is to give a deed with covenants of seisen, covenants against encumbrances, and the like, a tender of a deed,

[2] Champion v. Joslyn, 44 N. Y.
653; Uslow v. Mitchell, 26 Mich.
500.

[3] Mayo v. Knowlton, 134 N. Y.
254, s. c. 31 N. E. 985.

[4] Bell v. Ballance, 1 Dev. (N. C.)
391.

[1] Crominger v. Crocker, 62 N. Y.
151; Dunham v. Pettee, 4 E. D.
Smith, 500.

[2] Dunham v. Pettee, 4 E. D.
Smith, 500. It is held frequently
that a vendor is not bound to remove an incumbrance until the
vendee makes a demand for performance. Irvin v. Bleakly, 67
Pa. St. 25. But such a rule does
not apply to cases where the vendor makes the first offer.

though properly executed and containing the required covenants, is of no avail as a tender of performance if the vendor
has not the title.[1] So, where the covenant is to give a "good
and sufficient deed,"[2] or "a lawful deed of conveyance,"[3] or
a deed "conveying and assuring fee simple,"[4] the vendee
must convey an indefeasible title. Mr. Chief Justice Kent
said: "A covenant to execute a good and sufficient deed of
a piece of land, does not mean merely a conveyance good in
point of form. That would be a covenant without substance.
But it means an operative conveyance—one that carries
with it a good and sufficient title to the land."[5]

It was held in several New York decisions in the early
part of the last century that a contract with a covenant for
"a good and sufficient deed" was satisfied by a tender of a
deed, which was sufficient in point of law to pass whatever
title the vendor had; that the words used, denote merely
the quality of the deed, and had no reference to the title
to be conveyed.[6] And similar decisions have been made in
other states where the contract under consideration called
for "a good and sufficient deed"[7] or "a good and sufficient
deed of warranty."[8] But the rule announced in the authorities here referred to is a departure from the common law,
which is, that in every executory contract for the sales of
land, there is, whatever may be the language in which the
agreement is couched, an implied undertaking to make a
good title, unless such an obligation is expressly excluded
by the terms of the agreement. In later decisions in New

[1] Porter v. Noyes, 2 Greenl. 22,
s. c. 11 Am. Dec. 34; Judson v.
Wass, 11 Johns. 525; Fletcher v.
Button, 4 N. Y. 396; Pomeroy v.
Drury, 14 Barb. 418; Hill v. Ressegieu, 17 Barb. 162; Atkins v.
Barrett, 19 Barb. 639.

[2] Fleming v. Harrison, 2 Bibb.
171, s. c. 4 Am. Dec. 691. See
Kelly v. Bradford, 3 Bibb. 317, s.
c. 6 Am. Dec. 656; Frazier v.
Boggs, 37 Fla. 307, s. c. 20 So.
Rep. 245; Shouse v. Doane, 21 So.
Rep. (Fla.) 807.

[3] Dearth v. Williamson, 2 Ser.
& Raw. 498, s. c. 7 Am. Dec. 652.

See Wilson v. Getty, 57 Pa. St.
270.

[4] Traver v. Halsted, 23 Wend.
66. See Latimer v. Capay, 70
Pac. Rep. (Cal.) 82.

[5] Clute v. Robinson, 2 John. 613.

[6] Gazley v. Price, 16 Johns. 267;
Parker v. Parmele, 20 Johns. 130.

[7] Brown v. Covillaud, 6 Cal.
566. See Green v. Covillaud, 10
Cal. 322; Barrows v. Bispham, 6
Halst. 110.

[8] Aiken v. Sanford, 5 Mass. 494.
See Tinney v. Ashley, 15 Pick.
546; Joslyn v. Taylor, 33 Vt. 470;
Preston v. Whitcomb, 11 Vt. 17.

York, the decisions referred to were criticised and ultimately overruled, practically if not expressly, and the common law adhered to, and it was held that a covenant to execute a good and sufficient deed of conveyance, means that the vendor must have a good title or the vendee may refuse to receive a deed.[9] And a preponderance of the adjudication, where similar contracts were under consideration, are in harmony with this principle of the common law.[10]

Where land is sold at auction in separate lots, and several lots are purchased by one person, a failure of title as to one or more of the lots will not give the purchaser a right to reject a tender of a deed conveying those lots to which the seller has a good title, the purchase of all the lots not being one entire transaction.[11]

§ 230  Rejecting a deed where land is encumbered — Not bound to search the record—Retaining purchase money to care for attachment.—If there is an encumbrance on the land, a deed may be rejected.[1] And if the grantee accepts a deed in ignorance of an existing encumbrance, he may reject it on discovering that there is an encumbrance.[2] And, it has been held that the grantee is not bound to search the records for defects of title before the sale is executed by a conveyance.[3] If the land had been attached on mesne process, it has been held that a tender of a deed is good if the vendor is willing that the vendee retain a sufficient amount of the purchase money to indemnify him against such attachment.[4]

[9] Fletcher v. Button, 4 N. Y. 396, Burwell v. Jackson, 9 N. Y. 535, Penfield v. Clark, 62 Barb. 584.

[10] Young v. Wright, 4 Wis. 163, s. c. 6 Wis. 127, Abendroth v. Greenwich, 29 Conn. 356, Lounsbery v. Locander, 25 N. J. Eq. 554, Bateman v. Johnson, 10 Wis. 1, Davis v. Henderson, 17 Wis. 108, Park v. McAllister, 14 Ind. 12, Fleming v. Harrison, 2 Bibb. 171, s. c. 4 Am. Dec. 691, Stone v. Fowle, 22 Pick. 166, Packard v.

Usher, 7 Gray 531, Day v. Burnham, 11 S. W. Rep. (Ky.) 807, See Mead v. Fox, 6 Cush. 202.

[11] Van Eps v. Schnectady, 12 John. 435.

[1] Conway v. Case, 22 Ill. 127, Jerome v. Scudder, 2 Rob. (N. Y.) 171, Pursley v. Good, 68 S. W. Rep. (Mo. App.) 218.

[2] Porter v. Noyes, 2 Greenl. 221, s. c. 11 Am. Dec. 31.

[3] Fletcher v. Button, 1 N. Y. 396.

[4] Borden v. Borden, 5 Mass. 67, s. c. 4 Am. Dec. 32.

§ 231.  **An inchoate right of dower an encumbrance.**—An inchoate right of dower is such an encumbrance as will render a tender of a deed in which the wife had not joined, ineffectual, if the contract is such that the vendor is bound to convey a good title, free and clear of all encumbrances.  In a case where the vendor was to give "a good and sufficient deed in law to vest him with the title of the said farm of land, with the appurtenances," a tender of a deed in which the wife had not released her dower was held insufficient to defeat an action for damages for nonperformance of the contract.  The court said: "If the plaintiff's wife had a contingent life estate in one third part of the farm, the defendant had not a clear and absolute title.  If this claim of dower was not inconsistent with the title to be vested in the defendant, it would be difficult to maintain that any other life estate in the same in reversion or remainder, or any judgment or other lien thereon would be incompatible with it, and the title might thus be embarrassed and weakened until it had lost all its value and strength."[1]  In all such cases the legal estate in fee is liable to be defeated in part by the right of dower in the vendor's wife.[2]

There are cases holding a possibility of dower is not an encumbrance.[3]  That within a sense of a covenant, a settled fixed encumbrance is meant.[4]  And there is a case which holds that where the contract is "to give a deed of the premises" a tender of the deed in which the wife had not joined is good.[5]  But the question arose in an action in assumpsit by the purchaser to recover back the money paid upon the contract after he had gone into possession under the agreement, and the court adopted a strict construction, holding that the agreement, being silent as to the defendant's wife uniting in the conveyance, and the agreement not specifying "that the defendant should by deed, vest the title to the land sold in the plaintiff," it would be an interpolation

[1] Jones v. Gardner, 10 Johns 266.  See Porter v. Noyes, 2 Greenl 22 s c 11 Am Dec 31

[2] McCreery v. Davis, 28 L R A (S C) 655; Given v. Marr 27 Me 212, Bigelow v. Hubbard, 97 Mass 95, Harrington v. Murphy 109 Mass 299, Holmes v. Holmes 12

Barb 137, Griffith v. Maxfield, 39 S W Rep (Ark) 852

[3] Bostwick v. Williams, 36 Ill 65

[4] Powell v. Monson, 3 Mason, 355

[5] Ketcham v. Evertson, 13 John 358

to say that the defendant agreed that his wife should join in the deed. But this principle is irreconcilable with the common-law. Leaving out all question of the particular wording of an agreement to convey the land, which expressly or impliedly negative the right to require the wife to unite in a conveyance, the rule is now well settled, both in England and America, as before stated, that in absence of an unambiguous agreement to the contrary in a contract to convey land, the implied undertaking is to make a good title.

§ 232. **Title must be merchantable—Lis pendens—Adverse possession—Abstract showing fee simple title.**—The title of the tenderor must be merchantable. The law does not compel a purchaser of real property to take a doubtful title, but the courts act upon a moral certainty, and a purchaser will not be permitted to object to the title on account of a bare possibility.[1] A discussion of the defects which will render a title unmerchantable belong more properly to the subject of vendor and purchaser, and cannot be discussed here without a digression. If a *lis pendens* has been filed and a suit commenced, a vendee may reject the deed.[2] A party cannot be required to assume a lawsuit, even though he could not have properly rejected a deed owing to mere threats to bring suit where the claim disclosed was only a bare possibility of a right or interest. It may be observed that where a vendor is to convey an unincumbered title in fee, a title by adverse possession may constitute a marketable title.[3] But it has been held, where a contract requires the vendor to exhibit an abstract showing fee simple title to the land, that a tender of a deed when the title depends upon adverse possession is not a performance of the covenant.[4]

§ 233. **Readiness and ability required where the creditor is absent from the place of payment.**—The same ability, readiness

[1] Miller v. Cramer, 26 S. E. Rep. (S. C.) 657. See Hedderly v. Johnson, 42 Minn. 443.

[2] Joslyn v. Schwend, 85 Minn. 130.

[3] Barnard v. Brown, 4 Det. L. N. 44. 70 N. W. Rep. (Mich.) 1038, citing O'Connor v. Huggins, 113 N. Y. 521, Foreman v. Wolf, 29 Atl. Rep. (Md.) 837, Tewksbury

v. Howard, 138 Ind. 103, s. c. 37 N. E. Rep. 355, Elder v. McClaskey, 17 C. C. A. 251, s. c. 37 U. S. App. 1, 199 70 Fed. Rep. 529, and many other cases.

[4] Toompson v. Dickerson, 68 Mo. App. 535, citing Noyes v. Johnson, 139 Mass. 436, Reynolds v. Borel, 86 Cal. 538.

and willingness on the part of a person seeking to discharge himself from an obligation to pay money or perform a duty, is no less important when the other party is absent from the place of performance. If a debtor was ready at the time and place with the amount of money due upon the contract, he may plead that fact, as he would plead a tender, in bar damages, and by bringing the money into court save himself from costs.[1] Where a party was ready with the deed at the appointed time and place and would have tendered it but for the evasion of the other party, it was held to be a good tender.[2] An obligor, when the obligee is absent from the state, can discharge himself from the necessity of making a personal tender by going at the appointed time to the place designated for performance, with the deed or other instrument ready for delivery, and there making inquiries for the obligee. It is not convenient to consider, at this time, the variations in the rule as to the place of tender, when no place is designated by the parties. But the rule is imperative that wherever the place of performance may be, whether expressed in the contract or fixed by law, a party cannot escape the consequences of a default nor claim the benefit of a tender, unless he be ready to perform at the time and place. And it does not make any difference whether the creditor is designedly absent or unavoidably so. This rule applies with greater force to a tender of chattels, for the reason that the title to the articles can be vested in the vendee, by the act of the vendor in the absence of the vendee as well as when he is present. Although the debtor, by being ready at the appointed time, at the place designated in the contract, or at the place fixed by law, in the absence of the creditor with the money or thing to be delivered, may plead that fact as he would a tender, yet, if the absence is not for the purpose of avoiding a tender, such readiness will have no greater effect than merely barring interest and damages, and will not have the effect of discharging a lien or working a forfeiture.[4]

[1] New Hope D B Co v Perry, 11 Ill 467, Haxton v Bishop, 3 Wend 13

[2] Borden v Borden, 5 Mass 67, s c 4 Am Dec. 32

[3] Tasker v Bartlett, 5 Cush 359

[4] Southworth v Smith, 7 Cush 391

**§ 234. Actual production of the thing to be delivered.**—At common law, in addition to the foregoing requisites, in order to make a valid tender of either money or chattels, the thing must be actually produced and offered to the party entitled thereto.[1] It has been said that the object of requiring the actual production of the money is that the sight of it will tend to induce the party to whom it is offered to accept it, and thereby prevent litigation.[2] True, this might be a potent factor in swaying the minds of some, but certainly not all. On reflection it would seem that the better reason for the rule is that the production and offer are inseparable requisites, constituting the very essence of a tender. In strictness of law, a tender is a production and manual offer of the money or thing to be delivered. If the thing be not actually produced, the offer then is merely a proposition to produce and deliver the article if the other party signifies a willingness to accept it; which is not enough. If a proposition constituted a tender, such an offer might be for the purpose of sounding the creditor with the object of claiming the benefit of a tender if it is rejected, and with the intention on the part of the tenderor of not allowing the property to go out of his possession in any event. The intent which a party must have at the time of making a tender is to discharge himself of his obligation, by then and there delivering the article. To do this, he must place the money or property in such a position that his control over it is relinquished for a sufficient time to enable the tenderee, if he so desires, to reduce it to possession by merely reaching out and laying hold of the money or thing.[3] By thus placing it within the power of the tenderee to reduce the thing to possession, the tenderor has done all that lies in his power to perform, and if refused, he is discharged of all liabilities resulting from a default, and entitled to all the benefits of an actual performance

---

[1] 9 Bacon's Abr Tit Tender (B), Holt v Brown, 63 Iowa, 319, s c 19 N W Rep 235 Brown v Gillmore, 8 Greenl 107, s c 22 Am. Dec. 223, Deering Har Co v. Hamilton, 83 N W Rep (Minn)

11, Schrader v Wolfling, 21 Ind. 348

[2] Finch v Brook, 1 Bing (N C) 253, Holladay v Holladay, 13 Or. 523; Krause v Arnold, 7 Moore, 59, 2 Greenl on Ev § 602.

[3] Sands v Lyons, 18 Conn 18

A person is not bound to say whether or not he will accept the money or thing till it is produced.[4] It is universally held that a mere verbal offer to pay is not a tender.[5] Where a third party who had been requested to take certain shares of stock which were sold to be delivered, according to custom, on the following day, declined to accept the stock, and the brokers sent a letter to the purchaser fixing a time in which he was to take the stock or it would be sold, it was held not to be a sufficient tender to warrant a resale of the stock on the purchaser's account and holding him for the deficiency.[6]

§ 235. **Manner of producing and how offered—In bag or purse —Concealed about the person—In safe, desk or money drawer— Holding the money in the hand—Laying it down—Throwing money upon the ground.**—In regard to the manner of producing the money the rule formerly was, that the money must be produced and counted down,[1] but there has been a relaxation of the ancient rule in respect to the necessity for a count of the money by the tenderor at the time of making his offer The rule is laid down in Coke on Littleton, thus· "The feoffee may tender the money in purses or bagges, without shewing or telling the same, for he doth that which he ought, viz to bring the money in purses or bagges, which is the usual manner to carry money in, and then it is the part of the party that is to receive it to put it out and tell it."[2] And this is the rule which is everywhere followed.[3] The bag or purse said to contain the money must be actually produced and in sight, capable of immediate delivery It will not do to have it in "a pocket or place about the person, concealed from the party,"[4] nor in a safe, desk, money drawer, or other place where the tenderee can not lay hold of it without some further act on the part of the person offering to pay It is impossible to

[4] Bakeman v. Pooler, 15 Wend 637

[5] Bakeman v Pooler, 15 Wend 637, Liebbrandt v Myron Lodge, 51 Ill 81, Schrader v Wolflin, 21 Ind 338; Bacon v Smith, 2 La. Am 441.

[6] Johnson v. Mulvy, 51 N Y. 634.

[1] Appleton v Donaldson, 3 Pa St 381.

[2] Co Litt 208a

[3] Behaly v Hatch, Walker (Miss ) 369, s c 12 Am Dec 570, Thorn v Mosher, 20 N J Eq 259, Wing v Davis, 7 Me 31, Wade's case, 5 Co Rep 115, Reed v Golding, 2 Man & Sel 86

[4] Bakeman v Pooler, 15 Wend 637; Strong v Blake, 46 Barb 227

define a rule as to the manner of proffering the money that would be applicable in every transaction, but ordinarily the money, after being produced, ought to be placed upon a table, counter, desk or other place within the convenient reach of the creditor.[5] This rule, as far as it may be called a rule, must of necessity be varied to suit the situation of the parties.

A tender would be good if the money was held in the hand and actually offered to the creditor.[6] In a great many cases, as where the tender is made in the street, retaining the money in the hand would be the only practical way of offering it. In such case the conduct and declarations of the party offering the money must be fair, open, and unequivocal, so as to convince the creditor that, by reaching out his hand in a like manner the debtor will freely yield the possession of the money. If held in the hand under such circumstances it is considered as produced, for the creditor had the opportunity to reach out and take it from the hand of the debtor. True, it would appear that the tenderor had not, under the strict rule, relinquished his dominion over it, but as the intent of the party must be to deliver the money or thing, the danger that the tenderor's offer is not in good faith, or of his changing his mind and withdrawing the money from reach when held in the hand as compared to the case where the money is placed by him on a table or desk, is one of degree only. For, in the latter case, it is usual for him to stand so near that he ordinarily has it in his power to seize the money before the creditor could reduce it to possession. After the money is produced, if it is refused, it need not be laid down, for it would be laid down only to be taken up again. Throwing money, held loosely in the hand, upon the ground, or in at a door, is not a good tender. A creditor is not bound to hunt up and count the money thus scattered by a debtor. If contained in a bag or purse, and the creditor had but to stoop and pick up the bag or purse, in absence of authority, we would say the tender would be good. If refused by the creditor, and the debtor goes away without resuming the actual physical possession of it and it is lost, he must stand the loss, as the tender would not be kept good

---

[5] Curtis v. Greenbanks, 24 Vt. 536, Hartsock v. Mort, 76 Md. 281.

[6] Rains v. Jones, 4 Hump. 490.

**§ 236. Actual production waived when.**—The books abound in the general statement that the actual production of the money may be dispensed with by some positive act or declaration of the party to whom the tender is made, and in the use of this general statement, the authorities are uniform; but generalities always lead to considerable uncertainty and doubt, and more particularly is this so when they relate to an exception to a general rule. So, it will be difficult to determine the limit of this relaxation of the rigid rules as to the making of a tender. Dallas, Ch. J., said "To constitute a legal tender, the money must be actually produced, unless the plaintiff dispense with the tender by expressly saying the defendant need not produce the money, as he would not accept it."[1] But the rule is even broader, and seems now to be well settled, that the actual production and proffer of the money is dispensed with if the party is ready and willing to pay the same, but is prevented by the party to whom it is due merely declaring that he will not receive it.[2] So the actual production of money is excused if the party to whom the offer is made does what is equivalent to an express waiver of it;[3] as by refusing to remain until the money is counted, or until it is produced. Thus, where A in proceeding to B's house meets B. and says, "I have got the money here to pay you," specifying the claims, and put his hand into his pocket to take out the money, and while doing this B. said, "I want nothing to do with such cut-throats as you," and walked rapidly away, it was held to be a good tender.[4]

It is dispensed with if the creditor orders the debtor away or repulses him. Thus where a debtor, having a sufficient amount of money with him, informed his creditor that he was come to pay, and the creditor said, "Get away; I will have

[1] Krause v Arnold 7 Moore, 59, s. c 17 Com. L Rep 70 See Diskinfore v Shee, 4 Esp N P 68, Westmoreland v Dewitt (Pa) 18 Atl 724, s c 25 W N C 103

[2] Odum v Rutledge, etc Ry. Co, 94 Ala 188, Thorn v Mosher, 20 N. J Eq 257, Appleton v Donaldson, 3 Pa St 381, Farnsworth v Howard, 1 Coldw 213, Rudolph v Wagner, 36 Ala 698,

Hazard v Loring, 10 Cush 267, Wood v Bungs 48 Atl Rep (Del) 189, Pinney v Jorgenson, 27 Minn 26, Stephenson v Kirkpatrick, 65 S W Rep (Mo) 773

[3] Ashburn v. Poulter 35 Conn 552. Thomas v Evans, 10 East. 101

[4] Sands v Lyons, 18 Conn 18 See Leatherdale v Sweepstone, 3 C & P 342

nothing to do with it," it was held not necessary to exhibit the money or make a more formal offer of it.[5] So, where a mortgagor, with the amount of the mortgage debt, went to the house of the mortgagee and attempted to enter the house, saying, "I've got the money to pay those mortgages, and I want those mortgages," whereupon the mortgagee thrust him out and shut the door saying, "I have nothing to do with you," the tender was held sufficient.[6] The actual production is dispensed with if, while the debtor is in the act of producing it, or is about to do so, the creditor refuses to receive the money, not on the ground that it is not produced, but upon some collateral and distinct ground; as where the party to whom the offer is made declares that the one offering to pay the money did not owe it, and assured him that he was mistaken in supposing that any claim was set up to his land.[7] So, if one to whom the offer is made denies the existence of the contract, or repudiates it,[8] or declares that the time for payment has gone by, or denies that the debtor has a right to redeem,[9] or asserts an absolute ownership of the goods to obtain the possession of which the offer is made; or does that which is equivalent to an assertion of absolute ownership, refuses to deliver the goods, in general terms, without assigning any reason for it whatever, the waiver of the actual production and the proffer of the money is complete.[10] So, telling the debtor that it is no use and that he must see his (the creditor's) attorney,[11] or that he (an agent) has no authority to receive the money when he in fact had the authority,[12] or refusing to give up the goods unless certain charges, not constituting a lien on them, be first paid,[13] the actual production of the money is waived.

Where an act is to be done by the other party simultaneous with the payment of the money, as the delivery of the deed or any other instrument, or property, and the grantee or

[5] Meserole v. Archer, 3 Bosw 376

[6] Sharp v Todd, 38 N J Eq 324

[7] Koon v Snodgrass, 18 W. Va 320

[8] See Abrams v Suttle, Bush L. 99

[9] Bender v Bean, 52 Ark 132

[10] Wagenblast v. McKean, 2 Giant Cas 393

[11] Ex parte Dank, 2 De G. M. & G. 926, 22 L J, Bank, 73

[12] Smith v Old Dominion, B. & L Assn., 119 N C, 257.

[13] Wesley v. Norman, 31 Minn. 599

person who is to pay the money is "ready, desirous and eager
to perform," and had the money within reach and under his
control, but the other party insisted that the money be paid
first, the actual production of the money is excused.[14] So, it
has been held that the manual offer of a deed is unnecessary
if the vendor had it ready and in sight, and was willing to
make a delivery of it on receiving payment from the vendee
and so stated to the latter, who declared that he was unable
to make payment.[15] Where a party goes to the place designated for payment, at the time appointed, with the money or
thing to deliver it, and the person who is to receive it is not
present, the money or thing need not be produced.[16] Whether
or not the actual production of the money or thing, at the
time of the offer to deliver it, was dispensed with, is a question of fact to be determined by the jury.[17]

The foregoing exceptions to the rule requiring the actual
production of the money, is founded upon the well known
principle that the law does not require that to be done which
manifestly would be a vain and idle ceremony; and also upon
the equitable rule that a party is not allowed to take advantage of an act or an omission by another, when such act
or omission was designedly caused by himself. It may be
added that a party relying upon a waiver must himself be
ready to perform, and in that frame of mind that he would
have received the thing which the other party was bound to
deliver.

§ 237.  **What does not amount to a waiver.**—The actual production of the money is not dispensed with by a bare refusal
to receive the sum proposed, and demanding more. Where
a debtor said to the attorney of the creditor that he was
come to settle a certain account, but he claimed the balance
was £5, 5s., which he said he was ready to pay, but produced
no money, and the attorney stated that he could not take
that sum, as his clients claimed was £8, this was held to be
no tender, for there should have been an offer to pay, by

---

[14] Parker v. Perkins, 8 Cush.
318.

[15] Lawrence v. Miller, 86 N. Y.
131.

[16] Morton v. Wells, 1 Tyler
(Vt.) 384.

[17] Finch v. Brooks, 1 Bing. N.
C. 253; Guthman v. Kearn, 8 Neb.
502, s. c. 1 N. W. Rep. 129, 2
Greenl. Ev. § 602, 2 M. & S. 86,
s. c. 12 Eq. C. L. 35

producing the money, unless that was dispensed with.[1]  Even where a person offered to pay £7, 12s , and said that a third person had the money for that purpose, and the third person, being present, put his hand into his pocket to take out his pocket book to pay the sum, but the other party desired him not to do so, as £8 was demanded, the court held that it should have been produced.[2]  In another English case, where an attorney had collected £10 for his client, which, on going home, he left with his clerk, who stated to the client, on the latter calling for the money, that he had £10 for him, but the client refused to receive anything less than £16, 8s. 11d , the amount of the whole demand left for collection, and the clerk did not produce and offer the £10, on a plea of tender and proof of the above facts, a verdict for the plaintiff was not disturbed.[3]  Lord Ellenborough, C J , in considering the case said: "The actual production of the money due, in moneys numbered, is not necessary, if, the debtor having it ready to produce and offering to pay it, the creditor dispense with the production of it at the time, or do anything which is equivalent to that."  In a case which arose in New York, the court in referring to that case, said "The equivalent act spoken of by Lord Ellenborough is something more, it would seem, than a bare refusal to receive the money proposed to be paid, because the sum was not large enough; for that was done by the creditor in that case, and yet the tender was held to be insufficient"  The court said, further, in reviewing the decisions, that "the circumstance of demanding more than was proper, was not considered an act equivalent to dispensing expressly with the production of the money.'[4]  The same rule is approved of in other American decisions,[5] and it may be said that the law is now settled that a refusal of the sum offered on the ground that more is due, does not amount to

---

[1] Kishinfore v Shee, 4 Esp N P 68  See Lamar v Sheppard 84 Ga 561 s c 10 S E Rep 1084 See also Stickel v Standley, 17 N W Rep (Iowa) 489

[2] Krause v Arnold 7 Moore, 59

[3] Thomas v. Evans, 10 East 101

[4] Dunham v Jackson, 6 Wend. 22  See Griswold v Jackson, ——, when the same tender was established by additional proof

[5] Farnsworth v Howard, 1 Coldw 215; Wagenblast v McKean, 2 Grant's Cas 393; Brown v Gilmore, 8 Greenl 107, s c 22 Am. Dec 223

an express or implied waiver of the actual production and offer of the money.

§ 238. **Naming the sum offered—Burden of proof.**—In making a tender of money, whether the actual production be dispensed with or not, the tenderor must name the sum which he tenders. Thus, where the person who made the tender had two bank notes twisted up in his hand, enclosing four sovereigns and 19s. 8d. in change, making the precise sum intended to be paid, and the party, without opening it, informed the creditor of the amount, the tender was held good. Best, C. J., said: "If he had not mentioned the amount, I think it would not have done." [1] So, in another case, a debtor in passing his creditor said: "I want to tender you this money, * * * for labor you have done me;" and at the same time holding in his hand a sum equal to the indebtedness, but named no sum, it was held insufficient. [2] So, in those cases where the sum due is exclusively within the knowledge of the creditor, and he neglects or refuses to inform the debtor of the exact amount due, an offer to pay the debt will not amount to a tender unless the debtor names a definite sum which he offers. Whether a sum is tendered in a purse or bag, or is proffered in the hand, or otherwise, it is the business of the creditor to count it to see if there is enough to satisfy his demand. [3]

But the offer would not be a good tender if the debtor did not in fact have required sum. A party who desires to make a tender must, at his peril, provide himself with the amount he intends to offer. That the debtor actually had the sum offered at the time, however carried, is a fact requiring proof, and a refusal of the tenderee to receive or count the money does not dispense with the necessity for such proof. In a case where a bag containing the money was thrown upon a counter, and the tenderee did not offer to count it, and the agent of the tenderor, who made the tender, gave it as his belief that there was sufficient coin in the bag to pay the amount due, it was held to be a tender. [4] But this does not

[1] Alexander v Brown, 1 C & P. 288

[2] Knight v. Abbott, 30 Vt. 577. Contra State v Spicer, 4 Houst (Del.) 190

[3] Behaly v Hatch Walk (Miss) 369, s c. 12 Am. Dec 570

[4] Conway v Case, 22 Ill 124

seem to be enough. The proof ought to be positive as to the amount. It is a fact peculiarly within the knowledge of the debtor, or his agent when the debtor does not make the tender in person.

**§ 239. A tender must be unconditional—Right to exclude presumption that more is due.**—Where a person is to perform an act, the obligation to perform which does not depend upon any concurrent act to be performed by the other party, as where money is to be paid in liquidation of a debt, or specific articles are to be delivered absolutely, where the consideration has passed or where credit has been extended to the purchaser and the object is to discharge himself of the obligation, the money or thing to be delivered must be tendered unconditionally.[1] The nature of a tender as implied by the terms itself, is, that it is an offer to deliver the money or thing absolutely without conditions, terms, or qualifications, and the current of authorities—which is believed to be uniform—hold that a tender clogged with any conditions whatever, either expressed or implied, is not good, in those cases where the party who is to receive the thing tendered is not required to move in the matter. A tender must be of a specific amount and must be offered to be paid without annexing any terms or conditions.[2] Nevertheless every person who makes a tender does, in effect, try to get rid of the demand by a payment of only the sum proffered—a part of it—for the whole demand. Which, "means that the amount tendered, though less than the plaintiff's bill, is all that he is entitled to demand in respect to it."[3]

A tender is valid if it implies merely that a given sum is offered as being all that is admitted to be due,[4] and a tenderee will not preclude himself from recovering any balance remaining, by accepting an offer of part, accompanied by expressions

[1] Storey v Krewson 55 Ind 397, Coghlan v So Car R Co, 32 Fed Rep 316; Stanford v. Bulkley, 30 Conn 344, Elderkin v. Fellows, 60 Wis 339 s c 19 N W Rep. 101, 9 Bac Abr Tender (B), Perkins v Maier, 66 Pac. Rep. (Cal) 482, Chapen v Chapin, 36 N. E. Rep (Mass) 746; Jennings v. Major, 8 C. & P. 61; Peacock v Dickerson, 2 C & P. 51 N, Te Poel v Shutt, 78 N W Rep (Neb) 288, McEldon v. Patton, 93 N W Rep (Neb) 938

[2] Pulsifer v Shephard, 36 Ill 513

[3] Henwood v Oliver, 1 Gale & D 25 (2 C & P 51 N)

[4] Bowen v Owen, 11 Q. B. 131.

that are implied in every tender.[5]  It has been held that "The person making the tender has a right to exclude presumptions against himself, by saying, 'I pay this as the whole that is due.'"[6]  A party may tell his creditor that the sum offered is all that he considers to be due,[7] or is all that is due.  It has been said that, "This differs from an offer upon the condition that it shall be received only as closing the matter."[8]  The expression, "I am come with the amount of your bill," when accompanied by a statement of the sum offered, does not vitiate the tender.[9]  But the statement by the party, on offering a given sum, that he has "come to settle," although thought, in an English case, not to be inconsistent with a good tender,[10] yet such a statement would seem to imply that he had come to close the transaction entirely by a payment of the sum offered.  In another case, somewhat similar, the party offering the money said, "I have called to tender £— in settlement of R's bill," and it was held that it was for the jury to determine whether it was conditional or not.[11]  Where a party tendered three dollars and ten cents in payment of a note, "saying that he tendered said sum as the balance due upon said note," it was held to be merely an assertion of what he claimed to be due and an identification of the demand upon which he made the tender, that the language used was unequivocal, only expressing the intent and purpose with which every tender is made.[12]  The illustrations given are dangerously near the dividing line between conditional and unconditional tenders, and such expression ought to be avoided in making a tender.

§ 240.  **There must be a distinct form of condition.**—To make a tender conditional there must be a distinct form of condition.  It is not enough that the person making the tender says, "I assert this to be all that is due."  He must say in effect: "Take this in full discharge, or take nothing."[1]  If the

---

[5] Henwood v. Oliver, 1 Gale & D. 25 (2 C & P 51 N)

[6] Brown v Owen, 11 Q B 131, S P Davis v Dow, 83 N. W Rep (Minn.) 50

[7] Robinson v Ferriday, 8 C. & P. 752.

[8] Foster v Drew, 39 Vt. 51.

[9] Henwood v Oliver, 1 Gale & D. 25 (2 C & P 51 N)

[10] Read v Golding, 2 M. & S. 86

[11] Eckstein v. Reynolds, 2 Nev. & P 256

[12] Preston v Grant, 34 Vt. 201 s p Foster v Drew, 39 Vt 51 See Davis v. Dow 83 N. W Rep (Minn.) 50.

[1] Henwood v Oliver, 1 Gale & D 25 (2 C & P 51 N)

tenderor implies by his declaration, that if the other party takes the money, he is required to admit that no more is due, the tender will be conditional.[2] Thus, sending a check with a statement in the body of the check, "Balance account railing," is not a good tender.[3] So, where the sum offered is to be accepted in full discharge of all demands,[4] or "in full of his demand,"[5] or "as a settlement,"[6] or "in full settlement,"[7] or "in full satisfaction,"[8] or "in payment and extinguishment of the creditor's lien," the offer is not a tender. Where a note was payable in neat stock, a declaration, "If you will take forty eight dollars in full for the note, I will bring the stock forward," was held an insufficient tender, as being conditional[9] Where the defendant stated that, "I showed him five hundred dollars, and told him he could have it for his claim," the tender was held bad[10] So when a party took out his pocket book and said there was fifteen dollars in it which he would pay for the services, a tender was not made.[11] Offering a sum as a half year's rent, was held to be a conditional tender, for, if taken, it would have been an admission of the amount of the rent due[12] It is everywhere held that where the tender is made as being all that is due,[13] or as payment in full, it is not good[14]

In such cases, the question resolves itself into whether, in an action of the residue, proof of the payment and acceptance by the plaintiff under the circumstances would be proof that the whole debt was paid  If the sum offered "is to be taken

- Henderson v Cass Co, 107 Mo 50, Moore v Norman, 52 Minn 83, Evans v Judkin, 4 Camp 156; Wood v Hitchcock, 20 Wend 47.

[3] Hough v May, 4 Ad & El 954

[4] Wood v. Hitchcock, 20 Wend. 47, Strong v Harvey, 3 Bing 304, 11 Moore 72; Draper v Hitt, 43 Vt 439

[5] Clemant v Thornton 2 C & P 50

[6] Mitchell v King, 6 C & P 237.

[7] Martin v Bott, 46 N E 151

[8] State v Carson City Sav Bank, 17 Nev 146, 50 P Rep 703

[9] Brown v Gilmore, 8 Greenl 107

[10] Tompkins v Batle, 11 Neb 147, s c 38 Am Rep 361, 7 N W. Rep 747

[11] Elderkin v Fellows, 60 Wis 339, s c 19 N W Rep 101

[12] Hasting v Thorley, 8 C & P 573

[13] Field v Newport, 3 H & N. 109, Sutton v Hawkins, 8 C & P 259

[14] Moore v Norman, 52 Minn. 83, Sutton v Hawkins, 8 P & C 259, Thomas v Evans, 10 East 101; 9 Bac Ab. Tender (B); 3 Stark Ev 1393, Peacock v Dickerson, 2 C & P 51 N

in full of all demands," or, "as all that was due," or, "for what
the defendant owed the plaintiff," and is taken, "it must al
ways be a question of fact, whether it was by way of com
promise, received in full satisfaction, though the plaintiff, on
trial, should establish his claim to a greater sum." [15]  It is a
general rule that any proposition, when accepted, is to have
the force and effect which the party accepting knew the party
making it intended it should have.  A tender is an admission
that the money or thing tendered belongs to the tenderee,
and in those cases under consideration, where the tenderor
must move independently to discharge his obligation, he immediately becomes a wrongdoer, by withholding so much as
he admits to belong rightfully to the tenderee; and the excuse offered for the nonpayment,—that the tenderee would
not relinquish his claim for greater sum—is no excuse at all,
for, having admitted the sum tendered to be due absolutely,
there is no controversy as to that sum, and consequently it
has nothing to do with any other claim beyond that sum
which can be litigated independently.  In such case, to hold a
tender good, the acceptance of which would preclude a re
covery of any ulterior sum, would be to allow the tenderor,
notwithstanding his own wrong, all the benefits of a tender,
while the tenderee would be deprived of his money and
forced to bring an action to recover it, unless he choose to
accept the proposition with the force and effect the tenderor
intended it should have

§ 241. **Whether a tender is conditional or unconditional is
not necessarily a question of law.**—The question whether a
tender is conditional or unconditional is not necessarily
for the court.  If the language used in making a tender admit
only of one construction, it is properly a question of law   If
the meaning is not clear, it is a question of fact for the court
or jury as the case may be   In a case where in making a tender, the party representing the tenderor used these terms
"I have called to tender £8 in settlement of Reynold's account," Lord Denman, C J., left it to the jury whether it
was conditional or unconditional, but observed that, if the
words "in settlement" merely meant "in payment," the tender was good.  The jury found for the defendant.  On an ap

[15] Miller v. Holden, 18 Vt  337

peal the court refused to disturb the verdict, observing that "there is enough ambiguity to make the matter fit for the jury and they have decided it."[1] The supreme court of Vermont has said that the language used in making a tender must be interpreted as it was used with relation to the previous transactions between the parties, to determine correctly whether its effect is to affix a condition to the offer, or merely to explain what the party claims and intends that the tender will cover.[2] Where the facts bearing upon the question of a tender are uncontradicted the question whether a tender has been made is purely a question of law[3]

§ 242. **The amount offered must be admitted to be due—Denying the debt—Offer by way of a boon—To buy peace—As a compromise—With reservation**—A tender must be of a specific sum which the tendoror admits to be due. Offering a sum and saying "I pay you this but I do not owe it" is bad. So, making a protest that he was not liable for the full amount of what he tendered.[1] When a creditor called upon his debtor to receive payment, and while he was counting the money the debtor declared that the claim was extortionate, it was held that the creditor was justified in withdrawing from the premises, and that there was no tender[2] There must be no denial of the debt. If the money or thing is offered by way of a boon,[3] or to buy peace, there is no tender. A sum offered by way of a compromise,[4] or "to avoid litigation" is not good.[5] A tender of the amount of a legacy, coupled with the reservation for a decision of the question of the right of the legatee to interest on the legacy, was held bad[6]

It may be observed that, where the full amount of the claim is offered, accompanied by a protest by the party making the

[1] Eckstein v. Reynolds, 7 A. & E. 80 2 N. & P. 256, s. p. Marsden v. Goode 2 C. & K. 133

[2] Foster v. Drew, 39 Vt. 51

[3] Wheelock v. Tanner 39 N. Y. 481

[1] Wood v. Hitchcock 20 Wend. 47, Simmons v. Wilmott, 3 Esp. R. 91, 2 Phil. Ev. 7th Ed. 134. See Thorp v. Burgess, 8 D. P. C. 603

[2] Harris v. Mulock, 9 How. Pr. 102

[3] Kuhn v. Chicago etc. Ry., 65 Iowa 528, s. c. 22 N. W. Rep. 661, 2 Greenl. Ev. Sec. 605

[4] Elderkin v. Fellows, 60 Wis. 339, s. c. 19 N. W. Rep. 101, Latham v. Hartford, 27 Kan. 249

[5] Kuhns v. Chicago, etc., Ry. Co., 65 Iowa 528

[6] In re Wallace's Estate, 5 N. Y. Supp. 31

offer, that he does not owe the debt, or a part of it, an acceptance of it would close the transaction; the entire claim demanded being paid. But a debtor has no right to cast upon
his creditor the imputation that he is exacting an unjust
claim, and at the same time expect the law to confer upon
him the benefits that would accrue by reason of valid tender
and refusal, when by his aspersions he prevented the sum
offered from being accepted. In those cases where the offer
of the thing is in the nature of a boon, or to buy peace, or as
a compromise, the conditions expressed or implied are preju
dicial to the creditor's rights; as proof of an acceptance,
under those circumstances, would estop the creditor from
asserting a claim for any sum beyond the amount received.

§ 243. **Offer under protest.**—There are decisions holding that
a tender under protest, reserving the right to dispute the
amount due, if it does not impose any conditions on the
creditor, is good. As when the mortgagee is in possession
and the mortgagor makes a tender of the amount claimed to
be due, and at the same time reserving the right to review
their account.[1] So, when the tender was in this form "If you
insist upon being paid the amount demanded before satis
factory explanations have been given, our clerk will hand you
a cheque this morning for the amount (£1,596 3s. 6d.), but
you must consider the payment as under protest, and our
clients will seek to recover back what is overpaid after
wards" it was held sufficient.[2] Sending a check for the
amount of a call, and at the same time protesting against the
payment upon certain grounds, and declaring that the money
must be held in trust until the cause of complaint is settled,
was held to be a good tender of payment, and that the con
cluding words imposed no obligation or liability on the
directors of the corporation.[3] So, where a debtor claimed
certain deductions from the amount claimed by the creditor,
which the latter would not allow, it was decided that the use
of the term "under protest" did not vitiate the tender.[4]

---

[1] Greenwood v Sutcliffe, 1 Ch
1, s c 11 C B 226

[2] Scott v Uxbridge Ry Co, 1
Law Rep C P 596, 12 Jur N.
S 602; 35 L J, C P 293, 14 W
R 893

[3] Sweeney v Smith, 38 L J
Chenc 146, 7 L R Eq 324

[4] Manning v Lunn, 2 C. & K.
13. See Atchinson, T & S. F
Ry v Roberts, 22 S W Rep
(Tex. Cir App.) ——, when freight

There are cases when a tender under protest would be peculiarly appropriate, and a means to attain justice, as where a party must pay a sum of money by a certain time to save a forfeiture, or to avoid a penalty, and the amount due is peculiarly within the knowledge of the other party, or the sum demanded contains items which he, in good faith, thinks is not a legal claim; and, where a party must pay a sum demanded to get possession of certain property, where it would be a hardship and hazardous to tender a less sum and evoke the aid of the law to obtain the possession

§ 244.  **Right to require a third party holding a demand to furnish proof of his authority to receive payment.**—Where an account, note or other instrument is in the hands of a third person for collection, the tender may properly be made conditional upon proof, by the third person, of his authority to receive the money on the debt  The tenderor, as we shall presently see, may require evidence of the authority of the agent, other than the statement of such person that he has such authority, for it is a well settled rule of evidence, that an agent's authority cannot be proven by his declaration alone.  Mere possession by the third person of the books of account, note or other instrument, would not, in connection with the agent's declaration, be sufficient proof—for their possession may have been fraudulently obtained, or they may have been the subject of larceny  However, the debtor must not be unreasonable in his demands for proof of authority. He may require competent evidence, and if it is furnished and he is still in doubt, he must forthwith seek his creditor and make a tender to him personally  Failing in this, he will not be heard to say that he made a valid tender.  If the debtor had previously acquired competent proof of the agency, such as written or oral declaration of the principal, and he chooses to make the tender to the agent, instead of his creditor in person, he cannot clog the tender with the condition that proof of authority to receive payment be furnished

A debtor is not bound to multiply his proof of payment by tendering the money or thing to an agent.  If he does so, in

charges were tendered under protest

a case where he can make a tender to his creditor personally, it is his own fault. In any subsequent action to recover the debt, the *onus* is upon him to prove payment to a duly author ized agent. In those cases where the creditor resides without the state or country, and for that reason a tender to him in person cannot be made, but he has an agent within the state, it would seem that a tender may be made to the agent con ditional on the delivery of a writing signed by the creditor, showing the agent's authority to receive the money or thing due on the obligation. In the case of a negotiable instru ment, a special endorsement "for collection" removes all grounds for controversy. The rule is not any different where the account, note or other instrument, is lodged with an attorney for collection, where suit has not been instituted by the attorney to recover the debt. In such case the relation of attorney and client is governed by the law of agency, and nothing is presumed by virtue of the agent being an attorney

§ 245. **Same subject—Production of assignment of a mortgage —Of an unindorsed note payable to a certain person or order. —**Where a note secured by a mortgage is in the hands of a third person who claims to be the owner, where the note is payable to the order of a certain person and is unindorsed, a tender of the sum due on the note may be made conditional upon the third party showing his right to receive the same, by producing an assignment of the note or a release of the mortgage [1] In any case where an instrument is made payable to a certain person or order, and the instrument is unindorsed or unassigned in writing, the debtor pays it to a third person at his peril. A payment made under such circumstances is no defence in a suit to recover the debt brought by the real owner. The reason for making a tender conditional applies with greater force, when the payee named in the instrument notifies the payor not to pay the money to such third person.[2] The debtor is not bound to assume the hazards of a dispute between the other two parties. When the obligation to pay money is on an account or on any written instrument the title to which does not pass by mere delivery, the tender may

[1] Kennedy v Moore 58 N. W. Rep (Iowa) 1066

[2] Kennedy v Moore, 58 N W Rep. (Iowa) 1066

always be coupled with a condition that the third person prove his title.

§ 246. Same subject—Requiring proof of identity of payee or indorsee when payment is demanded—Where the payor goes to the payee or indorsee.—A payor of a promissory note, bill of exchange, check or other instrument, payable to order, when the payee or indorsee named in the instrument is not known personally to the payor, as a condition of his paying the money, may lawfully require proof of the payee or indorsee that he is the person named in the instrument, and, withholding the money until such proof is furnished will not subject the payor to any liability for interest and costs. If the thing to be delivered is a chattel such withholding does not constitute conversion. Such requirement is a prudent precautionary measure. On the other hand, if the payor of such an instrument is desirous of discharging his obligation, and goes to the payee or indorsee, whom he does not know personally, to pay the money or deliver the chattel, he must satisfy himself, as best he can, as to the identity of the payee, if he is not satisfied with a verbal statement, as the latter is not required to go to any trouble to furnish evidence that he is the right person.

§ 247. Conditional upon the surrender of negotiable note.—It is a familiar rule well established, in regard to commercial paper, that when the note or bill is paid, the payor is entitled to have it delivered up, and, when it is withheld after payment, a suit in equity may be maintained to compel its surrender. Notwithstanding this undoubted right of the payor after payment, to have the possession of a negotiable instrument, the rule is not so well settled as to the right of a payor to make a tender of the amount due conditional upon the note being surrendered. Much confusion and uncertainty has arisen, from accepting as the law general statements pro and con, disassociated from the facts had under consideration. In New York it has been held, that a tender of the amount due upon certain bonds and matured interest coupons, in the exercise of an option to pay them before the due day, was properly made with a condition that the bonds and all coupons due and not due, be surrendered.[1] The court went further and said, by way of argument, "It is not disputed that one liable to pay money secured by a written instrument has the right, as the condition of tender of payment to demand the surrender of the instrument which is the evidence of the debt." So are the dictum of other courts.[2]

A rule permitting a payor of a negotiable instrument, when there is no dispute as to the amount due, to require a surrender of the instrument as a condition of the acceptance of a tender of the amount due, has much reason to support it. If it be not surrendered, such paper after payment, might be put into circulation, and although in such case, the law would protect all parties to a negotiable instrument against any liability to a person who became the holder after it fell due, yet the burden would be upon the payor to prove that the note or bill came to the hands of the holder after it had matured, or if the payment was made after maturity, then that the holder acquired it after such payment. A burden not warranted by the contract, and, to impose which on a payor who had actually paid the full sum due to the payee or indorsee of the instrument, would be a manifest injustice. Putting a negotiable instrument into circulation after payment, is a thing not altogether improbable, and if its surrender could not be required as a condition of the acceptance of the tender of the sum due, there would be danger that the payor, or other person liable thereon, would be required to pay it a second time, and the danger would be all the greater, where the instrument was made payable on or before a certain date, as in the case of the bonds referred to in the New York case. In such case as the latter, the instrument does not carry on its face any evidence that would apprise a purchaser that the person liable on the instrument had exercised his option, by paying the sum due before the time limited. Even after a partial payment, there is a possibility that the payor may be required to pay the face value of the note, in an action brought by a third person who is a *bona*

[1] Bailey v Buckhanan County, 115 N Y 297, s c 22 N E Rep. 155

[2] Stafford v Welch, 59 N H. 46, Storey v. Krewson, 55 Ind 397; Smith v. Rockwell, 2 Hill 402. See Wilder v Seelye, 8 Barb 408, where the question was the right of an indorser to require the delivery of a note as a condition of his paying it, Balme v Wambaugh, 16 Minn. 117.

*fide* holder for value, but there is more or less hazard in all human transactions which the law cannot guard against.

**§ 248. Same subject — Contrary rule.—** There are decisions which hold the converse of the principle announced in the cases considered in the preceding section, to be the law. Thus, where the payor sent his agent to the place designated, at the time specified for payment with the property to be delivered, with directions to deliver the property only on the conditions that the note be surrendered, it was held to be a conditional tender and for that reason the property was not ready at the time and place for delivery.[1] So, where a mortgagor refused to part with the money unless the note was surrendered, the tender of the money was held to be conditional, and did not bar an action of ejectment to recover the land under the mortgage deed.[2]

**§ 249. Same subject—Where the amount due is not agreed.—** The authorities are agreed, that where the parties are not agreed upon the amount that is due, and the tender is of a less sum than the creditor claims to be due, though in fact sufficient, the tender is not good, where the acceptance of the sum tendered is made conditional on the surrender of the note or other evidence of the debt. For the possession of the note, acquired under such circumstances, would be strong evidence, in the nature of an admission, that the note was fully paid. And, as we have seen, a "tender is not effectual as such if it be coupled with such conditions that the acceptance of it, as tendered, will involve an admission by the party accepting it that no more is due." In a well considered case in Minnesota, where it appeared that a larger sum than that tendered was in good faith claimed to be due, the court said that by offering to pay the money only upon the condition that the notes be delivered up, the debtor insisted upon a condition, the acceptance of which would seriously compromise the right of the holder to recover any more, even though the sum tendered was in fact less than the amount due, and, it was held that such a tender was insufficient to discharge

[1] Robinson v. Batchelder, 4 N H 40

[2] Holton v. Brown, 18 Vt 224 See Balme v. Wambough, 16 Minn 117

the lien of the mortgage given to secure the payment of the notes; that "The defendant should not be heard to assert that a mere offer to pay a specific sum, less than was supposed by the other party to be due, has the effect of payment, so as to discharge the mortgage, when the offer was burdened with a condition."[1]

§ 250. Same subject—Correct rule.—In conclusion it may be said that where there is no dispute as to the amount due on a negotiable instrument, and it is in the possession of the owner at the time of the tender, its surrender may be demanded by any person liable upon it, if its surrender is not made a condition of the acceptance of the tender of the amount due. Demanding a note, but making its surrender a condition of payment, does not make a tender conditional.[1] If the amount due is in controversy, the offer must be to pay the money absolutely without annexing any terms or condition whatever. Should there exist such distrust of the holder, on the part of the payor, that the tender is made conditional that the note be first delivered up, or that the holder give his promise that he will surrender it after payment, the tender would be bad. At most the implied contract is merely to surrender the instrument at or after payment and not before the payment, and in absence of any declaration by the holder to the contrary the law presumes that he will surrender it. If the note is lost and it is not within the power of the owner to produce it, a tender may be made conditional upon the owner furnishing an indemnity, such as is required by the law merchants when a demand is made for payment of a lost bill or note to protect the payor against any subsequent liability on the instrument in case it turns up in the hands of another person. The same indemnity may be required in case the owner claims the note has been destroyed, for the payor is not bound to rely upon the assertion of the holder, that the note is not negotiated but destroyed.

§ 251 Same subject—Where the tender is made by a surety endorser, drawer, acceptor, &c.—The discussion in the foregoing sections was confined mainly to a tender made by a

[1] Moore v Norman, 52 Minn
84; s p Bank of Benson v Hove,
45 Minn 40

[1] Buffum v Buffum, 11 N H
451 Stafford v Welch 59 N H
46

payor of a negotiable note, but there is another class of persons liable on commercial paper, who, from their position, are treated with much more consideration. The class refer red to comprise endorsers, guarantors and sureties on notes and bills, and drawers and acceptors of bills of exchange. As to these, if the payment of the instrument by any one of them ended the transaction as to all parties, and the question was simply with respect to their liability after payment to a bona fide holder, their case would not be different from that of a payor who makes a tender of the sum due upon such an instrument. But they are, ordinarily, paying the debt of an other, and ought not to be embarrassed in making out their title to the note or bill as against the maker or acceptor, or in securing their evidence of payment as against a drawer as the case may be. The rule is well settled that when a surety, guarantor, endorser, or an acceptor, or drawer's liability has become absolute and fixed a tender of the sum due, when there is no dispute as to the amount due, may be made by such persons to depend upon the surrender of the note or bill.[1] Lord Tenterden, Ch. J., in a suit by an indorsee against an acceptor said: "The acceptor paying the bill has a right to the possession of the instrument for his own security, and his voucher and discharge, pro tanto in his account with the drawer. If upon an offer of payment the holder should refuse to deliver up the bill can it be doubted that the acceptor might retract his offer or retain the money?"[2] When the note or bill is lost or destroyed, an endorser, or any one standing in that relation whose liability has been fixed by a tender of sufficient indemnity by the holder at the time of the service of the notice of dishonor, or of making the demand, may require that such indemnity be surrendered to him as a condition of the owner's acceptance of the sum tendered.

The rights, duties and liabilities of those secondarily liable upon commercial paper in reference to the right of such person to have the possession of the note or bill surrendered to them, as a condition of the acceptance by the holder of their tender of the amount due, are considered more frequently in the books at least in cases arising on lost or destroyed bills or notes, and a comprehensive examination of those decisions,

[1] Wilder v. Seelye 8 Barb. 408       [2] Hansard v. Robinson 7 B. & C. 90

will, it is believed, go far to sustain the foregoing, as an unalterable rule, in cases where the amount due is not questioned.[3] But here also the implied contract is to surrender the instrument after payment, and not before, so that the party offering to pay cannot lawfully insist that it be first delivered up.

**§ 252. Conditional upon the surrender of a non-negotiable note.**—The reasons which can be urged so forcibly in regard to the right of one liable upon a negotiable instrument, to make a tender of the sum admitted to be due, conditional upon afterwards receiving the instrument, do not apply to non negotiable paper. Such instrument, after payment by the maker, becomes harmless as against him, wherever it may go, and a tender is not good, if it is clogged with a condition that the possession of such instrument be surrendered to the payor.[1]

**§ 253. Demanding a receipt.**—The most familiar example of a conditional tender is an offer to pay a certain sum conditional upon receiving a receipt for it. It is everywhere held that a debtor cannot insist upon a receipt in full in respect to the particular claim upon which the tender is made, or a receipt in full for all demand. On this the authorities are in harmony.[1] Accepting a sum tendered and delivering a receipt in full, under such circumstances, would be prima facie evidence that the debt was paid in full and that whatever differences of opinion may have existed as to the exact sum due, the parties had arrived at an understanding and had settled

[3] Hansard v Robinson 7 B & C 90; Smith v Rockwell 2 Hill 482 Rowley v Ball, 3 Cow 303, Story on Bills of Exchange Sec 449

[1] See dictum to contra, Balme v Wambaugh 16 Minn 117

[1] Butler v Hinckley, 17 Colo 523, Wood v Hitchcock 20 Wend 47; Griffith v Hodges, 1 C & P 419, Glasscott v Day 5 Esp 48; Jacoway v Hall, 55 S W Rep (Ark) 12 Doty v Crawford, 17 S E Rep 377, Richardson v Boston C Laboratory, 9 Met. 12;

Bowen v Owen 11 Q B 131 Hepburn v Auld, 1 Cranch 321 Siter v Robinson 2 Bailey (S C) 271 Finch v Miller 5 C B 128 Cole v Blake Peck's Nisi Prius 179, Foord v Noll 2 D N S 617 s c 12 L J, C P 2' Higham v Baddely, Gow 213 In West v Farmers Mut Ins Co 90 N W Rep (Io) 523 it was held that Code (Io) 1873, § 3063, providing that a tenderor may demand a receipt for the money tendered did not authorize him to demand a receipt in full for the amount paid over  This involves an admission, which, as has been shown, if insisted upon is fatal to a tender, as it would not leave the creditor free to persist in his claim for more, without overcoming the receipt by evidence that the amount of the claim was liquidated and not in dispute, or that he was mistaken or misinformed as to the amount actually due. A tender is vitiated by coupling it with a demand for a receipt merely for the sum offered.[2] And there is no distinction made between demanding such a receipt where the sum due is agreed upon, and the tender is of that sum, and, where a less sum than that claimed to be due is offered and the demand is for a receipt for such sum  A creditor is not bound to furnish his debtor with written or other evidence of a payment  If a receipt could be required, no different reason can be assigned why the creditor should not be required to produce reputable witnesses at the time of the tender, with which the debtor may thereafter prove payment. If a creditor could not write, or writing material could not be had at the place of the tender, the creditor could be kept out of the money indefinitely  If a debtor for any reason wants to have evidence of a payment other than his own testimony, he should take witnesses with him at the time he goes to pay the money  Where a tender was made by enclosing a check in a letter and no objection was made as to the medium, but merely to the amount, the tender was held not to be vitiated by a request that a receipt be sent back  Here, the court thought, by putting the check entirely out of his power a request for the receipt to be returned to him was not a condition[8]  Merely asking the question, "Have you got a receipt?" has been held not to be fatal to a tender.

---

[2] Holton v Brown 18 Vt 224; Kitchen v Clark, 1 Mo App 430, Roosevelt v Bull's Head Bank, 45 Barb 583, Sanford v Bulkley, 30 Conn 344  In Brock v Jones, 16 Tex 461 the rule holding that a demand for a receipt vitiates a tender is criticized but the case of Richardson v Jackson, 8 M. & W 298, referred to as showing the unsoundness of the rule is a case where the tender was rejected because the amount was thought to be insufficient  Subsequently the creditor sought to change his ground of objection by claiming that the tender was bad by reason of a receipt having been demanded which he could not do

[8] Jones v Arthus 8 D P C 442 B C

**§ 254. Where a receipt or release is stipulated for—Receipt required by law.**—Where a contract expressly provides for a delivery of a release of all demands a tender may be made with a condition that a receipt or release be delivered, and the creditor will be confined to other reasons for rejecting the tender than the one that a receipt is demanded. Where the statute requires a receipt to be given, as in the case of payment of taxes, a tender of the amount of the tax due will relieve the taxpayer from a liability for penalties, even though a tender is made conditional upon a receipt being furnished.[1] In England, under an old statute which required a stamped receipt to be given, it was held that the debtor must bring a stamped receipt for the creditor to sign, and that a tender complied with a demand for a receipt without proving it was had.[2]

**§ 255. Demanding that the instrument be endorsed.**—A tender of the amount due to the holder of a note, check, or other instrument payable to bearer, conditional upon the holder endorsing the paper, is not good. Nor is an offer to pay the amount due on a note or other instrument payable to certain person, or to a certain person or order, by a joint maker, surety, or other person secondarily liable thereon, good, if coupled with a demand that the holder endorse the instrument. The possession of such an instrument by a joint maker, surety or other person secondarily liable thereon is prima facie evidence that such person has paid the same.

**§ 256. Demanding release of mortgage — An assignment.**—A tender of a sum upon a debt, the payment of which is secured by a mortgage on real estate, upon the condition that the mortgagee execute a release of the mortgage, is a conditional tender, and is ineffectual for any purpose. The rule is not any different in cases when the full amount conceded to be due is tendered, and those cases where the amount due is in dispute, and a less sum than that claimed by the mortgagee is offered. If a mortgagor, by reason of his distrust of the mortgagee, or for any reason, could require a release

---

[1] State v. Cent. Pac. R. R. Co., 30 Pac. (Nev.) 686.

[2] Laing v. Meader 1 C. & P. 257; Ryder v. Townsend 7 D. & R. 119.

in advance, no different reasons exist why the mortgagee
should not demand an intermediator whose duty it would be
to hold the release until he had received and telled the money,
or that each should choose an intermediator, and the two, a
third. The payment of a debt is always a condition precedent
to the discharge of the mortgage or the surrender of any
security. It is a condition inherent in every contract where security is given for the payment of a debt or the performance
of an act. If it were otherwise, there would be a time when
the mortgagee, after delivering the release, would be without
any security, and the mortgagor would have it in his power to
withdraw without paying over the money; an event, the prob-
ability of which would amply warrant the withholding of the
release until full payment was made, according to the contract. It is not presumed in law that the mortgagee will not
do his duty after receiving payment of his debt.

At common law, it is the duty of the mortgagee, after receiving full payment, to execute a release of the mortgage or
surrender the instrument. The statutes of the various states
of the Union requiring a release to be delivered after payment, are but declaratory of the common law. Courts of
equity will enforce a release. In a well considered case in Indiana, the subject is comprehensively and logically treated.
The court said: 'The appellees had no right to demand a cancellation of the mortgage as a condition to the tender—it
would in no way have strengthened their right nor placed
them in any better legal status—for the surrender of the note,
upon its payment, worked the destruction of all legal vitality
in the mortgage * * * We think a demand to cancel the
mortgage as a condition of the tender, is not different in
principle from demanding a receipt as a condition to the payment of the money. It would be the duty of the appellants,
after 'having received full payment of the sum' secured by the
mortgage to 'enter satisfaction on the margin or other proper
place in the record of such mortgage'" according to the
statute, "but they could not be required to do so, merely upon
a tender of the amount as a condition to their right to receive the money."[1] The court of appeals of Missouri said

[1] Storey v. Knewson 55 Ind.
197. In Loring v. Cook 3 Pick
18, the tender was made conditional upon the purchaser of the
equity of redemption releasing
his right. In Jewett v. Earle, 53

"There is no possible theory upon which plaintiff would have the right to demand a release of his mortgage or deed of trust, before making payment or tender of the secured indebtedness."[2] A purchaser of the equity of redemption, on a tender of the amount due, must not make it conditional on receiving an assignment of the mortgage[3] So, a subsequent lien holder in redeeming must not clog his tender with a condition that the prior lien be assigned to him. A party is entitled to subrogation only after payment. A tender is not payment and a senior lien holder is under no obligation to assign his security.[4]

§ 257.  Same subject—Decisions to the contrary.—There are decisions of various state courts, based on their statute, which seem to indicate that a tender may be made conditional on an entry of satisfaction[1] But the statutes do not bear

N. Y Supr. Ct 349 three dollars was tendered for a satisfaction piece, which was an implied demand for a satisfaction piece before the money would be left. In both of these cases the tenders were held bad So, in Wendell v The New Hampshire Bank, 9 N H 404, a tender, made on the condition that the mortgagee would reassign, was held bad See Potts v Plasted, 30 Mich. 149

[2] McCormick v McDonald 70 Mo App 389

[3] Lumpsden v Manson, 96 Me. 357.

[4] Frost v Yonkers Sav Bank, 70 N Y 553; Appeal of Forest Oil Co, (Pa) 12 A Rep 442, Day v Strong, 29 N Y 505, Lumsden v Manson, 52 Atl Rep (Me) 783

[1] Salinas v. Ellis 26 S Car 337 In Halpin v. Phoenix Co, 118 N Y 165, s c 23 N E 482 it was decided that a tender of a mortgage debt is not invalidated by being conditional upon the mortgage being satisfied The court said by the way of argu-

ment, "Where there is no dispute as to the amount of the debt, a tender may always be restrictive by such conditions as by the terms of the contract are condition precedent or simultaneous to the payment of the debt or proper to be performed by the party to whom the tender is made." This applied to certain facts, is good law, but here it is a misapplication A release of a mortgage is never, unless made so by express stipulation, a condition precedent or even a simultaneous condition of receiving payment of the mortgage debt. The court cites Wheelock v Tanner, 39 N Y 481, Cass v Ilgenbotam, 100 N Y 253, s c 29 Hun 406, Sanders v Winship 5 Pick 259; Ocean Nat Bank v Fant, 50 N Y 479, Cutler v. Goold, 43 Hun 516 Bailey v County of Buchanan 115 N Y. 207; Smith v Rockwell, 2 Hill 482, all of which do not support the rule they announce, that a tender is not invalid by being made conditional upon the mortgage being satisfied  San-

such a construction, and right reasoning does not support the doctrine. If a mortgagee in good faith claimed more to be due than the sum tendered, and such sum should prove to be sufficient, where such a rule obtained, to refuse would be disastrous to him, although he may offer to accept the amount and credit it upon the note.

To comply with the demand by surrendering the security, would be an admission on his part that no more is due, which as an express or implied condition to the acceptance of the tender is always fatal. The mortgagor hazards nothing. The mortgage is but an incident to the debt, the payment of which is a full and complete discharge of the mortgage. Unlike negotiable instruments, a transfer does not preclude any defence the mortgagor may have to it. He may show that the debt is paid or is tainted with usury. While on the other hand a refusal by the mortgagor of an unconditional tender of the full amount due (when made on the law day at common law or before foreclosure under some modern decisions) is at the risk of a loss of his security, interest on the debt after the tender, and subjecting himself to a liability for costs in a suit to cancel the mortgage, and any penalty the law may provide for a refusal to discharge the mortgage of record.

§ 258. **Demanding a release of a chattel mortgage or surrender of the property.**—In the case of chattel mortgages the tender must not be made with the condition that the mortgagee

---

ders v. Winship, being the only case fairly supporting such rule, and there such a holding was not necessary to the decision. In Wheelock v. Turner the discharge of the mortgage was by the bond a condition precedent to payment. See Hepburn v. Auld 1 Cranch 330. Cass v. Higenbotam was a case where the creditor refused to surrender collateral on the ground that it was claimed by the third party, and in Ocean Nat. Bank v. Fant the question was as to the liability of the indorser, where the notary, on making a demand for payment of the maker did not have the collateral to deliver up. So, in Cutler v. Gould the demand was for the surrender of certain collateral negotiable notes not due. In Bailey v. County of Buchanan, the debtor was exercising an option given of paying before maturity, and demanded the return of all notes due and not due. And in Smith v. Rockwell it was held that a maker or endorser was not bound to pay a negotiable promissory note without receiving it as their voucher—all cases governed entirely different rules.

execute a release or satisfaction of the mortgage, or, if the mortgaged property be in the possession of the mortgagee an offer to pay the debt is ineffectual as a tender if made on the condition that the property be first delivered. No different rule obtains in case of pledges. It has been said by way of dictum that "A tender made to procure the possession of property can hardly be called conditional because it is accompanied with a demand for the property."[1] But it was made to appear that the tender was refused upon another and different ground. If a demand for the return of the chattel is made in such manner that it clearly appears that the money will not be paid unless the chattel is first produced and delivered, the offer to pay the debt does not operate as a tender.

§ 259. **Demanding the return of collateral.**—When the payee of a note or other obligation demands payment of the maker he must, at the time of making the demand, tender any collateral security given to secure the payment of the debt,[1] and, on the other hand if the payor tenders the sum due, he is entitled to have the collateral security delivered up[2] But as in the case of other securities, a debtor must not insist that the collateral be first surrendered[3] A surety however after a default may make a tender of the debt conditional upon afterwards receiving the collateral Making a demand for the possession of chattels to which a person is entitled upon the payment of a debt does not make a tender conditional, and if a tender is accompanied by a demand merely the lien will be discharged[4] Where collateral has been levied upon or attached at the instance of a third person, a tender upon the condition that the creditor immediately afterwards surrender the collateral is not good The debtor would be requiring of the creditor the performance of that which might be an impossible condition. When a person is entitled to

[1] Moynahan v Moore 9 Mich 9 s c 77 Am Dec 168 See McEldon v Patton 93 N W Rep (Neb) 938

[1] Ocean National Bank v Fant, 50 N Y 474

[2] Cass v Higenbotam 100 N Y 253 reversing 29 Hun 406

[3] See Loughborough v McNiven 15 Pac Rep (Cal) 773 following the same case in 14 Pac Rep 369 which holds the contrary to be the rule

[4] Price in re 74 N Y Supp 624

have a note or any security surrendered after payment of the debt, he cannot make the tender conditional upon the creditor first promising to surrender the note or security after payment. A creditor is not bound to give any assurances that he will perform his contract

§ 260. **Imposing conditions in what cases — Right must be clear.**—By the common law all tenders were required to be unconditional, but this rule has been justly relaxed in reference to contracts executory on both sides, upon a correct view of the legal rights of the parties. A tender of performance may be accompanied by such conditions as are, by the contract, conditions precedent to be performed by the party to whom the tender is made. So, where there are mutual and concurrent acts to be performed, as where a deed was to be delivered at the time of making a certain payment, it was held that a tender of the money conditional upon the delivery of the deed was sufficient to put the vendor in default.[1] So, if a mortgagee, by express contracts, agrees to assign or to execute a release at the time of the payment, it is thought that a tender, coupled with a condition that the mortgage be assigned or satisfied, will be good.[2] So, where property is in the possession of a third party, and it is necessary to have an order from the vendor or bailee before such third person will surrender the property, a tender may be made conditional upon receiving such an order, as where certain logs are in possession of a boom company, and can not be obtained without an order from the creditor.[3]

If a vendor's lien is expressly retained in a conveyance, a tender of the amount secured by a lien, upon the condition that the vendor will furnish a release of the lien, has been held good, for, without such release there will be a cloud upon the vendee's title.[4] But the condition must be one that the

[1] Shouse v Dane 21 So Rep 805, 807 Harding v Giddings U C C A 508 s c 31 U S App 642 73 Fed Rep 335 Contra Morris v Continental Ins Co 42 S W Rep 171 De Grattenried v Menard 30 S E Rep (Ga) 560 Elder v Johnson 40 S E Rep (Ga) 51

[2] Wheelock v Tanner 39 N Y 481 4 Cranch 430 and Wendell v New Hampshire Bank 9 N H 404

Johnson v Cranage 45 Mich 14 (7 N W Rep 188)

[4] Engelbach v Simpson 12 Tex Civ App 188 s c 33 S W Rep 596

tenderor has a clear right to exact.[5] Where under a contract
of sale of land, the contract provided for the execution of a
mortgage securing deferred payments, but was silent as to
the giving of notes or other evidence of the indebtedness, an
offer of a deed upon condition that the purchaser will execute
notes, and a mortgage securing the same is not such a tender
of a deed as would require the vendee to execute any mort
gage at all.[6] Insisting on a cash payment when the contract
of sale does not require a cash payment to be made will
vitiate a tender of a deed.[7] So, a tender of the purchase
money coupled with a demand for a deed for more land than
the contract called for is not good.[8] Where, by a contract,
the consideration is to be computed after ascertaining the
acreage, a tender of a deed is not good which is coupled with
an implied demand for the payment of an amount, calculated
upon the basis of the acreage named in the deed without
proof that such acreage is correct.[9] Where more than one
piece of land is covered by a mortgage, and there is no agreement for a partial release, a purchaser of one parcel, who
has assumed the note representing the purchase price of the
parcel purchased by him, cannot require a release of the
mortgage as to his lot, as a condition to the acceptance of a
tender of the amount due on the note assumed by him  Such
a tender will not stop the running of interest.[10] So, a tender
is bad, which is accompanied by a demand that a mortgagee
shall give a full release, when he is not the holder of one of
the notes evidencing the mortgage debt, and the mortgagor
is aware that one of the notes had been transferred.[11]

A tender must not be made conditional upon the perform
ance by the tenderee of some act which is in no way connected with the transaction, but which is a collateral and
entirely distinct matter,[12] as a tender coupled with a demand
that the tenderee shall dismiss a suit which is not connected
with the subject of the tender,[13] or that the mortgagee secure

[5] See Odum v Rutledge, 94 Ala.
188

[6] Bruce v Doble, 52 N W Rep
(S Dak) 586

[7] Bieja v Payne, 94 Iowa 755,
s c 64 N W Rep 669

[8] Cornell v Hayden, 114 N Y
270

[9] Bidwell v Garrison 36 Alt
Rep (N J) 941

[10] Flake v Nuse, 51 Tex 98

[11] Redfern v Ulmery, 12 Ohio C
C 87

[12] See Park v Allen, 42 Mich
482 s c 4 N W Rep 227

[13] Rose v Ducan, 49 Ind 269

a lease to which the mortgagor is not entitled.[14] So, where a husband contracts for the sale of his interest in certain land, a tender of the purchase money with a condition that he will cause his wife to convey her dower interest is not good.[15]

§ 261. **Demand for withdrawal of protest.** —Where the holder of certain county bonds which contained a stipulation that they might be exchanged for new bonds, served a writing upon the county officials, when they notified him that the bonds could not be exchanged but that he must accept cash, protesting against the unlawful exercise of power in violation of law, it was held that a tender made subsequently, on condition that he withdraw his protest, which he refused to do but offered to accept the money, was bad, the court said that the protest, though uncalled for, constituted no reason for withholding the money; that paying the money under such circumstances did not constitute any admission that the plaintiff held any other valid claim against the county.[1]

§ 262. **Demanding the performance of an impossible condition** —Where mortgaged property or a pledge has been destroyed, or has been sold, and it is not within the power of the mortgagee or pledgee to restore the property, which fact is known to all parties, a tender of the amount of the debt, where the acceptance is made conditional upon the return of the property, is not good. The court said in such a case, that such an offer might as well never have been made, that it was a mere useless ceremony to call upon the mortgagee to per-

[14] National Bank v Leavanseler, 73 N W Rep 399 Tendering a larger sum than the amount due and accompanying it with a counter demand in writing upon the tenderee, has been held bad, both in respect to the amount tendered and the counter demand. The court holding that a tender must be unqualified by any circumstance whatever. Brady v Jones, 2 D. & R 305 It does not clearly appear, however, that the payment or allowance of the counter demand was made a condition of accepting the tender.

This, however, might be inferred.

[15] Kelsey v Crowther, 7 Utah 519 In such a case a court of equity would have no power, on the husband's contract, to compel the wife to relinquish her dower right. If the seller tendered a deed without his wife joining, it would not avail as a tender of performance, unless it appeared from the contract or attending facts and circumstances that the dower interest was not to be conveyed by his wife

[1] Henderson v Cass Co, 107 Mo 50

form an impossible condition precedent, as it could place the parties in no other or different position than they were, that such a tender gave the parties no greater rights than those already possessed.[1] So, where a tender to an attorney was made with the condition that certain notes pledged be then and there delivered up, when the party making the tender knew that the attorney did not have the notes, it was held not good.[2] So, an offer of money to a cashier of a bank in payment of a note drawn payable at the bank, on condition that the cashier surrender the note, when the tenderor was informed that the owner was absent with the note, was held insufficient to discharge the lien of a mortgage.[3] But being at the place of payment in absence of the payee with the money and keeping the tender good would stop the running of interest.

§ 263. **Demanding change—Waiver.**—A tender must not be made upon an implied or express condition that the tenderee furnish change for the difference between the amount offered and the amount actually due.[1] But the objection to the tender on the ground that change is demanded, may be waived by some declaration of the creditor dispensing with a tender of the actual amount due, Lord Kenyon said: "I take it to be clear beyond doubt that if the debtor tenders a larger sum of money than is due, and asks change, this will be a good tender if the creditor does not object to it on that account but only demands a larger sum."[2] So if the tender is refused solely upon any ground which would lead the debtor to believe that a tender of the exact amount would be refused, as where the creditor claims the tender comes too late, the objection is waived. But there is no waiver if the creditor refuse to receive the money without assigning any reason. When a

[1] Bank v Freott, 10 Mich 640
[2] Malone v Wright, 46 S W Rep 420
[3] Bilme v Wambaugh, 16 Minn 117
[1] Robinson v Cook 6 Taunt 336, Batterbee v Davis, 3 Camp 70, Brady v Jones, 2 D & R 305 Blow v Russell 1 C & P 365

[2] Block v Smith, Peakes N P C 88 s p Cadman v Lubbock 5 D & R 289 Sinders v Graham, Gow 111 Beans v — 5 M & W 306 7 D & P C 510 3 Tur 608 Richardson v Jackson 8 M & W 298 Peoples Ins Co v Crosby 57 Neb 282 s c 77 N W Rep 658
[3] Brady v Jones 2 D & R 305 Batterbee v Davis 3 Camp

note is payable in specific articles, an offer of property of greater value than the amount of the note, with the demand for the difference in money, is not a good tender.[4] In such case there could be no waiver of the objection to the tender. The condition imposed is that the payee pay for something, which is entirely different from returning change, which is in fact, merely returning a part of the money just handed over by the payor.

§ 264.  **Making a tender in writing.**—At common law, in order to make a valid tender of either money or chattels, the thing, whatever it is, must be tendered personally to the party entitled thereto, but in many states,[1] under the statute, an offer in writing to pay a definite sum of money, or to deliver a particular thing, takes the place of an actual production and proffer of the money to be paid or thing to be delivered [2] Such an offer is in fact not a tender, but merely a written offer to pay money, or of performance, in the lieu of the actual production of the thing. In all other respects the common law prevails [3] The authorities are agreed that such written offer dispenses merely with the actual production of the money or thing, that it does not relieve the party making the offer from the duty of actually having the money or other thing at hand [4] Statutory provisions relative to making tenders, which are in derogation of the common law must be strictly complied with.

§ 265.  **Depositing money at place of payment.**—Where a note or other obligation is drawn payable at a bank, a deposit in the bank on the day fixed for payment, of the amount due on such obligation, does not constitute payment, but is a suffi-

---

70 Block v Smith, Peake's N. P C 89

[4] Lamb v Lathrop, 13 Wend. 95

[1] Iowa California, Oregon, Utah

[2] Ladd v. Mason, 10 Or. 308, Halloday v. Halloday, 13 Or 523, Holt v Brown, 63 Iowa 319, s c 19 N W Rep 235, Casody v. Bos-

let, 11 Iowa 242, Chielovich v. Knauss, 11 Pac 781

[3] Kuhn v Chicago, etc, Ry, 65 Iowa 528 s c 22 N W Rep 661

[4] Ladd v Mason, 10 Or 308; Halloday v. Halloday, 13 Or 523, Shugart v Patter, 37 Iowa 422, Hayms v Bamberger, 36 Pac. Rep (Utah) 202; McCourt v. Johns, 53 Pac Rep (Or) 601.

cient tender to bar subsequent interest and costs.[1] The deposit must be special.[2] A general deposit, even to the credit of the payee, will not do, as that would substitute the credit of the bank for the money. It has been repeatedly held that having money in the bank, where the demand is made payable, sufficient to meet the obligation, is not a tender, but that the money must be in some way set apart and appropriated for the purpose of paying the obligation.[3]

Where the note is not left at the bank where it is made payable, and a deposit is made there, the bank does not become the agent of the holder of the note, but a bailee of the sum for the payor, with authority to deliver the money to the payee when he calls for it. Where a note was made payable at the counting room of a third person, the placing of funds in the hands of such third person for the purpose of paying the note, with authority given to pay the note when due from those funds, and the readiness of such third person, to make payment if the payee had attended to receive payment, it was held to constitute a good tender.[4] In this case the third person must continue ready. Here, as well as those cases where a special deposit of the money necessary to meet the obligation is made in the bank where it is payable, it is being ready with the money at the place of payment and not the deposit, which constitutes the tender. The deposit is only one way of keeping the tender good. The payor after being ready with the money at the time and place, is at liberty to make a special deposit elsewhere, or he may keep the money for the payee in his safe or some other place.

§ 266. **Making a tender by letter.**—A tender may be made by letter through the post. But money sent in that way is at the risk of the sender. Such an offer of payment does not become effectual as a tender until it actually reaches the debtor's hand, or the hand of some one authorized to receive the money. It will not avail a debtor that the money was mailed to the creditor prior to the time fixed for payment, if it does not in fact reach the creditor until after the time

---

[1] Hill v. Place, 5 Abb Pr N S 18; Wallace v McConnell, 13 Pet 136, Miller v Bank of New Orleans, 5 Wharton 503 s. c 34 Am Dec 571

[2] See Riley v Cheesman 77 N Y S 453, 75 Hun 387

[3] Myers v Byington, 34 Io 205

[4] Carley v Vance 17 Mass 389

has passed.[1]  If the money is not at hand within the time limited for payment, the creditor may bring his action, declare a forfeiture, or claim whatever right a failure to make payment on the day may give him.  The case is not different from that where a debtor sends a messenger who arrives too late   Where a creditor has sent a letter demanding a remittance by return mail, he cannot complain that the remittance is in the form of a money order or draft, for that is the way a prudent man would make a remittance   But a personal check would not be good, unless he was requested to remit by check   If a tender is made in the form of a check in a letter, and no objection is made to the medium but only to the quantum of the tender, it is good if actually sufficient in amount.[2]  Where, in answer to a letter demanding payment, the debtor sent a money order in which the creditor was described by the wrong name, the tender was held bad, even though the creditor was informed at the post office that he might have the money at any time by his signing it in the name of the payee

§ 267. **Tender in absence of the creditor.**—Where the time and place of payment of money or the delivery of any article is fixed by the contract, a tender then and there is good, although no person is there to receive the article   Where a note is payable at a certain time and place, a failure on the part of the payee to demand payment at the place does not excuse the payor from providing for payment at the time specified[1]  A tender is effected by setting apart the amount of the note for payment on a presentation[2]  In making a tender in the absence of the payee or vendee, the tenderor must fulfil his contract strictly, as nothing is waived in reference to the contract by the tenderee unless he be present

If specific articles are to be delivered, the things to be delivered in discharge of the contract must be separated and set apart so as to pass the title with as much care as where

---

[1] See Paine v. Bounton 82 N. W. Rep (Mich) 816

[2] Jones v. Arthur, 8 D P C 442 4 Jur 859 B C  See Lampasas Hotel, etc., v. Home Ins Co, 43 S W Rep (Tex) 1081

[3] Gordon v. Strange 1 Ex 477

[1] Myers v. Byington, 34 Iowa 205, New Hope D B Co., v. Perin, 11 Ill 467

[2] Schmidt v. Hoffman, 18 Misc (N Y) 225

the person who is to receive them is present and is about to take them into his actual possession. It has been said that where a person designedly absents himself from home for the fraudulent purpose of avoiding a tender, he will not be permitted to set up as a defence to an action, that no tender was made. In that case the court said: "The law does not allow a party to defeat another's right by fraud."[3] So, it has been said that a tender was excused, where a person bound to deliver a deed makes inquiries at the residence of the vendee, and had with him the deed, even though the absence was not for the purpose of evading the tender.[4] But the doctrine is not correctly stated. A tender must be made. Absence from the place designedly or unavoidably, only dispenses with the formalities of a tender. The doctrine is clearly stated in another case to the effect, that where one is bound to deliver a deed on a day certain, and at the day was ready with the deed, and would have tendered it, but for the evasion of the other party this is equivalent to a tender[5] In all such cases it is the being ready at the time and place which constitutes the tender. Producing the money and counting it down, or taking a deed from the pocket when there is no one at the place to receive it, would be a useless ceremony Such acts only as would be an idle ceremony are waived

§ 268. **How made when the creditor is absent from the state** — When the holder of a certificate issued on a mortgage or execution sale, is absent from the state and so continues up to the last day allowed by the statute in which to redeem, the debtor may, on that day, commence a suit in equity to

---

[3] Southworth v Smith, 7 Cush. 391

[4] Tasker v Bartlett, 5 Cush 359 See Johnson v Houlditch 1 Burr 578 when the court refused to allow the plaintiff any costs, on the defendant paying into court the amount due, although a technical right of action existed at the time the action was commenced, the plaintiff having kept out of the way to prevent a tender of the debt But here evidently the defendant was ready and willing and able to make the tender, and undoubtedly sought for the creditor at the proper time and place which would be in effect a tender

[5] Borden v Borden, 5 Mass 67 s c 4 Am Dec 32 See Mathis v Thomas 101 Ind 119 Hall v Whittier, 10 R I 530. Southworth v Smith 7 Cush 390 and Johnson v Houlditch, 1 Bur 578

redeem and make a tender in the complaint, and on that day deposit the money in court.[1] Subsequent encumbrancers, who have placed themselves in line for redemption by taking the necessary steps prescribed by statute, may, if the purchaser continues absent after the expiration of the time in which the debtor is allowed to redeem, make a tender in a like manner and pay the money into court. Such a course is not everywhere necessary. Most, if not all the states, have a statute which provides that the redemption money may be paid or tendered to the sheriff, clerk of court, or other officer as the case may require. A right of redemption, in such cases, being a statutory provision, must be strictly complied with by paying or tendering the money to the creditor or person authorized by law to receive it, or by bringing an action alleging the creditor's absence from the state, and paying the money into court, within the time limited for such redemption. The right being one of strict law, if the statute authorizing it be not complied with, nothing is acquired and the estate remains in the purchaser, and an absolute title to the property is vested in the purchaser merely by the afflux of the time limited by the statute.[2]

Where money is to be paid in discharge of a debt, or in fulfillment of a condition, or to prevent a forfeiture, and no place of performance is appointed, the general rule is that the one who is to pay must seek the creditor and make the tender to him, if he is to be found within the state. The courts sometimes relieve a debtor from the effects of a default in failing to make a tender to the creditor in person, but in order to be relieved from such default the debtor must show, in addition to being ready, able, and willing, that up to the last hour of the last day on which the business could be transacted, he sought diligently for the person who was to receive the money, but could not find him.[3] It is the debtor's duty to make inquiries for the creditor of those most likely to know his whereabouts.[4] Failing in this he will not be heard to say that it was impossible to make a tender to

[1] Trimble v Williamson, 49 Ala 525, Gardner v Black, 12 So Rep (Ala) 813 See Beatty v Brown 101 Ala 695

[2] Farnsworth v Howard, 1 Caldw 215

[3] See Southworth v Smith 7 Cush 390, Howard v Holbrook, 9 Bosw 237.

[4] Bancroft v Sawin, 9 N. E. Rep (Mass) 539 See Samuel v. Allen, 33 Pac. Rep 275.

the creditor in person. In such a case where a bill to redeem
from a foreclosure sale, disclosed that there were persons liv
ing in the same town with the debtor, who knew where the
mortgagee resided, the court said that the debtor should have
made inquiries of them, that "there was a duty resting upon
these persons to impart the information to him, and the
presumption is that they would have done so."[5]

If a vendee is a nonresident, a tender of a deed, provided
for in a contract of sale of the land, may be made by executing
and filing it with a bill for specific performance.[6] So, if the
vendor is a nonresident, the vendee may file a bill for the
specific performance and make a tender of the money in the
bill. In the latter case, although he is not required to pay
the money into court except in compliance with a decree, yet
the vendee must be ready, able, and willing to perform at the
time of commencing his suit, and in such cases, a tender
being a continuous thing, he must continue so up to the
time of paying the money into court in compliance with the
decree

§ 269. How made when redeeming from a mortgage or execution sale—Documents to be produced.—The method of redeem
ing land sold on an execution sale or mortgage foreclosure
sale, by the mortgagor or a subsequent encumbrancer, in the
several states is regulated by statute, and the statute must
be strictly complied with[1] If a junior lien holder desires to
redeem land sold on a mortgage or execution sale, in some of
the states, if not all, he must, prior to the expiration of the
time allowed the mortgagor or the debtor to redeem, file a
notice of his intention of redeeming, if from a mortgage sale,
with the register of deeds of the county where the land is
located, and if from an execution sale, with the clerk of
the court of the same county. Having done this the lien
holder is in line for redemption If the debtor or mortgagor
fails to redeem within the time limited by the statute,
the senior subsequent encumbrancer, if he desires to redeem,
must, within five days or such other time as the statute may
prescribe, after the debtor's or mortgagor's time to redeem

---

[5] Lehman v Moore, 9 So Rep
(Ala ) 500

[6] Watson v Sawyers, 54 Miss
64

[1] Prescott v Everts, 4 Wis 329

has elapsed, at the time he tenders the money, produce and exhibit to the sheriff or other officer authorized by law to receive the money and issue a certificate, or to the holder of the certificate of sale, for his inspection, a certified copy of the docket of the judgment, or the mortgage, or of the records or files evidencing the lien under which he claims a right to redeem, together with an affidavit of the amount of his claim. If the redemptioner is the holder of a third or later lien, then he must, within the time allowed him to redeem after his immediate prior encumbrancer's time has elapsed, at the time of his tender, produce such documents for the inspection of the next prior encumbrancer who has redeemed A purchaser at the sale, or subsequent redemptioner, is not bound to receive the money from one who does not comply with the statute. A complaint which does not contain an allegation that the plaintiff, in attempting to redeem, produced to the sheriff a certified copy of his mortgage and an affidavit showing the amount actually due, does not state a cause of action.[2] It has been held, where the statute required certified copies to be produced that the production of the original instrument evidencing his lien, with the certificate of record thereon, was a sufficient compliance with the statute[3] If the mortgagor or owner desires to redeem, the statutes in almost every state require such person to produce a certified copy of the deed of conveyance, or other instrument, or record evidencing his title, but here also, the production of the original instrument or original record, has been held to be compliance with a statute requiring certified copies[4] A mortgagor or owner need not produce all the deeds constituting his chain of title.[5]

§ 270　Same subject — Waiver of the production of documents — If a subsequent encumbrancer who is seeking to redeem goes to the sheriff or other officer authorized to receive the money, he must tender to the officer an affidavit stating the amount of his lien as is required by the statute, or the attempted redemption will be invalid The officer is in no sense the agent of the holder of the certificate of sale and

<hr/>

[2] Dunn v Dewey, 77 N W Rep (Minn) 793

[3] Tincom v Lewis 21 Minn 132

[4] Sandeson v Menage, 41 Minn. 314 s c 43 N W. Rep 66.

[5] Nopson v Horton, 20 Minn

cannot waive anything.[1] The original or any subsequent purchaser may dispense with the performance of any of the conditions which the statute has made for his benefit.[2] He may part with his interest in the land on such terms as he may deem proper. In a case where it was held that a purchaser, by accepting the money of a subsequent lien holder without objection, waived the necessity of producing an affidavit, the court observed: "If another creditor had afterwards attempted to purchase, it may be that the want of the affidavit would have been fatal to the plaintiff; for without an affidavit of the amount due on their judgment the creditor would not know how much money he must pay to acquire the right of the prior purchaser, and it would probably be sufficient for him to tender a nominal sum beyond the original purchase money and interest."[3]

§ 271. **Tender on executory contracts where mutual and concurrent acts are to be done.**—The same strictness as to the manner of making a tender, where the acts to be done by the parties are mutual and concurrent, does not obtain as in the case of a tender of a sum of money in payment of a debt. The authorities abound in the expression that an offer of performance is equivalent to performance, and when refused is an answer to a claim for damages[1]. And, where the expression is used in those cases where the contract under consideration is executory on both sides and the acts to be performed are mutual and concurrent, it is literally correct, if it be understood that an offer of performance implies the immediate existing ability to then and there follow up the verbal offer by a manual delivery of the thing offered. The rule applicable to such cases is clearly stated by Chief Justice Storrs, thus "Some misapprehension or confusion appears to have arisen from the mode of expression used in the books in treating of the necessity of a tender or offer by the parties, as

---

[1] Tincom v Lewis, 21 Minn. 132 See Bank of Vergennes v. Warren, 7 Hill 91; The People v. Livingston, 6 Wend. 526; The People v Covill, 18 Wend 598; The People v The Sheriff of Brown, 19 Wend 87; Waller v. Harris, 20 Wend 555, The People v Baker, 20 Wend 602.

[2] See Todd v Johnson, 50 Minn. 310, s. c 52 N W Rep 864

[3] The Bank of Vergennes v Warren, 7 Hill 91.

[1] Commission of Kensington v. Wood, 10 Pa St 93, Green v. Borough of Reading, 4 Watts 382; The Mayor v. Randolph, 4 Watts & S. 516

applicable to the case of mutual and concurrent promises. The word 'tender,' as used in such a connection, does not mean the same kind of offer as when it is used with reference to the payment or offer to pay an ordinary debt due in money, where the money is offered to the creditor who is entitled to receive it and nothing further remains to be done, but the transaction is completed and ended, but it only means readiness and willingness, accompanied with an ability, on the part of the parties, to do the act which the agreement requires him to perform, provided the other will concurrently do the thing which he is required by it to do, and a notice by the former to the latter of such readiness. Such readiness, ability, and notice, are sufficient evidence of, and indeed constitute and imply an offer or tender in the sense in which those terms are used in reference to the kind of agreements which we are now considering."[2] Such an offer being once made at the appointed time and place, no further offer is required until the other party manifests a willingness to comply with his obligation and demands the money,[3] or other thing to be delivered.

The same rule applies to all contracts where there are mutual and concurrent acts to be done, whether the subject-matter be realty or personal property. If a vendor is to deliver a deed and the vendee is to pay the purchase price simultaneously, a strict tender of a deed need not be made by the vendor if, on an offer to perform, he being ready with the deed, the other party declines to pay the money. So, the vendee by being ready with the money, need not produce and make a manual offer of it, if on the verbal offer, the vendor declines to convey.[4] The vendee is not required to part with his money until he has assurances that the vendor will hand over the deed; nor is the deed required to be delivered until the money is forthcoming simultaneously. An offer by either party, made in good faith and accompanied by the requisite ability to immediately comply with the offer, will, if refused, entitle the willing party to bring a suit to enforce specific performance, or an action to recover damages for the breach of the contract. And, on the other hand, such refusal will defeat an action for damages brought by the other party. So,

[2] Smith v Lewis, 26 Conn. 110; s p Hanson v Slavin, 33 Pac Rep (Cal) 266, Hampton v. Speckenagle, 9 S & R 212

[3] Washburn v Dewey, 17 Vt. 92

[4] Cook v Doggett, 2 Allen 439

in such contracts for the sale and delivery of personal property, neither party is obliged to part with his property or to make a formal unconditional tender of it, if, on an offer by one party to perform, the other refuses to pay the purchase price or to deliver the specific property as the case may be.[5] However, if the vendor cares to risk the solvency of the vendee, he may make a strict tender of the thing contracted to be delivered, and bring an action to recover the purchase price. If he elects to recover the purchase price, he must observe all the rules applicable to a tender of property in payment of a note, by delivering the property at the time and place agreed, and then and there setting it apart and designating it so as to pass the title. It has been held that where a purchaser fails to perform, or repudiates the contract, and the possession and title remains in the seller, the law requires him to treat it as his own and sue, if at all, for the damages he has sustained.[6] If the property had been, at the time of making the contract or previous to the day fixed for payment, selected so that nothing remained to be done, but the delivery and payment, the vendee may make a tender of the money and pursue and recover the property by an appropriated action.

§ 272. **Tender of specific articles—Separation and designation —Title.**—Where a note is payable in specific articles, or a contract is for the delivery of specific articles and there is no concurrent act to be performed by the obligee, and the obligor has but to deliver the articles to discharge himself of the obligation, the doctrine is firmly settled that the party who is to deliver them, must, at the time specified, have the articles at the place designated for delivery, and he must, at or before the time for delivery, designate the property so as to vest the absolute title to the property in the payee or vendee.[1]

5 See McEldon v. Patton, 93 N. W. Rep. (Neb.) 938, which seems to be to the contrary.

6 McCormick Harvesting Machine Co. v. Balfany, 81 N. W. Rep. (Minn.) 10

1 Schrader v. Walfin, 21 Ind. 238; McJilton v. Smizer, 18 Mo. 111; Bates v. Churchill, 32 Me.

31; Hughes v. Eschbooch 7 D. C. 66. A contrary rule was announced in Alabama in an early case, where the obligation was to pay "$60, in shucks" on a certain day. The payee demanded the shucks at the residence of the payor, who at the time had only a portion of the amount neces-

**If designated, by setting them apart before the day, they must continue ready and separate thereafter. If they become**

sary, stripped from the corn, which he offered to the payee, declaring that the residue would be ready as fast as they could be taken away. The payee insisted on having all delivered at one time at a point designated by him within a few feet of the payor's corn crib and within fifty rods of a house containing a large quantity of cotton seed and fodder. Assumpsit was brought to recover the amount of the note in money. It was held that the readiness of the defendant to perform his contract and to deliver the shucks whenever the plaintiff would remove them, was a good defence to the action. The court thought that it might have been inconvenient to the defendant and hazardous to the safety of his property by depositing the shucks at the place designated. An observation that was prompted undoubtedly, by the remark made by the plaintiff, that he wanted them at the place to burn, sell or do whatever he thought proper with them. Armstrong v Tait, 8 Ala 635. Here the court failed to distinguish between a willingness to perform and a readiness. This case seems to have been once at least cited with approval. The court there said "The rule laid down by the [trial] court as to separating and setting apart the property to be delivered in payment has been thought to be subject to some qualification arising from the particular kind of property. If it be such as not to be susceptible of designation or distinction from the other property of the same kind, or

would be liable to almost inevitable destruction from so separating it and setting it apart, or if so doing be dangerous and inconvenient to the defendant these considerations are supposed to form an exception to the general rule." Hughes v Prewitt 5 Tex 264. In this case corn was to be delivered "as wanted" a case where a vendor has a reasonable time to comply with a demand. An entirely different case from one where a note is payable at a stated time and place in specific articles. So, it has been held that where a machine was to be delivered at a designated place to the care of a certain person, a delivery of a machine of the kind contracted for at the place and to the person designated, together with a number of machines of a like pattern, was a sufficient tender, although the particular machine purchased was not tagged or marked with the owner's name. Ganson v Madigan 9 Wis 138. In the case here referred to, the appellate court in considering the instruction by the lower court to the jury, that the plaintiff was bound to show that one of the machines had been set apart for the defendant and marked with his name prior to the date of delivery—said "This strictness of proof might be required if the case turned upon the point whether title to any specific reaper actually passed to defendant. If one of them had been levied on as his, or if they had been destroyed, and the question was who was to bear the loss, it might be material to in-mingled with the other property of a like kind before the day for delivery arrives, they must be on that day again set

quire whether any one had actually been set apart and designated as the machine of the defendant, so as to pass the title." But the question is whether the plaintiff complied with the order by delivering to the person designated, a reaper of the kind designated. It appeared from the evidence that the defendant called at the place after the date fixed and was shown the reapers, but insisted on being shown one with his name on it, that he would not select one nor allow the agent to do so. The court thought that to allow a party having so ordered a reaper to refuse to take it, because among a number answering the description no particular one had his name marked on it, was too great refinement upon the technicality to be established as a practical business rule. But the mere fact that the buyer would not allow a reaper to be selected for him, does not make the case different from those cases where a buyer repudiates the contract, in which class of cases it is the universal rule that before the seller can maintain an action for the purchaser price, he must designate the property so that the title will pass. The supreme court of Pennsylvania has said that a distinction is made between those cases where the act of separation is burdensome and expensive or involves selection, and those cases where the articles are uniform in bulk and the act of separation throws no additional burden on the buyer. The case in which this statement was made was where a defendant

had ordered the plaintiffs, who were commissioned merchants, to purchase 400 hectolitres of nuts. The plaintiffs transmitted their order to their correspondent at Para, Brazil, who, to obtain the quantity ordered, were obliged to purchase two lots aggregating 582 hectolitres, which were mixed together and shipped in bulk according to the usual course of trade. Plaintiff invoiced to the defendant the quantity covered by the order. Here, the court said the duty of measuring the nuts and their removal from the vessel was upon the defendant and the nuts being of uniform quality selection was of no consequence. That the title to 400/582 of the entire bulk when delivered on board the ships, passed to defendants, and that in New York, a tender of 582 hectolitres, from which the defendant was invited to take his share, was good. Brownfield v. Johnson, 128 Pa. St. 254. The court referred to its decision in a former case where 5,000 barrels of oil was to be delivered at a certain time and place. Defendant offered the 5,000 barrels in 118 bulk cars containing 5,891 barrels and it was held that the plaintiff was not bound to set aside the precise quantity named in the contract before offering to deliver the oil. Lockhart v. Bonsall, 77 Pa. St. 53. Here, the defendant was bound to pump the oil from the cars into the tanks which were designated as the place of delivery. The points upon which the court in both of the cases seem to lay particular

apart. The promisor must perform his contract as far as it lies in his power to do. Proof that he was able at the time is no evidence of an intention to deliver the thing; nor, is proof that he had previous to the day, made preparation to fulfil the contract, any evidence of intention to deliver the property on the day specified. There must be such a complete designation of the particular thing, by pointing it out to the promisee, or by setting it aside or tagging it, that the prom isee may be able to pursue and recover the property itself - Proof that a demand was not made upon the promisor for the property to be delivered, does not constitute a tender, nor an excuse for not making one, where the promisor can discharge himself of his obligation without any concurrent act on the part of the promisee.[3] In all such cases where the time for delivery is fixed, the vendor or debtor becomes the first actor and must tender the article to save himself from becoming in default. Where the obligation is to be paid in services, the same principle applies, and the promisor is bound to tender the services on the day fixed by the agreement, independent of any request or demand on the part of the creditor.[4] Where a plaintiff in replevin must return the goods, an offer to do so, unaccompanied by a tender, is no defence to an action upon

---

stress, are that it was the duty of the defendant to remove the property from the vessel or car after its arrival at the place of delivery and that the separation put no additional burden on the purchaser But these cases are hard to distinguish from those cases where a certain quantity of brick lumber, hay or grain is to be delivered where it is not sufficient to have at the appointed time and place, a larger quantity than that named in the contract, without setting apart the required amount intended to apply on the contract The obligee may be bound to remove the goods in these cases The Pennsylvania cases are not analogous to those cases where a large quantity of wheat or other commodity is to

be delivered and no place for delivery is specifically provided for. In such cases it is the implied understanding of the parties that warehouse receipts of a solvent warehouseman, will be tendered, and that the warehouseman who ever he may be has the wheat or other commodity mingled with articles of like quality belonging to other persons The foregoing cases are in conflict with the weight of the authority and the facts not so different as to establish an exception to the strict rule announced in the text — McConnell v Hall, Brayt (Vt) 223

[3] Mitchell v Gregory, 1 Bibb 449 See Thaxton v Edwards, 1 Stew R (Ala) 524

[4] Deel v Berry 21 Tex 463

the bond, even though the sheriff declared he would not accept them.[5]

§ 273. **Having more than enough articles at place of delivery —Articles of promisor's manufacture—Pointing out the articles —Absence of vendee.**—Where the article to be delivered is lumber, brick, wood or other like articles, it is not enough that the promisor had more than enough of the particular commodity at the place to pay the note, and was ready and willing to deliver the quantity promised.[1] If the property to be delivered by the promisor, is an article of his manufacture, having it ready within the time limited for delivery, and set out in his shop, where it is the custom and usage of the particular trade for the purchaser to call at the place of manufacture and there receive the article bargained for, is a good tender[2] If the articles are ready for delivery, and the vendee, not being ready to receive them, requests that they be kept for him until he is ready, no further tender is necessary.[3] Where a contract for the delivery of specific property is indefinite, or is drawn in the usual way, custom and usage of the particular business may be proven to determine whether a proper tender has been made[4] If the articles are at the time at the place, mingled with a number of other articles of a like kind, and are capable of being designated by pointing them out, or by describing them by number, color or otherwise, as in the case of the machinery, implements, articles of furniture, and the like, the tender may be made in that way, if the tenderee be present But if the tenderee be not present and there are other things at the same place of a like kind, those intended for delivery should be tagged or otherwise marked with the owner's name so as to enable the tenderee to select out of the entire lot the particular articles belonging to him; or they should be selected and set out and apart from the other things there of a like kind

[5] Schrader v Wolflin, 21 Ind 238

[1] Wyman v Winslow, 11 Me 398, Coffin v Reynolds, 21 Minn 456; Banes v Graham, 4 Cow 152; Smith v. Loomis, 7 Conn. 110; Wilt v Ogden, 13 John 56

See Robinson v Batchelder, 4 N H 40

[2] Downer v Sinclair, 15 Vt 495

[3] Wheelcock v Tanner, 39 N Y 481.

[4] Clark v Baker, 11 Met 186

**§ 274. Live Stock—Articles sold in bulk.**—Where the thing to be delivered is live stock, the animals intended to be delivered upon the contract should be put into an inclosure, separate from other animals of a like kind, if practicable. But if the tenderor has but one lot or pasture, or it is not convenient to keep them for the tenderee in an inclosure, separate from other animals owned by him, he may make at the time fixed for delivery, in absence of the vendee, a temporary separation for the purpose of identification,[1] so, that when the tenderee calls for them, he may point out to him the exact animals; or he may execute a writing, describing them by color, sex or otherwise, if they are capable of being thus distinguished from other animals there, and have it ready for the tenderee or his agent as a guide for their action in selecting their animals. If the vendee be present at the time appointed for delivery, the vendor must then and there separate the animals to be delivered from other animals there, so that the vendee may remove his animals without the trouble attending a separation

When a person obligates himself to pay at a certain time and place, a given quantity of grain, hay or other commodity which is sold in bulk, he is bound to set apart such a quantity of grain, hay or other commodity as will be sufficient to pay the debt, so the creditor may know what part of the quantity in the warehouse he is to receive.[2] It is not necessary that the grain or hay "should be weighed and specially turned out " The quantity may be otherwise ascertained, at the risk of the person making the payment, and no turning out or change of position is necessary, further than to separate or set it apart so that it may be identified and removed by the owner[3]

**§ 275 Goods sold upon credit—Absence of promisee or vendee no excuse.**—If a vendor sells goods on credit, he must, at the

---

[1] See Bates v Bates Walker, 101, 4 c 12 Am Dec 572, where the note was for the payment of ten cows and calves Driving eleven cows and calves into a lot without making any separation of the ten, was held not a tender though the debtor stated that he was ready to pay the note

[2] Veazy v Harmony, 7 Me 91; Newton v Galbraith, 5 Johns 119, Bates v Churchill, 32 Me 31.

[3] Leballester v Nash, 24 Me 316

time and place fixed for delivery, set apart or otherwise designate for the vendee the articles so purchased. Unless this be done the vendor is in default. The same strictness as to the manner of making a tender obtains in such case, as where specific articles are tendered in payment of a note. If the vendee, before the time for delivery arrives, becomes insolvent, the vendor may rescind the contract and retain the goods.

Where the contract is for the delivery of specific articles at a certain time and place, they may be delivered there in the absence of the person who is to receive them, as well as if he was present, and in an action to recover the purchase price, it is in no defence on the part of the promisee that he was not there to receive them. The promisee is aware of the time and place fixed for delivery and he cannot evade his contract by being absent from the place on that day.[1] Nor is it any excuse on the part of the promisor that the promisee was not there to receive the property. It is not always convenient or even possible for a person who has contracted to receive goods at a particular time and place to be present to receive them. Sending an agent to represent him may be as impracticable or as much an impossibility as to be present in person, but accidents are sometimes indistinguishable from events encompassed through design, so, the law, to preserve uniformity and certainty, does not permit, in such transactions, the misfortune or carelessness of one to vary the contract so as to increase the burden or duties of the other. Rigid rules are on the whole better than uncertain ones. By requiring a promisor, by an unvarying rule, to bring forward at the time and place, the property to be delivered and designate it, is requiring of him, in the absence of the promisee, no greater burden or duty than he had contracted to do should the latter be present. By thus making the tender, he not only has done all in his power to perform his agreement, but by placing it within the power of the promisee to reduce the property to an actual possession by coming to the place at a subsequent time, he has not increased the burden of the latter. So, by permitting the promisor to fulfil his engagement in the absence of the other party, he is freed from the necessity of finding another buyer

---

[1] Barton v. McKelway, 22 N. J. L. 165.

and escapes the risk of loss through deterioration or destruction of the property not occurring through his fault. The rule is not different, in such cases, if the promisee be present at the time fixed for payment and declares he will not accept the articles. When there is no condition precedent, or concurrent act to be performed by the promisee, and the promisor has but to deliver the property in order to fulfil his contract, it is obligatory on his part to set apart for the promisee the quantity of the kind of commodity required to satisfy the note or other demand. Failing in this the promisee may recover the consideration paid. So, where there are conditions precedent, or concurrent acts to be performed by a purchaser, and he refuses to accept the goods, before the seller can maintain an action for the purchase price there must be such a delivery actual or constructive, as will pass the title and vest the ownership of the property in the purchaser.[2]

§ 276. **Symbolical delivery—Warehouse receipts—Seeing the property—Unconditional control—Lien for storage—Bills of lading —Wharf warrants—Bills of sale.**—There may be a symbolical delivery of specific articles if they are ponderous and bulky, such as cannot be conveniently passed from hand to hand. In such a case the law only requires such acts as will place the property completely at the disposal of the vendee, and which are in accordance with the nature of the business. If the contract specifically provides for the delivery at a particular place, or from the nature of the thing to be delivered, or of the contract, the law implies that it is to be delivered at a particular place, the thing must be delivered there, however ponderous or bulky the article may be. But where articles of merchandise or other commodity is trafficked in in large quantities, and no place is fixed upon for the delivery of the property, a tender may be made of warehouse receipts for the same.[1] In a case which arose in Illinois, where 5,000 bushels of oats were to be delivered, the court put a case thus, "A party selling 50,000 bushels of wheat, or other grain,

---

[2] McCormick Harvesting Machine Co. v. Balfany, 81 N. W. Rep. (Minn.) 10

[1] Hayden v. Demets, 53 N. Y. 126, Stokes v. Recknagle, 38 N. Y. Super. Ct. 368, Dunham v. Patter, 4 E. D. Smith 500; Dustan v. McAndrew, 10 Bosw. 135

in a large parcel, cannot be expected to employ all the wagons and drays in the city, on which to transport the grain to the residence of the purchaser for the purpose of a tender. That kind of business is not transacted in that way."[2] The vendee, however, has a right to insist upon seeing the property, and may refuse to receive the warehouse receipts until the property is shown to him.

The vendee must have the legal unconditional control of the property. The control of the property must not be subject to the will of a third party, as where a permit is required from a third party, or the goods are subject to a lien for storage, unless the warehouse receipts are accompanied by a permit, or some provision is made that will enable the vendee to receive the goods unincumbered by the lien,[3] as where the vendor offers to allow the vendee to retain a sufficient amount of the purchase price to discharge the lien.[4] It will not aid a vendor, in making out a tender, to prove that the warehouseman would have waived the lien. A tender of bills of lading properly assigned, dock or wharf warrants, delivery orders, deeds, or bills of sale of personal property, when the property is incapable of immediate manual delivery will enable the seller to maintain an action for the purchase price, or defeat an action for their non delivery.[5]

§ 277. **Opportunity for inspection—Time to ascertain if notes are genuine—Examining deed—Records—Advice of counsel—Examining money—Right to have time to make inquiries.**—Where an offer is made of specific articles, either upon a contract wholly executory or on one where the consideration is executed, the tenderee must be given a reasonable opportunity to examine and count them and make computation. Taking the goods in his hand and opening the packages for the purpose of inspecting them to see what they are, is not a delivery and acceptance; nor is it a delivery and acceptance where the tenderee is allowed to take the goods into his possession, for that purpose, and does not keep them an unreasonable time.[1] A common carrier must give the consignee an oppor-

[2] McPherson v Gale, 40 Ill 368, 426, Stokes v Recknagle, 38 N
[3] Dunham v Patter, 4 E D Y Super Ct 368
Smith 500          [5] Benj on Sales § 928
[4] Hayden v Demets, 53 N Y.   [1] Lyons v Hill, 46 N H 49

tunity to make a reasonable examination. By so doing he will not render himself chargeable for the goods, unless they are sent C. O. D. and he allows the consignee to take possession and is unable to secure them again. If the goods to be delivered are in packages or boxes, the tenderee must be allowed to open the packages for the purpose of the examination. Park, J., said "A tender of goods does not mean a delivery or offer of packages containing them, but an offer of those packages, under such circumstances that the person who is to pay for the goods shall have an opportunity offered him, before he is called on to part with his money, of seeing that those present for his acceptance are in reality those for which he has bargained."[2] Where the agreement is to pay in notes of third persons, the tenderee, if he request it, must be allowed a reasonable time to ascertain if the notes are genuine. So, where a deed is offered, the tenderee may take time to examine it and the records and to take advice of counsel. When insulting language was used towards a creditor so that he suddenly left the office of the debtor, without counting or examining the money offered him, it was held that the offer of the money did not constitute a tender, and that the creditor should have been given sufficient time to enable him to ascertain whether the money was of such description as he would be willing to receive[3]

In general, where money or any thing is tendered, the tenderor, if a request is made by the tenderee for time to consider, must give him a reasonable time to look over his papers and make computations, to consult his lawyer, to make inquiries whether a suit has been commenced and costs incurred, or any other inquiry or examination pertaining to the tenderee's rights in connection with the transaction in which the tender is being made. The tenderee must have opportunity for intelligent action.[4]

[2] Isherwood v. Whitmore, 11 M & W 347

[3] Harris v Mulock, 9 How Pr. 402

[4] Root v Brodley, 19 Mich 27, s c 12 N. W Rep 896, Proctor v Robinson 35 Mich 284, Chase v Welch, 45 Mich 345, s c 7 N. W Rep 895, King v Finch, 60 Ind 420, Bakeman v Pooler, 15 Wend 639, Waldrom v Murphy, 40 Mich 668

§ 278.  Good faith.—A tender must be made in good faith.
It must be definite and certain in character,[1] unequivocal and
capable of being understood as bona fide.[2]  A tenderor is
bound to act in a straightforward way and distinctly and
fairly make known his purpose without mystery or ambigu
ity.[3]  In view of the serious consequences to a creditor, such
as the loss of security or subsequent accruing interest, re
sulting from a refusal of a tender; and the temptation to
contrive colorable and sham tenders, not intended in good
faith, the evidence must be so clear and satisfactory as to
leave no reasonable doubt that the tenderor intended at the
time to make full and unconditional payment.[1]  If it can be
proven that a person who made a tender afterwards said that
he did not intend to let the tenderee have the money or other
thing tendered if he had manifested a willingness to accept
it, the offer will not amount to a tender.[5]  So, a jury will be
justified in finding that a tender is not in good faith if the
tenderor afterward applies the property to a purpose inconsistent with its application to the payment of the debt, as
where he converts it to his own use.[6]  So, it is evidence that
a tender is not in good faith if a debtor does not give a
creditor an opportunity to accept, as by departing from the
place of payment while the creditor, sheriff or other officer
is making computation or examining his books or papers, or
taking advice of counsel, or withdraws from the place when
he sees the creditor approaching, or takes away the money
before the creditor could lay hold of it, or is in undue haste,
requiring the creditor to accept at once and refusing him
time to consider the matter, or comes with great bluster
and abuses and vilifies the creditor for the purpose of arous
ing his anger and creating a disturbance, or menaces and
threatens him, or makes the offer at a time and place where
the money or goods could not readily be received and ex
amined, weighed or counted.

[1] Eastland v Longshorn, 1 Nott
& M 191, Pulsifer v Shephard,
36 Ill 513

[2] Selby v Hurd 51 Mich 1, s c
16 N W. Rep 180

[3] See Proctor v Robinson, 35
Mich 284

[4] Potts v Plaisted, 30 Mich
119

[5] Fesh v Holden, 17 Tex 408

[6] McPherson v Wishwell, 16
Neb. 625 s c 21 N W Rep 391

§ 279. **In equity—In admiralty.**—The expression, that tenders are not regarded with the same strictness in equity as at law, is found in many decisions. But the expression has been most frequently used by the courts, in considering those cases where a tender affects only the question of costs, or cases where a tender was not absolutely necessary in the first instance,[1] as where the contract required mutual and concurrent acts to be done by the parties, where a mere offer of performance by either party, accompanied by the requisite ability, is a sufficient tender of the performance. But wherever the person alleging a tender was under the contract the first actor, and the tender and refusal is the basis of the cause of action or defence, the tenderor, whether the action is at law or in equity, must show that in making the tender he complied with all the formalities of a tender. Tenders are *stricti juris*, and nothing is presumed in their favor If a tender is not legal, a court of equity will not support it; nor supply a defect of a tender against a rule of law.[2] In reference to the plea, it has been said, that if a party pretends to avail himself of the plea of tender in equity, because he could not make it at law, he ought to be held to as great strictness as he would be held at law.[3] The tenderee by doing some act, or by failing to specify his grounds of objection, may waive some of the formalities of a tender, but whatever act or omission on the part of a tenderee will be considered in equity as having dispensed with any of the formalities of a tender, is equally available for the same purpose when the tender is considered at law. The doctrine, however, of courts of admiralty, as to the manner of making tenders, is less stringent "Any real offer to pay by one then

---

[1] Where fraud is the grounds on which it is sought to rescind a contract, or to set aside a settlement, or a sheriff's sale and the like It is ordinarily sufficient if a tender is made in the pleadings Tarkington v Purris, 25 N E Rep (Ind) 879, Berry v American Cent Ins Co, 132 N Y 49, s c 30 N E 254, Weaver v Nugient 72 Tex 272, Clarke v Drake, 63 Mo 354; Whelan v Reilly 61 Mo 565, Kinney v

Kleinin 49 N Y 164 See Town of Springport v Teutonia Sav Bank, 84 N Y 403, and Castle v Castle, 78 Mich 298, s c 44 N W Rep 378

[2] Gammon v Stone, 1 Ves 337; Shotwell v Denman, 1 N J L 174, Arrowsmith v Van Harlingen, Cove 26. See Shields v Lozear, 22 N J Eq 447

[3] Taylor v Reed, 5 T B Monroe 36

ready and willing to pay is treated as a valid tender, without enquiry whether the money was produced or not, or in what form."[4] But the offer must be without condition, and should be renewed in the answer or distinctly made upon the record at some time during the progress of the litigation.[5]

§ 280. **Offering everything necessary to complete the transaction—Complying with statutory requirements—Documents requiring endorsements.**—A person making a tender must do and offer every thing that is necessary to complete the transaction. Thus under an agreement to sell an interest in a partnership, a tender of a bill of sale is not sufficient without a deed conveying all the retiring partner's interest in the real estate held by the firm.[1] If land is to be conveyed, the deed tendered must include all the land.[2] So, any statutory provision must be complied with. If a tender is made after suit brought and the statute requires the money to be brought into court, and notice of such deposit given, a failure to give such notice will render the tender invalid;[3] and a failure to return an answer containing other defences is not a waiver of the want of such notice. Where the thing to be delivered are certificates of stock which are transferred by indorsement and not upon the books of the company, in tendering such certificates they must be indorsed.[4]

[4] 2 Pars Shipp and Admr. 484
[5] Boulton v. Moore, 14 Fed Rep 922 See Dedeham v Vose, 3 Blatchf 44.
[1] Plath v Kitzmuller, 52 Cal 491

Jounce v Studley, 81 Me 431 18 Atl Rep 288
[3] Wilson v Doran, 17 N E Rep (N. Y) 688
[4] Hill v. Wilson, 88 Cal 92, & c 25 P 1105 See Munn v Barnum 24 Barb 283.

# CHAPTER VI.

## TIME AND PLACE OF MAKING A TENDER

### I TIME.

## II PLACE

## I. TIME.

§ 281. **The time when a tender may be made—At common law—Modification of the rule.**—At common law a tender of money which a party is bound to pay at a certain time and place must be made on the day fixed for payment,[1] and a tender cannot be made at any subsequent time so that it will defeat the cause of action.[2] Where a party, bound to pay at

[1] Hume v. Peploe, 8 East. 168; Doble v Larkin, 10 Exch. 776; Pool v Tunbridge, 2 M & W. 223; Poole v Crompton, 5 D. P C 168 In the last case the court was of the opinion that if the acceptor of a bill went to the house of the payee and could not find him, but afterwards tendered him the money, it would be unjust to say that the acceptor is liable to an action, and is not to be allowed to plead that tender But here the court overlooked the fact that if the acceptor went to the place of payment ready to pay but did not by reason of the payer's absence that this alone constituted the tender and should have been pleaded, and not a renewal or subsequent offer Dewey v Humphrey, 5 Pick 187 Maynard v Hunt 5 Pick 240, Wilder v Seelye, 8 Barb 108, City Bank v Cutter, 3 Pick 414, Tracy v. Strong, 2 Conn. 659, Powers v Powers, 11 Vt 262, Downman v Downman, 1 Wash 29 Under the old English practice, where the debt or duty was not discharged by a tender and refusal, the tenderor was required to plead the tender with *uncore prist* (that he has been since the tender and still is ready) together with *tout temps prist* (that he has been always ready). "In strictness a plea of tender is applicable only to cases where the party pleading it has never been guilty of any breach of his con-

tract." See 9 Bac Abr. Tlt. Tender II. See also 1 Chit. G. Pr. 508, 1 Sand Rep 336, N. 2 and 33 C N. P last ed 1 Seld. N. P 110, 2 Cow Ti 810; Haldenby v Tuke, Willes 632, cited in Wilder v. Seelye, 8 Barb. 108.

[2] Poole v Trumbridge, 2 M. & W 223, Hume v. Peploe, 8 East. 168, Whitlock v Squire, 10 Mod. 81, Dixson v Clark, 5 C B 365, Cotton v Godwin, 7 M & W 147, Suffolk v. Bank of Worcester, 5 Pick 106. The reason upon which the rule mentioned in the text was founded, was that after a default damages accrued, and the demand became either wholly or partially unliquidated, requiring judicial inquiry to determine the amount due In ordinary contracts for the payment of specific amount of money, the damages are merely the interest accruing after the default. And prior to the adoption of those statutes fixing what is termed the legal rate of interest, the rate of interest sometimes changed, thus making it necessary in case of default, to have the rate determined by a court or jury The courts early adopted the practice of ascertaining the rate, and referring it to the clerk or officer to make computation instead of sending it to the jury. See Hume v. Peploe, 8 East 168, Lord Ellenborough C J But in those commonwealths where a rate of interest, in case none be agreed upon, is fixed by

a certain time, neglects or fails, for any reason, to make payment at the time, the only course open to him, if the other party will not accept after the time, when sued, is to pay the money, together with interest and accrued costs, into court under the common rule.[3] In a proper case he may bring a suit in equity, make a tender in the bill of the amount due and interest, and pay the money into cor

The common law rule, that a tender cannot be made after a default, has been changed in some states by statute,[4] or by the decisions of the court of last resort.[5] In case of money demands where the amount is liquidated, or capable of being made so by mere computation, and the damages are merely the interest, the rule that a tender may be made after a default is now almost if not wholly universal And where such a rule obtains, a tender of the amount due, with interest to date, may be made at any time before suit, except in cases where time is of the essence of the contract, and the circumstances will not warrant a court of equity in relieving the party from the consequences of his default

§ 282. Tender after a default in a contract of sale—After date fixed for entry by lessee—On premium note before loss—Fare while being expelled—After a distress —A tender made by a vendee three months after the time for performance had expired, was held good, where time was not of the essence of the contract, and the vendor held the notes given for the purchase money, and gave no notice, actual or constructive, of his intention to claim the contract as abandoned, and there was no change in the circumstance of the parties[1] But a party cannot unreasonably delay performance. What would be a reasonable time depends upon the facts in each case A tender when made within a reasonable time, will be upheld only when it appears that damages have not accrued, and the moving party is not guilty of intentionally delaying performance. A party will not be permitted to trifle with the other party by delaying performance of his contract in hope

---

statute, the damages in ordinary money demands for the payment of a specific sum, are capable of being liquidated by mere computation In such cases the reason supporting the common law rule fails, and consequently the rule itself

[3] See Hume v. Peploe, 8 East 168

[4] Suffolk Bank v Worchester Bank 5 Pick 105

[5] See Tracy v. Strong, 2 Conn 659

[1] Young v Daniels, 2 Io 126

of gaining some advantage by ultimately repudiating it, or coming forward to perform as he may deem it to be to his interest.

Where the agreement was to let certain premises for a year from a certain date and the lessee to take certain fixtures at a certain valuation on entry, it was held that the lessee had a continuing right of entry, and a tender in payment of the fixture on an entry at a date subsequent to the commencement of the time was held not to be too late[2] Where an insurance policy contains a provision that the company shall not be liable for a loss occurring while a premium note is overdue and unpaid, a tender made on an overdue note, but before the loss occurred, was held good, the policy not providing for a forfeiture in case of nonpayment at maturity.[3] A tender or offer of the fare, while being ejected from a train for a refusal to pay, has been held not to render a continuance of the expulsion torteous[4] In case of a distress for damage feasant, the owner may tender amends until the animals are impounded, after that they are in the custody of the law and a tender comes too late.[5] It has been said that a "tender upon the land before the distress, makes the distress torteous, tender after distress, and before impounding, makes the detainer and not the taking wrongful; tender after impounding makes neither the one nor the other wrongful, for then it comes too late"[6]

§ 283. On promise to pay in chattels or money of fluctuating value—Stock subscriptions.—A promise to pay in chattels, or paper money of a fluctuating value, must be strictly complied with as to time. And a tender of the thing cannot be made before or after the day fixed for payment[1] A subscriber, who agrees with the promoters of a proposed corporation to pay a certain sum for stock on or before a certain day, is not bound to tender the money on or before the day if the corporation has not been organized Such organization is a condition precedent.[2]

[2] Edman v Allen, 6 Bing (N. C) 19.

[3] Continental Ins Co v Miller, 30 N E Rep (Ind App) 713

[4] Behr v Erie R Co, 74 N Y Supp. 1007.

[5] Pilkington's Case, 5 Co 152; 9 Bacons Abr. Tit. Tender (D)

[6] The Six Carpenters' Case, 8 Co. 132

[1] Powe's Admls v. Powe, 48 Ala. 113; Hoys v Tuttle, 8 Ark 124.

[2] Mainstee Lumber Co v Union National Bank, 32 N E Rep (Ill) 449.

**§ 284. Where mortgagee has declared the whole sum due— Tender before maturity of mortgage—Statute of limitation—Tender upon mortgage or in redemption after the debt is barred— Tender by junior lien holder.**—Where according to the terms of a mortgage, the principal sum becomes due and payable at once at the option of the mortgagee, if the interest is not paid at the time it falls due, a tender of the amount due as interest, after a default in the payment of such interest, is not a defence to any proceeding to recover the whole sum due.[1] After the mortgagee has exercised his option by declaring the whole sum due, he cannot retract so as to defeat a tender of the whole principal and interest in arrears.[2] A mortgagor cannot compel a satisfaction or reconveyance before the time fixed for payment, by tendering the full amount of the principal and interest then due [3]

Where there has been no foreclosure, and the mortgagee has been let into possession a tender may be made of the mortgage debt after it is due at any time before an entry, or ejectment is barred by the statute of limitation   Where time began to run against an ancestor, it will continue to run against infant heirs   So, if a mortgagee enters during the life time of a tenant for life, after the latter's death the time continues to run against the remainderman.  Infancy, absence from the state, acknowledgment of the mortgage, or whatever interrupts the running of the statute, will extend the time.  Devising money in case the mortgage should be redeemed, or commencing foreclosure, or keeping a private account of the profits, or conveying the land subject to the equity of redemption, or an acknowledgment of the mortgage as a redeemable interest in a letter to a friend, or a settlement between third parties recognizing the mortgage, or an assignment treating the estates subject to redemption, will interrupt the running of the statute of limitation [4]

In some states there are statutes limiting the time within

---

[1] Lantry v French, 33 Neb 524, s c 50 N W Rep 679

[2] Rice v Kahn, 70 Wis 323, s c 35 N W. Rep. 465

[3] Brown v. Cole, 9 Jur 290 See Sec 305, as to whether the principal and all the interest that would accrue to the due date can be tendered

[4] As to what will constitute a sufficient acknowledgment by the mortgagee to interrupt the running of the statute   See 7 Bac. Abr Title Mortgages, also cases cited by Boon on Mort § 162 N. 13

which a mortgage may be foreclosed. Where the period of limitation within which a mortgage may be foreclosed coincides with the period within which an action may be commenced to recover a legal estate in land, the courts have no difficulty either at law or equity in applying the period of limitation to the mortgage. But suppose the period barring a foreclosure is shorter than that barring an action to recover a legal estate, and a mortgagee is in possession after his remedy by foreclosure is gone. Can the mortgagor recover possession of his estate by writ of entry or ejectment, without tendering the amount of the mortgage debt? It would seem that a mortgagee who thus allowed his right to hold the mortgaged premises to lapse, must bear the consequence of his own laches and surrender the estate; although the books all declare that a mortgagee once in possession is entitled to hold possession until the mortgage debt is paid. Where the statute of limitation has not run against the mortgage, to save the estate a tender of the mortgage debt must be made, even though the statute has run against the debt. This is so whether the mortgagee is in possession or not.

The right of a junior mortgagee or any subsequent lien holder, to redeem, is complete on the maturity of the junior lien, and the statute of limitation as to such lien begins to run.[7] Here, the right to redeem (or more properly to pay the mortgage debt), on the maturity of the junior lien is to be understood as true only where the senior mortgagee is in possession and his debt is due. A junior lien holder, however, whether his debt is due or not, and regardless of who is in possession, may tender the amount due on the senior lien as soon as threats are made to foreclose it.[8] This is because

[5] In California the remedy upon the mortgage is barred at the same time as an action on the note (bearing the same time) to secure the payment the mortgage was given. Some of the states have statutes of limitation applying specifically to foreclosures of mortgages (Minn G S 1894 § 5141), but where no such statute is in force courts of equity follow the law limiting the time within which an action may be commenced to recover a legal estate, and apply a like limitation to suits founded upon equitable rights. Askew v Hooper 28 Ala 634

[6] Higman v Humes, 22 So. Rep (Ala) 574

[7] Boon on Mort § 162

[8] See Frost v Yonkers Sav Bank, 70 N Y 553 But see Higman v Humes 32 So Rep (Ala) 574.

a foreclosure may destroy the junior lien holder's investment and subject him to great embarrassment and damage in re deeming from other liens, and because of the impairment of his security on account of costs and expenses  Whether a senior mortgagee is in possession or not, if the mortgage has been foreclosed, a junior lien holder, although his claim is due, cannot make a tender of the amount bid at the sale, until the time allowed the mortgagor to redeem has expired, unless he has foreclosed his lien and acquired the legal estate.

§ 285.  **Tender after a foreclosure—To the mortgagee—Sheriff —** If there has been a foreclosure, a tender of the amount bid at the sale must be made within the time allowed by the court or by statute within which to redeem, even though the statute of limitations has run against the mortgage since the commencement of the foreclosure proceedings.[1]  After a fore- closure, unless it is a strict foreclosure, a tender of the amount bid at the sale may be made at any time before the sun sets on the last day fixed by the court, or allowed by statute, in which to redeem.  The redemption money being payable at any time within the period, the redemptioner, if he desires to redeem before the last day, should make a tender to the holder of the certificate in person (or to the sheriff), or give notice to the holder of the certificate, that on a certain day, at the latter's residence, he will make a tender

[1] When steps have been taken to sell land upon execution, but before the day of sale arrives, the statute has run against the judgment  the purchaser at the sale acquires no right, there be- ing then no enforceable judgment to uphold the sale  There is some analogy between such sale and a sale of land on a mortgage foreclosure where the statute of limitations runs as to the mort- gage between the commencement of the foreclosure proceedings and the sale thereunder  The dis- tinction, however, lies in the wording of the statute of limita- tion which in express terms give the right to commence original proceeding at any time within the period limited. not specifying that such proceeding shall be complet- ed within the times  Foreclosure proceedings and an action to re- cover a judgment for a sum of money are both original proceed- ings, and all that is required to uphold them is that there exist, at the inception of the proceeding, a cause of action, namely a lien in one case, and in the other a liability for a sum of money  The execution is merely a proceeding to enforce an existing right, which falls to the ground when the right ceases, or is in abey ance

of the amount due. And a tender there on the day specified, at a convenient time before the sun sets so that the money may be counted by daylight, will be good, whether the certificate holder be there to receive it or not. A sheriff, however, would not be bound to attend at his office at any particular time to receive the redemption money, as that might interfere with the performance by him of other official duties.

A time being limited by law or under authority of law, within which payment must be made, and the law also fixing the place, namely, at the residence of the holder of the certificate, a tender at the last convenient time before the sun sets on the last day, will be good without any notice, and whether the holder of the certificate be there to receive it or not. Going to the office of the sheriff or other officer, even at the last minute of the time allowed to redeem, with the money ready and willing to redeem, in the absence of such officer will not constitute a tender. The office of sheriff has its situs at the county seat, and is technically open for business during business hours, every business day in the year, and a redemptioner by diligence and patience has it in his power to make a tender to such officer in person, and knowing that the officer may be called away to attend to his official duties, he ought not to wait until the last minute limited and expect to find the officer. A subsequent encumbrancer in line for redemption may make a tender to the purchaser or next prior redemptioner at any time within the time allowed by statute for him to redeem, and the right to redeem within the statutory time cannot be defeated by the holder of the certificate of sale agreeing with the mortgagor to extend the statutory time as to him.[2]

In case of a pledge, the pledgor must tender the amount due within the time limited by statute, if there be such a time limited by statute, and if there be no time limited, then within a reasonable time after notice of the sale.[3]

### § 286. Absence of vendor or creditor from state.

Where a vendor agrees to convey land on the payment at a certain time of the residue of the purchase price, and before the time for payment arrives the vendor departs from the state where the contract is made, and continues absent for a long period of time, and the vendee has had no opportunity to make a

---

[2] Sager v. Tupper, 35 Mich. 134.    [3] See Swann v. Baxter, 73 N. Y. Supp. 336.

tender within the state during that time, in those states where absence from the state interrupts the running of th. statute of limitation, the vendee may tender the residue of the purchase price when the vendor returns to the state.[1]

§ 287. **When rent should be tendered.**—In absence of a stipulation fixing the time when rent is payable, it is due and payable monthly, quarterly, semiannually, or annually, according to the usage of the country. It is usual in leasing urban property such as stores, offices, and tenements, to reserve a monthly rent; and where a lease for a long term provides that the lessee shall pay a certain sum per month, it is understood that the rent is to be paid in monthly installments each month, and not at the end of the full term.[1] Where the leasehold is agricultural land, the rent is usually payable annually whether payable in money or produce. Cash rent, in absence of an agreement to the contrary, is payable at the end of the rent-paying period, and not in advance. Rent payable in produce should be paid within a reasonable time after the crops are gathered. If rent is payable in advance, the first payment should be made before entry. The lessee has the whole of the first day or day designated to pay subsequent installments in advance. If during the day, before payment is made, the tenant is ousted by the holder of a paramount title, he need not pay the rent.[2]

A clause in a lease providing for a forfeiture, in the event of a default by the lessee in the performance of his covenant, has been held not to be self operating, so as to make a forfeiture take place *ipso facto* upon the occurrence of the default.[3] It being for the benefit of the lessor, a tender of the rent at any time before the lessor has enforced the forfeiture would be a good defence.

Under a statute in force in Minnesota, which provides that

---

[1] Gill v. Bradley, 21 Minn. 15. In Houbie v. Volkening, 49 How. Pr. 169, a mortgagee, after the execution of a mortgage in the state of New York, went to Europe to reside. A tender made of all that was due, when papers in foreclosure were served upon the mortgagor, was held good, the mortgagee not having left any person in the state of New York to receive interest and installments as they fell due.

[1] Gibbens v. Thompson, 21 Minn. 398.

[2] Smith v. Shepard 15 Pick 99 s. c 25 Am Dec 432. See Taylor Landlord and Tenant, § 390 and Boon on Real Property, § 108 on the subject, generally as to time of payment.

[3] Westmoreland v. DeWitt, 130 Pa St 235.

in case of a lease of real property, and a failure of the tenant to pay the rent, and the landlord brings an action to recover the possession, the lessee, or those claiming under him, at any time before the expiration of the six months after possession has been obtained by the landlord on a recovery in the action, may pay the sheriff, or bring into court, the amount of the rent in arrears, with interest and costs of the action, and by performing the other covenants to be by him performed, he may be restored to the possession and hold the property according to the terms of the original lease.[1] Under this statute it has been held that if a lessee may pay the rent in arrears after being ousted, he may do so during the progress of the proceedings, and a tender may be made at the trial, or the money may be brought into court.

§ 288   On contracts providing for a forfeiture—Where note is not at the place fixed for payment.   Where a previous payment is sought to be forfeited under a contract providing for a forfeiture in case the party making the payment does not comply with his contract, the party against whom the forfeiture is sought to be enforced in order to defeat such forfeiture must show that he was reasonably diligent and endeavored to make a tender at or within the time limited.[1] It has been held that where a note or other obligation is made payable at a certain place as where a bank is designated as the place at which a note is to be paid the payor is not in default in not making payment until the note is received at the bank.[2] But in that case the question of default was in reference to whether the party bound to pay the note was entitled to specific performance.[3] If the payor wants to stop the running of interest he must be at the place at the time fixed ready and willing to pay the note and keep the tender good.

[1] 1894 G S Minn § 5865

[2] Wicholz v Griesgraber 70 Minn 220 George v Mahoney 62 Minn 370

[3] Bayley v Duvall, 1 Cranch C C 283, Sylvester v Holisch, 86 N W Rep (Minn) 736  See

Whiteman v Perkins 76 N W Rep (Neb) 547

[2] Ballard v Cheney 19 Neb 58 s c 26 N W Rep 587 Robinson v Cheney 17 Neb 673 s c 24 N W Rep 382

[3] See Brinman v Pickney 118 N Y 604

**§ 289. When a tender should be made by a drawer or endorser.**—A drawer or endorser of a bill undertakes to pay it, if the acceptor does not, on receiving proper notice of its dishonor. As he cannot know in every case who is the holder of the bill at the time it is payable, he is not bound to pay it until he finds that out; and a tender within a reasonable time after he has had notice of its dishonor, will be in time. Where a notice of dishonor was given on the 12th of the month, and the drawer tendered the money on the morning of the 13th, it was held to be in time.[1] It has been held that a tender may be made by an acceptor of a bill, after a demand on the day of maturity, and in such case he will not be liable for the protest fees.[2]

**§ 290. On non-interest bearing obligations—Demands payable in "sixty days"—"In sixty days from date"—"On or before"—"Within one year"—"In the month of February"—Days of grace.**—Where non interest bearing debts are made payable at the future time, as where goods are sold upon thirty or sixty days' credit, a tender of the amount due may be made at any time before the time of payment arrives. The delay is given for the benefit of the debtor, to enable him to acquit himself when he can, on or before the day. The giving of the time is for the indulgence of the debtor, and the creditor cannot sue before the day. A note payable in "sixty days" is payable at the end of sixty days from date.[1] The phrases "in sixty days"—"in sixty days from date"—"in sixty days from the date of the date" mean the same thing. If a note is made payable "on or before"[2] or "within one year" a tender may be made immediately after it is executed. Where a note was payable "in the month of February" in plows, setting aside the plows on the first day of January, at the place agreed, where they remained down to and through the month of May, was held a good tender.[4] Unless a promissory note or bill of exchange by express terms include days of grace, the note or bill is due and payable, in most of the states, three days after its due date, and a tender made before the last day, if rejected, is of no avail, unless the last day

[1] Walker v Barnes 7 Taunt 240 s c 1 Marsh 36
[2] Leftley v Mills, 4 T R 173
[1] Henry v Jones, 8 Mass 453
[2] Brent v Fennel 4 Ark 160
[3] Buffum v Buffum 11 N H 451
[4] Gilman v Moore, 14 Vt 457

of the three should be Sunday, or a legal holiday, in which case the tender must be made on the second day instead of the third  This is to avoid the giving of four days  If the last day of grace is Sunday and the second a legal holiday, the tender must be made on the first of the three days of grace.

§ 291.  **On demand obligations—Notice of intention of making a tender required when—Right of selection—Requiring selection—Due bill—Conditional sale.—**If a note is payable on demand, the maker may, at any time before a demand, make a tender of the amount due, which will have the same effect as if the note was made payable on a certain day, and a tender was made on that day[1]  But the tender must be made at the place agreed, or if no place be agreed upon  then it must be made at a reasonable place, and to the payee personally, or to his duly authorized agent.  If the payee has no agent, and is absent from the place of the payment or his place of abode, a tender may be made at his place of abode in his absence, but a reasonable notice should first be given to the payee by the payor of his intention of making a tender there, specifying the day when he will make it  A note given for the payment of a certain sum in specific articles, without mentioning the time or place, is payable on demand.[2]

Where the time is fixed for the delivery of goods, and the party who is to receive them has the right of selection, a tender of the goods must nevertheless be made at the time fixed for performance, whether a selection has been made or not.  In such case, a party who has the right of selection, and does not exercise such right within the time, is deemed to have waived it, and the other party must make the selection  But where no time is limited for delivery, and the party who is to receive the goods has a right of selection, a demand and selection becomes necessary before the vendor can be put in a default.  The demand must be such as will enable the vendor to tender performance according to the terms of the contract,[3] and the payor or vendor has reasonable time to comply with the demand  If the vendee does not make a demand and selection within a reasonable time, the vendor,

[1] Wooten v Sherrard, 68 N Car 334
[2] Rice v Churchill, 2 Denio 145
[3] Russell v Ormsbee, 10 Vt 271  See Townsend v Wells, 3 Day's R 327

by notice, may require him to make a selection, and after a reasonable time, or the time specified in the notice, if reasonable, has elapsed, and the vendee still neglects to make a selection, the vendor may make the selection and tender the articles so selected. In the case of a due bill payable in goods, the time within which a demand should be made for the goods will depend upon the use to which the goods are to be put, the kind of goods, and the custom and usage of the business. If the goods are perishable, the merchant cannot require the holder of the bill to take more at one time than he has a right to expect the holder could use without loss to him. The latter cannot require a merchant to continue in business for the purpose of furnishing goods on a due bill, and on the other hand, if the merchant desires to retire from business, and the goods kept by him are such that the holder of the due bill could not be expected to take and care for, at one time, the quantity necessary to satisfy the due bill, the merchant should tender the balance in the money at the time he retires from business. If the holder of the due bill has held it a sufficient time to have exhausted the amount by trading at the store according to his needs, in the usual course of business, without protest by the merchant he cannot be required to take more goods than his needs require, even though the merchant is on the eve of retiring from business. But if the merchant had previously requested the holder to exhaust his due bill as fast as his needs require, and there has elapsed sufficient time after the request, and before the time of discontinuing the business for the holder to have exhausted the due bill, or a part of it, by trading in the usual course of business according to his needs, and he has not done so, he must take the required amount in goods, and if he refuses he cannot recover the balance in money. However if the goods are not perishable nor likely to become stale, nor such that their value does not depend upon the then prevailing fashion; but are such as will not materially deteriorate within a reasonable time, and can be kept by the exercise of the proper care, as well by the holder of the due bill as by the merchant, then the holder of the due bill, upon reasonable notice may be required to take all the goods at one time on the merchant retiring from business. The law abhors perpetual obligations and in all such cases affords a way to close the transaction.

Where, upon a conditional sale of chattels it is agreed that the vendee is to have possession and to pay the purchase price within a time fixed, and the vendee after the purchase price has become due and remains unpaid, is permitted to retain possession, and the vendor receives a part payment, it is a recognition that the contract is still in force, and of the right of the vendee to acquire title to the property by payment of the residue of the purchase money in future, and a tender of the residue may be made at any time before the right is destroyed by a demand for the balance of the purchase money.[4]

§ 292   **On contracts with option to contract the term — Notice required** —If a note or other obligation is drawn payable "on or before" a certain time, or during a certain period, the option gives the debtor a right to contract the term at any time he may see fit by a payment or tender to the creditor personally, of the amount due with interest   If the party who ought to pay the money or deliver the goods desires to contract the term and he cannot find the creditor conveniently, he may give to the party to whom payment or delivery is to be made, notice that upon a certain day prior to the last day limited he will make the payment or delivery. So, like notice must be given where money or goods may be paid or delivered at a certain place at any time   According to Lord Coke. "If a man be bound to pay twenty pounds at any time during his life at a place certain, the obligor can not tender the money at the place when he will, for then the obligee should be bound to perpetual attendance, and therefore the obligor in respect of the uncertainty of the time must give the obligee notice that on such a day at the place limited, he will pay the money  and then the obligee must attend there to receive it  for if the obligor then and there tender the money  he shall save the penalty of the bond for ever   The same law it is if a man make a feoffment in fee upon condition, if the feoffor at any time during his life pay to the feoffee twenty pounds at such a place certain, that then, etc   In this case the feoffor must give notice to the feoffee  when he will pay it, for without such notice as is aforesaid, the tender will not be sufficient. But in both these cases if at any time the obligor or feoffor meet the obligee or feoffee at the place, he may tender the money." [1]

§ 293. On contacts where no time is limited—Reasonable time—On written notice.—Where an executory contract is silent as to the time of performance, a tender of performance must be made within a reasonable time.[1] This is the general rule at common law.[2] The law applies the same to him whose duty it is to first move in the matter, whether he be the seller or buyer. In such cases, as well as where the contract expressly provides that the thing is to be done within a reasonable time, a reasonable time is to be determined in each case by a view of all facts and circumstances attending the transaction.[3] What would be a reasonable time in any given case, is somewhat difficult to ascertain. It must of necessity be arbitrarily fixed after considering the situation of the parties at the time of the contract, the location of the property to be delivered relative to the place of the delivery and the necessary time required for the preparation.[4] If the contract is in writing, parol evidence is admissable of the facts and circumstances attending the transaction to determine what is a reasonable time.[5] Where payment was to be made on receiving written notice, it was held that a notice

---

[1] Co Lett. § 340. In Town v. Trow 24 Pick 168 the court observed that if this could not be done, the time being uncertain it would be impossible for the debtor to make a tender as the creditor might always avoid the place of payment and thus render his debt perpetual

[1] Atwood v Cals, 16 Pick 227 s c 26 Am Dec 657, Bass v White 65 N Y 568 Ellis v Thompson 3 M & W 445, Coleridge v Jenkins 92 N W Rep (Neb) 123

[2] Roberts v Beatty 2 Penn 63 If a payee of a promissory note agrees to receive property in pay

ment of a note and no time is fixed for its delivery the payee is allowed a reasonable time in which to tender the property Jones v Peet 1 Swan (Tenn) 293 In Conklin v Smith 7 Ind 107 s c 63 Am Dec 416 it is held that a purchaser at a sheriff's sale must tender the purchase money within a reasonable time

[3] See Newmark on Sales § 22 1 Addison on Cont § 320

[4] Robert v Mazeppa Mill Co, 30 Minn 413

[5] 2 Benj on Sales, 907 See also Newmark on Sales, § 232

which required payment to be made in a half hour was not a reasonable notice.[6]

§ 294. Same subject—Where a buyer departs without paying the price—Failure to withdraw an option.—Mr. Comyn in his work on contracts, said: "If two are agreed upon a price, and the buyer departs, without tendering the money, and comes the next day and tenders it, the other may refuse; for he is not bound to wait, unless a day of payment was agreed between them."[1] If no time is specified, in an executory contract, for the payment of the purchase price, the price must be tendered at the time of the delivery of the goods, deed, or other thing to be delivered. If the seller has a custom of extending credit for a limited time to regular customers, and goods have been delivered to such customer in the usual course of trade, he need not tender the purchase price until the customary time for payment arrives. There are fine distinctions drawn as to the time of performance when there is no time limited by express stipulation. An astonishing and curious lot of diversities are mentioned by Lord Coke, and are given in a subjoined note.[2]

[6] Prighty v. Norton 32 L. J. Q. B. 38

[1] 2 Comyn on Cont. 211

[2] Littleton in his Institutes of the Laws of England (s 337) puts a case of feoffment made upon condition that if the feoffor pay a certain sum of money to the feoffee then it shall be lawful for the feoffer and his heirs to enter, but if the feoffor die before the payment is made, a tender cannot be made by the heirs. For where the condition is that if the feoffor pay &c. this is as much to say as if the feoffer during his life pay the money &c. and when the feoffor dieth then the time of the tender is past. But otherwise it is where a day of payment is limited and the feoffer die before the day. Lord Coke in his commentary upon this section says this diversity is plain and evident and declaring that there are diversities worthy of observation proceeded with much subtlety as follows:

First between this case that Littleton here putteth of the condition of a feoffment in fee for the payment of money where no time is limited and the condition of a bond for the payment of a sum of money when no time is limited for in such a condition of a bond the money is to be paid presently that is in convenient time. And yet in case of a condition of a bond there is a diversity between a condition of an obligation which concerns the doing of a transitory act without limitation of any time as payment of money, delivery of charters or the like for there the condition is to be performed presently, that is in convenient

A person is under no legal obligation to withdraw an offer to sell property on certain terms after the expiration of a

time; and when by the condition of the obligation the act that is to bee done to the obligee is of its own nature locall, for there the obligor (no time being limited) hath time during his life to perform it as to make a feoffment, etc, if the obligee doth not hasten the time by request   In case where the condition of the obligation is locall, there is also a diversity, where the concurrence of the obligor and the obligee is requisite (as in the said case of the feoffment), and where the obligor may perform in the absence of the obligee, as to knowledge satisfaction in the court of the King's bench although the knowledge of satisfaction is locall, yet because he may doe it in the absence of the obligor, he must doe it in convenient time, and hath not time during his life

Another diversitie is, where the condition concerneth a transitory or locall act, and is to be performed to the feoffee or obligee, and where it is to be performed to a stranger   As if A be bound to B to pay ten pounds to C   A tenders to C and he refuseth, the bond is forfeited, as in this section shall be said more at large

Another diversitie is betweene a condition of an obligation and a condition upon a feoffment where the act that is locall is to be done to a stranger and where to the obligee or feoffor himselfe   As if one make a feoffment in fee, upon condition that the feoffee shall enfeoffe a stranger and no time limited, the feoffee shall not have time during his life to make a feoffment, for then he should take

the profits in the mean time to his own use, which the stranger ought to have, and therefore he ought to make the feoffment as soone as conveniently he may; and so it is of the condition of an obligation   But if the condition be, that the feoffee shall reinfeoffe the feoffor, then the feoffee hath time during his life, for the privities of the condition, between them, unless he be hasten by request, as shall bee said hereafter

Another diversitie is, when the obligor or feoffor is to enfeoffe a stranger, as hath been said, and where a stranger is to enfeoffe the feoffee or obligee, as if A enfeoffe B. of *Black*   upon condition that if C enfeoffe B of *White*   A shall re-enter, C hath time during his life, if B doth not hasten it by request and so of an obligation

But in some cases albeit the condition be collateral, and is to be performed to the obligee, and no time limited yet in respect of the nature of the thing the obligor shall not have time during his life to perform it   As if the condition of an obligation bee to grant an annuitie or yearly rent to the obligee during his life payable yearely at the feast of *Easter*, this annuity or yearly rent must be granted before *Easter*, or else the obligee shall not have it at the feast during his life, *et sic de similibus* and so was it resolved by the judges of the common plea in the argument of the Andrew's case, which I myself heard

reasonable time, and a failure to formally withdraw the offer, after the expiration of a reasonable time, will not validate a tender made thereafter according to the terms of the offer [a]

§ 295   On contract to perform "as soon as possible"—"Forthwith"—"Directly."—Contracts to be performed "as soon as possible," "forthwith," "directly," etc., like contracts to be performed within a reasonable time, require judicial investigation as each case arises, to determine whether the tender of performance, as to time, complies with the contract Where a manufacturer agreed to deliver goods "as soon as possible" it was held that the time "as soon as possible" meant as soon as the vendors could, taking into consideration their ability to furnish the goods ordered, consistent with the proper execution of prior orders.[1]  In a later case the term "as soon as possible" was construed, with reference to the facts in that case, to mean "that they would make the gun as quickly as it could be made in the largest establishment with the best appliances "[2]  Here, the court distinguished the two cases; observing that the possibility of delay occasioned by the vendor's execution of prior orders was one which the purchaser might reasonably be presumed to have taken into account, while a delay caused solely by the vendor's inability to secure competent workmen (the cause of the delay in the latter case) was not taken into account.[3]  It is evident that the period for performance when a thing is to be done "as

Lastly, When the obligor feoffor or feoffee is to doe a sole act or labour, as to go to *Rome Jerusalem &c* In such and the like cases the obligor feoffor, or feoffee hath time during his life, and cannot be hastened by request   And so it is if a stranger to the obligation or feoffment were to doe such an act, he hath time to doe it at any time during his life '

[a] Bowen v McCarthy, 48 N W Rep (Mich) 155

[1] Attwood v Emery, 1 C B N S 110

[2] Hydraulic Engineering Co, v McHaffie L R 4 Q B Div 670 C A

[3] See Newark on Sales § 231, Benj on Sales, § 911 912, Keer's notes referring to Rommel v Wingate 103 Mass 327, Attwood v Cobb 23 Mass (16 Pick ) 227 s c 26 Am Dec 657 Neldon v Smith, 36 N J L (7 Vr ) 148; Danforth v Walker 40 Vt 257 Blydenburg v Welsh 1 Baldw C C 331 Crocker v Franklin, &c Co 3 Sumn C C 530

soon as possible," must of necessity be fixed in each case by the court or jury, after taking into consideration the facts and the circumstances attending the transaction. Where goods were to be delivered "forthwith" and the contract provided that the purchase price was to be paid within four teen days from the time of making the contract, it was held that the goods were intended to be delivered within that time.[1] "Directly," "forthwith" and "immediately" means, ordinarily, that the thing will be done at once, without delay, but not instantly, and it is generally understood that they do not indicate as protracted a time as does the expression "within the reasonable time."[5]

§ 296. On contracts where time is of the essence of the contract.—Time may be of the essence of a contract by express stipulation, or it may arise by implication from the nature of the business, or the property, or the avowed object of the seller or purchaser.[1] So, time may be made of the essence of the contract, by notice, in advance of the time of performance, requiring prompt performance on the day fixed, or after default by notice requiring the party in default to perform on or before a certain time.[2] Where time is thus of the essence of the contract, the party whose duty is to first move in the matter must be punctual. So, also, must the other party when the time arrives for him to perform. In such cases a tender after the time will be unavailing if rejected,[3] unless there be circumstances which would warrant a court of equity relieving the party against the default. The Supreme Court of Illinois, in an early case, aptly stated the principles which govern the court of conscience, in cases where there has been a failure to tender a performance at the precise time fixed, thus: "We have always held that the doctrine of equity is compensation, not forfeiture, * * *

[4] Staunton v. Wood 16 Q B 638. In Rommel v. Wingate, 103 Mass 327, it was held that a defendant was not bound to accept, at a remote date a cargo of coal of 392 tons on an order for a cargo of 375 tons to be shipped immediately.

[5] See Addison on Cont § 320.

[1] Chenny v. Libby, 134 U S 68

[2] Austin v. Wack, 30 Minn 335

[3] Kentucky Distil Co v. Warwick, 109 Fed Rep 280; Pursley v. Good, 68 S W Rep (Mo App) 218. In the last case which was based upon an agreement with a privilege to recovery, it was held that a deed must be tendered within the time fixed or the right to recovery would be waived.

and in passing upon the facts and circumstances in each and every case, where the powers of this court are invoked for the enforcement of such strict legal rights, it will never disregard such facts and circumstances as excuse a strict performance at the day, to mitigate the rigor of a forfeiture, or absolve from it altogether. There may be, undoubtedly, in many cases, such circumstances as should restrain the vendor from the strict enforcement of the contract; and as will entitle the purchaser to a specific performance, although he may have failed of a strict compliance at the day. Numerous cases of this kind can be found in the books." [1]

§ 297. Same subject—Tender after default where the other party is also in default — After accepting a part — Leading a party to believe that the money will be accepted later.—If there is a precedent or concurrent act to be performed by the party who seeks to put the other in default, and he has not performed or was not at the time ready and willing to perform, a tender made by the other party within a reasonable time after default will be held good in equity.[1] So, if the question of time has been waived by accepting a partial payment after default, or the contract is otherwise treated as still subsisting, or the party has been led to believe that the money or thing to be delivered will be received at a subsequent time and he is not guilty of laches, a tender at the earliest time possible, or within a reasonable time after default, will be good. The court, of course, will give due regard to the question of damages, costs, and expenses of the innocent party, so that he may not lose anything by the delay of the other party.

§ 298. Same subject—A strict compliance required when—Notice requiring prompt performance.—There are cases where time being of the essence of the contract the stipulation as to time must be strictly complied with in equity as well as at law. Thus, where the thing sold is of greater or less value according to the afflux of time, or where the property is purchased for a certain purpose known to the other, as where property is to be conveyed on or before a given time and is to

[4] Steele v. Biggs, 22 Ill. 643.
[1] Hubbell v. Von Schoening, 49 Ill. 180.
N Y 326. Bishop v. Newton, 20

be used as a residence,[1] or where a right to reconvey and have
a return of the consideration is reserved,[2] or where stock is
to be delivered for shipment by a certain train, or perishable
property, or any property is wanted for a certain market day,
or time of the day, or any property is wanted on a certain day
to fill a contract; in all of which cases, and many more sim
ilar, a tender must be made at the precise time fixed in the
agreement. So, where time is made of the essence of a con
tract by one party serving upon the other, a notice requiring
performance to be made promptly on the day fixed, or on or
before a certain time if there is a default, the party receiving
such notice must tender performance promptly at the time
fixed,[3] if he is the party first to move in the matter, or if the
acts to be done are mutual and concurrent, he must be at the
time and place appointed, ready and willing to perform. The
party making a demand, in cases where there has been a
default, must give the party who is to perform a reasonable
time in which to fetch the money or goods from the place
where they are kept, providing that they are within a reason
able distance from the place of delivery. A party living in
New York would not be bound to wait until money or goods
could be brought from Chicago, or from a foreign country.

§ 299.  **Where the time to perform is limited by statute** —
Where the time within which a certain act must be done is
fixed by statute, as where time is limited in which to pay
taxes, or redeem from a tax sale, or a mortgage or execution
sale, a tender must be made of the amount due within the
time.[1]

§ 300.  **What constitutes a waiver as to time—Denial of benefit
of waiver to whom.**—If a tender of performance of a contract
is made after the day, and the tender is rejected upon some
other and untenable ground, the objection that it is too late
is waived.[1] But in a case when the vendor in a contract for

[1] Hipwell v Knight, 1 Y & C
115

[2] Pursley v Good, 68 N W
Rep (Mo App) 218

[3] Friess v Rider 24 N Y 366,
see Lewd v Smith, 41 N Y, 618

[4] Clower v Flemming, 7 S E
Rep (Ga) 278; Thomas v Nichols,

37 S E Rep (N C) 327  In the
last case it was held that where
a statute provided that a tax pay
er had until a certain day to pay,
a tender on that day was suffi
cient

[1] Cythe v La Fountain 51
Barb 190

the sale of land was in default and the time was extended to
a certain hour on a later day, a tender made at a subsequent
hour to the one appointed was held bad, although the vendee
stated as a reason for declining, not the lapse of time, but
waste of the premises.[2] The action was for damages for a
refusal of the vendee to perform. Here, the principle of
waiver of the objection as to time was limited to cases where
the party who made the waiver seeks to hold the other party
liable for a breach of the contract.[1]

§ 301. **When compensation must be tendered for land taken
under eminent domain.**—The time when compensation must be
tendered to the owner of land by a railroad company, mill
company, or other company or person exercising the right of
eminent domain, varies somewhat in the several states. In
almost every commonwealth, however, where a private corporation seeks to condemn land under the power of eminent
domain, the compensation must be paid or tendered before
the right to enter upon the land accrues. The owner is
entitled to have his day in court, before whatever tribunal
the statute may provide, and have an appraisement and
assessment of the damages, and payment or tender of the
damages. An entry upon the land before such adjudication
and payment or tender cannot be justified. A tender made
after an entry is no defence to an action of trespass.[1] If the
owner appeals from the decision of the appraisers, or of the
court awarding the damages, under some statutes the company may tender the damages assessed, and on paying the
amount into court, enter upon the land.[2] So, an entry may
be made after a tender of the amount of the award, notwithstanding a reassessment has been ordered. So, the company may tender the amount of the award and enter upon
the land and appeal upon the question of damages.[4] In all

[2] Hess v. Rider, 24 N. Y. 367.
See Gould v. Bank, 8 Wend.
562.

[1] Storer v. Hobbs, 52 Me. 144.

[2] See Colvill v. Langdon, 22
Minn. 565 when it was held that
a tender, pending an appeal from
an award, was not sufficient to
show a right to enter upon the

land. Possibly if the money had
been paid into court, the reasoning
of the court might have been
otherwise.

[3] Lessing v. Philadelphia &c.
Ry., S. W. & S. 459. Lake Erie
&c. Ry. v. Kinsey 87 Ind. 514.

[4] People v. Syracuse, 78 N. Y.
56.

such cases, if compensation is not tendered within a reasonable time, the proceedings will be deemed to have been abandoned.[5] A tender should be made before proceedings are instituted in court, in order to subject the owner to costs.[6]

Where the state, or any political subdivision, exercise the right of eminent domain, it is not necessary to pay or tender the compensation before the appropriation of the land[7] The reason upon which the rule is said to be based is, that all the taxable property in a town or municipality (or even a county) constitutes an adequate fund to which the owner may, without risk of loss, resort to compel payment.[8] As to the state it is presumed that it will always make just and equitable reparation to any citizen for any injury or loss suffered by him caused by it in the exercise of its sovereign powers. Although the payment or tender need not necessarily precede the seizure by the state, or any political subdivision under eminent domain, nevertheless the state must so proceed as to subject the land legally to its use, before the owner can be deprived of his property. It must proceed in the way pointed out by the statute and ascertain the value of the land before it can be appropriated to the use of the public.[9]

## § 302. Where a tender may be made on a Sunday—At common law—Statutory prohibition.

At common law it is not unlawful to follow one's ordinary calling or perform work and labor on Sunday, and contracts made on that day to be executed on that day or at any other time are valid,[1] unless

[5] Bensley v Mountain Lake Water Co, 13 Cal 306, s c 73 Am Dec 575

[6] Oregon Cent R Co v Wait, 3 Or 128

[7] Rexford v Knight, 11 N Y 308, Norton v Peck 3 Wis 714.

[8] Norton v Peck, 3 Wis 628, Smeaton v Martin, 57 Wis 374.

[9] Norton v Peck, 3 Wis 714, McCauley v Weller, 12 Cal 500. See Rexford v Knight, 11 N. Y. 308, Baker v Johnson, 2 Hill. 342; People v. Hayden, 6 Hill 359

[1] Amis v Kyle, 2 Yerg 31 s c 24 Am Dec 463, Sayles v Smith, 12 Wend 57; Merrett v Earle 29 N Y 120, Story v Elliott, 8 Cow 27, s c 18 Am Dec 423 And see subjoined note on the subject generally; And see also Coleman v Henderson, 12 Am Dec 290 and extensive note, s c Litt Sel Cases 171, Van Ripper v Van Ripper, 1 Southard, 156, s c 7 Am Dec 576 Benj. on Sales (3d Ed. Am Notes) § 723, et seq and cases cited See also Boynton v

expressly prohibited by statute. In Tennessee, in an action of covenant brought upon a sealed instrument for the payment and delivery of horses, six months after date, where the day of payment and delivery fell upon Sunday, and the defendant pleaded a tender and refusal, made on the day following, to which plea plaintiff demurred, the court, after reviewing the English cases and the history of the law upon this question, said: "These adjudged cases prove that, at common law, act not expressly prohibited might be done on a Sunday; and that contracts made, work and labor done, and even business of one's ordinary calling followed on that day, were not, on that account, ever considered by it illegal," and after considering the local statute, held that a tender of chattels on Sunday in performance of a contract, is legal both at common law and under the statute; and therefore the day for performance in that case falling on Sunday, a tender on the following day was too late.[2]

Under some statutes the performance of certain business transactions on a Sunday, under some circumstances, is interdicted, while under the other circumstances they may be lawfully done. There being considerable more than forty jurisdictions which have derived their manners, customs and laws from (or patterned after) England, with changes and modifications, it is necessary before making or refusing a tender where the contract was entered into on a Sunday, or the day for performance falls upon a Sunday, to carefully examine the local statute. In England it was enacted, that 'No tradesman, artificer, workmen, laborer or other person whatsoever' shall do or exercise any worldly labor, business or work of their ordinary callings upon the Lord's Day, or any part thereof (works of necessity and charity only excepted), * * * that no person or persons shall publicly cry, show forth, or expose to sale any wares, merchandise, fruits herbs, goods or chattels whatsoever upon the Lord's Day, or any part thereof upon pain," &c.[3] Under this statute and those similar to it, such as the one in Tennessee, it is held by the courts that the following of one's vocation on the Lord's Day is unlawful, while the same business transaction on

Page, 13 Wend. 125, Lyon v.          [2] Amis v. Kyle, 2 Yerg. 31, s. c.
Strong. 6 Vt. 219                 24 Am. Dec. 463
                                  [3] 29 Charles II. c. 7

a Sunday by two persons who do not make such business their vocation, would be lawful. The decision of the Supreme Court of Tennessee, holding that the tender of the horses on Monday, upon a contract to deliver them upon the preceding Sunday, to be too late, was based upon the ground that neither of the contracting parties were pursuing their ordinary calling.[4] Other statutes declare to be unlawful the making of contracts and the performance of work and labor on a Sunday,[5] regardless whether the particular labor or work pertains to the ordinary calling of the persons who may be engaged in performing such labor or making the contract[6] Where a contract is made with reference particularly to the performance on a Sunday of a particular thing, the doing of which on that day is declared to be unlawful, the contract is void whether it was entered into on a week day or on a Sabbath, and a tender by either party on a Sunday or at any other time, if refused, will not support a cause of action in favor of either.[7]

**§ 303. Same subject—Promissory notes and bills—Mercantile contracts—Where the last day of grace falls upon a Sunday—Where the last day of a period falls upon a Sunday.**—Where a bill of exchange, or promissory note is made payable a certain number days after date, and by computation the last day is found to be a Sunday, a tender made upon a following Monday is sufficient.[1] This rule, by the custom of merchants, is applied to all mercantile contracts, where by computation the day of performance is found to fall upon a Sunday. The law merchant is a branch of the common law used by

---

[4] Amis v. Kyle 2 Yearg 31, s c 24 Am Dec 463 See Drury v De Fountaine, 1 Taunt. 131, where a horse auctioneer was held not to be following his ordinary calling when he made a private sale of a horse on Sunday.

[5] Under these statutes works of necessity and charity are invariably excepted The sale of tobacco newspapers, drugs and medicines, on a Sunday, are also permitted by some statutes, notably in Minnesota

[6] See §§ 6513, 6517, 1894, G S Minn

[7] See Handy v St Paul Globe, 41 Minn 188, where the contract was in reference to advertising in a Sunday newspaper

[1] In Avery v Stewart, 2 Conn 69, s c 7 Am Dec 240 which seems to be a leading case, the rule was applied to non negotiable instrument, s p Barrett v Allen 10 Ohio 426 where the note was payable in woolen cloth at "fair wholesale factory price"

persons engaged in a particular calling, and in this respect at least it is a modification of that law.

A merchant thus escapes the necessity of attending at his place of business on Sunday to receive payments, or to receive merchandise on contracts where by computation the day of performance is found to fall upon a Sunday. By the law merchant, Sunday for the purpose of performing a contract is not regarded as a day, and should, as to that purpose, be considered as stricken from the calender.[2]

Where the last day of grace allowed on a bill or note falls due on a Sunday, a tender, by the same custom of merchants, must be made on the previous Saturday. Days of grace being an indulgence sanctioned by law, it is perfectly proper to require payment on the second day of grace to avoid giving four days.[3] In cases not falling within the common law as modified by the law merchant, or a statutory provision, a tender of performance must be made on a Sunday, if by computation the day for performance is found to fall upon that day.[4] Where, by statute, money is to be paid within a certain time, and the last day of the period happens to be Sunday, a tender must be made on the preceding Satur

---

[2] Salter v. Burt, 20 Wend. 205. In Saunders v. Ochiltree, 5 Porter 75, the note was made on Saturday and payable one day after date. In Kilgour v. Miles 6 Gill & J. 268. In the case of a non-negotiable note payable in merchandise which fell due upon a Sunday, the same rule was applied as is applicable to notes and bills upon which days of grace are allowed. The day of delivery was held to be on Saturday. See also Doremas v. Barton, 5 Bliss, 57, where it is held that where days of grace are waived, and the note falls due on Sunday, a demand and protest on Saturday is good and sufficient to hold the endorser.

[3] Avery v. Stewart, 2 Conn. 69,

Salter v. Burt 20 Wend 205. See Lindenmuller v. The People 33 Barb 560. The rule is applied also to legal holidays. See Kunz v. Tempel 48 Mo 75

[4] The rule that Sunday is not to be counted as a day, when the day for performance is found to fall upon that day, has been applied to contracts other than those governed by the law merchant. Thus where the rent fixed in a lease fell upon a Sunday a tender on the next day was held to be a legal performance. Warne v. Wagener, 15 Atl Rep (N J) 307. This in derogation of the common law. We are not informed whether or not in New Jersey such a tender is permitted by statute

day.[5] In some states by statute, the tender and payment may be made on the following Monday.[6]

§ 304. **Hour of the day when a tender should be made—Before the sun sets—Before midnight—Closing hour of business concerns, etc.**—The question of the hour of the day when a person may make a tender of money or chattels has commanded the attention of the courts on many occasions, and the decisions are sufficiently nice. A person who is to pay money, or deliver property, or to perform an act on or before a certain day, or on a certain day, has the whole of the day fixed, or the whole of the last day limited in which to perform. The party who is to receive, for his own protection has the correlative right of being present, counting the money, or examining the goods, and, therefore, that the entire transaction may be completed within the time, the tenderor must make his tender of the thing at such a reasonable hour that the tenderee may close the transaction by his count or examination, before the period for performance expires. It is thought by some authors,[1] that the time of day when the period for performance expires, depends upon whether the thing is to be done at a certain place, or anywhere. That is, if the place is expressly stipulated, it is enough if the tender be made at such a convenient time before the sun sets that the act may be completed by daylight, while, if no place be specified for performance, the tender may be made at a convenient time before midnight. Although such opinion is supported by authority,[2] yet it

---

[5] Pugsley v. Luther, 1 Wend. 42. In a case where a merchanic's lien expired on Sunday it was held that the principal of Avery v. Stewart (2 Conn. 69) was not applicable and that the lien must be strictly construed against the lien holder. Patrick v. Foulke, 45 Mo. 311.

[6] Bovey De Luttre Lumber Co. v. Tucker, 50 N. W. Rep. (Minn.) 1038. In Minnesota (§ 2230 G. S. Minn. 1894) and some other states, the statute provides that bills of exchange, drafts, promissory notes and contracts, due or payable or

to be performed on a Sunday or upon certain holidays shall be payable or performable upon the business day next preceding. So in Minnesota the statute in reference to computing time, provides that where the last day within which an act is to be done falls on Sunday, it shall be excluded § 5222 G. S. Minn. 1894.

[1] 2 Benj. on Sales 910.

[2] In Startup v. Macdonald, 46 Eng. Com. L. 623 s. c. 6 M. & G. 593 the court considered the question at length. In that case ten tons of linseed oil was to be deliv-

does not seem to be in harmony with the rule, that, in absence of a stipulation fixing the place for performance,

ered within a certain period No place for delivery was stipulated. A tender was made to the vendee personally on the last day, at half-past eight o'clock in the evening The jury found that the time was an unreasonable and improper time of the day for the tender of the oil Park, B, said "Upon a reference to the authorities, and due consideration of them, it appears to me that there is no doubt upon this question It is not to be left to the jury to determine as a question of practical convenience or reasonableness in each case but the law appears to have fixed the rule and it is this, that a party who is, by contract, to pay money or to do a thing transitory, to another anywhere on a certain day, has the whole of the day and if on one of several days the whole of the days for the performance of his part of the contract, and until the whole of the day or the whole of the last day has expired no action will lie against him for the breach of such a contract In such a case the party bound must find the other at his peril and within the t or limited if the other be within the four seas and he must do all that without the concurrence of the other he can do to make the payment or perform the act and that at a convenient time before midnight such time varying according to the quantum of the payment or nature of the act to be done Therefore, if he is to pay a sum of money, he must tender it a sufficient time before midnight for the party to whom the tender is made, to receive and

court; or if he is to deliver goods, he must tender them so to allow a sufficient time for examination and receipt This done, he has, so far as he could, paid or delivered within the time, and it is by the fault of the other only, that the payment or delivery is not complete But where the thing to be done is to be performed *at a certain place*, on or before a certain day, to another party to a contract, there the tender must be to the other party *at that place*, and as the attendance of the other is necessary at the place to complete the act, there the law, though it requires the other to be present, is not so unreasonable as to require him to be present for the whole day where the thing is to be done on one day or for the whole series of days when it is to be done on or before a day certain and, therefore, it fixes a particular part of the day for his presence; and it is enough if he be at the place at such a convenient time before sunset on the last day as that the act may be completed by daylight, and if the party bound tender to the party there if present, or if absent, be ready at the place to perform the act within a convenient time before sunset for its completion, it is sufficient; and if the tender be made *to the other party* at the place at any time of the day the contract is performed and though the law gives the utmost convenient time on the last day, yet this is solely for the convenience of both parties, that neither may give longer attendance than is necessary, and if it happened and the party who is to receive cannot be found and lives within the "four seas," the law fixes the place. In a case

that both parties meet at the place at any other time of the day, or upon any other day within the time limited, and a tender is made, the tender is good. See Bac. Abr. Tit. Tender (D.) (a.) Co. Litt. 202a This is the distinction which prevails in all cases—where a thing is to be done anywhere, a tender at a convenient time before midnight is sufficient; where the thing is to be done at a *particular place*, and where the law implies a duty on the party to whom the thing is to be done to attend, that the attendance is to be by daylight and a convenient time before sunset." 8 p. Smith v. Walton, 5 Del. 111 We do not find that the rule layed down by the court in Startup v. Macdonald, has been followed to any great extent, yet there is nevertheless a strong inclination on the part of the profession to accept the expressions and views of the ancient jurists as founded in wisdom, without stopping to find out whether the particular views expressed are in harmony with other branches of the law, or in fact founded upon reason, or deducible from the premises relied upon Park, B, in that case, seemed to think that where no place of payment was specified, it was payable anywhere. This is true if the debtor on the day can come up with the creditor So also is the statement that the debtor must, at his peril, find his creditor if within the four seas. But there has never been, so far as we are able to find, a time when, in absence of a stipulation fixing the place of payment, the law did not fix a place. If a

creditor leaves his abode and travels from place to place, the law has never required a debtor to abandon his business and keep his creditor in sight so that on the day for payment he may be able to make a personal tender But if the creditor has a place of residence at the time the contract matures, the debtor at his peril must find it, if within the four seas, and there make a personal tender, or in the absence of the creditor, be there with the money ready to fulfil his contract This is what is meant by the early commentators, when they say in absence of a stipulated place of payment, the debtor, at his peril, must find his creditor, if within the four seas There fore the distinction made in reference to sunset being the uttermost time for the payment when the place is fixed by the contract and midnight when no place is fixed by the contract, is not well grounded in reason Coke, in his commentaries on Littleton, said "But if the parties meet upon any part of the land whatsoever on the same day, the tender shall save the conditions forever for that time" Co Litt 202a And to the same effect is Bac Abr Tit Tender (D) This seemed to be relied upon by Park, B, for his conclusion that a tender may be made at any hour, even after sun set, if the debtor is able to meet with the creditor But this is not the correct conclusion to be de duced from Coke In Wade's Case 5 Co 114a, it is said "But if the both parties meet together any time of the same day, and the

which arose in Vermont, the court said: "That to make a tender good, the party must, at the latest time, on the last day of the term of the contract, before the sun sets, proceed to the dwelling house, or other usual place of abode of him to whom the tender is to be made, if no other place be provided by the contract, and there produce the money or goods, and offer to comply with the contract on his part." [3]

The general rule is, that a tender of money or goods must be made a sufficient length of time before the sun sets, so that the money may be counted or the goods examined by day light. [4] In Bacon's Abridgment, the rule is laid down, that, "although the party who ought to pay money, or deliver goods, has until the uttermost convenient time of the last day limited for payment or delivery to pay the money or deliver the goods, a tender is not good, unless there be, after it is made, time enough, before the sun sets, to examine and tell the money, or to examine and take account of the goods; for if a man should be compelled to receive either money or goods in the dark, there would be great danger of his being imposed upon." [5]

obligor or mortgagor, &c. make a tender in the place, &c to the mortgagee, &c and he refuses it, the penalty is forever saved, and he need not make a new tender by a convenient time before the last instant." In McClartey v Gober, 31 Iowa, 505, a tender of money made at about eight p m was held good, but the observation of the court, that it thought the time reason for the refusal was a desire to defeat the contract, discloses that the court's mind was swayed by reasons not strictly legal, and the case therefore is worthless as authority See Sweet v Harding, 19 Vt. 587; In Williams v Johnson, Litt. Sel. Cases, 84, a holding of the trial court, that a tender might be made at any time before midnight, was repudiated and the decision of the lower court reversed See Croninger v Crocker, 62 N. Y. 158

[3] Morton v Wells, 1 Tyler (Vt) 384; Wing v. Davis, 7 Me 31; Kendal v. Talbot, 1 A K Marsh. 237. See Williams v. Johnson, Litt. Sel. Cases, 84

[4] Williams v Johnson, Litt Sel 84, s c. 12 Am Dec 275. At common law, a demand for rent must be made at a convenient time before the sun sets on the day the rent is due A demand made at half past ten o'clock in the morning was held insufficient to entitle the lessor to re-enter without action Alcock v Phillips, 5 H & N 183. The common law rule has been generally adopted in the United States See Jackson v. Harrison, 17 Johns 70, McQueston v Morgan, 34 N H. 400, Colyer v. Hutchings, 2 Bibb 405; Jouett v Wagnon, 2 Bibb. 269; Johnson v. Butler, 4 Bibb 97

[5] 9 Bac Abr. Tit Tender (D); s p Sturgess v Buckley, 32 Conn.

It has been said that nature has formed, and convenience has pointed out the day, as the proper time for the trans action of the ordinary concerns of human life. Though night, as well as day, is a part of the natural time, and, for some legal purposes, is taken into estimation, yet it is not that portion of time which the law, founded in reason and consulting the convenience of mankind, has allotted for the tender of money or of goods, which a person may be bound by contract to pay or deliver.[6] One reason that the latter part of the day, rather than any other part of the day is appointed by law as the uttermost time in which to perform, is aptly stated by Coke, thus:—"By the express words of the condition the money is to be paid on the day indefinitely, and a convenient time before the last instance is the extreme time appointed by the law, to the intent that the one should not prevent the other, the one being sometimes there, and the other not, and the other being sometimes there, and not the other; and therefore the law appoints the extreme time of day, to the intent that both parties may certainly meet together; for the law, which always requires conveni ence, and is grounded on the experience of the sages, will not compel any of the parties to make an attorney, or repose confidence or trust in any other to pay it for him when he will do it himself (for *non temere credere est nervus sapientiae*)"[7] Another reason given in the books for the rule is, (and it applies in all cases whether the uttermost

18, Aldrich v Albee, 1 Greenl 120, Doe v Paul, 3 C & P 613. In Avery v Stewart, 2 Conn 69, Gould, J, said: "I cannot persuade myself that the rule requiring a tender to be made before sun set was ever meant to apply to cases, where the creditor is absent through the whole day. The rule was made for his convenience, that he might have a fair opportunity to examine, compute, and take an account of the money or other property tendered But if he will not appear at all at the place appointed, to avail himself of the benefit of the rule, he waives it for it can be of no pos

sible advantage to him. While at a distance from the place where the property is he can no more examine it by day-light than in the dark." It would seem here, that the court overlooked the fact that if the creditor was not at the place appointed at the proper time he would be in no position to claim a default by the other party, the debtor being first to act in the matter. See Kendall v Tabbot, 1 A K Marsh. 237

[6] Williams v Johnson Litt Sel Cas. 84

[7] Wade's Case 5 Co 114a, 2 Co Litt 202a. See Tiernan v Napier, 5 Yerg 410

times for performance be sunset, or is governed by the custom and usage of the particular business) that it is for the convenience of the parties that neither may be compelled, unnecessarily, to attend during the whole day [8] The length of time before the sun sets, when a tender should be made, depends upon the time necessary to count the money or examine the goods [9]

The law fixing the uttermost convenient time of the last day, before the sun sets, for performance, is for the convenience of the parties and neither can discharge himself in the absence of the other by being present and ready to perform before that time But if it so happens that both parties meet at the place at an earlier hour of the last day, a tender is good [10] So, where the place is not designated in the contract, and the money or thing may be tendered to the person who is to receive it anywhere, a tender to the person wherever he may be met with, at any earlier time of the day, will be good. The debtor must do all in his power to perform the contract; he must not only have the money or article promised in readiness to be paid or delivered to the creditor, but if the latter does not appear, the debtor must

[8] Hall v. Whittier, 10 R J 530, See 12 Am Dec 572n Fermin v Napier 5 Yerg 110

[9] In Hill v Grange 1 Plow 173, it was said that if the rent reserved was a great sum, as £500 or £1,000 the lessee ought to be ready to pay at such a convenient time before sunset, in which the money might be counted for the lessor is not bound to count it in the night after sunset, for if so he might be deceived In Wade's Case 5 Co 114a, a case is put of a person bound to pay £10 000 on a certain day, in which case it was thought sufficient if he tender it in bags, for it could not be counted in one day But there, the discussion is as to tendering money in a bag and who should take it out of the bag and count it We apprehend that where a person is to pay a $1 000,000 00, or any great sum, on a certain day, and it would take two or three days to count the money, that the party bound to pay would not have to tender it before the last day, even though it could not be counted by the tenderee personally in one day, but that the tenderor would be bound, however, to make a tender at the earliest possible time on the last day taking into consideration the business hours of the tenderee and possibly the hour of opening of the bank or other safe place where such a large sum is kept

[10] 2 Inst § 331, 9 Bacon s Abr Title Tender (D), Wade's Case, 5 Co 114a Aldrich v Albee, 1 Greenl 120, Hall v Whittier, 10 R I 530 See 12 Am Dec 572n

remain at the place in person, or by agent, till the sun has set, waiting for the creditor.[11] Although the uttermost convenient time before the sun sets is the legal time for a tender to be made, yet the money or thing is not completely due until the end of the natural day (midnight) and an action will not lie to recover the thing, or a forfeiture cannot be enforced until the full time has expired.[12] The rule limiting the time for payment to a convenient time before the sun sets, so that the transaction may be completed by day light may be varied by special agreement.

There is a remarkable dearth of authorities on the question whether a tender must be made at a convenient time before expiration of an earlier hour than sunset, which by custom and usuage in a particular business is the time limited for closing the daily business.[13] Where a contract provided for the delivery of stock at a specified day, it was held that a tender made at the uttermost convenient time of the day fixed, before the usual time of shutting the books, was good.[14] Afterwards when a similar case arose, and it appeared that there was more business that day than

---

[11] Aldrich v Albee, 1 Greenl 120, Tinckler v Prentice, 4 Taunt 549 Lancashire v Killingworth, 1 Ld Ry. 686, s c 12 Mod 529, 3 Salk 312, Com. 116. In Duckham v Smith, 5 T. B Mon 372, the proof was that the tobacco to be delivered was taken to a warehouse in wagons at nine o'clock in the morning, and was taken away in about an hour.

[12] This question has frequently arisen in cases where the controversy was, whether the heir or administrator was entitled to the rent of real estate, the lessor having died on the day the rent was due after the hour of sunset and before midnight. The early case gave it to the heir, on the ground that the rent was not in fact due until the last minute of the natural day. 3 Coke on Litt 202a See 1 Sand 287, and 1 P William, 178 In Stafford v Wentworth, 9

Mod 21, a life tenant, who had made a lease for years, died about two p m on the day the rent fell due and it was held under such circumstances where the tenant pays the rent to the remainder man, that the court would order it paid to the administrator But by statute, 11 Geo 2, C. 19, S 15, which provides that the administrator in such cases, may recover of the under tenant all or a portion of such rent as the case may be This is the equitable rule, although the rent may not be due until a certain time, yet it may be nearly all earned at the time of the death of the lessor. And the obligation to pay so much as is earned is certainly personal property

[13] See Sweet v Harding 19 Vt. 587, Sturgess v Buckley, 32 Conn 18

[14] Lancashire v Killingworth,

could be transacted before the regular closing hour and, for that reason the books were again opened after that hour, a transfer made before the regular closing hour was held not a good tender. The court observed that the general rule, which is that a tender must be made at the uttermost convenient time of the day, ought not to be broken through, except in case of necessity; and that in the present case there was no necessity to break through it, because, as the books were again opened in the afternoon, the tender ought to have been made at the uttermost convenient time before the shutting of the books in the afternoon.[15] A rule requiring the tender to be made at a convenient time before the expiration of regular business hours, where the tenderee is a large corporation, or other large concern, where it is necessary in order to bring the daily business to a close at a reasonable hour to close its doors at an early hour before the sun sets, would be convenient. The custom obtains, particularly in the villages and smaller cities, of keeping the shop and places of business open after the sun sets and until a late hour, and of doing business by lamp light, in such case a tender of money or goods after the sun sets, to the shop keeper while yet in his shop doing business, would be good, unless perhaps goods were tendered which required sunlight for a proper examination.

§ 305. **Premature tender—Rule of the civil law—At common law—Interest-bearing obligations—Days of grace—Rescission—Tender of principal and entire interest to end of term—Waiver.**—According to the civil law, where the right of requiring payment is deferred until the expiration of a term, and such distant day of payment is given exclusively for the benefit of the debtor, the latter may make a tender of the amount due before the time fixed for payment arrives.[1] But the rule at common law is thought to be directly the reverse.[2]

Salk. 624, s. c. 12 Mod 533, s. p. 9 Bac. Abr. Tit Tender (D).

[15] Rutland v. Batty, Stra 777, s. c. 1 Ld. Raym. 686. See Bac. Abr. Tit Tender (D)

[1] Pothier's Obl. p. II c. 3, art 3, § 2

[2] See McHard v. Whetcroft, 3 Har. & M. (Md) 85, where the condition of a bond was to pay a sum of money "at or upon' a certain day. In this case it was held that a tender before the day fixed was not premature The counsel who presented that side of the case claimed that the question was governed by the civil law, and admitted that the common

330 THE LAW OF TENDER. [§ 305

Contracts wherein it is expressly provided that the term may be contracted at the option of the debtor, as where the privilege is given to pay "on or before" are not here referred to. When it appears from the contract or the circumstances, that the term is appointed in favor of the creditor as well as of the debtor, as where a sum of money due on a note or other obligation, carried interest before the maturity, a tender cannot be made before the time for payment arrives.[3] Upon this question the common law and the civil law agree.[4] The right to refuse a tender in such cases seems to rest on the right of a creditor to keep his money at interest according to contract. It is a general rule that wherever a debtor would derive a collateral advantage, as where he would escape paying interest to the due day, it allowed to make payment before the full term expires, or would have the use of certain property, if allowed to re-enter or take possession of property on such payment, or, on the other hand the creditor would be deprived of the profits or advantages accruing by reason of the contract, between the time of the attempted payment and the end of the term as fixed by the contract, a tender before the day will be unavailing. According to Pothier the time of payment specified in a bill of exchange is deemed to be appointed in favor of the creditor who is the holder as well as the debtor. A promissory note entitled to days of grace is due and payable on the third day of grace, and the holder cannot be compelled to accept a tender thereon before the same is due. If the note bears interest, the holder is entitled to interest until payment is legally demandable.[5]

Where an option to rescind a contract or to repurchase is given to be exercised at the expiration of a certain time, a tender before the time is premature.[6] So, a tender of the purchase money before the time provided in the contract

law was different s p Quinn v. Whetcroft, 3 Har & M (Md) 136.

[3] Abshire v Corey, 15 N E. Rep (Ind) 685, Tillou v. Britton, 4 Halst 127, Saunders v Winship, 5 Pick 267, Kingman v. Pierce, 17 Mass 247; Moore v. Kime, 61 N W Rep (Neb) 736

[4] Pothier's Obl p II c 3, art 3 § 3

[5] Smith v Merchants' & Farmers' Bank, 11 Oh. C. C. 199

[6] Schultz v O'Rourke, 45 Pac (Mont) 634

for payment, will not put the vendor in default on the account of the non delivery of the deed.[7]

Where a mortgagor has an option of paying the whole or part of the principal and interest, at any interest paying period, a tender between the periods of the full amount of the principal and interest is unavailing.[8] Where there is no option given to the debtor allowing him to contract the term, is a tender good of the principal and the full amount of the interest which could accrue up to the time of payment fixed by the contract? In a case which arose in Wisconsin, the court said that the question was somewhat novel, and one upon which the authorities were not numerous, owing doubtless to the rarity of the occurrence as a matter of fact  The point was not decided, but the court asks the question—"Can it not be said that the creditor may have an interest in keeping his money invested upon security, rather than to have it in his own hands"[1]—and concluded by observing that it would seem as though he might have such interest, and might even arbitrarily or obstinately, and without advantage to himself, insist upon keeping it out according to contract, unless the rule of the civil law is to prevail.[9] In the absence of positive authorities, the rule would seem to be that a tender of the principal and all the interest that could accrue to the due date would not be good [10]

According to Pothier, "A term, is either of right or of grace: when it makes part of the agreement, and is expressly or tacitly included in it, it is of right; when it is not a part of the agreement, it is of grace; as if it is afterwards granted by the prince or the judge at the requisition of the debtor."[11] An effect common to both is the postponing the right of requiring payment, but with respect to a term of grace it stops the pursuit of the creditor, but does not exclude the right of the compensation  This term of

[7] Rhoyer v  Bila, 83 Cal, 51

[8] Di Silva v  Turner, 44 N. E. Rep (Mass) 532

[9] Moore v  Cord, 14 Wis. 231

[10] See Abbe v  Goodwin, 7 Conn. 377, and Brown v  Cole, 14 Sim. 427 (found later), where it is held that such a tender is not good. In Burgoyne v. Spurling,

Cro Car 283 and Hoyle v  Cazabat 25 La Ann 138, the right to pay before the day was not at the time questioned  In Scott v. Fink, 53 Barb 533, the agreement permitted such payment

[11] Pothier's Obl p II c 3 art. 3, Sec  1

grace is not known at common law. But there is a term in
the English and American law which bears some analogy to
it, as where a time is limited by a court of equity for the
doing of an act, as where a certain time is given by the court
within which a debtor may redeem, in which case a tender
of the amount due may be made at any time before the
day limited.[12] Where both parties treat a debt as then due,
but the tender is refused upon some other ground, the ten
deree cannot defend upon the ground that the debt was not
then due.[13]

§ 306. Tender before action — On unilateral contracts — Conversion—Replevin—Specific performance—Abandoning contract
—Rescission—Exception to the rule—After a discontinuance—
Action when commenced.—It has been said that no instance
can be found in the practice of the common law courts in
which a tender made subsequent to the commencement of
the action has been countenanced as a ground for a plea
of tender.[1] Unless authorized by statute a tender must be

[12] There was at common law,
terms that were somewhat analogous to the term mentioned by
Pothier   Littleton mentions a
custom of giving a day of grace,
or a day of courtesy to a tenant
The delay, however, was granted
by the court, "at the prayer of
the demandant or plaintiff in
whose delay it is, and never at
the prayer of tenant or defend
ant" Co Litt 135a   So, Sir
William Blackstone mentions days
of grace   Where a person was
summoned to appear at court, he
had three days of grace beyond
the day named in the writ, in
which to make his appearance;
and if he appeared on the fourth
day it was sufficient   The reason given for this indulgence was,
that "our sturdy ancestors held
it beneath the condition of a freeman to appear or to do any other
act, at the precise time appointed" 3 Bl Com 278. In these

terms of grace the analogy is
very slight. They have long
since become absolute. The days
of grace, now a matter of right,
but formerly an indulgence pure
and simple, given to the payor of
a promissory note or bill of exchange, bears also a slight analogy
to the term of grace by the civil
law, as does also the statutory
period allowed a mortgagor or
execution debtor, within which to
redeem   The mode mentioned in
the text of a court of equity fixing
the time within which a debtor
may redeem from a mortgage
comes nearer in analogy to the
manner of granting a term of
grace by the civil law, than any
other case to be formed in English
jurisprudence

[13] Wyckoff v Anthony, 90 N. Y.
142

[1] Levan v Sternfield 25 Atl
Rep (N J) 854

made before the commencement of the action.[2] No rule is better settled than this. The object of a debtor in making a tender is to discharge himself and escape the payment of damages and costs, and this cannot be done by delaying a tender of performance until after an action has been commenced and costs incurred. Where the contract sought to be enforced is unilateral, the rule is very strict, and the party not bound must show that he tendered performance on his part before bringing his action.[3] To lay the foundation for an action against a pledgee for conversion of the thing pledged, the pledgor must tender the amount of the debt on the day of maturity, and a tender made after the day the debt becomes due is not good.[4] After maturity of the debt he may lay the foundation for an action to redeem by a tender of the amount due. A tender, to change rightful into wrongful possession of property, and to be of avail in an action to recover such property, must be made before the commencement of the action.[5] Where a mortgagee is foreclosing under a statute, a tender may be made at any time before sale.[6]

In some of the states, as we have seen, where the payment of the purchase price and the delivery of the conveyance to real estate are simultaneous and concurrent acts, neither party can call for specific performance without first having tendered performance on his part.[7] And where such rule prevails the tender must always precede the action.[8] But

[2] Fishburn v Sanders, 1 N. & M 242, Simon v. Allen, 76 Tex 398, Berry v Davis 77 Tex 191

[3] Miller v Cameron, 1 L. R. A. (N J) 554.

[4] Butts v Burnett 6 Alb P N S 302. In this case, upon the maturity of the debt the pledgee could have sold the pledge, and he would only have been liable for the balance after satisfying his debt. A different rule would certainly apply when the statute prescribed a mode of disposing of pledges after giving notices. Woodworth v. Morris 56 Barb 97.

[5] Smith v. Woodleaf, 21 Kan. 717. See Marsden v Walsh, 52 Atl (R I) 684, where, in trover by a mortgagor, it was held that a tender of the mortgage debt before action was necessary, though the property had been attached by a third person at the instance of the mortgagee. See also Allen v Corby, 69 N Y Supp 7, where it was held that a tender before action was unnecessary, where the bailee demanded a much larger sum than that actually due.

[6] Davis v Dow, 83 N W Rep. (Minn) 50

[7] Chahoon v Hollenback, 16 W. & S 425 s c 16 Am Dec 587

[8] Snyder v Wolfley, 8 Serg & R 328

where a vendor has disabled himself from performing, or has repudiated the transaction, the willing party may treat the contract at an end, and bring an action to recover back what he has paid, or to recover damages for the breach of the contract, without making any tender or offer of performance before bringing the action.[9]

Where money or anything of value has been received on a contract, and the party receiving afterwards desires to rescind the contract on the ground of fraud, a tender of the thing received must be made to the other party as soon as the fraud is discovered.[10] But if the thing received is of no value in itself, as a due bill, bill of sale, promissory note and the like, the rule is not so strict, and if the rights and liabilities of the parties are in no way changed by the delay, a tender of the instrument made at the trial,[11] or even before a verdict will be good.[12] Where an action has been discontinued and another commenced, a tender made after the discontinuance and before the commencement of the second action is a tender before the action.[13] A tender by a plaintiff of the amount due on a judgment, before it is pleaded as a set-off, is a tender before action, though made after the action was commenced. A set off or counter claim is not in litigation until it is pleaded.[14]

Retaining an attorney to bring suit is not the commencement of an action. A tender between the time of the application for a writ and the time it is issued is a tender before the action.[15] So is a tender made after the attorney had drawn and sent off a declaration to be filed, but before filing or service.[16] Signing a summons is not the commencement of an action.[17] Under some of the statutes, delivering the summons or process to an officer for services is a commencement of the action. In Kansas, it was held that a tender made

[9] Bunge v. Koop, 48 N. Y. 225

[10] The Mich. Cent. R. Co. v. Dunham, 30 Mich. 128; Pangborn v. Continental Ins. Co., 67 Mich. 683, 35 N. W. Rep. 814.

[11] Sloam v. Shiffer, 156 Pa. St. 59, s. c. 27 Alt. Rep. 67, or even before a verdict will be good

[12] Schofield v. Shiffer, 156 Pa. St. 65, s. c. 27 Alt. Rep. 69.

[13] 3 Bl. Com. 304n 19, Johnson v. Clay, 1 Moore, 200

[14] Hassam v. Hassam, 22 Vt. 516

[15] Briggs v. Calverly, 8 T. R. 629

[16] Brown v. Fergeson, 2 Deno 196

[17] Kerr v. Mount, 28 N. Y. 659, Kelly v. West, 36 Super. Ct. 304

after the filing of a petition and the issue of process is not before the commencement of the action.[18]  As to when an action is commenced more has been said elsewhere.[19]

§ 307.  **Tender after action brought—A statutory right—Applies to what cases.**—A tender after an action has been commenced can only be made under a statute authorizing it.[1] Such a tender does not bar the further prosecution of the action, but if otherwise sufficient it stops interest, and subjects the plaintiff to subsequent costs.[2] It may be proven at the trial by oral testimony.  In New York and some other states, a tender may be made at any time before the commencement of the trial, after the trial it comes too late.[3] It appears that, in Tennessee, it may be made after an appeal has been taken.[4] If, after an action has been commenced, the plaintiff agrees to take notes or anything else in payment of his claim, a tender of the notes or other things agreed upon is not a tender after the action brought, but a tender upon an agreement made after the action was commenced.[5]

A statute authorizing a tender at any time before judgment was held not applicable to cases where the plaintiff is bound to make a tender previous to suit to have a standing in court.[6]  In Vermont, an action of ejectment after a forfeiture to recover the possession of real estate conveyed by mortgage, is considered an action to recover money in which a tender may be made under the statute of the amount due at any time before the three days before the setting of the court to which the writ is returnable.[7]  In Mississippi, an action of replevin to recover chattels sold upon a conditional

[18] Smith v Woodleaf, 21 Kan 717

[19] See § 201

[1] Snyder v Quarton 17 Mich 211 10 N. W. Rep 204; Kelly v West 36 N Y Super Ct 304, Sweetland v Tuthill, 54 Ill 215. Gill v Lathrop 39 Me 434; Hull v Peters, 7 Barb 331  See Farr v Smith, 9 Wend 338 s c 21 Am Dec 162

[2] Sweetland v Tuthill, 54 Ill 215 Wagner v. Heckenkamp 84 Ill. App 324, Le Flore v. Meller, 64

Miss 201, Columbian Bldg Assn v Crump, 42 Md 192

[3] Houston v Sledge, 101 N Car 640 Pell v Chandos, 27 S W Rep (Tex Civ App) 48

[4] Freeman v Napier, 5 Yerg 410

[5] Emmons v Meyers 8 Miss. 375  See Heirn v Carron, 11 S & M (Miss) 361

[6] Farquhar v Iles, 39 La Am 871

[7] Powers v Powers, 11 Vt 262

sale, is considered somewhat in the same light, and a tender under the statute of the amount due and accrued costs, was held to fix the purchaser's right as though payment had been made before suit [8] In New York, under a statute there in force, allowing the same defences in summary proceedings as may be interposed in a court of record, it was held that the statute did not authorize a tender of rent due to be made and pleaded during the pendency of the proceeding, as the statute authorizing a tender to be made in an action pending in a court of record could be made only where the "complaint demands judgment for a sum of money only." [9]

Where a statute permits a tenant, against whom an action to recover the premises for the non payment of the rent is pending, during the pendency of the action or within a certain time after a recovery of possession by the landlord in the action, to pay into court all rent in arrear, interest, and costs, and retain or recover the possession as the case may be, a tender of the amount required while the action is pending, or afterwards within the time limited, is insufficient to give the tenant any right to retain or recover the possession.[10] When a minor may redeem from a sale of his land for taxes, within one year after he attains his majority, he may tender the amount due the purchaser, pending an action of ejectment against him by such purchaser, if within the year [11] In such case if the year has not expired, he may make a tender after judgment. A general rule as to the class of actions covered by the statutes in which a tender may be made, cannot be satisfactorily formulated, but it may be affirmed as a general principle that a tender may be made after an action brought in all cases where a tender might have been

---

[8] Le Flore v Miller, 64 Miss. 204 Citing Helm v. Gray, 59 Miss 51, when it was said, "It is settled in the actions mentioned (i e replevin and detinue) it is admissible to inquire into the state of the title at the trial (Wells on Replevin 196). * * * The rule is general in all actions that the plaintiff must have the right to recover at the commencement of the suit and at the trial."

[9] Stover v Chase, 29 N. Y Supp 291, s c 9 Misc Rep 15 citing the statute § 731, and Code of Civ Pro, § 2244

[10] Wilcoxen v Hybarger 38 S W (Tex) 669. See 1894 G. S. Minn. § 5865 See Wickolz v Griesgraber, 70 Minn 220 and George v. Mahoney, 62 Minn. 370, to the contrary. See Sec 287, ante

[11] Price v. Ferguson, 6 So Rep (Miss) 210

made before the action was commenced, excepting cases where a tender is necessary to the cause of action, and cases where a tender is necessary to prevent a forfeiture [12]

§ 308. **Computing time—Excluding first day—Including last day—Fractions of days.**—It is a general rule, that where a thing is to be done at the expiration of a certain time from or after a given day, or after the happening of a certain event, that the given day or the day of the happening of the event, is to be excluded and the day for performance included [1] Thus where a bequest is made conditional upon the beneficiary doing a certain thing within six calendar months after the testator's death, the day of the death is to be excluded.[2] The rule excluding the first day and including the day of performance, has been generally adopted in the computation of the time, where by a statute, money is to be paid or any act done within a given time.[3] In some states the statutes specifically prescribe this manner of computing time.[4] Under a statute allowing a tender of damages and costs to be made at any time "until three days before commencement of the term," at which the action is returnable, both the day on which the tender is made and the first day of the term are excluded [5]

The rule for computing time where money is to be paid, or anything is to be done at the expiration of a certain time from the doing of a certain act, is not entirely settled. According to some authorities the day of the act is to be included,[6] while other authorities are to the contrary holding that

---

[12] Whiteman v Perkins 76 N W Rep (Neb) 547

[1] Good v Webb, 52 Ala. 452, Roehner v The Knickerbocker, Life Ins Co, 63 N Y 160, Woodbridge v Brigham, 12 Mass 102, s c 7 Am Dec 85, Avery v Stewart, 2 Conn 69; Hadley v. Cunningham, 12 Bush 402, Sand v Lyons 18 Conn 18

[2] Lester v Garland, 15 Ves. 248, s. p Sands v Lyons, 18 Conn 18

[3] Biglow v Willson, 1 Pick 485. In computing three years after

entry for condition broken, within which a mortgagor may redeem the day of entry is to be excluded, and in such a case a tender made on August 15th, 1828, when the entry was made on August 15th, 1827 was held good in Wing v Davis 7 Me 31

[4] 1894, G S Minn s 5222

[5] Willey v Laraway, 64 Vt 566, s c 25 A Rep 435

[6] Bellasis v Hester, 1 Ld Raym. 280 Hadley v Cunningham, 12 Bush 402, Batman v Megowan, 1 Met (Ky) 547; Pearpaint v Gra-

22

the day of the act must be excluded.[7]  But the weight of the
authorities appear to establish the rule that the day of the
act is to be included.  In computing time fractions of days
are counted as days.[8]

§ 309.  **Fixing the time—Enlarging or accelerating the time
by parole when.**—Where no time is fixed for performance the
parties may fix a time.  If the time is specified in a simple
contract the parties may by a parole agreement enlarge the
time.[1]  So, the time may be accelerated by a parole agreement.[2]  The time for a performance of a contract under a
seal, before any breach of it, cannot be extended by parole
where the agreement to extend the time is executory.[3]  After
a breach of a sealed instrument it may be modified as to the
time, or wholly rescinded by an executed parole agreement
founded upon a sufficient consideration.[4]

## II. PLACE.

§ 310.  **The place where a tender may be made—General rule.**—
The place of making a tender is frequently of much importance in determining whether a party bound to do a certain
thing has complied with his obligation.  It is a general rule
that if a contract be to pay money or to deliver goods at a
certain place, a tender can only be made at that place,[1] as the

ham, 4 Wash. C. C 420, Arnold v.
United States, 9 Cranch, 104;
Blake v. Crowninshield, 9 N. H.
304

[7] Weeks v. Hull, 19 Conn. 376;
Bemis v. Leonard, 118 Mass. 502.
But in the last case, the English
authorities cited (Lester v. Garland, 15 Ves. 248; and Webb v.
Fairmanner, 3 M & W 473), as rejecting the doctrine of the earlier
English cases that the day of the
act is included, do not sustain the
position taken by the Massachusetts court.  The question under
consideration in the first case, was
as to the mode of computing time,
where an act was to be done within a certain time from the happening of a certain event, and in the

latter case goods were to be paid
for in two months.

[8] See Sands v. Lyons, 18 Conn.
18.

[1] Keating v. Price, 1 Johns Cas
22, s c 1 Am. Dec 92, and cases
referred to in note.  Friess v.
Rider, 24 N Y 367.

[2] Anderson v. Moore, 145 Ill.

[3] Allen v Jaquish, 21 Wend.
628; Eddy v Graves 23 Wend 84;
Dodge v. Crandall, 30 N. Y. 307.

[4] Dodge v Crandall, 30 N. Y.
307, and see cases cited  Fleming
v. Gilbert, 3 Johns. 528.

[1] Sanderson v. Brown, 14 East.
500; 9 Bac Abr Tit. Tender (C),
Pothier Obl 502; Roberts v Beatty, 2 Pen. & Watt 63; Adams v.
Rutherford, 13 Or. 78

place is made part and parcel of the contract. A tender at the place is sufficient though the one to whom it is to be made be absent at the time.[2] In a case where horses were to be delivered at Lexington, evidence of a tender of horses at the vendee's house in the country was held not admissible.[3] Where a tender to the person is not necessary, as where a place of payment is fixed by the contract, or the law fixes the place, as in the case of rent issuing out of land, a tender to the person is good unless objected to on that ground.[4] Littleton says, "Where the place of payment is limited, the feoffee is not bound to receive the payment in any other place but in the same place so limited. But yet if he does receive the payment in another place, this is good enough and as strong for the feoffor as if the receipt had been in the same place so limited, &c."[5] If a promissory note or other obligation to pay money, or property, is payable at either of the two places, it is sufficient for the payor to be at either, at the time fixed for payment, with the thing to be delivered. Where no place for payment is appointed in the instrument, and it is afterwards orally agreed that payment may be made at a specific place, a tender at the place agreed on will be sufficient.[6]

§ 311. **Payable in a town or city generally.**—If a negotiable promissory note is made payable in a town or city generally, without pointing out any particular place in the town or city and the payor has there no dwelling house, or other place of abode, or a place of business, and the payee on the day of payment does not know whether the payor is then at the place, or his whereabouts if then there or the payor has there a place of residence or business but the payee or holder is unable to find such place, it is sufficient to be any where in the city or town on the day with the note ready to demand payment. In such a case where a bill was payable in London generally, it was thought that an attempt to search for the

---

2 Judd v Ensign, 6 Barb 258

3 Price v Cochran. 1 Bibb. (Ky ) 770

4 Crop v Hamilton, Cro Eliz 48. See Hunter v Le Coute, 6 Cow 728, and Slingerland v. Morse, 8 Johns 370

5 Co Litt Sec 343

6 See Whitewell v Johnson, 17 Miss 449, Bank of America v. Woodworth, 18 John R. 315, s c. 19 John R 391 See State Bank v Hurd, 12 Mass 172, as to when a demand may be made.

payor in such a city as London would have been without object or effect.[1] In such case it is the duty of the payee or owner to make diligent search for the payor's residence or place of business. He should enquire of those who would be most likely to know, as merchants in the same business, or of those whom he knows to be relatives, or friends, or employee, &c. If there be a directory, he should search there for the address. On the other hand, in like case, if the payor has no abode or place of business it is sufficient for him to be any where in the town or city named on the day fixed ready with the money to discharge the note. He being held to the exercise of good faith and fair dealing

Where a non negotiable note, or any contract to pay money other than negotiable notes, is drawn payable in a town or city generally and the payee has there no abode or place of business, or the payee has there an abode or place of business, but the payor cannot by the exercise of reasonable diligence and inquiry find it, being ready on the day fixed for payment with the money to discharge the obligation at any place in the town or city will be a sufficient tender If goods sold, or goods due on a note, are to be delivered in a town or city generally, and the vendee or payee has there no abode or place of business, which fact is known to the vendor or payor in advance of the time for performance, the latter should apply to the former to know the particular place in the town or city where he will have the goods delivered and they should be delivered at the place designated But if the vendor or payor knowing that fact was unable to find the other party, or he did not know that the other party did not have an abode, or place of business in the town or city designated as the place of delivery, the vendor or payor on coming to the town or city, with the goods to discharge his contract, and no one coming to point out a place of delivery, may select some suitable place and then deposit the goods and notify the other party as soon as possible where his goods may be found. In such case, if the vendee or payee has an abode or place of business in the town or city named as the place of delivery, it is implied that the articles will be delivered at his residence, if he has no place of business, and vice versa, or if he has both an abode and place of business.

[1] See Boot v Franklin, 3 Johns 208, and 3 Kent's Com 96

at either one or the other as may be determined by the
nature of the article, or the known purpose for which the
thing is wanted.  If the things to be delivered are wanted
for shipping, as live stock or merchandise, it is implied that
the chattels are to be delivered at some yard, or warehouse,
to be designated by the vendee or payee, and if the latter is
absent or for any reason fails or neglects on a request to
point out the place, the vendor or payor may select a suitable
place and there leave the stock, or merchandise, and notify
the other party where they are.

§ 312.  **Where the time but no place is appointed for the payment of money—Not bound to go out of the state.**—At common
law, with respect to the payment of money, where the time
but no place of payment is specified, the rule is stated generally to be that the debtor must seek his creditor, if within
the "four seas" and make a tender to him.[1]  Without qualifi

---

[1] Littleton, according to Sir Edward Coke, said: "Also, upon such
a case of feoffment in mortgage,
a question hath been demanded in
what place the feoffor is bound to
tender the money to the feoffee at
the day appointed, &c  and some
have said upon the land so holden
in a mortgage, because the condition is depending upon the land.
And they have said that if the
feoffor bee upon the land there
ready to pay the money to the
feoffee at the day set, and the
feoffee bee not then there, then
the feoffor is quit and excused of
the payment of the money, for
that no default is in him  But it
seemeth to some that the law is
contrary, and that default is in
him, for he is bound to seek the
feoffee if hee bee then in any
other place within the realm of
England  As if a man be bound
in an obligation of 20 pound upon
condition endorsed upon the same
obligation, that if he pay to him
to whom the obligation is made
at such a day 10 pounds then the

obligation of 20 pounds shall lose
his force, and bee holding for
nothing; in this case it behooveth
him that made the obligation to
seek him to whom the obligation
is made if he bee in England and
at the day set to tender to him the
said 10 pound, otherwise he shall
forfeit the sum of 20 pound com-
prised within the obligation, &c
And so it seemeth in the other
case, &c

And albeit that some have said
that the condition is depending
upon the land, yet this proves not
that the making of the condition
to bee performed, ought not to be
made upon the land, &c  no more
than if the condition were that
the feoffor at such a day shall
do some special corporal service
to the feoffee, not naming the
place where such corporal services shall be done  In this case
the feoffor ought to do such corporal service at the day limited to
the feoffee, in what place soever
of England that the feoffee bee,
if he will have advantage of the

cation, it would seem that the tender must be made to the obligee in person and failing in this the obligor would be in

condition, &c. So it seemeth in the other case. And it seemes to them that it shall bee more properly said, that the estate of the land is depending upon the condition, than to say that the condition is depending upon the land, etc." Commenting upon this, Lord Coke observes. "Here and in other places, that I may say once for all, where Littleton maketh a doubt, and setteth down several opinions and the reasons, he ever setteth down the better opinion and his own last, and so he doth here. For at this day this doubt is settled, having been oftentimes resolved, that seeing the money is a summe in grosse, and collateral to the title of the land, that the feoffor must tender the money to the person of the feoffee according to the later opinion, and it is not sufficient for him to tender it upon the land." Co. Litt. Sec. 340. There is scarcely a rule of law in the whole of the English and American jurisprudence that has been stated more frequently in the books, than the rule given in the text, and, it would be hard to find one stated with any more unerring generality. From the earliest time to the present, the courts and text writers who have treated of it, have gone on stating the general rule, without qualification, to be that, in absence of a stipulated place for payment of money, the debtor must seek his creditor if within the "realm," "four seas," "England," or the "state," etc., and make a tender to him. It has been long settled, that where no place is selected by the parties, at which

the payment may be made, the law fixes the place (Niles v. Culver, 8 Barb. 209) and, it is now a matter of little importance, in the United States at least, whether the general statements adverted to, ever obtained without qualification. Elsewhere we have expressed our belief that the law has always fixed a place of performance, where the contract was silent on that point. Sec. 304, note. In the following cases and many more, some reference to the rule may be found. Startup v. McDonald, 6 M. & G. 624, s c 46 Eng. Com. L 624, Cranley v. Hillary, 2 Maul. & Sel 122; Francis v. Deming, 59 Conn. 108; Hoys v. Tuttle, 8 Ark. 124; King v. Finch, 60 Ind 420; Smith v. Smith, 2 Hill. 351, Littell v Nichols, Hard, 71, Galloway v. Smith, Litt Sel Cas. 133; Grieve v. Annin, 1 Halst 461, Chambers v Winn, Saeed. 166; Currier v. Currier, 2 N. H. 75, Townsend v Wells, 3 Day. 327, Frenchot v. Leach, 5 Cow. 506, Lent v. Padelford, 10 Mass 230. See Bac. Abr Tender C, Co Litt. 210a (Sec 340) Littleton said, "And therefore it will be a good and sure thing for him that will make such feoffment in mortgage to appoint an especial place, where the money shall be paid, and the more especial that it bee put, the better it is for the feoffor," and Lord Coke referring to this, observed, "Here is a good counsell and advice given, to set downe in conveyances everything in certainitie and particularitie for certamitie is the mother of quietude and repose, and incertainitie is the cause of default. It is believed, however, that the early commentators referred to those persons having a domicile in England, and that the tenderor was bound to go to any part of England wherever the tenderee had his domicile. But the strict rule, if it ever obtained without qualification, has been modified, and it is now sufficient if the debtor seek his creditor at his place of residence, if within the realm, and there make a tender.[2] A debtor is not bound to go out of the realm to find his creditor. In the United States the debtor is not bound to go out of the state in which the contract was made.[3] The states, in this respect, are treated as foreign countries.

If no place be specified in the contract for the payment of money, or delivery of portable articles, the law fixes the place, and parole testimony is not admissible of a prior, or contemporaneous parole agreement fixing the place.[4] But the parties may by a subsequent parole agreement, agree upon a place of performance,[5] or change the place of payment or performance.[6]

If a party desires to redeem land from an execution, or mortgage sale, or from a sale under any lien, and the law fixes a time within which such a redemption may be made, and such a redemption is sought to be made prior to the last day limited, the redemptioner must seek the holder of the

---

variance and contention; and for obtaining of the one, and avoiding of the other, the best means is, in all assurances, to take counsel of learned and well experienced men, and not to trust only without advice to a precedent. For as the rule is concerning that state of men's bodies, *Nullum medicamentum est idem omnibus*, so is the state and assurance of a man's land, *Nullum exemplum est idem omnibus.*" Co. Litt. Sec. 342.

[2] Grussy v. Schneider, 55 How. Pr. 188. Stoker v. Cogswell, 25 How. Pr. 274, Roberts v. Beatty, 2 Penn. 63 (specific articles). See Smith v. Smith, 25 Wend. 405. The Code Napoleon, according to Mr. Chippman, provides "That if no particular place be named at

which payment is to be made, then tender shall be made to the creditor himself, or at his house, or at the place selected for the execution of the agreement." Chips. on Cont. 75.

[3] Houbie v. Volkening, 49 How. Pr. 169, Gill v. Bradley, 21 Minn. 15. Santee v. Santee, 64 Pa. St. 473; Allshouse v. Ramsay, 6 Whart. 33. Tasker v. Bartlett, 5 Cush. 359. Howard v. Miner, 20 Me. 330. Jones v. Perkins, 29 Miss. 139. Young v. Daniels, 2 Iowa, 126.

[4] La Farge v. Rickert, 5 Wend. 187. Niles v. Culver, 8 Barb. 209.

[5] Frenchot v. Leach, 5 Cow. 506. See Smith v. Smith, 25 Wend. 405, s. c. 2 Hill, 351.

[6] Miles v. Roberts, 34 N. H. 254.

certificate wherever he may be within the state and make a
tender to him in person, or seek the sheriff or other officer
authorized by law to accept the redemption money and make
a tender to him. If the redemptioner cannot come up with
the holder of the certificate any where conveniently, he may
give notice to him that at a certain time, at the residence of
the holder of the certificate, he will make a tender of the
money. But he is not authorized to give the sheriff notice,
and require him to attend at his office at any particular time,
as that would interfere with the movements of the sheriff,
and might interfere with the latter's performance of other
official business. In such case the time being limited, and
the place being fixed by the law, if the redemptioner waits
until the last day, he must attend at the residence of the
holder of the certificate at the last convenient time before
the sun sets, with the money, ready and willing to make the
redemption. Where a tender and a demand are necessary
before a grantee will be entitled to a deed, the grantee's
ignorance of the grantor's residence will not excuse a tender.[7]
If no place for payment be fixed, a tender anywhere to the
person entitled to it is good.[8]

A debtor, in seeking his creditor for the purpose of making a
tender, must exercise extraordinary diligence, and the utmost
good faith. He need only search for his place of residence,
and he should inquire of those most likely to know the place
of residence, such as agents and tenants, relatives of the
creditor, or those whom the debtor knows to be intimate
friends of the creditor. Where a bill to redeem disclosed that
there were persons living in the same town who knew where
the mortgagee resided, the court held that they should have
made some inquiries, that "there was a duty resting upon
these persons to impart the information to him and the
presumption is that they would have done so."[9] In a case
where the trial court found that the vendor could have found
the plaintiff by the exercise of reasonable diligence and good
faith, it was held that the defendant could not claim the

---

[7] See Sage v. Ramsey, 2 Wend
532.

[8] See Hunter v. Le Conte, 6 Cow.
728, Slingerland v. Morse, 8
Johns 370

[9] Lehman v. Moors, 9 So. Rep.
(Ala.) 590, s p Bancroft v. Sea-
man 9 N E Rep (Mass) 539

position of a vendor who could not find the vendee, for the purpose of making a tender of performance.[10]

**§ 313. Where no place is appointed in a negotiable note.—** To the rule that in contracts for the payment of money where the time, but no place of payment is fixed, the debtor must at his peril seek his creditor at his place of residence if within the realm, and make a tender to him, there is an exception. Negotiable promissory notes pass from hand to hand in the commercial world, and a payor has no means of knowing in whose hand his note will be on the day fixed for payment, and, where the place of payment has not been designated in the instrument, the owner, on the day fixed for the payment, must seek the payor at his residence, or other place of abode, or at his place of business, counting house, or office, and demand payment, or the demand may be of the payor personally, wherever the holder of the note may come up with him. From this it follows that being ready with the money to discharge the note, either at his place of abode or place of business, will constitute a tender. If a present-ment be made at one place and the money is at the other, the payor, if at the place of presentment, may take a reasonable time to fetch the money, or the holder of the note may repair with the payor to the other place, and there receive it. But the latter cannot be required to go with the payor to such other place to receive the money, for in such case it being a personal demand, the payor must get the money, for he ought to have the money with him at the place to discharge the note. It is only when he is absent from the place of presentment, or from both places, that having the money ready to discharge the note at one place, even though the presentment is at the other, will save a default. Would a payor on learning that presentment of the note had been made at his abode in his absence, when he had the money ready at his place of business, be required to seek out the holder and deliver over the money? The payor not being required to keep sufficient funds at both places, and, having sufficient money at one place to pay the note constituting a tender where no personal demand is made, it would seem that all the payor need do would be to keep the money safely for

[10] Teaild v Smith, 44 N. Y. 618

the holder of the note, to be paid over whenever he may call for it. This would seem to be a just rule, inasmuch as the payor might not learn by a presentment of a note at a place where he is not, who the holder is. The like rule applies to cases when both the abode and place of business are in the same town or city, and where the place of business is in one town or city and the place of residence in another, or in the country, if both are within the same state. If between the time of making a negotiable note, and when it becomes due, the payor changes his place of abode, or place of business, to another place in the same state, where no place of payment is named in the note, it is payable at the payor's new abode or place of business, and must be presented there in order to charge an endorser.

§ 314. **When neither time nor place is appointed.**—If neither time nor place be fixed in a contract for the payment of money, it is payable on demand,[1] at the debtor's place of residence or place of business. But a tender may be made anywhere, and at any time, when the parties are together.[2] In all cases where neither the time nor place is fixed, if the debtor desires to make a tender, he must seek for his creditor and make a tender to him. If the debtor cannot come up with his creditor at the place of his residence or place of business or anywhere else, after due diligence, it would seem a just rule to then allow the debtor to give notice to his creditor, that at a certain day he intends to make a tender at the latter's place of residence or place of business, although it has been said, that only in cases where the place but no time is fixed in a contract can the debtor require his

---

[1] In Deel v. Berry, 21 Tex 463, the court thought that where no time or place was specified in a contract for the payment of specific articles, there was a diversity of opinion as to whether the creditor must demand payment or the payor seek the payee and offer to perform. Elsewhere it appears that we have come upon the statement that the payor must **tender** performance within a reasonable time, but the weight of the authority is that the payor is not in default until a demand has been made, and he is then unable to comply with his contract. See Litt Sec 337, for a general discussion of the subject. There, exceptions to the rule are given.

[2] See Town v. Trow, 24 Pick 168, citing Fraunces's Case, 5 Coke, 92; Hunter v. Le Conte 6 Cow 728; Slingerland v. Morse, 8 Johns 370.

creditor to appear at any particular time so that a tender can be made.[3] Such notice enables the debtor to fix a time when he can terminate his contract, and if the creditor does not see fit to be present at the time fixed, he cannot be heard to complain. It is a general rule that where the time for performance is fixed, either in the contract, or by subsequent notice, a tender at the place agreed, or at the place fixed by law, or in the notice, as the case may be, is good, whether there be any one at the place to receive it or not.[4]

§ 315. **Tender made in the street.**—A tender of a sum in satisfaction of a claim in litigation,[1] or of a mortgage,[2] has been held not good if made in the street, when the creditor, by reason of the place, was without means of ascertaining the amount due. But a tender by the debtor of the whole sum demanded by his creditor, by pulling out his pocket book and offering to pay it if the creditor would go into a public house near by, has been held sufficient.[3]

§ 316. **Taxes, public dues—Debts due from the state.**—All taxes and public dues must be tendered to the proper officer at the place appointed by law for the receipt of such public moneys. Debts and other obligations owing by the government—national, state, or any other political subdivision,—need not be tendered at any place other than at the office of the disbursing officer authorized by it to discharge such obligations

§ 317. **Rent to be tendered where.**—According to Sir William Blackstone, "Rent is regularly due and payable upon the land from whence it issues, if no particular place is mentioned in the reservation, but in case of the king, the payment must be either to his officers at the exchequer, or to his receivers in the country."[1] Sir Edward Coke, in his commentaries upon Littleton, in considering the particular place upon the land where rent is demandable, and consequently payable, says "If there be a house upon the same, he must demand the rent at the house. And he cannot

---

[3] Town v Trow 24 Pick 186
[4] See Smith v Smith, 25 Wend 405, s c 2 Hill, 351, which appears to hold to the contrary.
[1] Chase v Welsh, 45 Mich. 345.

[2] Waldrom v. Murphy, 10 Mich. 668
[3] Reed v. Golding, 2 Mau. & Sel. 86.
[1] 2 Black Com 43  See Walter v Dewey, 16 Johns 222.

demand it at the backe doore of the house but at the fore
doore, because the demand must ever be made at the most
notorious place. And it is not material whether any person
be there or not. Albeit the feoffee be in the hall or other
part of the house, yet the feoffor need not but come to the
fore doore, for that is the place appointed by law, albeit the
doore be open If the feoffment were made of a wood only,
the demand must be made at the gate of the wood, or at some
highway leading through the wood or other most notorious
place. And if one place be as notorious as another, the
feoffor hath election to demand at which he will, and albeit
the feoffee be in some other part of the wood redie to pay the
rent, yet that shall not avail him." So, he says "If the rent
be reserved to be paid at any place from the land, yet it is in
law a rent, and the feoffor must demand it at the place
appointed by the parties, observing that which has been said
before concerning the most notorious place"[2] What has
been said, he observed, is to be understood when the feoffee
is absent, for if the feoffee cometh to the feoffor at any
place upon any part of the ground at the day of payment, and
offer his rent, albeit they be not at the most notorious place,
the feoffor is bound to receive it.[3] Elsewhere Littleton, in
the text concerning the place of payment, lays down the rule,
that where a yearly rent is reserved, and for a default of
payment a re entry, &c., the tenant need not tender the rent,
when it is behind, but upon the land because this is a rent
issuing out of the land[4] By this is meant, that if there be
neither a tender of the rent, nor a demand by the feoffor, on
the day, there, then it is due and payable every day there
after, and the feoffor having failed to make a demand at the
day, before he can claim a dissesin, he ought to go to the land
out of which the rent issues, and demand the arrears of the
rent[5] And, consequently, the tenant need not tender the
rent in arrears until it is demanded upon the land[6] As has

---

[2] Co Litt Sec 325.

[3] Co Litt Sec 325n

[4] Co. Litt 341.

[5] Co. Litt 233

[6] 8 Bac Abr. 185, citing Maund's
Case, 7 Co 20, 2 Roll Abr 427.
Littleton, in several places, in the
chapter entitled, "Of Estates upon
Conditions," makes mention of a
diversity as to the tender of rent
which is issuing out of the land,
and of the tender of a sum in
gross, which is not issuing out of
any land, relative to the place of
making a tender Co Litt Sec
340, 341 Keeping 'n mind that

been said, a tender to the person off the land is good.[7]

Where corporal service is reserved, the tender must be to the person to whom the service is due.[8] If the rent reserved is payable in *kind* at such a place in a town or city as the lessor may appoint, and no appointment is made, it is the duty of the lessee to call upon the lessor before the time for delivery arrives, and demand to know where he will appoint to receive it, and there it must be delivered. This is the rule applicable to debts payable in specific articles which are cumbersome and bulky, where the time, but no place, is designated in the contract. Although not necessary to the decision this was the view taken of it by the court, in a case arising in New York; there, the rent which in that case was to be paid in wheat, was to be delivered in Albany, at a place to be selected, etc. The court went further and in a dictum gave it as its opinion, that as the wheat must be delivered in Albany, and the landlord could not be found, a delivery of the wheat at any place in Albany would probably be sufficient.[9] But where no place is designated for the payment of rent in kind, the produce is to be delivered on the land.[10]

§ 318. **On contracts of bargain and sale—At the place where the goods are at the time of the sale—At residence of vendor.—** If no place be designated for the delivery of goods sold, the general rule is that the goods are to be delivered at the place where they are at the time of the sale.[1] Goods sold by a

---

all rent must issue out of the land, that is as a profit, and that a sum in gross is a sum of money collateral to or independent of an estate in land, that is in no way depending upon the land to produce the sum, as a loan of money, the payment of which is secured by a grant of land in mortgage, there will be no difficulty in arriving at a conclusion that Littleton is not speaking of two kinds of rent. He is considering the manner of complying with the condition of the various grants of land upon condition.

[7] Cropp v Hamilton, Cro. Eliz.

48. See Hunter v. Le Conte, 6 Cow 728 See Sec 310.

[8] Co. Litt. Sec. 304.

[9] Lush v Duse 4 Wend 313

[10] See Remsen v Conklin, 18 Johns 450, and Lush v Duse, 4 Wend 313. Neither Littleton nor Coke make any distinction between money rent, and rent payable in kind, but speak of rent issuing out of land generally. According to Blackstone, all rent, whether it be a money rent, service, or specific articles, must issue out of the land 2 Black Com 41.

[1] 2 Kent Com 505.

merchant, wares by a mechanic, or produce by a farmer, are
to be delivered at the store, shop, farm, or granary, where
the articles are deposited, or kept.[2]  Pothier, in reference to
a sale of a thing certain said: "If I have sold the wine of my
vineyard to a merchant, the delivery ought to be made in my
repository where the wine is: he should send there for it, and
load at his own expense; my obligation is to deliver it to him
where it is, and I am not obliged to take up, but merely to
give him the key, and permit him so to do."[3]  If the articles
sold are indeterminate, whether the vendor has such articles
on hand, or must manufacture them, or procure them else
where, and he has no place of business, or shop, where such
articles are kept or manufactured by him, then his place of
residence is the place where the tender must be made.  The
early French law is stated by Pothier thus  "If the debt is
not of a specific thing  but of anything indeterminate, as a
pair of gloves, a sum of money, a certain quantity of corn,
wine, &c., the payment in the case cannot be where the thing
is  because the generality of the engagements prevents there
being any such place, where must it then be?  The law above
cited decides, that in this case payment should be made at
the place it is demanded *ubi petitur*, that it is to say, at the
domicile of the debtor."[4]

§ 319.  **Change of residence by vendor—By payee.**—If the
merchant, mechanic, or farmer, before the time for delivery

---

[2] Miles v. Roberts, 34 N. H. 254;
Chambers v. Winn, Sneed 166;
Dandridge v Harris, 1 Wash 328;
Sheldon v. Skinner, 4 Wend 525,
s c 21 Am Dec. 161.

[3] Pothier on Oblig 512

[4] Pothier, Oblig. 513

According to Pothier, under the
French law, where the debtor and
creditor reside near each other,
as if they live in the same town,
and the thing due consists of a
sum of money, or anything else
that may be carried, or sent to the
creditor without expense; where
these two things occur, payment
should be made at the house of
the creditor  He said: In this case

the debtor owes his creditor this
compliment which costs him nothing.  But this is given as an exception to the general rule stated
by him, that where an indeterminate thing, as a pair of gloves,
a sum of money, a certain quan
tity of corn, wine, &c., the pay
ment should be at the place where
demanded, that is to say, at the
domicile of the debtor.  Pothier,
Oblig. 513  He makes no distinction between vendors and debtors
He designates both as debtors,
hence the law as stated by him
applied to contracts of sale, obli
gations payable in specific articles,
and ordinary money demands.

arrives, transfers the property to another place in the same state, or another state, the vendee is not bound to go to such other place to receive them.[1] Where the agreement was to pay sixteen dollars in one year, for a wood clock, or interest on that sum, and the clock uninjured, and afterwards the vendor moved out of the state, it was held that the vendee was not bound to deliver the clock at a place different from that at which he received it.[2] So, where a son had given bond to pay his widowed mother a certain annuity, it was held that he was not bound to deliver the articles wherever she might go.[3] Where a note was executed at Jackson, Mississippi, and no place of payment was designated, it was decided that the presumption was that it was payable there, that the debtor was not bound to go out of the state to make a tender.[4] A term of years was limited upon an estate located in Ireland, to raise £12,000 for the portion of certain daughters  The parties at the time of the agreement resided in England.  It being a sum gross, and not a rent issuing out of the land, it

[1] Pothier practically conceded that the goods might be carried to another place, he said, "If the debtor, after the sale, has transferred the thing from the place where it was, to another place from which the carriage would be more expensive to the creditor, he may demand, by way of damages, what the carriage costs, more than it would have cost if he had remained in the place where it was before the sale; as the debtor ought not by his act to prejudice the creditor."  Pothier on Oblig. 512. This might be a just rule, if it was optional with the creditor to refuse the goods, or go for them and claim the damages  But if no option was given, and the creditor was bound to fetch the goods away wherever they may have been carted, then the debtor has it in his power to inject into the transaction an unliquidated claim, over which there might be much controversy.  The distance may not be increased by the transfer of the goods, yet the creditor may be inconvenienced in that he may so arrange his business that he may be able to bring the goods from the original place of delivery, on his return from a more extended journey  If the goods could be removed at all they could be removed to another place after the debtor had made any convenient arrangement for taking them away  Many other reasons might be suggested why there should be no departure from the rule that the goods must remain and be tendered at the place where they were at the time of the making of the contract.

[2] Barker v. Jones, 8 N. H. 413.

[3] Santee v Santee, 64 Pa. St 173

[4] Jones v Perkins, 29 Miss 139, s c 64 Am Dec 136. See Allshouse v Ramsay 6 Whart 331, Gill v. Bradley 21 Minn 21; Houble v. Volkening, 49 How. Pr. 169.

was held that the money ought to be paid in England, where the contract was made.[5] A payee, after a note was executed which contained a stipulation that it might be discharged in personal property, changed his place of residence. The payor elected to pay the note in property and tendered the property to the creditor at the place where he then lived, who offered to receive it at the place where he lived at the time the note was given. The debtor, not making a tender at the latter place, was held to be in default.[6] But the payor, where the contract is a non-negotiable money demand, as we have seen, where the payee acquires a new domicile in the same state, must make a tender of the sum due at the payee's place of residence (or to him personally) at the time the demand falls due.

§ 320. **Usage of trade—Previous course of dealing.**—To the general rule, that goods sold, are to be delivered at the place where they are at the time of the sale, or at the store, shop, farm, or residence of the vendor, as the case may be, where the contract is silent as to the place of delivery, there are exceptions arising from special contracts or special circumstances, custom, and usage, &c., "It will be proper to keep in mind that the *place* of performance, where the contract is silent in that respect, is a mere *rule of construction* to supply that omission; and that, therefore, this rule should be predicated on the supposed understanding of the parties when forming their contract"[1] It is therefore a matter of compact or a matter of law.[2] The usage of trade or previous course of dealing between the parties will sometimes fix the place of delivery. If it is the custom of a particular business on receiving orders for goods from purchasers residing within or without the state, for the seller to forward the goods to the purchaser, it is sufficient to deliver the goods at the warehouse of a carrier to be forwarded.[3]

---

[5] Co Litt 210b.

[6] Borah v. Curry, 12 Ill. 66.

[1] Wilmouth v Patton, 2 Bibb. 280

[2] Galloway v Smith, Litt Sel C 133

[3] In Huxham v Smith, 2 Camp 21, a merchant abroad ordered goods of a shop keeper residing in London, to be put on board a ship lying beyond the limits of the city. The shop keeper sent them from his shop to be shipped in pursuance of the order, and the question was where the debt arose, and whether a suit could

**§ 321.  Commodities subject to inspection, &c.**—If the commodities sold are subject to be inspected at a public warehouse,[1] or weighed by a public weighmaster, or guaged, or surveyed, in absence of a specific agreement it is implied that the articles are to be delivered at some warehouse, scale, or boom, where the purchaser usually receives such articles if known to the seller, if not known to the seller at the time or made known later, then at same warehouse, scale, or boom selected by the seller.

**§ 322.  On contracts to pay on demand—At residence—At place of business.**—If a note or other obligation is payable in specific articles on demand, and no place for payment is fixed by the contract, a demand must be made at the residence of the debtor, if he has a known place of residence within the state, and a tender there by the obligor will be good.[1] But if the note be payable in lumber and the obligor has a lumber yard,[2] or is the note of a merchant payable in goods, or a mechanic payable in his wares, and it is payable on demand, or which is the same thing, the creditor has a right of selection, the law implies that the lumber yard, store, or shop, as the case may be, is the place of payment agreed upon by the parties.[3] Mr. Chipman puts a case thus. If a merchant give a due bill to A payable in goods, and no time or place of payment be designated, the due bill contains an acknowledgment that A has paid him in advance for the amount in goods therein expressed, and a promise is implied on the part of the merchant, that whenever A shall call at his store, and present the due bill, he will deliver to him such articles as he shall select out of the goods on hand. The store of the merchant

---

be maintained in the Mayor's court of London to recover the debt. Lord Ellenborough said there was a delivery as soon as the goods were put in course of conveyance. Here it would seem that a delivery to a carrier would be sufficient.

[1] See Chambers v Winn Sneed 166

[1] Chambers v Winn, Sneed 166, Wilmuth v Patton, 2 Bibb 280. An obligation which is silent

both as to time and place is to be performed on demand. See also Vance v Bloomer, 20 Cow 196. The demand may be made at the residence of the obligor in his absence. Mason v Briggs, 16 Mass 453

[2] Rice v Churchill, 2 Denio, 145

[3] Rice v Churchill, 2 Denio, 145, Mason v Briggs, 16 Mass 452, Hughes v Prewitt, 5 Tex. 264, Goodwin v Holbrook, 4 Wend 377

is the place of payment." [4]  So, where property is to be delivered at a valuation, in absence of a stipulation as to the place of payment the creditor is bound to receive it at the debtor's house, [5] or place of business, if it be articles dealt in by the debtor.  If a demand is made for property at any other place than at the store, shop, or farm of the obligor, he may take a reasonable time to fetch the property from where it is and tender it where demanded, or he may offer to make the payment at the place fixed by law, and the holder of the note must repair to that place to receive the article. [6]  The like rules apply to obligations to pay money on demand, as apply to contracts to pay in specific articles, or contracts to deliver specific articles on demand which are portable.  If the goods to be delivered on demand are ponderous, they are to be delivered where they are at the time of entering into the contract, no place being mentioned [7]

§ 323.  **On contracts payable in specific articles—Services—** Where a note is payable in specific articles, and the time for payment is fixed but no place, the common law rule is that the articles, if portable, must be tendered at the place of residence of the creditor   That is at the place where the creditor resided at the time the note was executed [1]  In Kentucky the contrary obtains and a tender made at the residence of the debtor is good [2]  If a blacksmith, wheel

<hr>

[4] Chip. on Cont 28

[5] Dandridge v Harris 1 Wash. 326

[6] See Rice v Churchill, 2 Denio, 145   An officer with an execution, who demands property attached and held to respond to the judgment at any place where the property is not, must repair to the place where it is to receive it Scott v Crane 1 Conn 255

[7] See Higgins v Emmons, 5 Conn 76

[1] Chip on Cont 25, Borah v Curry, 12 Ill 66 Morey v Lake 3 Minn 392, Goodwin v Halbrook, 4 Wend 380, La Farge v Rickerts 5 Wend 187 Wagner v Dickey, 17 Ohio, 139

[2] Chambers v Winn, Sneed 166 Galloway v Smith, Litt Sel Cas 133, Letcher v Taylor Hard 79, Wilmouth v Patton, 2 Bibb 280 Grant v Groshow, Hard 85, Littel v Nichols, Hard 66   The Kentucky rule was recognized in an early Missouri case (Dameron v Belt, 3 Mo 213), though it was found not necessary to follow it in that case as the obligor elected to make and plead a tender  The court held that having elected to make a tender instead of waiting for a demand, he must have made it at the dwelling house of the vendee   Some of the Kentucky cases cited as establishing a contrary rule were obligations pay

wright, &c, be bound to pay a certain sum in work, and he has a shop where he is accustomed to labor, the inference is, in absence of a stipulated place, that it was the understanding and intent of the parties that he should perform such labor at his shop. But if he be a journeyman, and the payee has a shop, the inference would be that he is to perform such labor at the shop of his creditor.[?] If neither the payor nor payee have a shop, or the payor be a carpenter, painter, or other mechanic whose labor is not exclusively performed in his shop, or a mason who does not perform his work in a shop at all, then the labor is to be performed at any place within the state, that the payee shall appoint.[?]

§ 324   **On contracts to deliver ponderous or bulky articles.—**
At what place are specific articles to be delivered that are ponderous and bulky? Lord Coke in his Commentaries upon Littleton laid down the rule that "if the condition of a bond or feoffment be to deliver twenty quarters of wheat, or twenty loads of timber, or such like, the obligor or feoffor is not bound to carry the same about and seek the feoffee, but the obligor or feoffor before the day must go to the feoffee and know where he will appoint to receive it, and there it must be delivered. And so note a diversity between money and thing ponderous, or of great weight."[?] This rule is still the law applicable to notes, bonds and other obligations for the payment of specific articles that are cumbersome,

able on demand (Chambers v Winn. Walmouth v Patton) where a tender may be made at the dwelling of the debtor on a demand being made for payment. According to an early Illinois decision under a statute there in force, if the payee had not a known place of residence in the county at the time the contract was executed, or has a known place of residence but the property is ponderous, then the party may tender the property at the place where the maker resided at the time the contract was entered into. See Borah v Curry, 12 Ill. 66.

See Currier v Currier, 2 N. H. 75.

¹ Tribue v Kay, 4 Bibb 226.

² Co. Litt. 211b, Chip. on Cont. 27. Miles v Roberts, 34 N. H. 254, Cheney's Case, 3 Leon. 260, Currier v Currier, 2 N. H. 75, Roberts v Beatty, 2 P. & W. 63, Morey v Lake, 5 Minn. 392, Barnes v Graham, 4 Cowen, 152, s. c. 15 Am. Dec. 394, Sheldon v Skinner, 4 Wend. 525, s. c. 21 Am. Dec. 161. La Farge v Rickert, 5 Wend. 187. Deed v Berry, 21 Tex. 463, England v Witherspoon, 1 Hayw. 361.

where the time for payment has been specified but the contract is silent as to the place. The creditor need not wait for a request to be made. He may appoint the place immediately after the execution of the note, as well as at any other time, because such appointment and notice is for the benefit of the debtor, enabling him to more readily perform his contract.[2]

If the debtor inquires of the creditor at what place he will receive the articles and the creditor designates a reasonable place, and one within the contemplation of the parties,[3] they must be tendered at the place. "If the creditor cannot be found, if he refuses to appoint any place, or, which is much the same, to appoint a reasonable place, the debtor may himself select any suitable and reasonable place, and a delivery there, with notice to the creditor, if he can be found, will discharge the contract."[4] If the debtor does not inquire of his creditor where he will receive the articles, a readiness at his own dwelling house, on the day appointed, will not avail him as a defence.[5] In Maine, the common law rule, that the payee of a note payable in specific articles, if cumbersome, must seek his creditor prior to the day of delivery, if within the state, and ascertain from him where he will receive the goods, has not only been adopted, but the rule also that if the creditor resides abroad, the foreign domicile does not absolve the debtor from the obligation of ascertaining from him, if he can, where he will receive the goods, and failing in that, of designating the place himself and making the tender there.[6] Where creditor, on removing from the state leaves an agent, it is the duty of the debtor to call upon the agent to appoint a place for receiving the articles.[7] If the creditor does not leave an agent to attend to his affairs, the general rule is that the debtor may select the place of delivery.

[2] Aldrich v. Albee, 1 Green, 120, S C 10 Am Dec 15

[3] Barnes v Graham, 4 Cow. 452, S C 15 Am Dec 394

[4] Miles v Roberts, 34 N. H 254, Chip on Cont 25, Bac Abr Title Tender (C), Howard v Miner, 20 Me 325.

[5] Bean v Simpson, 16 Me 49

[6] Bixby v Whitney, 5 Greenl 192, White v Perley, 15 Me 470

[7] Santee v Santee, 64 Pa St 473

**§ 325.  Property illegally seized—Property received by bailee.—**
To restore property illegally seized [1] and carried away, it
must be tendered at the place where it was when taken.
As the wrong doer may not be able to meet the owner at the
place where the goods were when taken, he should, particularly if the property be such as would require immediate
care, as in the case of live stock or perishable property, noti
fy the owner of his intention to restore the property at the
place at a certain time, or in any case notify the owner as
soon after the delivery that harm cannot possibly befall the
property before the owner by the exercise of ordinary dili
gence can take charge of it.  While it is true, generally, that
property illegally seized may be returned to the place where
it was when taken, yet this, under some circumstances, as
where the property is taken from a person other than the
defendant, is qualified, for the reason that the party from
whom it was taken may himself have been in the wrongful
possession, or in possession temporarily as a bailee, as where
goods are seized while being removed by a drayman from
one place to another,[2] or where horses are taken from a
livery barn while there merely as transients   In such cases
the property must be tendered at the residence of the de
fendant.  The same is true if the articles are taken from
the defendant while going to or from his house, or while
temporarily absent anywhere in the state

Where a person receives hogs on his farm to be fattened
upon shares, after the contract is performed as to fattening,
the share falling to the original owner must be tendered at
the place where the hogs were received, no other place being
agreed upon.[3]  So, where articles are delivered to a bailee,
for storage, or to have work done on them, in absence of any
agreement as to place of re delivery they are to be delivered
at the place where they are stored, or the shop where the
work was done, providing it is the warehouse or shop con
templated by the parties at the time of the delivery of the
articles

[1] Powers v. Florance, 7 La Am.
524

[2] Coldwell v Arnold, 8 Minn
265.

[3] Sheldon v Skinner, 1 Wend
525 s c 21 Am Dec. 161

**§ 326. On a rescission.**—If a person desires to rescind a contract by returning money received thereon, or a deed, mortgage, note, or other instrument, he should seek the other party and make a tender to him personally, if he can be found, otherwise the tender should be made at the latter's residence or place of business, and give notice of such rescission as soon as possible. If the articles to be returned are specific articles, it is sufficient to return them at the place where received,[1] and if the manner or place of delivery be not such as to apprise the other party of the rescission, notice of such rescission and of the return of the property should be given as soon as practicable.[2] Leaving a horse in the yard of the vendor without any notice of an intent to rescind the contract has been held not a rescission[3] Where the person to whom it is desired to restore property has since removed from the state, or is a transient, having no known place of abode within the state, and the articles are such as naturally belong to a warehouse they may be left at a warehouse, subject to the other person's order and the latter notified where they are,[4] or, they may be kept by the vendee ready for the vendor, whenever he may call for them, and notice given to him of the rescission, and a request made to take them away, or which is the same thing, that the goods are held subject to his order.

**§ 327. Bank notes where payable.**—Bank notes which circulate as money are payable at the counter of the bank responsible for their issue, but where the holder of a bank note demands payment at the counter of the bank, and payment is refused, the bank, desiring to discharge itself thereafter, must seek the holder and make a tender to him personally[1] The tender ought to be made at a reasonable place, thus, the holder ought not to be required to accept the money at a place where there would be a great danger of his being

[1] Paulson v Osborn, 27 N. W. Rep (Minn) 203 s c 37 Minn 19. See McCormick Har Machine Co v Knoll, 78 N W Rep (Neb) 394, and cases cited

[2] See Buchman v Harvey, 12 Ill 338

[3] Thayer v Turner, 8 Met 553
[4] Angell v Loomis, 55 N W Rep (Mich) 1008
[5] Hubbard v Chenango Bank, 8 Cow 88

robbed, or at any other place where he could not convenient
ly care for the money, or keep it safely.[2]

**§ 328.  By an executor where—By legatee.**—In an ancient
England case it was held that if no place of payment be
fixed in a will which directs the payment of money, there
must be a request to pay money, for the executor is not
bound to seek all England over for the legatee[1]  A devisee
who accepts a devise, subject to a legacy of a certain sum
annually charged on the land, becomes a debtor by reason
of the land for the legacy; and like any other debtor is
bound to pay without a demand, and must tender the money
or specific articles if portable, where no place is appointed,
at the residence of the legatee, that is at the place where he
resided at the time the legacy took effect.[2]  If no place be
appointed, and the articles are ponderous or bulky, the de
visee should seek the legatee and request him to appoint a
reasonable place[3]

[2] The rule fixing a place of making a demand is the same whether
the thing be specific articles services or money  and are alike ap
plicable to contracts when the
place of delivery is fixed by law,
and where the place is named in
the contract  Lord Coke says that
where A  by deed agrees to pay B.
£100 at Rotterdam in Holland up
on the first requisition the demand
may be made at any other place
besides Rotterdam, and if the demand be made in England or at
Dort  which is 10 miles from Rotterdam it is good for he ought to
have reasonable time to pay it
after the demand, having respect
to the distance of the place  He
adds  "But if the demand should
be limited to Rotterdam, perhaps

he would never come then"  Co
Litt  210b)

The rules in reference to the
place of making a demand in no
wise govern or fix the place of
making (See Higgins v  Emmons,
5 Conn  76) a tender of the thing
demanded  except to allow the
payor where the demand is not
made at the place of payment, to
pay at the place demanded if he
so desires

[1] (1651) Anonymous Brownl &
G  16  See Pickering v  Pickering,
6 N  H  120

[2] See Pickering v  Pickering, 6
N  H  120, Wiggins v  Wiggins, 43
N  H  561, Veasey v  Whitehouse,
10 N  H  409

[3] See Wiggins v  Wiggins, 43 N
H  561

# CHAPTER VII.

## BY WHOM AND TO WHOM A TENDER MAY BE MADE

## I BY WHOM MADE

§ 329. **In general—Where right is personal—Services to be performed—By debtor—Joint debtor—Any party to a bill or note—Sub-lessee—Assignor of contract**—Where money is to be paid or an act performed, a tender must be made by the party whose duty it is to pay the one or perform the other  Whenever the right to make payment is personal, as where a person is entitled to some right during his life, by reason of the payment, a tender cannot be made by his heirs or personal representatives  Littleton puts a case of a feoffment upon condition, that if the feoffor pay a certain sum of money to the feoffee, then it shall be lawful for the feoffor and his heirs to enter, and the feoffor die before the payment made, a tender by the heirs of the feoffor is void. Here no time is limited and when the feoffor dies then the time of the tender is past. "But otherwise it is where a day of payment is limited, and the feoffor die before the day, then may the heirs tender the money as is aforesaid, for that the time of the tender was not past by the death of the feoffor"[1] So may the executor of the feoffor. If services are to be performed and the relation between the employer and employee is confidential, or the employment is by reason of the ability, skill, or experience of the employee, or by reason of the confidence reposed in the employee's integrity, a tender of the services cannot be made by any one representing the employee either before or after the latter's death

Where a debt is owing by a firm, a tender by one partner is a tender by all. A tender may be made by one of two or more joint debtors for and on behalf of all, or it may be made by all, but a tender made jointly with another person who is not entitled to make a tender is not good[2] So a tender of the amount due upon a mortgage or contract of sale may be made by a joint tenant, tenant in common, or any person having an interest in the property subject to the mortgage or contract[3] A joint tender cannot be made where the interests are not joint, but several[4] After maturity, any party to a bill or note may make a tender of the amount due thereon. So may a surety on a bond or other obligation. Where a lessee has sublet the premises in violation of the contract a tender of the rent by the sublessee may be refused[5] An assignor of a contract, on a failure of the assignee to take and pay for the goods to be delivered thereon, may make a tender of the amount to be paid and take the goods[6] unless the vendor agreed to the substitution of the assignee in place of the vendee and re-

---

[1] 1 Inst § 337

[2] Bender v Bean, 52 Ark 132

[3] Poehler v Reese, 78 Minn 71

[4] Bigelow v Booth, 39 Mich

622. Hall v Norwalk Ins Co, 57 Conn 105

[5] Pneu v Deponelly, 8 La Ann 399

[6] Dustan v McAndrew, 44 N. Y. 72

leased the latter. Where a person agrees with a married woman to convey to her certain lands on payment by her of a debt due from the husband, the insolvency of the husband and his inability to perform will not defeat the right of the wife, and on a tender being made by her she will be entitled to specific performance.[7]

**§ 330. Personal representatives — Assignees and receivers — Third person who has assumed the debt of another.**—Where the right of tendering is not personal, a tender may be made by the personal representatives of the debtor. If the estate is liable for the debt the tender must be made by the personal representatives. In some cases, however, it may be made by the heirs. Where property had been assigned for the benefit of creditors, a tender made by the widow of the debtor was held to have been made by a stranger, but that if it had been made by her as administratrix, the tender would have been good.[1] A tender by an executor in accordance with the directions in a will, of a deed executed by the testator in his life time, is good.[2]

Assignees and receivers of bankrupts may make a tender of money in satisfaction of liens on the bankrupt's property belonging to the estate, or in redemption of such property sold to satisfy a lien.[3] They should, however, first obtain an order of the court authorizing them to make the payment. An assignment does not take from the debtor his right of making a tender, and a lien holder has no right to refuse a tender made by him.[4] A third person who has agreed, for a consideration, to pay the debt of another, as where a vendee in a deed assumes a mortgage, or any property is transferred under an agreement that the transferee shall pay the debt of the transferrer, the former, whether a trustee or a purchaser, being liable to the debtor upon such agreement, may tender the amount of the debt.[5]

7 Washburn v Dewey, 17 Vt 92

1 McDougald v Dougherty 14 Ga 570

2 Reaich v Swinehart 11 Pa St 233, S C 51 Am Dec 540

3 Davis v Dow, 83 N W Rep (Minn ) 50

4 Trimble v Williamson 49 Ala 525

5 See Bell v Mendenhall 71 Minn 331 and cases cited

§ 331. Lienors—Sureties and endorsers when—Junior lien-holder—Purchaser who does not assume mortgage debt.—The question of who may make a tender arises most frequently in cases where it is sought by the payment to discharge a lien, or redeem from a sale under it. Where there has been no attempt to foreclose a lien, only the debtor, or one standing in the relation of surety, endorser, and the like, who are secondarily liable for the debt, or one whose property is subject to the lien, and who stands in the relation of a surety, may make a tender. One who has acquired the property which is subject to the lien, either by foreclosing a junior lien and acquiring the equity of redemption, or by conveyance from the mortgagor,[1] stands in place of the debtor as far as the lien is concerned, and may make a tender of the debt. The tender is good even though he does not state in what capacity he is acting, if no questions are asked.[2] Such tender does not render the purchaser personally liable for the debt.

In New York it is held that where mortgaged premises are conveyed to a purchaser subject to the mortgage, but without any assumption of the debt by him, the land is, as between the mortgagor and purchaser, the primary fund for payment and the purchaser cannot make a tender that will discharge the lien of the mortgage. The purchaser of the equity of redemption, in such cases, is a stranger to the debt. He owes no debt, and therefore can only redeem the land by actual payment.[3] A junior mortgagee or lien holder cannot make a tender of the amount due upon a senior mortgage or lien until steps are taken to foreclose it.[4] Declaring the mortgage debt to be due and threatening to foreclose is sufficient. A junior lien holder has a right to prevent the costs of a foreclosure being incurred.

§ 332. By redemptioners—Who are.—The persons who may make a tender in redemption of lands sold under a mortgage foreclosure, in the several states, are usually designated by statute and are in general divided into two classes. First, the mortgagor or those deriving an interest through him by purchase, heirs and devisees, and executors or administra-

[1] Bradley v. Snyder, 14 Ill. 263.
[2] Johnston v. Gray, 16 S. & R. 361.
Harris v. Jex, 66 Barb. 232.
Noyes v. Wyckoff, 30 Hun 466.
[4] Frost v. Yonkers Sav. Bank, 70 N. Y. 553.

tors of the one dying seized of the mortgaged premises A tenant for life or for years, provided their estate was carved out of the fee subsequent to the execution of the mortgage, may make a tender. So may one acquiring an easement subsequent to the mortgage. A tenant in dower or by the courtesy or a jointress, where their inchoate interest attached subsequent to the creation of the mortgage lien may make a tender in redemption of the property. This is so where they have joined in the mortgage. It has been held where the dower interest is inchoate, that the wife may protect her interest in the mortgaged property by tendering the amount due upon a judgment lien [1] And upon the same principle she may make a tender of the amount necessary to redeem from a mortgage sale whether she joined in the mortgage or not Where the mortgagor's estate in land has terminated, either by a strict foreclosure,[2] or by conveying it away, or by sale in satisfaction of another lien, he cannot redeem from a senior or other lien, but as long as any right of redemption from a sale under a junior lien remains in the mortgagor or owner, he may redeem from a foreclosure sale made upon any senior mortgage or lien Where a mortgagor who is personally liable for the debt, sells the property, and the amount of the mortgage constitutes part of the purchase price and the purchaser allows the mortgage to be foreclosed and the premises sold for less than the mortgage debt, the mortgagor may redeem notwithstanding he has parted with his legal title to the property. The guardian of an infant heir idiot, insane person, or spendthrift may make a tender for his ward *Second*, creditors having liens, legal or equitable whose lien would be affected by the foreclosure, providing they have complied with the statutory requirements may make a tender in redemption of property sold under a senior lien. The assignee of the lien may make a tender If, after a mortgagee or lien holder has filed a notice of intention to redeem, he assigns his mortgage or lien, the assignee may redeem under the notice so filed [3] A second mortgage made and filed in the interval between the attachment of the

[1] Roberts v Meighen 74 Minn 274

[2] Da Silva v Turner 14 N E Rep (Mass) 532

[3] Boyes v De Luttre Lumber Co, 50 N W Rep (Minn) 1038

equity of redemption on mesne process and the sale on execution, may redeem from the execution sale.[4] A subsequent lien holder is entitled to make a tender in redemption of property sold on a senior lien, and it makes no difference at what time subsequent to the senior lien the junior lien attached. Thus, where the last day of the year from the confirmation of the sale fell on a Sunday, a mortgagee, whose mortgage was executed on Monday following, was allowed to redeem.[5] A judgment creditor who has acquired a lien by levying upon chattels, may redeem from a mortgage which is a lien prior to his lien.[6] A second mortgagee in possession of chattels, when the first mortgagee has brought replevin on tendering the amount due on the first mortgage is entitled to a judgment for the return of the property.[7] The holder of a tax title which is not subject to a mortgage cannot make a tender of the mortgage debt.[8]

§ 333    Attorney — Agent — Joint agent — Divulging name of principal — Proof of authority — Time to ascertain if authority exists — Where money is to be paid or goods delivered, not withstanding the right may be personal, a tender may be made by an attorney, agent, clerk, servant or other person authorized to make it on behalf of the debtor or the one who is to deliver the goods. A person, except in a few cases, may always employ a third person to transact his business. The tender being that of the principal, it may be made by an infant or whomsoever the principal may see fit to authorize to represent him regardless of the agent's individual status at law. The agent must be provided with the necessary funds.[1] Where it is agreed between a debtor and his creditor that a third person shall pay the debt out of certain money he owes the debtor, a tender by such third person is a tender by and on behalf of the debtor.[2] Such tender, however, does not discharge the debtor nor make the third person liable to the creditor in absence of an express agreement to assume

[4] Biglow v Wilson, I Pick 487
Bovey v De Laittre Lumber Co 50 N W Rep (Minn) 1038
[5] Lambert v Miller, 38 N J Eq 117
[6] Williamson v Gottchalk, 1 Mo. App 425

[8] Sinclair v Learned, 51 Mich 325 s c 16 N W Rep 672
[1] See Wyllie v Matthews, 11 N. W Rep (Iowa) 242
[2] Keystone Lumber Co v Jenkinson 37 N W Rep (Mich) 198

the debt. Where two or more persons are appointed agents to pay certain money, a tender by one of the joint agents is sufficient,[3] providing he is acting for all. Where a tender is made by a third person, the creditor must be informed in whose behalf it is made, if not so informed the tender is invalid.[4] A tenderee may insist on competent proof of the agent's authority, and may take a reasonable time to ascertain that the person making the tender is in fact authorized to make it.

§ 334. **Infant—Guardian—Next friend—After marriage of female infant—Idiot.—**An infant has no authority to make a tender in his own behalf, nor can he empower an agent or attorney to act for him. He cannot authorize another to do that which he cannot do himself. Where lands of an infant have been sold to satisfy a mortgage or judgment, the general guardian of the minor must make the redemption[1] To this rule there is an exception. If an infant has no general guardian, and is of tender years, that is under the age of fourteen, the tender may be made by the natural guardian In England, according to a very ancient case, a mortgagor, one Maynard, died leaving surviving him his son and heir, being within age. Afterwards at the day of payment limited by the mortgage, a stranger at the instance and request of the mother of the heir, tendered the money to the mortgagee, who refused it It was held by the court "that the same is not a sufficient tender to redeem the land * * * for it is found by the jury, that the heir at the time of the tender was within age, generally, not particularly of six or ten years, &c., then it might well stand with the verdict, that the heir at such time was of the age of 18 or 19 years, at which age he is by law out of the ward of his mother, or any other *prochein amy,* in which case it is presumed in law, that he has discretion to govern his own affairs, and in this case the mother is but a stranger, for the law hath estranged the mother from the government of the heir, but if the jury had found that the heir at the time of the tender was of tender age, viz, within the age of fourteen years, in which

---

[3] St Paul Div Sons of Temperance v Brown, 11 Minn 254

[4] Mehler v Newham, 32 Cal 168

[1] See Jones on Mortg § 1062

case by law he ought to be in ward, in such case the tender had been good." [2] If a mother of an infant of tender age die leaving an estate and a husband surviving her, or such infant receives an inheritance from another person, the father in absence of a general guardian, may make a tender for the minor. If the parents are divorced, the one having the legal custody of such infant may interpose as his next friend and make a tender. We have not found any decisions holding that where both parents of an infant heir of tender years are dead, and he has no general guardian, any other relative may act as his next friend in making a tender. It would seem a just rule which would permit a grandparent, uncle, or other relative having the care and custody of the infant, to interpose as his next friend for the protection of his estate. A master to whom a minor is apprenticed has no authority to make a tender for him, a parent being alive. It is a general rule that a minor under the age of fourteen years, cannot select a guardian, hence it is not only proper but prudent that under that age, in absence of a general guardian, his guardian by nature, or if they be dead then some near relative should have power to act for him. After arriving at the age of fourteen, although the guardian by nature can continue to exercise control over the person of the infant, he has the right of selecting a guardian to look after his prudential affairs and he must do so [4]

2 Watkins v Ashwick 1 Cooke's 132 s c. Cro Eliz 132 See Co Litt 206 b

3 See Commonwealth v Keidig 1 Serg & R (Pa) 366

4 In Brown v Dysinger, 1 Rawle (Pa) 407, a tender was made by an uncle of a minor, the mother and natural guardian being alive The court observed "It is true, he had not at that time been legally appointed the guardian of the minor, but he was his uncle, and surely one so near in blood may lawfully interpose as his next friend We think an infant ought not to lose his inheritance, merely because he has no guardian, his uncle or next friend may act for him, he did so here, the tender by him was well made." This case illustrates in exceptional cases how the courts are prone to extend a rule of law to prevent hardship While, in this case the exception proved beneficial to the minor, yet, so would an exception to the rule announced in the text, which would allow a stranger in some cases, to act for a minor Ignoring well defined and long established rules, by creating exceptions, or ignoring the rules altogether render the law uncertain, and on the whole creates more litigation and hardships than if the courts would adhere to the

A minor on arriving of age may disaffirm or repudiate those transactions concerning his estate which were not authorized by law, and it is therefore of the utmost importance to a tenderee, where a tender is being made by and on behalf of an infant, that the tender be made by one having the cloak of legal authority to act for the minor. A tender made by any one else, however beneficial it may be for the minor, may be rejected. A rule is laid down in Coke on Littleton, that "if the heir be an idiot, of what age soever, any man may make a tender for him in respect of his absolute disability, and the law in this case is grounded upon charity." [b]

In those jurisdictions where a husband is entitled to the control and custody of the wife's property, the marriage of a female ward with an adult ousts the general guardian of his control of the infant wife's estate, excepting possibly, where the guardian is testamentary and the will explicit. The law, while settled that the husband is entitled to the control of the estate of his infant wife, yet it is not uniform or well settled that the marriage *ipso facto* determines the authority of the guardian. In some jurisdictions he must first apply to the court for an order transferring it to him, while elsewhere, it is thought that the marriage of its own force superseded guardianship. The marriage of a male ward does not oust the guardian from his control of the estate of the minor, whatever be the age of the wife. If a male and female infant marry the guardian of the husband assumes control of the estate of the infant wife. In the United States, in the several states under the married woman's statutes, the foregoing in reference to the adult husband of an infant wife superseding her general guardian in the control and management of her property, could not well apply. Under such statutes, where an adult woman has

---

strict letter of the law especially where the business could be as easily done and the same ends attained by conforming to the law as it is. In this case the uncle or mother of the minor could have seen to it that the tender was made by the proper person. When courts undertake to create exceptions to general rules or ignore them, in order to prevent hardship resulting from ignorance of the law they open a wide field for speculation as to what the law will be held to be in a given case.

[b] Co. Litt. 206 b.

equal rights with men, in reference to her property, the law ought to be, if it is not, that the marriage of an infant female with an adult, does not transfer the authority of her general guardian to the husband, but leaves the management of her estate with her guardian until she attains her majority. Upon this subject the laws are not uniform or well settled, and local statutes and decisions should be carefully examined before making a tender in behalf of a married female infant. In some states the statute provides that marriage emancipates a female infant.

§ 335. **Stranger—Who are—Supra protest.**—A tender by a mere stranger is invalid,[1] whether made in his own behalf or as a mere volunteer for the debtor. Littleton in his Institutes of the Laws of England, according to Sir Edward Coke, said, in reference to a tender to a mortgagee, "that he is not bound to receive it at a stranger's hand. But if any stranger, in the name of the mortgagor or his heirs (without his consent or privity) tender the money, and the mortgagee accepteth it, this is a good satisfaction, and the mortgagor or his heirs agreeing thereto may re-enter into the land, *omnius ratihabilio retro trahitur et mandato aequiparatur.* But the mortgagor or his heirs may disagree thereto if he will"[2] The objection to a tender that the one making it had no interest in the matter, or if claiming to represent another, that he was not authorized to act for the person entitled to make payment, is not waived even though no objection is made to the tender upon that ground at the time it was made.[3]

Any person who has an interest in the condition upon which the right of tendering is based, such as one who would share in the loss occasioned by a failure to make a tender are not accounted strangers.[4] An inhabitant of a town or other political subdivision whose property is liable to seizure and sale to satisfy a poor rate, or any public dues, has such a direct interest in the consequences of a tender that will entitle him to make it[5] Would a tax payor

[1] Mahler v Newbauer, 32 Cal 168, McDougald v Dougherty, 11 Ga 570, Sinclair v. Learned, 51 Mich 335, s c 16 N W Rep 672

[2] Co Litt 207 a

[3] Contra Lampley v Weed, 27 Ala 621

[4] 2 Inst 207

[5] Kincaid v School District, 11 Me 188

who would be liable to pay an increased rate, by reason of
a default in the payment of the obligations of a town, city,
or county, have such an interest as would enable him to
make a tender of the amount due and compel a transfer of
the obligation to him? It would seem that he would have
such right if he waived the question of a breach of the condition as to himself. Unless he did this for a reasonable
time at least, there being a default, he would at once have
it in his power to subject the public to the same costs as
the original holder, which costs spread over all the property
would not save him or the public anything. There is an
exception to the general rule that a stranger has no right
to pay or discharge the debt of another. By the law merchant a stranger to a bill of exchange may make payment
*supra protest* for the honor of the drawer, acceptor, or endorser, or for all and acquire a right to reimbursement.

### II To Whom Made

§ 336. **To creditor—Person designated in the contract—Bearer
—Holder of unendorsed note—Personal tender unnecessary
when.**—A tender must be made direct to the creditor,[1] or
to the person designated in the contract,[2] or to some one
duly authorized to receive on behalf of the creditor the
money or thing contracted to be delivered. A tender to the
holder of a note is good though the note is subsequently assigned.[3] The holder of a note payable to bearer is the proper
one to whom a tender should be made, and an answer setting
up that he did not know who was the owner, but that he
was ready and willing to pay the same at the place of payment named in the note, without alleging a tender sets up
no defence.[4] Payment cannot with safety be made to one
who has possession simply of an unindorsed bill or note.[5]

The general rule is, that where a contract for the payment
of money, or the delivery of portable specific articles at a
day certain, does not specify the place of payment, the money
or other thing must be tendered personally to the person to
whom the money or thing is due. But as a debtor may not

[1] Hornby v Cramer, 12 How
Pra 490. See Grussy v Schneider 50 How. Pra 134
[2] Te Poel v Shutt 78 N W
Rep (Neb) 288
[3] Ashue v Covey, 113 Ind 484
[4] Bronson v Chicago R Isl &
Pac Rv, 40 How Pr 18
[5] Doubleday v Kress 50 N Y
110

be able to find his creditor when the day arrives for payment, the law wisely allows, in such cases, a tender to be made at the residence of the creditor in the absence of the creditor.⁰ If no one be present to whom the tender may be made, then a personal tender is excused, and the debtor, by being there at the last hour of the day on which payment is to be made, at a convenient time before sunset and continuing there until the sun sets, ready to make the payment, will have made a sufficient tender. A creditor is charged with notice that the money will be tendered at the day and at the place designated by law. The same rule obtains in cases where both the time and place of payment are specified in the contract, and the creditor is not there at the time to receive payment. A personal tender is excused in either case whether the creditor is unavoidably detained from the place or is intentionally absent.

§ 337. **Joint mortgagees or obligees—Tenants in common—Partners.**— A tender to one of several joint mortgagees,[1] or obligees,[2] or purchasers,[3] is good. A tender of one gross sum to several creditors whose claims are several, when they were all assembled, was held to be good, when they refused to receive the amount, merely insisting that more was due.[4] Where tenants in common appear and contest certain proceedings without objecting to the proceedings on the ground that it should be against them severally and not jointly, a tender in such proceedings made to one of them was held to be good.[5] Where a debt is owing to a firm, a tender to one partner is a tender to all.[6] But one partner has no implied authority to settle in any other way than for cash, and the amount due must be tendered in cash even though one partner may offer to off set his indebtedness against the amount due the firm. The party paying a debt due a partnership in that way, runs the risk of having the transaction re-

[1] See Judd v. Ensign, 6 Barb 258 Smith v. Smith, 25 Wend 405, Wagner v. Dickey, 17 Ohio 439

[1] Flanigan v. Seelye, 53 Minn 23

[2] Dawson v. Ewing, 16 S & R 371

[3] Prescott v. Everetts, 4 Wis 329, Carman v. Pultz, 21 N Y 547 See Dodge v. Deal, 28 Ill 303

[4] Black v. Smith, Peake 121

[5] Dyckman v. City of New York, 5 N Y 434

[6] Prescott v. Everetts, 4 Wis 329.

pudiated by the firm or other partner. The question of one partner's authority to receive goods or other thing in satisfaction of a debt due the firm, depends upon the scope of the partnership business, but wherever a valid agreement can be made by one partner to accept something else in lieu of cash, in discharge of a debt due a firm, a tender of the thing to one partner under such agreement will of course be good.

§ 338. **An assignee of contract — Notice of assignment — Where an assignment of mortgage is not recorded — Assignee under an option to repurchase—Assignor when.—**Where a mortgage, note, or other obligation has been assigned, the tender must be made to the assignee, provided the debtor has actual or constructive notice of the assignment.[1] Where the assignee of a mortgage, or the grantee under a conveyance from the purchaser at an execution sale has gone into possession, the creditor is charged with notice of the assignment, and the tender must be made to the assignee or grantee.[2] If an assignment of a mortgage has not been placed upon record as required by statute, and the mortgage refused to state to whom he has assigned the mortgage, a tender to the mortgagee is good.[3]

Where on the sale of land a right to repurchase is reserved, and the land is subsequently sold subject to the agreement, on electing to exercise the option, the tender should be made to the then owner of the land[4] So, where a grantee of land has notice that the grantor is under bond to convey the land to another for a specific sum, the tender may be made to the grantee[5] But, in such case if the party entitled to a conveyance desires to lay the foundation for an action for damages, the tender ought also to be made to the party agreeing to convey On a failure of an assignee of a contract to perform on a tender and demand for per

[1] Flanigan v Seelye, 53 Minn 23 See Wilson v Doran, 17 N E Rep (N Y) 688, and Smith v Kelley, 27 Me 237

[2] Wing v Davis 7 Me 31, Camp v Simon 34 Ala 126

[3] Fritz v Simpson, 31 N J Eq 436 See Noyes v Clark 7 Paige Ch 179, s c 32 Am Dec 620 and Stafford v Welch, 59 N H 46

[4] McLaughlin v Royce 78 N W Rep (Io) 1107

[5] St Paul Div Sons of Temperance v Brown, 9 Minn 744

formance by the other party, a tender must be made to the assignor, as the latter has a right to perform for his assignee and may do so,[6] if within his power.

§ 339. Assignee or receiver in insolvency.—If a debtor has made an assignment for the benefit of his creditors, or a receiver has been appointed for his property, the payment must be made to the assignee or receiver. But in such cases, a valid tender cannot be made, that is such a tender as will discharge a lien, release a surety, and the like. The contract is not with the assignee or receiver; he is but the hand of the court to receive the money when it comes due. It is not like the case of two contracting parties, where one is held bound when the other has performed his part of the contract according to its terms, or has offered to perform but has been prevented by the act of the other. If such was the case, an ignorant or unscrupulous officer might destroy the value of the assets in the custody of the court by refusing to receive the proper amount due, thereby releasing the liens or other security.[1] But if a debtor makes an offer of payment which in other cases would be a valid tender, and keeps the money for the assignee or receiver, separate and apart from his other funds, ready to hand over whenever the assignee or receiver calls for it, the debtor will be exonerated from the payment of interest after the date of the offer. A party has a right to avoid payment of future costs, damages, and penalties, by offering to perform his contract at the appointed time and place, regardless of who may have acquired the right to receive the thing to be delivered.

§ 340 Corporations—What officer.—In making a tender of money or anything due a corporation, it must be made to the officer authorized to receive the money or other thing. Where a debt is due a bank, or payable at a bank, the tender ought to be made to the cashier or receiving teller or his assistant. A tender of an amount due a building and loan association to its local secretary and treasurer, was held to have been properly made.[1] There is no uniform rule or cus-

[6] Dustan v. McAndrew, 10 Bosw. 135.

[1] Prague v. Greenlee, 22 Gratt. 724.

[1] Smith v. Old Dominion B & L. Assn., 119 N. C. 257, s. c. 26 S. E. Rep. 40.

tom relative to what officer of a corporation has authority to receive money due it, but ordinarily the tender ought to be made to the officer in the active general management of its business affairs. If the tender is not made to the right officer, the creditor at that time ought to be informed of that fact. A tender to a president of a corporation of the amount due on an assessment upon the stock, was held good when made at the office of the company and no objection being made that the president did not have authority to represent the company.[2]

§ 341. **Agent — Clerk — Servant** — A tender to an agent authorized to receive payment has the same effect as a tender to the creditor in person.[1] Authority to receive payment of a demand implies the power to accept a part payment to apply upon it.[2] A tender to an agent of a less sum than that demanded by the principal, whether tendered unconditionally, or as all that is due, and the agent in refusing neglects to object to it on that ground, even though the less sum is in fact all that is due is not good. An agent having no authority to compromise a debt due his principal, could not by waiver make that a valid tender, which would not be binding if accepted. Where there is a dispute as to the amount due, the principal should be given an opportunity to accept a less sum. Where an agent is sent to demand a specific sum on an unliquidated claim, a tender to such agent of a less sum, is not a legal tender to the creditor.[3] But a tender to an agent has been held good, where the agent was instructed not to receive the money until certain conditions were complied with, which conditions if annexed to the acceptance of the tender by the principal would not have been a good excuse for his refusing the tender.[4] A debtor is under no obligation to make a tender to an agent, and he may make it to the creditor or to the agent at his election.[5]

2 Mitchell v Vermont C Co 67 N Y 280

1 Goodland v Blewith 1 Camp 178, Moffatt v Parson 1 Marsh 55, Post v Springsted, 49 Mich 90, s c 13 N W Rep 370 See Fletcher v Dougherty, 13 Neb 224, King v Finch, 60 Ind 420

2 Whelan v Reilly 61 Mo 565
3 Chipman v Bates 5 Vt 143
4 Crowford v Osman 51 N W Rep (Mich) 284
5 Hoyt v Hall 1 Bosw (N Y) 12, Hoyt v Byrnes 11 Me 475

unless the contract specifically provides that the money or thing is to be delivered to an agent. Where a managing clerk had been told not to receive certain money, the demand having been previously placed in the hand of an attorney, and the clerk on the sum being tendered, refused to receive it, assigning such reason, it was held to be no valid objection to the tender.[6] If a creditor removes from the state and leaves an agent to attend to his business, and the debtor has notice of such agency, it is the duty of the debtor to make a tender to the agent at the appointed time and place. The creditor should, however, provide the agent with a receipt signed by him, or written evidence of the agency, as the debtor ought not to be required to assume any risk in his proof of agency. A tender to an agent has been held good where the debtor believed the agent to be the real party in interest.[7]

A person who makes a tender or payment to a third person claiming to represent the creditor is bound, at his peril, to ascertain the nature and extent of the agent's authority. The burden is upon the debtor who has made a tender or payment to a person assuming to be agent, if the agency be denied, to prove that the party alleged had authority to receive the payment.[8] When a person assuming to be an agent demands payment of a debt due his principal, the debtor may require competent evidence of such third person's authority to receive the money, which if not furnished will excuse a tender of the money then and there to the agent, but such failure to furnish evidence of the agent's authority will not excuse a tender to the creditor in person, or at the place of payment in his absence. If the debtor chooses he may take a reasonable time to ascertain the agent's authority, but the debtor cannot take such time for the purpose of extending the time of payment. He must be ready at the appointed time and place to make payment to somebody. Where the money is due on a note or other written instrument, the debtor may insist upon seeing it, for if the instrument has been withdrawn by the principal, the agent's authority to receive payment ordinarily ceases

[6] Moffat v. Parson, 5 Taunt. 307.

[7] Conrad v. Druids, 64 Wis. 258. S. C. 25 N. W. Rep 24.

[8] See Garnett v. Myers, 91 N. W. Rep (Neb) 400

with such withdrawal.[9]  If a debtor goes to an agent to make payment, where he could as well have gone to the creditor, the agent is under no legal obligation to furnish evidence of his authority beyond his own statement to that effect, and a failure to furnish evidence will not excuse a tender either to the agent or principal.

The general rule is, that a tender to a clerk in a store of the amount due for goods purchased at such store, is equivalent to a tender to the proprietor.[10]  The presumption is that a clerk or agent who sells goods has authority to receive payment for them.  In those stores where the clerks act merely as salesmen, and the money is required to be paid to the cashier, a tender must be made to the cashier.  It has been held that where a person demands the payment of money at his office, such demand amounts to authority for the clerk there to receive payment, and in the absence of the creditor, a tender to the clerk is good.[11]  A tender to a traveling salesman is not good unless he is expressly authorized to receive payment.  Such authority, however, may be implied from the fact that other payments were made to him and credited by the principal without objection.

Where the day but no place of payment is specified and the creditor cannot be found for the purpose of making a tender to him personally, and the debtor is compelled to make the tender at the residence of the creditor in his absence, can a tender be made to a servant or other member of the creditor's family?  In New York, in a case where upon inquiry at the creditor's house, the debtor was informed that the creditor had "gone east" and where it appeared from the circumstances, that the creditor by being voluntarily absent, intended to render it impossible for the debtor to make a valid payment, it was held that a tender to the creditor's family was valid.[12]  In a case which arose in England, (the master being at home), the debtor sent a sum of money by a servant to the creditor's house, who gave it to the creditor's servant, who retired and appeared to go with the money to his master and returned with the answer that his

9 Smith v Kidd, 68 N. Y. 130
10 Hoyt v Byrnes, 11 Me 475
See Moffatt v Parson, 5 Taunt 307
11 Kirton v Braithwaite, 1 M & W 310; 5 D P. C 101, 2 Gale 48
12 Judge v. Ensign, 6 Barb (N Y) 258.

master would not receive it, it was left to the jury to say
whether the money had been tendered, and the jury found
that it had. Lord Kenyon said, "that in the common transactions of life, this kind of intercourse, by the intervention
of servants, must be allowed, and that if the money was
so brought to the house of the plaintiff, and delivered to his
servant, who retired, and appeared to go to the master, it
was evidence to be left to the jury, from which they might
infer that a tender was made." [13] It is to be observed that
the foregoing decisions were based upon exceptional circumstances. It is not to be doubted that a rule permitting
a tender to be made on the day for payment, at the creditor's
house, to a servant or other member of the creditor's family, would be in some cases convenient to both the debtor and
creditor. But reasons why the rule should not obtain out-
weigh the convenience. A creditor may employ a servant
for the performance of domestic duties and yet be unwilling
to trust him with sums of money; so, a debtor may not be
able, upon a hurried visit, to determine who are the servants
and members of his creditor's family, and ought not, therefore, to be required, in absence of the creditor, to take any
risk, by depositing a sum of money with an entire stranger.
While a creditor is charged with notice, in such cases, that
the money will be tendered on the day at his home, yet it
may not be convenient or possible to be there, and equally
as inconvenient or impossible to provide a reliable agent to
represent him at the time, and he ought not to be subjected to the risk of a loss of his money by having it left
with any one the debtor may find there, who may not even
be a member of the family or of his household. The rule,
that the debtor by being at the home of his creditor, at the
last hour of the day on which to make payment, at a convenient time before sunset, ready and willing to pay over
the money, when he is required to make a personal tender
and is unable to do so by reason of the creditor's absence,
is the correct rule, and one that leaves neither party any
worse off. The debtor has but to keep the money safely for
his creditor to exonerate himself, and the creditor has but to
call for his money to receive all that is his due. In a case
arising in New York subsequent to the last case but one

[13] Anonymous 1 Esp (N P C) 349

above referred to, a tender to a servant, at the mortgagee's residence, without proof that she was actually or apparently authorized to receive the money, was held to be insufficient.[1] But in this case the mortgage was past due, and it does not appear that any notice was given of an intention of making a tender at that time.

§ 342. **Attorney.**—A debtor may make a tender to an attorney with whom a demand has been lodged for collection.[1] If a creditor has held an attorney out as authorized to receive payment upon a certain demand, the debtor may rely upon the authority until he has notice that it is withdrawn, and in absence of such notice a tender to the attorney whose authority has in fact ceased but who still assumes authority will be good. If at the time the debtor makes an offer of payment to an attorney, he disclaims all authority to receive payment, the debtor must go to his creditor and make a tender to him.[2] But such disclaimer must be in accordance with the truth that the agency never existed or has been revoked, and it will not defeat a tender if the agency or authority in fact exists.[3] To receive payment must be within the scope of the attorney's authority. A tender of the mortgage debt to an attorney who had been employed for the sole purpose of seeing that the mortgage sale was conducted fairly was held to be insufficient.[4]

If an attorney demands that payment be made at his office, and at the time the debtor comes there the attorney is absent, he is bound by the acts of his clerk or the person he allows to represent him, and a tender to his clerk at his office is good.[5] Where an attorney wrote a letter stating that the debt due his client "must be paid to me" on the next day, and the debtor on going to the office of the attorney

[1] Jewett v. Earle, 53 N. Y. Super. Ct. 349

[1] Billiot v. Robinson, 13 La. Ann. 529, Salter v. Shove, 60 Minn. 483, McIniffe v. Wheelock, 1 Gray 600. See Thurston v. Blaisdell, 8 N. H. 367

[2] Wilmot v. Smith, 3 C. & P. 453

[3] McIniffe v. Wheelock, 1 Gray 600

[4] Tuthill v. Morris, 81 N. Y. 94

[5] Wilmot v. Smith, 3 C. & P. 453 Katon v. Braithwaite 1 M. & W. 310, 5 D. P. C. 101, 2 Gale 48. A tender was made to a boy in the attorney's office who refused to receive the money unless a charge for writing the letter was also paid.

made a tender to a writing clerk, who said that he could not take the money as his employer was out, it was held not a good tender, as not being made to a person having authority to receive the money. But the court observed that if he had asked that payment be made "at my office," a tender to any person in the office carrying on the business there would have been sufficient." In a case where a tender was made to a managing clerk of an attorney, who at the time disclaimed authority from his master to receive the money on the debt, it was held insufficient. The court said, although a party puts his case into the hand of his attorney, who thereby becomes authorized to receive payment, it by no means follows that all the attorney's clerks have such authority.[7] Calling at the office of an attorney prepared to pay, when the attorney is at home sick, was held not to meet the requirements of the law, that the debtor should have called at the abode of the attorney or on the debtor. Before suit has been commenced on a demand, the law of principal and agent govern the relation of attorney and client. If an attorney is authorized to receive payment of the whole debt, his authority not being specially limited, he may receive a part to apply upon the demand, but without express authority he cannot compromise his client's claim, and therefore, in absence of such authority a tender of a less sum than the amount claimed, even though the less sum is in fact all that is due, is not good.

Where after suit has been commenced the court has imposed costs as a condition of granting any favor, as opening a default and the like, a tender of such costs to the attorney is sufficient.[10] So a judgment for costs, which under a statute or order of the court must be paid before a party will be entitled to a second trial, may be tendered to the attorney. After judgment, the authority of the attorney of the successful party continues, usually for two years, for the purpose of enforcing the judgment, and a tender of the amount of the judgment made to the attorney within that

Watson v. Hetherington, 1 C. & K. 6.

[7] Bingham v. Allport, 1 N. & M. 398.

Francis v. Deming, 59 Conn. 108.

Whelin v. Reilly, 61 Mo. 565, Rodges v. Kouze, 81 N. C. 164.

Wolf v. Canadian Pac. R. R. Co. 89 Cal. 332.

time will be good unless the judgment debtor has notice that such authority has been withdrawn. An attorney's authority, like that of an agent, cannot be proven solely by the statement of the attorney.

**§ 343. Bank where note is payable.**—Where an instrument by its terms is made payable at a particular time, at a certain bank, counting house, or other place, it amounts to a stipulation that the holder will have it at the bank or other place when due, and that the obligor will produce there the funds to pay it. It is the general custom in such cases where the obligation is made payable at a bank, for the holder to lodge the instrument with the bank for collection, so that the party bound for its payment can call there and take it up. Specifying a bank as a place of payment, how ever, does not constitute the bank the agent of the holder of the instrument[1] A note drawn payable at a bank need not be left there. The party may not care to trust the solvency of the bank. Where the instrument is not lodged with the bank, any sum received by the bank to be applied upon the instrument is received as the agent of the payor and not as the agent of the payee.[2] If the instrument is lodged with the bank to be delivered to the payor on its payment, the bank is a proper person to whom a tender can be made, and in absence of the creditor from the bank it should be made to the bank. If the instrument be not left with the bank and the creditor be absent, a personal tender is excused, providing the obligor is at the place at the ap pointed time, with the money ready to make the payment[3]

**§ 344. Sheriff—Clerk of court—Officer in replevin—Officer holding execution—Procedure if refused.**—Where property has been sold under a foreclosure of a mortgage, a party desiring to redeem may tender the amount necessary to effect the redemption to the sheriff who made the sale, or to his successor in office.[1] Where real property is sold under execu

---

[1] Cheney v Libby, 134 U S 68, Adams v Hackenback Imp Co, 44 N J L 638; Mahon v. Waters, 60 Mo 167

[2] Ward v Smith, 7 Wall 447

[3] Adams v Hackenback Impro Co, 44 N J L 638

[1] Thompson v Foster 21 Minn 319

tion, the tender of the amount necessary to redeem may be made to the sheriff who made the sale or to the clerk of the court of the county where such real estate is located. The right to make a tender to the clerk of court or sheriff is purely statutory. It is for the convenience of the debtor, but he may, if he prefers, make the tender to the purchaser.[2] The sheriff or clerk acts merely as an officer, and is in no sense the agent of either party, and his acceptance or rejection of a tender will not prejudice the rights of either party. Under a statute making the sheriff or constable in replevin the judge of whether property had been injured while in the defendant's possession under bond, a tender of the property, on a judgment for plaintiff, should be made to the sheriff or constable.[3] Where an execution is in the hands of an officer, a tender of the money or thing to be recovered should be made to the officer. But the tender, in any case where an officer is authorized to collect money, need not necessarily be made to the officer, for wherever a payment to an officer is good, a payment or tender to the party entitled to receive it from the officer is good. If the sheriff or creditor refuse a tender, the only way to make it effectual, is to bring the money into court and move for and obtain an order to enter satisfaction upon the record.[4] When an officer is entitled to fees after an execution is in his hand, the debtor cannot escape paying such fees by making a tender to his creditor. If the creditor accepts the money without collecting such fees, he must pay them.

§ 345. **Personal representatives—Guardian—Trustee.**—Where a debt or anything is due to the estate of a deceased person, the tender must be made to the personal representatives. A tender to a person before he qualifies as executor is not good.[1] The death of a person fixes the status of his property as of the date of his death. But after a foreclosure of a lien, the death of the lien holder will not prevent an absolute title vesting in his heirs merely by the afflux of time. If, however, there is not sufficient time between the

[2] Armstrong v. Pierson 5 Iowa 317

[3] Childs v. Wilkinson, 40 S. W. Rep. (Tex. Civ. App.) 749

[1] Jackson v. Law, 5 Cow. 248

[1] See Todd v. Parker, 1 N. J. L. (Coxe) 45

date of the death of the lienor and the last day allowed
the debtor to redeem, to appoint an administrator, a tender
will be excused. The debtor must show, however, if his
right to pay the money later is questioned, that he was
willing and able and ready on the last day on which a re
demption could be made, to pay the money, and would have
done so but for the death of the lienor. Personal representa
tives are trustees, either appointed by, or whose appointment
is sanctioned by the court having jurisdiction of estates of
deceased persons, and are, therefore, officers of the court.
Like receivers and assignees, in the management of the
estate they have very little discretionary power, being but
the law's representative authorized to collect the assets and
distribute them pursuant to law under the order of the
court. Between them and debtors of the deceased, there
exists no contractual relation, and the same reason supporting the rule that a lien or surety is not discharged by a
refusal by an assignee or receiver, of an offer of payment
which would be a valid tender if made to the creditor in
person, apply with equal force to an offer of payment made
to an executor or administrator. However, in an ancient
case in England, it was held that a tender by the owner,
of the amount due, to the executor of the pawnee, which she
refused, was as good as payment and that the special prop
erty in the goods pawned was revested and that the owner
could bring trover or conversion.[2]

A tender of the amount due a minor, spendthrift, or an in
sane person under guardianship, must be made to their
guardian. If a guardian *ad litem* or next friend has recov
ered a judgment in favor of a minor or other person under
disability, a tender of the amount due should be made to
their general guardian if they have one at the time of the
tender. In absence of a general guardian, then the tender
may be made to the guardian *ad litem* or next friend who
acted in the matter, or to the attorney employed by them to
prosecute the action. What has been said in reference to
the effect of a refusal of a tender by assignees, receivers and
personal representatives, also apply to a refusal by a guard
ian. Money due a beneficiary should be tendered to the
trustee.[4]

[2] Ratcliff v. Davis, Cro. Jac. 244;
[4] Chanoon v. Hollenback, 16
Am. Dec. 587, Hayward v. Mun
ger, 14 Iowa 516. See Hursh v.
Phillips, Cro. Eliz. 755.

# CHAPTER VIII.

## KEEPING A TENDER GOOD

**§ 346 General rule—Effect on interest and costs—Interest commences to run from what time on a failure to keep the tender good**—It is a general rule that wherever the debt or duty remains after a tender, the tender to be available must be kept good. In such cases the obligation to keep the tender good is as essential to the legal efficacy of the tender as the offer of the money.[1] It must be kept good in order to

---

[1] McCalley v Otey, 90 Ala 302, Odum v Rutledge, etc Ry Co 94 Ala 488 Bullock v Cross 16 Colo 162, Kortright v Cady 23

Barb 490 Warbuiy v Wilcox, 2 Hilt 121 Nelson v Loder 132 N Y 292 s c 55 Hun 173, Matthews v Lindsay 20 Fla 952

escape paying interest subsequent to the tender, and costs in case an action is subsequently brought to recover the sum due. A failure to keep a tender good, not only sets the interest to running from the time of such failure, but it will run uninterruptedly from the maturity of the debt, or other time provided for in the instrument.[2] If a valid tender has been made on a non interest bearing obligation, a failure to comply with a subsequent demand for the money, or a failure to keep the tender good where no demand has been made, will set the interest to running at the legal rate from the due date.

§ 347. Necessary when right to possession continues until payment—Where title to land remains in vendor—Option of vendee.—Where the right to the possession of property continues until payment, as where a mortgagee on default asserts his right under the mortgage by taking possession,[1] a tender thereafter of the amount due will not support an action of trover or replevin unless the tender be kept good. So, where the purchase price of goods sold has been duly tendered to a vendor who has retained the possession, and the latter is wrong in refusing it, nevertheless the right of possession remains in the seller until payment "Nothing short of payment, or its legal equivalent, *tout temps prist*, can deprive the defendant of the right of possession."[2] A tender of the balance due upon a contract for the purchase of land where the legal title remains in the vendor, must be kept good and the money brought into court, if the vendee desires to enforce the contract by a bill for specific performance[3] But where a tender has been made of the purchase price of goods or of land, and it has been refused the

Tuttill v Morris, 81 N Y 94
Jones v Mullnix, 25 Iowa 198,
Saum v La Shell, 45 Kan 205,
Dodge v Pearcy, 19 Hun 278,
Mohn v Stoner, 11 Iowa 115, Musgat v Pumpelly 1 N W Rep
(Wis) 410, Barker v Brink, 5
Iowa, 481, Pulsifer v Shepard, 36
Ill 513, Craig v Robinson, 67 N
Y Supp 969, Balm v Wambough,
16 Minn. 117, Lloyd v O'Rear,
59 S W Rep (Ky) 483

[2] Tate v. Smith, 70 N C 685

[1] Smith v Phillips, 47 Wis 202,
s c 2 N W Rep 285, Blain v
Foster 33 Ill App 297 See Long
v Howard, 35 Iowa 148 See also
§§ 375, 376, 377

[2] Summerson v Hicks 134 Pa
St 566

[3] Scheaff v Dodge, 33 Ark 346
See Murray v. Nickerson, 95 N
W. Rep (Minn) 898, to the contrary

purchaser may, if he desires, bring an action to recover damages, without keeping the tender good.[4]

§ 348. Necessary in replevin when — Rescission — Audita querela — Where tender is to third person — In action on administrator's bond — Where a plaintiff in replevin alleged the wrongful seizure of goods by a tax collector, and relied upon a tender of all that was due as entitling him to a return of his goods, it was held that he must be continually ready to pay the sum tendered.[1] A party who makes a tender to rescind a sale must keep the tender good.[2] A tender of the amount due upon an execution must be kept good to entitle the execution debtor to relief by *audita querela*.[3] Where a party is entitled to some right by reason of making a certain payment to a third person, as where land is granted to a railroad company on condition that the company pay a certain sum to a city on a certain date, and a tender is made and the city refuses it, the tender must nevertheless be kept good.[4] In an action against an administrator and sureties on his bond to recover a distributive share of the estate, a tender of such share by the administrator is of no avail as a defence, unless the tender is kept good.[5]

§ 349. Where a tender is made by a mortgagor after a default — On the law day — After a foreclosure. — At common law, a tender after default in the payment of a mortgage debt does not discharge the lien of the mortgage, and to be available in an action to redeem, or as a defense in foreclosure, where the cause of action or defence is based upon such tender, it must be kept good. Nothing short of payment will divest the mortgagee of the legal title. Under the common law, if, on the due day, a mortgagor tenders the amount due on the mortgage debt to the mortgagee and he refuses it, the mortgage lien is discharged. So, the same effect is produced by a tender of the mortgage debt at any time before a foreclosure, in most of those commonwealths where prevails the modern doctrine that the legal title remains in the mortgagor until divested by a foreclosure. Where a mortgage

4 Thomas v. Mathis, 92 Ind. 560.

1 Miller v. McGhee, 60 Miss. 903. See § 383.

2 O. Riley v. Surei, 70 Ill. 85.

3 Perry v. Ward, 20 Vt. 92.

4 State v. Illinois Cent. R. Co., 33 Fed. 730.

5 Rainwater v. Hummel, 79 Iowa, 571.

25

lien is thus discharged by a tender, the mortgagor may plead the tender to defeat a foreclosure, or the recovery of the possession of the property by the mortgagee, without keep ing the tender good.[1] But this rule is not universal.[2] How ever, if the debt remains, the tender must be kept good if the debtor desires to escape paying interest subsequent to the tender, and costs of an action brought to recover the debt. A tender made after a foreclosure and before the time to redeem has expired must be kept good to be effectual as the basis of an action to redeem commenced after the time to redeem had expired.[1] The same rule applies if the action is commenced before the time to redeem has expired

§ 350. **Unnecessary where debt or duty is discharged—A** surety **—Where no personal obligation exists to pay the money—Void and voidable contracts.**—If a debt or duty is discharged by a tender and refusal, the tender need not be kept good for a party is not bound to continue ready to pay a debt or per form a duty of which he has been discharged.[1] Where a surety tenders the amount due on his principal's obligation and it is refused, he is discharged, and he need not keep the tender good So, where there exists no personal obligation on the part of one making a tender, as where a person exe cutes a mortgage, or delivers property in pledge as security for the debt of another, a tender made to secure the release of the mortgage, or the surrender of the property, need not be kept good The owner of such property stands in the relation of a surety Where a contract is void or voidable, as being against public policy, or where it is within the statute of frauds, or for want of consideration, a tender made upon such contract need not be kept good, such tender not validating such contract.

§ 351. **Unnecessary when—Exception where tendeior seeks equitable relief —**In cases where the cause of action or de fence is based upon an alleged default, and the thing sought

---

[1] Kortwright v Cady, 21 N Y 354; Potts v. Plaisted, 30 Mich 150, Stewait v Brown, 48 Mich 387

[2] Matthews v Lindsay, 20 Fla 962 See Danghdill v. Sweeney, 11 Ala 310, Bailey v Metcalf, 6 N H 156, Dunn v Hunt, 63 Minn 184

[1] Dunn v Hunt, 63 Minn 484, S C 65 N W Rep 948

[1] 9 Bac Abr. Tit Tender (II)

to be obtained by the action is damages [1] or the enforcement of some collateral right, the defendant (or plaintiff) need not plead *tout temps prist*, nor make a profert of the money in court. As in replevin, a plea of tender to an avowry or cognizance, need only go to the extent of alleging that before the distress, a tender was made and refused.[2] The same rule applies in replevin by a mortgagee, where the lien of the mortgage has been discharged by a tender and refusal; to actions by a vendor to recover property sold on a conditional sale,[3] and to suits to foreclose a real estate mortgage or any lien[4] To the general rule that where the lien is discharged by a tender, the tender need not be kept good in order to be of avail to the debtor, there is an exception. A tender, when it is made the foundation of an action in equity, must be kept good, or it will be wholly ineffectual; as where an action is commenced, based upon a tender and refusal, to compel the execution and delivery of a satisfaction of the mortgage,[5] or a cancellation of record,[6] or to set aside a tax sale and cancel the certificate.[7] In such case it does not matter whether the lien was discharged or not, or whether a suit would lie independent of any tender The exception to the general rule applies alike to a plaintiff or a defendant. A defendant who invokes the equitable powers of the court to cancel the security in whole[8] or in part,[9] on the ground that a tender of the debt had been made, must keep the tender good In Michigan, in a case where the lien of the mortgage had been discharged by a tender, where the defendant consented to have such decree made in the case as would be just, the court decreed that the debt should be paid within three months, and in default of payment the premises should be

[1] Bonaparte v Thayer, 52 Atl Rep (Md) 196, Ashley v Rocky Mt Tel Co, 61 Pac Rep (Mont) 765

[2] Hunter v Le Conte, 6 Cow. 728

[3] Christenson v Nelson, 63 Pac Rep (Ore) 648

[4] Kortright v Cady, 21 N Y 343

[5] Halpin v Phoenix Ins Co, 118 N Y 166; McGhee v. Jones, 10 Ga 127, Foster v Meyer, 24

N Y Supp 16; Nelson v Loder, 132 N Y 292, McNeil v Sun, etc Co, 78 N Y Supp 90

[6] Tuthill v Morris, 81 N Y 94, Parker v Beasley, 116 N C 1, s c 33 L. R. A 231

[7] Lancaster v De Hadway, 97 Ind 566

[8] Brunich v. Weselman, 100 N Y 609

[9] Werner v Tuch, 127 N. Y. 217, s c 27 N E Rep 845, 5 N Y Supp 219

sold.[10] The same strictness as to a tender obtains in such cases, as at law. A complainant in equity, who relies for relief upon a tender, must allege all the facts substantially, which are necessary in pleading a tender at law.[11] If a lien is discharged by a tender, a defendant desiring the benefit of it must go no further in his answer than to set up the tender as a defence. If any equitable relief is sought the maxim "He who seeks equity must do equity" at once applies. Where, however, a mortgagee, whose mortgage lien has been discharged by a tender, is foreclosing the mortgage by advertisement, there being no statutory or other provision for interposing a defence in such cases, the mortgagor, without keeping the tender good, may apply to a court of equity for an injunction, restraining the mortgagor from proceeding with the foreclosure

§ 352. **Burden of proof—Amount to be kept where more than is due was tendered.**—The burden of proof is upon the person alleging a tender to show that he has kept the tender good.[1] A tender of a sum of money in discharge of a debt, is an admission that the amount offered is due, but it is not conclusive, and if too much had been tendered, no obligation is created to keep good the whole amount tendered.[2]

§ 353. **Specific articles—Tenderor cannot abandon the property.**—A tender of personal property in compliance with a contract of sale and delivery, or in payment of a chattel note, if valid, vests the absolute title to the thing tendered in the tenderee, and the tenderor is discharged from his contract. Unlike a tender of money, a tender of property need not be

---

[10] Ferguson v Popp 42 Mich 115 s c 3 N W Rep 287 See Clark v Neuman 76 N W Rep (Neb) 802 where a vendee was resisting a foreclosure of the vendor's lien on the ground of a tender but did not bring the money into court It was held that it was error to decree a conveyance from the vendor to vendee, without requiring the money to be paid in by a certain day

[11] McGhee v Jones 10 Ga 127 Dunn v Hunt, 63 Minn 484 Call v Scott, 4 Call 402

[1] v Howard 35 Iowa 118 See Sanders v Bever, 152 Miss 144, Davis v Parker 14 Allen 94

[2] Able v Opel 21 Ind 280 See Martin v Bott, 46 N L Rep (Ind App) 154 to the contrary citing Ansem v Byrd, 6 Ind 475 and Moon v Martin, 55 Ind 218 See also Tucker v Buffum 16 Pick 46

kept good.[1]  In a case where it was contended by the plaintiff that the defendant must aver that he had abandoned the property, or that he had kept it for the plaintiff, to be delivered when he demanded it, the court observed: "Money can be kept without expense, and with little comparative risk; not so as to bulky articles.  If one contracts to pay another twenty horses at a specified day, buys them and has them ready to deliver at the day, and the other party refuse to receive them, would it be reasonable that he who had contracted to deliver the horses, should keep them for an indefinite length of time ready to deliver to the other party on demand, or should abandon them, in order to be discharged from liability on his contract?  I think not."[2]  The tenderee must resort to the specific articles tendered, and the person in whose possession they are, holds them as bailee and at the tenderee's risk.[3]  Because the tenderor is discharged from his contract, it does not follow that he may abandon or destroy the property tendered;[4] on the contrary he is bound to take care of the property, though at the risk and expense of the creditor.[5]

It is now well settled that if a tenderor, after a refusal to accept chattels, or where the tenderee fails to attend at the time and place fixed for delivery, retains possession of them, it is as the bailee of the tenderee.  There is no undertaking to care for the property, except that arising by law from the fact of the tenderor retaining the possession.  Although the thing tendered is to be kept at the risk and expense of the tenderee, yet the tenderor is only required to keep them with ordinary care.  Notwithstanding the right to a reasonable compensation for his services in the care of the property, and reimbursement for the necessary expense incurred in and about its preservation, the obligation for the safekeeping of the property resting upon the tenderor is no greater than that of a bailee in the case of a mere naked deposit without

---

[1] McPherson v. Wiswell 21 N. W. Rep. (Neb.) 391.  See Mitchell v. Merrill 2 Blackf. (Ind.) 89, Mitchell v. Gregory 1 Bibb 449

[2] Goulard v. Zachariah, 1 Stew. (Ala.) 272

[3] Slingerland v. Morris 8 Johns. 370

[4] Gale v. Snyam, 21 Wend 274

[5] Sheldon v. Skinner 4 Wend 525.  Mr. Kent in his Commentaries said that the debtor may abandon the goods, but the weight of authority is to the contrary.  2 Kent's Com. 509

reward.  A tenderor need not keep the articles tendered in
his immediate possession; the obligation resting upon him
in case the property is left on his hand is not to abandon or
destroy it.  If unable to keep the articles, or he does not
care to, he may place them in a warehouse, or other suitable
place, in the care of a third person, subject to his order or the
order of the tenderee.[6]

§ 354.  **Option of tenderor on rejection of chattels** —The
American doctrine applicable to contracts of sale, now well
settled, is, that where the goods tendered have been rejected,
or the vendee is in default in not attending at the time and
place appointed to receive them,—his presence being neces
sary to complete the transaction,—the vendor, if he elects to
stand upon a tender of the goods, has the choice of either of
two methods to indemnify himself.  "(1) He may store or
retain the property for the vendee, and sue him for the
entire purchase price  (2) He may sell the property, acting
as the agent for this purpose of the vendee, and recover the
difference between the contract price and the price obtained
on such resale"[1]  So, he may treat the contract as broken
and at an end, and sue for the difference between the market
price at the time and place of delivery and the contract price,
but this pertains more to the question of an abandonment of
a tender.  If the vendor resells the property, which he ought
to do if the goods are perishable, all that is required of him
is, that he act with reasonable care and diligence and in good
faith[2]  Mr Kent said that the usage was for the vendor to
sell the goods at auction;[3] but such a custom is not uni
versal, in fact it does not appear to be obligatory anywhere.
The rule as to a resale, is not different in those cases where
specific articles are tendered in payment of a note drawn pay
able in such articles.  If the goods are rejected, or the cred
itor does not go to the appointed place to receive them and
they are perishable, the debtor must not allow them to perish
without making a reasonable effort to sell them for the
creditor[4]  The tenderor, however, is not required to make

[6] Dustan v. McAndrews, 44 N.
Y 72

[1] Dustan v McAndrews, 44 N
Y 72, Newmark on Sales, § 391
The law in England, on the ques-
tion of resale is different  See

Benjamin on Sales § 1051 et seq
[2] Dustan v McAndrews 44 N.
Y 72
[3] 2 Kent's Com 504
[4] See Miller v Mariner's Church,
7 Greenl 57

any great sacrifice of his time or incur expense, in order to save the pocket of his creditor.

**§ 355. Exception to the rule that a tender of specific articles need not be kept good.**—There is a class of specific articles which, if tendered in compliance with a contract, must be kept safely for the tenderee,[1] and in an action where the tender is pleaded, they must be brought into court. In a case where a note, bond and mortgage were tendered under an agreement, in settlement of a note, and on a refusal they were destroyed, the court said "It is sufficient to say that the tender here is not governed by the rule applicable to specific chattels, it is like a tender of money, or thing that may be brought into court. In such case the defendant must plead that he has always been and still is ready with the money or thing tendered, and it must be in court on the trial".[2] In a case arising in Illinois, the tenderor of certain bonds, having gotten into a dispute with his solicitors who retained the bonds, and he was unable to produce them at the time they were needed, it was held that the ability of the appellant to deliver the bonds is an essential element in the tender of which he claims the benefit. If his ability to surrender them is lacking, then the tender necessarily fails.[3] So, a party offering bills for redemption at a bank, by taking them away upon the refusal of the bank to redeem them, charges himself with their safekeeping until the agreement should be performed, whether by means of legal proceedings or otherwise.[4] A party tendering a deed or any instrument, where he relies upon the tender as the basis for relief, must keep the instrument ready to comply with a demand on the part of the tenderee should he change his mind. Where a second note, for the true amount, was to be substituted for the first note when the exact amount should be ascertained— it was held, that a failure of the payee, after a tender of the second note to an endorser with notice of the agreement, to keep the tender good, did not effect the right of the maker

---

[1] Gile v. Suydam, 24 Wend. 274.

[2] The Brooklyn Bank v. De Grauw, 23 Wend. 342. s. p. Fannin v. Thompson, 50 Ga. 614.

[3] Saunders v. Peck, 131 Ill. 407, s. c. 25 N. E. Rep. 508.

[4] Racine County Bank v. Keep, 13 Wis. 233.

to urge such agreement in an action on the original note. It being no part of the maker's duty to keep the tender good[5]

## § 356. Manner of keeping a tender good—Medium.

To keep a tender good the party making it must keep the money so that he may produce it when demanded. Where it is necessary to be kept good, it must be a continuous tender. It must be kept open for the acceptance of the other party whenever he expresses a willingness to accept it.[1] It must be kept open by a continuing readiness, a mere willingness is not sufficient.[2] It must be kept good in money.[3] A tender of a check if accepted would at most only operate as a conditional payment, and where a tender of a check is rejected, and pending a suit the bank fails, the tender is not kept good, even though the check had been certified and is kept for the tenderee.[4]

It is not necessary that the identical money tendered be kept.[5] But the same money or money of like kind must be kept on hand.[6] Money of like kind means money of like legal tender quality. If a tender be made of a sum in gold coin, only gold or its equivalent in other legal tender money can be used in keeping the tender good. A tender in one thousand dollars in gold coin cannot be kept good by substituting subsidiary silver coin, such as half dollars, quarters, &c. Bank bills will not do; nor silver or gold certificates as they are not a legal tender, and are good in making a tender only when no objection is made to them on the ground that they are not a legal tender. Any money to which a valid objection could be urged if tendered, cannot be used in keeping a tender good to replace money to which no valid objection could be taken. But a tender of money that is not a legal tender (where no objection is raised as to its quality) may be

[5] Murray v. Reed 48 Pac (Wash) 343

[1] Voss v. McGuire, 26 Mo App 452, Gray v. Angier 62 Ga 596, Aulger v. Clay, 109 Ill 487, Matthews v. Lindsay, 20 Fla 962, McCalley v. Otey, 90 Ala 302, Dunn v. Hunt, 63 Minn 484, Coghlan v. South Car R Co. 32

Fed Rep 316 Dodge v. Lenz 49 Hun 277 Call v. Scott 4 Call 402

[2] Slingut v. Pattee 37 Iowa, 422 Dunn v. Hunt, 63 Minn 484

[3] Aulger v. Clay, 109 Ill 187

[4] Larsen v. Breen, 12 Colo 480

[5] McCalley v. Otey, 90 Ala 302, Colbey v. Stevens 38 N H 191, Thompson v. Lyon 40 W Va 87

[6] Dunn v. Hunt 63 Minn 484

kept good by keeping a like amount of legal tender money. A tender of one thousand dollars in gold coin or any legal tender money, may be kept good by keeping part of it in subsidiary coin, providing the amount of subsidiary coin is within the limit for which it is a legal tender, the balance must be kept good with money of full legal tender quality. The reason that the identical pieces of money need not be kept is, that in law, at all times, one dollar is the equivalent of every other dollar of like legal tender quality. No good purpose can be served by a debtor substituting one dollar for another, and the strict rule, that the identical pieces of money tendered must be kept for the tenderee, ought to prevail.

§ 357. **Same subject—Money or thing how kept.**—A tender may be kept good before an action is commenced based on a tender, or before a defence is interposed based on a tender, by the tenderor keeping the money in his possession.[1] If a person who has made a tender keeps the money in his possession he must not use it for his benefit.[2] Using the money tendered amounts to a withdrawal of the tender.[3] Where a bank made a tender, and on its refusal mingled the money with its other funds, and used it in its ordinary business, it was held that the tender was not kept good.[4] Money tendered in payment of one bond, when refused, cannot be used in making a tender upon a second bond, a third, &c.[5] Where a tender is made by a third person in behalf of the creditor, and the party to whom the money belonged used it in whole or in part the tender was held to be invalidated.[6] Borrowing money for the purpose of making a tender, and on its being refused returning it to the lender, vitiates the tender.[7]

[1] Rice v. Kahn, 70 Wis. 323, s. c. 35 N. W. Rep. 465. Longbridge v. Iowa Life Ins. Co. 50 N. W. Rep. (Ia.) 568.

[2] Gray v. Angier 62 Ga. 596, Giles v. Hall, 2 P. Wms. 378, Bissell v. Howard 95 U. S. 580, Werner v. Tuch, 127 N. Y. 217, Stow v. Russell 36 Ill. 33, Thayer v. Meeker 86 Ill. 471. The Columbian Bldg. Assn. v. Crump 42 Md. 192, Nintz v. Lober 1 Duv. 304.

[3] Aulger v. Clay 109 Ill. 487, Ruley v. Metcalf 6 N. H. 156,

Voss v. McGuire 26 Mo. App. 452, Frink v. Pickens 69 Ala. 369.

[4] Roosevelt v. Bulls Head Bank, 45 Barb. 579.

[5] Quynn v. Whitecroft, 3 Har. & M. 352. See Lamprey v. St. Paul Ry. Co. 91 N. W. Rep. (Minn.) 555 where in an action for specific performance such a tender was held good.

[6] Werner v. Tuch, 127 N. Y. 217.

[7] Park v. Wiley, 67 Ala. 310, Dunn v. Hunt 63 Minn. 484.

There are a few authorities holding that because money when tendered and refused, does not, as do specific articles, become the absolute property of the person to whom it is tendered, the party making it is at liberty to use it as his own, and that all that he is under obligation to do is to be ready at all times to pay the debt in current funds.[8] What the opinion of the court was, in each of those cases as to what would constitute a readiness, is a matter of conjecture. However, the weight of authority is, that the money must not be used by the tenderor. Being financially able to pay the money at all times is not sufficient.[9] If a tender is made by an agent, he must keep the money subject to the tenderee's order.[10] The agent must not use the money, or mingle it with his own money, and if he does so it amounts to a conversion of it. Where money that has been tendered and refused is left in the possession of a third person, the risk of it being converted,[11] is upon the tenderor and not upon the tenderee.

§ 358.  **Same subject—Depositing money tendered in a bank.—** It is not necessary that a person who makes a tender should keep the money on his person ready to be paid the instant it is demanded. He may deposit it in a bank or other place for safekeeping.[1] And the better opinion is, that it should be set completely aside, whether it be deposited somewhere or kept in the possession of the tenderor. The money must not be deposited in a bank to the credit of the person making the tender.[2] A general deposit of money in a bank creates the relation of debtor and creditor between the bank and the depositor. The depositor parts with the title to his money, and accepts the credit of the bank in lieu thereof. The de

8 Curtis v. Greenbank, 24 Vt. 536, Woodruff v. Trapnall, 7 Eng. (Ark.) 640. In Shield v. Lozear, 22 N. J. Eq. 447, the court reviewed the authorities, but without approving or disapproving of the tenderor's use of the money in that case. See Cheney v. Bills, 74 Fed. 52, s. c. 20 C. C. A. 291, 36 U. S. App. 720.

9 Saunders v. Bevers, 152 Mass. 111.

10 Rice v. Kahn, 35 N. W. Rep. 465.

11 Dent v. Dunn, 3 Cin. p. 296.

1 Dunn v. Hunt, 63 Minn. 484; Ritchie v. Ege, 59 N. W. Rep. (Minn.) 1020.

2 Nelson v. Loder, 55 Hun. 173. See Riley v. Cheesman, 27 N. Y. Supp. 153, s. c. 75 Hun. 387.

posit converts the fund from ready money to a chose in action.[3] Being a loan to the bank, the case is no different from that where the money is used for the purpose of making a loan to an individual. So, the money must not be deposited in a bank, by a general deposit, to the credit of the tenderee. A creditor cannot be compelled to accept the credit of a bank in lieu of money. The rule is not different where the note or other obligation is drawn payable at a bank. Drawing a note in that way does not make the bank the agent of the payee. But if the note is left there for collection, then the money may be paid direct to the bank as agent. It must not be deposited to the payee's credit. In such case when paid to the bank, it does not matter to the payor whether the money is set aside by the bank for the payee, or is passed to his credit. If a payor of a note or bill, which is drawn payable at a bank, calls at the bank on the day fixed for payment ready to pay it, but does not find the instrument there, he may make a special deposit of the money there, to meet the note when it is presented.[4] But this is not obligatory, he may keep the tender good by retaining the money in his possession, or he may deposit it elsewhere for safe keeping. Wherever deposited the deposit must be special, so that the identical money will be kept safely for the tenderor and so he may reclaim it and deliver it to the tenderee when demanded. It may be deposited in that way to be delivered to the tenderee, but the latter is under no obligation to call for the money. If the tenderor wants to sustain his tender he must reclaim the money and deliver it to tenderee when demanded, or pay it into court as the case may be.[5] Whether it is a special deposit subject to the order of the depositor, or to the order of the tenderee, it is a trust fund, and does not pass with the general assets of the depositary, in insolvency to a receiver.[6] Where a tenderor makes a special deposit with a bank or third person, it does not constitute payment [ ] lace the money at the risk of the tenderee.[7]

If [ ] nd is converted, stolen or destroyed, the tender is not k[ ] good. Money which has been used in making a ten-

[3] Boon on Banking, Sec. 10

[4] See Wallace v. McConnell, 13 Pet. (U. S.) 136

[5] Baker v. Fourth N. H. Turnpike, 8 N. H. 509

[6] Capital Bank v. Coldwater Bank, 69 N. W. Rep. (Neb.) 115

[7] Benton v. Roberts, 2 La. Ann. 243

der, if refused, is subject to levy by creditors of the tenderor, and if deposited it may be attached by garnishee or trustee process.[8] If taken to pay another debt of the tenderor, and he has no other money of like kind on hand, the tender is not kept good. So, if money is thus attached and the tenderor, on a demand by the tenderee for the money, is unable to secure its release, the tender is not kept good although the tenderor ultimately secures the release of the money. Where a sum of money is tendered and refused, an agreement that the sum tendered shall be deposited in a bank, so that if the tenderee changes his mind he can receive the money there, does not bar an action, it being only an agreement as to where the tender may be sustained[9]

§ 359. **Statutory provisions—Consignation.**—Under an early Iowa code, where the payee of an instrument is absent from the state when it becomes due, and there is no one authorized to receive the money at the place of payment, the payor was permitted to deposit the money with the clerk of the district court of the proper county.[1] In California, under the Code, where an offer of performance is refused, the money may be deposited in a bank.[2] But this statute merely prescribes a mode of extinguishing a debt or obligation. The offer need not necessarily be a legal tender. A legal tender, nevertheless, may be made,[3] and when made it may be kept good according to the rules of the common law.[4] In South Dakota under the statute, the money may be deposited in a reputable bank, in the name of the creditor, and notice of the deposit given to the creditor.[5] In Louisiana, a tender of money or notes, if refused, must be followed by a consignation of the money or notes.[6] According to the civil law, a consignation could only be made after an effectual offer of payment

---

[8] Stowell v Reed 16 N H 20.

[9] Baker v Fourth N H Turnpike 8 N H 509

[1] Young v Daniels, 2 Iowa 126, Code Sec 958

[2] See Thompson v Superior Court, 51 Pac Rep (Cal) 863, where it is held that a claim that the creditor avoided a tender was no excuse as the party could have extinguished his obligation by an offer and deposit under the code

[3] Sayward v Houghton 51 Pac Rep (Cal) 853

[4] See William Wolff Co v Canadian Ry Co, 56 Pac Rep (Cal) 453

[5] Stakke v Chapman 83 N W Rep (So Dak) 261

[6] Walker v Brown, 12 La Ann 266.

Formally, the creditor was summoned to appear immediately before a judge, who thereupon directed a consignation at a particular time and place, notifying the creditor to be present; but the practice was subsequently changed, so that it was sufficient to specify in the summons that the consignation would be made at a particular time and place, the previous order of the judge being dispensed with. If the consignation and notice is thereafter adjudged to be valid, such judgment relates back to the time of the consignation, and the effect is that the debtor is thereby absolutely discharged. If a specific article is to be delivered at the place where it is, there may be a summons to take it away, and upon default of the creditor or vendee, the debtor may obtain an order from the judge to deposit it in a different place, if he wants to occupy his rooms in a different manner.[7]

§ 360   Must be kept good by bringing the money into court when.—Where an action at law or a suit in equity is commenced based upon a tender and refusal, or a tender which must be kept good is pleaded as a defence, the tender must be kept good by bringing the money into court according to the rules of the common law, at the time of bringing the action or interposing the defence.[1] This rule is universal. More at length will be said in a subsequent chapter upon the necessity of bringing money into court.

§ 361   Services—Duty of employee after his tender of services is refused.—If a person is bound by a contract to perform certain services, and on the day set for performance, or commencement of performance, he tenders performance and his tender is refused, or he has entered upon his duties and is

[7] 1 Pothier's Obl. Art. 8

[1] Daughdrill v. Sweeney, 41 Ala. 310; Bailey v. Metcalf, 6 N. H. 156; Rahn v. Warnbough, 16 Minn. 117; Riley v. Cheesman, 27 N. Y. Supp. 153, s. c. 75 Hun 387; Wallace v. McConnell, 13 Pet. 136; Rice v. Kahn, 70 Wis. 323, s. c. 35 N. W. Rep. 465; The Brooklyn Bank v. De Grauw, 23 Wend. 342; Werner v. Tuch, 127 N. Y. 217, s. c. 27 N. E. Rep. 845; Halpin v. Phoenix Ins. Co., 118 N. Y. 165; Smith v. Phillips, 2 N. W. Rep. (Wis.) 285; O'Riley v. Surei, 70 Ill. 85; Vallette v. Bilinski, 68 Ill. App. 361, affirming 167 Ill. 564; Perry v. Ward, 20 Vt. 92; Long v. Howard, 35 Iowa, 148; Sratington Bangor Syndicate v. Sewer 12 Mont. Co. L. Rep. 162; Deacon v. Central Iowa Ins. Co., 63 N. W. Rep. 673.

discharged, the party tendering such services, e who is so discharged, may forthwith sue for a breach of the contract, or wait until the full term, or any wage paying period has expired, and recover a sum equal to the stipulated wages for the period then past. In the latter case the employee must be ready during the whole term for which he seeks to recover, to perform the services contracted for[1] While it is stated generally to be the duty of the employee to hold himself in readiness, during the whole term, to render the services according to the contract, yet the rule is not without a very important qualification. He must not voluntarily be idle. It is the duty of a person who has tendered his services in accordance with his contract and they have been refused, not to be idle and trust to his action for entire remuneration. "In all cases of breach of contract, it becomes the *active duty* of the party injured to make reasonable exertion to render the damages resulting therefrom as light as possible."[2] In accordance with this wise rule, the law makes it the active duty of an employee, in case of a breach of his contract of employment by his employer refusing his services, to endeavor with reasonable diligence to procure employment elsewhere. It has been said "His obligation in that respect was one of *ordinary* but *active* diligence. * * * If voluntarily idle, he failed in his legal and moral duty, as the law regards such conduct a fraud upon his employer."[1] He must hold himself in readiness only when he cannot, with reasonable diligence, secure other employment of like kind, or work in another line which he is accustomed to do, in the city, town or other place where he resides. He is not bound to leave his home and accept employment at a distance in order to lessen the damages. The employee need not forego making a contract to serve another, for a term covering the same period during which he was to serve under the contract which was broken. And his inability to discontinue work under the new contract and resume work for his former employer on demand of the latter, will not relieve the former

[1] Johnson v Trinity Church, 11 Allen 123. See Polk v Daily, 4 Daly, 411.

[2] Polk v Daily, 4 Daly 411, Hamilton v. McPherson, 28 N Y 76

[1] Polk v Daily, 4 Daly, 411 See Shannon v. Comstock, 21 Wend 156, Huntington v Ogdensberg, 33 How 416, Dillen v Andrews, 13 N Y 237.

employer of his liability for the difference between the wages he was to pay and the wages the employee receives from his new employment, for, perchance, the employee may be unable to secure employment without entering into a contract for a certain term, and, again the employee is not bound to confine his contracts of hire to jobs from day to day, in expectancy that he may be called upon to work for a person who had broken his contract by rejecting his proffer of services. That the employee does procure other employment is a benefit to the person rejecting the proffer of services, of which the latter cannot complain. The former being held merely to good faith in accepting, at the time, the highest wages offered him in his particular calling. He has a right, for a reasonable time, to seek employment of the same character.[4] He is not, however, bound to accept a contract for a longer period than that specified in the contract which was broken, and may accept other employment at a less salary.[5] The obligation to show that the employee could have procured other employment is upon the employer.[6]

[4] Simon v. Allen, 76 Tex. 398; Griffin v. Brooklyn Ball Club, 73 N. Y. Supp. 864.

[6] Thompson v. Wood, 1 Hilt. 93; Costigan v. The Mohawk & H. R. R. Co. 2 Denio 608; Hein v. Wolf, 1 E. D. Smith 70.

# CHAPTER IX.

## THE CONSEQUENCES OF A TENDER AND REFUSAL

§ 362.　**A tender does not discharge the debt—Title to the money in whom—Statute of frauds**—In no case where there is a direct cause of action, will a tender and refusal discharge a debt or duty.[1] A direct cause of action exists wherever there is a privity of contract between the tenderor and tenderee as in the case of a book account, or any bond, contract or promise made by one person with another, to pay him a certain sum of money, or where a like promise is made to perform certain services. A tender and refusal in such case is no bar to an action. In the case of an unaccepted tender of money, no property in the money tendered vests in the party to

9 Bac Abr Tender (P) Coll v Green 10 S & R 11, Hall v Place 7 Robt 389, Kelly v West, 36 N Y Super Ct 304, Gracy v Potts, 4 Baxter 395, Curtis v Greenbank 24 Vt 356, Haynes v Thom 28 N H 386; Town v Trow, 24 Pick 168 Co Litt 209 a Howard v Hunt 57 N H 467 Colton v Oakland 70 Pac Rep (Cal) 225 Memphis v City of Aberdeen 27 So Rep (Miss) 608, Hoskins v Doughertys, 69 S W Rep (Tex Civ App) 103

whom it is made, and it may be seized by an officer on process against the party who made the tender.[2] An unaccepted tender will not take a contract out of the statute of frauds.[3]

§ 363. **Stops the running of interest—Damages.**—If the debt remains after a tender and refusal, the effect when lawfully made and maintained, is to discharge the debtor from a liability for interest subsequent to the tender.[1] A tender, otherwise valid, will bar the recovery of subsequent interest, whether made on the due day or at any time thereafter, before action is commenced to recover the debt or enforce a forfeiture. So, in those states where the statute permits a tender to be made after an action is commenced, a valid tender made and maintained according to the common law, will bar the recovery of interest after the tender. If an extension of the time be given within which a redemption may be made, a tender pursuant to the agreement will stop the running of interest.[2] A tender and refusal of a legacy may be urged in a surrogate's court, in bar of interest subsequent to the date of the tender, the same as if suit had been brought to recover the legacy at law.[3] The recovery of interest is barred, whether the rate be stipulated, or is fixed by law and would accrue as damages, *ratione detentione debiti*. Interest which has accrued prior to a tender is not discharged. A refusal of a valid tender of a debt or duty, if the tender be kept good, defeats the recovery of damages that would accrue subsequent to the tender by reason of non-payment or non performance.[4]

[2] Stowell v. Reid 16 N. H. 20, Thompson v. Kellogg 23 Mo 281

[3] Hershey v. St Paul 66 Minn 449

[1] Engelbach v. Simpson 12 Tex Civ App 188 s c 33 S W Rep 596, Riley v. McNamara 18 S W Rep 141 Town v Trow 24 Pick 168 Balm v Wambaugh 16 Minn 117 9 Bac Abr Tender (P), Thayer v Meeker 86 Ills 474 Wallace v McConnell 13 Pet 136 Cockrill v Kirkpatrick 9 Mo 697 Rudolph v Wagner 36 Ala 698 Curtis v Greenbanks 24 Vt 536 Brown v Simons 45 N

H 213, Wheelock v Tanner, 39 N Y 481 Gray v Potts 4 Baxter 395 Hamlett v Tallman 30 Ark 505 Sweatland v Squire Salk 623 Loomis v Knox, 60 Conn 343 Minkel v Belscamper, 51 N W Rep (Wis) 500, Lloyd v O Rear 59 S W Rep (Ky) 483 See Thiel v Conrad 21 Lt Ann 214

[2] McNeil v Call 19 N H 403

[3] Morgan v Valentine 6 Dem Sur 18

[4] Town v Trow 24 Pick 168 Curtis v Greenbanks 24 Vt 536, Wallace v McConnell, 13 Pet 136

§ 364.  **Bars the recovery of costs when—Rule not affected by statute—Costs in equity—Where a tender upon one of two causes of action is found sufficient.**—The authorities abound in the general expression, that a valid tender, if refused, bars interest subsequent to the tender, and costs in case an action is commenced to recover the debt [1]  But a tender and refusal will not bar the recovery of costs, unless the tender is kept good by bringing the money into court at the time of commencing the action, or interposing a defence where the tender is relied upon as a defence and is such that it must be kept good  It is the bringing the money into court that saves the costs.[2]  Those statutes, which award costs to a defendant who has brought money into court and prevails in his plea of tender, are imperative,[3] and prevail over other statutes awarding costs to one party or the other under certain circumstances  Thus a statute which provides that a defendant who appeals from a justice's judgment and does not reduce the amount of plaintiff's recovery one half or more, shall pay the plaintiff's costs, does not apply, if the defendant succeeds in reducing the amount of plaintiff's recovery to the amount of his tender, although the judgment appealed from is not reduced one half.[4]  Statutes awarding costs to a party who has brought money into court in support of his plea of

---

[1] Hamlet v Tallman, 30 Ark 505, Gracy v Potts, 4 Baxter, 395, Randolph v Wagner 36 Ala 698 Hull v Place 7 Robt 389, Rand v Wiley, 29 N W Rep 814, Leis v Hodgson 1 Colo 393 Collier v White 67 Miss 133  See Memphis v City of Aberdeen 27 So Rep (Miss) 608

[2] Cockrill v Kirkpatrick 9 Mo 697; Cornell v Green 10 S & R 14  See ch. XV on bringing money into court

[3] Redmin v Thomas 39 Mo App 113  In this case it is also held that the statute does not deprive the court of its discretionary power in cases where the tender is found insufficient

[4] In Michigan a statute permitting the circuit court in its discretion, to withhold or award cost on a partial reversal of a judgment in an appeal from a judgment of a justice court, was held not to apply where the judgment awarded by the appellate court although in form given against the defendant for damages, was in fact in his favor is maintaining his plea of tender  That another statute which expressly provided that in such cases the defendant shall pay no costs accruing after a tender but shall recover them rendered it inconsistent with any discretion in the matter  Wilcox v Loflin 44 Mich 35, s c 5 N W Rep 1091 Comp L Secs 6180 6181

tender, on his plea being found true, are merely declaratory
of the common law.

Where money is brought into court under a plea of tender
and the party alleging the tender prevails in his plea, the
party who refused the tender, whether he be the plaintiff or
defendant, must pay the costs of the other party.[5] Courts
of equity are no less strict than courts of law in this respect.[6]
Although a court of equity, under its general powers, except in a case governed by specific statute, has authority to
award or withhold costs in its discretion, yet where there is
a clear right to costs, by reason of a wrongful refusal of a
tender, an equity court will not relieve a party, thus in the
wrong, of a liability for costs.[7]

If separate tenders are made upon two causes of action
and refused, or upon one cause of action and not upon the
other and the two causes are afterwards joined in one
action, and the plea of tender upon one of the two causes of
action is found for the tenderor, the latter, by keeping the
tender good and bringing the money into court, will escape
paying interest on the cause of action upon which the issue
was found for him and the witness fees and other taxable
costs incurred by the plaintiff in support of that particular
cause of action.[8] But the plaintiff will be entitled to recover
his costs and disbursements as to the cause of action upon
which he prevailed. The defendant, however, is entitled to
a judgment or offset for disbursements incurred by him in
successfully maintaining that his tender was sufficient.
It has been held that where the right to take an appeal is
made to depend on the amount in controversy, a tender
maintained according to the common law, will bar the right
if the difference between the amount sued for and the sum
tendered is below the statutory amount.[9]

[5] Columbian Bldg. Assn. v.
Crump, 42 Md. 192.

[6] Gage v. Du Puy, 137 Ill. 652.
See Boardman v. Marshalltown,
105 Iowa 445; Rucker v. Howard,
2 Bibb. 166.

[7] See Elliott v. Parker, 72 Iowa,
746; Hendee v. Howe, 33 N. J. Eq.
92. See also Binford v. Boardman, 44 Iowa 53, where it is held
that where the tender was not ab-

solutely necessary the court may
apportion the costs. In New
York, under the statute, it appears to be discretionary. Pratt
v. Ramsdell, 16 How. Pr. 59.

[8] See Hatch v. Thompson, 67
Conn. 74.

[9] Griffin v. Harriman, 74 Iowa,
436; Young v. McWald, 57 Iowa,
101.

**§ 365. What is a more favorable judgment.**—A more favorable judgment, such as would saddle a tenderor with costs, must be for a sum greater than the amount of the principal and interest at the date of the tender. Interest subsequent to the tender cannot be added to bring the total over the sum tendered as keeping the tender good precludes the recovery of such interest. In case the tender is proven to be good in form, or is admitted to be such and the dispute is solely as to the amount due, the question then is how much was due at the date of the tender. Costs and disbursements and other expenses which follow a judgment in ordinary cases cannot be added to the sum found due, in order to increase the amount of the recovery beyond the sum tendered and shift the liability for costs. In equity, if the tenderor maintains the issue as to the amount, but the tenderee is granted some equitable relief denied to him by the tenderor, the judgment is more favorable to the tenderee than that conceded by the tenderor and the disbursements and costs, if allowed follow the judgment as if no offer had been made

**§ 366. Tender of amends.**—The effect of a tender of amends for damages resulting from a tort, allowed under the statute in some of the states, is restricted solely to the right of the plaintiff to recover the costs of the action. The tender can not be pleaded in bar nor be given in evidence to the court or jury. The court is to take notice of the tender and to act on it in the taxation of costs[1] Under some statutes if the verdict is for no more than the sum tendered, the plaintiff is entitled only to the costs prior to the tender and must pay those of the defendant. Under other statutes the plaintiff under such circumstances cannot recover any costs but must pay the defendant's costs and disbursements[2] In a case arising in Vermont under such a statute the court observed "It is apparent to us that the object of the statute was to enable the defendant, in such cases, to pay money into court, to answer the plaintiff's claim"[3] We do not find this view adverted to in subsequent cases in that state, but if it is not the rule it ought to be. In such cases the court has no means of knowing a tender had been made, or that it has

1 Spaulding v Warner 57 Vt 654 Adams v Morgan, 39 Vt 302 Sweet v Wilber 35 Vt 132    2 G S Minn Sec 5406    3 Smith v Miller, 35 Vt 132

been kept good, and the question of whether a tender of the amount claimed to have been tendered, was in fact tendered, is open to dispute when the time comes to tax the costs. Unless, perhaps, the court tries an issue as to the tender after the jury retires, or after they have delivered their verdict, or determines it upon affidavits on motion before a taxation. According to Sir William Blackstone,[4] under several statutes, particularly 2 Geo. II. c. 19, in cases of an irregularity in the method of distraining, and 21 Geo. II, c. 21 in case of mistake committed by a justice of the peace, a tender of sufficient amends to the party injured is a bar of all actions, whether he thinks proper to accept such amends or no. In the United States, in many of the states under the statute, a tender may be made of amends for the commission of a tort with like effect. At common law a tender to constitute a bar must be pleaded and proven, and when a tender of amends may be pleaded in bar of the action, the common law rule requiring money tendered to be brought into court applies.[5]

Unless the money be required to be brought into court, the plea being in bar of the action, it would amount to a payment and satisfaction of the damages without being so in fact.

§ 367. **Upon an accord—Two views—Points in common.**—The authorities are divided on the question whether an accord with an unaccepted tender of satisfaction is a defence to an action on the original contract. A creditor's mere promise to receive from his debtor, in discharge of his demand, the promissory note of the latter, or a less sum in payment than the full sum due, without more, is a *nudum pactum*,[1] and a tender of the note or the lesser sum is insufficient to bar an action for the whole sum.[2] It has been held very frequently, and the rule appears to be well founded in reason, that when the new agreement entered into is to be in full satisfaction of the debt, and it imposes a new duty on the

[4] 2 Bl. Com. 16.

[5] Under a statute which merely confers the right to make a tender, the common law governs the mode of procedure, and limits the legal effect of the tender. Bacon v. Charlton, 7 Cush. 581.

[1] Smith v. Keels, 15 Rich. 318.

[2] Clifton v. Litchfield, 106 Mass. 38. Leeson v. Amundson 58 N. W. Rep. (Mich.) 72.

debtor, which is or may be burdensome to him or beneficial
to the creditor, a new consideration arises out of the new
undertaking and sustains the agreement. In such case the
new contract, when entered into, constitutes the accord and
satisfaction  And a tender of the thing agreed to be paid
within the time specified, will bar an action on the original
contract, and when maintained interrupts the running of
interest, and saves the debtor harmless from the costs in
an action on the new agreement. Thus, where the new
agreement is to receive goods in satisfaction of the debt,
a tender of the goods within the time agreed will be good.[1]
So, when payment is to be made at a different place, as
where the new agreement provides for the payment in New
York, of $1,500 in satisfaction of a $2,000 demand payable
in Mississippi[4] Or if the new agreement is to give security
or additional security, or provides for payment by a third
person, or substitutes the individual liability of one of sev
eral persons jointly liable, for all, or is a composition with
creditors,[5] or a compromise of a claim where there exists
a *bona fide* controversy as to the liability or amount due,
rendering it a proper matter for a judicial investigation, as
where the claim is unliquidated or uncertain in character,
a tender of the thing agreed to be received according to the
terms of the agreement is good even where the amount or
value of the thing stipulated for is less than the original
claim[6] Decisions supporting a rule to the contrary are
numerous, and it is difficult to determine which rule the
weight of authority supports. An agreement to take gov
ernment bonds in satisfaction of a debt has been held to be
no defence to an action for the recovery of the debt, unless
a tender of the bonds in pursuance of the agreement be
accepted[7] So, a tender of performance on an agreement
to surrender land in satisfaction of the mortgaged debt, was
held to be no defence to an action upon the bond[8] A re

[1] Bradshaw v Davis 12 Tex
336; Rose v Hall, 26 Conn 392 s
c 68 Am Dec 402

[4] Jones v Perkins 29 Miss 139
s c 64 Am Dec 136

[5] Stewart v Langston 30 S E
Rep (Ga) 35

[6] Story on Contracts, Sec 982b,
3rd Ed , Hehn v Carrow, 11 S &

M 361, Addison on Contracts
Sec 378, Cartwright v Cooke 23
Com L Rep 308, Good v Chees
man 22 Com L Rep 42  See
Case v Barber, Sir T Rym 450

[7] Smith v Keels, 15 Rich 318

[8] Russell v Lytle 6 Wend 390
s c 22 Am Dec 537

fusal of a tender upon an accord, where a judgment creditor agreed to accept a part of the judgment debt in land and the balance in money, was held not to be ground for specific performance.[9] So are many other decisions to the effect that an executory accord with tender of performance is no bar to an action on the original agreement.[10]

On two points the authorities do seem to be practically in unison—(1) After a debt is due, any agreement then made whereby the creditor is to accept a less sum in satisfaction of his claim, without more, is a *nudum pactum*, and whether the tender is accepted or unaccepted it does not bar an action on the original obligation. (2) Where an agreement is entered into whereby a sum certain is to be paid in satisfaction of a claim about which there existed a *bona fide* controversy as to the liability or the amount due, rendering it a proper matter for compromise and adjustment, a tender according to the agreement is a satisfaction of the original claim.

§ 368. **Consequences of a tender and refusal upon the lien of a real-estate mortgage—Tender made on the law day—Effect of a failure to make a tender on the law day under the old law—Common law as modified by equity—Remedy of mortgagor—Tender after default.**—If a debt is secured by a mortgage upon land, a tender of the amount due on the mortgage debt, on the law day, at common law, extinguishes and discharges the mortgage as effectually as if the tender had been accepted.[1] This is the law at this day everywhere. A tender

[9] McKean v. Reed, Litt. Sel. Cas. 395, s. c. 12 Am. Dec. 318.

[10] Bank of Brooklyn v. De Grauw 23 Wend. 342, s. c. 35 Am. Dec. 569; Crane v. Maynard 12 Wend. 408; Daniels v. Hallenbeck 19 Wend. 410; Hawley v. Foote 19 Wend. 517; Fulton v. Alcott 16 Barb. 598; Osborn v. Robbins 17 Barb. 483; Dolson v. Arnold, 10 How. Pr. 530; Russell v. Lytle 6 Wend. 390, s. c. 22 A. Dec. 537; Watkinson v. Inglesby, 5 Johns. 392; Gahoney v. The German Ins. Co., 48 Mo. App. 185; Allen v. Harris 1 Ld. Raym. 122,

James v. David, 5 T. R. 141. See Perdew v. Tillma 88 N. W. Rep. (Neb.) 123.

[1] Mitchell v. Roberts, 17 Fed. Rep. 776; Moore v. Cord 14 Wis. 231; Merrett v. Lambert 7 Paige, 344; Post v. Arnot 2 Denio, 344; Salinas v. Ellis, 26 S. C. 337; Cordon v. Constantine Hydraulic Co. 76 N. W. Rep. (Mich.) 142; Scheriff v. Dodge 33 Ark. 346.

Littleton in his Institutes of the Laws of England (Sec. 338), said "And note that in all cases of condition for payment of a certain summe in gross touching

at the day complies with the condition of the mortgage, and the mortgaged estate reverts to the mortgagor by the express terms of the mortgage deed. The time and place of payment being fixed, a mortgagee must know in advance that a tender of the debt will be made at the time and place fixed and should be ready to receive payment of his debt when lawfully tendered to him, and he cannot complain of a loss of his security if he refuses it. If the mortgagee is in possession, the mortgagor's remedy is by writ of entry or ejectment. Under the ancient common law, on a failure of a mortgagor on the law day to pay the mortgage debt or perform the duty, to secure which the mortgage was given, the estate was forfeited absolutely, however great might be the value of the estate compared with the mortgage debt. But the courts of equity, early in the development of equity jurisprudence, to prevent such manifest hardship, while still recognizing the rule that the mortgage conveyed a legal estate and that on a default it was forfeited at law (at least to the extent of recognizing the mortgagee's right to the immediate possession), ingrafted upon the law of mortgages a right to redeem, technically called an equity of redemption; which continues until cut off by the statute of limitations or by a foreclosure. Indeed the equity of redemption is now so deeply ingrafted upon the law of mortgages and so cherished as one of the bulwarks against the oppression and exactions of lenders, that a mortgagor can not, by inserting a stipulation in the mortgage or by a separate agreement at the inception of the mortgage, deprive himself, his heirs and creditors, of the right of redemption. Wherever the common law rule, thus modified, prevails, a tender may be made after a default, but a tender or even payment after a default is not sufficient to retransfer or divest the mortgagee of the legal estate. The rule is based upon the theory that the mortgage is a conveyance of a legal estate, defeasable only upon payment at the day specified, and that after a default, the defeasance having become inoperative, it takes something more than a mere

lands and tenements if lawful tender be once refused, he who ought to tender the money is of this quit, and fully discharged forever afterwards." And Lord Coke in his notes said "This is to be understood that he who ought to tender the money is of this discharged forever to make any other tender."

tender or payment to re-transfer the legal estate. This is termed by some writers the legal and equitable theory of mortgages. After a refusal of a tender of the mortgage debt made after a default, the mortgagor's remedy is by a bill in equity to redeem,[2] and the only effect of the tender, if kept good, and the money brought into court, is to stop the running of interest and subject the mortgagee to the costs of the suit.[3]

§ 369. **Rule which obtains in some states where the legal and equitable theory of a mortgage prevails.**—In many of those states[1] where prevails the legal and equitable theory of mortgages, a tender of the mortgage debt after a default, where the tender is kept good, is held to divest the mortgage lien. In Illinois, the Supreme Court said: "We think the preferable rule is, where the tender is made after the day the debt secured by the mortgage is due, to require that it shall be kept good in order that it may operate to discharge the mortgage."[2] As between the common law rule, that a tender after default, if kept good, goes only to the question

[2] Mainard v. Hunt, 5 Pick. 489. Bailey v. Metcalf 6 N H 156, Smith v. Kelly 27 Me 237 Howe v. Lewis 14 Pick 329

[3] Shields v. Lozier, 34 N J L 496

[1] According to Mr Pomeroy (See 1187) the states adhering to the legal and equitable theory of mortgages with some variation as to remedies &c. are Alabama Arkansas, Connecticut, Delaware Illinois Kentucky, Maine Maryland Massachusetts Mississippi, Missouri New Hampshire New Jersey North Carolina, Ohio Pennsylvania Rhode Island Tennessee Vermont Virginia and West Virginia

[2] Crain v. McGoon 86 Ill 431, s p Parker v. Beasley 116 N C 1 s c 33 L R A 231, Landis v. Saxton, 89 Mo 375 s c 1 S W Rep 359, see Diet v McClung v Missouri Trust Co 38 S W Rep

(Mo) 578, Henderson v. Glencoe, 11 S W Rep Mo 650 Marshall v. Wing 50 Me 62, Smith v. Kelly, 27 Me 237 Stocton v. Dundee Mantg Co 22 N J Eq 56, Mainard v. Hunt 5 Pick 489, Mathews v. Landis 20 Fla 962

In Daughdrill v. Sweeney 41 Ala 310 it is held that a bill to redeem is without equity unless the tender is kept good and the money paid into court but, see McGuire v Van Pelt 55 Ala 344 where it is held that in an ordinary bill to redeem a tender is not necessary the right springs out of the mortgage In Carlin v. Jones, 55 Ala 624 it is held that Daughdrill v. Sweeney is overruled by McGuire v. Van Pelt each of these cases was a bill in equity to redeem cases where a tender only goes to the question of barring the recovery of subsequent interest and the costs

of interest and costs, &c., and the rule just mentioned, that
a tender, if maintained, destroys the estate of the mortgagee,
there is in practice, a distinction without a very material
difference, in so far as the real cancellation of the mortgage
of record is concerned. In either case the amount of the
mortgage debt at the time of the tender, must first be
brought into court before the mortgagor, either as a plain
tiff or as a defendant, can obtain any affirmative relief dis
charging the mortgage of record, or before relief would be
denied to the mortgagee.

§ 370. Rule governing the effect of a tender and refusal where
the equitable theory of a mortgage prevails.—In New York,
Michigan, Minnesota and perhaps some other states,[1] the
common law has been changed so that the mortgage deed
does not convey a defeasable legal estate, but merely creates
a lien for the security of the debt analogous to that created
by a pledge of chattels. This is the equitable theory of mortgages. In some of the states, though not in all, where this
modern doctrine prevails, the time is extended so that a
tender made at any time after the law day and before a fore
closure will discharge the lien of the mortgage as effectually
as payment or tender on the law day at common law, and
the tender need not be kept good or the money brought
into court.[2] In those states, as long as the mortgagee's
interest continues a mere lien, a lawful tender will destroy
it. Thus, if the mortgagee is proceeding by statutory foreclosure to enforce payment of his claim, a valid tender of the
principal, interest and costs, at any time before the sale of

[1] Mr. Pomeroy in his work upon
equity jurisprudence (Sec. 1188),
besides the states above named
gives as adopting the purely equitable theory of mortgages, California, Colorado Florida, Georgia,
Indiana, Iowa, Kansas, Louisiana,
Nebraska, Nevada Oregon, South
Carolina, Texas Utah Wisconsin.
[2] Davis v Dow, 83 N W Rep
(Minn) 50, Caruthers v Humphrey 12 Mich 270, Van Husin v
Kanouse, 13 Mich 303, Ferguson
v Popp 3 N W Rep (Mich) 287,
Salinas v Elles, 26 S Car 337,

Mankel v Belscamper 54 N W
Rep (Wis) 500, Kartwright v
Cady 21 N Y 343, Nelson v
Todel 132 N Y 292. In Green v
Fry, 93 N Y 353, a tender of an
installment before an action is
commenced to foreclose was held
to discharge the lien of the mortgage to the extent of the install
ment. See Merritt v Lambert, 7
Paige 344. A sale of mortgaged
premises subsequent to a tender
has been held irregular and fraudulent. Jackson v Crafts, 18
Johns 110.

the premises, if refused, discharges the lien of the mortgage.[3] Where the mortgage is being foreclosed in equity and there is a statute permitting a tender to be made in such cases after action brought, the mortgagor, if he desires to escape paying subsequent interest and costs, must make a tender, and if it is refused bring the amount tendered into court, or if there is no statutory authority for making a tender after action brought the mortgagee may apply to the court to be allowed to bring the sum due into court or wait and comply with the decree of the court.

§ 371. **Same subject—Remedy of Mortgagor—Not necessary to keep the tender good when—A tender invoking the equitable powers of the court—Restraining a statutory foreclosure—Discharging lien of record.**—A tender which discharges the lien is an absolute defense to a suit to foreclose the mortgage. If the mortgagee has gone into possession, the mortgagor, or those claiming under him, may bring an action to recover the possession. If the mortgagee enters for the breach of one condition, there being several, and a tender has been made of the condition which has been broken, the mortgagor will be entitled to a judgment for possession, unless the mortgagee in his answer sets up his right to hold the possession for the breach of another condition[1] In all those cases where a lien is discharged by a tender and refusal, the tender to have that effect need not be kept good. A lien once discharged, cannot be revived by a failure to keep the tender good. Although in equity a plaintiff or defendant who relies upon a tender, if he invoke the equitable powers of the court, will be required to make the tender good. But this is because the court, having acquired complete jurisdiction over the parties and the subject matter, seizes the opportunity to do justice between the parties by applying the maxim, "He who seeks equity must do equity." Having once waived his strict legal defence by a submission to the equitable powers of the court, his legal defence is beyond recall (unless possibly the court would allow an amendment), and the case proceeds to a decree of foreclosure as if no tender had been made, except as to the effect on the interest and costs if shown to have been

3 See Hartley v Totham, 1    1 Sanders v Winship, 5 Pick
Keys 222                  259

kept good. However, where a mortgage lien has been discharged by a tender and refusal, equity will grant a perpetual injunction restraining a statutory foreclosure without requiring payment of the mortgage debt, the mortgagor not having an adequate remedy at law.[2]

If a lien is discharged by a tender there is no forfeiture and no occasion for a bill to redeem, there being nothing to redeem from. However, the fact remains that the mortgage is still an apparent lien of record. In Wisconsin, under the statute, where payment or a valid tender has been made of the mortgage debt, the mortgagee on a tender to him of the necessary fees, is required under pain of a penalty to discharge the mortgage of record.[3] Where the lien is discharged by a tender of the mortgage debt, equity will not decree a satisfaction of the mortgage of record, unless the mortgage debt be paid. But the mortgagor being in a position to assert his strict legal rights, a decree in a suit to foreclose, that the plaintiff is not entitled to any relief, or if the mortgagee is in possession, a judgment in ejectment that the mortgagor is entitled to the possession of the mortgaged premises, will have the same effect as a formal decree discharging the mortgage of record. So a perpetual injunction granted to restrain a statutory foreclosure, where the lien has been discharged by a tender,[4] will have the same effect. In all such cases a certified copy of the judgment or decree should be filed in the office of the Register of Deeds of the county where the mortgage is recorded

§ 372. **A tender by a junior lien holder — Demand for an assignment—Equity compelling an assignment—Subrogation.—** A tender may be made by a junior mortgagee[1] attaching creditor[2] or any subsequent lien holder, but a tender made by a subsequent encumbrancer will not operate as a discharge of the prior lien, unless such is the clear intent of the party making it "He must make an absolute tender of payment, which if received will discharge the debt and the incumbrance"[3] A tender, accompanied by a demand for an

[2] See Daugherty v Byles 41 Mich 69, s c 1 N W Rep 919

[3] Moore v Cord 14 Wis 231

[4] See Daugherty v Byles 1 N W Rep (Mich) 919

[1] Sager v Tupper 35 Mich 134

[2] Felknor v Hazelton 35 Atl 1051

[3] Frost v Yonker's Sav Bank 70 N Y 553.

assignment of the lien, is not intended to discharge the lien, but to procure a transfer of all rights under it.[4] In New York, and perhaps some other states, a tender of the amount due on a prior incumbrance by the holder of a junior lien, if refused, will give a tenderor a standing in equity to compel an assignment on bringing into court the amount of the debt, interest and costs incident to the debt and lien.[5] Although the weight of authority appears to support the rule that a subsequent lien holder who has paid the senior mortgage debt, must rely upon his equitable assignment and general right of subrogation,[6] yet, when a tender is refused, and the junior lien holder is forced into an equity court to protect his rights, there would appear to be no valid reason why such lien holder who pleads the tender and brings the money into court, when he asks it, either as a plaintiff or defendant, should not have a decree requiring the senior lien holder to execute a formal assignment of his lien.

§ 373. **A tender by a stranger—A purchaser who has not assumed the mortgage debt.**—A tender by a mere stranger will not discharge the lien of a mortgage. Where mortgaged premises are conveyed to a purchaser subject to a mortgage, but without any assumption of the debt by him, a tender by such owner of the equity of redemption, will not discharge the lien.[1] As between the mortgagor and the purchaser of the legal estate, the mortgage debt is part of the consideration and the land is the primary fund for the payment of the mortgage debt. Hence a purchaser cannot be permitted to discharge the lien of the mortgage by a mere tender without payment. If he desires to pay the mortgage debt so as to free his land, and the mortgagee refuses the money, he has his remedy in equity to compel a discharge of the mortgage, and by keeping the tender good, and bringing the money into court for the purpose of the payment, he stops the running of

[4] Nelson v. Loder 55 Hun 173, Day v. Strong 29 Hun 305, Frost v. Yonker's Sav Bank 70 N Y 553 Proctor v. Robinson, 35 Mich 284, Brown v. Simons 15 N H 211

[5] Day v. Strong 29 Hun 505

Frost v. Yonker's Sav Bank 70 N Y 553 Nelson v. Loder, 132 N Y 292 Ellsworth v. Lockwood, 42 N Y 90

[6] Pomeroy Eq Jur 1214

[1] Harris v. Jex 66 Barb 232 Noyes v. Wyckoff, 30 Hun 464, (Chattel Mortgage)

the interest, and subjects the mortgagee to the costs of the suit. Or, in a suit to foreclose he may plead the tender as a defence and bring the money into court with like effect.

§ 374.—A tender after a foreclosure.—However great may be the variance in the authorities, as to the effect of a tender of the mortgage debt after default and before a foreclosure, resulting from a blending of, or a change in the several states in the two theories in respect to mortgagees, the authorities are as a unit as to the effect of tender after a foreclosure. The effect of a foreclosure and sale is to vest in the purchaser a legal title to the property, subject, in all cases except where a strict foreclosure is allowed by law, to a right of redemption by the mortgagor, to be exercised within the time limited by statute, or within a time appointed by the court. The estate of a purchaser and the right of redeeming, are the same as that of the mortgagee and mortgagor after a default at common law, after the right of redemption had been engrafted upon that law by the equity courts, except that, at common law, after the mortgagee has taken possession, the right of redemption continued until extinguished by the statute of limitations, unless the mortgagee sooner obtained a decree in equity, limiting the time within which the mortgagor shall pay the debt. Mr. Chancellor Walworth said "Where the mortgagor's interest in the land is reduced to a mere equity of redemption, an actual payment, and not a mere tender or offer to pay, then becomes necessary, to discharge the legal and equitable title of the mortgagee," and that the statute fixing the period within which to redeem did not change the principal.[1] The only effect of a tender and refusal after foreclosure, and before the time to redeem has expired, is to preserve the right of the redemptioner to have the redemption perfected, if such right be seasonably asserted.[2] But to preserve such right beyond the time limited

---

[1] Merrett v. Lambert, 7 Paige, 344, s p. Scobee v. Jones, 1 Dana (Ky.) 13, Adams v. Kobbe, 6 B Munroe 384; Schroeder v. Lahman 28 Minn 75; Post v. Arnot, 2 Demo, 344, Smith v. Anders, 21 Ala 782; Dunn v. Hunt, 64 Minn 164, s c 65 N W 948, Scales v. Thompson, 12 Ala 309; Pollard v. Taylor, 13 Ala 604, Ransom v. Pellon, 9 Hump 271, Heptum v. Kerr, 9 Hump 728, Thornhill v. Gilmer, 4 S & M 153, Watson v. Hannum, 10 S & M 521, Raub v. Heath, 8 Blackf 575.

[2] Schroeder v. Lahman, 28 Minn 75.

within which the redemption may be made, and to have the effect of barring interest and throwing the costs upon the purchaser, the tender must be maintained. A bare tender before the last day will not extend the time in which to redeem.

§ **375. Consequences of a tender and refusal upon the lien of a chattel mortgage—Tender made on the law day—Acceptance of a tender made after default—Equitable modification of the common law as to right of redemption—Tender after possession taken or demand made by mortgagee.**—The effect of a tender on the law day of a debt which is secured by a chattel mortgage, is the same as that of a tender under the common law of a debt secured by a mortgage on real estate. Like a real estate mortgage under the common law, a chattel mortgage conveys a legal estate, defeasable upon the payment of the debt at the day appointed.[1]  Under a chattel mortgage, the

---

1 By some text writers, a chattel mortgage is said to be a conditional sale which becomes absolute upon the mortgagor's failure to perform the condition. Pomeroy's Eq. 1229. Jones on Chat. Mortg. 1. But a conditional sale familiar in the United States and a sale by way of mortgage common in England or a formal chattel mortgage in the United States, are very different things. True, the terms 'grant, bargain, sell, assign, transfer and set over' or "grant and convey" are used in a mortgage of chattels. So the same or other words of similar import are used in a mortgage of real estate. A transaction termed a conditional sale is one of bargain and sale, pure and simple conditional, however, that the title shall remain in the vendor until the purchase price be paid. The title must first be in the vendor and there the title remains until the condition is complied with. There is no 'right of redemption" on the vendor resuming possession. To create a chattel mortgage there must first be a debt, or duty, or a sum of money to be paid. It may arise out of a bargain and sale just completed, or be a debt created long antecedent or it may be a gratuity. The title to the property mortgaged must be in the mortgagor, and it is transferred conditionally, that is it will revert on the performance of the condition. In equity there is always a right of redemption. There is now absolutely no similarity between a chattel mortgage and a conditional sale, except, possibly, a similarity in the terms used in making the grant. Under the old common law where there was no right of redemption and the possession passed to the mortgagee there was some reason in calling a mortgage of chattels a conditional sale but the reason has long since ceased to exist in the United States at least.

27

mortgagee is entitled to the immediate possession, although a change of possession is not absolutely essential to the validity of the instrument. After a default, if the mortgagee has not the possession, he may take the chattels into his possession forthwith. At law, after a default, he is not bound to restore the property on a tender.[2] A tender at the day revests the legal title in the mortgagor according to the condition of the mortgage.[3] So will the acceptance of a tender made after default, such acceptance being a waiver of the forfeiture. A mortgagor of chattels being unable at law after a default, to recover the possession of his property, courts of equity, as in the case of a mortgage of real property, established the practice of relieving against the rigor of the law, and the doctrine is now well settled, that, notwithstanding the mortgagee's legal title and right of possession after a default, a right of redemption remains in the mortgagor, enforceable by a suit to redeem, if commenced within a reasonable time, and before the right is destroyed by a valid public sale of the property. A tender, in such case, is not absolutely essential to a bill to redeem, but if one is made and relied upon, to have the effect of barring subsequent interest and throwing the costs of the suit upon the mortgagee, it should be kept good and the money brought into court.

As to the effect of a tender after a default, on the lien of a chattel mortgage, the authorities are not agreed. In some of the states it is held that after default and possession taken by the mortgagee or a demand therefor, a mere tender will not have the effect of revesting the title in the mortgagor, whether the tender be kept good or not.[4] The mortgagor is left to his remedy in equity to redeem,[5] and the effect of a tender, if one is made and kept good, is merely to bar the recovery of subsequent interest, and saddle the costs of subsequent proceedings upon the mortgagee. In Wisconsin, it has been held, that when a mortgagee on a default asserts his right under the mortgage by taking possession of the mortgaged property, a tender made there

[2] See Weeks v. Baker 152 Mass 20 s c 24 N E Rep 905. Burtis v. Bradford, 122 Mass 129.

[3] Thompkins v. Battie, 11 Neb 117 s c 7 N W 249

[4] See Patchin v. Pierce 12 Wend 61

[5] Jackson v. Cunningham 28 Mo. App 351 Boyd v. Beaudin 11 N W Rep (Wis) 521

after did not have the effect of discharging the lien and re-vesting the mortgagor with the legal title, the tender not having been kept good.[6] Subsequently the same court held, where after possession was taken by the mortgagee and a tender was made and kept good by bringing the money into court, that the tender operated to effectually discharge the mortgage, and a judgment in replevin was awarded the mort-gagor.[7] If a mortgagee, deeming himself unsafe, takes pos-session of the mortgaged property, or is about to do so before the debt secured by the mortgage falls due, he thereby con-fers upon the mortgagor the right to pay the debt, and a tender of the amount due, kept good and the money brought into court, will divest the lien of the mortgage.[8]

§ 376. Same subject — Tender after default and before pos-session taken, or a demand made, does not discharge the lien—Con-trary rule obtains where—Rule in Michigan and Oregon—Massa-chusetts.—There is some conflict in the authorities as to the effect of a tender made after default and before the pos-session of the property has been taken by the mortgagee, or a demand made by him for it. In some of the states, notably Alabama, Illinois, Missouri, Nebraska, and perhaps some others, a tender after the law day or before the mortgagee takes possession does not operate to extinguish the title of the mortgagee unless kept good.[1] In a case arising in Min-

[6] Smith v. Phillips, 47 Wis. 202, s. c. 2 N. W. 287.

[7] Vreeland v. Waddell, 67 N. W. Rep. 57. See Ganshe v. Milbrath, 69 N. W. 990.

In Roberts v. White, 146 Mass. 256, s. c. 15 N. E. Rep. 568, the court said: "It is difficult to see how any tender after suit brought can avail the defendant, but if it can under any circum-stances it must be a tender fol-lowed by bringing the money into court for the plaintiff's use" cit-ing Stover v. McGraw, 11 Allen, 527; Brackett v. Wallace, 98 Mass. 528.

[8] Rice v. Kahn, 70 Wis. 323, s. c. 35 N. W. Rep. (Wis.) 465.

[1] Frank v. Pickens, 69 Ala. 369; Commercial Bank v. Crenshaw, 103 Ala. 497; Shaver v. Johnston, 62 Ala. 37; Welsh v. Phillips, 54 Ala. 309; Maxwell v. Moore, 95 Ala. 166; Knox v. Williams, 24 Neb. 630, s. c. 39 N. W. 780; Thomp-kins v. Batie, 11 Neb. 147, s. c. 38 Am. Rep. 361; Gould v. Armagost, 65 N. W. Rep. (Neb.) 1064; Blaine v. Foster, 33 Ill. App. 297; Wool-ner v. Levy, 48 Mo. App. 469; Patchin v. Pierce, 12 Wend. 61; Noyes v. Wyckoff, 30 Hun 466.

In Nusgates v. Pumpelly, 46 Wis. 660, s. c. 1 N. W. Rep. 410, the court held that the effect of a tender of the mortgage debt by a mortgagor who has remained in

nesota, where after the law day, a tender was made of the sum due upon the mortgage note, and the mortgagee thereafter brought an action in replevin to recover the mortgaged property, the court, at some length, considered the statutory provisions in force in that state, relative to chattel mortgages, and the rights, privileges, and remedies of the mortgagor of real and personal property, and the distinction between the two classes of mortgages. It said: "The distinction is therefore more in theory than in practice. If this be so, why should a different effect be given a tender made of the amount of the debt in the one case than in the other? We can discover no reason for the distinction which commends itself, and no reason is suggested in the decision cited by the respondent, except that based upon the technicality before referred to, that a mortgage upon real estate is a mere lien, while a mortgage on personal property vests the legal title thereof in the mortgagee. This is not satisfactory, and, in analogy with the rule laid down in case of real estate security, which is well supported on principle and authority, we are of the opinion that the effect of a tender of the amount of a debt secured by chattel mortgage, though made after maturity, is to extinguish and discharge the lien, the debt only remaining, and that it is not necessary to keep the tender good by depositing the money in court in case an action is thereafter brought by the mortgagee to obtain possession of the chattels." So, in Michigan and Oregon, a tender of the full amount of the mortgage debt after default and before a foreclosure, destroys the lien of the mortgage, and the mortgagor without keeping the tender good may bring an action in replevin to recover the property,[1] or trover for its value.[4] The Michigan and Oregon courts have gone further than the courts in Minnesota, as it appears from an examination of their decisions that a tender

---

possession after condition broken if the tender be kept good by bringing the money into court is a good defence to an action by the mortgagee to recover the possession. See Sims v. Canfield 2 Ala. 555.

4 Moore v. Norman 43 Minn. 428.

1 Daugherty v. Byles, 41 Mich. 69 s. c. 1 N. W. Rep. (Mich.) 919, Stewart v. Brown, 48 Mich. 383 s. c. 12 N. W. Rep. 199, Flanders v. Chamberlain 24 Mich. 305, Bartel v. Lope 6 Or. 321.

4 Fry v. Russell, 35 Mich. 229.

after the mortgagee has taken possession effects a discharge of the lien.[5] In these states the interest of the mortgagee before the foreclosure is a mere lien

In Massachusetts,[6] under a statute which provides that on a tender or payment of the amount of the mortgage debt together with all reasonable and lawful charges and expenses incurred in the care and custody of the property, or otherwise arising from the mortgage, and the property is not forthwith restored, the person entitled to redeem may recover in an action of replevin, or may recover in an action adapted to the circumstances of the case such damages as he may sustain by the withholding thereof, it was held, that a mortgagor redeems when he tenders the sum due, that the statute gives a payment or tender at any time before foreclosure, the same effect upon the rights of the parties in the property which a payment or tender would have had if made when the debt was due.[7]

## § 377. Refusal to restore mortgaged property—Remedies of the mortgagee—Defence when the mortgagor is in possession—Enjoining mortgagee from selling—Replevin or trover will not lie when—A tender an equitable defence when.

Where the lien of a chattel mortgage has been discharged by a tender and refusal, whenever made, and the mortgagee has the possession of the mortgaged property and refused to restore it, or he has not the possession at the time the tender was made, but

---

[5] A late decision in Minnesota has extended the rule in that state so that a tender made after the mortgagee had taken the possession discharges the lien. Davis v. Dow, 83 N. W. Rep. 50.

[6] Pub. St. Mass. Ch. 192, Sec. 6.

[7] Weeks v. Baker, 152 Mass. 20, s. c. 24 N. E. Rep. 905. The court refers to Roberts v. White, 116 Mass. 256, s. c. 15 N. E. Rep. 568, which considered such a tender set up as a defense to an action of replevin brought by the mortgagee, and disposes of the apparent conflict by saying that in the latter case, the statute which it is now considering was not referred to. The statute referred to in the text contemplates a tender or payment at any time before foreclosure whether the mortgagee has taken possession or not, while in Roberts v. White, the conclusion to be drawn from the language is that such a tender is no defence to an action of replevin brought by the mortgagee, unless the tender was kept good and the money brought into court. It is clear that under the statute after the mortgagee has acquired the possession, but before he has effected a sale of the property, such tender will discharge the lien.

seized the property after such tender had been made, he is
guilty of a conversion[1] And the mortgagor may maintain
trover to recover its value, or bring replevin to recover the
property, and, as has been said, the right to recover posses
sion is absolute, and the title does not oscillate between
the mortgagor and mortgagee according to their subsequent
change of conduct in reference to the tender.[2] Such tender is
an absolute defence to any action the mortgagee may bring
to recover the property.[3] A judgment creditor of a mort
gagor of chattels may redeem from the mortgage which is
prior to the execution issued on his judgment and levied upon
the chattels, and on a refusal of a tender of the principal,
interest and reasonable and lawful expense incurred in and
about the sale, he may enjoin the mortgagee from selling the
chattels under the mortgage[4] Where a mortgagor is not
re invested with the legal title by a tender and refusal, he
cannot maintain replevin or trover to recover the property
or its value[5] In some states the code permits equitable de
fences to be interposed in actions at law, in which case the
mortgagor may plead a tender in an action of replevin by
the mortgagee, although it did not have the effect of dis
charging the lien, provided, however, that he has kept the
tender good and brings the money into court

§ 378. **Consequences of a tender and refusal upon the lien
of a pledge—Separate tender where distinct lots are pledged—
Title in whom — Rule as to title — Where a chose in action is
pledged** — A tender of a debt for which property is pledged
as security, extinguished the lien and the pledgor may re
cover the pledge in replevin, or its value in trover or other
proper form of action,[1] without keeping the tender good-

[1] Rice v Kahn 85 N W Rep
(Wis) 165.

[2] Weeks v Baker 152 Mass 20,
s c 24 N E Rep 905

[3] Knox v Williamson, 39 N W
Rep 787

[4] Lambert v Miller, 38 N J
Eq 117

[5] Smith v Phillips 17 Wis 202,
s c 2 N W Rep 285, Gauche v
Milbrath, 69 N W Rep (Wis)
999

[1] In trover the damages would
be the value of the security at the
time the pledgee refused to give
it up after deducting the amount
of the debt Hancock v Frank
lin Ins Co, 114 Mass 155. See
Ball v Stanley, 5 Yerger 199 s c
26 Am Dec 263, where it is held
that the pledgor may recover full
damages without any abatement
on account of the debt Here the
pledgee is left to his remedy to

Where distinct lots of wheat are deposited as collateral security for separate advances, a tender of an amount of money sufficient to pay all advances and charges on any number of the separate lots, and a refusal, constitutes a conversion, and an action for damages may be maintained for the specific lots demanded.[1] In such case, each deposit constitutes a separate pledge. A tender of a part of a debt, will not have the effect to divest the lien on any part of the property pledged.[2]

A pledge differs from the modern chattel mortgage, in that it need not be in writing but may be created by delivery merely, and that as a general rule the title does not pass to the pledgee. But in the case of a pledge of chose in action, the title passes in so far as to enable the pledgee to enforce collection, or to take other legal steps to make the pledge effectual. As between the pledgor and pledgee, however, as long as the pledgee remains in possession, the title or general property in the chose in action remains in the pledgor, and a valid tender will destroy the lien of the pledgee as effectually as if the pledge was any other kind of property. Unlike chattel mortgages the character of the pledge or lien is not changed by default. A default gives the pledgee a right to proceed in a legal way by notice and sale or in the mode prescribed by the contract to make the security available for the purpose of satisfying his claim, and until such sale or proceeding, the pledgor's right and interest in the property remains the same after a default is it is before and a legal tender after default will discharge the lien of the pledgee as effectually as if made on the day the debt became due, and such tender need not be kept good.[3]

## § 379. Same subject—Relation of the parties to the property after the lien is discharged — Retaining the pledge to secure

recover the debt. This is not the rule in the code states.

[2] Appleton v. Donaldson, 3 Pa. 381; Ratcliff v. Davies Cro. Jac. 244; Coggs v. Barnard 2 Ld. Raym. 909; Mitchell v. Roberts, 17 Fed. Rep. 776; Norton v. Baxter 41 Minn. 146; Jones v. Rohilly, 16 Minn. 320; Loughborough v. McNevin 21 Cal. 250; Cass v. Higinbotham 100 N. Y. 248.

Nelson v. Robson, 17 Minn. 284.

[4] Appleton v. Donaldson 3 Pa. St. 381; Biglow v. Young 30 Ga. 121.

[5] Hyams v. Bamberger 36 Pac. (Utah) 202; McCalla v. Clark, 55 Ga. 53.

another debt—May waive the tort and sue for the money had and
received when—Consequences of the pledgor demanding equitable relief—Restraining a sale on application of a surety—By a
subsequent purchaser.—Where the lien is discharged by a ten
der and refusal the parties stand in relation to the property
pledged as though payment of the debt had been made, and
as though no pledge had been made and the creditor had ac
quired the property by wrongful act[1] The pledgee has no
right to retain the collateral as security for another debt due
him from the pledgor.[2] If the pledgee, after a valid tender,
disposes of the collaterals, the pledgor may waive the tort
and bring an action for money had and received[3] It is a gen
eral rule that a pledgor, whose tender has been refused, will
not be granted affirmative relief of an equitable nature, unless he has kept the tender good or at least comes before a
court in an attitude of willingness to pay what is due from
him[4] But an injunction restraining the sale of a pledge, after
a valid tender by the pledgor, would undoubtedly be granted
on the application of the owner of the property, where it had
been pledged to secure the debt of the pledgor,[5] whether the
pledgor kept the tender good or not. So, where a third per
son, subsequent to the making of the pledge, acquires rights
in the property, and a valid tender is made by the pledgor
and refused, a court of equity will enjoin the pledgee from
enforcing the pledge[6] In both these cases the owner or the
one acquiring an interest in the property owes nothing to the
pledgee and is not chargeable with fault because the debtor
does not keep the tender good

§ 380. Consequences of a tender and refusal upon lien of a
bailee—Of freight charges—Storage charges, &c.—Upon a mechanic's lien—Attorney's lien.—A tender of freight charges to
a common carrier, if refused, discharges the lien of the carrier, and replevin may be brought for the recovery of the
goods, without keeping the tender good    It has been held

---

[1] Ball v Stanley, 5 Yerger, 199,
s c 26 Am Dec 263

[2] Hathaway v Fall River Natl
Bank 131 Mass 14, Mitchell v
Roberts 17 Fed Rep 776

[3] Hancock v Franklin Ins Co,
114 Mass 155

[4] See *Obiter* Norton v Baxter,
41 Minn 145, Citing Tuthill v
Morris, 81 N Y 94

[5] See Mitchell v Roberts 17
Fed Rep 776

[6] Norton v Baxter 41 Minn
146

that a tender of the freight charges, less the amount of the damages done to the goods by the carrier in transportation, if refused, entitles the owner to bring replevin.[1] But such a rule violates the general principle that neither party may make an estimate of unliquidated damages. A valid tender and refusal of freight charges, under a statute in force in Texas, renders the carrier liable for certain damages for each day's detention of the goods.[2] In admiralty, after tender and refusal of the charges for freight, the consignee may abandon the cargo to the vessel and sue for its value.[3] The same effect upon the lien, results from a tender and refusal of the amount due a warehouseman for storage charges, or a mechanic for bestowing labor or furnishing material in repairing property intrusted to his care for that purpose,[4] or the charges due any other kind of a bailee, as result in the case of a valid tender to a pledgee or a common carrier, and the bailor is entitled to pursue the same remedies without keeping the tender good. In all cases the bailee must resort to his action to recover his charges.

A valid tender of the amount due a material man, mechanic or laborer, for material or labor furnished in and about the construction or repair of a building or other improvement on real estate, for which the statute gives a lien, if refused, will discharge the lien, whether made at or after the debt is due, or after the lien has been filed, and whether made by the contractor who had purchased the material or labor, or by the owner of the property. If a tender is made of the amount due from a contractor, for which a lien is given, and it is refused, the material man, or laborer to whom the tender was made, must look to the contractor for his pay. A tender by the owner of the amount due in such case, does not make him personally liable for the debt. The property on which the labor is bestowed, in such case, stands somewhat in the relation of a surety. A tender made after an action to foreclose has been commenced is of no effect unless authorized by statute, and then it would have such effect only as the

---

[1] Bancroft v. Peters, 4 Mich. 619, see Boggs v. Morton, 13 B. Monroe, 239.

[2] Atchison &c. Ry. Co. v. Roberts, 22 S. W. Rep. 183.

[3] The Reben Doud, 16 Fed. Rep. 800.

[4] See Mitchell v. Roberts, 17 Fed. Rep. 776, Ball v. Hanley, 5 Yerg. 199, Moynohan v. Moore, 9 Mich. 9.

statute gave it. In such cases, when an action is commenced, the cause of action as it existed at the time of bringing the action, measures the right of the plaintiff, and no act done thereafter by the defendant can be pleaded or given in evidence to change such rights, unless expressly authorized by statute. Where an attorney has a lien upon the papers in his possession belonging to his client for the sum due him for professional services, or upon a judgment for the amount due him in obtaining judgment, a valid tender of the sum due in either case will discharge the lien.

§ 381.  **Tender by bailee or receiptor.**—A valid tender of personal property to the bailor by the bailee or receiptor, terminates the particular contract of bailment under which the goods were delivered,[1] and thereafter the goods are held at the risk and expense of the owner, and the bailee is chargeable with only ordinary care.

§ 382.  **Upon the lien of taxes—Selling the property after a tender—Tender before the tax becomes delinquent—After it is delinquent—Upon a tax judgment—Certificate of sale—Purchaser's estate terminates.**—A tender of the amount due for taxes, and a refusal by the collecting officer to receive the sum tendered, deprives the officer of all authority for further action, and makes every subsequent step illegal and void.[1] A tax payer who has tendered the amount of tax due by him, has in all things, performed his obligations to the state. In such case, a lawful tender of payment is equivalent to actual payment,[2] and a sale thereafter is void.[3] The effect is the same whether the amount due is tendered and refused before it has become delinquent, or is tendered and refused after it has become delinquent. A lawful tender of the amount due on a tax judgment and a refusal of it, amounts to a satisfaction of the judgment.[4] Such a tender is the equivalent of payment in its effect upon a certificate of sale.[5] Where the amount necessary to redeem from a tax sale is tendered

[1] Haynes v. Thom 28 N H 386

[1] Poindexter v. Greenhow 111 U S 270

[2] Green v. Brook 28 Fed Rep 215

Atwood v. Weems, 99 U S

183. United States v. Lee 106 U S 196

[4] Woodruff v. Trapnall, 10 How 190

[5] Poindexter v. Greenhow 111 U S 270

to the purchaser and refused by him, his estate terminates thereafter.[6] However, if the owner comes into equity for relief—to have the sale set aside and cancel the certificate, or redeem—basing his right to such relief upon a tender, he must keep the tender good and bring the money into court.[7]

**§ 383.  Same subject—Restraining a sale—May bring replevin, detinue or trover when—Liability of collector to the state—Mandamus to compel collector to receive whatever the statute declares is receivable for taxes—Enforcing issuance of certificate of redemption.—**The tax payor making such tender, if it is refused, may obtain an injunction restraining a sale of the land, or may bring action to recover the possession if it has been sold and possession taken by the purchaser.[1] If personal property has been seized by a collecting officer after a valid tender of the amount due, the owner may bring replevin, detinue or trover to recover his property or its value.[2] He is entitled to have the remedy which the law gives to every other citizen, not himself in default, against a wrongdoer, who under color of law, but without law, disturbs and dispossesses him.[3] By seizing property after a lawful tender of the tax due, the collecting officer ceases to be an officer of the law and becomes a private wrong-doer. In such a case the court observed. This is simply a case in which the defendant, a natural private person, has unlawfully, with force and arms seized, taken and detains the personal property of another.[4]

There being no personal liability for the payment of a tax, and a valid tender and refusal discharging the lien, thereby rendering all proceedings to enforce it illegal, the tax is thus lost to the state; and a tax collector, who refuses a valid tender of a sum due for taxes whereby it is lost to the state, is liable to the state for the amount thereby lost. A state has authority to provide that taxes due it may be

6 Bender v. Bein, 12 S. W. Rep. (Ark.) 241.

Lancaster v. De Hadway, 97 Ind. 565.

7 Cooley v. Irwin, 18 Wall. 549.

2 In Miller v. McGehee, 60 Miss. 903, it is held that in replevin against a tax collector where the owner of goods relies upon a tender of the taxes he must show a continuous tender up to and during the trial.

3 See Poindexter v. Greenhow, 114 U. S. 270.

4 Poindexter v. Greenhow, 114 U. S. 270.

paid in whatever it may see fit; and where a tax collector refuses a tender of interest coupons, or anything else by statute made receivable for taxes, the tax payer has a remedy by mandamus to compel him to do so.[5] So, mandamus will lie to compel a county treasurer or other officer to issue a certificate of redemption, if he refuses to issue such certificate on a tender of the full amount of the tax due.[6] But in such cases the tax payor is seeking affirmative relief, and will be required to make the tender good.

§ 384.  **Tender of amount due on a judgment—Proceedings when refused—Pleading the tender as a defence when—Enjoining the collection of a money judgment in replevin—Enjoining the enforcing of judgment by execution—Of use for purpose of a redemption.—**A tender will not satisfy, nor extinguish the lien of a judgment.[1] A judgment is by law the final of all controversies between litigants, by the means of which society speaking through its courts and officers give to its citizens their just dues when denied them, and terminates further resistance. If a tender satisfied a judgment, it would satisfy the debt, for the judgment is in fact the debt. If a judgment had a separate and distinct entity from the debt, a tender which would discharge the judgment and leave the debt, would simply result in a renewal of the litigation to recover the debt. Such is not the aim of the law. So, if the lien of a judgment upon any property be discharged by a tender, a debtor by successive tenders, if he had more than one piece of property, might thus free all his property and thus prevent a speedy satisfaction, and thereby defeat the aim of the law. If a judgment debtor refuses to accept the amount due on a judgment and satisfy it, a motion for an order of satisfaction is the proper remedy.[2] Such order will be granted on the money being brought into court. A tender of the amount due on a judgment, where it is kept good, may be pleaded in bar to a *scire facias* to revive the judgment.[3] So such a tender, if kept good may be pleaded in defence to an action on the judgment. In replevin, if the defendant ten

---

[5] Hartman v. Greenhow, 102 U. S. 672. Antoni v. Greenhow, 107 U. S. 769.

[6] People v. Edwards, 10 N. Y. S. 335 s. c. 56 Hun 377.

[1] Law v. Jackson 9 Cow. 641 s. c. 5 Cow. 248. Rother v. Monahan, 60 Minn. 186.

[2] Callahan v. Gilman, 2 N. Y. S. 702.

[3] Carr v. Miner, 92 Ill. 604.

ders the property described in the judgment, and the plain
tiff refuses to accept it, the latter may be enjoined from
proceeding under execution to collect the value of the prop
erty.[1] In any case, if, after a valid tender of the amount due
on a judgment, and the tender is maintained, the judgment
creditor attempts to enforce the judgment by execution or
persists in using it for the purpose of redeeming land of his
debtor from a sale on a prior lien, a court will enjoin the
creditor from such use of the judgment as an abuse of the
process of the court, or of the statutory right of redemption.[2]

§ 385. **Effect of a tender upon the lien of an execution upon
real estate—After a sale—Lien upon personal property—Remedy
of judgment debtor—Lien of an attachment.—** A tender and refusal of the amount due upon an execution which has been
levied upon real estate, will not discharge the lien of the
execution. A subsequent sale of the premises, however, is
wrongful,[1] and, if the tender is kept good, it will be vacated
on application to the court where made within a reasonable
time. Or, if the tender is kept good, and there is time
enough, the sale may be enjoined. The judgment being a
lien, which cannot be discharged except by actual payment,
nothing short of acceptance of the amount tendered, or the
equivalent, tendering the amount due and keeping it good
and bringing the money into court in a direct application
to satisfy the judgment, will suffice. Until this is done, all
proceedings to enforce the judgment, though the proceedings
may be inequitable are valid. After a sale of real estate
upon execution, the judgment and execution is satisfied to
the amount received at the sale, and a tender thereafter must
be in redemption of the property. The purchaser gets the
legal title, subject to statutory right of redemption. A ten
der after sale, if refused, must be kept good in order to
preserve the debtor's right to redeem.[2]

[4] McClellan v. Marshall, 19
Iowa 561, Freeman on Executions. See 436.

[5] Rother v. Monahan, 60 Minn.
18. See Mason v. Sudam, 2
John's Ch. 172.

[1] Mason v. Sudam, 2 John's Ch.
172.

[2] See Abraham v. Holloway, 11
Minn. 156, see also Legro v. Lord,
10 Me. 161, where it is stated in
the syllabus that such a tender is
sufficient to revest the title to the
property without a deed of conveyance from the purchaser.
But a careful analysis of the case

A lien of an execution upon personal property levied upon, is incidental, and accessorial to the debt, and a tender of the amount due upon the execution together with costs, and its refusal, will discharge the lien.[3] If the officer refuses to restore the property, the owner may maintain replevin therefor without keeping the tender good. A sale of the property under the execution is wrongful, and an action for conversion will lie against the sheriff in case he refuses it and proceeds with the sale.[4]

A tender will not discharge the lien of an attachment, although a tender of the amount due and the increased costs on the judgment, if kept good, would render any further proceedings under the judgment wrongful. The law has provided other ways for dissolving attachments[5]

§ 386. Liability of a surety—Surety as a joint maker—Property pledged for the debt of another—Accommodation note—Endorser's liability after a tender.—A valid tender of the amount due upon an obligation, by the principal to his creditor, and the latter's refusal to receive it, operates as a discharge of the surety, even though the tender be not kept good[1] This is so, even where the surety appears upon the face of the note as a joint maker, if the holder knows the party to be in fact a surety[2] So, the surety is discharged if he makes a valid tender of the amount due and the creditor refuses to receive the money or thing tendered After a debt is due, the surety has the legal right to pay the debt and at once proceed against the principal debtor In such a case, the court said "It necessarily follows that he is entitled to have the money

shows that the money was accepted and a deed given not to the original owner, but to his son, so that the case is worthless as an authority on this subject

[3] Parmenther v Fitzpatrick 11 N Y S 748

[4] Tiffany v St John, 65 N Y 314, Freeman on Executions Sec 19

[5] Chase v Welch, 45 Mich 345, s c 7 N W Rep 895

[1] Smith v Old Dominion B L Assn 110 N C 257, s c 26 S F

Rep 40, Wilson v McKey 83 Ind 110, Randal v Tatum 33 Pac 433 Griswold v Jackson, 2 Edw. Ch 400 Dunn v Hunt 63 Minn 484 Brant on Suretyship, Sec 295 Musgrave v Glasgow 3 Ind 31 Cmrack v Packard. 29 Cal 194 Sears v Van Dusen 25 Mich 351, McQuesten v Noyes 6 N H 19, Joslyn v Eastman 46 Vt 278 Johnson v Mills 10 Cush 503 See Clark v Sickler 64 N Y 231

[2] Fisher v Stockebrand, 26 Kan 565

accepted by the creditor in order that he may proceed. It is the duty of the creditor to receive it, and a gross violation of the duty and good faith on his part to refuse, thereby interposing an insurmountable obstacle in the way of the pursuit of the surety of his most prompt and efficient remedy."[3] So, where the property of one party is pledged as security for the debt of another, or mortgaged, as where a wife mortgages her property to secure the debt of her husband, a tender and refusal of the amount due, discharges the lien upon the property pledged or mortgaged, without keeping the tender good. The owner of the property stands in the relation of a surety.[4] If an accommodation note is put up as collateral security, the maker of such note is in effect a surety, and a valid tender to the creditor of the amount due on the principal obligation, discharges the maker of the accommodation note from his liability thereon.[5]

Concerning the reasons why a surety is discharged by a tender and refusal, Mr. Justice Mitchell, speaking for the Supreme Court of Minnesota, said: "The rule is well settled that if the principal, after the debt is due, duly tenders payment and the creditor refuses to receive it, the surety is discharged. One of the reasons sometimes assigned for this rule is that the transaction amounts to a payment of the debt, and a new loan to the principal. But doubtless the main reason for the rule is that the contract of suretyship imports entire good faith and confidence between the parties in regard to the whole transaction, and any bad faith on part of the creditor will discharge the surety. The refusal of the creditor to receive the money is a fraud on the surety which exposes him to greater risk. After the debt is due and payable, the creditor cannot by his unjustifiable refusal to accept payment compel the surety to continue responsible for the future acts of the principal as his debtor or bailee of his money. If it were otherwise, the creditor would have it in his power to keep the surety liable indefinitely."[6] A tender, however, to have the effect of releasing the surety must be

[3] Hayes v. Josephi, 26 Cal. 535. See Halsey v. Flint, 15 Abb. Pr. 367.

[4] Smith v. Old Dominion B. & L. Assn. 119 N. C. 257, Wood v. Babb 16 S. C. 127, King v. Bald-

win 2 John's Ch. 554, Strong v. Wooster 6 Vt. 536, Mitchell v. Roberts 17 Fed. Rep. 776.

[5] Appleton v. Donaldson, 3 Pa. St. 381.

[6] Hull v. Warner 79 N. W. 669.

one that the creditor would be required to accept. An offer of part of the debt will not release the surety,[7] even *pro tanto*. A creditor is not bound to accept payment of his claim by piece meal. So, where the obligation is a money demand, a tender of property and a refusal of it by the creditor will not relieve the surety,[8] even though the surety stands by and offers to take the property off his hands and pay full value for it.[9]

A guarantor's liability may be discharged by a valid tender of the amount due and a refusal by the creditor to receive it. So, it would seem, that a tender of the amount due upon a negotiable instrument on the law day, if refused, would discharge an indorser. The indorser's contract relative to payment is, that the maker will upon due presentment of the note, pay it at maturity. That, if, when duly presented, it is not paid by the maker, he will upon due notice of its dishonor pay the same. If a maker of a note offer to pay it at maturity he has done all that the indorser's contract implies. That the tender is not received so as to constitute payment is the fault of the holder and the loss or increased hazard should fall upon the one whose fault it is. But the like effect would not be produced by a tender by the maker and a refusal by the holder, after the dishonor of the paper and the indorser's liability is fixed by notice. The indorser's contract being, that in case the maker does not pay at the day, he will do so on receiving the proper notice, after such default and notice, that which was a contingent liability becomes absolute, and a tender by the maker of the money due and its refusal, would no more discharge the indorser's absolute liability than such a tender on the part of the indorser would discharge it.

§ 387. **Same subject — Surety upon an official bond** — The authorities are at variance upon the question of the effect of a tender and refusal, upon the liability of the sureties upon official bonds. In Ohio, it was held, that where a sheriff having collected money on execution, absconded with the money, having previously made a tender of it to the party

---

[7] McCann v Dennett, 13 N. H 528

[8] Williams v Reynolds 11 La 230

[9] Wilson v McVey, 83 Ind 108

entitled, who refused to receive it, such tender and refusal was no defence in an action against the sureties upon the sheriff's official bond. In that case the court said "The principle of discharge arising from an act done by the creditor prejudicial to the surety, does not apply. An ordinary suretyship is a mere contingent obligation, for the payment of money, in default of the principal. The securities upon an official bond guarantee the faithful performance of official duty. The payment of money, and other acts done by the creditor, injurious to the surety, may discharge the one, but the faithful and honest performance of official duty alone can fulfil the condition of the other. The fact of the tender and refusal does not convert the official trust into a mere private liability for a money demand. The obligation to pay over money received by a sheriff in his official capacity, continues an official duty until performed by payment to the party entitled. As long, then, as the obligation to pay continues an official duty, so long were the securities responsible for its violation, upon their official bonds * * * They (the securities) can find no excuse in the fact that the injured individual has not been cautious to fortify himself against official misconduct. Their undertaking is that there shall be no such thing as official misconduct." [1]

In Minnesota, where a sheriff received some $1,800 upon a redemption from a mortgage sale at which the plaintiff was purchaser, the sheriff made a tender of the sum so received to the plaintiff who refused to receive it. Afterwards, the plaintiff, changing his mind, made several demands for the money, but in each case the sheriff refused to pay it over. The sheriff upon entering upon the performance of the duties of that office, furnished the usual bond with sureties, conditional that he would well and faithfully in all things perform and execute the duties of sheriff. The action was against the sureties. Mr. Justice Mitchell, for the court, reviewed the law, and the reasons therefor, relative to a discharge of a surety upon unofficial obligation under like circumstances, and said "We fail to see why the same acts on the part of the creditor which would release a surety on a private bond would not also release a surety on a sheriff's official bond," and confessed his inability to understand the

---

[1] State v. Alden, 12 Ohio, 59.

28

reasoning of the Ohio court, unless it meant that no act or conduct on the part of creditors or other private parties interested in the official conduct of a sheriff would release the sureties on his bond until and unless the sheriff has fully performed his whole duty in that regard by paying the money to the party entitled to it, "a proposition which we think will be found to be without support in any other adjudicated case." (Referring to the Ohio case.) It was held that the sureties were released from liability by the refusal of the plaintiff to receive the money when tendered by the sheriff.[2]

Notwithstanding the profound learning and pre eminent ability possessed by the late Justice Mitchell, we are constrained to say that the decision of the Ohio court appears to be supported by the better reasoning. There is no privity of contract between a sheriff holding money as such for a litigant, and the latter. The money comes into the sheriff's hand as an officer of the law. He is the arm of the law that reaches out and affects that adjustment of the pecuniary affairs of men which the law, acting through the courts, has decreed. It is the sheriff's duty, as such sheriff, to keep the money or property safely, and no dispute or bickering as to the correct amount, or as to the sheriff's right to receive the money at the time he did, will relieve him of that duty. Unless the arising of a dispute and consequent refusal of the party to receive it, changes the holding from that of an officer, to that of a private individual. Which cannot be. Nor is there any privity of contract between the sureties upon an official bond, and a litigant, whose affairs a sheriff or other officer may be called upon to adjust. The voluntary contractual relation, peculiar to a suretyship in unofficial transaction, and which calls for that absolute good faith and fair dealing with the surety, is wanting in the case of an official bond where the liability to a private person is one created solely by law.

§ 388. **Loss of the sum due where the lien is discharged** — A lawful tender of a sum of money, the payment of which is secured by a mortgage, after the statute of limitations has barred the recovery of the debt but before the statute has run against the mortgage, will divest the mortgage lien and

2 Hull v. Warner, 79 N. W. 669.

consequently result in the loss of the debt. So, after a tender by the owner of the equity of redemption, which discharges the lien, where there is no personal obligation on his part to pay the money, an action cannot be maintained to recover the sum tendered.[1] In every case, where there is no personal obligation to pay money, as where trustees execute a mortgage to raise a portion, or where a person without any loan, debt or duty proceeding, executes a mortgage for the payment of a certain sum to another in the nature of a gratuity or gift, and the sum is tendered according to the condition, but it is refused, the lien is discharged and the party to whom the money was to be paid has no remedy therefor.[2] So, where a mortgagor dies and the mortgagee relying upon the security, neglects to file his claim against the estate within the time specified by statute, a proper tender by the heir or executor, if refused, will discharge the lien and consequently cause the loss of the mortgage debt to the mortgagee.[3] So, the same result will be produced if a mortgagor of exempt property is discharged in bankruptcy of his personal liability on the mortgage note, and he afterwards makes a valid tender of the amount due upon the mortgage debt and it is refused.

According to Lord Coke: "If a man make an obligation of 100 pounds with condition for the deliverie of corne, or lumber, &c., or for the performance of an arbitrement, or the doing of any act, &c., this is collateral to the obligation, that is to say, is not parcell of it, and therefor a tender and refusal is a perpetual barre."[4] It is generally true, that if a person enters into a bond to do something for the benefit of another which was not incumbent upon him to do at the time of entering into the obligation, or, being bound by one instrument to pay a certain sum or perform a duty, enters into another agreement, whereby, if he pays a less sum or performs another thing, the former instrument shall be void, a tender according to the condition, if refused, will be a perpetual bar to an action upon the obligations. The reason of this is, that in the former case there is no personal obligation on the part of the obligor on the bond in the first instance, and the bond being collateral to and merely incident

---

[1] Long v Howard, 35 Iowa 148. Co Litt Sec 209b

[2] See Co Litt Sec 335

[3] Co Litt Sec 335

to the duty, it is satisfied by the tender and refusal. So, in the latter case, the second agreement constituting a defeasance of the first instrument, if performance is tendered and refused, the condition is complied with in so far as it lay in the power of the obligor to do, hence, it satisfies the first, while the amount to be paid or duty to be performed in the second instrument, is collateral to and not a parcel of the original sum or duty, it is also discharged by the tender and refusal.[5] In all such cases the tender does not amount to payment or performance of the debt or duty, but is equivalent to payment or performance so far as satisfying and discharging all things collateral to and incident to the debt or duty. The loss of the debt or other thing is occasioned by reason of there being no remedy remaining after a tender and refusal, to enforce payment of the debt or performance of the duty.[6]

§ 389. **A tender of a deed does not pass the title—Recovery of purchase price — License to occupy revoked when — Incumbrance upon the land.**—A tender of a deed in compliance with a contract for the sale of land, does not pass the title to the vendee   A refusal of a deed entitles the vendor to recover the purchase price in an action at law.[1] If the vendee has been let into possession, a refusal of a valid tender of a deed revokes the license to occupy the land and the vendor may maintain ejectment to recover the possession [2]  It is no defence that there is an incumbrance upon the land not assumed by the vendee where there is a balance of the purchase money due over and above the amount of the incumbrance not assumed.  He should specify his objection and give up the possession of the land   If the vendee does not want to give up the possession, he should state his objection at the time of the tender of the deed and offer to pay the balance due on the incumbrance being discharged, or tender all of the purchase money to be paid at the time of the

5 See Co Litt Sec 335 et seq, and 9 Bac Abr Tender (F), for several cases of peculiar and complicated nature, where a party "hath no remedy by the common law to have his money because it shall be accounted his own folly

that he refuses the money, when a lawful tender of it was made unto him"

6 9 Bac Abr Tender (F)

1 Richards v Edick 17 Barb 265

2 Pierce v Tuttle, 53 Barb 155

delivery of the deed, except a sum sufficient to discharge the incumbrance.[3]

§ 390. **Declaring a forfeiture—Right to the purchase money —Loss of collateral rights—Effect where the legal title is retained by the vendor—Tender of performance after a rescission.**—A tender by the vendee of the amount due upon a contract of sale of land and a refusal deprives the vendor of the right to declare a forfeiture.[1] By refusing to accept he does not forfeit his right to the money tendered, but he loses all collateral benefits or securities. If the legal title has been transferred to the vendee, the latter is in a position to act on the defensive, and can plead the tender and refusal to defeat a foreclosure of the lien, without keeping the tender good. So, where merely the possession has been delivered, the vendee may plead a tender and refusal as a defence to an action to recover the possession. But where the vendor retains the legal title, it has been held that a tender of the amount due, and its refusal, did not discharge the vendor's lien, and that the vendor could not be divested of his legal title except upon actual payment, and that in bringing a bill for the title, the tender should be kept good and the money brought into court.[2] In such case, an equity court would not decree a specific performance unless the vendee could show he had not abandoned the tender, and was still willing to pay what was equitably due. It has been held that a refusal of a deed gives the vendor a right to rescind, though the deed was defective, if no objection was taken to the deed on that account.[3] If a vendor is in default in not executing a deed on a tender of the purchase price, and the vendee elects to rescind the contract by a tender of a quit claim deed of the land, and demanding a return of the installments already paid, a subsequent offer of performance will not relieve the vendor from the effect of his default.[4]

[1] Viele v Troy & Boston R R., 20 N Y 187, Pierce v Tuttle, 53 Barb 155

[2] Hill v Carter 59 N W Rep (Mich) 413, Loomis v Pingree, 43 Me 299

[3] Scheaff v. Dodge 33 Ark 346

See Harle v Smith, 113 Cal. 656, s c 45 Pac (Cal) 872.

[3] Hoskins v Dougherty, 69 S W Rep (Tex Civ App) 103

[4] Woodruff v Semi Tropic L & W Co 87 Cal 275, s c 25 Pac Rep 354

§ 391. **Effect of a tender of specific articles upon contract of sale—Upon chattel note.**—The rule is now well settled, if indeed it has ever been unsettled, that in case of an executory contract of sale of specific articles whether they are to be paid for upon delivery or not, and in cases where a note or other obligation is payable in specific articles, a tender of the thing contracted for, at the time and place agreed, though refused to be accepted by the vendee or promisee, is a satisfaction of the demand, an absolute discharge of the contract, and a bar to any suit upon it,[1] A tender of specific articles is analogous to a consignation under the civil law, where the debtor is discharged.[2] The title to the property tendered vests absolutely in the vendee or promisee,[3] and the vendee or creditor

---

[1] Lamb v Lathrop, 13 Wend 95, Singerland v Morris, 8 Johns R 370, Mitchell v Morrill, 2 Blackf. 87, Robbins v Luce, 4 Mass 474, Barney v Bliss, 1 D Chip 399, Dewey v Washburn, 12 Vt 580, Downer v Sinclair, 15 Vt 495, Hayden v Demets, 53 N Y 426

There is a small volume extant published in 1822 entitled 'An Essay on the Law of Contracts for the Payment of Specific Articles," by Daniel Chippman, which contains much valuable information on this subject

[2] See Sheldon v Skinner, 4 Wend 528

[3] DesArts v Leggett, 16 N° Y 582, Dewees v Lockhart 1 Tex 505, McPherson v Wiswell 21 N W Rep (Neb) 391, Dowagiac Mfg Co. v Higinbotham 91 N W Rep (S D) 330, Mitchell v Morrell, 2 Blackford (Ind) 87, s c 18 Am Dec 128, Curtiss v Greenback, 24 Vt 536, Mitchell v Gregory, 1 Bibb 449

In Schrader v Wolffin 21 Ind 333, after the plaintiff in replevin had suffered a non suit he offered to return the property, the court said we see no reason why a tender in this case should not stand upon the same ground as a tender in the case of an ordinary agreement for the delivery of chattel Games v Manning, 2 Green (Io) 251, 2 Kent's Com 508

In Weld v Hadley, 1 N H 295, the contrary was held to be true that where a tender of specific articles is refused, the party to whom they were tendered acquired no property in them, though the tender discharged the contract But the decision stands alone among modern authorities a judicial comet, as it were Under the ancient English Common Law most undertakings for the payment of money or property were in the nature of penal bonds and if there was a breach of condition the whole penalty was forfeited and could be recovered in an action at law This form of instruments being oppressive to the debtor, the courts held creditors to great strictness and created an exception to the general rule, to the effect that if the article tendered according to the terms of the condition was not accepted the penalty of the bond was saved, the debtor or obligor must resort to the specific articles, and may recover them from the person in whose possession they are, and for this purpose, if they are withheld, may maintain replevin, or detinue, or conversion, or trover for the value, as he may elect[4]

§ 392. Option of vendor after a tender of chattels is refused—Must not abandon the goods—Vendee a bailee when—Recovering the purchase price.—The vendor, on a tender of the chattels being refused, may treat the contract as at an end, and keep the property and sue for the difference between the contract price and the highest market price at the time of the refusal; or he may treat the property as that of the vendee, and resell the same, acting as the agent of the vendee, and recover of the vendee the difference between the contract price and the amount realized by the sale[1] He must conduct the sale openly and fairly, and at public auction after notice to the vendee A private sale, however, would be good if the articles were sold at the prevailing market price. If they be not such articles that have a regular market price, then it must be shown that the chattels were disposed of at a reasonable price If the goods are perishable, the party making the tender ought to make a reasonable effort to sell them The vendor or debtor after a refusal of his tender, although discharged from his contract, is not relieved from all further care of the property He must not abandon them[2] But this

was discharged, and the thing tendered was forfeited and the creditor was left without remedy, either upon the contract or for the thing tendered (see McJilton v Smizer, 18 Mo 111) But this law was changed by the statute of 8 & 9 Wm & M. which made a penal bond a mere security for the sum really due or for damages actually sustained so that a tender in performance of the conditions of a penal bond and a tender in performance of a simple contract were analogous This is the law in the United States and there is at this day no case where the property is lost to a creditor by

a tender and refused by him to receive it

[4] Rix v Strong 1 Root 55, Mitchell v Gregory 1 Bibb 449, Hughes v Eschbach 7 D C 66, Bates v Bates 12 Am Dec 572

[1] Hayden v Demets, 53 N Y 426

[2] McJilton v Smizer, 18 Mo 111; Gale v Suydam 21 Wend 274

In Sheldon v Skinner, 4 Wend. 525 turning hogs fattened on shares into the street after notice to the other party to take them, was held to be a breach of duty for which the other party may recover damages

See Kent's Com 509, where it

does not mean that he may not leave them at the place of delivery, after taking all needful precaution to preserve them against destruction. If the thing to be delivered is portable and very valuable, there is a moral as well as a legal obligation to place it in some secure place for the vendee or creditor, or leave it with some reliable person to be delivered to the owner,[3] if he does not care to, or cannot well keep the property in his own possession. This would be prudent, for he may have judged erroneously as to the validity of his tender. The vendee or creditor must be present before he can be charged with a waiver of any defects in that respect In the event of the tender being proven insufficient he would continue liable on his contract, and if so unwise as to abandon the property it may be a loss to him

If the vendor or debtor elects to retain the property in his possession, subject to the demand of the vendee or creditor, he does so as the bailee of the other party, and at the latter's risk and expense. Thereafter the new relation of bailor and bailee subsists in place of that of debtor and creditor[4] On a tender and refusal of the property the vendor may, when the time for payment arrives, bring his action to recover the purchase price from the purchaser or his sureties[5]

§ 393. Vendor's lien—Vendee's remedies—Divesting title where transaction is a conditional sale—Statutory lien—Tender of installment.—The lien of a vendor of personal property, where the vendee is not to have the possession until payment, is not discharged by a tender of the purchase price[1] If the property has been designated so that the vendee may identify it, on the refusal of his tender he may bring replevin, and by keeping the tender good and bringing the money into court, thus obtain the property ; or he may abandon the goods to the vendor and bring an action to recover the difference between the contract price and the market price at the time of the refusal of the tender. A tender of a part of the pur

---

is stated that the party tendering chattels on their refusal, may abandon them, but the weight of authority is to the contrary

[3] Bement v Smith, 15 Wend 493

[4] Lamb v Lathrop, 13 Wend

95, Desarts v Leggett 16 N Y 582 2 Kent Com 508 509

[5] Kemble v. Walles, 10 Wend 371

[1] Summerson v Hicks 134 Pa St 566

chase price, where the sale is one entire transaction, will not transfer the title to a part of the goods.[2] Where the property has been delivered to a vendee, under a conditional sale providing that the title shall remain in the vendor until the purchase price be paid, a wilful and unjustifiable refusal of a valid tender of the balance due will divest the vendor of the legal title, and he must pursue his ordinary remedy to recover the purchase price.[3] So, in the ordinary sale and delivery of personal property where the title passes on the completion of the sale, a tender of the unpaid purchase price will divest the vendor of any statutory lien he may have on the goods for such deferred payments. But the refusal by the vendor of any installment due will not divest the vendor of his title, or lien on the property for the balance due, but merely stop his pursuit of the property to enforce payment of the installment which has been refused.

§ 394. **Distress for rent—Cattle taken damage feasant.**—The effect of tender in cases of distress for rent in arrears, or where cattle are taken *damage feasant*, is stated in The Six Carpenter's Cases thus: 'It was resolved *per totam curiam*, that not doing cannot make the party who has authority or license by the law a trespasser *ab initio*, because not doing is no trespass; and, therefore, if the lessor distrains for rent, and thereupon the lessee tenders him the rent in arrears &c. and requires his beasts again, and he will not deliver them, this not doing cannot make him a trespasser *ab initio*. * * * So, if a man take cattle *damage feasant*, and the other offer sufficient amends, and he refuses to redeliver them, now if he sues a replevin, he shall recover damages only for the detaining of them, and not for the taking, for that was lawful * * * Vide the Book in 30 Ass. Pl. 38, John Matrever's case, it is held by the court, that if the lord or his bailiff comes to distrain, and before the distress the tenant tenders the arrears upon the land there the distress taken for it is tortious. The same law for *damage feasant*, if before the distress he tenders sufficient amends * * * Note, reader, this difference that tender upon the land before the dis-

[2] See the New York Co. v. Flynn 55 N. Y. 653

[3] See Le Flore v. Miller 64 Miss 204 see, also, Christenson v. Nelson 63 Pac Rep (Or) 648

tress, makes the distress tortious, tender after the distress, and before the impounding, makes the detainer and not the taking wrongful, tender after the impounding, makes neither the one or the other wrongful; for it comes too late, because then the case is put to the trial of the law, to be there determined. But after the law has determined it, and the avowant has return irreplevisable, yet if the plaintiff makes him a sufficient tender, he may have an action of *detinue* for the detainer after; or he may, upon satisfaction made in court, have a writ for the re delivery of the goods."[1]

§ 395. **Effect of a tender on bond with a penalty—Note—Contract providing for a forfeiture—Fines.—**By the ancient common law, on a default in the conditions of a penal bond, the amount of the penalty became the debt, and because of this hardship upon the debtor, the courts held the creditor to great strictness, and maintained that on a tender according to the terms of the condition, and a refusal, the penalty was saved, the obligor discharged, the thing tendered forfeited, and the creditor had no remedy, either on the contract or for the thing tendered. But this oppressive rule, at a very early date in England was changed by statute, so that a bond with a penalty merely secured what was actually due, whether liquidated or unliquidated, and on a default, the obligee could only recover so much as was actually due Thereafter a tender and refusal was not a discharge upon any bond with condition for the payment of money,[1] or a bar to an action upon such bond. This is the law everywhere in the United States.[2] Where by the terms of a note or other obligation, a certain sum is to be added in case it becomes necessary to bring an action to recover the debt, the right to the additional sum accrues only on commencing the action, and if before action, a tender is made of the sum due, the right to the penalty is gone, even though the tender is not kept good.[3]

It is a universal rule that for the purpose of avoiding penal

[1] The Six Carpenter's Cases, 8 Co 142; Davis v Henry 63 Miss 110 Hunter v Le Conte, 6 Cow 728 Smith v Goodwin 4 B & A 413 See Tiffany v St John, 65 N Y 314

[1] See Haynes v Thom, 28 N H 386 and McJilton v Smizer 18 Mo 111

[2] Manny v Harris, 2 Johns 24

[3] Pinney v Jorgenson 27 Minn 26

ties or forfeitures, or the loss of any rights or privileges, a valid tender is the exact equivalent of payment or performance. Where a society declares a contract forfeited and refuses to receive an assessment from a member when it is tendered, a subsequent failure to tender assessments will not effect his right to recover on the contract.[4] Where a company loans money to be repaid in weekly installments, a failure to pay one installment when due, which rendered the member liable to a fine, and a refusal to pay the fine, does not render the borrower liable for subsequent fines, if he tenders the subsequent weekly installments as they come due.[5] If a party who is to give security for the faithful performance of a contract, performs a part without giving such security, and it is accepted, such acceptance is a waiver of the right to security as to the part performed, and there is no ground for declaring the contract at an end, and a tender thereafter of security for the performance of the balance of the contract, if refused, entitled the willing party to damages for non performance.[6]

§ 396  **Effect of a tender where the right to rescind is reserved — Where grounds for rescission exist — Fraud discovered after a tender.**—Where a party has a right by the terms of a contract to put an end to a bargain by returning what he received under it, a valid tender of the thing received will restore his original title to the property parted with. Any violence in repossessing the property will not divest the title of the one rescinding.[1] The effect of a tender or offer to place the other party in *statu quo*, where the right of rescission is not expressly reserved in the contract, but there are grounds for a rescission, is to give the party rescinding a standing in equity to compel a rescission or at law to recover what he has parted with under the contract, or it places him in a position to plead a rescission as a defence in any action that may be commenced by the other party. A tender of the thing due upon a contract will not prevent a rescission

4 Beatty v Mutual R F L Assn 75 Fed Rep 65 citing Meyers v Ins Co 73 N Y 516 and Miesell v Ins Co 76 N Y 115

Pentz v Citizens' Fire Ins Co 35 Md 73

5 Cornwell v Haight 21 N Y 462

6 Moore v Shenk 3 Pa St 13

of the contract for fraud discovered after the tender has been made. A tender of performance before the fraud is discovered can in no sense be taken as an affirmance of the contract. So, a tender will not estop a party from claiming that a contract is void, or avoiding a voidable contract, or urging a failure of consideration.

**§ 397. A tender creates a right of redress—Must not be abandoned.**—A tender of performance by a vendor or vendee of real or personal property, or by an employer or employee, bailor or bailee, and a refusal, gives to the willing party a right to invoke the remedial powers of the courts, either for specific relief or for pecuniary remuneration, as the facts may warrant. The topic of redress for breach of contracts is covered by volumes of legal works on "Specific Performance of Contracts," "Measure of Damages," &c., and the reader must look there for a full discussion. Considering here that part of the topic of redress, relating to the right of redress and the kind, would be at the risk of repetition, as every illustration of a tender given in the text, in the class of cases referred to, came before a court in a controversy involving the right to redress and the remedy, resulting from the tender, and some mention, either directly or indirectly, is there made to them. It may be repeated that a tender and refusal fixes the right to redress, but in no sense fixes the extent of the damages

At common law, after a contract is broken, a tender will not be effectual to bar an action for damages. But in some states, in reference to contracts for the payment of money the common law has been changed by statute, in others by the decisions of the courts, so, that a tender made of the whole sum due after default, may be pleaded in an action subsequently brought, in like manner and effect as if such tender had been made punctually on the day fixed for performance[1] In all jurisdictions, where a tender may be made after a default, whenever the right to damages accrues by reason of the non-performance of a duty, if the value of the services or duty be stated and in the nature of liquidated damages, or fixed by law and capable of liquidation by mere computation a subsequent tender in money, of the amount stated or fixed

[1] Suffolk Bank v Worcester Bank, 5 Pick 105

by law, with interest at the legal rate computed from the time of the breach, takes away the right to further damages.[2] A person liable upon a promissory note or any instrument may, when a valid tender of the amount due thereon is refused, maintain a suit in equity against the holder for its possession.[3] In order that a tender may be available and have the effect the law gives to it, either as the ground for specific relief, or for pecuniary remuneration, or as a defence, it must not be abandoned, but must be continually insisted upon, and where an action is brought, it must be pleaded by the party relying upon it.

§ 398. **Eminent domain—Water dues—After a petition in insolvency—After indictment for embezzlement.**—In Georgia, under a statute there in force, a tender of an award, duly made and continued, in proceeding under the power of eminent domain, is equivalent to payment in its effect upon the right of the corporation to enter upon the land and prosecute the work of construction.[1] In Colorado, by statute, a person who has taken and paid for water during prior years, and has not ceased to do so with intent to procure water elsewhere, may on payment or tender of the proper amount compel the irrigation company from whom he has theretofore taken water to give him the preference over new applicants.[2] Where a petition in insolvency has been filed by a creditor to have a debtor declared insolvent, the debtor being admitted to be insolvent, a tender of the amount due the petitioner will not bar the petition, unless the debt set out in the petition is the only one outstanding, or unless all the creditors have consented, knowing of the insolvency. The petitioners would have no right to accept payment in full without the consent of all.[3] A person indicted for embezzlement or for receiving a deposit in a bank knowing the bank to be insolvent, cannot defeat the prosecution by tendering the amount of money lost, to the party losing it.[4]

[2] It has been held that a tender will not bar the action but merely the right to subsequent damages and costs. Huntington v. Zeigler, 2 Ohio St. 10. See Johnson v. Clay, 7 Taust 186.

[3] Strofford v. Welch, 59 N. H. 16.

[1] Oliver v. Union Point, 9 S. E. Rep. 1086.

[2] Northern Colo. Irrigation Co. v. Richards, 45 Pac. 123.

[3] In Re Williams, 1 Low. 406, 29 Fed. Cases 1322.

[4] Meadowcroft v. People, 163 Ill. 56, s. c. 35 L. R. A. 176.

**§ 399. Ignorance of the law no excuse for refusing a tender —Relying upon the decision of the highest court—Unconstitutional law—Refusal must be unqualified—Good faith—Unwilling to accept.**—A creditor cannot avoid the effect of a refusal of a lawful tender on the ground that he was ignorant of the law, but where a tender was refused by a creditor on the ground that the money offered was not a legal tender, the creditor relying upon the decision of the highest judicial tribunal in the land to the effect that the money was not a legal tender as applied to such contracts, which decision was, after the tender, overthrown by the same court, it was held that the tender did not discharge the lien of the mortgage given to secure the debt, and that *"ignorantia juris non excusat"* did not apply.[1] It would seem that a tenderee may refuse that which is declared not to be a legal tender by the highest judicial tribunal in the land, although in fact such, and not to be subjected to the harsh consequences of a refusal, while a tenderor, according to well established principles, may not make a tender of that which is declared to be a legal tender by a law which is unconstitutional, although not declared so until afterwards

The question of the discharge of a lien by a tender and refusal has been thought to depend somewhat upon the good faith of the party refusing. It has been said "It is the rule undoubtedly that a tender discharges the security, * * * but to produce such a serious and heavy consequence the refusal must have been unqualified and unaccompanied by any *bona fide* claim of right, which was supposed by the party to justify his refusal The claim of right may have been one that could not be supported in law, still, if it was believed in, and was not put forward as a cover for a wrong purpose, it is sufficient to prevent the forfeiture of the security"[2] But the doctrine here stated is too broad the question of good faith is taken into consideration in most cases, to determine whether some request on the part of the tenderee, such as requesting time to ascertain his rights, or whether costs have been incurred and the like, is,

[1] Harris v Jex, 55 N Y 421 The tender made after the decision of Hepburn v Griswold, 8 Wall 605 and before it was reversed by Knox v Lee, 12 Wall 457.

[2] Union Mutual Life Ins Co v Union Mills Plaster Co 37 Fed Rep 286 s c 3 L R A. 91

or is not put forward for the purpose of delay or to avoid accepting the tender. In Missouri, it is held that a mortgagee is bound to take notice of the rights of the mortgagor, and that in refusing a tender, the question of the good faith of the mortgagee is immaterial.[1] The refusal need not be in direct terms, it is sufficient to discharge the lien if the mortgagee is unwilling to accept the money and does not.[4] As to what constitutes a refusal more is said elsewhere.[5]

[1] Campbell v. Seeley, 13 Mo. App. 21. In Michigan, the equity courts it would seem, on a cursory examination of their decisions have gone further than the courts of any other state in treating with indulgence a party who has rejected a tender. But a more analytical examination discloses that the observations of the court, in each case were not absolutely necessary to the decision of the case. Thus, in Renard v. Clink, 51 N. W. Rep. 692 the assignee of the mortgage having foreclosed without first placing the assignment upon record believed she was the absolute owner of the mortgaged premises, but nevertheless was willing to accept the principal interest and costs and even offered to take the money tendered as far as it would go. The mortgagor tendered the principal and interest and insisted that it be received in full payment and discharge and afterwards insisted that the lien was discharged by the tender. Such a tender being conditional would not have the effect of discharging the lien in any event. But here there was not a refusal but on the other hand an offer to accept. The discussion of the question of a party being in some cases relieved against a mistake of law was unnecessary, and although considered at some length, in view of the other facts considered by the court, it could not have been the sole ground of overruling the defendant's claim that the lien was discharged.

In Myers v. Hart, 40 Mich. 517 the mortgagor filed a bill in equity to set aside a mortgage sale and asked that the premises be relieved from mortgage lien. The court found that the mortgagee was mistaken as to his legal rights, but was acting in good faith and refused to enforce the statutory penalty for failing to discharge the mortgage of record, and decreed that the mortgagor pay the mortgage debt as a condition to relief. In this case as well as in Canfield v. Conklin 41 Mich. 371 s. c. 2 N. W. Rep. 191, the mortgagor came into equity seeking affirmative relief, a case where the courts of equity invariably require the complainant to do equity. The question of good faith was considered mainly in the latter case at least in connection with the statute which provided for a penalty "for wilful and knowingly wrongful refusal to discharge the mortgage."

[4] Ferguson v. Popp, 3 N. W. Rep. (Mich.) 287.

[5] Ch. XI.

§ 400. **Benefits derived from a tender by the party refusing—Where not pleaded—Distinction between a tender and an offer of compromise—Waiver of forfeiture.—**We have thus far considered principally the effect of a tender and refusal relative to the benefits derived by the party making it, and the corresponding deprivations of the one refusing There remains to be considered the benefits which the party refusing derives from a tender. The chief advantage to a tenderee to be derived from a tender is gained by reason of the tenderor pleading it But in absence of the plea a party may prove that the defendant made an unconditional tender of a certain sum on the demand in controversy Such tender is an admission of a liability but it is not conclusive. Its weight is to be considered by the court or jury over against a subsequent denial of all liability, or an assertion of a liability for a less sum than that tendered The defendant is not precluded from stating his reasons or object in making the tender, that it was his desire to close the transaction and avoid litigation; or that at the time he thought the tender was necessary to save certain rights, or that it was made under the mistaken belief that the sum was due[1] By being made without reservation, tacit or express, that no advantage shall be taken of the offer, the plaintiff may prove the fact and thereby gains some advantage from it by adding some weight to his other testimony, if nothing more In Minnesota, under a statute allowing a tender to be made in actions founded on tort, if the tender is refused, it cannot be pleaded or given in evidence to the court or jury[2]

An unconditional tender differs from an offer of money by way of a compromise Evidence of the latter is inadmissible An offer to compromise in reality admits nothing except that there is a dispute, and the party tendering the money by way of a compromise may claim that nothing is due The law encourages compromises Men must be permitted to offer to purchase peace, without prejudicing themselves if the offer should not prove successful, and such offer may be made in order to stop litigation, without regard to whether anything is due or not "[3] On the contrary it has been held

---

[1] Ashuelot v Cheshire, 60 N H 756

[2] 1894 G S Minn Sec 5106

[3] Latham v Hartford 27 Kan 249, 1 Greenl Ev Sec 192 Talmage v Third Nat Bk 91 N Y 531

that where a laborer leaves his employer without the latter's consent, before his term of service has expired, and the employer, while denying his liability, offers to pay *pro rata* for the services rendered, and makes a tender of the amount which would be due at that rate, the employer, both by the offer of payment and tender, waives the forfeiture of the wages for the services performed.[4] A tender of payment or part payment will not validate a contract void under the statute of frauds.[5]

§ 401. **Conclusive admission when—Amount of verdict—Judgment—Introduction of evidence unnecessary.**—It is frequently stated in general terms, perhaps oftener than otherwise, that a tender is a conclusive admission that the amount tendered is due, and that the party in whose favor the tender is made, is entitled to that amount. While the tender *is* the admission, the foundation upon which the rule rests, yet the statement is inaccurate. It does not in fact become conclusive until the tenderor makes it a matter of record. The rule has been comprehensively stated thus: "A plea of tender is an unequivocal admission of the justice of the plaintiff's claim to the extent of the sum tendered. So conclusive is the admission that if the tender is refused, and the parties proceed to trial and it shall turn out that the plaintiff was not legally entitled to anything, the plaintiff shall have a verdict for the sum tendered."[1] A verdict should not be against

[4] Patnote v. Sanders, 41 Vt. 66.

[5] Edgerton v. Hodges, 41 Vt. 676.

[1] Roosevelt v. New York & C. R. R. Co. 45 Barb. 554; s. p. Supply Ditch Co. v. Elliott 10 Colo. 327; Phoenix Ins. Co. v. Readinger, 44 N. W. Rep. (Neb.) 864; Wright v. Howell 35 Iowa 288; Johnson v. Clay 7 Taunt. 486; Fisher v. Moore 19 Iowa 84; Cobbey v. Knapp 23 Neb. 579; s. c. 37 N. W. 485; Babcock v. Hawes 37 Iowa 109; Murray v. Cunningham 10 Neb. 170; s. c. 4 N. W. Rep. 319, 956; Huntington v. Banks, 6 Pick. 340; Cox v. Brain, 3 Taunt. 95; Martin v. Whistler,

62 Iowa, 416; s. c. 17 N. W. Rep. 593; Schnur v. Hickox, 45 Wis. 200; Woodward v. Cutter 33 Vt. 49; Davis v. Millandon 17 La. Ann. 97; Eaton v. Wells 82 N. Y. 576; Brown v. Fink, 4 Jones L. 378; Monroe v. Chaddick, 78 Ill. 429; Bacon v. Inhabitants of Charlton 7 Cush. 581; Wagonblast v. McKean, 2 Grant 393; Sugart v. Pattee 37 Iowa 422; Phelphs v. Rathbon 30 Iowa, 231; Simpson v. Carson 11 Or. 361; Latham v. Hartford 27 Kan. 249; McDaniels v. Upton 45 Ill. App. 151; Metropolitan Nat. Bank v. Commercial Bank 71 N. W. Rep. (Io.) 26. See Turpin v. Gresham 106 Iowa,

the admission, and a judgment entered on a verdict to the effect that the plaintiff had no cause of action,[2] or is for a less sum than that admitted to be due by the plea will be reversed;[3] but the judgment may be for more. Where the complaint contains only one cause of action, a plea of tender leaves open only the question whether the plaintiff is entitled to recover a greater sum. If the plea meets only one cause of action in a complaint the question of the right to recover a greater sum is confined to the cause of action which the plea meets, and the plea in no wise affects the other causes of action set out in the complaint. The plaintiff is entitled to the amount tendered and pleaded, without introducing any evidence.[4]

§ 402. Plea of tender admits what.—The plea of tender in effect admits the defendant's liability on the contract or cause of action to which the plea relates, so that a promise to pay the debt of another need not be proved to be in writing;[1] or that the plaintiff is an apothecary,[2] or a duly licensed physician, or that the defendant was negligent. In fact the tender and plea dispenses with proof of everything that would otherwise be necessary to enable plaintiff to recover upon the obligation or cause of action sued upon,[3] or to enable him to recover in the capacity in which he sues to the extent of the sum admitted to be due by the plea. So it precludes the defendant from introducing any evidence as

187, s c 76 N W Rep 680, where a tender was made on a note of an installment falling due after action brought. A tender was set up by way of supplemental pleading. It was held that the plea of tender being needless it was no admission that any thing was due at the time of commencing the action

[2] Brayton v The County of Delaware 16 Iowa 44, s p James T Harr Co v Hickock 45 Ill App 504

[3] Phelphs v Kathron 30 Iowa 231 s p Bump v Schwartz 56 Iowa, 611, s c 10 N W Rep 99 Denver, &c R R Co v Harp 6

Colo 420 See Spence v Owen County 117 Ind 573 where no evidence was given to the jury of the amount which was alleged to have been tendered by defendant —held plaintiff could not complain on account of the verdict being for a less sum

[4] Metropolitan Nat Bank v Commercial State Bank 74 N W Rep (Iowa) 26

[1] Middleton v Brewer Peake 15

[2] Wilks v Langridge 2 H & W 250

[3] Bacon v Inhabitants of Charlton, 7 Cush 581

to contributory negligence on the part of the plaintiff, either as to the merits of the action or in mitigation of damages.[4] Where an administrator has been ordered to pay a certain sum of money to an heir, a tender and plea of that sum establishes his liability to pay the sum.[5] So, if a purchaser of real estate promises to pay an incumbrance, a tender and plea is an admission of the debt.[6] But a plea of tender does not prevent a defendant from establishing his counterclaim for the amount of plaintiff's claim above the amount tendered.[7]

§ 403. **No admission of all the alleged grounds for recovery.**— The tender admits the amount tendered to be due, but it does not, however, admit all the alleged grounds for recovery. In an action for rent, a plea of tender together with a general denial does not admit that the defendant used the premises described during all the time, nor that he used them at any time.[1] In an action against a town on an account annexed, for the care and board of a certain person for a certain period at fifty cents per week, a tender of an amount equal to the stipulated rate for a part of the time, does not preclude the defendant from proving that the plaintiff did not board the person during the remaining portion of the time.[2] So, where a defendant pleaded a tender of a certain sum generally and the complaint contained two counts, which combined exceeded the amount tendered, he is not estopped to show that the sum tendered is the amount of the debt.[3] A defendant, for the purpose of preventing a recovery of more than the amount admitted to be due by his plea of tender, may plead and prove that the plaintiff has no cause of action, that he is not damaged; or the contract is not in writing and void under the statute of frauds, or that the plaintiff is not an apothecary,[4] or a duly licensed physician, or attorney.[5]

[4] Bacon v. Inhabitants of Chilton 7 Cush. 583

[5] Rainwater v. Hummel 79 Iowa 571 s. c. 44 N. W. Rep. 814

[6] Cobbey v. Knapp 37 N. W. Rep. (Neb.) 485. See Sec. 502

[7] Young v. Borgone 66 Pac. Rep. (Wash.) 135

[1] Griffin v. Harriman 74 Iowa 436 s. c. 38 N. W. Rep. 139

[2] Howlett v. Holland 6 Gray 418

[3] Sawyer v. Baker 29 N. H. 525

[4] Willis v. Langridge, 2 H. & W. 250

[5] See Sec. 503

§ 404. **Effect of a tender which is authorized by statute—Unauthorized tender—Insufficient tender—Tender must accord strictly with cause of action.**—A tender authorized by statute has the same force and effect when pleaded, as a tender at common law[1] Thus where cattle had been taken *damage feasant* and the plaintiff, under the statute, pleaded a tender of amends in his replication, it was held that the plaintiff admits of record that he was liable for the trespass complained of, and that the cattle were lawfully taken and held *damage feasant*, through plaintiff's fault and wrong.[2] So, where a tender is made and pleaded, in a case where one cannot be legally made or pleaded, as in the case of an offer of a sum upon an unliquidated claim, it is an admission of record and dispenses with the proof necessary to enable the plaintiff to recover, unless he goes for a greater amount of damages. But such a tender will be unavailing to save costs[3] So, a tender which is insufficient, in that it was conditional, or the money was not produced, or the money was not a legal tender, has, if pleaded, the same force as an admission, as a valid tender[4]

A tender and plea to have the effect of an admission must accord strictly with the cause of action set out in the complaint Thus, where heirs were sued for money alleged to have been received by the ancestor, it was held that an allegation that the only money so received was Confederate money and of which a tender was made, was not such a tender and plea as would authorize a judgment against them for the amount, or preclude them from pleading prescription against the demand[6]

§ 405. **Proceedings where tenderee elects to accept—Conclusive as to what amount—Asserting another defence after a tender**—If a tender is pleaded to the whole case and not to any

---

[1] Bacon v Inhabitants of Charlton, 7 Cush 581

[2] Miller v Gable 30 Ill App 578 See Bench v Geffery 1 Ill App 283

[3] Taylor v Chicago Ry Co, 76 Iowa 753 s c 40 N W Rep 84, Frink v Coe, 4 G Green 555, s c 61 Am Dec 141, Woodward v Cutter 33 Vt 49, Roosvelt v New York &c R R Co 45 Barb 554,

Cilley v Hawkins 48 Ill 308 See Turpin v Gresham, 76 N W Rep 110 r 680

[4] Denver v Harp 6 Colo 420 See Breen v Texas R Co 50 Tex 43

[5] Denver &c v Harp 6 Colo 420, Eaton v Wells, 82 N Y 576

[6] Southern Mut Ins Co v Pike, 34 La Ann 825

particular matter pleaded, the adverse party is, if he chooses
to accept it and it is essential to his right, entitled to a judgment for the amount admitted to be due.[1]    But ordinarily,
the party for whom money has been brought into court is
entitled to it without any judgment therefor.    If the money
has not been brought into court, and there is no counterclaim
or prayer for affirmative relief interposed by the defendant,
or no other cause of action is set out in the complaint, or if
there is another and the plaintiff chooses to abandon it he
may at any time move for an order for judgment on the plea
of tender    It is the plea on the part of the tenderor that
concludes him.    As to the amount due, it is conclusive only
as to the amount stated in the plea, which he is still willing,
ready and able to pay    If more was tendered than is set
forth in the plea as being due, the tender is not conclusive as
to the surplus, and the tenderor may show that no more was
due than the sum admitted to be due in his plea.[2]    It has
been held, in a suit in equity to redeem and for an accounting,
that where a defendant refuses to receive a sum tendered,
and puts the plaintiff to his proof of the balance due there
can be no reason why the plaintiff should be bound by the
sum tendered, if by mistake and ignorance of the facts he
tenders a larger sum than was actually due.[3]    So, where
$35,000 was tendered to secure the possession of certain se-
curities, and on that sum being refused $16,000 was tendered,
it was held not conclusive on the plaintiff, that the defendant
has a lien for $16,000.[4]    In an action to recover the possession
of certain premises on a default in payment of interest, the
defendant alleged payment made under a subsequent agreement whereby the interest was to be paid in work, also that
before suit he made a tender of the amount due, it was held,
that where there is a dispute, and a party makes a tender to
avoid imperiling his interests, he may, after suit is brought,
assert any other existing defence.[5]

§ 406.    **No non-suit after a plea of tender** —Where a tender
has been pleaded by a defendant in a case where the tender
must be kept good, and the money has not been brought into

[1] Wolmerstadd v. Jacobs, 61
Iowa, 372, s c 16 N W Rep 217
[2] Abel v Opel 21 Ind 259
[3] Tucker v Buffum 16 Pick 46

[4] Talmage v Third Nat Bk, 91
N Y 531
[5] Hill v Carter, 59 N W Rep
413

court, the plaintiff cannot be non-suited.[1] The reason is, that the defendant by his plea of tender, has conclusively admitted that the plaintiff is entitled to the amount set out in his plea, and being entitled to that much without the introduction of any evidence, or regardless of whether he has a cause of action or not, he must be given a judgment for the amount, or the judgment for dismissal would be in effect a decision against the admission But the rule is otherwise where the money has been brought into court, as we shall presently see [2]

---

[1] Harding v Spicer, 1 Camp  [2] Ch XV
327 Contra Anderson v Shaw,
3 Bing 290, s. c 11 Moore 11

# CHAPTER X.

## ACCEPTANCE OF A TENDER

**§ 407. In general—A willingness to accept.**—The acceptance of a tender of the money due upon any obligation vests the title to the money absolutely in the creditor, constitutes payment and discharges the debtor forever from his liability. To constitute payment it requires the express acceptance on the part of the creditor, or such acts as would be construed to be an acceptance, holding the creditor to absolute good faith and fair dealing. Payment implies an acceptance and appropriation of that which is offered by the debtor to his creditor.[1] If money which has been tendered, is left with the creditor against his will, and he afterwards refuses to give it up, such a refusal amounts to an acceptance.[2] Intimating a willingness to receive money offered without actual reception of it does not constitute payment. A notary went to an acceptor of a bill and demanded payment, the latter uncovered a large quantity of dimes and half dimes lying on

[1] Barker v. Bank 5 Iowa 484    [2] Rogers v. Rutter 11 Gray 410

the table, and told the defendant there was the money for him. The defendant ran his hand over the money and mixing the coin somewhat, said, "I suppose I shall have to take it, and I will go to my office to get bags for it." On returning a few minutes later he found that the money had been levied upon as the property of the acceptor. In an action against the notary for the amount of the bill, alleged to have been paid to him, it was held not to be a payment but only a tender.[a]

§ 408. **Receiving a part offered in satisfaction of the whole demand—Payment pro tanto—Accord and satisfaction—Under protest as to sufficiency — Acquiescence or dissent by debtor.** —The term tender, as used in the books, denotes a legal offer, one which one party is under obligation to make and the other bound to accept or suffer certain consequences for his wrong It is an offer to do those things in the fullest sense, which the obligor by his contract undertook to carry out. An offer of a less sum than that which is due, is not what the obligee undertook to do, and is no tender. The acceptance of a smaller sum than is legally due, does not satisfy the whole debt, but is considered a payment *pro tanto*.[1] The payment of a part of what is legally due upon a liquidated claim, furnishes no consideration for the creditor's relinquishment of his claim to the residue, whether it is offered as the whole sum due and accepted as such or as a part and accepted in full satisfaction So, an offer of a sum of money in satisfaction of a claim which is open and unliquidated, does not constitute a tender, unless the making of the tender is authorized by statute. In such a case, as well as in those cases where the sum due upon a contract is in controversy, if a party makes an offer of a certain sum in payment of the claim and attaches to his offer the condition that the sum, if taken, must be received in full satisfaction of the claim in dispute, and the other party receives the money, he takes it subject to the condition attached to it and it operates as an accord and satisfaction.[2] This has been said

---

[1] Thompson v Kellogg, 23 Mo 281

[1] Duluth v Knowlton, 42 Minn 229, Patnote v Sanders 41 Vt. 66; Myers v Byington, 34 Iowa 205

See Leeson v Anderson 58 N W Rep (Mich ) 72

[2] Foster v Drew, 39 Vt 51; Donohue v Woodbury 60 Mass 150, s c 52 Am Dec 777, Cotter

to be the effect, even though the party at the time of receiving it, declares that he will only receive it in part satisfaction of the claim.³ The same court in a later case, reported in the same volume, held, that where a debtor tenders a sum of money in full for all legal demands against him upon account, and the creditor receives the money protesting that it is not sufficient, but saying that he will take it and pass it to the debtor's credit and the debtor does not dissent from this course, the acceptance of the money tendered did not bar the creditor's right to recover such sum as may be found due him exceeding the amount received.⁴ In such a case whether the offer or tender, if accepted, will constitute an accord and satisfaction, will depend upon whether the debtor persists in his claim. The same court just referred to in a later case, said, "If he (the creditor) takes it his claim is cancelled, and no protest, declaration, or denial of his, so long as the condition is insisted on, can vary the result."⁵

§ 409. **Prescribing terms of acceptance—Rule at law—In equity —Creditor put to an election when—Becomes matter of contract when.**—The creditor cannot, against the consent of the debtor, prescribe the terms of acceptance.¹ Where a creditor had agreed to accept notes secured by a deed of trust, in payment of a balance due him, on a tender of the notes, and deed of trust, took them but declared that they would not be received in satisfaction but only as collateral, and held them notwithstanding the protests of the debtor that they were delivered as a tender in full satisfaction, and that if retained they must be taken as tendered, it was held that the tender being made on the express condition and under protest to the effect that if retained it must be in full satisfaction, it was the creditor's duty either to accept the tender on the terms prescribed or to have returned the notes and deed of trust,

---

v. O'Connell 18 Iowa 552, Fuller v. Kemp 30 L. R. A. 785, s. c. 33 N. E. Rep. (N. Y.) 1034, Latham v. Hartford, 27 Kan. 249, Vermont St. B. Convention v. Ladd 4 Atl. (Vt.) 634

⁵ McDaniels v. Lapham 21 Vt.
222

⁴ Gassett v. Andover, 21 Vt. 341 See Perin v. Cathcart, 89 N. W. Rep. (Io.) 12

⁵ Preston v. Grant, 34 Vt. 201 s. p. Rosema v. Porter, 70 N. W. Rep. (Mich.) 316

¹ Hoyt v. Sprague 61 Barb. 497, Perin v. Cathcart, 89 N. W. Rep. (Iowa) 12

and not having done so, the creditor was bound by the term of the tender as prescribed by the debtor[2]  If the sum offered upon certain terms and conditions, is taken without words of assent, the acceptance is an assent *de facto*, and the party is bound by it[3]  "The mere act of receiving the money is an agreement to accept the same on the conditions upon which it was offered"[4]  The same rule as to the acceptance of a conditional tender, prevails in equity as at law.  It is sufficient that when the money is offered a *bona fide* controversy exists in relation to the matter, that the claim is of an unliquidated or uncertain character.[5]  Where a tender or offer is thus made, the party to whom it is made, has no alternative but to refuse it or accept it upon such a condition,[6] and must accept it as made or it must be rejected[7]  If a conditional tender is made and accepted, it becomes a matter of contract[8]

§ 410.  **Acceptance of original sum after right accrues to demand a larger sum—Reservation—Ticket fare—Train fare.**—Where a vendee agrees to pay a certain sum on a day certain, and in case of default, a larger sum, an acceptance by the vendor after default of the lesser sum is a waiver of his right to the greater sum, unless the acceptance is on the express condition that he will only receive the lesser sum as a part payment  So, where a common carrier of passengers is entitled to charge a sum in addition to the regular ticket fare, when a passenger goes aboard its cars without procuring a ticket, an acceptance by the conductor  with full knowledge of the purpose for which it is tendered  of the regular ticket fare from a passenger  for his passage between two points is a waiver of the right to charge the additional sum[1]  But when a passenger goes aboard a train, and pays to the conductor the sum demanded by him, and the sum paid is less than the train fare, the conductor on discovering his error,

[2] Adams v Helm 55 Mo 468
[3] Donohue v Woodbury 6 Cush 148
[4] McDaniels v Bank of Rutland 29 Vt 230  McDaniels v Lapham 21 Vt 222
[5] McDaniels v Bank of Rutland 29 Vt 230

[6] Rosema v Porter 70 N W 346 s c 3 Det L N 869
[7] Hanson v Todd 10 So Rep 354
[8] Bickle v Beseke 23 Ind 18
[1] Du Laurans v The First Div St P and R R R 15 Minn 49

may rightfully demand the balance of the fare up to the limit of the train fare, and upon the passenger's refusal to pay the balance, he may be required to leave the train.[2]

**§ 411. After a forfeiture—Waiver of objection as to time—Reservation as to damages.**—If, after a forfeiture, a mortgagee of personal property, receives payment of his debt, it is a waiver of the forfeiture and his title to the property is extinguished,[1] and the mortgagor may assert his title at law, although before payment he could only avail himself of his equity of redemption.[2] An acceptance of a tender is a waiver of the objection that it comes too late.[3] So, after default, the acceptance of a part of the money or goods to be paid or delivered, is a waiver of the objection that the thing was not tendered within the time agreed,[4] unless the acceptance be qualified by a reservation of the right to claim damages for the delay.[5]

**§ 412. Waiver of objection as to place—Quality of the money—Money received how accounted for—Acceptance under protest as to quality.**—An acceptance of a tender is a waiver of any objection that could have been taken to the place of tender, or to the quality of the money tendered.[1] Where money is tendered and received without a special agreement for any distinction in computing or accounting for the same by reason of the kind of currency in which the payment was made, it must be accounted for and credited by the number of dollars paid.[2] A person cannot retain any particular form of money received in payment and credit it upon the debt at

[2] Wardwell v. Chicago M. & St. P. Ry. Co. 49 N. W. Rep. (Minn.) 206, overruling Du Lamans v. First Div. St. P. & P. Ry. Co. supra, upon the point that the conductor cannot retain out of the sum received the fare of the passenger from the point when he entered the cars to the station where he is ejected.

[1] Nost v. Clary 47 N. Y. 425; Patchin v. Pierce 12 Wend. 61; Tighton v. Shapley 8 N. H. 359.

[2] Jones on Chattel Mortgages Sec. 633.

Adams v. Helm 55 Mo. 468; Stow v. Russel 36 Ill. 33.

[4] Emery v. Tingley 1 Idaho 695; Minneapolis Threshing Machine Co. v. Hutchins 67 N. W. Rep. (Minn.) 807.

[1] See Lampasas Hotel Co. v. Home Ins. Co. 43 S. W. (Tex.) 1081 where a draft was sent and retained.

[2] Stark v. Coffin 105 Mass. 328; Bush v. Biddge 11 Allen 367; Stanwood v. Flagg 98 Mass. 124

a value not assented to by the other party.[1] Where United States treasury notes were presented for payment and the holder demanded gold coin in payment, which demand the Secretary of the Treasury refused to comply with, but tendered the required number of dollars in legal tender notes, which the creditor under protest accepted and surrendered the treasury notes, it was held in an action against the United States to recover the difference in the market value of the gold and the legal tender notes, that the protest being unauthorized by law, it had no efficacy to qualify the voluntary surrender of the treasury notes, and by such surrender independent of the question whether or not the notes received were legal tender, the creditor waived all claim to the difference.[4] So, when a party entered into a contract to erect a building for a certain sum, to be paid in gold or silver coin, a tender and an acceptance of United States treasury notes, though under written protest, was held a complete satisfaction of the debt.[5]

§ 413. **Counterfeit money — Forged paper — Qualification of rule.**—An acceptance by a creditor of that which he supposes to be money, but on examination afterwards, it is discovered to be counterfeit, is not a waiver of the right to recover the sum due in money.[1] A counterfeit of money, is not money, and its acceptance will not constitute payment. The acceptance of counterfeit money, the character of which was unknown to the debtor and creditor, will save a forfeiture, if the debtor on receiving notice of the defect promptly replaces it with good money. If that is tendered as money, which is known by the debtor to be counterfeit, the tender

[1] Gilman v. Douglas, 6 Nev. 27. See Walkup v. Houston, 65 N. C. 501, and Mitchell v. Henderson, 63 N. C. 643.

[4] (1875) Savage v. United States, 92 U. S. (2 Otto.) 382.

[5] (1870) Gilman v. Douglas, 6 Nev. 27. See Evers v. United States, 5 Ct. of Cl. 509, when under a special act of Congress, certain claims were to be paid in gold it was held where a claimant in receiving paper money declared that he would receive it only at its value and retain his claim for the difference between paper money and gold, that if the debtor without objection allows him to take the paper money, he impliedly assents to the creditor's proposal.

[1] Markle v. Hatfield, 2 Johns. Rep. 455. Gates v. Winslow, 1 Miss. 63. Contra. See 5 Rep. 115, cited in 9 Bac. Abr. Tit. Tender B.

will not save a forfeiture, even though it be accepted. In such a case the debtor commits a crime against the state as well as defrauding his creditor. The modern authorities support the rule that payment received in forged paper of a third person, or in any base coin, is not good, and the creditor may recover upon the original obligation.[2] But there is a qualification engrafted upon the general rule:—the notice of the forgery and a return of the paper must be within a reasonable time, and any neglect in this respect will absolve the party who has in good faith, delivered such paper, from responsibility.[3] Any delay in ascertaining the genuineness of the paper, is such negligence as will endanger the right of the party paying such forged paper to recover from the party from whom he secured it. Where a bank (or private person) receives, as genuine, forged or altered notes purporting to be its own, and redeems them or passes them to the credit of a depositor who acts in good faith, it is bound by the payment or credit thus given.[4]

The same rule applies to the acceptance and payment by a drawee of a bill of exchange—the drawer's handwriting being a forgery.[5] And, also, to the acceptance and payment by a bank of a forged check drawn upon it.[6] In case of a forged check, the court said, "Some of the authorities decide that

---

[2] Markle v. Hatfield, 2 Johns. 455; Young v. Adams, 6 Mass. 182; Jones v. Ryde, 5 Taunt. 488; United States v. Bank of Georgia, 10 Wheat. 333; Bruce v. Bruce, 5 Taunt. 495.

[3] In Smith v. Mercer, 6 Taunt. 76, the acceptance was a forgery and a week elapsed before the forgery was discovered and notice given. The plaintiff was not allowed to recover. In Gloucester Bank v. The Salem Bank, 17 Mass. 33, the court said, "the true rule is, that the party receiving such notes must examine them as soon as he has the opportunity, and return them immediately. If he does not, he is negligent, and negligence will defeat his right of action." Here, some fifteen days

elapsed before the notes were examined and their doubtful character discovered. See Kenneth Ins. Co. v. Bank, 70 S. W. Rep. (Mo. App.) 173, and cases cited.

[4] Bank of the United States v. Bank of Georgia, 10 Wheat. 333.

[5] Price v. Neale, 3 Burr. 1355; Smith v. Chester, 1 D. & E. 654; Barber v. Gingell, 3 Esp. 60; Bass v. Clive, 4 M. & S. 15.

[6] Kenneth Ins. Co. v. Bank, 70 S. W. Rep. (Mo. App.) 173, citing McKeen v. Bank, 74 Mo. App. 288; Bank v. Whitman, 94 U. S. 347; Frank v. Bank, 84 N. Y. 213, s. c. 38 Am. Rep. 501; Bank v. Barnes, 65 Ill. 69, 16 Am. Rep. 576; Bank v. Bank, 81 Ga. 597, s. c. 7 S. E. Rep. 738, 2 L. R. A. 96.

the acceptor is bound, because the acceptance gives a credit to the bill. * * * But the modern cases certainly notice another reason for his liability, which we think has much good sense in it, namely, that the acceptor is presumed to know the drawee's handwriting, and by his acceptance to *take this knowledge upon himself*."[7]  Mr. Justice Story recognized this rule as the correct one in a case where a bank received as genuine forged notes purporting to be its own, and passed them to the credit of the depositor and afterwards refused to pay the deposit.  After an extensive review of the cases he said "Considering, then, as we do, that the doctrine is well established, that the acceptor is bound to know the hand writing of the drawer, and cannot defend himself from pay ment by a subsequent discovery of the forgery we are of opinion that the present case falls directly within the same principles  We think the defendants were bound to know their own notes, and having once accepted the notes in ques tion as their own, they are concluded by their act of adop tion and cannot be permitted to set up the defence of forgery against the plaintiffs"[8]

§ 414  **What may be accepted by sheriff or other officer—Agent or attorney**—A sheriff, or other officer, authorized by law to receive payment for a purchaser in redemption from a mortgage or execution sale, or to receive payment on an execution or in satisfaction of a judgment cannot receive anything in payment except legal tender money or its equiva lent in other lawful money.  And an acceptance by the officer of a bank check does not constitute payment or save a for feiture[1]  The same rule applies to an acceptance by an agent or attorney  More upon this subject may be found elsewhere in considering the question of a tender of bank checks

§ 415.  **Chattels—Duty of tenderee—Opportunity for inspection—Latent defects.**—On a tender being made of chattels, it is the duty of the party who is to receive them, to then and there

---

[7] Levy v The Bank of the United States 1 Binn 27
[8] Bank of the United States v Bank of Georgia 10 Wheat 333 Gloucester Bank v The Salem Bank 17 Mass 33  See Sec 92

[1] Thorn v San Francisco 4 Cal 127  See Sanderson v Menage 41 Minn 314, s c 43 N W Rep 66 to the contrary
[2] Sylvester v Holasek 86 N W Rep (Minn) 336

make an examination to determine the quality and quantity, and reject or accept them, unless the time and place will not permit, owing to the character of the goods. Thus, diamonds, silk or other articles which require sunlight to determine the color or quality could not with safety be examined by artificial light, and the party receiving may take the goods into his possession and retain them for the purpose of such examination. If the articles are delivered in packages, the tenderee may take them into his hand and open them for the purpose of inspecting them. A consignee is entitled to a reasonable opportunity to examine the packages brought to him, ascertain the quality of the goods before he determines whether to accept them or not, and a reasonable detention of them for that purpose cannot be regarded as an acceptance."[1] If the goods are accepted and they prove to be defective in quality by reason of latent defects, the vendee may rescind the contract and return the goods (although this is not universal), or keep them and sue for damages. This subject belongs more properly to a work upon the law of sales of personal property and the reader is referred to those works for a full discussion.

§ 416. **Acceptance of whole or part of demand after action brought—Effect on right to costs.**—It is a general rule that the rights of the parties in an action at law must be determined as they existed at the time of commencing the action except as far as they are changed thereafter unfavorably to the plaintiff's cause of action either by his own acts or by operation of law. It has always been the practice, and very properly so, to allow all discounts and payments made up to the time of trial but not so as to destroy plaintiff's cause of action and entitle defendant to cost.[1] Costs allowed by statute in such cases are merely incident to the debt and whatever discharges the debt will discharge the costs,[2] and if the plaintiff voluntarily impairs or discharges his cause of action after action brought, by accepting a tender or by

[1] Lyons v. Hill 46 N. H. 49. 2 Parsons on Cont. 325 Percival v. Blake 2 C. & P. 514.

[1] Hudson v. Johnson 1 Wash (Va.) 10 Brooks v. Phoenix Mut. Life Ins. Co. 46 Blatchf. C. Ct. 182.

[2] Bendix v. Annesley 12 Barb. 192 s. c. 27 How. Pr. 181. See McIntyer v. Carrer 2 W. & S. 392.

compromise or release, that fact may be set up in the answer, or supplemental answer if such impairment or discharge occurs after issue joined, and if proven it will relieve the defendant of his liability for costs in whole or in part, as determined under the statute by the judgment subsequently entered. It has been said that the acceptance of a tender after an action has been commenced, should be considered analogous to the case of bringing money into court, in reference to the costs of the action.[3] But there is this distinction, however, and that is that if the amount of the debt, principal and interest, be brought into court without accrued costs, the plaintiff may proceed to judgment upon the admission and recover judgment for the amount paid in, and his entire costs (or, in some commonwealths merely a judgment for costs), while in the other case if the amount of the principal and interest due be accepted after action brought, the plaintiff by such act destroys his right to any costs,[4] even his right to those that had accrued prior to the payment. The reason being that in the former case, the plaintiff, having good cause to sue, ought not to be charged with the costs by reason of any act of the defendant, while in the latter case he voluntarily impairs or destroys his cause of action. If a less sum than the whole amount due be accepted after action brought, and the balance due is less than the sum for which costs are allowed in the court in which the action is pending, the amount of the judgment for the balance, and not the amount sued for, will determine the right of the plaintiff to costs under the statute. Thus, where after action brought to recover $77.45 the defendant paid $55.00 on account and promised to pay the balance at a subsequent time, but failing to pay the balance as promised, he served an answer setting up the agreement. Plaintiff moved to strike out the answer as frivolous and for judgment, which motion was granted and a judgment was entered for the balance due without costs. Held, that the costs followed the debt, and a sum having been accepted which reduced the amount of the judgment below $50.00 the plaintiff was not entitled to costs.[5] So, after a cause is removed from the state court to the Federal Court

[3] Hudson v Johnson, 1 Wash (Va) 10

[4] Bendit v Annesley, 12 Barb

192 s c 27 How Pr 184 Shaut v Southern, 10 Iowa 115

[5] Rice v Childs 28 Hun 303

the acceptance of a tender of a sum which reduces the
amount in controversy to less than $500.00 deprives the
plaintiff of his right to costs.[6] The plaintiff, however, at the
time of accepting the tender may reserve his right to costs.
The acceptance should be upon the condition that it shall in
no way whatever affect his right under the judgment to the
full amount of the costs, he, however, to credit the defendant
upon execution, or satisfy the judgment, to the amount he
had received on account of the debt.[7] An acceptance of a
tender after action brought, of the full amount of the debt
exclusive of costs, will not entitle the defendant to costs
unless the plaintiff attempts to collect the costs to which he
had not reserved the right

[6] Brooks v. Phoenix Mut Life
Ins Co, 16 Blatchf C Ct 182.

[7] Bonner Brick Co. v Canda
Co. 42 N Y Supp 14, s c 18
Misc 681 citing Watson v Depey-
ster 1 Caines, 66, Johnson v
Brannin, 5 Johns 268, Stewart v
Price 2 Paige 604, Warfield v.
Watkins 30 Barb 395, Bendit v

Annesley 12 Barb 192, 27 How.
Pr 184, Keeler v Van Wie, 49
How Pr 97, Rice v Childs, 28
Hun 303 See Eaton v Wells 82
N Y 576 And upon the sub-
ject generally,—Abb Tr Brief, p.
414 Sec 502, Styles v Fuller, 101
N. Y 622, 4 N E 348, Ferris v.
Tannebaum, 15 N Y Sup 295

# CHAPTER XI.

## REFUSAL OF A TENDER

**§ 417. Acts and declarations amounting to a refusal.**—Whenever a creditor is present at the time the debtor is seeking to comply with his contract, and uses unequivocal language in rejecting the tender, such as will convey to the mind of a person of ordinary intelligence the fact that the money or thing tendered will not be accepted under any circumstances, or until certain declared requisites are complied with, there is no occasion for a conflict of opinions as to what constitutes a refusal of the tender, and any subsequent controversy between the parties turns squarely upon the effect of the tender and refusal. There are, however, numerous cases where the courts, in determining the effect of the conduct of the creditor, were called upon to apply those equitable principles and doctrines commonly invoked to prevent one party by his own wrong from gaining a technical and unconscionable advantage over another. Although the courts in rendering the decisions, did not in express terms say that the conduct of the creditor constituted a refusal of the tender, they however, did hold that the conduct of the creditor amounted to a waiver of the formalities of a tender, which harmonize with the general doctrine that the conduct of a creditor in preventing a formal tender amounts to a refusal of it. Any deliberate act on the part of a creditor that prevents his debtor from making a formal tender to him is equivalent to a refusal. Thus, where a creditor avoids a tender by designedly absenting himself from the appointed place,[1] or being at the place he withdraws therefrom for that purpose,[2] or declares that nothing is due him,[3] or makes a demand for a larger sum than that due, in a manner that it amounts to an announcement by the creditor that it will be useless to tender a smaller sum[4]

If a party to whom money is due makes, in advance of the day, a statement that he will not receive it if tendered, and such statement be not withdrawn before the day for payment arrives, or makes any declaration, as when he claims a forfeiture of the contract, or that he will hold the property mortgaged until another debt entirely independent of the mortgage is paid, such statement or declaration amounts to a refusal of the tender[5] So, if he denies his liability,[6] or denies the existence of the contract.[7] If the payment of the purchase price and the delivery of certain stock are to be simultaneous acts, and the purchaser at the time named in the contract offers to take and pay for the stock, a failure to respond to that offer excuses a formal tender, and therefore it is equivalent to a refusal of it. So, where the creditor says, "There have been costs made and you have got to settle with my attorney"[8] Where a party has disabled himself from performing his contract,[9] as by selling the property to another, or making a voluntary assignment in

[1] See Hall v. Whittier, 10 R. I. 530

[2] Gilmore v Holt, 4 Pick 237, Southerland v Smith 7 Cush 391, Stafford v Welch, 59 N. H. 46

[3] Lacy v Wilson, 24 Mich 479

[4] The Norway 11 Jur N. S. 892 13 W R 1085, 13 L. T. N S 50 3 Moore P C, N S 245

[5] Vreeland v Waddell, 67 N. W. Rep (Wis) 51; Root v Johnson, 10 So. Rep (Ala) 293, Hoyt v Sprague, 61 Barb 497, Dorsey v. Barber, Litt Sel Cas 204, s c 12 Am Dec 296

[6] Mattocks v Young, 66 Me 459, Blair v Hamilton, 48 Ind. 32.

[7] Dufty v Patten, 74 Me 300; Koon v Snodgrass, 18 W. Va. 320

[8] Ashbum v Poulter, 35 Conn. 553

[9] Woolner v Hill, 93 N. Y 576, Hawley v Keeler, 53 N Y 114

bankruptcy, the refusal is complete. So, by replying in the negative to an inquiry if anything by way of a tender or performance would be required.[10] Where a person is wrongfully prevented from redeeming certain premises from a mortgage sale, the effect is the same as if he had made a formal tender before the time to redeem had expired and it had been refused.[11]

Where a creditor avoids his debtor for the purpose of evading a tender, or disables himself from performing his part of a contract or makes any declaration, or so conducts himself that it is evident that a formal tender would be an idle ceremony, all the rights that would accrue to the debtor by an express refusal of a tender flow from such acts. The debtor must, however, in order to claim these rights, act in perfect good faith and have in his possession or under his immediate control the requisite amount of money or other property of the kind required with which to perform his part of the agreement, for if it is proven that the debtor was himself in default in this respect, he will acquire no rights, whatever may have been the motive of the creditor in evading or otherwise preventing a tender. When a creditor keeps out of the way of the debtor to prevent a tender, and then commences a suit to recover the amount due him, such suit will be stayed upon payment of the amount due without cost.[12]

§ 418 **What does not constitute a refusal.**—Creditors are frequently called upon abruptly to receive payment of their claims by a debtor, who arbitrarily insists upon an immediate acceptance. In case of a hesitating or ignorant creditor who is apprehensive that he may not receive the last penny due him, or that he may lose some valuable right, controversies often arise as to whether the tender was in fact rejected, and the question becomes complicated. In view of the serious consequences which result from a refusal to accept a tender, such as the loss of a lien, release of a surety, or the destruction of a right to damages which in many instances is equivalent to the loss of the debt, the proof must

10 Wollner v Hill 93 N Y 576, Holmes v Holmes, 9 N Y 529, Smith v Podlon, 87 N Y 594

11 Kling v Chelds 30 Minn 309 12 Noyes v Clark, 32 Am Dec 620, Gilmore v Holt 4 Pick 257

be clear that it was deliberately and intentionally refused.[1]

The effect of a refusal of a tender, like forfeitures, is always regarded with disfavor by the courts, as it is in many instances an unconscionable advantage gained over an honest but over cautious creditor. If a creditor is abruptly and unreasonably urged to a decision, he may lawfully take a reasonable time to consider what are his rights. He is not bound to know at his peril at all times what is due upon his claim, and the authorities are unanimous in holding that the creditor may insist upon a reasonable opportunity to ascertain that fact. Thus, it was held in Michigan in a case where a sum was tendered to a woman engaged in the occupation of pulling weeds in her door yard, which tender she refused because she thought considerable more was due her, that "a woman engaged in her ordinary occupation is not bound at her peril to know at all times what is owing to her, and to be ready to determine forthwith, without opportunity for examination and computation, whether she will accept any particular sum that is tendered to her. She must have reasonable opportunity to satisfy herself what are her rights."[2] It was proven that the sum tendered to her was in fact insufficient in amount, but the foregoing observations of the court are sound in principle and embody the general rule. "'The refusal of a tender must be absolute;' to refuse 'Till I consult my attorney' is not a refusal at law."[3] So, where a note had been left with an attorney for prosecution, and a tender was thereafter made to the creditor who stated that he did not know but some costs had been made, and refused to accept the sum offered until he ascertained that fact, it was held that "the party was entitled to a proper time to inquire without being subjected to the penalty of a refusal. Even had the money been produced, and he in good faith had replied, 'Before I take the money, I must first satisfy myself whether a suit has been commenced. I don't wish to hazard being put to costs by receiving payment.' The witness would have been bound to wait his inquiry; that could not be a refusal."[4] So in a case where a man was infirm and

[1] Moore v Norman, 43 Minn 428, Tuthill v Morris 81 N Y 94

[2] Root v Bradely 49 Mich 27, s c 12 N W Rep 806, s p Post

v Springstead 13 N W Rep (Mich) 370

[3] King v Finch 60 Ind 420

[4] Bakeman v Pooler, 15 Wend 639

nearly blind, was approached in the street after banking
hours, and urged to accept a sum tendered as due upon two
mortgages, and to execute satisfactions, which he refused to
do, stating that he would be at the bank in the morning, the
court said. "In such a case a man who is perfectly well—and
far more a man both sick and nearly blind—cannot be held
to have unreasonably refused a tender, if he merely desires
a reasonable time and a reasonable place to determine his
conduct."[5] Each case must be determined by the court tak
ing into consideration the reasonableness of the time or
place and the circumstances under which the tender was
made, and the conduct of the parties as to their good faith.

§ 419. **Renewal of tender—Subsequent request for the money
—Information as to amount due—Waiver.**—Where the time or
place of a tender is unreasonable, as in the case of a tender
made in the street after banking hours, or where it is known
or ought to be known to the tenderor that the tenderee has
not the note or mortgage at hand from which to make com
putation, or in the case where the tenderee cannot then and
there execute a discharge required by law to be given if one
is insisted upon, and the refusal to receive payment at the
time, is upon any or all of these grounds, the tender must be
renewed at a subsequent reasonable time or place. But
when a reasonable time is requested to enable the tenderee
to ascertain his rights, or that he cannot himself make the
computation, the delay is on his account and for his benefit,
and he must subsequently apply to the tenderor for the
money or thing tendered, otherwise the tenderor would be
kept renewing his tender to no purpose. The request for
time must not be for the purpose of gaining any advantage
by the delay. If the offer to pay was in good faith, and the
tenderor at the time of such offer actually had in his im
mediate possession a sum of money in legal tender, which he
supposed to be sufficient to cover the entire claim, the ten
deree will not be allowed to acquire any advantage. When
the sum tendered proves, on computation, to be insufficient
in amount, the tenderor, on such subsequent application,
must be informed of the exact amount required, and given
an opportunity to produce that sum; it being presumed that

[5] Waldron v Murphy, 40 Mich 668

if objection had been made at the time of the tender, to the
sum tendered as insufficient in amount, the tenderor would
have produced the larger sum. If on investigation of his
rights the tenderee decides not to receive the money, or what
is the same thing, does not make known any decision at all,
the tenderor may elect to stand on his previous tender, or
he may make a fresh tender, taking care to tender enough
to cover the entire claim. The request by the tenderee for
time to ascertain his rights, operates as a waiver of the ob
jection to all formalities and requisites of the tender which
could have been then and there complied with by the ten
deror, had timely objections been made thereto, such as the
actual production of the money, or that the sum produced
was insufficient in amount, or to the kind of money when the
kind was made known to the tenderee. But it must appear
that the tenderor was otherwise ready, willing and able to
make a legal tender.

§ 420. **Stating ground of refusal.**—It is a general rule that
a tenderee in rejecting a tender, if he assigns any reasons
for doing so, is bound to state all his reasons for refusing
the money or the thing tendered  Justice and fair dealing
require this to be done. If one reason be assigned and
not another, it is reasonable to suppose, and the tenderor
would so take it, that but for the objection assigned the
tender would be accepted  and if a tenderee was permitted
to assign a reason not well founded, and afterwards shift
his position to an objection that is well founded, he could
always entrap the tenderor by objecting to the tender on
some ground impossible of performance, or which he knows
the tenderor will not comply with   Almost every objection to
a tender, excepting that it comes too late, is based upon
grounds which can be overcome, and a debtor, who in good
faith is attempting to comply with his contracts according
to his judgment and understanding, should not be allowed to
lose valuable rights, or to be subjected to damages, or any
unnecessary hardships, by reason of the creditor's silence
and superior knowledge of what are his rights: when by a
frank statement on the part of the tenderee of all the reasons for refusing the tender, the tenderor could have then
and there overcome the objections and closed the transaction.
If, by an error in judgment, or in computation, a tenderor

offers to the tenderee a less sum than is actually due, or a less sum than the tenderee thinks is due him, and he puts his refusal upon the ground that more is due, the tenderor can then offer a larger sum, and whether the larger sum is rightfully or wrongfully exacted, his debt is paid. But, if he refuses to increase the amount of his offer, and elects to stand upon his tender of the less sum, he has not been misled in any way, and if his tender is subsequently proven to be insufficient, he has no one but himself to blame for his error. So, an objection at the time a tender is made that the money is not a legal tender, can be overcome by the tenderor procuring and offering money which is a legal tender. So, an objection to the right of the person making the tender to act for the debtor, if made at the time, enables the agent to produce proof of his authority or to notify the debtor to make the tender in person. While if the objection be on some other ground, and the amount, medium &c., could be afterwards questioned, the tenderor would be misled. Requiring a creditor to comply with the foregoing rule, does not impose upon him any hardships, nor take from him any acquired rights; but promotes justice and fair dealing and thereby obviates much needless litigation, which is the true aim of all sound law.

§ 421. **Waiver of formalities—Actual production of money.**— When a tenderee does not state his reasons for rejecting a tender, he waives all the formalities of the tender. Thus, where a debtor actually has the money in a purse or bag in his hand, and is in the act of taking it out, a declaration that it will not be received, excuses the actual production of the money.[1] The tenderor will not be required to perform the idle ceremony of producing and offering the money or other thing contracted to be delivered, if the tender is rejected not upon the ground that the money is not produced but upon

---

[1] Thorn v. Mosher, 20 N. J. Eq. 257; Hanna v. Phillips 1 Grant 253; Dorsey v. Barber Litt. Sel. Cases 204, s. c. 12 Am. Dec. 296; Scott v. Railway Co. 21 Minn. 323; Farnsworth v. Howard, 1 Calder 215; Bellinger v. Kilts 6 Barb. 273; Stone v. Sprague, 20 Barb. 509; Brewer v. Fleming, 51 Pa. St. 102; Wesling v. Noonan 31 Miss. 599; Hazard v. Loring 10 Cush. 267; Lacy v. Wilson 24 Mich. 479; Terell v. Walker 65 N. C. 91; Green v. Barney 36 Pac. Rep. (Cal.) 1026; Walsh v. St. Louis Expo., 101 Mo. 50; Dickinson v. Dutcher, Brayt. (Vt.) 104

some collateral and entirely distinct ground,[2] as where a
debtor goes to the house of his creditor with the required
amount of money in legal tender notes for the purpose of
paying his debt, and the creditor declares that he will take
nothing but gold or silver,[3] or where one party, without
objecting to the tender, declares he will not perform according to the terms of the contract and prescribes other terms,[4]
or that he (the vendor) cannot convey a title to the stock,[5]
or that the time for the payment of the money or the delivery
of the article had expired.[6]  So, where a sum was tendered
as due upon a coupon note, and refused because the principal
note was not paid, it was held that the production of the
money was excused.[7]  In a case where the amount tendered
was not entirely sufficient in amount, and the amount due
was not known to the tenderor, but was within the exclusive
knowledge of the tenderee, who refused to inform the tenderor of the exact amount due and did not demand a larger
sum, it was held that such facts were sufficient to go to the
jury as to the question of a waiver of an actual production
of a greater amount.[8]

It has been held, however, that a bare refusal to receive
the amount due and demanding a larger sum does not dispense with the actual production of the money.[9]  So where
a creditor does not refuse the money, or interpose any objection to it, or intimate that the production of it will not be
required, but merely refers his debtor who has come to pay
his debt to his attorney saying that it is but a step to his
office, the production of the money is not waived.  A bailee
by refusing to deliver grain on the ground that the grain
belongs to another person, waives the formal requisites of a
tender of storage charges and grain receipts required by the
Minnesota statute.[10]  The California code requiring all ob-

2 Koon v. Snodgrass, 18 W. Va.
320.
3 Hanna v. Ratham, 43 Ill. 462.
4 Chamberlain v. Block, 55 Me.
87.
5 Wheeler v. Grice, 10 N. Y.
584.
6 Wood v. Babb, 16 S. C. 427;
Roberts v. Mazeppa Mill Co., 30

Minn. 413; Chamberlain v. Block,
55 Me. 87.
7 Whelan v. Reilly, 61 Mo. 565.
8 Nelson v. Robinson, 17 Minn.
284.
9 Dunham v. Jackson, 6 Wend.
22; Wagenblast v. McKean, 2
Grant's Cas. 393.
10 Wallace v. Elevator Co., 37
Minn. 464.

jections to the "mode" of making an offer which can be then and there obviated, to be made or they will be waived, is held to apply to conditional offers.[11]

**§ 422. Waiver of objection as to time—Right to damages—Refusal without assigning any reason when.**—A party to whom performance is due may waive his right of action for a breach, and accept a performance of the contract; and where a tender is made after a breach of a contract to deliver goods, the objection that it comes too late is waived, if a refusal to accept is based solely on the ground that the goods are unmerchantable.[1] Where a tender is otherwise sufficient, the waiver of the formalities of a tender is a waiver of a strict performance of the contract, even if time is of the essence of the contract.[2] The right to recover damages is also waived.[3] In New York, in a case before the court of appeals, it was held that where a vendor makes default and thereafter tenders performance, the vendee was not bound to accept performance or assign any reason for nonacceptance, and therefore it was immaterial whether he assigned a true or false reason.[4] But the case referred to was brought by the party in default to recover stipulated damages. The time having been extended to accomodate the vendor he defaulted a second time, but later made a tender which was rejected upon the sole ground that waste had been committed, which was not true. It is in general true, that where a party makes default upon any contract, and particularly where time is by express terms of the essence of the contract, or the thing to be delivered is of a fluctuating value, or there is a forfeiture on default, or title or some right vests merely on the afflux of time, and the party comes later and makes an offer of performance, the other may reject it without assigning

---

[11] Koloed v Gordon, 51 Pac. Rep 1115 The objections required to be made under the code are mere rules of evidence and effect merely the right to costs A failure to object to the amount offered does not estop the plaintiff from insisting on the full amount due Colton v Oakland, 70 Pac Rep (Cal) 225

[1] Guild v Bank, 8 Wend 562 s c 24 Am Dec 91, Adams v Helms, 55 Mo 468, Buck v Buck, 18 N Y. 340, Cythe v La Fontain 51 Barb 190

[2] Hanna v Rotekin, 43 Ill 462
[3] Gould v Banks, 8 Wend 562 s c 24 Am. Dec 91
[4] Friess v Rider, 24 N Y 367

any reason. Unlike objections to other requisites of a tender, the objection could not be overcome and the defect remedied by the party tendering performance, however plainly stated the objection may be. In this, the party offering performance can not possibly be in any way imposed upon or misled by the silence of the party refusing, as to his reason for so doing. An objection made at the time of a tender that it comes too late may be of no avail, particularly in contracts concerning reality, if time is not of the essence of the contract and the creditor or party to whom performance is due has neglected to claim a forfeiture of the contract. This, however, is because the old contract is in effect modified as to the time of performance, by the laches of the party who is to receive, and he is estopped from asserting that the contract no longer subsists.

§ 423. **Waiver of the objection as to the amount tendered.—** A tender of a less sum than is due will not invalidate a tender, if no objection be taken to the amount, but the tender is refused upon some collateral ground.[1] A failure to tender a "carriage fee" to which an irrigation company is entitled, will not render invalid a tender of the water rentals, where the refusal to receive the sum tendered is based solely upon the nonpayment of certain illegal royalties.[2] A party succeeding to a vendor's rights, in an action for specific performance by such purchaser of the land, will not be allowed to dispute the sufficiency of a tender by the vendee, when the vendor refused the tender on the ground of an alleged forfeiture of the contract, and not upon the ground that the amount offered was too small.[3] In Iowa, the Supreme Court, in construing a section of the code of that state[4] which provides that any objection to the currency, or instrument, not taken at the time of the tender will be deemed to be waived, held, that the clause "objection to the money" referred to the kind of money and not to the amount, and that by neglecting to object to the tender on account of the sum being

[1] Oakland v Appegath, 67 Cal 86, Graves v McFarlane, 2 Coldw 167 Flanders v Chamberlain, 24 Mich 305, Brewer v Fleming 51 Pa St 102, Gauche v Milbrath, 69 N W Rep (Wis) 999

[2] Northern Colo Irrig Co v. Richard 15 Pac Rep 423

[3] Thayer v Meeker, 86 Ill. 470

[4] Code 1873, Sec 2107

too small did not preclude the tenderee from denying the sufficiency of the tender on that account.[5] Under the rule that a debtor must, at his peril, tender the full amount due, it would seem that, if a tender of a certain sum is refused without assigning any reason and the sum offered is too small, there would be no waiver of the objection to the amount.

§ 424. **Waiver of objection to medium—Checks—Bank bills—An objection cannot be disregarded.**—A tender, to be wholly unobjectionable as far as the medium of payment is concerned, must be made in the legal tender money of the realm, but if a tender be made in bank bills, or any lawful money which is current at par, and no objection be taken at the time of the tender to the medium of payment on the ground that it is not a legal tender, the objection is waived.[1] An agent or clerk authorized to receive payment can waive the objection to the medium of payment, to the same extent as the principal,[2] provided, however, the money tendered be lawful money, that is something recognized by law as money. If a vendee or debtor tender his check on a bank to the vendor or creditor for the amount to be paid, and it is refused, not because it is not lawful money but upon some collateral and distinct reason, as where he, the vendor, had sold the goods to some one else, the objection to the medium of payment is waived.[3] So, where no objection was made to a tender of a bank check on the ground that it was not money, but the objection was to the form of the check, that it was not certified to; and the tenderor was given time to get it certified, which he did, and again presented the check within a short time thereafter, it was held that the tender was good, the right to demand money being waived.[4] But where the objection is to a particular check, and a request is made for an

[5] Chicago etc. R. Co. v. Northwestern U. P. Co. 38 Iowa 377; McWhirter v. Crawford, 72 N. W. Rep. (Io.) 505. Under a former statute (St. 1860, Sec. 1898) a failure to object to the amount was fatal to any subsequent objection on that ground. Hayward v. Munger, 14 Iowa 516; Guengerich v. Smith, 36 Iowa 587; Sheriff v. Hull, 37 Iowa 174.

[1] Polglass v. Oliver, 2 C. & J. 15, S. C. 29 Tyr. 89.

[2] Hoyt v. Byrnes 11 Me. 475.

[3] McGrath v. Gegner 26 N. Rep. 502; Jones v. Authur S. Dowl. Pr. 112; Mitchell v. Vermont Co. 67 N. Y. 280.

[4] Duffy v. O'Donovan 46 N. Y. 223.

other drawn in a particular way, as where the request is that it be drawn payable to one member of a firm instead of the partnership, and the request be not complied with, there is no waiver of the objection to the check. The creditor being under no obligation to receive the check, the debtor must comply with his request,[5] or tender that to which no objection can be legally made.

Mere silence on the part of a creditor as to the medium of payment is generally held to be a waiver of the objection to current bank bills, for the reason that they constitute the common currency of the country, and are, by all classes paid out and received as money, but it was said by the Supreme Court of Ohio, that the reason did not fully apply to the bank check.[6] A specific objection to a tender because it is made with a check, or with bank bills, or any money not a legal tender, cannot be disregarded by the court or jury, even though the real motive for refusing the tender is to get rid of the contract.[7] The rule is well established that a person's legal rights cannot be disregarded no matter what may be the motive for insisting upon such rights.

§ 425. **Waiver of objection that agent did not produce his authority—Waiver of costs—Lien—Objection that more than the sum due is demanded—Defect in deed—Note.—**An objection that the agent making the tender did not produce his authority is waived unless proof of his authority is called for at the time of the tender.[1] Where a creditor makes no claim for costs, and the debtor does not know that costs have been incurred, an objection that the amount tendered is insufficient to pay the debt waives all claims for costs.[2] If a tender is made of a sum to secure the possession of certain property, and the party in possession of it has another lien but claims to retain the property on a different ground and makes no mention of it the lien is waived. This is so held in cases of demands for the possession of chattels where the holder's refusal to deliver them is based upon a ground distinct from that giving a

Murphy v. Gold 3 N. Y. S. 804

[6] Jennings v. Mendanhall 7 Ohio St. 257

[7] DeCamp v. Feay 5 Sar. & Raw. 223

[1] Lampley v. Weed, 27 Ala. 621

[2] Haskell v. Brewer 11 Me. 258

right to a lien." But such will not be the effect of a general refusal, where the omission is merely to make a statement of the particular grounds on which the lien rests.[4] If a vendor, on tendering a deed, demands payment of more than is due him, and no objection is made at the time on account of the amount demanded, and an offer is not made to pay anything, the objection to the tender because of such a demand is waived.[5] Where there is a defect in a deed which is fatal to the tender if objected to on that ground but which can be remedied if pointed out an objection to the tender on that ground is waived unless taken at the time the deed is tendered.[6] On appeal, in order to support the judgment, the court will indulge in the presumption that the objection to the tender was not based on the defect, but upon some untenable ground or no ground at all. However, the objection to the deed is not waived, and the vendor is bound to furnish such a deed as the contract calls for. Where the agreement was to pay in notes, and the creditor was given an opportunity to examine them, and refused the tender on the sole ground that he had changed his mind, it was held that all objection to the notes on account of the place of payment mentioned in them was waived.[7]

**§ 426. No waiver unless the tenderee is present—Sheriff, clerk of court or agent may waive what.—**Where the time and place for payment of money or the delivery of property are fixed by the contract, a valid tender may be made at the appointed time and place in the absence of the tenderee, but it behooves the tenderor to comply strictly with the contract as to the kind and quality of money or thing to be delivered, as there cannot be any waiver of any defect in the tender in this respect, unless the tenderee is present and has an opportunity to object to the tender on that account. Thus where the tenderor is at the appointed place with a check drawn upon his banker for the full amount of his debt, a tender is

[3] Weeks v Goode 6 C B (N S) 367 Judah v Kempt, 2 Johnson's Cas 411 Boidman v Still, 1 Camp 410.

[4] See Everett v Coflin, 6 Wend 603, and Buckley v Handy, 2 Miles 449

[5] Hannan v McNickle 83 Cal 122

[6] Carman v Pultz 21 N Y 547 See Gilbert v Mosier 11 Iowa 498 which is based on a statute

[7] Sleslnder v Bresler 68 N W Rep (Mich) 128

not made,[1] for there is no presumption, in such cases, that the tenderee, if present, would accept the check in lieu of the actual money. The same is true if the money is not a legal tender. So, a vendor in making a tender in the absence of the vendee, must, at his peril, designate and set apart for the vendee a sufficient quantity of the kind of articles called for by the contract, and if there is any default in this respect, the vendee will not be estopped from asserting that a tender was not made. Even in those cases where the tenderee is present, if the tenderor does not produce and exhibit the money, or state the kind of money he has with him in his purse or bag, or make known the kind of property he has at hand to deliver, the tenderee may show that the money was not a legal tender, or that the property was not the kind specified in the contract. There can be no estoppel without knowledge of the defects.[2]

If a tender is made to a sheriff, clerk of the court or other officer authorized by law to receive the money, by a person seeking to redeem from a mortgage or execution sale, and the tender is refused upon any ground, the creditor may nevertheless urge the objection that the alleged tender was made by offering a check for the amount due. The officer is not the agent of either party, and his acts do not estop the creditor from urging the objection that the medium offered was insufficient. The same rule applies to a tender of a check to an agent, as neither an officer nor an agent is authorized to receive a check in payment, and a failure to object to a check which the creditor has a right to reject if received by the officer or agent, cannot possibly create a waiver.

§ 427. **Changing ground of objections** — A creditor who has placed his objection to the sufficiency of a tender upon a certain ground is precluded from afterwards placing his refusal upon another and different ground.[1] If a creditor

[1] Sloan v. Petrie 16 Ill. 262.
[2] Waldron v. Murphy 40 Mich. 668.
[1] Hill v. Carter 59 N. W. Rep. 413; Lathrop v. O'Brien 37 Minn. 175 s. c. 58 N. W. Rep. 987; Railway Co. v. McCarthy, 96 U. S. 258; Monahan v. Moore 9 Mich.

9 s. c. 77 Am. Dec. 468; Wallace v. Elevator Co., 37 Minn. 464; Wyckoff v. Anthony 90 N. Y. 442; Stokes v. Recknagle 6 Jones and S. 368; Harriman v. Meyer 45 Ark. 37; Richardson v. Jackson 8 M. & W. 298 s. c. 9 D. P. C. 715; Cole v. Blake, Peck's N. P. 179,

was permitted to shift his objection to a tender from one ground to another, on discovering that the one specified was untenable, a debtor would never know, with any certainty, the real objection. The reason stated would often serve as a cover to conceal the real objection. Whatever may be the intention of the party making the objection, he must, in all subsequent controversies, be confined to the ground stated. But in applying the above rule, it is important to distinguish between those objections going to the formalities of a tender—which are merely technical—and other objections which if made known may be readily overcome at the time,—and those objections pertaining to the readiness and ability of the tenderor to perform his part of the contract. The latter are never waived. The rule confining the tenderee to the specific objection made by him, is based upon the ground that by his declaration he interrupted the tenderor and prevented him from proceeding further and complying with the other formalities, or rendered a further tender of performance a vain and useless ceremony

§ 428.  **Extent of the waiver.**—The formal requisites of a tender may be waived, but in order to establish a waiver, there must be an existing capacity to perform[1] The cardinal principle of a tender is that it is a substantial performance, which cannot be true if the tenderor is not ready at the time of his offer with the money or thing to be delivered. It follows, even though a tender has been rejected upon some ground which is not well taken, that the tenderee is not precluded from afterwards raising the objection that the tenderor was not ready and able to perform  This, although an apparent exception to the rule stated in the preceding sections, is not in reality an exception at all  By being unable to deliver the money or thing specified at the time of his offer, the tenderor is in default and a tender is not in fact made  When the amount offered in payment is insufficient and no objection

Ricketts v Buckstaff, 90 N W Rep (Neb) 915  This seems to be much the same as that which obtains in the action of claim and delivery under the code practice or trover at common law, where a defendant is not permitted to set up any reason for not delivering the property, other than the one assigned by him at the time of the demand  Holbrook v White 24 Wend 169

[1] Eddy v Davis, 40 Hun 637. s e 22 N E Rep 362

is made to the offer on that account, there is no waiver unless the party making the tender has other money in his possession, either at hand or at a place from where he may fetch it before the time for payment expires, with which he could have overcome the objection, if made, by producing the required amount. Having a part, but being unable to produce the residue, is as fatal to a tender as is an inability to produce the whole. To make a waiver complete, where no objection is taken to the offer as insufficient in amount, the tenderor must show, not only that the tenderee did not object to the tender on that ground, but that he had the amount offered at hand within easy reach. If he had the money elsewhere the refusal was of a verbal offer merely and not of a tender. But it is not necessary in order to establish a waiver of the objection that the sum tendered is too small, to show that the balance between the amount tendered and the amount actually due was at hand. All that is necessary is to show that he then had other money with which to supply the deficiency had any objection been made to the offer on that account, and could have produced it within the time limited for payment. The presumption is that the tenderor would have secured such funds and renewed the tender within the time. That the tenderor can borrow the residue is not sufficient.

It is in general true that if a vendor or debtor produce and offer to the vendee or creditor that which is not called for by the contract, as where a kind of goods different from that contracted for is produced and offered in satisfaction of a contract of sale and delivery, or something that is not money (excepting bank checks) is offered in satisfaction of a debt, the vendee or creditor, as the case may be, is not bound to state his objections, and the mere fact that he mentions certain ground of objection to the offer is not of itself a waiver of the other grounds not mentioned. Thus where an offer is made of an accepted order in payment of an amount agreed to be paid in cash the objection that cash was not tendered is not waived by mentioning other objections, and failing to object to it on the ground that an order instead of cash was tendered.[2] Where the contract is "to make a warranty deed free and clear of all incumbrances," an agreement

2 Hall's Appeal 67 Conn 585 s c 35 Atl 524

to accept a deed without making any objection to an incumbrance is not a waiver of the defect of want of title[1] So, the failure of a purchaser to object to a tender of goods on the account of a lien for storage thereon is not a waiver of that objection.[1] In all such cases, to constitute a waiver it must be shown that the party had knowledge of the incumbrance or liens and expressly waived the objection[5]

§ 429. **Same subject.**—By neglecting to require a person claiming to act for another to prove his authority, and rejecting the tender upon any other ground, does not prevent the tenderee from showing that the offer was made by a stranger, and for that reason there was no tender. The tenderee may also show, notwithstanding he rejected the offer, that it was not in good faith, and that the tenderor did not intend to deliver the money or thing offered had he attempted to take it So, where a tenderee neglects to object to the terms of a deed or other instrument on the ground that it does not conform to the contracts, as he was required to do by an early Iowa statute,[1] or to be precluded from afterwards objecting to the sufficiency of the tender, the estoppel only goes to the extent of preventing a forfeiture of the contract and saves the tenderor from subsequent damages and costs, but it does not excuse the tenderor from furnishing another deed or instrument in terms as required by the contract. So, a tender of a less amount than is due, if not objected to on that ground, relieves the debtor from liability for further interest and costs, but it does not prevent the plaintiff from recovering whatever principal sum may be found due[2] The operation and extent of a waiver of the objection that the tender comes too late, is limited to those cases where the party who made the waiver seeks to hold the other liable for a breach of the contract and is not extended so as to give a tenderor who is grossly in default in point of time, an action for a penalty[3]

§ 430. **Consequences of a refusal.**—At common law, a wilful and unjustifiable refusal to accept a lawful tender when

[1] Porter v Noyes, 2 Green 22 s c 11 Am Dec 31

[4] Dunham v Pattee 1 E D Smith 500

[5] Porter v Noyes, 2 Green 22,

Dunham v Pattee, 1 E D Smith 500

[1] Rev St. 1860 Sec 1818

[2] Sheriff v Hall 37 Iowa 174

[3] Priess v Reider, 21 N Y 367

made on the law day, discharges a lien given to secure the payment of the debt. In New York, Michigan, Minnesota, and perhaps some other states, the common law rule is modified as to time, so that an unjustifiable refusal of a valid tender, made at any time after default and before a foreclosure, has the same effect. In no case does the refusal of a tender discharge the debt or duty, but only the damages which would accrue by reason of the non payment of the one or the non performance of the other[1] A refusal of a tender, however wanton and vexatious, is not an illegal act from which positive and consequential damages flow, and to sue for a debt previously tendered is not actionable.[2] The question of the good faith of a party refusing a tender, where the refusal is unqualified, is immaterial.[3] Where a conductor on a street railway declined to receive an old coin, because he, in good faith believed it to be counterfeit, it was held no excuse for relieving the railroad company from liability for damages for the wrongful expulsion of the passenger[4] The subject of the consequences of a refusal of a tender is considered more fully in a preceding chapter[5]

---

[1] Town v Trow 24 Pick 168, 9 Bac Abr Tender (I)

[2] Kramer v Stock 10 Watts 115 See Hill v Pettit 66 S W Rep (Ky) 188.

[3] Campbell v Seeley, 13 Mo App 23

[4] Atlanta St Ry Co v Keeny, 33 L R A (Ga) 824

[5] Ch IX

# CHAPTER XII.

## SUBSEQUENT DEMAND.

§ 431.  **Manner of making—Precise sum—Greater sum—Less sum—Principal—On what account—Two demands—Sum legally due —** A subsequent demand for a sum tendered must be made upon the debtor personally, so that he may have an opportunity of complying with the request  Sending a letter demanding the thing tendered is insufficient.  In an English case, Ld. C. J. Abbott said· "I have a very strong opinion against considering a letter written by plaintiff's attorney, demanding the sum tendered, as evidence of a demand to support plaintiff's issue  I think that at the time of the demand, the defendant should have an opportunity of paying the money demanded."[1] In relation to a subsequent demand, made for the purpose of avoiding a tender, the rules are very strict.[2] The authorities are unanimous in holding, that a demand, to avoid a tender, must be of the precise sum tendered; and, if a larger sum is demanded, the debtor may disregard it.[3] Unless this was required, the tender would be avoided by a refusal to pay a sum which the debtor had not admitted to be due by his tender. Lord Ellenborough said "A creditor, to do away with the effect of a tender, must demand only the sum before tendered, or the debtor would be put to the necessity of repeated tenders, and would thus be harassed to no sort of purpose."[4] Where a plaintiff replied a previous demand of the sum tendered, on which the defendant took issue, proof of a demand of a larger sum was held not to support the issue, a demand of the precise sum must be proved.[5] To the rule that the precise sum tendered must be demanded, there is an exception. A creditor is not required to demand more than is due, and if more is tendered than is due, he may demand the sum due.[6] Although the general rule is, that the demand must be for the exact sum tendered, yet the creditor need not, necessarily, state the amount in exact figures. Any language may be used, which will inform the debtor, and leave no doubt in his mind as to the particular sum requested. Thus, if a creditor should say, "I am come to get the money which you tendered to me yesterday," it would be sufficient. Cases very frequently arise, where the creditor does not know of his own knowledge the exact sum tendered, as where the tender is made to an agent, or where the offer is made to a sheriff or other officer in attempting to redeem from a mortgage or execution sale. In which case it would be sufficient to say, "I am come for the redemption money which you tendered to the sheriff," specifying the transaction. Such language, where there is but one transaction of the kind between the parties, or where the transaction is designated, would leave no doubt in the mind

[1] Edwards v. Yeats Ry. & Mood 360, criticising Hayward v. Hague, 4 Esp Rep 93

[2] Town v Trow, 24 Pick 168

[3] Thetford v. Hubbard, 22 Vt 440, Mahan v Waters 60 Mo App 167,

[4] Spybey v Hide, 1 Campb 181

[5] Rivers v Griffith, 5 B & A 630

[6] Dean v Jones 4 B & A 517, s c 1 N & M 393

of the creditor as to the exact sum wanted. The debtor is bound to know what sum he had tendered. It is always a fact particularly within his knowledge, and is presumed so, even where he sends an agent to make the tender. If the tender has the effect of stopping the running of interest, the demand must be for the principal alone.[7]

A person making a tender must state specifically on what account it is made,[8] and, to render a demand effectual the same information is required on the part of the creditor. He must state clearly, if there is more than one sum due, which sum he is demanding."[9] A creditor may make a demand for the amount tendered on two or more demands, but he should take pains to explain at the time how the amount demanded is made up. Such a demand is merely a simultaneous demand of the several debts. If a debtor tenders a sum in payment of two or more distinct claims, which is refused because it is considered insufficient in amount to cover all the claims, and the amount of one of the claims being agreed, the creditor may demand a sum sufficient to cover that claim, the amount of which is not in dispute specifying the claim, and the debtor would have no right to withhold that amount. Nor, has he a right to withhold the whole amount tendered when demanded, if that much be actually due. The fact that a creditor claims more than the debtor thinks is due, can furnish no excuse for withholding the amount he thinks is due. Nor can the withholding of the amount due or admitted to be due be lawfully used as a club to compel a creditor to relinquish what the debtor may consider an exorbitant claim. The debtor always finds that such excuse for not delivering the sum demanded is wholly disregarded on his pleading a tender in an action to recover the amount claimed. In which case he must pay the amount tendered into court for the use of the plaintiff, or suffer a judgment to go against him for the amount admitted to be due by his plea, with interest and costs.

The demand must be for the sum legally due. Thus, where a tender had been made and refused and an action thereafter

7 Mahan v. Waters, 60 Mo. 167.  9 Cabeen v. Winston Clo. Lhz
8 Coore v. Callaway, 1 Esp. Cas  200
115. Warner v. Harding, Latch
70.

commenced to recover the amount due, which was dismissed, it was held by Lord Kenyon that a demand for the amount for which the action was brought and half of the costs of the suit, which the defendant had agreed to pay, was not a proper demand for the reason that the agreement to pay the costs was *nudum pactum*.[10] Where, in the meantime the statute of limitations has run against one of two or more sums included in a tender, the demand must be for the amount of the claim constituting a valid demand.

§ 432   Same subject—May negative implied admission that no more is due—Renewing tender unnecessary when —By saying that the demand must be *modo et forma*, it is impliedly asserted that the money or thing tendered, if paid on a subsequent demand, must be received as tendered. But to this there is the limitation that the creditor may negative any implied admission that no more is due. In a case where the whole debt, being £11 6s., the debtor tendered £5 1s. and the creditor demanded the whole amount instead of the amount tendered; Lord Ellenborough said, if the plaintiff had demanded the smaller sum, this would have been no admission of that being all that was due to him. He might have said 'I take so much, and will bring an action for the residue.' In this way the plaintiff would not have been considered as abandoning any part of his right."[1] Where a creditor claims a larger sum than that tendered, and the demand is for the larger sum the debtor is under no obligation to make a fresh tender of the sum previously offered. As it had been once refused, and the creditor then demanding the whole of the demand originally claimed to be due him, the debtor would have no reason to believe that the sum formally tendered would be accepted.[2]

§ 433.   Same subject—Tendering a release—Deed, note, mortgage, &c —Limitations upon the rule —Where the law requires a satisfaction of a lien to be given on payment of the debt, such satisfaction must be offered or tendered at the time of making a subsequent demand. The same principle applies where any instrument, as a deed, bond, note or mortgage is

[10] Cogle v. Callaway, 1 Esp Rep 115

[1] Spybey v Hide, 1 Camp 181
[2] Spybey v Hide, 1 Camph 181

contracted to be delivered on payment of a sum. A demand
for a sum tendered is ineffectual unless accompanied by a
proffer of the instrument. If the sum tendered was in pay
ment of a note, on a subsequent demand, where the note has
been lost or destroyed, the holder must, at the time of the de
mand, tender indemnity as required by the law merchant in
case of lost or destroyed bills and notes. So, if chattels are
pledged, or collaterals of any kind are taken as security, the
demand must be accompanied by an offer to surrender the
pledge. If the chattels be bulky or ponderous, a symbolical
delivery may be made, as the surrender of warehouse receipts,
etc. The question whether a release or surrender of the secur
ity, or the note, or other instrument could or could not have
been required as a condition to the tenderee receiving the
money at the time of the tender, is not to be taken into consid
eration in connection with the subsequent demand. If the
full amount was actually tendered, the creditor violated his
contract by refusing the money, and on a demand, being the
moving party, he must offer to surrender to his debtor that
which he is entitled to receive on payment  The offer to
surrender the security, however, may be upon the condition
of first receiving payment  The general rule that the note
or other instrument to be delivered, or a satisfaction of the
lien, or the property pledged, must be offered or tendered
at the time of making a subsequent demand, applies to cases
where the full amount admitted to be due is tendered  If a
less sum than is admitted to be due is tendered, the creditor
has an undoubted right to that sum, and a right also to hold
the note and any security given, to secure the payment of the
residue  In cases of real estate mortgages, by the payment
of the sum tendered on demand, when the creditor insists on
holding the security to ensure the payment of any balance
claimed to be due, the debtor does not hazard anything, but
places himself in a better position than he would be in, if the
effect of his tender is destroyed by a demand and refusal
If he complies with the demand, and the sum paid over is
in fact sufficient to extinguish the debt, he may then plead
payment to defeat a foreclosure, or, either as a plaintiff or de
fendant, he may plead it as a foundation of a cause of action
in equity for affirmative relief. The debtor also avoids pay
ment of interest and damages on the sum paid, and, if suc
cessful, subjects the creditor to the payment of costs; and

in some states to a statutory penalty for refusing to execute
the release. But in reference to chattels that are pledged,
the benefits of a payment on a subsequent demand, and the
pledgee retaining the property, are not so apparent. The
effect of a refusal to comply with the demands, as to interest
and damages, is the same. Yet, in many cases, the debtor
had better subject himself to the possible liability for inter
est and damages, in case the tender should prove to be insufficient in amount, and adhere to his conditional tender, than
to hazard a loss of both his property and money by trusting
to the solvency of the creditor. In any case where the law
requires a release to be executed, or property to be surrendered, it is only upon a tender of full payment.

§ 434. **Same subject—Where instrument is not at hand—
Waiver—Renewal of tender necessary when—Prompt action on
option—Unnecessary to apply to agent—Good faith.**—Where a
creditor notifies his debtor generally that he is ready to
receive the money and execute the release, deed, or other
instrument, or surrender the pledge or collateral security,
and the debtor does not then object to the demand on the
ground that the article engaged to be surrendered is not at
hand, but promises to pay later, for the reason that the sum
tendered is not in his immediate possession, or for any other
reason, he waives the defect in the demand, and he must,
at his peril, make another tender. Where the demand is
made by an agent and such promise is given, he may produce
and deliver the money or thing to the agent, if the agent's
authority be continued for that purpose, but if the agent's
authority had ceased in the meantime, or he is unable to
find the agent, the debtor must, within a reasonable time,
seek          editor and make the payment, as the former tender i          'ed by the notice and promise to pay. In such
cases          a debtor is given an option to pay, and he takes
no exception to the place or manner of making the demand,
but promises to pay the sum previously tendered, he must
act promptly on the option, and it is no excuse that he cannot
find the agent. In such case he must be even more diligent
in enquiring for and seeking the creditor personally, than he
is required to be in making the tender in the first instance.
A creditor, who has signified a willingness to accept a sum
previously tendered, is presumed to be in readiness to receive

it within a reasonable time, or until the option is otherwise withdrawn within such time; while on the other hand, an agent, and more especially attorneys at law, are presumed to have other duties to perform besides holding themselves in readiness and always accessible to receive a particular debt. Although a demand by an agent who exhibits his authority on request, will, if not complied with, avoid the tender, yet the debtor, on a subsequent promise to pay the amount tendered, is not bound to apply to the agent in the first instance, but a failure to apply to him for the purpose of ascertaining the whereabouts of the creditor, or to ascertain if his authority to receive the money still exists when the creditor cannot be found by the debtor, would be evidence of an abandonment of his option. A demand must be in good faith, and if it can be shown that the creditor did not intend to take the money or thing tendered if produced, the demand will not avoid the tender.

§ 435. **By whom made.**—A tender may be made to an agent authorized to receive the money. So a subsequent demand for a sum tendered may be made by an agent or by anyone having authority to receive payment, and such demand and refusal will do away with the effect of a tender as fully as if made by the creditor in person. But it must appear that the person making the demand was properly authorized to receive the money[1] In an early case, where it appeared that a clerk to an attorney had been sent to demand the money, Lord Kenyon said, that the statement of the clerk that he had been sent by his master to demand the money was not a sufficient evidence of authority to receive, and therefore the debtor was justified in refusing to pay the money[2] Where the demand is made by a person other than the creditor, the debtor may refuse to comply with the request until proper authority to receive payment be shown. The debtor has a right to require absolute proof of the authority of the person making the demand to receive payment. If the thing tendered be personal property, refusing to deliver the article without proof of the authority of the person demanding it, does not constitute conversion. The rule in this respect is

1 Coore v Callaway, 1 Esp 115    Coles v Bell, 1 Campb 478 N
2 Coore v Callaway, 1 Esp 115.    See Pimm v Grevil, 6 Esp 95

not distinguishable from that applicable to demands consid
ered in actions of trover, where the demand for the thing is
not made by the owner, but by another person on his account
In such cases, proof that the defendant refused to deliver the
article on the ground that he does not know to whom it be
longs, and therefore retains it until that is ascertained; or
that the person who applies is not properly empowered to
receive it, or until he is satisfied by what authority he ap
plies, is not evidence of conversion[1] The rule is the same,
and the reason supporting it, as that applicable to the pay
ment of the money in the first instance  A debtor who pays
money or delivers property to a third person on a verbal
assurance by such person that he has authority from the
owner, does so at his peril  Although a payment to such
person, when the authority actually exists, would be a legal
compliance with the demand  The burden of proving pay
ment to one duly authorized by the creditor to receive it,
falls upon the debtor whenever the owner does not receive
the money or thing demanded  and a dispute arises   to
the authority of the person who claimed to represent the
creditor  Payment to a third person multiplies the debtor's
proof, and he may refuse to pay to anyone coming under any
circumstances, except the creditor  But the refusal must
be upon the ground that he will pay the creditor personally
This would not constitute a refusal to comply with the de
mand  But in such case the debtor must be diligent in seek
ing the creditor and making payment  If the debtor does not
object to paying to an agent  but insists upon proof of his au
thority to receive payment, if it be verbal merely  it would
seem that he may insist upon written or verbal assurances
from the creditor that the person applying for the money or
thing tendered represents him  When a creditor sends a
third person, under such circumstances to make the demand,
the debtor is not bound to make any inquiries or hunt up
evidence of the agent's authority.  If the person demanding
the thing tendered produces written authority, the debtor
may take a reasonable time to satisfy himself that the writ
ing is genuine  When, on demand, objection is not then made
by the debtor to the right of the person making it to receive
payment, or he is not requested to produce or prove his

Solomons v  Dawes  1 Esp  83

authority, objection cannot afterwards be made that the agent did not produce proof of his authority. In such case if the agent had either written or verbal authority, the demand destroys the effect of the tender

If the person who made the demand was not at the time authorized to make it, the demand is ineffectual, even though the creditor may seek to ratify the act. A demand made by a stranger has no effect, and it makes no difference whether the debtor questioned his authority, or refused to pay upon some other ground. Where a tender was made to an attorney with whom a claim had been lodged for collection, and was of a less sum than the amount claimed, on a subsequent demand by the attorney for the amount tendered, he must, on request, produce or prove his authority to accept the less sum, in case the demand be made by way of a compromise. The general authority of an attorney does not extend to compromising claims for his client. Where a release or discharge is required to be given, the demand must be made by some one authorized to give the debtor a discharge.[1] If the creditor, after a tender, sells his demand, makes an assignment in insolvency, or dies, the demand must be made by the transferee, assignee or personal representative, and evidence of the authority of the person making the demand, to receive payment, must be furnished if requested by the debtor.

§ 436 On whom made—Debtor—Joint debtor—Surety—Guardian—When of minor—Stranger—Personal representative—Assignee—Depositary.—Where a person has the power to appoint an agent, the tender may be made by an agent appointed for that purpose; but a demand for a sum tendered must be made on the principal and not on the agent. In a case which arose in Missouri, where the tender had been made by an attorney and a subsequent demand made on him for the amount tendered, the court in considering the case said "But there is another objection, the demand, if any, was made of the attorney and not of the debtor. A tender may be made by an agent, or to an agent where he is authorized to receive the money, but a demand ought to be made personally of the debtor, in order that he may have an opportunity

[1] Code v Bell, 1 Camp 178 N

for paying the money demanded." [1]  An agent's power to act is limited by the instructions and authority delegated to him by his principal  If his instructions be merely to go to the creditor and offer to pay him a sum of money, on doing so and it is refused, the agent has then done all that he was employed to do.  An application by the creditor to the agent would, in nearly every case, result in a declaration being made by the agent that he had nothing more to do with it  Justice and common sense would require that a creditor, who in good faith thinking more was due or for other reasons, had refused a sum tendered, should not be required to perform an idle ceremony  by applying to the agent whose authority to act might prove to have ceased with the offer  He is not  therefore, the agent or representative of the debtor for the purpose of responding to a demand for the money which he may have tendered  So in Massachusetts it was held that the demand must be made upon the debtor and not upon anyone else  It is frequently the case that the money, after a tender and refusal, is deposited with a third person or in a bank, and notice given of the deposit.  This does not relieve the debtor on a demand  from the necessity of producing the money  The creditor is not bound to make a demand on the depositary  It has been held that where the tenderor did not ask for delay till he could produce the money 'but relied upon his exemption from such demand and the duty of the plaintiff to call upon the depositary of the money,' that he erred 'and was guilty of a refusal which entitled the plaintiff to judgment '

Where a tender is made by two on a joint contract  a subsequent application to one of them is sufficient to support a replication alleging a demand on both defendants [4]  The same rule would obtain in case of a tender by the obligors on a joint and several obligation  A demand upon one of a firm would be good  So a demand on the president or other managing officer of a bank or corporation would be sufficient  Where the debtor resides in another state or country, the demand must be made on him personally, even though the tender was made within the state and by an agent  A tender

[1] Berthold v Reyburn 37 Mo 586

[2] Town v Trow, 24 Pick 168

[3] Town v Trow 24 Pick 168

[4] Pearse v Bowles 1 Stark 323,

9 Bac Abr Tender (H)

by a surety, and a refusal, releases him, and any demand thereafter must be of the principal debtor, for, the surety being released by the refusal, is under no obligation to keep the tender good. A demand must be made upon the guardian of a minor, spendthrift, or insane person, and not upon the ward. If the minor has no guardian, the demand should be of him if he had authority to make the tender. Where a tender is made by the next of kin, or by anyone acting under cloak of legal authority for a minor, the demand must be of the one making the tender. Where a tender is made by a stranger on behalf of an idiot, a subsequent demand for the sum tendered must be made on the stranger. Where a debtor, after a tender, dies or becomes insane, the demand must be made upon the personal representatives or guardian as the case may be. The personal representatives or guardians, in such cases, having no authority to respond to a demand for a sum tendered by the debtor, the creditor is bound to wait until an order authorizing the payment is obtained of the court having jurisdiction. If, after a tender, the debtor makes an assignment in bankruptcy, or is adjudged a bankrupt, a demand on the assignee, receiver or trustee for the sum tendered will be of no avail. By the deed of assignment or order of adjudication, all the debtor's property becomes subject to claim of all the creditors, and by that fact the tender is abandoned. But if it is a benefit to the estate, and the creditor is willing to await the making of an order allowing the payment, such order will ordinarily be made.

Where there are local statutes providing for a deposit of money, which has been tendered and refused, in a bank or other depository, the demand may be on the depositary designated by the statute. In the case of personal property which has been tendered and refused, or which has been tendered in the absence of the tenderee, if the thing tendered has been deposited in a warehouse or other place for safe keeping, and notice given of the place of storage, the demand should be made of the person in charge of the property. By the tender the title in the thing passed to the tenderee, and it is his duty to demand and recover his property of him in whose possession it then is. The general rule as to money demands is, without exceptions, that the demand must be on the persons upon whom the law imposes the obligation of keeping the tender good.

§ 437.  **Time when demand may be made.**—A debtor, where the tender must be kept good, must always thereafter be ready to pay, and, if, at any time before the statute of limitation has run against the claim, he is requested to pay and neglects or refuses to do so, that avoids all tenders made before the request.[1]  The demand may be made at any hour of the day or night, but if made at an unreasonable hour, the debtor may take such reasonable time in which to comply as the nature of the business, the circumstances and situation of the parties will warrant   If an immediate compliance with a demand could be required of a debtor, an obdurate and unscrupulous creditor would have it in his power to avoid any tender   A creditor who has refused a tender has no right to impose any unnecessary burden or hardship upon the debtor in consequence of his own wrong in not receiving payment of his claim.  If the demand be made at an unreasonable hour  and an immediate compliance is insisted upon, the debtor may refuse to comply at that time, and offer to pay it at another and reasonable time, such refusal will not avoid the tender   A demand on a subsequent day, after sunset, has been held to be an unreasonable hour.[2]   A demand for the sum due, made prior to a tender, has no effect. A replication that the sum tendered was part of a larger sum due  which larger sum was demanded before the tender was held bad.[3]

§ 438.  **Place where demand may be made.**—It is elsewhere shown that the demand must be made upon the debtor personally  and it follows as a logical sequence that the demand may be made upon the debtor wherever he may be found.  As regards the place where the demand should be made, the case is not very different in principle from that of a tender  where no time or place for payment is fixed by the contract   The demand may be made anywhere and at any time, when the parties are together  and if the creditor desires to make a demand, he must find the debtor for that purpose   The debtor cannot restrict the other party to a particular time

1 Vose v  McGuire, 26 Mo App 152

2 Tucker v  Buffum 16 Pick  46

3 Brandon v  Newington, 3 Q B  915

or place for making a demand, any more than a creditor can appoint a time and place for making a tender, where no time or place is fixed by their agreement.[1] Although the demand may be made at any place, it does not necessarily follow that the debtor must produce and deliver the thing tendered in stanter. He is not required to keep the money or thing tendered on his person, or in his immediate possession, he may keep it at his residence, or place of business, or, if a large sum, he may make a special deposit of it in a bank, or place it in a safety deposit vault, or other place for safe keeping. If the demand be made in the public highway or at any other place, at a distance from the place where the money or other article is kept, the debtor is entitled to have a reasonable time to produce and deliver it where the demand was made, or he may insist upon accompanying the creditor to the place of deposit if at a place reasonably near, or if the money or property was payable at a particular place, he may insist on accompanying the creditor to that place and there making the delivery, unless the demand be made at the place where the money or thing tendered is kept, or the creditor offers to accompany the debtor to the place of deposit, otherwise a debtor would be bound to deliver money or property at a place other than that stipulated in the contract.

§ 439. **Opportunity to comply.**—Where a creditor prevents performance of a contract by refusing to accept the money or the thing tendered, and afterwards demands it at any time or place, the debtor is entitled to a reasonable opportunity to comply with the demand.[1] When money is left with a depositary and the demand be made after business hours he may take until the opening of business on the next secular day to comply. A demand made at the debtor's house some six or seven miles from the bank where the money had been deposited, by a solicitor who refused to wait while the debtor would go and get the money, was held insufficient and did not entitle the plaintiff to recover interest.[2] A creditor would not be bound to wait an unreasonable time for the debtor to comply, as where the demand is made at one place and the money is at a great distance from the place of pay-

---

[1] Town v Trow, 24 Pick. 168.
[2] Town v Trow, 24 Pick. 168.
[1] Stafford v Welch, 59 N H
[1] Gibb v Stead, 8 B. & C. 528.
[2] Sharp v Todd, 38 N J Eq.
321.

ment. If a debtor cannot leave his employment for any rea
son, until a certain hour, or is at work on something which
might be damaged if left uncompleted, he may insist on
making payment at a subsequent reasonable time. By failing
to object at the time of the demand, to the time or place, the
debtor waives all defects, and cannot afterwards be heard
to say that the time or place was unreasonable. On a subsequent demand, if the debtor does not then ask for time
to produce the money on the spot, or insist on accompanying
the creditor to the place of deposit or place of payment, but
promises to pay at a subsequent time, which is expressly
or tacitly assented to, he must, at his peril, seek the creditor
and make another tender within the time limited. The
debtor cannot compel the creditor to attend at a subsequent
time and at a different place to receive the money.

When the notice is given by the creditor generally, that
he will receive the money, no time being mentioned, and the
right to have time to fetch it from the place of deposit for
the purpose of an immediate compliance with the request, is
not insisted upon, the debtor must use due diligence in making another tender to the creditor wherever he may be
found, for the option may be withdrawn after the lapse of a
reasonable time. What would constitute a reasonable time,
in such case, would depend upon the time of day the demand
was made, the distance to the place of deposit, if the money
had been deposited anywhere for safe keeping, and the
whereabouts of the debtor at the time of the demand.

§ 440. **Demand how complied with—Kind of money—Excuse
for non-compliance—Chattels in warehouse—Unnecessary to comply when.**—If gold or silver coin or their equivalent is used
in making the tender, on a subsequent demand, if the tenderor produced and offered to the creditor an equal sum in
bank notes or other money which could have been objected
to at the time of the tender, the creditor may reject the
money. If bank notes or other moneys subject to objections
was tendered, any legal tender money may be produced on
the demand, and no objection will lie to the money produced.
As a general rule, it is a sufficient compliance with a demand
to offer the same money or money having the same legal
tender qualities as that tendered. The demand is, in effect,

32

an offer to accept the kind of money previously offered. Where the debtor, on a subsequent demand, produces an equivalent amount in any kind of money, which is received without objection, it then becomes immaterial whether the money, as to kind, was or was not kept according to the ordinary rules of keeping a tender good. It would seem, however, that a person does not waive those facts of which he had no knowledge, and subsequently, on learning that the tender had not been kept good, he would be entitled to recover interest and damages accruing between the time of the tender and the demand, which in many cases would amount to considerable. The tenderor must not use the money for his own benefit and if he conceals that fact from the tenderee at the time of the demand he must make it good

It is not a sufficient reason for the refusal, that the money when demanded had depreciated and ceased to be a circulating medium, nor that it was lodged with the clerk of the court in a former suit[1] Nor is it any defence to show that the money tendered had been deposited with a third person, and that the person making the demand was told he could get the money by applying to the depositary[2] Where chattels which have been tendered, are stored in a warehouse or left in the care of a third person, it is a sufficient compliance with a demand to inform the tenderee where the chattels may be found If it is necessary, in order to secure the chattels, that a warehouse receipt be surrendered, or an order given for the goods, the tenderor must surrender the one or give the other. Where a contract of sale of goods is executory on both sides, and the goods tendered are refused or retained because of a failure of the vendee to pay the purchase price, the vendor may elect to retain the goods as his own, in which case he need not respond to a demand

§ 441. **Effect of a failure to comply with a demand—Where lien or duty is discharged by a tender—Lien or duty revived when —Liability of surety.**—It has already been shown that in all cases, excepting those where the obligation or lien is discharged by the tender and there is no personal obligation to pay the debt accompanying the mortgage or lien, the tender

[1] Rose v Brown Kirby (Conn)   [2] Town v Trow, 21 Pick 168

must be kept good. It necessarily follows that a subsequent demand and a refusal to deliver the money or thing tendered, where the tender is required to be kept good, destroys the effect of the tender.[1] "It is therefore necessary that the person making the tender, should always hold himself in readiness to meet a subsequent demand for the money or thing tendered, because the party to whom it is due has a right to call for it at any time, and if he fails to deliver it on request, he loses the benefit of the tender."[2] As long as the vendee continues in possession of the goods tendered, he is bound to deliver them on demand. A neglect to do so constitutes a conversion of the goods. Where a tender has the effect of discharging a lien or duty, whether the debt remains or there exists no personal obligation to pay the money secured by the lien, the foregoing doctrine as to the effect being lost by a failure to comply with a subsequent demand, is regards the right to insist that the lien or duty is discharged, does not apply. However, where a subsequent offer to accept the money or article tendered, and surrender the security, is in the nature of an offer of compromise, a failure to insist on the tender and promising to pay, opens up the former transaction, is a waiver of all rights acquired under the tender and in effect revives the lien or duty.[3] Where a lien is created as security for a sum of money, for the payment of which there is no personal obligation, opening up a former transaction where an alleged tender had been made, on a subsequent demand, is a recognition of the right of the tenderee to demand and receive of the honor the money due on the lien. Such a state of facts was under consideration in an action of assumpsit to recover upon the common money count, the amount secured by a mortgage. In making the demand, an attorney's fee previously claimed to be due was waived by the mortgagee, thus making the

[1] Manny v. Harris 2 Johns 24, Rose v. Brown Kirby 293, s. c. 1 Am Dec 22, Carr v. Miner, 92 Ill 604 Nantz v. Tober 1 Duv 304 Hambell v. Tower 14 Iowa 530 Rainwater v. Hummel, 79 Iowa 571 s c 44 N W Rep (Iowa 914, Frank v. Pickens, 69 Ala 369, Cupples v. Galligan 6 Mo App 62, Sloan v. Petrie, 16 Ill 262, Columbian Bldg Ass'n v. Crump, 42 Md 192

[2] Town v. Trow 24 Pick 168; Rose v. Kline, 26 Mo App 452

[3] Coit v. Houston 3 Johns Cas 243

[4] Barker v. Parkenhorn, 2 Wash 112

demand clearly an offer of compromise, and the mortgagor by taking a satisfaction offered and stating he would take his own time in which to pay the amount demanded, furnished the consideration to support a recovery upon the money count.[5]

A bare promise to pay the amount tendered, on a subsequent demand, where the debt remained, would not be a waiver of the right to insist upon the discharge of the lien or duty. A failure to insist on a tender, and opening up the former transaction by a debtor, would not re establish the liability of a surety, nor revive the lien on property the owner of which stands in the relation of a surety. A debtor is at liberty to waive any right arising in his favor out of a wrongful refusal of money or goods that he had tendered to his creditor; but the refusal, if the tender was valid, discharged the surety, or the lien on the property of another pledged to secure the payment of the debt, and any act of the principal debtor would not extend to the surety so as to bind him.

§ 442. **Starts interest running from what time—Non-Interest bearing obligations—Revival of right to damages.**—On sums of money carrying interest a tender stops the running of interest from the time of the tender. A subsequent demand and a refusal or neglect to comply with the demand, starts the interest to running, not from the date of the demand but from the date of the tender.[1] This rule is stated differently in Bacon's Abridgment There it appears, that on a demand, if the money be not thereupon paid, interest begins again to grow from the time of the demand.[2] But the better legal reasoning would be—and it is in harmony with the current of authorities holding, where the tender is abandoned, that interest may be recovered for the whole period—that the interest should not be intermitting. On a subsequent demand, a refusal amounts to a withdrawal of the tender, and such withdrawal relates back to the time it was made. A tender does not start interest to running on a non interest bearing obligation. By tendering the amount due the debtor has done all in his power to comply with his agreement, but,

---

[5] Fry v. Russell, 35 Mich 229  
[1] Tate v. Smith, 70 N. C 685.  
[2] Bac. Abr Tender (F)

by refusing a subsequent demand for the money, he places himself in the wrong, and interest at the legal rate begins to run from the date of the demand, the rule being the same as that applicable to non interest bearing demand notes. The ancient law that a tender was a bar to an action on a bond with a penalty, was founded upon the theory that the penalty upon a forfeiture became the debt, but in England this was changed by statute, and in the United States the courts have justly changed the rule so that the law now is, that on payment of the sum named in the condition, the court will order satisfaction  So, that a tender of the sum stated, or of the balance actually due in case of a penal obligation, cannot now be said to take away the remedy on the obligation.[3]  A tender and refusal takes away the right to damages on account of the non-payment of the debt, and this right may be restored by a demand subsequent to the tender and a refusal[4]  The amount due being stated, or in the nature of liquidated damages, the right thus restored would be the right to recover damages accruing since the date of the tender.  Ordinarily the damages in such cases would be interest at the legal rate on the amount actually due

§ 443.  **Does not admit a valid tender was made—Admits the amount tendered was the entire sum due when—Pleading.**—By making a subsequent demand the creditor does not thereby admit that there was a valid tender, or that there was any tender made at all.  Thus, where a tender is claimed to have been made to a sheriff, clerk of court, or other officer authorized by law to receive money in redemption from mortgage or execution sales, which tender is alleged to have been refused by the officer, a subsequent demand by the holder of the certificate of sale, on the debtor for the amount necessary to redeem, would not be such an admission.  In such case the creditor does not know, except from hearsay, in what manner the tender was made.  And in a suit to redeem based on such a tender, where it is claimed that a valid demand had been made, or an application for an injunction to restrain the mortgagee from foreclosing by advertisement, or where

---

[3] See Manning v Harris, 2 Johns 24          [4] See Manning v Harris, 2 Johns 24

the tender is relied upon as a defence to a foreclosure in a suit in equity, the mortgagee may show that a legal tender was not made. The same is true where the tender is made to a creditor personally. If it be a case where a lien or duty would be discharged by a valid tender, and the tender is not sufficient in law to affect that result, an offer to accept the sum tendered and release the lien, which is in the nature of a compromise and which the law favors, or an offer merely to accept the sum tendered, would never be made if such offer resulted in the destruction of the security. Such offer or demand not being complied with, the creditor may enforce payment of his debt, or the performance of the duty by a foreclosure of the lien, or appropriate proceedings on the bond or other obligation. In cases where a sum is tendered as all that is due, the demand being unliquidated, or there exists a controversy as to the amount due, a subsequent demand and acceptance of the sum without objection to the amount, or reservation of the right to claim more, is an admission that the sum received is all that is due

A plaintiff in order to have the benefit of a subsequent demand and refusal must plead it affirmatively in his reply[1] On a replication of a subsequent demand, the demand is not proved by the mere fact of the bringing of the action to recover the money[2]

[1] Mahan v. Waters, 60 Mo 167, Dixon v. Clark, 5 C B 365, Cotton v. Goodwin, 7 M & W. 147,  Brandon v. Newington, 3 Q B. 915
[2] Johnson v. Clay, 7 Taunt 486

## CHAPTER XIII.

### ABANDONMENT OF A TENDER.

§ 444.  **Failure to keep the tender good—Using the money.**—In all cases where the debt or duty remains after a tender, a failure to keep the tender good is an abandonment of the tender  The party making the tender must keep the money in his possession or under his immediate control, so that it may be delivered over on a demand being made therefor. This is imperative, and a slight deviation from the strict rule destroys all rights under the tender  Where the lien is destroyed by the tender, and the debt or duty remains, an abandonment only destroys the defence to the recovery of the interest and damages, and not the defence to the foreclosure of the lien.  The question of abandon arises most frequently in cases where the person making the tender afterwards uses a part or all the money as his own  It has been said that a debtor, by using the money, virtually withdraws his tender [1]  So, a tender was held to have been abandoned, where the money was tendered on behalf of the cred-

[1] Alger v  Clay, 109 Ill. 187, Gray v Angier, 62 Ga 596, Stow v Russell, 36 Ill 33; Bissell v Heyward, 96 U S 580, Giles v. Hart, 3 Salk 343

itor by a third person to whom it belonged, and the latter afterwards used the money.[2] So, where it appeared that the money tendered was afterwards mingled with the funds of the tenderor—a bank, and used by it in its ordinary business, even though the bank had in its vault at all times sufficient funds to meet a demand, the tender was held to be abandoned.[3] Where the money tendered was borrowed from a bank for the express purpose of making the tender, and on its refusal, was immediately returned and repaid to the bank, it was held, in a suit to redeem from a foreclosure sale based on the tender, commenced after the expiration of the time allowed by the law in which to redeem, that the tender was ineffectual for any purpose, and that the mortgagor stood precisely as if no tender had ever been made.[4] Where a party wishing to rescind a sale of a jack on the ground of fraud, tendered him back to the seller, and on the latter refusing to accept him, the purchaser, instead of leaving the jack at the seller's stable or upon the premises, took him home and used him as his own, it was held that the tender was abandoned and that his remedy was an action for damages.[5]

§ 445.  **Non-compliance with a subsequent demand—Notice of withdrawal—Failure to insist upon the tender—Subsequent offer of judgment.**—A neglect to comply with a subsequent demand is an abandonment[1] The duty resting upon the party making the tender is to keep the money safely and to respond to a demand. "A neglect of the duty or disabling himself from performing it is an abandonment of the tender."[2] After a refusal, an express notice that the tender is withdrawn, or that the creditor cannot have the money, even though the identical money be kept on hand and the party afterwards on reconsideration notifies the creditor that the money is ready for him, the tender is abandoned. Whatever benefits accrue by reason of the tender are destroyed by the notice and cannot be revived. A second tender must be

[2] Werner v. Tuch, 127 N Y 217

[3] Roosevelt v. Bull's Head Bank, 45 Barb 579

[4] Dunn v Hunt, 63 Minn 484; s c 65 N W Rep 948, s. p Park v. Wiley, 67 Ala 310

[5] McCullough v Scott, 13 B Mon. 172.

[1] Carr v Miner, 92 Ill 604

[2] Frank v Perkins, 69 Ala 369.

made if not too late in point of time. A tender may be abandoned by subsequently failing to insist upon it.[3] Thus, in an action of trover to recover the value of a vessel pledged to secure a loan of a sum of money, the defendant, being entitled to certain advances made on account of repairs, on a tender refused to produce his account, declaring that he would not receive the money, but on a subsequent day and before suit brought, he did furnish the plaintiff with his account, who thereupon made the objection that it was extravagant, without objecting to opening the transaction of the former day, it was held that the plaintiff could not recover in trover. By failing to stand upon the tender and refusal, and merely questioning the accuracy of the account, he opened up the former transaction, and he was bound at his peril to again tender as much as he thought the defendant was justly entitled to receive.[4] So, in a case where the tender had been rejected because the sum tendered did not include an attorney fee claimed to be due according to the terms of the mortgage, and on an offer subsequently made to discharge the mortgage on receipt of the amount actually due, the mortgagee waiving the attorney fee, the mortgagor instead of relying upon his tender, took the discharge offered, and at the same time declared he would take his own time to pay, it was held that the tender was withdrawn.[5] It has been said that by filing a written offer of judgment, the question of a tender is waived.[6]

**§ 446. Failure to comply with subsequent promise—Receiving the money back—Taking the thing tendered away—Neglect to comply with decree.**—If, on a subsequent demand, the tenderor

[3] Nelson v Estate, 50 Atl Rep (Vt) 1094.

[4] Barker v Parkenhorn, 2 Wash 142

[5] Fry v Russell, 35 Mich 220 The facts mentioned in the text arose in an action of assumpsit to recover on the common money count, the sum due upon the mortgage It appeared that there was no collateral agreement or personal obligation to pay the money secured by the mortgage. A re-covery was had on the ground that the offer to waive the attorney fee and discharge the mortgage was in the nature of an offer to compromise, and by receiving the discharge, the mortgagor recognized the right of the plaintiff to demand and receive of him the amount due upon the mortgage.

[6] Gregg v. Berkshire, 62 Pac Rep (Kan App) 550

promises to pay the money but fails to produce it, he cannot fall back upon his tender and plead it as a defence in bar of interest and damages. A tender is abandoned by requesting a return and receiving the money tendered[1] So, where, after a tender of certificates of stock, and at the same interview, the tenderor said that he desired to consult his lawyer, and promised to return shortly, and thereupon departed with the certificates of stock, the tender was held to have been withdrawn.[2] A failure or neglect to comply with the terms of a decree setting aside a foreclosure,[3] or a decree allowing a redemption is an abandonment of the tender.

§ 447. **Depositing money tendered in bank—Intent.**—The intent of the party making a tender, in reference to keeping it good, is immaterial, and the reception of any evidence to prove intent is error.[1] Thus, it does not infrequently happen that the tenderor, with the express intent of keeping the tender good, and with the utmost good faith, makes a general deposit of the money tendered with a bank or other depositary. This is an abandonment, and it makes no difference whether the deposit be made in the name of the party to whom the tender was made or in the name of the person making the tender In the former case the money passes beyond his control by his attempted substitution of the credit of the depositary for his own debt, and in the latter case, by the general deposit, he loans the money to the depositary, and the credit of the depositary becomes substituted for the money[2] The rule is not different where the party depositing the money is, at all times, financially able to pay the money[3] An abandonment arises even where the deposit is special,

---

[1] State v. Illinois Cent R Co, 33 Fed. Rep 730

[2] Currie v. White, 7 Robt 637

[3] Cupples v Galligan, 6 Mo App 62

[1] The intent referred to is the intent of a party making a tender to keep it good If it can be shown that a person who had made a tender, stated that the tenderee could not have the money if he wanted it, or used equivalent expressions, it would be material as going to show that the tenderor's intent was to abandon the tender, and if such an intent be proven, the fact that he still had the identical money on hand would be immaterial

[2] Boon on Banking, Sec 40 See Rainwater v. Hummel, 44 N W Rep (Io) 814, where the depositary failed, and the tenderor was unable to respond to a demand

[3] Sanders v. Bryer, 152 Mass 141, s c 25 N. E. Rep 86.

and accompanied by the express direction to keep the money intact, where the depositary converts the money to his own use, or it is destroyed or stolen.

**§ 448. Acts inconsistent with ownership of tenderee—Conversion—Tenderee's remedies.**—In the case of an unaccepted tender of chattels, the tenderor may so deal with the property that it will amount to a withdrawal of the tender  If the tenderor retains the possession, he must care for the property as that of the tenderee.  In this respect, "there is an obligation resting upon him which he cannot disregard, and if he does disregard it, he loses the advantage the law would otherwise give him  *  *  *  If they be promissory notes, he cannot collect and use for himself the interest accruing on them, for such would be in conflict with the right of the other owner—would be a conversion, and equivalent to a withdrawal of the tender and a destruction of all rights under it."[1]  If the article be such that will be consumed by use he cannot use it.[2]  The general rule is that any act upon the part of the tenderor inconsistent with the ownership of the party to whom the tender was made, amounts to an abandonment of the tender.  Where, after a refusal, the tenderor converts the article tendered to his own use, and the purchase price has been paid, the tenderee may elect to treat the conversion as an abandonment of the tender, and bring an action to recover the damages for a breach of the contract, or he may bring trover for its value.  On bringing an action of trover, the tender must stand as made, that form of action being inconsistent with the claim that the tender was withdrawn  The conversion could only take place after a valid tender had passed the title to the plaintiff  The latter action would, in many instances, be more favorable to the plaintiff, the recovery not being limited to the value of the article at the time fixed for delivery, but to the value at the date of the conversion or demand  Upon the other hand, where the conversion consists in converting the thing tendered into cash, waiving the tort, and suing upon the implied promise, in many instances, would be advantageous to the defendant,

[1] Fannin v Thompson, 50 Ga. 614    [2] Fannin v Thompson, 50 Ga 614

as he would then have the right of set-off, and the right to pay the money into court.[3]

§ 449.   **Abandoning the property.**—Where the property is perishable, or is such as require housing or to be otherwise protected from injury or destruction, liable to result from exposure to the elements or other natural causes, or is such as, owing to its value, would be particularly liable to be stolen, or is a horse or other animal requiring food and which if not secured will wander abroad and become lost to the owner, the tenderor, after a refusal to accept the property tendered, or which is the same thing, on a failure of the tenderee to attend at the time and place appointed by the contract for delivery when his presence is indispensable to the care and control of the property, must not abandon the property.  He should, in all such cases, either dispose of the property by resale, or, if he does not care to retain the article in his own possession, store it for the vendee, and notify him where his property may be found.[1]  And it may be stated, as a general rule, that if the tenderor wilfully abandons the property so that the same is destroyed, lost or stolen, the tender is abandoned, and the tenderee may sue for a breach of the contract.  If the articles be bulky or ponderous, the same duty to properly protect them when they are susceptible to damage from the elements or other cause, rests upon the tenderor as where the articles are portable   Thus, a load of hay, unless properly stacked or housed, is as liable to damage from inclement weather (but not necessarily to the same extent) as is a case of silks left unprotected on a wharf or other place   It is to be observed, however, that a delivery of ponderous articles at the place designated at the time specified, in the absence of the vendee, and going away and leaving them, where the articles are such as do not require immediate attention, and cannot be seriously affected by exposure to the elements for a time at least, as timbers castings, heavy machinery and the like, does not constitute an abandonment of the articles, and the tender, if otherwise

[3] Cooley on Torts, p. 92, citing Young v Marshall 8 Bing 43

[1] Chancellor Kent in his valuable Commentaries stated the converse to be true, that the debtor may abandon the goods so tendered but neither the authorities which he cites, nor reason or justice, bears him out   2 Kent Com 509

sufficient, stands, though the articles are immediately stolen or destroyed.

**§ 450.  Neglecting to dispose of perishable property.**—If the property tendered be perishable, such as provision that must be immediately consumed, or anything that requires labor and attention to preserve it for future use, and it is marketable, the vendor must make a reasonable effort to dispose of the property for the benefit of the vendee  A failure to make any effort to effect a sale of it would be a flagrant disregard of the moral and legal obligation which one citizen owes to another, not to increase unnecessarily, because it lies in his power, the burden of one liable to loss on account of his own wrong.  Such conduct would constitute gross neglect, and would be equivalent to a withdrawal of the tender. Mellen, C. J, in an analogous case, in a terse *dictum* laid down the principle which it seems governs such cases; he said: "The purchaser of perishable goods at auction, fails to complete his contract.  What shall be done? Shall the auctioneer leave the goods to perish, and throw the entire loss upon the purchaser?  That would be to aggravate it unreasonably and unnecessarily.  It is his duty to sell them a second time, and if they bring less, he may recover the difference, with commission and other expenses of resale, from the first purchaser.  If the party entitled to the benefit of the contract can protect himself from loss arising from a breach, at a trifling expense, or with reasonable exertion, he fails in his social duty, if he omits to do so. regardless of the increased amount of damages for which he may intend to hold the other contracting party liable "[1]  The tenderor, in this respect, is to be governed by the rules of sound business methods.  Thus, a vendor of fruits, vegetables, or fresh meats and the like, who had engaged to deliver his commodities at a public market or elsewhere, will not be heard to say that he deposited the perishables in the street, or that he left them unprotected and undisposed of elsewhere, relying upon his cause of action against the vendee to recover their value, when with little trouble and expense, he could have disposed of them on the

[1] Miller v  Mariners' Church, 7 Greenl. 51

market. And the rule ought not to be different, whether the consideration was executory or executed, or whether the vendee was intentionally absent or unavoidably detained elsewhere; or, when he is present and refuses to receive them. The vendor's conduct should be that of a discreet and prudent man, for peradventure he might fail in his proof of a lawful and valid tender.

§ 451. **Gross neglect of the property.**—The obligations resting upon a tenderor when he remains in possession of the article after its proffer and refusal, are those of a bailee. He must not suffer the article to become depreciated or lessened in value resulting from any act of his [1] Whether there are any authorities defining and classifying this species of bailment, the author is not prepared to say. The least care which the law would impose and by the use of which a bailee could hope to escape liability in any case, would be reasonable care, and, it would follow as a necessary concomitant that gross neglect or wilful acts, resulting in the damage or destruction of the property, would be equivalent to a withdrawal of the tender, giving a right to recover on the contract as fully as if a tender had not been made in the first instance

§ 452. **Destruction of the property—Tenderee's remedies —**A tender is withdrawn when the thing tendered is destroyed, or the tenderor otherwise put it without his power to respond to a demand   Thus, at the time of taking a note payable at six months, the payee agreed to surrender it, provided the maker, before maturity, gave a satisfactory acceptance at six months, and such acceptance was tendered, and on its being refused it was thereupon destroyed by the acceptor, who had personally made the tender, this was held to be a complete revocation of all that had been done by way of performance   Cowen, J, said, by an act of destruction or mutilation he undoes all that he had performed. If it be destroyed, or its value impaired by the act of the tenderor because not accepted, it was a wrong which the tenderee, in his election, may treat according to the apparent intent, which is to take back and annul all that has been done. It was held that the payee could elect to sue upon the note, or upon the

---

[1] Fannin v Thompson, 50 Ga 611

acceptance, and that an action upon the note, brought previous to the expiration of the second period of six months, was maintainable.[1] So, in a case where a note, bond, and mortgage had been tendered in settlement of a note, and they were destroyed after the tender and a refusal, a recovery was had upon the original note; the court holding that in such a case the defendant must plead that he has always been and still is ready with the money or thing tendered.[2]

**§ 453.  When a tender may be withdrawn—Of goods—Services —Duty of employee.—**As regards the rights of vendors of chattels where the contract is executory on both sides, and the purchase price is to be paid on delivery, although the same consequences as to the title result from a valid tender, the setting apart and tender of the articles give only a right to the property in them but not the right of possession without payment.[1] In such cases the rule is different, the vendor may withdraw the tender if he does not care to risk the solvency of the vendee. On a sale of chattels "upon the refusal of the vendee to accept and pay the price, the vendor, upon proper notice, may sell the property and recover the difference. He may elect to retain the property as his own and sue for the difference between the contract and the actual price."[2] This rule was applied in a case where the contract was to construct a sulky. The sulky was refused and it was held that the vendor had an election, to resell and recover what he had lost by the resale, or keep the property for the vendee, and recover the whole original price agreed.[3]

There is an obvious distinction between the sale of chattels and contracts to sell labor and services. In the latter case the right of electing to stand on the tender is abridged, and justly so. The laborer or bailee presents himself and offers to perform, but his hirer declines the services. It is his duty to sell them to another or convert them to his own use. He must not lie idle for the length of time which performance would have required, when other avenues of employment are

---

[1] Gayle v. Suydam 24 Wend. 271

[2] The Brooklyn Bank v. DeGauw, 23 Wend. 342

[1] 2 Kent Com. 492. See Simpson v. French, 25 How. Pr. 465;

Billings v. Vanderbeck, 23 Barb. 554

[2] Hiden v. Dements, 53 N. Y. 426

[3] Bennett v. Smith, 15 Wend. 493

open to him. If a tender was equivalent to performance in
all respects, he might safely lie idle; but going only to the
right of action and not to the measures of damages, inten
tionally lying idle would be such a gross fraud that the damages would be merely nominal. A person, however, is not
required to accept employment of an entirely different kind.
Thus, a person employed to superintend a railroad, in order
to relieve the pocket of an employer is not bound to take up
the business of a farmer or merchant;[4] nor would the mate
of a steamboat be required to accept employment as a deck
hand; or a seamstress that of a nurse or house servant; nor
would the party whose services had been refused be required
to change his place of residence. or to accept any employment
requiring his continued absence from his family, even though
the employment which he could enter upon is of the same
character as that which he had contracted to perform[5] To
pursue the subject of abandonment further would be at the
risk of repetition. A careful analysis of the rules bearing
upon how the tender is kept good, and applying the strict
rule, will enable the practitioner, in a given case, to determine whether the conduct of the tenderor after the rejection
of the money or thing amounts to an abandonment

§ 454. **Conclusion of law—Finding on the facts.**—An aban
donment of a tender is a conclusion of law to be drawn by
the court from the acts of the party making the tender, and
in cases where it is within the province of a jury to determine
the facts, a special finding should always be taken on the
facts relied upon to show the abandonment, otherwise a gen
eral verdict in favor of the party pleading the tender will in
clude a finding that those facts were not proven, and unless
clearly against the evidence the verdict would not be disturbed. Any act of the tenderor in his care of the money or
property being shown, which is inconsistent with the absolute
ownership of the person to whom the tender was made, the
conclusion that the tender was abandoned must follow.

[4] Costigan v Mohawk, &c, R
R Co, 2 Den 607.
[5] See Litherberry v Odell, 7

Fed. Rep 641; Sedgwick on Dam-
mages, sec 207, Fuchs v. Koerner,
107 N. Y 529

## CHAPTER XIV

### PLEADING AND PROOF.

**§ 455  Must be pleaded—Kind of plea** — A valid tender and a refusal is held, and very properly so, to effect certain results beneficial to the debtor and detrimental to the creditor. A debtor is bound, not only by his contract but by law, to a strict performance of his agreement up to and until it is extinguished by payment, and if he desires to avail himself of any benefits to be derived from any act of his or of his creditor short of full payment of the principal, interest and costs, and the right of the creditor, until such full payment is received, to enforce the contract to the strict letter by any collateral right he may have for that purpose, he must plead the tender and refusal.[1] It is an affirmation plea,[2] whether it is the foundation of a cause of action, or the foundation of a defence, otherwise the defendant or plaintiff would not be apprised of the grounds of the opposition to his recovery It is a fundamental rule of pleading that a litigant must notify his opponent on paper, of every issuable fact which he intends to establish by evidence. A litigant cannot well anticipate affirmative matter, while he may anticipate and be prepared to meet the few things that may be given in evidence under a negative plea, which go usually to the non existence of the thing or right in the first instance. Whatever legal rights a party may have acquired by his own act or by the act of another, may be waived by him by an affirmative declaration or by silence, so as to leave the rights of another wholly unimpaired. Therefore, if a tender be not pleaded, the benefits accruing by reason of the tender are waived It is a plea in bar.[3] It was originally considered in nature of a dilatory plea and construed with strictness, but is now, every where, looked upon as a fair and honest plea to the merits of the action,[4] though it is still construed with strictness It must be specially pleaded in a justice court as well as in a court of record[5] A defendant may plead a tender and payment of the money into court in a former action, and on proving a payment in that action to the clerk, he will be entitled to a judgment in such subsequent action[6]

§ 456. **At what time a tender may be pleaded** — A plea of tender ought to be included in the pleading in the first instance, but under a sufficient showing the court, in its discretion, may allow an amendment setting forth the tender If a tender is permitted by statute to be made after action brought, and it is one that cannot be given in evidence under

[1] Hughes v Eschback. 7 D C 66, Shereding v Gaul, 2 Dall 190. Barker v. Brink, 5 Iowa 481, Hegler v Eddy, 53 Cal 597, Meredith v Santa Clara Ass'n, 56 Cal 178

[2] Park v Wiley, 67 Ala 310

[3] It is a plea in bar of damages *ultra*, and not in bar of the action Ayers v Pease, 12 Wend 393, Wheeler v Woodward, 66 Pa St 158, Huntington v Zeigler, 2 Oh St 10, Sheehan v Rosen. 12 Pa Super Ct 298

[4] Kilwick v Maidman 1 Burr. 59. Moore v Smith, 1 H Black 369, Tidd's Pr 475

[5] Griffin v Tyson 17 Vt 35

[6] Robinson v Gaines. 3 Call (Va) 243

a general denial, or is a tender made in rescission after action
brought, if made after the answer is served, it ought to be
set out in a supplemental answer. It may be pleaded after
an order is made overruling a demurrer and leave given to
plead to the merits of the action.[1] If the plaintiff amends,
but does not include any new items in his account, a tender
which was not pleaded in the original answer cannot be set
out in the answer to the amended complaint, without leave
granted to amend the answer in that particular. Under the
ancient law in England, it was held that a tender must be
pleaded within four days, and before a general imparlance,
but the strictness of the rule, after a time, was relaxed, and
the rule established that it might be pleaded after the four
days, and after an imparlance. After the granting of the
indulgence (to imparle) to the defendant was abolished by
statute (if indeed the rule was not that way before) the
time of pleading a tender was governed by the same rules
as applied to the pleading of any new matter, which rule
now obtains. A tender which was not pleaded in an action
in a lower court cannot be pleaded after an appeal has been
taken.[2]

### § 457. Cannot be proven under a general denial—Exception.—

It is a general rule that a tender cannot be proven under a
general denial.[1] But under a statute in New Hampshire
which allowed a party to give evidence of any special matter
under the general issue, it was held that evidence of a tender
was admissible under that plea.[2] So, in Vermont, under the
statute which permitted a tender to be made at any time
before three days before the sitting of the court to which the
writ was returnable, it was held that evidence of such a
tender might be given in bar under the general issue.[3] Sim-

---

[1] See Tiernan v Napier 5 Yerg
410, where the plea was allowed
after a judgment on a writ of inquiry was set aside

[2] Grover v Smith, 165 Mass
132, Bickett v Wallace, 98 Mass
528, McDaniel v Upton 45 Ill
App 151, Johnson v Triggs, 4
Green 67; Chipman v Bates, 5
Vt 143, Griffin v Tyson, 17 Vt
35; Seibert v Kline, 1 Pa St 38

[1] Robinson v Batchelder, 4 N
H 40, Schrader v Wolfin, 21 Ind
238

[2] (1859) Colby v. Stevens, 38 N.
H 191 See Bliss v. Houghton, 16
N H 90

[3] Powers v Powers, 11 Vt 262,
Woodcock v Clark, 18 Vt 333,
May v Brownell, 3 Vt 468, Pratt
v Gallup, 7 Vt 344; Smith v Wilbur, 35 Vt. 133, Adams v Morgan,

ilar statutes are in force in other states.[4] To the general
rule that a tender must be pleaded in order that the one
making it may receive the benefit thereunder, there is an
exception. When the tender is collateral to the action, as
having operated to extinguish or suspend the plaintiff's title
to the specific property sued for, it need not be pleaded to
such action.[5] So, under a complaint alleging ownership and
right to immediate possession of personal property, a plaintiff, in proof of such ownership may show his redemption of
the property by a tender to the defendant, a pledgee, the
amount secured by the pledge thereof.[6] On the other hand
under a general denial of ownership, the defendant may show
that the tender was insufficient to discharge his lien as
pledgee.[7]

§ 458. Inconsistent pleas.—A plea of tender of a sum due
upon a contract and a denial of the right of action for the
sum, are inconsistent pleas, and must not be joined,[1] nor
should the plea of non assumpsit or *non est factum* and a tender be joined,[2] nor that the plaintiff is an alien enemy and a
tender;[3] nor that the contract is void as usurious and a
tender, when the whole debt, tainted with usury, is forfeited.
But a plea of tender of the principal and a plea of usury may
be joined when the interest only is forfeited. If the cause
of action be founded upon a casual or involuntary trespass
or any action for damages where the statute allows a tender
to be made and pleaded, the defendant may deny that the

39 Vt 302, Spaulding v Warner
57 Vt 651, Nelson v Estate, 50
Atl Rep (Vt) 1094

4 Warren v Nichols 6 Met 261,
Bickell v Wallice 98 Mass 528
See Dunlop v Funk, 3 Har & M
(Md) 318 and Snyder v Quinton,
17 Mich 211

5 Hill v Carter, 59 N W Rep
(Mich) 413, Powers v Powers 11
Vt 262, McDaniels v Reed 17 Vt
674, Woodcock v Clark 18 Vt
383 See Christenson v Nelson
63 Pac Rep (Or) 648

6 Jones v Rahilly, 16 Minn 320

7 Jones v Rahilly 16 Minn 320

1 Dobie v Larkin, 10 Exch 776,
MacClellan v Howard, 4 D & E
194 Dowgall v Bowman, 3 Wils
145, Alderson v Dodding Barnes
359 Blagton v Delaware County
16 Iowa 14, Livingston v Har-
son, 2 E D Smith 197, Davis v
Millander, 17 La Ann 97 Hitch
v Thompson, 67 Conn 74 See
Griffin v Harriman 74 Iowa 436

2 Jenkins v Edwards 5 T R
97, Orgell v Kempshead 1 Taunt
479, Union Bank v Ridgeley 1
Har & G (Md) 107

3 Shombeck v De La Cour, 10
East 326

plaintiff was damaged and also plead a tender of amends.[4]
He may prove that the defendant was not damaged at all
for the purpose of defeating a recovery of any sum beyond
the sum tendered.

§ 459. **Consequence of pleading a tender** —A plea of tender
admits the amount tendered to be due the plaintiff, and that
he is entitled to a judgment for the amount.[1]  If the money
tendered be paid into court, and the plaintiff accepts it forthwith as all that is due, or goes for more, and the issue is
found for the defendant, the latter is entitled to a judgment
for his costs.  The effect of pleading a tender is considered
more fully in the chapter entitled, "Consequences of a tender
and refusal."[2]

§ 460. **What must be alleged — Actual production — Waiver
—Performance of condition—Time—Place.**—The general rule in
reference to pleading a tender is, that every requisite which
is necessary to the validity of a tender must be shown to
have been complied with, otherwise the plea, for want of
showing that the party tendering has done all that was in
his power to pay the debt or perform the duty, is not good.[1]
There must be an allegation showing an actual production of
the money and an offer of it, or an excuse for its non-produc-
tion.[2]  An allegation that a certain sum was refused without
alleging an offer, or a general statement that a tender was
made is not enough.[3]  That a tender was made is a conclusion
of the pleader merely, and is as defective as a general aver-

[1] Martin v. Kesterton 2 Bl. Rep. 1093; Gerung v. Manning, Burnes 366

[1] Babcock v. Harris 37 Iowa 409; Gray v. Graham 8 Iowa 425; Young v. Borzone, 66 Pac. Rep. (Wash) 135; Williamson v. Chicago Ry. Co. 68 Iowa 673.  In the last case it was held that, on a motion in arrest of judgment, the defendant could not claim the complaint did not state a cause of action

[2] Secs. 402, 403, 502, 503

[1] 9 Bacon's Abr. Tit. Tender (H); Lancashire v. Killingworth, Salk. 624

[2] Dickenson v. Hayes 26 Minn. 100; McGhee v. Jones, 10 Ga. 132

[3] Indiana Bond Co. v. Jameson, 56 N. E. Rep. (Ind. App.) 37; see Dickenson v. Hayes, 26 Minn. 100

[4] See McNeil v. Sun, &c. Co. 78 N. Y. Supp. 90 where it is held that a denial of an allegation that a sum was "duly tendered" raises an issue

ment of fraud. He must state the facts which constitute a
legal tender.[5] A plea of performance of a condition must
show the manner of performance. If the condition to be per
formed is a specific act, a special performance must be
averred.[6] An exception to the general rule is, where the mat
ter is of so intricate and complicated a nature, or embraces
such a variety of minute circumstances, that a particular
statement would violate the rule of pleading prohibiting pro
lixity.[7] The time the tender was made must be set forth with
definiteness.[8] Thus, an averment that the money was ten
dered "on or about the first day of March" is bad, although
such a plea has been held good as against a general demurrer.[9] It must be shown to have been made before the
commencement of the action.[10] If the party entitled to re
ceive the thing tendered was present at the time, or was
represented at the time and the place by an agent, it is
sufficient to state that the tender was made to him on a cer
tain day without specifying the time of the day. But if the
party who is to receive, be absent from the place of per
formance, it is not enough for the plaintiff (or defendant) to
allege that he was ready at the day and place, and offered to
transfer the stock, deliver the articles, or pay the money,
etc., he must allege the tender to have been made at the
uttermost convenient time of the day fixed for performance.[11]
A plea "that he was ready on the day, but neither the plain
tiff, nor anyone on his behalf attended with the vessels to
receive it," was held ill for want of a statement of the time

[5] Cothran v Scanlan 34 Ga
555, Indiana Bond Co v Jameson,
56 N E Rep (Ind App) 37

[6] Tinney v Ashley, 15 Pick.
546

[7] Tinney v Ashley, 15 Pick 546

[8] Downman v Downman 1
Wash 26, Vance v Blair, 18 Ohio,
532; Shank v Groff 15 W Va
543 See Schwartz v Evans Co,
75 Tex 198 which was a case
where it appeared that time was
not of the essence of the contract See Sec 304 and cases
cited.

[9] Haile v Smith, 45 Pac (Cal)
872 See Schwartz v Evans, 75

Tex 198 It would seem, accord
ing to the forms subjoined as an
appendix to Mr Chitty's treatise
on pleadings, that the tender may
be alleged to have been made
about a certain day 3 Chitt 19
956 But such a rule if it ob
tained would not be good law

[10] Jacobs v Oren, 18 Pac (Or)
131, Cope v Bryson, Winst L
112, Winningham v Redding, 6
Jones, 126

[11] Lancashire v Killingworth,
Salk 624, s c 12 Mod 529, Duck
ham v Smith, 5 T B Mon 372

of day the obligor attended.[12] It is not sufficient for the pleader to state that he was there shortly before the setting of the sun, he must plead that he was there long enough before to have counted the money,[13] or examined the goods by daylight. When a plea was to the effect, that in the month of May, 1809, he was ready and prepared, and willing to deliver to the plaintiff, or his agents or assignees, at the place of embarkation at Brownsville, the quantity of 1,920 gallons of good merchantable proof whiskey, in good tight barrels, according to the tenor and effect of the said condition, but that the plaintiff was not then and there ready to accept the same, etc., it was held bad. In such case, to secure the benefit of a readiness to perform, the party must aver that he was ready and prepared at the last convenient hour of the last day of the month.[14] When a person was bound to pay a certain sum to a person on coming of age, a plea of payment in the words of the bond was held bad on a special demurrer, because it did not state the time, place, and manner of performance; and yet, said the court, the plea unquestionably covered every hour of the time after the obligee became of age.[15] Where a note or other obligation is payable in articles of a fluctuating value, the tender must be alleged to have been made on the day of the maturity of the obligation.[16] So, the place where the tender was made must be set out with particularity.[17]

§ 461. Same subject—Amount—Denial of amount.—The party pleading a tender should state in his plea the precise sum offered.[1] It is not sufficient to say that a sum of money was offered;[2] nor that a tender was made of a sum sufficient to discharge the debt, without specifying any particular sum. Thus, when it was alleged in the complaint that the plaintiff

[12] Jowett v. Wagnon, 2 Bibb. (Ky.) 269. See Tranter v. Hibbard, 56 S. W. Rep. (Ky.) 169, where an averment that "he was then ready, able and willing to deliver the stock in satisfaction of the note," but that the note was not presented at the bank, was held insufficient.

[13] Tinckler v. Prentice, 4 Taunt. 549.

[14] Savary v. Goe, 3 Wash. 140.

[15] Hulsey v. Carpenter, Cro. Jac. 359.

[16] See Lanier v. Trigg, 6 S. & M. 641, s. c. 45 Am. Dec. 293.

[17] See Trabur v. Kay, 4 Bibb 226.

[1] Bothwell v. Millikan, 104 Ind. 162; Goss v. Bowen, 104 Ind. 207.

[2] Bailey v. Troxell, 43 Ind. 432.

was ready and willing and offered to pay the amount actually
due and owing on the mortgage before foreclosure, it was
held that the allegation was utterly insufficient to make out a
tender because it did not show a production of the money and
an offer of it to the defendant, nor any excuse for its non
production, and because the amount which plaintiff was ready
and willing and offered to pay was not stated.[1] A plea of
tender of one half of the amount of the note is bad, unless
it contains an allegation that the tender was of the amount
due.[4] So, a plea of a tender of a certain amount that is due
the plaintiff is bad, as referring to the amount due at the
date of the plea, and not at the date of the tender.[5] A plea
was held good which stated, as to £10 parcel of the sum sued
for "the defendants say that they were always ready and
willing to pay the same, and that before suit they tendered
and offered to plaintiff, to pay the same to him, but he re
fused to receive it; and the defendants bring into court the
£10 ready to be paid to plaintiff."[6] If a tender is made under
a statute authorizing a tender after action brought, in plead
ing it there must be an averment of a tender of a specific
amount upon the debt and a certain amount for cost.[7] It is
not necessary to specify what part of the sum offered is to
cover the interest, as accrued interest constitutes a part of
the debt. Even where the amount due is particularly within
the knowledge of the other party, as when a mortgagee is in
possession and the mortgagor is entitled to an accounting if
he makes a tender he should first apply to the mortgagee to
know the balance due, and plead a tender of the exact bal
ance stated to be due. A tender of a less sum is at his peril.
If he is not informed of the amount due on such application,
he should offer and plead a tender of some specific sum, and
whether it is subsequently found to be sufficient in amount
or not, if kept good, the mortgagee will suffer a loss of the
interest subsequent to the tender and must pay the costs of

[3] Dickerson v Hayes 26 Minn
100, Soice v Huff 102 Ind 422

[4] Frost v Butler, 58 N H
146

[5] Sussman v Mason 10 Misc
(N Y) 20  See McCalley v Otey,

104 Ala 169, Smith v Anders 21
Ala 728

[6] Smith v Manners, 5 C B N
S 634

[7] Eaton v Wells 82 N Y 576,
Walsh v Southworth 2 L M &
P 91, 6 Exch 150  See Young v
McWard 57 Iowa, 101

the action. However, in such cases, and those similar, a mere offer to pay what is due without naming any sum, will, if pleaded, be sufficient to give the party a standing in equity, but it will not stop the running of interest, and not being a tender, awarding or withholding costs would be within the discretion of the court. If property was to be delivered, the exact quantity offered must be alleged, and if property of a certain value was to be delivered, or a certain sum was payable in property, or in money or property, the value must be stated positively. An allegation in an action upon a covenant to pay $196, in money or negroes, that a negro, who two disinterested persons valued at $196, was offered in payment, was held bad as not alleging the value.[8]

Where the complaint contains several counts or causes of action, the better practice is to make and plead a separate tender to each count or cause, for if the tender, as made on some of the counts, proves to be sufficient in amount and fall short as to the other counts, he would escape the payment of interest subsequent to the tender, on the amount set out in those counts where the tender was sufficient. So, he would save himself harmless from the costs of the opposite party, incurred in attempting to disprove the tender, and be entitled to credit for taxable costs necessarily incurred in establishing his tender. But a party may make and plead a tender of one sum upon all the counts, and run the risk of it being held insufficient in amount as to all. Where an action was brought to recover for use and occupation, work and labor, money lent and money paid, and for money due on an account stated, the defendant interposed several pleas without distinguishing the counts, to all but £7, parcel of the money in the declaration, and as to the £7 a tender and payment of that sum into court. The plaintiff joined issue upon the tender, it was held, that proof of a single tender of £7 in respect of the use and occupation satisfied the plea of tender.[9] Such a pleading, however, before the tender is traversed would be open for a motion to make it more definite and certain. A plea of tender to a part of an entire claim, is not good without, in the same plea, in some way, disposing of the residue of the claim, by alleging payment,

[8] Johnson v. Butler, 1 Bibb (Ky.) 97

[9] Robinson v. Ward, 8 Q B 920, 10 Jur 109 15 L J Q B 271

set-off, or in some way showing that no more than the sum
tendered was ever due, or some other defence; [10] otherwise
the residue will stand admitted, and the plea would be bad
as alleging an offer of part only. In trespass, if the defend
ant pleads a tender of a certain sum being sufficient amends,
the plaintiff should deny that he tendered the sum named, or
allege that the sum was insufficient, and not that he did not
tender sufficient amends. [11] An allegation of a tender of a
large sum, to wit, £100, being a sufficient sum to discharge a
lien, which is traversed, does not put in issue a tender of any
other greater or less sum than the sum specified, notwith
standing it was alleged under a *videlicit*. [12] A replication,
that before the time of the tender, a larger sum was owing
and was demanded and refused, is no answer to a plea of
tender of a smaller sum [13] A reply alleging that accrued
costs were not included in the amount tendered, when the
tender was made after action brought, has been held good [14]

§ 462. **Same subject — Kind of money — Of chattels — Quality
—Deed.**—The party alleging a tender must describe the
money sufficiently, so that the quality may be determined
from the pleading. [1] An allegation that he tendered a certain
sum in money, or lawful money, is insufficient for the reason
that money is a generic term, including everything that circu

---

[10] Dixon v Clark, 5 C B 365
See Cotton v Goodwin, 7 M &
W 150; Tyler v Bland 9 M &
W 338, Jourdain v Johnson 2 C
M & R 570 Where a defendant
pleaded a tender of £55 6 s a part
of the sum claimed in the declaration, and the plaintiff in his replication alleged that a larger sum
than the £55 6 s was due upon
one entire count inclusive of, and
not separate and divisible from
said sum of £55 6 s, and the defendant, in his rejoinder alleged
that he had a set-off to the extent
of such larger sum, except the £55
6s so tendered It was held that
the rejoinder was bad and that the
set off should have been pleaded

in the first instance   Searles v
Sadgrove, 25 L J 15

[11] Williams v Price, 3 B & Ad
695

[12] Marks v Lahee 3 Bing N C
408 4 Scott 137

[13] Brandon v Newington 3 G
& D 194 2 Q B 915, 7 Jur 60,
12 L J Q B 20 43 E C L R
1035, condemning Cotton v Goodwin, 7 M & W 150 and Tyler v
Bland 9 M & W 570 See Hes
keth v Fawcett 11 M & W 356

[14] Hampshire Bank v Billings,
17 Pick 87

[1] Ralph v Lomer, 28 Pac 760,
3 Was St 101; Goss v Bowen,
104 Ind 207, Downman v. Downman 1 Wash 26

lates as money whether a legal tender or not.[2] He should aver that he tendered a certain sum in gold coin, or gold or silver coin, or greenback, legal tender money of the United States. If two or more forms of money go to make up the total, he need not aver the specific amount of each, but if there is any statutory limitation upon the quantity of any form of money affecting its legal tender qualities, there must be proof that the amount of that form of money which went to make up the total, was within the limit. If any form of money not a legal tender was offered, he must state the kind and allege facts constituting a waiver as to the medium of payment. If a tenderor intends to rely upon a tender of a kind of money not a legal tender and to pay that money over and none other, he must allege that he has been always ready to pay that very money, otherwise if he alleges a tender of money generally, he must bring into court that which is legal tender money at the time of the plea.[3] A declaration upon a note payable in good bank notes is bad, if it does not contain an averment that they were of par value.[4] So, if a note is made payable in bank notes a plea of tender of bank notes must allege that they were current.[5] In an action on a note payable in the notes of a particular bank, as of the chartered banks of Mississippi, the defendant may plead that he tendered those notes without alleging they were at par.[6] If an obligation is drawn payable in good commercial paper, the party alleging a tender should state that the notes were good and further, that he had indorsed them so as to transfer the legal title.[7]

If a plea of tender is of chattels or other things upon an obligation, the articles tendered must be so described that they can be distinguished and known, and the kind tendered must be alleged. If articles are to be appraised by one or more

[2] Magraw v. McGlynn 26 Cal 420

[3] Downman v. Downman, 1 Wash 26

[4] McNairy v. Bell 1 Yerg 502, & c 24 Am Dec 454, Smith v Elder 7 S & M 507

[5] Bonnell v Comington 8 Miss (7 How ) 322

[6] Smith v Elder, 15 Miss 507

[7] As against a demurrer, it has been held that an averment that defendant had tendered the notes was sufficient. Eichholtz v Taylor 88 Ind 38

[8] Nichols v Whitney, 1 Root, 443

[9] Lilienthal v McCormick 86 Fed Rep 100

persons, a plea of tender is bad which does not show that he procured the required number of persons to attend and appraise the articles, or if particular persons were to value them, that he procured their attendances and appraisal, and that the articles in their opinion were of the value fixed by the contract.[10] If the articles were to be of a certain quality, as merchantable, the vendor must allege that they were merchantable. The kind of deed tendered must be stated.[11]

§ 463. Same subject — Offer — Readiness and willingness.— A plea of readiness, or willingness without alleging an offer, is not good, for it is the tender or offer that is traversable and not the readiness, or willingness.[1] Thus, in an action for rent the defendant pleaded that on the day the rent became due he was ready to pay it. This was held bad for want of an allegation of an offer.[2] Where a vendee sought to recover the purchase money already paid, on a failure of the vendor to convey, an allegation that he had 'been ready and willing during all the time aforesaid, and has offered to accept and take said conveyance, pursuant to said agreement, and to pay the balance of said purchase money," was held an insufficient averment that he tenders the balance of the purchase money. That besides a readiness and willingness there must be a production, and an offer to pay the balance due on the other party performing the requisite condition.[3] So, in assumpsit on a note payable in ten thousand feet of good merchantable pine boards, on October 1st, 1819, at the defendant saw mill, a plea that at the time and place appointed, defendant had the said boards sawed and prepared for payment of the said note, and were ready then and there to have paid the same, and remained at said mill throughout the said day and until sundown, for the purpose of delivering said boards to the plaintiff, but that he did not come to receive them, and that the said boards ever since have been and still are, ready for the plaintiff at the said mill if he

10 Bohannous v Lewis 3 T B Mon 376, Stockton v Creager, 51 Ind 262

11 McCulloch v Dawson 1 Ind 413, Haile v Smith, 113 Cal 656, Bateman v Johnson, 10 Wis 1

1 9 Bac Abr Tit Tender (H) - Cole v Walton 3 Lev 46; or Clole v Watson 2 Lev 209, Dickenson v Hayes 26 Minn 100

3 Englander v Rogers, 41 Cal 420; Newby v Rogers, 40 Md 9

will take them, was held bad, a plea of willingness not being sufficient.[4] In such cases, the payee or vendee not being present, the pleader must set out that the articles were set apart for him, which is as far as he could go in his absence. The court observed, in the case of the note payable in boards, "that a formal offer to perform in the absence of the creditor has been usually adopted, and is called in the books a tender in law, and is so pleaded." If the tenderee was present it is sufficient to allege that the articles were pointed out to him, if capable of such designation.

§ 464. **Same subject—Refusal—Exception** — A party making a tender can derive no benefit therefrom unless it is refused by the other party, therefore, the averment of a refusal is necessary if the party whose duty it was to receive the thing, was present. The presence of the other party is sufficiently shown by the averment that the offer was made to him. In an action for money upon a contract for building a house, the plaintiff alleged that he made a tender of building the house. This was held to be insufficient because he did not aver that the defendant refused to allow him to build it.[1] The refusal, as well as the tender, is traversable.[2] But if the party who is to receive the money or other thing was absent from the place of payment at the time, and no one was there to represent him, it is sufficient, in addition to the averment of the readiness and willingness, to allege that the other party did not come to the place.[3]

§ 465 **Pleading a tender in equitable actions** — In equity, where a tender is the foundation of the cause of action, without which the suit could not be maintained, the complaint must aver all the facts which are necessary in pleading a tender at law.[1] It has been said that in some of the states

---

[4] Barney v. Bliss, 1 D. Chip (Vt.) 399, s. c. 12 Am. Dec. 696. See Smith v. Loomis, 7 Conn. 115.

[1] Peters v. Opie, 2 Saund. 346.

[2] 9 Bac. Abr. Tit. Tender (H) 1. See Chip on Cont. 108 when it is said that a failure to allege a refusal is considered a defect in form only and the defendant can take no advantage of it, except by special demurrer.

[3] Tea v. Exelby, Cro. Eliz. 889, Lancashire v. Killingworth, Cro. Eliz. 775, 1 Ld. Ry. 686, Huish v. Phillips, Cro. Eliz. 754.

[1] Sharp v. Wyckoff, 39 N. J. Eq. 376, Shields v. Lozus, 7 C. E. Gr. 447, Cotham v. Scanlan, 34 Ga.

a more lax rule prevails in equity than at law. Unfortunately the authorities have fallen to some confusion, owing, doubtless, to a failure of the courts to distinguish between those cases where the tender is important only as bearing upon the question of costs, where the rights of the party is not dependent upon a tender,[2] and those cases where the tender affects a particular result such as the discharge of a lien, release of a surety, etc., where it is the very foundation upon which the right to relief rests.[3] The rule requiring an offer to do equity is not universal, being required in some jurisdictions and not in others. Such offer, when required, is not a plea of tender; but an offer or an averment showing a willingness to comply with the decree of the court. It does not take the place of a tender which ought to be made before suit.[4]

§ 466. **Where concurrent acts are to be performed.**—Where concurrent acts are to be performed by the parties to a contract, the party suing for damages for the non performance by the other party, or for specific performance, is only required to aver that he was ready and willing to perform the agreement on his part, and that the defendant was requested to perform the agreement on his part but refused and neglected to do so. In such cases an offer on the part of the party making the demand is implied, and a refusal and neglect to comply with the demand dispenses with any other offer[1] The refusal of one party to perform, in such cases, is a waiver of performance, and it is sometimes said to be a waiver of a tender,[2] but the expression is inaccurate, as an offer of performance, where there are concurrent acts to be performed by the parties, is not, strictly speaking, a tender

555; Tyler v Reed, 5 T. B Mon (Ky) 36, McGehee v Jones, 10 Ga 127, Lumpsden v Manson, 96 Me 357; Sheets v Shelden, 7 Wall 417

[2] See Webster v Frevet 11 Ill 254, Board v Henneberg, 41 Ill 179; Binford v Boardman, 44 Iowa, 53, Breitenbach v Turner, 18 Wis 140, Palmer v Palmer, 72 N. W Rep. 322, s c. 4 Det L N

649, Cain v McGimon, 36 Ala 168

[3] See Dunn v Hunt, 63 Minn 484

[4] Dotterei v Freeman 88 Ga 186

[1] Tinney v Ashely 15 Pick 546, St Paul v Brown, 9 Minn 157 Stevenson v Maxwell, 2 N Y 115, Smith v Lewis, 26 Conn 110

[2] Martin v. Merritt 57 Ind 34

**§ 467. Plea of tender met by general denial—Demurrer—Motion to make more definite and certain.**—The plea of tender may be met by a general denial, and under it the plaintiff may prove any fact done, or omitted, that will show that the alleged tender was insufficient in law. But if it be alleged specifically, that it was insufficient, by reason of being conditional, or that the amount was insufficient, etc, the tender will be held sufficient if the issue is found for the defendant upon that point. The plea must be met by a reply or the tender will be admitted.[1] It is to be doubted whether the vice in pleading, termed a negative pregnant, peculiar to denials of time, value, payment, etc., in other cases could be urged against a denial of specific amount tendered, or the time a tender was made, for the reason that the exact amount, and the exact time, are material.

If a plea of tender is insufficient, as when it imports a conditional tender,[2] or fails to state the time, or does not state it with certainty,[3] or that the defendant was always ready and willing to pay the money since the time of tender,[4] the defect should be taken advantage of by demurrer.[5] Where leave is granted to file a new plea in an appellate court, such plea is demurrable if it does not show that a tender relied upon in the lower court was pleaded in that court.[6] So, if a tender is shown by the complaint to be necessary, and it is not pleaded, the defect may be taken advantage of by demurrer.[7] Where the allegations are indefinite and uncertain a motion may be made to make more definite and certain.[8]

**§ 468. When uncore prist is pleaded—Tout temps prist.**—If the debt or duty is discharged by a tender and refusal, it is sufficient merely to plead the tender and refusal.[1] So, when

---

[1] Davis v Henry, 63 Miss 110

[2] Hall v The Norwalk F Ins Co, 57 Conn 105

[3] Halle v Smith, 45 Pac 872

[4] Lanier v Trigg, 6 S & M 641; Clough v Clough, 26 N H 24

[5] Gardner v Black, 98 Ala 638

[6] Brickett v. Wallace, 98 Mass 528

[7] Rennyson v Relfsnyder 11 Pa Co Ct 157

[8] Bateman v Johnson, 10 Wis 1

[1] 1 Inst 207, 2 Co Litt Sec 335 N 101; Cotton v Clinton, 1 Cro 755, 9 Pac Abr Tit Tender (II) 2

ever a lien or some collateral right is discharged by the
tender and refusal, in an action wherein the creditor is seek
ing to collect the debt, or take advantage of the alleged fail
ure to perform the duty, by resorting to a foreclosure of the
lien or enforcement of the collateral right, if the tenderor
elects to stand merely upon the defensive without seeking
any affirmative relief, it is sufficient, without more, to plead
the tender and refusal.[2] But when the debt or duty is not
discharged by the tender and refusal, it is not enough for
the party who pleads the tender, in an action brought by
the other party to recover the debt, or damages for a failure
to perform the duty, to plead the tender and refusal alone,
but "he must also plead that he is yet ready to pay the
money," or perform the duty.[3] According to the old books,
where the debt or duty arose at the time of the contract, and
was not discharged by the tender and refusal, it was not
enough for the party pleading the tender to plead the tender
and refusal with *uncore prist*, but he must also plead *tout
temps prist*  Formally the plea of tender with *tout temps prist*
was applicable only where the party pleading the tender had
never been guilty of any breach of his contract   He was
required to plead in addition to the tender and refusal with
*uncore prist*, not that he has been ready and willing to pay
from the time of the tender but that he was always ready
from the time the obligation became due[4]  The authorities

-Hunter v  Le Comte 6 Cow
728  See Sec  351

[2] 2 Co  Litt  Sec  335  9 Bac
Abr  Tit  Tender (D) 2  Ferrell v
Lacy  31 So  Rep  (Ala) 109  Wil-
der v  Seelye  8 Barb  108

[3] Hume v  Peploe 8 East 168,
9 Bac  Abr  Tit  Tender (D) 3
Dixon v  Clark  5 C  B  365  Haldenby v  Tuke  Willes 632  Downman v  Downman  1 Wash  29
Giles v  Hart  Salk  622  was an
action of  *indebitatus assumpsit*
and *quantum meruit*  The plaintiff alleged a request on such a
day and place and that the defendant refused to pay  The defendant pleaded that at such day,
before the request  he tendered
and the plaintiff refused  and that
afterwards he was always ready
and tenders the money into court.
Plaintiff demurred because the defendant had impuled  and be
cause it is not pleadable in as
sumpsit  and because here was no
answer to the special request  Et
par Holt C  J  "When the agree
ment is to pay at a certain time
tender at that time  and always
ready is a good plea  but when
the money is due and payable im
mediately by the agreement  the
party must plead *tout temps prist*
from the time of the promise
But this cannot be after an impar
lance, for by that it appears he
has not always been ready  other

seem to have fallen into confusion concerning this question. But whatever the ancient rule may have been, now a tender may be made in cases when the sum due is definite and certain, at any time after the obligation falls due and before an action has been commenced to recover upon it, and whenever the tender and refusal has the effect of barring the damages, it must be a continuous thing, and it is necessary to allege in the plea, not only that the money was tendered, but that the defendant ever has been since the tender and still is ready and willing to pay the same.[1] And where the amount alleged to be due is uncertain, as where a sum is alleged to be due by reason of the breach of a contract, the defendant, in order to prevent a recovery, must allege and prove that he made a tender on the day the obligation fell due, and that he ever has been since the day ready and willing to perform his agreement. Where it is necessary to keep the tender good, the rule in equity in reference to pleading *uncore prist* with *tout temps prist* is no less strict than at law.[2] In a suit to redeem, a complaint was held sufficient which stated

---

wise it no importance then he might have pleaded *tout temps prist* notwithstanding the special request had in the declaration because it was immaterially alleged there. So in debt though the plaintiff lay a special the defendant may plead *semper paratus*, and pray judgment *de dampnis*. And the plaintiff may reply a special request to show the defendant was not always ready. So in the principal case. Yet there is a difference between debt and assumpsit, for in debt the damages are but accessory, but in assumpsit, are the principal. Therefore in debt the defendant may plead in bar of the damages, but in assumpsit the defendant ought to plead *always ready*, with a *profert in curia*, and demand judgment *de ulterioribus dampnis*."

Walker v. Walker, 17 S. C. 329. Wilson v. McVey, 83 Ind.

... Shugart v. Patter, 37 Iowa, 122. Barker v. Brink, 5 Iowa, 481. Town v. Trow, 24 Pick. 168. McCalley v. Otey, 90 Ala. 302. Cothran v. Scanlan, 34 Ga. 555. Dunn v. Dewey, 75 Minn. 153. 2 Greenl. Ev. Sec. 600.

"Cothran v. Scanlan, 34 Ga. 555. A plea of *tout temps prist*, after a demurrer is somewhat contradictory for the reason that if the debtor was always and still is ready and willing to pay the money or perform the duty he ought not to be concerned about the defects in his adversary's pleading. However under the old common law the court upon the particular circumstances of the case, after a decision upon the demurrer gave the defendant leave to plead as of a former term, or compelled the plaintiff to declare as of a subsequent term. Roberts v. Hughes, Barnes, 459. 9 Bac. Abr. Tit. Tender (H) 3.

34

that the plaintiff "has always since the making of the tender aforesaid, been ready and willing to pay said sum of money, so tendered as aforesaid, to the defendant, and said plaintiff still is ready and willing so to do, and now brings the same into court for that purpose, and hereby offers to pay the same." [7]

The title to specific articles passes to the obligee by the tender, and the obligor has no further concern about them, other than the duty resting upon him to leave them in some safe place for the obligee, or in case he retains the articles in his possession, to care for them as a bailee, and in pleading a tender of chattels it is not necessary to plead *uncore prist* [8] The reasons upon which the rule, resting the title of the property in the obligee, and relieving him of the necessity of continuing ready, as in the case of a tender of money, is founded, is, 'that they be *bona peritura*, and it is a charge for the obligor to keep them.' [9]

§ 469. Where a profert in curia is pleaded.—Whenever the debt or duty is not discharged by a tender and refusal, and the tender is made the ground of the cause of action or defence, the tenderor must plead the tender and refusal with *uncore prist* (or *uncore prist* together with *tout temps prist* as the case may be) together with a *profert in curia*. A plea of tender which fails to allege a payment into court sets up no defence [1] A plea of tender of money without *profert in curia* is bad on demurrer [2] The *profert in curia* is not a traversable part of the plea [3] It requires no evidence to prove it, and all questions relating to a failure to make the profert good or to the disposition of the fund when brought in are dealt with summarily by the court as a matter of practice. The pleader

7 Thompson v Foster, 21 Minn 319

8 Slingerland v Morris 8 Johns 379, Mitchell v Gregory, 1 Bibb 449, Mitchell v Merrill 2 Blackf (Ind) 89 Contra Miller v McClun 10 Yerg 245

1 Horn v Lewin Ld Raym 639 Crown v Epstein 1 N Y Supp 69, Ralph v Lomer, 28 Pac Rep 760 3 Was St 401, Jacobs v Owen 18 Pac Rep (Or) 431,

Shugart v Pattee 37 Iowa 422; Sheredine v Gaul, 2 Dall 190, Wescott v Patton 51 Pac Rep (Colo App) 1021; Hill v Place, 5 Abb Pr N S 18, Agnes v Pease 12 Wend 393 Warren v Nichols 6 Met 261, 9 Bac Abr Tit Tender (H) 4 See Sec 482

2 Gilpatrick v Ricker 82 Me 185

Planter v Lehman 26 Hun 371

should allege the facts as they are. If the money has been already paid into court, the plea should contain the allegation "and the said defendant avers that he the said defendant hath paid the said sum of £— into court　*　*　* in this action so depending as aforesaid, ready to be paid to the said plaintiff, if he will accept the same," or, if it has not been paid in previously, the allegation, "and he now brings the same into court here ready to be paid to the said plaintiff if he will accept the same."[4]

§ 470. **Prayer for judgment.**—Where the debt or duty is discharged by a tender and refusal, the plea of tender ought to conclude with a prayer of judgment for the defendant, as in such cases the action is barred forever[1]. If the tender and refusal go no further than to discharge the damages, the debt remaining, the plea should conclude with the prayer that the plaintiff take nothing, for in this case, if the thing tendered be money, the plaintiff has only to withdraw from court the money there for him, or if it be property he can take the property where it is.[2] If the damages are barred and there is no duty to continue ready, as where a vendor of chattels in an executory contract, on a tender and refusal, may elect to consider the contract at an end and he so elects, the plea of tender should likewise conclude with a prayer that the plaintiff take nothing. If a lien be discharged, in an action to foreclose the lien the plea of tender should conclude with a prayer to the effect that it be adjudged and decreed that the plaintiff is not entitled to the relief demanded.

§ 471. **Proof of a tender—Burden of proof—Strict proof required.**—A plea of tender is an affirmative plea, whether relied upon as a cause of action or as a defence, and whether interposed at law or in equity.[1] And the burden of proof

---

[4] 3 Chit Pl 921 Post Sec 182 See Durham v Landerman, 15 Pac Rep (Okla) 15 where it is held that the allegation "plaintiff here tenders into court all legal taxes that the court may find due" was sufficient under the statute requiring the money to be deposited at the trial or when ordered by the court.

[1] Bac Abr Tit Tender (H) 1.

[2] 3 Chit. on Pl 955. See Giles v Hart Salk 622, and see Karthaus v Owings 6 Har. & J. 134.

[1] Park v Wiley, 67 Ala 310

rests on the party alleging the tender.[2] The authorities are practically unanimous in holding that, in view of the serious consequences resulting from the refusal of a tender, such as the loss of interest, or the destruction of all collateral rights, which often amount to the absolute loss of the entire debt, "and in view of the strong temptation which must exist to contrive merely colorable or sham tenders, not intended in good faith," the evidence should be so full, clear, and satisfactory, as to leave no reasonable doubt that the one to whom it is made will understand it at the time to be a present, absolute and unconditional tender in payment and extinguishment of the debt or claim.[3] Where a plaintiff testified that he made a tender, which was denied by the defendant, and the plaintiff offered no evidence in corroboration, though a third person was present at the time of the alleged tender it was held that the evidence was insufficient to show a tender.[4]

§ 472. What must be proven—Ability, readiness and willingness.—The party relying upon a tender, whether the actual production of the thing is dispensed with by statute, as when a tender may be made in writing, or the actual production is dispensed with by some act on the part of the party to whom it is made, must prove that he was able, ready and willing to pay at the time of the offer.[1] Where the proof showed that no money was produced, but that the debtor informed the creditor that he then had the money ready to pay, and the creditor refused to accept it, it was held error to exclude evidence that the debtor had the money with him ready to pay.[2] Proof of a mere willingness is not sufficient. Ability and readiness means having then and there within reach, or under control, the money or thing so that it may be

[2] Tuthill v Morris 81 N Y 94, Lawrence v Stagg, 10 R I 58; Park v Wiley, 67 Ala 310, Calley v Otey 99 Ala 584

[3] Potts v Plaisted, 30 Mich 149, Bank of Benson v Hove, 45 Minn 40 Proctor v Robinson 35 Mich 284, Engle v Hall 45 Mich 57 s c 7 N W Rep 239, Shotwell v Denman 1 N J L 174, Adams v Greig 85 N W Rep

(Mich) 1078, McCormick v Lithenthal, 117 Fed Rep 89 See Kerney v Gardner, 27 Ill 162

[4] Butler v Hannah, 15 So Rep (Ala) 641 Here, both witnesses were examined by deposition

[1] Ladd v Mason, 10 Or 308, Pulsifer v Shepard, 36 Ill 516

[2] Penny v Jorgenson, 27 Minn 26

immediately handed over, or the possession surrendered, should the creditor signify a willingness to accept it. Evidence that the debtor was financially able to pay will not do.[3] Nor that he had at the time money on deposit in a bank,[4] even though the parties are then in the bank. Unless the money is drawn, the depositor has only a chose in action, the obligation of the bank to pay, which is not money. Nor is evidence that a third party would have loaned the money for the purpose of the tender, sufficient, unless it be also proven that the third party was present with the money and said that he would let the debtor have it for that purpose. Nor is it sufficient to show that he had money in the next room, or that he could have brought it from any other place.

If the things to be delivered are chattels, the debtor or vendor must show that he was ready with them at the time and place of delivery, and that they were set apart or otherwise designated.[5] To have them elsewhere would not be a readiness. If a deed or any instrument is to be delivered it must be executed and ready at the time of the offer and evidence of that fact given. So, if the party intends to pay by a bank check, he must show that the check was drawn and signed, and the revenue stamp affixed and canceled if the revenue laws require it. If a note of a third party was tendered, proof that it was endorsed, or if to be taken at the risk of the transferee that it was endorsed so as to transfer the title must be offered.[6]

§ 473. **Same subject — Amount — Quality — Appraisal —** If money is tendered, whether it is produced or not, the debtor must show that he had the exact amount or more at hand,[1] and that he stated the amount he offered. If a greater sum is tendered than was due, it must appear that it was offered as the sum due, or in payment of a less sum without requiring the creditor to return any of it; or if change was demanded, that no objection was taken to the tender on that account; if chattels, that he had the exact quantity, or a

See Hawley v Mason 9 Dana 32

[4] Myers v Byington 34 Iowa, 205

[5] Hambell v Power, 11 Iowa, 580

[6] See Eichholtz v Taylor, 88 Ind 38

[1] Bank of Benson v Hove, 45 Minn 40

larger quantity which he offered in satisfaction of the con
tract for a less quantity. As to the latter, the reasons are,
that the required quantity must be set apart so that the
title may pass to the tenderee, and, that the tenderee is not
bound to go to the trouble and expense of separating the re
quired quantity from a greater quantity; it being his duty
merely to receive, and not to assist in getting the articles
ready for delivery.

The debtor must show affirmatively the quality of the
money.[2] That it was a legal tender. If bank notes, or other
lawful money not a legal tender, or a bank check was ten
dered, the debtor must show a waiver, by proving that no
objection was taken to the medium. If lawful money not a
legal tender be offered, the jury or court must find that the
creditor waived all objections to the quality of the money.
A finding that "the lawful sum of $1,059.79 in money" was
tendered, is insufficient. There is a wide distinction between
"lawful sum in money" and "legal tender."[3] Any money
which is recognized in law as money and circulates as money,
is lawful, although a person may not have to accept it. Evi
dence of a tender of a promissory note due from the plaintiff
to the defendant, will not support a plea of tender of the sum
due on the debt.[4] If one hundred dollars is tendered, a part
of which is gold and a part silver, or minor coins, the evi
dence must show that the amount of each kind was within
the limit for which each is a legal tender. As to a tender
of chattels, the burden of proving the quality and condition
of the articles is upon the obligor. Evidence that the goods
are unmerchantable is admissible to prove that the tender
was not a legal performance of the agreement.[5]

If the contract calls for an appraisal, an appraisal in strict
accordance with the contract must be proven. Or if the stat

---

[2] In Koehler v. Buhl, 94 Mich
496, s c 54 N W Rep 157, the
defendant being unable to state
whether the money tendered was
green backs or national bank
notes, the trial court refused to
allow any further evidence on the
question whether a tender had
been made. On appeal, this was
held error on the ground that a
tender of bank notes is good un
less objected to on the ground that
they are not a legal tender

[3] Martin v. Bott, 46 N E Rep
(Ind.) 151.

[4] Carey v. Bancroft, 14 Pick
315

[5] Gould v. Banks 8 Wend 562.
s c 24 Am Dec 90

ute requires the articles to be inspected, surveyed or gauged, that the statute has been complied with must be affirmatively shown.[6]

**§ 474.  Same subject—What was said and done—Time of tender —To whom made—Actual offer—Refusal.**—The debtor must adduce proof of what was said and done, not that he tendered the money or goods. A tender is a conclusion to be drawn from the acts of the party making the offer. It must be shown upon what account or accounts the money was offered, if there is more than one cause of action set out in the complaint. If made after action brought what part, if any, was to cover the costs. The time the tender was made must be proven. If a party was not sure on which of two dates he made a tender and the last date was too late, it will not be presumed that he made it upon the first date mentioned, as nothing is presumed in favor of a tender. If no one was at the place appointed to receive the thing it must be shown that he was at the place a sufficient length of time before the sunset to have counted the money or examined the goods by daylight, and that he remained at the place until after the sun had set. So the actual production of the money must be made to appear, or that the production was dispensed with, by showing that the creditor was not there to receive it, or if present that he refused to receive it upon some ground other than a bare refusal of the sum offered, and demanding more. The debtor must prove that he made the tender to the party entitled to the money or thing offered. If made to an agent, the burden of proving the authority of the agent to receive the money or the property is upon the debtor or vendor. He must show that he made an actual offer, and not a mere proposition to pay.[1] That the tender was unconditional, or if conditional then that there was a waiver. In fact everything necessary to constitute a valid tender must be established by proof in the first instance, by the party relying upon it, nothing being presumed in his favor. The debtor must also prove a refusal by the creditor. To specify each step here, in the proof required, is at the risk of

---

[6] Jones v. Knowles 30 Me. 402     [2] Adams v. Greig 85 N. W. Rep
[1] Shotwell v. Denman 1 N. J.     (Mich.) 1078

a repetition of the chapter on the manner of making a tender. There, will be found cases illustrating what will and will not constitute a valid tender.

§ 475. **What rules govern proof of tender—Limited to pleading.**—Aside from the strict proof required, which goes mainly to the weight of the evidence, all the other rules of evidence relative to the competency, relevancy and materiality, apply in the case of proof of a tender as to any other fact necessary to be proven. An entry of an offer and refusal made by a clerk of the plaintiff's attorney, since deceased, in a day book kept for the purpose of entering daily transactions, is admissible in evidence to prove a tender.[1] A person is limited in his proof to whatever he has alleged in his pleading, and a person cannot aver payment or performance, and then in his proof be allowed to excuse his non-performance by showing a tender and refusal.[2] Nor upon the other hand is a plea of tender supported by evidence of an excuse for not making one,[3] or that the making of the tender was waived[4] or that the tenderor was able to perform. If the money was not produced, facts constituting a waiver must be adduced. A waiver of the production of the money, or a tender, cannot be established by requiring the defendant to state whether he would have received the money if a tender had been made, and it is error to admit his answer that he would not have received it.[6]

§ 476. **Proof of keeping tender good.**—Where a tender must be a continuous thing, that is kept good, the one who pleads the tender has the burden of showing that, at all times between the time of the tender and the time of the trial or the time when the money was paid into court, he has held in

---

[1] Marks v. Lahee, 3 Bing. N. C. 408, s. c. 4 Scott, 137.

[2] Duckham v. Smith, 5 T. B. Mon. 372; Barker v. Brink, 5 Iowa, 481; Grieve v. Amm, 6 N. J. L. 461.

[3] Sharp v. Golgan, 4 Mo. 30.

[4] See Holmes v. Holmes, 9 N. Y. 525, where it is stated in the syllabus that evidence of a waiver of a tender is competent and suf-

ficient to support a plea of tender. But the opinion discloses that there was merely a waiver of the production of the money. A waiver of any of the formalities of a tender is not a waiver of a tender, and there the evidence, in fact, supported the plea of tender.

[5] Hawley v. Mason, 9 Dana, 32.

[6] Bluntzer v. Dewees, 79 Tex. 272, s. c. 15 S. W. Rep. 29.

readiness a sum of money equal to the sum tendered,[1] or the sum actually due, separate and apart from his other funds. But it is not necessary to prove that the identical money tendered was kept on hand[2] Money of like legal tender qualities is sufficient.

**§ 477. Question for jury—Finding of the court—Verdict.**—The question as to whether the tender was sufficient is for the jury, but whether or not the money has been brought into court, as alleged, is for the court to determine[1] A finding that "the plaintiff ever since said tender has been ready, willing and able to pay the amount necessary to redeem from said mortgage sale," and a second finding that "the tender made by the plaintiff to the sheriff on said 5th day of October, 1893, was not kept good," are inconsistent The first finding according to its import, means that the tender was kept good Where conflicting the cause will be remanded for a new trial[2] A finding that all the allegations of the answer are untrue excepting the one alleging a tender of $60, but that that sum "was and is wholly insufficient in amount" is a finding that the tender was not good.[3] A verdict in favor of the plaintiff, for the sum alleged to have been tendered, does not of itself show that the tender and deposit were found to be true, so as to entitle the defendant to his costs The jury may have based its verdict upon the admission in the answer, and not upon any proof of tender. The defendant should take a special finding upon that issue[4]

[1] McCalley v Otey 12 So Rep (Ala) 406 See Saunders v Byer 152 Mass 141

[2] Colby v Stevens 38 N H 191

[3] Post Sec 186

[2] Dunn v Hunt, 63 Minn 484, s c 65 N W Rep 948

[3] Shaffer v Willis 56 Pa Rep (Cal) 635

[4] Jacobs v Oren 30 Or 593, s c 48 Pac Rep 431 See Gamble v Sentman, 68 Md 71

# CHAPTER XV.

## BRINGING MONEY INTO COURT.

**§ 478 Bringing money into court on a plea of tender in actions at law.**—Bringing money into court is the act of depositing money in the hand of the proper officer of the court for the purpose of satisfying a debt or duty [1] The practice of bring money into court in support of a plea of tender is of ancient origin Sir Edward Coke in his Commentaries upon the Institutes of the Laws of England by Littleton mentions the practice He said "If an obligation of an hundred pounds be made with condition for the payment of fifty pounds at a day, and at the day the obligor tender the money, and the obligee refuseth the same, yet in action of debt upon the obligation, if the defendant plead the tender and refusal, he must also plead that he is yet ready to pay the money, and tender the same into court" [2] The practice has since

[1] 1 Bouv Law Dic 207 See Leavitt v. De Launay, 4 Sandf. Ch 180

[2] Co Litt. 207 a. The first edition of Sir Edward Coke's Commentaries upon Littleton was published in his life time, in 1629.

been followed, and now, whenever a tender is made and the
debt remains, a plea of tender in an action at law to recover
the debt must be accompanied by a *profert in curia.*[1] A statutory provision allowing a tender to be made in writing, such
as is in force in Iowa and Oregon, does not change the rule
in this respect. The common law rule in reference to keeping
the tender good and bringing the money into court applies[1]
The practice extends to actions for the recovery of an un-

[1] Mohn v Stoner, 11 Iowa, 30,
Same v Same, 11 Iowa, 115, Sheredine v Gaul, 2 Dall 190, Soper
v Jones, 56 Md 503; Felkner v.
Hazelton, 38 Atl Rep 1051, Park
er v Beasley, 116 N C 1, State
v Briggs, 65 N C 159, Bailey v
Metcalf, 6 N H. 156; Becker v
Boon, 61 N Y 317; Frost v Flanders, 37 N. H 549, Allen v
Cheever, 61 N H 32, Jarboe v
McAfee, 7 B Mon 279 Shugart
v Pattee, 37 Iowa 122; Hill v
Place, 5 Abb Pr N S 18, Gilker-
son v. Smith 15 W Va 44, Wing
v Hurlburt, 15 Vt 607, Pratt v
Gallup, 7 Vt 344; Brock v Jones,
16 Tex 461, Took v Bonds 29
Tex 119; Fishburn v Sanders, 1
N & M 242, Hamlett v Tallman,
30 Ark 505, Park v Willey, 67
Ala 310, Cullen v Green, 5 Hart
17 Robinson v Games 3 Call
243; Eddy v O'Hara, 14 Wend
221, Brown v Fergeson 2 Denio,
196, Bailey v Bucher, 6 Watts, 74;
Clark v Mullinix 11 Ind 532,
Booth v Comegys, Minor 201,
Ratan v Drew, 19 Wend 304,
Hayward v Munger, 14 Iowa 517,
DeWolf v Long 2 Gilman, 679,
Jeter v Littlejohn 3 Mur 186,
Spann v Baltzell, 1 Fla 301,
Coghlan v South Car R Co 32
Fed Rep 316 Warrington v Pol-
lard 21 Iowa 281, Eastman v
Town of Rapids, 21 Iowa 590,
Jones v Mullinix 25 Iowa, 198,

Phelph v Kathron, 30 Iowa, 230,
Hasley v Flint, 15 Abb Pr 367,
Mahan v. Waters, 60 Mo 167;
Phoenix Ins Co. v. Overman, 32
N E Rep (Ind. App.) 771, Authur
v Authin, 38 Kan 691; McDaniel
v Upton, 45 Ill App 151 A tender in an action at law but tried
by agreement, in equity, must be
kept good by a deposit of the
money in court. West v Farmers' Mut Ins Co, 90 N W Rep
(Iowa) 523

[1] Mohn v Stoner, 11 Iowa, 30,
Same v Same 11 Iowa, 115, Johnson v Triggs, 4 G Gr 97, Warrington v Pollard, 21 Iowa, 281,
Shugart v Pattee 37 Iowa, 122
In Missouri, under an old statute
which provided that in all actions
where, before suit brought, tender shall be made and full payment offered, and the party to
whom such tender shall be made,
shall refuse the same, and yet afterwards will sue for the debt, he
shall not recover any costs in such
suit, but the defendant shall recover costs as if judgment had
been given in his favor upon the
merits, it was held that the common law was changed and that it
was not necessary after a tender
to bring the money into court nor
to show that the defendant had
always been ready to pay; the
tender before suit brought only effecting the matter of costs (1852)
Klein v Keyes 17 Mo. 326

liquidated sum in cases where the statute permits a tender to be made.[5] A tender of the amount due upon an execution must be kept good by bringing the money into court, on an application for an *audita querela*,[6] or for relief by way of a motion. An action of detinue, or a suit in equity, based on a tender and refusal of the amount of the debt, cannot be maintained to recover a note and mortgage given to represent and secure the debt without bringing into court the amount admitted to be due.[7] In all those commonwealths where a tender and refusal does not have the effect of extinguishing the mortgage security unless kept good, the money must be deposited in court at the time of commencing an action or interposing a defence based upon the tender.[8] A tender of money by a party who has broken his covenant must be kept good by bringing the money into court, in order to avail him in an action brought for such breach.[9]

In general, a surety being bound by a collateral undertaking incident to the debt is discharged by a tender and refusal, and when sued he need only plead the tender and refusal without bringing the money into court; but if the undertaking be to pay a debt of record, as where a surety undertakes to pay the judgment that may be awarded on an appeal, either for the principal and costs, or merely the costs, in order that a tender may amount to payment, the money must be brought into court for the party to whom it is due.[10] In such cases where judgment goes against the principal, the liability of the surety is not contingent but fixed and definite and of record, not depending upon the result of any future litigation based upon an alleged default of the principal.

The thing tendered need not be brought into court in support of a plea of tender and refusal, where the thing sought to be recovered is not the thing contracted to be delivered, as where damages are sought to be recovered for an alleged breach of a covenant to deliver property.[11]

[5] See Solomon v. Bewicke, 2 Taunt 317

[6] Perry v. Ward, 20 Vt 92

[7] Commercial Bank v. Crenshaw, 15 So Rep (Ala.) 741

[8] Woolner v. Levy 18 Mo App. 469; Campbell v. Seeley V. 38 Mo App 301, Landis v. Saxton, 89 Mo 382. See Musgates v. Pumpelly 16 Wis 600

[9] Nelson v. Orne, 41 Ill 18

[10] Halsey v. Flint 15 Abb Pr 367

[11] Mitchell v. Gregory 1 Bibb 449

§ 479. **Bringing money into court on a plea of tender in suits in equity.**—If a tender and refusal is made the basis of a cause of action in equity, in cases where, but for the tender and refusal, the right to relief at the time of commencing the action would not have existed, the amount tendered must be brought into court. In a suit to restrain a sheriff from selling certain lands upon execution, on the ground that a tender had been made to him of the full amount due, the court said: "He should have brought the money into court and deposited it with the clerk when he filed his bill, so that the other party might at any time have accepted the tender, and put an end to the litigation. This is indispensably necessary as well in courts of chancery as in courts of law."[1] So, where there is an attempt to redeem from a statutory foreclosure of a mortgage or other lien (where the statute provides that in order to redeem the amount bid at the sale must either be paid or tendered to the purchaser) by a tender of the amount due, in suit to redeem based upon the tender and a refusal, the amount tendered must be brought into court.[2] So, where the heirs of a mortgagor brought a writ of entry against the mortgagee in possession, alleging a tender and refusal, it was held that the money must be brought into court.[3] So, where the tender and refusal affects the discharge of a lien, if made the basis of affirmative relief, either by a plaintiff or by a defendant, the tender must be kept good and the money brought into court, even though the tender and refusal may be pleaded as a defence without keeping the tender good or bringing the money into court.[4]

But where the right to affirmative relief is not dependent upon a tender and refusal, in an action to obtain such relief or where such relief is asked by a defendant, and a tender and refusal is pleaded, it is not necessary to bring the money tendered into court. Thus in an action to foreclose a mortgage or other lien, a tender may be set up to defeat a fore

[1] De Wolf v. Long 7 Ill. 679, Doyle v. Teas 4 Scam. 268, Shields v. Lozier, 22 N. J. Eq. 447.

See Alexander v. Caldwell 61 Ala. 550.

[2] See Ritchie v. Ege, 59 N. W. Rep. (Minn.) 1020, to the contrary.

[3] Bailey v. Metcalf, 6 N. H. 156.

[4] Werner v. Tuch, 127 N. Y. 217, s. c. 27 N. E. Rep. 845. Foster v. Mayer 24 N. Y. Supp. 46, Cobbey v. Knapp, 37 N. W. Rep. 485, Clark v. Neumann, 76 N. W. Rep. (Neb.) 892.

closure and for equitable relief, without bringing the money tendered into court.[5] So, bringing money into court is not required where the action is to redeem from a mortgage or trust deed.[6] In all such cases, before foreclosure the right of paying the debt and having a discharge of the mortgage or other lien exists independently of any tender and such right may be invoked without a tender.[7] The action in such cases, although termed a "suit to redeem" is in fact one to compel the mortgagee to accept the amount of the mortgage debt, and to discharge the mortgage of record. The term applied to the suit and the term designating the relief, namely "redemption" are, since the adoption of the equitable theory of mortgages, misnomers. It is unnecessary to bring money into court where the real foundation of the cause of action is some committed or threatened wrongful or fraudulent act of the defendant, as where an action is commenced after a tender to set aside an unauthorized sale under a trust deed,[8] or to restrain a sheriff from executing a deed, where, at the time of the sale, he neglected to make a memorandum of such sale so as to take the same out of the statute of frauds.[9] So, where a tender has been made in rescinding a contract on the ground of fraud, it is unnecessary to bring the money into court at the time of filing the bill to rescind, although it should be brought in before the relief is granted.[10] Where the covenants are dependent, the rule that a strict and unconditional tender followed by bringing the money into court is necessary in order that the tender may be regarded as payment at the time does not apply to the offer or tender of performance required in some jurisdictions before bringing a suit for specific performance of a contract for the sale of land.[11] In all such cases a tender or offer goes only to the

Mankel v. Belscamper, 54 N W Rep (Wis) 500 Breitenbach v. Turner 18 Wis 148

[6] Hayward v. Munger 14 Iowa, 516, McCalley v. Otey, 90 Ala 302 Catlin v. Jones 55 Ala 624 See McGuire v. Van Pelt 55 Ala 344, overruling Dinghdrill v Sweeney 11 Ala 310

[7] See Beebe v. Buxton 99 Ala 117

[8] Whelan v. Reilly 61 Mo 565

[9] Ruckle v. Barbour, 48 Ind 274

[10] Miller v. Louisville &c Co, 83 Ala 274

[11] Webster v. French 11 Ill 254 Bradford v. Foster 87 Tenn 4 Livingston County v. Henningberg 44 Ill 179 McDaniel v. Kimbrell 3 Green 335 Dill v. Hazeltigg 15 Ind 576, citing Hunter v. Bales, 24 Ind 299 Irving v. Gregory 13 Gray 215;

question of barring interest and costs  But the rule that the money need not be brought in is not universal.[12]

Where a tender of the amount due is a bar to a collateral remedy, as where a lien is discharged by a tender and refusal, such tender may be pleaded as a defence in a suit to enforce such remedy without bringing the money into court.[11] But, as we have seen, if a defendant goes further and asks for affirmative relief, it will be granted solely upon the condition that he does equity; namely that he bring into court the amount admitted to be due on the mortgage. Equity goes further and enforces payment by awarding a decree of foreclosure. Having neglected to insist upon his strict legal right and submitting his case to the equitable powers of the court, the court applies the maxim—"He who seeks equity must do equity."

§ 480. **Where it is unnecessary to bring money into court.**— Where a tender is made for the purpose of discharging goods from a lien and it is refused, it is not necessary in an action to recover the possession of the goods to bring the amount tendered into court [1] If an administrator has tendered to an heir or devisee the amount coming to him, or to a creditor of an estate the whole sum due or a dividend decreed to be paid, he has performed his duty and an action on the probate bond cannot be maintained, even though the administrator neglects to bring the sum thus tendered into court [2] It is sufficient to show that there was not any forfeiture of the bond when the action was brought. If a sum is tendered which,

Lynch v. Jennings, 43 Ind. 276, Gardner v. Randell, 7 S. W. Rep. 781, Sparm v. Sterns, 18 Tex. 556, Burk v. Boquet, 1 Dessaus 142 Louther v. Anderson, 1 Bro Ch 347, Hunter v. Daniel, 4 Hare, 3, Eng Ch 420, Washburn v. Dewey, 17 Vt 92. See Jarboe v. McAlle's Heirs, 7 B Mon 279, and Lampre v. St Paul &c Ry Co, 91 N. W Rep (Minn) 29

[12] Schearff v. Dodge, 33 Ark 340.

[13] Simpson v. French, 25 How

Pr 464, Moynahan v. Moore, 9 Mich 9, s c 77 Am Dec 468, Hill v. Carter, 59 N. W Rep (Mich) 413, Exchange Fire Ins Co v. Norris, 26 N Y Supp 823, s c 76 Hun 527, Cass v. Higenbotam 100 N Y 248, Kortright v. Cady, 21 N. Y 363, Loughborough v. Nevine, 74 Cal. 250

[1] Wagenblast v. McKean, 2 Giant s Cas 393 See Evansville R. Co v. Marsh, 57 Ind 505

[2] Potter v. Cummings, 18 Me 55

in an action by the tenderor upon the obligation, is a proper
set off, it is not necessary to bring the money tendered into
court. Thus, where, after a tender of the premium due upon
a life insurance policy, an action is brought to recover upon
the policy, the amount of the premium theretofore tendered
need not be brought into court but may be deducted from the
sum recovered.[3] The reason for bringing money into court
has been said to fail where the money has so notoriously de
preciated as to have become of no value.[4] Unless accounted
for as on hand or lost or destroyed without fault of the
tenderor, such a rule would enable a tenderor to dispose of
the notes at a time when they were of value and escape his
liability by showing that at the time of the plea they were
valueless

§ 481.  Object of bringing money into court.—The object of
bringing money into court on a plea of tender is to keep the
tender good, and place the money where the party entitled
to it may receive it at any time, should he change his mind
A tender does not satisfy the demand, it merely stops the
running of interest if kept good   After a tender is made
the money justly belongs to the creditor and it should be at
all times accessible to him[1]  So, also, by bringing the money
into court where there has been a previous tender of it, the
defendant, providing his tender is proven sufficient, is enabled
to escape paying the costs of the action.[2]  A tender, not hav
ing the effect of satisfying the demand, there is no way for
the plaintiff to secure his dues in his action except by a
voluntary deposit in court of the sum due, or through the
coercive machinery of the law   So, that unless the defendant
voluntarily deposit in court the sum tendered, from whence
the plaintiff may take it by the mere asking  the machinery
referred to must of necessity be kept in motion to recover
that which the defendant was once willing to deliver but
which he might withhold should the right to pursue his prop
erty be denied to the creditor.  If he does not voluntarily
come forward with the money he is in default and he loses

[3] Schwartz v. Germania Life
Ins Co, 18 Minn 448
[4] Ieter v. Littlejohn, 3 Mur. 186
[1] Johnson v Triggs, 4 Green
97

[2] Stowell v Reed, 16 N H. 20,
s c 41 Am Dec 714 Huntington
v Zeigler, 2 Ohio St 10

the benefit of his previous offer, and must pay the interest and costs. The plaintiff by his action having transferred the controversy to the court, the defendant is enabled by bringing into court the amount he concedes to be the plaintiff's dues, to relieve himself from further responsibility for the sum. Thereafter he need only establish that his offer conformed to the requirements of a valid tender, and that it was continuous, and confine his defence to plaintiff's claim to any ulterior sum. The defendant having been cast in suit, there is no more convenient way of placing the sum tendered at the disposal of the plaintiff and at the same time protecting himself from the consequences of the litigation, than by surrendering the subject of the litigation to the immediate control of the court to which the plaintiff has submitted his cause.

§ 482. **Pleading where money is brought into court on a plea of tender.** — A plea of tender, as we have seen, where the debt remains, to be good must allege the tender and refusal with *uncore prist*, or *uncore prist* and *tout temps prist* together, with *profert in curia*[1] The plea must be to the effect that the money has been brought into court or that he now brings it in, and a plea of tender will not be considered unless this is alleged. A plea that "defendant now brings the money into court" means that the money was brought in with the

[1] Soper v. Jones, 56 Md. 503, Carley v. Vince, 17 Mass. 389

[2] 3 Chit. Pl. 921. Hall v. Place 5 Abb. Pr. N. S. 18. 36 How. Pr. 26, same. Booth v. Comegys Minor 201 Slack v. Price 1 Bibb 272 Seldon v. Roof 55 N. J. Lq. 608 Eddy v. O'Hara 14 Wend 221 Greeley v. Whitehead 35 Fla. 523 Bailey v. Bucher 6 Watts 74 Brickett v. Wallace 98 Mass 528 Sheredine v. Gaul 6 Dall 190 Foster's Succession 51 La. Ann 1670

[3] Kuthans v. Owings 6 H. & J. 139 Robinson v. Games 3 Call (Va.) 243 See Christian v. Na-

-tional Life Ins. Co, 101 Ala. 634, s. c. 14 So. Rep 374 where it was held that there was no prejudice in sustaining a plea of tender which fails to allege that the defendant "now brings into court" where another plea in the same count is in legal form and the proof is conclusive that the money was paid into court when the plea was filed. See also Diebold Safe Co. v. Holt 4 Okla 479 where it is held that after judgment the objection to the plea on the ground that it did not contain an allegation of payment into court, came too late

answer.[4] It is not necessary to allege that the money brought in is the identical money tendered.

As to the necessity of pleading a tender with a *profert in curia*, it has been said, where money is payable at a fixed time and place and a tender is made, that the defendant should not be driven to plead it, as the plea of tender requires the money to be brought into court, and therefore if the defendant be compelled to plead, he must transport his money to the court however distant, though he may have always had it ready at the place where and when only he had promised to pay it.[5] But the decisions so holding are few and in conflict with the current of authorities. The rule may be stated to be whether a time and place be fixed by the contract or not that the party if he relies upon a tender must plead the tender with a *profert in curia*, and he must take the money and deposit it in the court in which the action is pending, wherever it may keep its office for the transaction of its ministerial duties.[6]

§ 483. **Manner of bringing money into court on a plea of tender.**—Money may be brought into court in two ways, namely, upon a plea of tender in an action to recover a debt for damages where a tender in such cases may be made, and upon a rule or order of the court.[1] A rule or order of the

[4] Noldon v. Root, 35 N. J. Eq. 408.

[5] See Mitchell v. Mitchell, 2 Blackford 87, s. c. 18 Am. Dec. 128, which was a tender of personal property. The court in considering the question referred to Sanders v. Bowes, 14 East 500, Rowe v. Young, 2 Broad & Bing. 165, Gully v. Springer, 1 Blkf. 257, and Palmer v. Hughes, 1 Blkf. 328, which appear to be decisions upon the old question whether a plaintiff in his declaration in cases where the demand is a promissory note or bill and the like should aver a demand at the place or whether it should be left to the defendant to plead a tender at the place.

[6] See Curley v. Vance, 17 Mass. 388, where the plea was that at the day and place he was ready with the money, etc., which was held bad for the want of a *profert in curia*.

[1] It has been said that the power of a clerk of court to receive payment of a judgment in his office exists at common law. Commercial Ins. Co. v. Peck, 73 N. W. Rep. (Neb.) 152. But the current of authorities are to the effect that the clerk has no such power. Lewis v. Cockrell, 31 Ill. App. 476. Seymour v. Haines, 104 Ill. 557. Chinn v. Mitchell, 2 Metc. (Ky.) 92. Mazyck v. M'Ewen, 2 Bailey (S. C.) 28. See Curry v. Thomas, 8 Port. (Ala.) 293. The

court is necessary (1) in all cases where the money brought in is in the nature of a deposit to abide such disposition of it as the court may deem equitable upon the final determination of the action upon its merits, and (2) in actions to recover a debt where the amount which ought to be paid is certain or capable of being made certain by computation and the defendant having been cast in suit, desires, in order to save subsequent interest and costs, to confess all or a part of plaintiff's claim. In the latter case, depositing money in court is termed "Bringing money into court upon the common rule," of which more will be said presently. Where a tender has been made and pleaded with *uncore prist*, the party pleading it has a right to bring the money into court because it constitutes a part of his plea of tender [2] The practice is for the party pleading the tender, on filing or before serving the plea, to deliver the money to the clerk of the court or other officer authorized by law to receive it for the court. In England, formerly, and the same practice at present obtains here, the officer to whom the money is delivered receipts for it in the margin of the plea [3] An order of the court authorizing the deposit where a tender was pleaded in an action to recover a debt, has been obtained owing doubtless to confounding the practice with that of bringing money into court upon the common rule and the practice of allowing money to be brought into court in equity to abide the event of the suit, but such an order is unnecessary [4] Bringing money into court in an action to recover a debt where a tender with *uncore prist* and *profert in curia* are pleaded, as observed, is a part of the plea, a legal right, and mandatory upon the part of the pleader regardless of any rule or order of the court [5]

clerk cannot receive the amount of plaintiff's claim before judgment Ball v. State Bank, 8 Ala 590, Governor v Reed, 38 Ala. 252, Windham v Coats, 8 Ala 285, Baker v. Hunt, 1 Wend 103

[2] Murray v Windley, 7 Iredell's Law, 201, citing Sellon's Pr. 305 See Curry v Thomas, 8 Port (Ala) 293, and Neldon v Root, 55 N J Eq 608

[3] Tidd's Pr 672

[4] See Phelps v Town, 14 Mich 374

[5] Bringing money into court in support of a plea of tender is a practice which has obtained in the English common law court from time immemorial, and in America from the beginning whenever a court was erected to administer the laws derived from the mother country It would seem that, concerning the subject

In those cases where the money brought into court is in the nature of a deposit to abide the final determination of the action, whether it is brought in in a case where a tender is pleaded or upon an offer or tender in the bill, an order for leave is necessary for the reason that being brought in

of pleading a tender with *profert in curia*, which, throughout several centuries the courts have repeatedly been called upon to consider all points as to the mode of procedure in bringing the money into court would have been long ago resolved and the practice clearly pointed out, but such is not the case, and there is no more difficult and perplexing subject. The adoption of the more modern practice of bringing money into court upon the common rule, and the still more modern practice of allowing money to be brought into court in equity to abide the result of the suit has through the frequent confounding of the practice in those cases with that under a tender tended to render the practice under a tender more obscure Sir William Blackstone did not elucidate the practice of paying money into court in support of a tender In considering the plea of confession by way of *payment of money into court*, he dismisses the subject of bringing money into court in support of a plea of tender thus—"which is for the most part necessary upon pleading a tender" and then continues with the consideration of the practice of paying money into court after action brought, for he mentions the necessity of bringing in the costs theretofore incurred a thing unnecessary where a tender is pleaded with *profert in curia* 3 Bl Com 304 Mr Tidd in his work entitled "The Practice of the

Courts of King's Bench and Common Pleas, etc.," has made no mention of the mode of paying the money in further than to mention the officer to whom the money must be paid I Tidd's Pr 673 The supreme court of Pennsylvania has said that to enable a defendant to recover costs upon a plea of tender, he must not only have tendered the amount due but must have obtained a rule to enable him to bring the money into court Harvey v Hackley 6 Watts, 264 The correct practice is indicated in a negative manner It is true by decisions of the supreme court of Massachusetts and of North Carolina In the former state the court said "The payment of money by plaintiff to the clerk of court it not appearing to have been upon any tender averred in the bill and substantiated by proof, and not being made under any rule or in pursuance of any order of the court cannot effect in any manner the rights of the parties" Hart v Goldsmith 1 Allen, 145 In the latter state the court observed "In no case can the defendant after failing to make a tender at the proper time and pleading it in a proper manner, bring money into court but upon a rule first obtained" Murray v Windley 7 Iredell's Laws, 201, citing 1 Sellon's Pr 305; Mazyck v M'Ewen, 2 Bailey 28; Hart v Goldsmith 1 Allen (Mass), 145 See Currie v Thomas S Port (Ala) 293; Levan v Steinfeld 55 N J L 41

conditionally, it is necessary that it be placed at the disposal of the court subject to the conditions attached, and this cannot be done in any other way than upon a motion for leave to bring it in for the purpose specified. The court must guard against bringing money in, in cases where it is not necessary, as a practice of allowing litigants to deposit money with the clerk for the court whenever they see fit, would be to make the court the custodian of all moneys due, and throw upon the officers of the court the risk incident to the care and safe keeping of the thing deposited, which in many instances would be great

§ 484. **At what time money may be brought into court.—** On a plea or answer setting up a tender the money must be brought into court at the time of filing the pleading[1] If the practice is to serve the pleading upon the adverse party and file it later, which may be done in some of the code states, then the money must be deposited in court before serving the plea or answer The common law rule requiring the money to be brought into court at the time of filing the plea setting up the tender is changed by statute in some of the states In Kansas, it is held sufficient if it is deposited at the time of the trial or when ordered by the court;[2] in Oklahoma, when ordered by the court;[3] in Maine, it is the practice to bring it in on the first day of the term.[4]

[1] Shields v Lozier 22 N J Eq 117 Gilkeson v Smith, 15 W Va 44 De Wolf v Long, 7 Ill 679, Franklin v Ayer, 22 Flo 663, Neldon v Roof, 55 N J Eq 608; Whittaker v Belvidere Co, 55 N J Eq 674, 2 Jones on Mortg Sec 1095 Keyes v Roder, 1 Head 19, Warren v Nichols, 6 Met. 261, Commercial Bank v Crenshaw, 103 Ala 497 See The Serapis, 37 Fed Rep 436, where it is held that the money, under the rules of the court must be deposited with the clerk before answer, plea or claim filed In a justice court where a defendant is summoned to appear on a certain day and answer the complaint of the plaintiff, the practice is the same as that which obtains under the common law In courts of record and the money must be brought in on the return day on filing the answer setting up the tender Keyes v Roder, 1 Head 19

[2] Authur v Authur, 38 Kan 691, German Am Ins Co v Johnson, 49 Pac Rep 972

[3] Gray v Styles, 49 Pac Rep. 1083

[4] Reed v Woodman 17 Me 13 This was a case where the tender was made under a statute after action brought Pillsbury v Willoughby 61 Me 274, Fernald v Young 76 Me 358, Gilpatrick v Ricker, 82 Me 185 See Sargent v Slack, 47 Vt 674

Where money is brought into court upon a plea of tender it is presumed to be brought before the court, and it has been said that it cannot be brought in in vacation.[5] Whatever may have been the practice formerly, it is evidence that courts of record, as now constituted, are always open to litigants for the purpose among other things, of commencing their actions and advancing them to issue, so that now in theory as well as practice, depositing money with the clerk where it constitutes a part of the plea, is bringing it before

---

[5] Curtis v. Thomas, 8 Port. 293. Under the ancient common law an action was commenced by the delivery of an original writ issued in the name of the king out of the court of chancery containing a summary statement of the cause of action, which writ was addressed to the sheriff of the proper county requiring him to command the defendant to satisfy the claim and on his failure to comply to summons him to appear before one of the courts of common law there to account for his non compliance. The sheriff was commanded to have the writ in court on a certain day with his return, which day was called the return day, and it was always a day during term time. If the defendant did not appear he was brought into court by means of other writs issued out of the common law court to which the original was returnable. These processes were also returnable in term time. The various kind of writs obtainable to enforce appearance we need not enumerate. After the actual appearance of the defendant the pleadings were all made up in open court on the return day or during the term. At first the pleading was oral, later it came to be done on paper. The practice of compelling an actual appearance except in a few cases was in time discontinued, and a formal entry of an appearance by the defendant or by his attorney for him in the office of the court was sufficient. The ancient practice of delivering the pleadings in open court came also in time to be changed so that they were by the parties or attorneys mutually delivered out of court or filed with the clerk. Without tracing the various changes which took place in the practice from the time of the use of the original writs and the enforced appearance and the oral pleading to the modern common law practice in reference to appearance and pleading it is sufficient to observe that the pleadings were nevertheless throughout the various modifications of the practice entitled as of the return term and were supposed to be brought into court at that time if not delivered or filed with the clerk before the term. It will be seen that bringing money into court when the plea of tender was oral or when the plea was delivered on paper in open court being a part of the plea the money was of necessity brought before the court in term time and the theory still obtains that the pleading is done before the court, though not now in open court in term time.

the court, though the court may not then be sitting for the trial of causes. The clerk as such, can have no custody of money except for the court, and his office is always open for the transaction of the ministerial duties of the court among which is receiving and filing pleas.[6]

§ 485.  **Notice of bringing money into court.**—Notice that the money has been paid into court should be served with the plea.[1]  The averment that "he now brings the same into court here ready to be paid to the said plaintiff if he will accept the same," has been held not to be a notice that the money had been actually paid in; that it was a mere *profert in curia*[2]  But such notice may be contained in the plea, as where the pleader alleges the fact to be that the money had been there tofore paid into court.  If the plea is not accompanied by a notice that the money had been paid into court, it may be disregarded,[3] but the plaintiff, by proceeding without objecting that no notice was served, waives the irregularity[4]  In New York, where the service of notice of the payment of money into court in cases where a tender is made after action brought is not a matter of practice under the regulation of the court but a part of the prescribed statutory procedure, it was held that a plaintiff may waive the service of the statutory notice, but that a failure to return an answer containing several defences, among them a tender before suit, or otherwise raise the question before trial, was not a waiver of the right to insist on the trial that the money paid in was not a good tender after suit brought by reason of the fact that the statutory notice was not given.[5]

[6] See Phelps v Town, 14 Mich 374

[1] Sheridan v Smith 2 Hill, 538, Wilson v Doran, 110 N Y 101, Taylor v Brooklyn El R Co 7 N Y Supp 625  In Missouri where, under the statute, the money may be paid to a constable, no notice is required Crawford v Armstrong 58 Mo App 214  The rules governing a tender at common law are not applicable to a tender under the statute  Vass v McGuire, 26 Mo App 452

[2] Planter v Lehman, 26 Hun, 374

[3] Sheridan v Smith 2 Hill, 538

[4] Wilson v Doran, 110 N Y 101, Planter v Lehman, 26 Hun 374

[5] Wilson v Doran, 110 N Y 101

§ 486. **Proof that money has been brought into court.—** The plea of *profert in curia* is a present averment to be accompanied by an act of which the court takes notice as done in its presence and shown by its own records in the action[1] No evidence of the deposit of the money is required as it is a part of the plea. That the money is in court is ascertained in the same way as is the fact that a *profert in curia* is pleaded, namely, by an inspection of the records.[2] If a tender may be made under a statute by depositing the money in court, the court will inform itself whether the money has been brought in without the aid of a jury.[3]

§ 487. **Bringing money into court a matter of practice.—** The *profert in curia* is not a traversable part of the plea of tender. It is not involved in the issue and is not a question proper to be litigated on the trial.[1] Bringing money into court is a matter of practice, and questions relating to it are dealt with accordingly.

§ 488. **Consequences of a failure to bring money into court on a profert in curia—Waiver—Extent of waiver—Judgment non-obstante verdicto —** A plea of tender without the *profert* being made good by the actual deposit of the money in court is a nullity and it need not be replied to by plaintiff[1] Money which has been tendered, though not accepted, is in contemplation of law set apart and held for the tenderee by the party making the tender It follows the plea in which he tenders and offers to bring the money into court, and until the money is brought in and placed in custody of the law, the defence is unavailing[2] A plea of tender with *profert in curia* must not be confounded with the practice in equity of making a tender in the bill or answer and offering to bring the money into court, in cases where it is sufficient merely to offer to do equity and abide the order and decree of the court There, it is usually brought in or paid direct to the opposite party

---

[1] Gilpatrick v Ricker, 82 Me 185

[2] See Knox v Light 12 Ill 86 Neldon v Roof 55 N J Eq 608

[3] Newton v Ellis 16 Wis 210

[1] Sheridan v Smith, 2 Hill, 538, Gilpatrick v Ricker, 82 Me 185

Planter v Lehman, 26 Hun 374.

[1] Sheridan v Smith 2 Hill 538; Gilpatrick v Ricker 82 Me 185; Gilkinson v Smith, 15 W Va 44.

[2] Hamlett v Tallman, 30 Ark 507

in compliance with the decree. An application at the commencement of the action by the party desiring to make the deposit is seldom refused, as bringing it in is without prejudice. So in some cases resting upon particular facts, it may be ordered to be paid in to abide the final determination of the suit. Where a plea of tender with *profert in curia* is pleaded, and the *profert* is not made good, the pleading should be returned by the plaintiff.[1] Under the New York Code, which requires a notice of the deposit of the money in court to accompany the plea of tender, it was held, in a case where the answer was returned as a nullity because the notice required by the statute had not been given and the money had not in fact been brought in, that returning the answer as a nullity was in accordance with the practice before the code took effect.[2] The plaintiff may sign judgment as for want of a plea,[3] but this can be done only where the plea of tender goes to the whole issue. Where the answer contains more than one defence it cannot be returned. The other defences must be replied to if such as require it, and disposed of by a trial upon the merits. But the plea of tender may nevertheless be treated as a nullity, and there is no waiver by retaining the answer for the purpose of replying to the other defences.[6] A motion should be made to strike out the plea of tender.[7] A judgment signed as for want of a plea, where the plea of tender goes only to a part of the action, will be set aside as irregular.[8]

Where a plaintiff pleads a tender with a *profert in curia* and fails to make good the *profert* the summons or writ cannot be returned. If the plea of tender constitutes the foundation of the cause of action and but for the tender the cause of action would not exist, the defendant should move for judgment. If there are causes of action set forth in the com

[1] Planter v. Lehman, 26 Hun 374.

[2] Simpson v. French 25 How. Pr. 464.

[3] Tidd's Pr. 612, Pether v. Sheldon, Str. 368, Chapman v. Hicks, 2 Comp. & M. 633, 9 Bac. Abr. Tit. Tender (I) Becker v. Boon 61 N. Y. 317, Rosenbaum v. Greenbaum 65 N. Y. Supp. 212. Supreme Tent v. Hammers, 81 Ill. App. 560.

[6] Becker v. Boon 61 N. Y. 317. See Wilson v. Doran 110 N. Y. 105.

[7] Morrison v. Jacoby, 114 Ind. 84.

[8] Chapman v. Hicks 2 D. P. C. 641 s. c. 2 C. M. & R. 633.

plaint other than the one based on the tender, or the plea of tender with *profert in curia* affects merely the interests and costs, a motion should be made, based on such irregularity, to strike out the plea of tender, and an answer interposed to the remaining part of the declaration." Where, on a bill to redeem alleging a tender and offer to pay the redemption money into court, the court on the refusal of the plaintiff to comply with an order to bring the money into court, dismissed the bill, it was held, there appearing other equities in the bill aside from the tender alleged, that the plaintiffs were entitled to an answer and an investigation of the facts.[10] In all such cases the efforts should be confined to getting rid of the plea of tender, as the plaintiff is not entitled to a judgment embracing the whole issue, nor is he entitled to split up the action in advance of a final judgment and take judgment upon a confession of a part of one cause of action or a confession of one of several causes joined in the same action.

Bringing money into court is a requirement for the plaintiff's benefit,[11] and he is entitled to have the money paid into court before he takes issue on the plea.[12] Where the *profert in curia* has not been made good, and the plaintiff prefers to have the money under his control rather than sign judgment or move to have the plea stricken out, he may apply for an order directing it to be paid into court *nunc pro tunc*, and in default that the plea be stricken, &c.[13]

A failure to make good the *profert in curia* is not fatal to a plea of tender. It is an irregularity to be dealt with summarily by the court.[14] Being a requirement in favor of the plaintiff he may waive it,[15] and if he neglects to bring the irregularity to the attention of the court and takes issue on the plea of tender he does waive it.[16] The waiver, however, is

9 See Polk v. Mitchell, 85 Tenn. 633 where it is held that the objection that the money tendered did not accompany the bill, if tenable, should have been taken by demurrer. See also Carley v. Vance 17 Mass 389

10 Mabey v. Churchwell, 2 Coldw 63

11 Storer v. McGaw, 11 Allen, 527

12 Shepherd v. Wysong 3 W Va 16

13 Richmond &c R Co v. Blake, 49 Fed Rep 904

14 Gilpatrick v. Ricker, 82 Me 185

15 Storer v. McGaw, 11 Allen, 527

16 Shepherd v. Wysong, 3 W Va 16 Storer v. McGaw, 11 Allen, 527, Woodruff v. Trapnell,

of the right to sign judgment as for want of a plea, or to have the plea of tender summarily stricken out, as the case may be. The plaintiff still has the right to object to the irregularity upon motion for an order requiring the money to be brought in,[17] and in default that the plea be stricken out; or he may apply for leave to withdraw his reply and to sign judgment, or to have the plea of tender stricken out. So, he may at the trial object to the introduction of any evidence in support of the plea of tender, or ask that the jury be instructed to disregard the evidence of the tender or which amounts to the same thing, that instructions be given them as to the consequences of the money not being brought into court.[18] After issue and verdict is found in favor of a defendant, the plaintiff is entitled to a judgment *non obstante veredicto*, if it appears that the money has never been brought into court.[19] An objection and exception to the action of the trial court in omitting to instruct the jury as to the effect of bringing money into court to keep the tender good, raises the point that the tender was not kept good by bringing the money into court, and the point may be urged on an appeal.[20]

Where a plea of tender with *profert in curia* goes only to the question of interest and costs, without the money being brought into court, "it would be a waste of time to try the issue of tender, inasmuch as, if the tender be established by

12 Ark 689, Kelley v West 36 N Y Super. Ct 304, Knight v Beach 7 Abb Pr N S 241; Wood v Rabe, 20 J & S 479, Warren v Nichols, 6 Met 261, Wilson v Doran 17 N E Rep 688, Sheridan v Smith, 2 Hill 538, Earl v Earl 16 N J L 273, Gilpatrick v Ricker 82 Me 185, Witherbee v Kinsterer 11 Mich 359 s c 2 N W Rep 15 See Whittaker v Belvidere Co 55 N J Eq 674, where it is held that if the money is not brought in at the time of filing the answer no notice need be taken of a subsequent deposit

17 In Knox v Light, 12 Ill 86, the defendant refused to comply with the order of the court to pay the money into court, and thereupon judgment was entered for the plaintiff See Becker v Boon 61 N Y 317 as to the power of the court to order the money paid into court after answer

18 Freeman v Fleming, 5 Iowa, 460 See Dunbar v DeBoer 44 Ill App 615, and Monroe v Chaldeck 78 Ill 429

19 Porchelmer v Holly, 14 Flo 239 Claflin v Hawes, 8 Mass 261 See Ryerson v Kitchell 2 N J L 168

20 Dunbar v DeBoer 44 Ill App 615

verdict, it would be unjust to give judgment for the defend
ant and leave plaintiff's admitted debt unpaid," and where
a plaintiff neglects to take advantage of the failure to make
good the *profert in curia*, the court, on its own motion, may
interfere to save its own time from waste on immaterial issues,[21] and by order require the money to be deposited with
the clerk, and on default strike out the plea of tender or ex
clude the evidence offered thereunder.

If the money is brought in before the plaintiff moves for
relief the irregularity is cured.[22] If on the trial the tender
is proved to have been continuous by keeping the money for
the plaintiff, and it is thereupon handed to the clerk, the
irregularity is cured and the tender before action is estab
lished.[23] Where, on a plea of tender with *profert in curia*
in a police court, the money was offered to the plaintiff in
open court, who refused to receive it on the ground that he
was entitled to a larger sum, and the money was not in fact
placed in the custody of the court, and the defendant ap
pealed, and in the appellate court properly pleaded the *profert*
and paid the money into court, it was held that it was then
too late for the plaintiff to object to the irregularity in the
lower court.[24] The same rule would undoubtedly be applied
in like cases on appeals from a justice's court, or on appeals
from any inferior court where the pleadings may be amended
or recast in the appellate court, and a trial had *de novo*.

§ 489  **In what courts money may be brought in on a plea
of tender.**— At common law, money may be brought into court
in support of a plea of tender in all courts of record, at law,
in equity and in admiralty. It has been doubted whether the
practice of pleading a tender with *profert in curia* as applied
to courts of record, obtained in a justice's court.[1] In view of

[21] Gilpatrick v. Ricker, 82 Me
185. See Freeman v. Fleming, 5
Iow 460

[22] Gilpatrick v. Ricker 82 Me
185. See Freeman v. Fleming, 5
Met 264.

[23] Sheridan v. Smith 2 Hill
538, Painter v. Lehman, 26 Hun,
374, citing Knight v. Beach 7
Abb Pr N S 241

[24] Storer v. McGaw, 11 Allen,
527

[1] People v. Banker, 8 How Pr.
258 See Jonson v. Nabring, 50
Ala 392 where it is held that the
statute requiring money to be
paid into court on a plea of tender
applied to a court having a clerk
and not to a justice's court

the decisions upon the question there is now no reason for any doubt.[2] It has been said that the rule requiring money to be paid into court is just as imperative in actions commenced before a justice of a peace, where the pleas are oral, as it is in actions in the circuit court.[3] The question of the right to bring money into court in an action in a justice's court, ought certainly to be at rest in all those commonwealths, where, by statute, the courts of justice of the peace are vested with all the power, in reference to the exercise of jurisdiction within its limits, as are usual in courts of record.[4] The practice is now usually extended to police courts,[5] and all inferior courts exercising civil jurisdiction

§ 490. **Disposition and control of money in court pending an appeal—Removal of cause from State to Federal court.**—On an appeal from a *nisi prius* court the money remains in the trial court, and the appellate court has no control over the money, or over the trial court in regard to it except as may be determined in its judgment and order remanding the cause for further proceedings.[1] But where the trial is *de novo* in the appellate court, as in the case of an appeal from a judgment of a justice's court, the money should be sent up by the justice with, and as a part of his return.[2] So, by analogy, where an action is removed from a state to a federal court, money in the former court in the action should accompany the papers, so as to be in the immediate custody of the court assuming jurisdiction and where only further proceedings may be had

§ 491. **When a court of equity will order money to be brought into court.**—A court of equity may require a party who is seeking to set aside a foreclosure under a power before pro

[2] Keyes v. Roder, 1 Head 19, Nelson v. Smith, 26 Ill. App. 57, Seibert v. Kline, 1 Pa. St. 38, Phelps v. Town 14 Mich. 374

[3] McDaniel v. Upton, 45 Ill. App. 151

[4] See Philip v. Town 14 Mich. 374

[5] Brickett v. Wallace, 98 Mass. 528

[1] Califano v. McAndrews 51 Fed. Rep. 301

[2] Nelson v. Smith, 26 Ill. App. 57 Brooks v. Lawyer 61 Ill. App. 366. See Seibert v. Kline, 1 Pa. St. 38 and Phelps v. Town 14 Mich. 274, Waide v. Joy, 45 Iowa 282.

ceedings under it have been perfected, to bring the amount apparently due into court, as a condition of granting a continuance of an injunction.[1] In general, in order to support an order to deposit money in court pending an action in equity, and before the final decree there must be a clear and explicit admission in the answer, or admission in the suit, that a specific sum is due,[2] and that he who has it has no equitable title thereto.[3] There must be no uncertainty as to the amount due or doubt whether in the progress of the cause it may not turn out that no part of the claim should be paid.[4] The admission may be in the answer or one made upon an examination before a master.[5] The admissions must be admissions in the suit,[6] and by the party bound to pay so that it will not be open to subsequent controversy.[7] Where it is clearly admitted in the answer that the money is held by the defendant as a trustee, the admission is sufficient upon an interlocutory application, for making an order requiring the money to be deposited in court. An application for an order requiring money to be brought into court was refused where it was based upon an affidavit of an accountant that from an examination of the schedules and books of the defendant he found a certain sum was due.[8] The order to deposit the money may be made upon the application of the party entitled to it, or one who has some interest in the final disposition of the fund,[9] or upon the court's own motion.

A final decree should always be made conditional and the money ordered to be deposited in court in all cases where the party entitled to the relief prayed for, is found to be indebted to the other party on account of the transaction,[10] and this

[1] Schwartz v Sears Harr 440

[2] Coursen v Hamlin 2 Duer 513 McTighe v Dean 22 N J Eq 81

[3] McKim v Thompson 1 Bland 150 See Francis v Collier 5 Madd 75

[4] Schwartz v Sears Harr 440

[5] Coursen v Hamlin 2 Duer 513

[6] McTighe v Dean 22 N J Eq 81

[7] McKim v Thompson 1 Bland 150

[8] See Mills v Hanson, 8 Ves 68 Roe v Gudgen Cooper's case 304

[9] McKim v Thompson, 1 Bland 150

[10] Johnson v Huhing 18 N E Rep (Ill) 786 citing Gage v Nichols 112 Ill 271, Gage v Schmidt, 104 Ill 107, Phelps v Harding 87 Ill 442 See Lampicy v St Paul &c Ry Co 91 N W Rep (Minn) 29

should be so whether the party praying for the relief alleged
a tender, or a tender was not made. It has been said that
an order requiring money to be paid into court is not appeal
able for the reason that if a party could suspend the effect
of the order by appealing and filing an appeal bond, then he
could in effect prevent the court from going further than
barely demanding security for the payment of the money.[11]
This subject and the one considered in the next section have
no place in reality in a work on tender.

§ 492. **Bringing money into court by a stakeholder—By a
garnishee—By a defendant where there is an intervenor or claim
ant.**—Money in the possession of a stake holder, or other dis
interested party, such as a garnishee, trustee and the like,
to which he does not assert any right and which has become
the subject of litigation, may, on the application of a party
to the action claiming an interest in the fund or on the
application of the party in possession of such fund, be
ordered to be paid into court to abide the final deter
mination of the action.[1] A party indebted upon a
contract in a sum admitted to be due, but to which
sum there is more than one claimant whose claim of
right arose subsequent to the making of the contract, is it
has been said, virtually in the position of a stake holder, and
when all the claimants are before the court he will be allowed
to deposit the money in court.[2] If a person holding money or
property as bailee or custodian or otherwise, to which there
are two or more claimants, desires the benefit of a statute
permitting him to deposit the money or property with the
clerk of the court and be relieved from any liability on ac

---

[11] McKim v Thompson 1
Bland 150 See 2 Wait's Pr 595,
for a more extended discussion of
the subject of a court ordering
money to be paid into court before a final decree

[1] Successors of John S. Thompson, 14 La Ann 810

[2] Aetna Bank v United States
Life Ins Co 25 Fed Rep 531
Under a statute where material
men and laborers on a delivery
of an attested account are en-

titled to have the amount of their
claim withheld by the owner out
of money due the contractor, and
the claims presented exceed the
amount due, it was held that the
owner might institute an action
against the claimants for the pur
pose of having the amount due
from him distributed among the
claimants by order of the court,
and for that purpose may depo it
the amount due from him in court
Clark v Saloy, 2 La Ann 987

count thereof, or the benefit of proceedings by interpleader in equity, must not assert any claim to the property or voluntarily contest the asserted right of the claimants in the action brought to recover it. If he does so he waives the right to invoke the statute or claim any protection under the interpleader, and will be bound by the judgment against him[1] It has been held that a deposit in court by a defendant of a sum of money (including interest and costs) to abide the result of a controversy between the plaintiff and certain intervenors claiming the amount, not being a tender, and the plaintiff not able to take it, the defendant was not thereby discharged of his liability to pay further interest and costs.[4]

But it would seem that, if the money be paid in for the plaintiff, unconditionally, and not to abide the result of the controversy between the plaintiff and the intervenor, the fact that the latter is contesting plaintiff's right to the fund, ought not to continue the plaintiff's liability for subsequent interest and costs. This, undoubtedly, would be the rule if it was a case where money may be brought into court upon the common rule, and the defendant was allowed to withdraw his answer and bring the money in under that rule. A garnishee must actually pay the money arrested in his hand into court, in order to stop interest, a mere tender into court is not sufficient[5]

§ 493. **Bringing money into court upon the common rule—History—Manner of bringing it in.**—The practice of bringing money into court upon the common rule is said to have been first introduced in the reign of Charles II, and the first motion for leave to bring money into court is credited to Mr Sargent Leving, when Kelynge was Chief Justice of the King's Bench[1] The practice was introduced for the purpose of giving a defendant who had neglected to make a tender, an opportunity of satisfying the debt to recover which the action had been commenced, and, where a tender had been

[3] Austin v March 90 N W Rep (Minn) 384

[4] DeGoer v Keller, 2 La Ann 196, Alexandrie v Saloy, 14 La Ann 327

[5] Long v Johnson 74 Ga. 1

[1] Giles v Hart 1 Ld Raym 255 White v Woodhouse 2 Str 787 Tidd's Pr 669, 9 Bac Abr Tit Tender (K), Foote v Palmer, Wright 336 Levan v Sternfeld, 55 N J L 41

made, to enable a defendant to avoid the hazard of pleading a tender occasioned by the difficulty of proving a technical tender.[2] Mr. Chitty observed that it is advisable for the defendant, unless he be certain that before the commencement of the action he made a legal tender that can be safely pleaded in bar, to pay money into court.[3] The same object is attained by a defendant in bringing money into court upon the common rule, as upon a plea of tender with *profert in curia*; namely, immunity from the payment of further interest and costs which would otherwise accrue after the time of the tender or deposit, and disposing the money so that the plaintiff may take it when he will. Sir William Blackstone said, it is itself a kind of tender to the plaintiff.[4]

Where the dispute is not whether anything is due but how much is due the plaintiff, the defendant may have leave to bring into court any sum of money which he thinks will cover such portion of plaintiff's claim as can be proved against him, together with such costs as have been theretofore incurred by the plaintiff. Having resolved to confess such portion of the plaintiff's claim, he obtains from the court a rule in the following terms    That unless the plaintiff accept the sum paid into court, together with costs which have accrued up to the time of payment, in discharge of his claim, then the sum so paid in shall be struck from the declaration, and paid out of court to the plaintiff, and the plaintiff, upon the trial, shall not be permitted to give evidence for the sum brought in.[5] And a defendant after failing to make a tender at the proper time and pleading it in a proper manner, cannot bring money into court but upon first obtaining such rule allowing him to do so.[6] Depositing money with the clerk

---

[2] White v Woodhouse, Str 787, 9 Bac Abr Tit Tender (K), Tidd's Pr 669, Boyden v Moore, 5 Mass 365, Levan v. Sternfeld, 55 N J L 11   In Letherdale v. Sweepstone, 3 C & P 342, Mr Chief Justice Tenderden said "The plea of tender is a practice so seldom successful that I am always sorry to see a plea of tender on the record, because I know from experience that it is seldom made out"

[3] 3 Chit Pr p 684
[4] 3 Bl Com 304
[5] Levan v Sternfeld 55 N J L 11, 1 Tidd's Pr 669, 9 Bac Abr Tit Tender (K), Hallet v East India Co, 2 Burr 1120 Bank of Columbia v Sutherland 3 Cow 336

[6] Murray v Windley 7 Iredell's Law, 201, citing 1 Sellon's Pr 305, Ruckes v Palsgrave, 1 Camp 557 N, Keith v Smith, 1 Swan 92, Baker v Hunt, 1 Wend 103,

after the commencement of an action without a rule or order is not a payment to the creditor or to any one authorized to receive it for him.[7] The clerk takes it in his individual capacity as the mere agent of those who intrust him with the money.[8] The deposit is not only an irregularity but as to the plaintiff an absolute nullity. As observed by the supreme court of Tennessee—"can he [the defendant] insist that the plaintiff shall proceed at the peril of costs when there is nothing upon the record that orders it."[9] The deposit does not in any manner affect the rights of the parties and it remains the money of the party paying it in and subject to his order.[10] Without a rule or order the plaintiff must have a verdict.[11] It has been said that the court may recognize the money in the possession of the clerk as a fund in court, but this cannot be, for the reason that the custody of money by a clerk without an order directing its deposit is merely that of a private person, and it can no more be recognized as a fund in court than could money in the possession of an attorney for one of the parties. A deposit of money in court in support of a plea of tender which is proven to be insufficient, in that the offer was made after the action was commenced, or is proven to be insufficient in some other respect, does not on such failure of the defendant to substantiate his plea have the force and effect of a deposit of money upon the common rule. Such a deposit has no effect upon the costs of the action or subsequent accruing interest.[12]

§ 494. **In what cases money may be brought into court upon the common rule.**—At common law, bringing money into court upon the common rule is allowed in actions upon contract to recover a debt, where the amount due is certain or capable

Cope v Bryson, 1 Winst 112 Winningham v Redding, 6 Jones' Law (N C), 126

[7] Alexandrie v Salog, 11 La Ann 327 Levan v Sternfeld, 55 N J L 41, s c 25 Atl Rep 854

[8] Commercial Inv. Co v. Peck, 3 N W Rep (Neb) 152

[9] Ruble v Murray, 4 Haywd 27.

[10] Hart v Goldsmith, 1 Allen, 45. This was a deposit with the clk in a suit in equity and not by a defendant at law, but a rule requiring an order allowing the deposit is the same in equity as at law, although the consequences are not necessarily the same

[11] Levan v Sternfeld 25 Atl Rep 854 Ruckes v Palsgrave, 1 Camp 557, n, Currie v Thomas, 8 Port (Ala) 293

[12] Levan v Sternfeld, 55 N J L 41

of being ascertained by mere computation[1] It must be a case where a jury, after determining that the plaintiff is entitled to recover upon the whole or a part of his cause of action, has no sort of discretion as to the amount, but must arrive at the amount of their verdict by computation Money may be brought into court upon the common rule, with one exception, in every action to recover money, where at common law, a tender might, before the action was commenced, have been made. The only exception to be found in the books is in an action of debt wherein the plaintiff cannot recover less than the sum demanded, as upon a judgment.[2] And the reason appears to be that the controversy once having been settled by litigation, the amount due is no longer open to question, and that, being settled and of record, the law has wisely provided that, although the defendant may tender to the plaintiff the amount of the debt, he cannot get rid of the result of the litigation except by actual payment, consequently the plaintiff is entitled to have the old record satisfied, either by payment or by the substitution of a new record, and the defendant, having neglected to satisfy the old record before the action was brought thereon, must move the court to stay proceedings in the new action, upon his satisfying the judgment by the payment of the amount due thereon, together with the costs then incurred in the new action, or submit to have a new record with the addition of taxable costs incurred   Money may be brought into court upon the common rule in *qui tam* actions, where a tender before action brought cannot be made. A tender in such actions cannot be made for the reason that the wrongdoer cannot know for a certainty who will first institute the proceedings to recover the penalty   After action brought, the statutory penalty being fixed and certain, the court will grant leave to bring the money into court upon the common rule.[3]

The rule permitting money to be brought into court upon the common rule does not apply to an action to recover dam

[1] Govenor v Sutton, 4 Dev. & Bat. 484.

[2] Fishburn v Sanders 1 N & M 242, 9 Bac Abr Tit Tender (P), citing Burridge v Fortesque,

6 Mod 60, 7 Mod 114   See also 1 Tidd's Pr 670

[3] 9 Bac. Abr. Tit Tender (P), citing Webb *qui tam* v Poulter, Stra 1217; Stock v Dage 2 Black Rep 1052, Tidd's Pr 541

ages for the commission of a tort;[4] or to actions for the recovery of damages for dilapidation;[5] or to actions for damages for the breach of a contract,[6] where the sum sought to be recovered is uncertain and in the nature of unliquidated damages, unless the right be given by statute. The cases falling within the various classes of common law actions where money may be brought into court upon the common rule, all turn upon the cardinal principals, whether the sum sought to be recovered be certain or is capable of being reduced to a certainty by computation, where the court or jury has but to determine whether the plaintiff is entitled to recover upon all or a part of his cause of action; or there is an element of uncertainty rendering it a fit case for a judicial investigation and inquiry not only as to the right to recover but also as to the amount. In the former case leave to bring money into court is granted, while in the latter case it is not permitted, for, as observed by Chief Justice Mansfield, where the money which ought to be recovered cannot be ascertained by computation, but does in some measure depend upon the judgment of a jury, it is reasonable that the plaintiff should be at liberty to have such judgment, without being liable to costs in case it should be against him.[7] Therefore, notwithstanding the action may sound in damages, leave will be granted to bring money into court upon the common rule if there is that certainty about the sum that ought to be recovered as will dispense with the judgment of a jury upon that question. Thus, in an action of assumpsit upon a charter party, where two of the breaches assigned were for the non payment of money due for freight, and the non payment of money due for demurrage, leave was granted to bring money into court upon these counts for the reason that both the freight and demurrage due could be ascertained by computation.[8] So, in assumpsit against a common carrier for not delivering goods, where the latter gives notice that he will not be answerable for damages beyond a certain sum unless

[4] Johnson v Crawford, Phill. L (N C) 342

[5] Salt v Salt, 8 Term R 47

[6] Hodges v Lichfield, 2 Dowl 741, s c 3 M & S 201; Strong v Simpson 3 B & P 14, Squire v Archer, 2 Stra 906

[7] Hutton v Bolton, 1 H Black. 299 n

[8] Hallett v East India Co, 2 Burr. 1120

the goods are entered and paid for at a greater rate, the defendant, on an affidavit of the giving or publication of such notice, may have leave to bring into court a sum equal to the sum limited in the notice. In an action to recover for the loss of a trunk, which in point of value was full £50, where upon an affidavit of the defendant stating that he had published a notice limiting his liability to £20, for parcels &c., a motion for leave to bring money into court was granted, Lord Mansfield said "In the present case Defendant truly says, 'I am by express stipulation liable only for £20, and am ready to pay it to you.' What is the question on the merits? Is it true? If so, he is right; if not, he pays the costs. As to notice of the advertisement, it is open to be tried." [9]

In England during the reign of William IV,[10] by statute a defendant, except in certain cases, was permitted to bring money into court in actions to recover unliquidated damages, and the practice in reference to such actions appears there to be still permitted and regulated by statute. But in the United States the practice of bringing money into court in such actions, as upon the common rule, has not been established in many (if any) of the states, although in many of the states under the statute, a tender may be made after action brought, in actions to recover damages for the commission of a tort, and the money so tendered may be brought into court in support of the plea of tender. Which tender when well pleaded and proven is attended by the same consequences as is a deposit of money under the common rule, although it lays upon the defendant the burden of proving a valid tender. So, in many of the states, statutes are in force permitting a defendant to offer judgment for so much of plaintiff's claim as he thinks can be proven against him and such offer has the same effect upon subsequent accruing interest, or damages, as the case may be, and costs, as a deposit in court of the sum admitted to be due upon a plea of tender or upon the common rule. Bringing money into court in an action to recover unliquidated damages, though

---

[9] Hutton v. Boulton, 1 H. Black. 299, n.

[10] According to a note in Tidd's Pr. 671, 24 Geo. II, Ch. 14 See 4 is the first statute allowing money to be brought into court in an action for general damages.

brought in under a rule of the court, unless permitted by statute will not affect the rights of either party, and in estimating the damages a jury can take no notice of a sum of money brought into court for the use of the plaintiff.[11] It has been held that where money is brought into court where it cannot be properly brought in, the plaintiff should move to discharge the rule. A defendant may bring money into court upon any or all of the counts in a declaration, providing they fall within the rule requiring certainty in the amount which ought to be recovered. If there are several causes of action or breaches set forth in a declaration, and as to some of them the defendant may bring money into court, but as to the others it is not permissible, he may have leave to bring money into court upon some of the counts only.[12]

**§ 495. In what courts money may be brought into court upon the common rule.**—Money can only be brought into court upon the common rule at law and in admiralty. The practice seems to be confined to courts of record. It is not permitted in equity for the obvious reason that bringing money into court is for the express purpose of giving a defendant an opportunity to accept the money and put an end to the litigation. In equity, even in cases where a money judgment may result from the litigation the court must adjust the equities upon one or both sides of the case, and consequently the deposit would not terminate the action. The proper way to save further costs in such cases, if there be no defence is to interpose an answer consenting to a decree being entered for the relief demanded and obtain leave to deposit the sum

[11] Johnson v Crawford Phill L (N C) 312 It has been held that although bringing money into court in an action for damages is irregular if the plaintiff takes it out, he thereby waives the irregularity and he cannot have judgment unless he recovers more than the sum brought in Griffith v Williams, 1 Term Rep 710 But the decision is bad as the payment amounts to an admission that that much is due the plaintiff and because the defendant chooses to make it in that way rather than admit a liability to the same amount in the answer the plaintiff ought not to be subjected to the risk of costs any more than he would be on account of an admission of a liability in an answer

[12] Hallet v East India Co, 2 Burr 1120

due in court for the plaintiff. But even this would not end
the litigation unless the sum demanded was specific.

**§ 496. Amount which should be brought into court upon the
common rule—On a plea of tender—Costs—Amending the rule as
to amount.—**A defendant may bring into court, upon the
common rule, whatever sum of money he sees fit, and where
there are two or more causes of actions set forth in the com
plaint, he may bring money in upon one or upon any number
of them. Where there are several causes of actions or
breaches set forth in the complaint, and the defendant in
tends to bring money into court, it would be safer to specify
upon what cause or breach, or what causes or breaches he
intends the payment to apply, and in the latter case how
much is meant to be applied to each. But such course is not
necessary, and the money may be brought in generally upon
the whole or any number of the claims.[1] But if one of the
causes of action is based upon a bill or note, the plea of
payment into court should specify how much of the money
so brought in is to be applied upon the bill or note, and if
the whole note or bill is not covered, there should be a de
fence interposed to the residue. The reason for this is stated
to be that the plea of payment into court is in the nature of
a plea of *non assumpsit* as to the residue of the claim not
paid in and is inapplicable to a cause of action based upon a
bill or note.[2] However, if the plaintiff joins issue on such a
plea, the defendant may interpose any defence which is ad
missible under the general issue.[3]

Under the modern practice, in the United States at least,
a defendant must bring into court the costs of the action up
to the time of the application,[4] and the costs necessary to
dispose of the action of record, including the fee of the clerk
for receiving and paying out the money. It is an elementary
rule that after an action has been commenced upon an exist-

[1] Marshall v. Whiteside 1 M. &
W. 192, Jourdain v. Johnson, 2 C.
M. & R. 564, s. c. 1 Gale, 312

[2] Jourdain v. Johnson, 2 C. M.
& R. 564

[3] Finleyson v. MacKinzie, 3
Bing. N. C. 824

[4] Goslin v. Hodson, 24 Vt. 140
In Whipple v. Newton, 17 Pick.
168, where two actions were pending upon the same cause of ac
tion the court held that the plaintiff was not bound to accept the
sum sued for and costs of one
action

ing cause of action, a defendant cannot by a payment to the plaintiff out of court, deprive him of any of his taxable costs without his consent, and in those jurisdictions where, under the statute, a money judgment at law carries with it the taxable costs including an attorney fee, it would seem that a defendant in such actions must bring into court, in addition to the costs above mentioned, the attorney fee to which the plaintiff would be entitled in the event of a judgment in his favor, in absence of such payment, for as much as the amount paid in.[5] He must bring the costs into court even though the plaintiff should proceed with the action and recover no more than the amount paid.[6] So, on a plea of tender after action brought, the costs of the action already incurred must be brought into court along with the amount admitted to be due.[7] Bringing money into court upon the common rule, or on a plea of tender after action brought, is without effect upon the question of costs unless it is specified how much of the money brought in is in payment of the claim and how much is meant to cover the costs.[8] If the defendant fails to bring in the costs he will not be entitled to subsequent costs.[9]

Where the money is brought into court upon the common rule, interest down to the date of bringing the money in must be paid,[10] and if the interest has not been paid the plaintiff may proceed for the balance due.[11] A defendant must take care, at his peril, to bring into court enough money to cover the principal, interest and costs. A discrepancy of forty one cents on an account amounting to more than one hundred fifty six dollars was held to be fatal.[12] The amount which is to be brought into court upon the common rule must be mentioned in the rule or order. After issue is joined,

[5] Duckwell v. Jones, 156 Ind 682

[6] State Bank v. Holcomb, 7 N J L 193

[7] The Serapis 37 Fed Rep 436; Hillard v. The Good Hope, 40 Fed Rep 608; Summerson v. Hicks, 142 Pa St 344; Burt v. Dodge, 13 Ohio, 131

[8] Hillard v. The Good Hope 40 Fed Rep 608

[9] Summerson v. Hicks, 142 Pa. St 344. See McI'ldon v. Patton, 93 N W Rep (Neb) 938. In this case the amount of the claim was brought in upon an alleged tender. The defendant failed in his proof.

[10] Mercer v. Jones, 3 Campb 477

[11] Kidd v. Walker, 2 B & Ad 705

[12] Boydon v. Moore, 5 Mass 365

leave will not be granted to amend the rule, nor will another rule be made permitting an additional sum to be brought in.[13] In a case where such an application was made, the court observed "That this was a subterfuge of the defendant, to try if the plaintiff would accept less than is due, and as he would not do so, he now wants to bring more money into court.[14] If too much is paid in upon one count and too little upon another, the defendant will not be permitted to change the excess over.[15] Paying money into court will not deprive the plaintiff of his right to amend, and the defendant must pay in enough to meet any recovery under any amendment the plaintiff may lawfully make.[16] In case of bringing money into court upon a plea of tender, the defendant need bring in no more than was tendered, for if the tender be proven to be sufficient the costs must be borne by the plaintiff.[17] If the amount tendered be insufficient, bringing into court a greater sum will not cure the defect. A defendant in such case should bring the money into court upon the common rule. While a plea of tender of a certain sum, under some circumstances, will be supported by evidence of a tender of a greater sum, yet a plea of tender of a certain sum cannot be supported by proof of a tender of a less sum, even though no more than the less sum be due, and it necessarily follows that the exact sum alleged to have been tendered must be brought into court.[18]

## § 497. When a motion for leave to bring money into court should be made.

A motion for leave to bring money into court

---

[13] Green v. Beaton, Barnes 286.

[14] Swan v. Freeman Barnes 282. See 9 Bac. Abr. Tit. Tender (K).

[15] Reed v. Mutual Ins. Co. 3 Sandf. (N. Y.) 54.

[16] Hill v. Smith 34 Vt. 535.

[17] The Scrapis, 37 Fed. Rep. 436; Beaver v. Whiteley, 3 Pa. Co. Ct. 613.

[18] It is stated in Martin v. Bott, 46 N. E. Rep. 151, in positive language that the amount tendered must be brought into court, and any deduction therefrom is fatal to the tender, but it is contrary to the general rule that a defendant is under no obligation to keep the tender good by holding himself in readiness to pay the full amount tendered if less be actually due. So its effect is an admission is not conclusive the defendant being concluded only by the amount pleaded. A defendant, therefore, should plead a tender of the amount actually due, and sustain his plea by proof of a tender of a larger sum, and bring into court the amount admitted to be due by his plea.

upon the common rule should be made before answering. It is sometimes made after issue joined, but not without first obtaining leave of the court to withdraw the answer and re plead, which usually would be granted upon terms. In those states where amendments to the pleadings are allowed with in a certain time as of course, a motion for leave to bring money into court may be made within the time limited, upon a showing that an amended answer setting up that fact will be served within the time. If the time to amend as of course has expired, leave to amend must first be obtained. So, upon a proper showing, after the granting of a new trial, a motion to amend and for leave to bring money into court may be granted.[1] Permission to amend the pleading and leave to bring money into court may be had upon the same motion

## § 498. Before whom a motion for leave to bring money into court must be made—Practice—Failure to make profert.

The motion for leave to bring money into court is a motion of course. In England under the old common law practice the rule was drawn up during term time or within a week of the end of the term by a subordinate officer of the court, on the motion papers being left with him, after a week from the end of the term a judge's order for drawing up the rule was required.[1] In the United States, the practice appears to be, both in the common law and code states, for the party desiring to bring money into court in satisfaction of so much of plaintiff's claim as he is willing to pay, at all times to apply to the court for an order allowing him to bring it in. The motion is usually made, when made at the usual time before pleading before a judge at chambers, and the motion is based upon the complaint and a mere formal written applica- tion for the order, setting forth the particulars as to what cause of action if it is not to be paid in generally the money is to be applied and specifying how much is for costs.[2] No affidavit need accompany the motion papers.[2] The rule or order must be entitled in the action and if not properly en- titled it will be discharged on motion.[3] If after obtaining

[1] See Tidd's Pr 672

[1] 1 Tidd's Pr 672 This prac- tice seems to have been changed by recent acts of parliament

[2] 3 Bl Com 304

[3] Satterthwaite Admx v Wat- ford Barnes 280

the rule, the defendant fails to make profert, the plaintiff will not be liable for costs.[4]

## § 499. At what time money may be brought into court upon the common rule.

—The money must be brought into court before filing or serving the answer. Although a defendant has obtained the common rule for bringing the money into court, he cannot bring it in after he has pleaded. In a case where the defendant neglected to bring the money in before pleading, the rule was discharged.[1] A defendant has been allowed to withdraw his demurrer and bring money into court.[2] The right to withdraw the plea and bring money into court was denied by some of the early cases,[3] but the practice of allowing a plea to be withdrawn and a deposit of money upon the common rule came eventually to be adopted. But it is not a right as of course. If a plea be withdrawn the case stands as if the defendant had not in fact pleaded, so that in this case the money is brought in before the defendant has pleaded. Money cannot be brought into court upon the common rule after the judgment is regularly entered. So, where a judgment had been vacated, upon terms and pleading the general issue, a motion for leave to bring money into court upon the common rule was denied.[4]

## § 500. Pleading where money is brought into court upon the common rule.

—Bringing money into court upon the common rule must be pleaded in all cases, and a copy of the rule should be annexed to the plea or otherwise served upon the plaintiff's attorney.[1] Bringing money into court upon the

[4] Grover v. Elkins, 3 M. & W. 216.

[1] 9 Bac. Abr. Tit. Tender (L), citing Straphon v. Thompson, Barnes 281.

[2] Littledale v. Bosaquet, Barnes 162.

[3] 9 Bac. Abr. Tit. Tender (L) citing Salmon v. Aldrich, Barnes 349. See Usher v. Edmunds, Barnes 344.

[4] 9 Bac. Abr. Tit. Tender (L), citing Burgess v. Pollamounter, Barnes 281, Hatfield v. Baldwin, 1 Johns. 506.

[1] 1 Tidd's Pr. Levan v. Steinfeld 55 N. J. L. 41. On an examination of the authorities in order to avoid becoming confused upon the subject of pleading a payment into court upon the common rule, some attention must be given the subject historically. Prior to the report of the English common law commissioners and the Statute of 4 Wm. IV. which embodied provisions suggested by the commissioners a payment of money was not pleaded but it was carried out by a rule of court wholly outside

common rule does not constitute a defence to the action, for, in general, a defence relates to the status of the cause of action at the time of commencing the action, or some impairment by the plaintiff's own act occuring since the commencement. Bringing money into court is in its very essence a confession with tender of satisfaction, and when pleaded it is not in defence to, nor in bar of the action, but in bar to the further maintenance of the action. It has been said that a defendant after having obtained the common rule for bringing money into court upon one count, cannot demur to any other count in the declaration, as the object of the rule permitting money to be brought into court is to put an end to the action.[2] Where the defendant has no defence to any portion of plaintiff's demand, he may obtain a rule or order for bringing the amount of the demand and cost into court and have a stay of proceedings. So, if he has no defence to one of two or more causes of action he may have a rule for bringing into court the amount alleged to be due upon the particular cause, together with costs and have a stay as to that cause. As to the remainder the plaintiff will be at liberty to proceed as he thinks fit.[3]

Where the plea of payment is upon the whole declaration, the remaining portion of plaintiff's demand not covered by the plea of payment should be met by a denial. So, where the plea of payment is to a part of plaintiff's demand, the residue of the demand should be met by other pleas by way of confession and avoidance as payment and the like. The latter pleas should be confined to those causes of action or parts denied, and first exhausted and then the plea of payment interposed to the residue or part confessed, so that in any case the other pleas or defences, together with the rule or order and the plea of payment into court will constitute a complete answer to plaintiff's entire demand.[4] Where a part of one cause of action which was admitted by

---

of the record. The statute above referred to required it to be pleaded. For a historical review of the subject see opinion of Williams J. (opinion given at *nisi prius*) 13 L. R. Q. B. Div 597

[2] See 9 Bac. Abr. Tit. Tender (M) and cases cited.

See 9 Bac. Abr. Tit. Tender (M) Hallet v. East India Co., 2 Burr 1120.

[4] Levan v. Sternfeld 55 N. J. L. 11. Tittersall v. Parkinson, 16 M. & W. 752.

the plea of payment into court, was left unanswered, it was held, though all the other issues were found for the defendant, that the plaintiff was entitled to nominal damages upon the whole record.[5] A plea of payment into court of a less sum than the amount of a note or bill, in absence of some answer to the residue, is bad on a special if not on a general demurrer.[6] And such a plea has been thought to be ill in *assumpsit* as well as in debt, for the reason that the plea of payment into court admits the larger sum to be *prima facie* due, and the part paid in does not satisfy the whole of the sum thus admitted to be *prima facie* due.[7] So, a plea of payment into court, in an action where the declaration contains a count on a bill or note and the general count, of a sum upon the whole declaration, less than the entire demand but more than the amount of the bill or note, without answering as to the residue, was thought to be bad on demurrer for the reason that so much of the money paid in as would cover the bill or note cannot necessarily be ascribed to the bill or note.

A plaintiff after receiving a plea of payment of money into court is put to an election. He is at liberty to reply to the same by accepting the sum so brought into court, in full satisfaction of the demand or cause of action in respect to which it was brought in, or he may reply that the defendant is indebted to him (or that he has sustained damages as the case may be) in a greater sum. The plaintiff must reply to the plea of payment within the time for replying whether he takes the money out or not.

§ 501. **Proof that money has been brought into court** upon the common rule.—That money has been brought into court upon the common rule can only be proven by the production of the rule for bringing it in.[1] It being a matter of record the record is the best evidence.

---

[5] Fischer v Aide, Exch T T 1838, Leg. Obs No 468 Cited in 1 Chitty's Prec 367, n

[6] Armfield v Burgin, 6 M & W 284

[7] Jourdoin v Johnson, 2 C M & R 570, s c 1 Gale, 312

[1] Israel v Benjamin, 3 Camp 40 Here it was proposed to examine the attorney who took the money out Rubble v Murray, 4 Hayw (Tenn 27, 1 Tidd's Pr 674, 3 Starkie on Ev. 828.

§ 502. **Consequences of a profert in curia, and of bringing money into court upon the common rule—As an admission.**—We have heretofore had occasion to consider the effect of a plea of tender as an admission of the cause of action,[1] and as what was there said is also applicable, in actions to recover a debt, to bringing money into court both in support of a plea of tender and upon the common rule, some repetition is unavoidable. The effect as an admission, of bringing money into court, in both cases is the same, and to avoid further repetition, they will be in this connection considered together. Bringing money into court in support of a plea of tender in an action to recover a debt, and bringing money into court upon the common rule, is a solemn judicial admission of record, conclusively admitting that the plaintiff is entitled to the amount thus paid in and that the defendant owes the plaintiff such amount.[2] It admits that the plaintiff has a cause of action, that the amount paid in is due upon the cause of action set forth in the complaint, and that the plaintiff's claim is just.[3] If there is but one contract, or duty, or specific wrongful act or omission set out in the complaint or count, to which the deposit relates, it operates as an admission of that contract, duty or wrongful act or omission.[4] Where two or more causes of action or

[1] Ch. XIV. See also Ch. IX.

[2] Murray v. Cunningham, 10 Neb. 167, s. c. 4 N. W. Rep. 349, 953; Dillenback v. The Rossend Castle 30 Fed Rep 462, Beach v. Jeffery, 1 Ill App 283, 1 Greenl Ev. Sec 205 Sweetland v. Tuthill, 54 Ill 215; Griffin v. Hartman 71 Iowa 436, Mohan v. Waters 60 Mo 167. A failure to bring the money in does not make the admission any less distinct and unequivocal Roosevelt v. New York Cent. Ry Co, 45 Barb 554

Horsburg v. Orme. 1 Campb 58 n. Burrough v. Skinner 5 Burr 2629, Watkins v. Towers, 2 T R 275; Wilson v. Railway Co, 8 Iowa 673, s. c. 27 N W Rep 16. Currier v. Jordan 117 Mass

200. See Lloyd v. Walkey 9 C & P 771 which was an action for damages for killing a cow. Held, after payment into court defendant could not prove that he did not kill the cow. See also Speck v. Phillips 5 M & W 279, where evidence in mitigation of damages was held inadmissible after payment into court.

[3] Williamson v. Bailey 78 Mo 636

[4] Bacon v. Charlton 7 Cush 581 Mayer v. Smith 4 B & Adol 680 Yate v. Willan 2 East 134; Wilson v. Doran 110 N. Y. 101, s. c. 30 Hun 88 Huntington v. American Bank 6 Pick 340; Mellish v. Allnutt 2 M & S 106, Middleton v. Brewer. Peak 20; Cox v. Brain 3 Taunt 95; Seaton

counts are set forth and the plea of payment into court is
to the whole declaration, the rule is stated in general terms
to be, that the defendant thereby admits all the causes of
action, leaving only the question of the amount due to be
determined.  Unless the plaintiff elects to apply the whole
amount upon one or more of the causes of action, in which
case the remaining causes will not be admitted.

There is a limitation upon the admission in some cases
where money is brought into court generally, in an action
where the declaration contains two or more causes of action
or counts.  Where, in each cause of action or count, a special
contract is set out, or a specific wrongful act or omission is
alleged by which an injury is done to a person or a single
article of property, the admission by a general payment upon
the whole declaration goes to all the causes of action or
counts to the same extent as if the payment into court had
been made in an action where the declaration contained but
one count based on a special contract, &c, in which case the
plaintiff is not called upon to prove either cause of action in
order to recover the amount paid in; but in assumpsit where
the declaration contains the common money counts; or the
common money counts and a count specific in its nature as
for use and occupation of certain premises, and in actions
of tort in which tender and payment into court is allowed,
where the allegation is general, by charging, for instance,
the conversion of several articles; a tender and payment
into court only admits a liability to the amount paid in upon
some one or more of the several causes of action or counts,
but it is not an admission of any particular contract or a
debt upon any one of the counts, nor does it admit a liability
upon all of them, and if the plaintiff does not accept the sum
so paid in in full satisfaction, but goes for a larger sum, he
must prove the contract or the tort as well as a greater

Watson 11 Eng C L 270, Johnson v Columbian Ins Co 7
Johns 315

6 Cox v Brain, 3 Taunt 95,
Fischer v Alde Exch L T 1838,
Leg Obs No 468 Goff v Harris,
5 M & G 573  See Chitty's

Pierced 367 N Jones v Hoar, 5
Pick 285 Huntington v Ameri
can Bank 6 Pick 340, Governor
v Sutton, 4 Dev & Bat 181

6 Hubbard v Knous, 7 Cush
558

7 Cook v Hartle 8 C & P 568

amount of damages.[8] If the payment was not intended to be made upon all the counts, an amendment of the rule will be allowed so as to apply it to a particular count or counts.[9]

A payment into court supersedes the necessity for all that proof which a plaintiff would otherwise be required to produce in order to recover the amount paid in.[10] It admits the existence of the contract;[11] the execution of a deed, dispensing with the testimony of attesting witnesses.[12] It obviates the necessity of proving the promise to be in writing;[13] of proving the handwriting of the drawer of a bill of exchange or check.[14] It admits that the contract was made with the party alleged.[15] Such payment is an admission of the existence of a contract in every transaction which is capable of being converted into a contract by assent of the parties. Thus, where a person in the possession of the goods of another, sells all or a part and keeps the residue in specie, and is sued for goods sold and delivered, a payment into court admits the transaction to have been converted into a contract.[16] It admits the implied contract, dispensing with the proof of a conversion in an action for money had and received; or occupancy of the premises in an action for use and occupation.[17] Payment of money into court admits that the plaintiff is entitled to it in the character in which he sues;[18] that the plaintiff is a merchant in trade,[19] that he is an apothecary,[20] a physician,[21] an attorney, an

[8] Bacon v. Charlton, 7 Cush 581, Hubbard v. Knous, 7 Cush 556 Kingham v. Robins 5 M & W 94 Archer v. English, 1 M & G 873 Stapleton v. Nowell 6 M & W 9 Perren v. M Ry Co 11 C B 855

[9] Andrews v. Palsgrave 9 East 325 and see 9 Bac Abr Tit Tender (N) citing Jones v. Hoar 5 Pick 285 and Huntington v. American Bank 6 Pick 340

[10] See Bacon v. Inhabitants of Charlton 7 Cush 581

[11] Bennett v. Francis, 2 B & Pul 550 Randall v. Lynch 2 Camp 357

[12] Randall v. Lynch, 2 Camp. 352

[13] Middleton v. Brewer, Peak 20

[14] Gutteridge v. Smith 2 H Black 374

[15] Walker v. Rawson 5 C & P 486 Noble v. Pignant 162 Mass 275

[16] Bennett v. Francis, 2 B & Pul 550

[17] Currier v. Jordan 117 Mass 260

[18] See Tuson v. Batting, 3 Esp 192

[19] Brown v. Fink 3 Jones L 378 s c 48 N C 378

[20] Shearwood v. Hay 5 A & E 83

[21] Lipscombe v. Holmes, 2 Campb 441

37

administrator; an executor; a guardian; a trustee, &c.; that the plaintiff is a corporation or a partnership as the case may be.[22] After paying money into court a defendant cannot allege a non joinder.[23] It admits plaintiff's right to maintain the action in the court in which he sues;[24] that the court has jurisdiction of the subject matter and of the person of the defendant;[25] that the action was not prematurely brought.[26] Such payment admits that the conditions of an undertaking were complied with;[27] that the goods delivered were of like quality as the sample,[28] that there was no interruption of defendant's rights;[29] that a condition precedent has been complied with;[30] that the amount paid in was due at the date of the commencement of the action,[31] that there was a breach of the contract as alleged;[32] that the defendant is liable to the plaintiff in the character in which he is sued, as administrator, &c.[33] If several defendants pay money into court, there being but one contract, they cannot set up the defence that one of them was not a party.[34] Such payment has the force and effect of an estoppel.[35] A defendant cannot claim that the instrument was insufficiently stamped,[36] or that less is due than the amount paid in, or that nothing is due,[37] or that the title is not in the plaintiff.[38] If the difference between the

---

[22] Walker v. Rawson, 5 C. & P. 186.

[23] Dolby v. Ives, 3 P. & D. 387.

[24] Miller v. Williams, 5 Esp. 19.

[25] Miller v. Williams, 5 Esp. 19.

[26] Harrison v. Douglas, 3 A. & E. 396. See Letcher v. Taylor, Hard. 85, where it is held that where a demand is necessary an omission to aver a demand is not cured by a plea of tender.

[27] Watkins v. Towers, 2 T. R. 275.

[28] Liggett v. Cooper, 2 Stark. 103.

[29] Cox v. Brain, 3 Taunt. 95.

[30] Harrison v. Douglas, 3 A. & E. 396.

[31] Gibboney v. German Ins. Co., 48 Mo. App. 185, Harrison v. Douglas, 3 A. & E. 396.

[32] Wright v. Goddard, 8 A. & E. 144, Dyer v. Ashton 1 B. & C. 3. See Lechmere v. Fletcher, 3 Tyr. 455.

[33] Lacy v. Walrond, Adam 3 Hodg. 215, 3 Bing. N. C. 841.

[34] Ravenscroft v. Wise 1 C. M. & R. 203.

[35] Herman on Estoppel. See 836.

[36] Israel v. Benjamin 3 Campb. 40, Randel v. Lynch, 2 Campb. 357.

[37] Wilson v. Railroad Co. 27 N. W. Rep. 916, Mahan v. Waters 60 Mo. App. 167.

[38] Broadhurst v. Baldwin 4 Price, 58.

amount of plaintiff's claim and a set off is paid in, the defendant cannot dispute the amount of plaintiff's claim though the plaintiff may defend against the set-off.[39] So, if the plaintiff in his complaint alleges a contract to pay an agreed price for a specific article, a payment into court precludes the defendant from denying the sum originally due.[40] In other words a defendant cannot interpose any defence for the purpose of defeating plaintiff's right to all or any part of the sum paid into court.[41] Bringing money into court upon a plea of tender, though the tender be proven to be insufficient, has the same force and effect as an admission, as a payment into court in cases where the tender is sufficient.[42] A payment by a defendant to the plaintiff, pending an action, of a part of the demand to recover which the action was brought, is not equivalent to a deposit of money in court as an admission of the cause of action.[43] Such payment has no more force or effect as an admission, than has a payment before the action was commenced. Bringing money into court by virtue of a statute, does not, it is said, admit the cause of action.[44]

§ 503. **Extent of the admission** —Bringing money into court, as has been shown, admits a liability to the amount paid in, dispensing with all that proof which a plaintiff would otherwise be required to produce in order to recover the amount paid in, but it admits nothing more, and a defendant may dispute his liability ultra such payment[1] upon any ground consistent with an admission of the original cause of action.[2]

[1] Williamson v. Bailey, 78 Mo. 636.

[40] Cox v. Brain, 3 Taunt 95.

[41] See Hosmer v. Warner, 7 Gray 186.

[42] Schnur v. Hickcox, 45 Wis 200.

[4] Galloway v. Holmes, 1 Dougl (Mich) 330.

[44] 3 Stark Ev. 829, citing 13 East 202.

[1] Simpson v. Carson, 11 Or 361; Bouve v. Cottle, 143 Mass. 310; Sherwood v. Hay 5 A & E 383; Mellish v. Allnutt, 2 M & S 106;

Lacy v. Walrond, 3 Hodg 215, Spalding v. Vandercock 2 Wend 431, Davis v. Mellandon, 17 La. Ann 47. A tender does not confer upon the plaintiff a right of action for a larger sum than that actually tendered, and cannot be construed as an admission of a debt due beyond that sum. Simpson v. Ruth 2 B & P 355.

[2] Wilson v. Doran, 110 N. Y. 101. See Mead v. Wyndham, Bunb 100 where it is held that after payment into court a plea of *non assumpsit* is not allowed

Where money is brought into court upon one cause of action or count, it is no admission of any allegations as to the other causes of action or counts,[1] and as to them the defendant may plead the statute of limitation, or other defence.[4] Bringing money into court on a cause of action based upon a promissory note payable by installments, is only a admission that the amount paid in is due upon the note, it does not preclude the defendant from pleading the statute of limitation as to a further sum claimed to be due upon the note. If paid in upon a particular item of an account sued upon it admits nothing as to the other items in the account, and the defendant, notwithstanding the payment, is free to deny the character in which the plaintiff sues and the justice of his claim.[6]

Payment of money into court generally does not admit that all the terms of a contract were complied with, and the defendant may show that the goods were not loaded according to the terms of the policy.[7] Such payment upon a count stating a total loss in an action upon an insurance policy does not preclude the defendant from showing that the loss was not total.[8] A tenant, by bringing money into court, will not be precluded from showing that the landlord's title has been extinguished, for such sum may be due for rent which accrued prior to the transfer of the title.[9] Where it is alleged that goods were sold to be paid for at the market, or at the average price of the season, bringing money into court

[1] Baillie v Cazalet 1 T R 579 Charles v Braaker, 12 M & W 743, Wolmerstadt v Jacobs, 61 Iowa 374 s c 16 N W Rep 217

[4] Helber v Hallet Barnes 286, Mead v Wyndham, Bunb 100, Long v Greville 1 D & R 632, Wilson v Doran, 110 N Y 101

[5] Reid v Dickens, 5 B & A 499 See Collver v Willock, 12 Moore 557; Morgan v Rowland, 41 L J Q B 187; Bateman v Pender, 2 G & D 790

[6] Brown v Pink 3 Jones, 378, 48 N C 378

[7] Mellish v Allnutt, 2 M & S 106 See Griffin v Harriman 74 Iowa, 136

[8] Rucker v Palsgrave 1 Campb 557 See Donnell v Columbia Ins Co, 2 Sumner 366

[9] See Griffin v Harriman, 74 Iowa, 136 s c 38 N W Rep 139 where it is held, in an action for rent, that the plea of tender and payment into court together with a general denial, did not admit all the alleged grounds for recovery and therefore did not admit the defendant used the premises during the time named or that he used them at any time. But this decision seems to be based upon the fact that the general denial was pleaded

does not admit the price to be as stated.[10] Although bringing money into court admits that the amount brought in belongs to the plaintiff, yet it does not admit that there is a contract between the parties where none exists, and a defendant to defeat a recovery of a further sum may show that the plaintiff had not acquired title to the cause of action.[11] So, if an account sued upon contains any items for which a defendant is not liable, such as goods sold to a wife where the law does not raise an implied promise on the part of the husband to pay for them, a payment of money into court generally does not admit a liability on the part of the husband to pay for such items.[12] So, such a payment will not prevent a parent or guardian from showing that the goods furnished a minor were not necessaries; nor preclude a minor from availing himself of the defence of infancy, as the money paid in may be for necessaries.[13] Where a plaintiff sets forth in his complaint multifarious and inconsistent demands, a payment into court of a sum insufficient to meet all the demands, cannot be applied by the plaintiff to prove such of the demands as he may elect.[14] Although a defendant is held to have admitted the contract sued upon by a payment into court, yet to recover damages ultra the plaintiff must show a breach of the contract stated, which he cannot do by showing a breach of a different contract, hence a defendant may show a material variance between the contract alleged and the real contract.[15] So, a payment into court does not admit that the plaintiff was the owner of the thing to recover the value or price of which the action was brought. Thus a defendant may show that goods purchased of a broker were not the goods of the plaintiff;[16] that goods alleged to have been lost at sea were not the goods of the assured.[17]

---

[10] Bac. Abr. Tit. Tender (N), citing 2 B & A 116, S P 1 Tidd's Pr 676

[11] Wilson v Doran, 110 N Y, 100 Cox v Parry 1 T R 464 See Hennell v Davis, 1 Q B 367

[12] See Seaton v Benedict 2 M & P 66

[13] Hitchcock v Tyson 2 Esp 481 n See Dilk v Keighley, 2 Esp 481

[14] Tidd's Pr 676

[15] See Mellish v Allnutt, 2 M & S 106

[16] Blackburn v Scholes 2 Campb 341

[17] Cox v Perry, 1 T R 464 If brought in by two defendants, the plaintiff in order to recover damages ultra the sum brought in, must prove a joint obligation Archer v English, 1 M & G 873 See Stapleton v Nowell, 6 M & W 9

Bringing money into court only admits a legal demand. Where money was brought into court generally, in an action by an innkeeper against a candidate to recover upon two demands, one of which was for provision furnished to a voter upon defendant's request, which was illegal because it was against the law for a candidate to furnish provision to any voter, the court said "It is to be observed that such payment is only an admission of a legal demand." [18] As a plaintiff is put to the proof of the entire damages suffered by him, in order to establish that he is damaged to a greater amount than the sum paid into court, it necessarily follows that the defendant may show that the plaintiff was not damaged to the extent of the amount admitted to be due or that he was not damaged at all.[19] The full amount of damages alleged not being admitted by a payment into court of a less amount, the defendant may show any stipulation limiting the amount of the damages. In an action to recover damages for a breach of a contract of carriage occasioned by a loss of the goods, it was held that the defendant might prove notice to the plaintiff that he would not be liable above a certain sum unless the goods were entered at a higher valuation and paid for as such, that the notice did not alter the contract for safe carriage, but merely limited the amount of the damages for a breach of the contract.[20]

§ 504. **Money belongs to whom—In actions at law to recover a debt.**—Bringing money into court on a plea of tender or upon the common rule, conclusively admits that the money so brought in belongs to the party for whom it was paid in [1]

18 Ribbans v Crickett, 2 B & P 264

19 See Taylor v Brooklyn El Ry, 119 N Y 561

20 See Starkie on Ev 830, citing Clark v Gray, 6 East 564

1 Parker v Beasley, 116 N C 1, s c 33 L R A 231, Vose v McGuire, 26 Mo App 452 Halpin v Phoenix Ins Co 118 N Y 165, s c 23 N E Rep 482, Cox v Robinson Stia 1027, Reed v Armstrong, 18 Ind 209, Soule v Holdridge, 20 Ind 209, Supply

Ditch Co v Elliott 10 Colo 327 Murray v Bethune, 1 Wend 191 Le Grew v Cooke 1 B & P 332 Wheeler v Woodward, 66 Pa St 158 Costs paid into court to render a witness competent are absolutely and irrevocably paid Clement v Bixler, 3 Watts 248 A deposit of money to cover an award in condemnation proceedings cannot be diverted by the depositor or his creditors, but must remain subject to the order of him for whom it was deposited

It is a payment on record, a solemn judicial admission, and the party paying it in cannot have it back though it afterwards appear that he paid it wrongfully;[2] or that he paid it in by mistake,[3] or that nothing was due,[4] or that the plaintiff had not been damaged in any amount,[5] or that the plaintiff had not acquired title to the cause of action. It belongs to plaintiff although he had no notice of the payment[6] It belongs to the party for whom it was paid in, absolutely, and no part of it will be ordered repaid to the defendant whether it is found that plaintiff is entitled to a greater or less sum;[7] or the plaintiff is non suited, or defendant has a verdict;[8] or whatever may be the fate of the action,[9] unless,

Stoltz v. Milwaukee Co. 88 N. W. Rep. 919. See Brown v. Railway Co. 89 N. W. Rep. 105 where it is held that after prosecuting a proceedings to obtain a right of way to a final determination the party instituting the proceedings is estopped to repudiate or abandon them

[2] Malcolm v. Fullerton 2 T. R. 645; 1 Tidd's Pr. 674 citing 2 D. & E. 645

[3] Vaughan v. Barnes 2 B. & P. 392; Phelps v. Town 14 Mich. 374

[4] Roosevelt v. New York &c. Ry. Co. 45 Barb. 554

[5] Taylor v. Brooklyn El. Ry. 119 N. Y. 561

[6] Murphy v. Gold 3 N. Y. Supp. 561

[7] Cass v. Higenbotam 100 N. Y. 248; Sweetland v. Tuthill 54 Ill. 215; Logue v. Gellick, 1 E. D. Smith 398; Berkheimer v. Geise 82 Pa. St. 64. In Vaughan v. Barnes 2 B. & P. 392, where a rule was granted calling upon the plaintiff to show cause why part of the money paid into court should not be refunded it having been shown that the plaintiff was not entitled to as much as was paid in the court said "Almost every defendant pays something

more into court than he believes to be due that he may be certain of covering the just demand and consequently if the court were to attend to the present application there would be no end of motions of this kind"

[8] 1 Tidd's Pr. 674; 9 Bac. Abr. Tit. Tender (N), Wilson v. Doran, 39 Hun 90; Rhodes v. Andrews, 13 S. W. Rep. (Ark) 122; Taylor v. Brooklyn El. Ry., 119 N. Y. 561

[9] Schnur v. Hickcox 15 Wis. 200; Cilley v. Hawkins 48 Ind. 576; Wilson v. Doran 39 Hun 90; 110 N. Y. 101; Slack v. Brown, 13 Wend. 390; Becker v. Boon 61 N. Y. 317; Dillenback v. The Rossend Castle 30 Fed. Rep. 462; Coglan v. South Car. Ry. Co. 32 Fed. Rep. 316; Black v. Rose 11 S. C. 278; Kansas City Tr. Co. v. Neiswanger 27 Mo. App. 356; Califrino v. McAndrews 51 Fed. Rep. 300; Jenkins v. Cutchens 2 Miles (Pa.) 65; Le Grew v. Cooke, 1 B. & P. 332; Fox v. Williams 66 N. W. Rep. (Wis.) 357; Crockey v. Martin Barnes 281; Murray v. Bethune 1 Wend. 191; La Fisher v. Kitchingham Barnes 281, the plaintiff having died before trial, defendant moved to have the

perhaps, it is made to appear that some fraud or deceit had been practiced upon the party paying it in.[10] A plaintiff in proceeding after a deposit simply runs the risk of paying defendant's costs, if the recovery falls short or is for no more than the amount paid in, while the defendant takes the risk of losing the amount paid in in the event of his succeeding in the action.[11] He pays it in at his peril.[12] It has been said that, "The prudence of paying money into court, is one of the most anxious points on which counsel can be asked to advise, * * * but whatever course be adopted, it must be followed by all its legal consequences."[13]

Money which has been tendered, in cases where it must be kept good is in theory the money of the tenderee, but such tender, nevertheless, does not vest the title to the particular money tendered, or any money, in the tenderee,[14] and until it is accepted by him or paid into court, it is subject to the claim of the creditors of the tenderor and may be levied upon and appropriated in payment of their demand. Paying it into court has the force and effect of an acceptance,[1] the court representing both parties. It is then beyond the reach of the creditors of the tenderor.

§ 505. Same subject—In equitable actions.—While the rule that a party pays money into court at his peril is unquestionably applicable to all such payments upon the common rule, and in support of a plea of tender in actions to

---

money in court paid back to him, but the court refused the application. So in Knapton v. Drew Barnes 279 the defendant having died, the court refused an application to have the money in court paid to the executor. See Murray v. Bethune 1 Wend 191. According to Bac. Abr. in an action against an executor, if money has been brought into court upon the common rule and the plaintiff is afterwards non-suited, or there is a verdict against him, the defendant shall have the money out of court again because being an executor he might not know whether his testator was indebted to the plaintiff or not. 9 Bac. Abr. tit. Tender (N)

[10] See Dicta. Vaughan v. Barnes 2 B. & P. 392

[11] Taylor v. Brooklyn El. Ry. 119 N. Y. 561 s. c. 23 N. E. Rep 1106 7 N. Y. Supp. 625

[12] 3 Bl. Com. 304. Vaughan v. Barnes 2 B. & P. 392

[13] Broadhurst v. Baldwin. 4 Price 58

[14] See Stowell v. Reed 16 N. H. 20. s. c. 41 Am. Dec. 714, where it is held that the tenderee cannot maintain trover for the money

[15] See Taylor v. Brooklyn E. Ry. 119 N. Y. 561

recover a debt, is it applicable to a payment into court in support of a plea of tender in equitable actions or actions at law where the tender must be unconditional and where the money paid in is not the thing sought to be recovered? The strict rule was held to apply in a case where plaintiff, in rescinding a contract, tendered to the defendant one hundred dollars which he had received to close the bargain. The judgment which was for the plaintiff also awarded the money to him. On an appeal that part of the judgment awarding the money to the plaintiff was reversed, the court holding that the tender and payment into court of the money tendered, was a conclusive admission that the amount paid in was due the tenderee, and that the money belonged to him absolutely, whatever may be the fate of the action, and that the fact that the tender was not essential to plaintiff's right of relief did not make the case an exception to the rule.[1] So, the strict rule was recognized as applicable in equity to an unconditional payment into court as a tender, by Hammond, J., in a case before the circuit court for the western District of Tennessee.[2]

It is true that the strict rule if applied in equity in suits to redeem based upon a tender and like cases at law, where the tender is the foundation of the cause of action and where it must be kept good by bringing the money into court, would sometimes appear to result in the tenderor losing both the property and the money so paid in; yet there is much to support such a rule. (1) A plaintiff or defendant who pays money into court which he previously tendered, is presumed to know his legal rights, and afterwards if it is demonstrated that at the time he paid the money into court he had no right

---

[1] Fox v. Williams 66 N. W. Rep. (Wis.) 357 s. p. Hoffman v. Stemman 4 N. Y. St. Rep. 627

[2] Cresar v. Capell, 83 Fed. Rep. 135. See Putnam v. Putnam 13 Pick. 139. The report of this case is very unsatisfactory. It does not appear that the action was based on a tender. In Dunn v. Hunt 78 N. W. Rep. 1110 which was an action to redeem from a statutory foreclosure, based upon a tender the trial court impound-

ed enough of the money paid into court to satisfy defendant's costs. The author as one of his grounds for an affirmance contended that the order impounding the money was without prejudice to the plaintiff for the reason that by the payment the entire sum brought in was lost to the plaintiff and that the defendant was taking his costs out of his own money. From this view the court dissented.

to the property, it cannot be said that he loses the property in the action, for he then had no property interests involved to be lost, for it is universally conceded as a truism that a judgment merely declares the status of the property or rights involved, as of the date of the commencement of the action, and the award is so made. So, that in such actions if the party and his counsel cannot truly discern his rights, it is his own fault. The risk which he assumes in bringing the amount tendered into court is no greater than the risk assumed by a defendant who pays money into court in an action to recover a money judgment where it may be proven that nothing was due the plaintiff, or that he did not own the cause of action, or was not damaged, &c. (2) A litigant who solemnly makes the admission that he owes a certain sum to his opponent by paying the money into court for him does so to obtain the advantage which by law follows such deposit. He says, "I tender you this money: it is yours, I do not want it; here it is; I will enforce my rights." If he was permitted to recover the money after strenuously insisting until defeat overwhelms him that the money belonged to the other party, and that something else was his, the payment would be no evidence of good faith. He would run no risk of loss while harrassing and annoying his opponent, and laying upon the latter, by the tender and deposit in court, the risk of paying costs, loss of interest, &c. If in such cases a party after being defeated is permitted to say: "I was mistaken. I thought I owed the money but find I do not. I made the deposit to obtain what I thought were my rights, having in good faith done this the court ought now to relieve me of all risk and hand back the money I paid voluntarily," what good would solemn judicial admissions be? Litigants would not hesitate to make such admissions as evidence of good faith and to give color to any fancied or pretended claim of right, if the money they hazard is not hazarded at all but merely awaits their reclaiming. (3) It is a voluntary payment made with full knowledge of all the facts? Those cases

³ Voluntary Payment. "The general rule on this subject (though it has its exceptions like other general rules) is that ignorance of the law with full knowledge of the facts under circumstances repelling all presumption of fraud and imposition furnishes no ground either in law or equity to rescind agreements or reclaim money paid voluntarily under a claim of right, or set

in equity or at law, where the right of action is not dependent upon a tender and the money is allowed to be brought
into court conditionally or to abide the event of the action,
are not here referred to.[4]

§ 506.  **Application of the payment.**—The general principle
governing a payment of money between the parties out of
court, in cases where it is to a creditor holding two or more
demands which are due, which permit the creditor in absence
of an application of the payment by the debtor to a particular demand, to apply it upon any demand then due which
he may see fit, is applicable to a payment of money into
court; and where money is brought in generally in an action
to recover upon two or more causes of action, the plaintiff
may apply it upon whichever cause of action he pleases and
such application by the plaintiff will have the same effect as
an admission of the cause of action to which the payment
was applied, to the same extent as if the defendant had
directed the application of the payment.[1]  But there is a
limitation to the rule, the payment cannot be applied by the
plaintiff so as to make it evidence of any particular ground
upon which the claim is based.  Thus, where a total loss was
alleged to have occurred by stranding, it was held that the
payment did not admit a total loss by stranding as the loss,
consistent with the allegation, might have resulted from
other means.[2]  So, where money is paid in generally in an

aside solemn acts of the parties"
2 Kent's Com. 191.  Money paid
*bona fide* and with full knowledge
of the facts cannot be recovered
back though there was no debt
Clark v. Dutcher, 9 Cow. 674.
'The presumption is that every
man is acquainted with his own
rights provided he has a reasonable opportunity to know them
And nothing can be more liable
to abuse than to permit a person
to reclaim his property upon the
mere pretense that at the time of
parting with it he was ignorant
of the law"  Rankin v. Morti-
more 7 Watts 372, s. p. Storrs

v. Baker 6 John Ch 169  "A
payment is voluntary, if made by
a party informed of all the facts
connected with the subject matter
of the payment, and under influence of no duress or coercion,
even though it may be accompanied by a written or verbal protest  Shane v. City of St Paul
26 Minn 543

[4] See Lynch v. Jennings 43 Ind
276, Duckwell v. Jones, 58 N. E.
Rep (Ind App) 1055

[1] Gutteridge v. Smith 2 H
Black 374, Goddard v. Cox, Bull
N. P. 174

[2] Everth v. Bell 7 Taunt 450

action containing the common money counts, the payment cannot be appropriated so as to admit any particular ground of recovery.[1] So, there is an exception to the rule; a plaintiff cannot apply the payment to an illegal demand;[4] nor to one for which the defendant is not liable, as in the case of goods sold to a married woman, or a minor, where there is no implied promise on the part of the defendant to pay for them; nor can it be applied to a claim barred by the statute of limitation,[5] and proceed with the action and recover upon the legal demand or demand upon which the defendant is solely liable. Where money may be brought into court upon some of the counts and not upon the others, the payment can only be applied to those counts upon which it can be properly made.[6]

§ 507. **Taking money out of court—Effect—Judgment unnecessary.**—Money brought into court on a plea of tender in an action to recover debt, and money brought in upon the common rule, may be withdrawn by the plaintiff at any time. It may be taken out of court by the plaintiff though he replies that the tender was not made before action,[1] or that the amount is insufficient;[2] or that there was no tender made; or that he subsequently demanded the money and it was refused.[3] Such tender or payment being required to be unconditional, the plaintiff may take the money out at any time before or after issue joined, either as a part payment or in full satisfaction of the demand or cause of action in respect to which it had been paid. And the court will not before a verdict retain the money on the chance of a verdict going for defendant, in order to secure the payment of the latter's costs.[4] But where an application is made to with

[3] See Bacon v. Charlton, 7 Cush. 581

[4] Ribbans v. Crickett 2 B & P 364 In this case it is said that bringing money into court will give an illegal or invalid contract no validity

[5] Seaton v. Benedict 2 M & P 66 Hitchcock v. Tyson 2 Esp 481, n, Dilk v. Keighley, 2 Esp 481 Long v. Greville 3 B & C 10 S C 4 v & R 636, Cox v.

Parry 1 T R 464, Naish v. Tatlock 2 H B 319

[6] Cotterel v. Apsey, 6 Taunt 122

[1] Le Grew v. Cooke, 1 B & P 332

[2] Murphy v. Gold 3 N Y Supp 304

[3] Tidd's Pr 672

[4] Le Grew v. Cooke, 1 B & P 332

draw money in court in full satisfaction of the demand, either before or after issue joined on the plea of tender, or after issue joined on the sufficiency of the amount brought into court upon the common rule, or after verdict against the plaintiff, the court, if objection be made thereto, will not allow the money to be taken out of court without satisfying defendant's costs  At common law the withdrawal of the money in court in no way affects the right of the plaintiff to proceed with his action to recover the balance between the amount paid in and the amount alleged to be due.  It is no ground for a dismissal of an appeal,  or for a summary dismissal in the lower court.⁶  In Tennessee and Alabama, where by statute a plea of a tender of money or of a thing in action must be accompanied by a delivery of the money or thing in action to the clerk of the court, it is held that if the plaintiff withdraws the money he does so in full satisfaction of his entire demand.⁷

Where a defendant paid into court the full amount which the plaintiff could have recovered under his declaration, together with costs, and the money was taken out of court by the plaintiff, it was held, that in absence of proof that the plaintiff took the money in full satisfaction of his claim he was not precluded from filing new counts and recovering an additional sum.⁸  Where, in an action on a policy of insurance, the plaintiff sought to recover for a total loss, or a return of the premium in case he could not recover on the policy, and the defendant paid the amount of the premium into court which plaintiff took out after informing defendant that he intended to go for a total loss; it was held that the

---

McCulley v Otey 103 Ala 469

Humphrey v Merritt 51 Ind 197

⁷ Hanson v Todd, 10 So Rep (Ala) 354  Gardner v Black, 12 So Rep (Ala) 813  Jonathan Turner's Sons v Lee Gin 38 L R A (Tenn) 549  These statutes requiring the money to be brought into court and deposited with the clerk are merely declaratory of the common law (see Hanson v.

Todd) and in no way change that law, as the statutes impose no terms or conditions whatever  The effect of a withdrawal is declared by the courts of those states is opposed to the common law rule and the construction is contrary to the effect given a tender where the right to make one is merely conferred by statute, where the common law as to the mode of procedure and effect of the tender is held to govern

⁸ Hill v Smith 34 Vt 535

plaintiff was not precluded from proceeding for a total loss.[9] Where money has been brought into court on a plea of tender, and the plaintiff accepts it as a part payment, he is entitled to have the money out of court without a judgment therefor.[10] So, where money is brought into court upon the common rule and the plaintiff elects to take it in part payment, a judgment for the money is unnecessary. The reason is that judgment cannot be entered by piece meal. An order directing the payment to the plaintiff is a sufficient record of its disposition until the whole controversy is disposed of by a final judgment.

§ 508. **Same subject—How withdrawn.**—The money is in the custody of the court as a court, and not in the custody of the judge, clerk, or other officer of the court as such; and money in court can only be paid out upon the rule or order of the court.[1] A court commissioner or other officer vested with the powers of a judge at chambers has no authority to dispose of funds in the custody of the court and an order made by a court commissioner authorizing the withdrawal of funds in court is an absolute nullity, and on motion will be stricken from the files.[2] When paid out under a void order, the money, as far as the rights of the parties are concerned, is still in court and it behooves the clerk to get it back.

In England, formerly, under the practice which came to be adopted after the report of the Common Law Commissioners, the plaintiff under a general rule of court was entitled to have the money paid out to him merely upon a production of a copy of the rule or order, if any, for paying it in, and the plea of payment. More recently, in England, in an attempt to simplify and mend the practice, both in reference to bring

9 Sleigh v Rhinelander, 1 Johns 192. 9 Bac Abr Tit Tender (K) See Tidd's Pr 672

10 Walmerstad v Jacobs, 61 Iowa 374, s c 16 N W Rep 217

1 Schunn v Hickcox 45 Wis 200 Baker v Boon 64 N Y 332, Roosevelt v Railway Co, 45 Barb 554

2 In Dunn v Hunt 78 N W Rep 1110 at *nisi prius*, the plain-tiff on learning that the decision was adverse to him applied to the court commissioner for leave to withdraw the money deposited in court, who thereupon made an order which in terms directed the clerk to pay it over On motion of the defendant this order was stricken from the files by the court as a nullity

ing money into court on a plea of tender, and upon the common rule, numerous rules, both parliamentary and judicial, regulating the payment of money in and out of court have been adopted. So, that there now, from an examination of the rules, orders and decisions, the practice seems to be in greater confusion than ever. In the United States no attempt which may be termed comprehensive appears to have been made in any state by statute to regulate and change the common law practice of bringing money into court on a plea of tender and upon the common rule and withdrawing it. Indeed courts of record, except in a very few cases, have not attempted to regulate the practice of paying money in and out of court by their general rules and orders. In absence of any general rule of court pointing out the procedure in taking money out of court, it can only be withdrawn upon an order obtained upon a special motion for that purpose. No execution is necessary.[2] In equity the usual practice is to proceed by petition and not by motion. That it should be by petition is not material unless the petitioner wishes to offer to accept the money upon certain conditions.[4] As to the notice to be given, the practice is somewhat obscure. However, withdrawing money from court, as far as the procedure is concerned, is purely a matter of practice which may be regulated by the court by its general rules and order or left to be governed by the general practice in reference to motions and orders, which in the latter case at least would require notice to the defendant. This was held to be the practice in an action against the clerk for the money, where the question of the manner of fixing the liability of the clerk was under consideration.[5] In equity, money in court can only be withdrawn after notice to all parties interested in the fund or its application. In any case the clerk not being an interested party, is not entitled to notice. The motion may be brought on for hearing according to the prescribed practice of the court, and it may be heard in term time in open court or at chambers, or during vacation at chambers,

See Hornish v. Ringin Stove Co. 89 N. W. Rep. (Io.) 95 where a separate action in the same court was instituted to have money in another action paid upon the judg-

ment in that action, was treated as a motion in the former action.

[4] See Caesar v. Copell, 83 Fed. Rep. 135, and authorities cited.

[5] Schnur v. Hickcock, 15 Wis. 200.

but always before the judge sitting as the court. In equity, on an application for leave to withdraw money in court, the party applying must produce the certificate of the clerk or other officer having the immediate custody of the fund, showing the amount of the fund, how invested, and the claims that have been made thereon, so that the proper order may be made to enable the applicant to obtain the fund.[6]

§ 509. **Effect of taking money out of court in equity.—** The rule as to the effect of a withdrawal of money in court in actions at law, does not apply in equity to those cases where the cause of action is not founded upon a tender, but exists independently of any tender, and the failure to make one affects merely the question of costs. Here, the tender if made, is usually conditional on the performance by the other party of some act which is alleged to be a condition precedent or concurrent act with the payment, and whether the money be deposited in court on a plea of tender, or on a plea of tender into court, it is usually deposited conditionally, to be paid out to the other party on the performance by him of the conditions, or to abide the event of the action. In such cases the deposit in court is not a matter of absolute right but rather goes by favor, and the party paying it in may attach such conditions to the withdrawal as he may deem himself entitled to have performed. If the conditions are within the scope of the relief demanded, the court, prior to a final decree, cannot disregard the conditions by ordering the money paid out absolutely. Hence a party will not be allowed to withdraw money paid into court conditionally in such actions, as his own absolutely, in advance of a judgment, without complying with the conditions attached to the deposit, or admitting the other party's right to have the relief, to obtain which the deposit was made, or that such withdrawal shall not preclude the opposite party from urging any defence or asserting any right to the same extent as if the money had remained in court.[1] In other words the tender and payment into court being conditional it must be accepted

6 See Hulbert v. McKay, 8 Paige, 651 which was merely a question of disposing of the sur- plus money on a mortgage sale

1 Caesar v. Copell, 83 Fed Rep 45

as made. It is more in the nature of a security for a final judgment than as an offer of immediate amends.[2]

A court of equity having acquired jurisdiction of the parties and the subject matter, in its decree, may disregard the conditions attached to the deposit, and award the funds to whichever party it justly belongs, and after a final decree the court will allow the money to be withdrawn from court only under the terms of the decree. A court, however, cannot apply money deposited in court for a purpose different from that for which it was deposited. Thus, where a defendant tendered seventeen dollars and fifty cents and a mule, in rescission of a contract exchanging mules, and seized the other mule, which the plaintiff thereupon sequestered, and the defendant under a plea for a rescission deposited the money tendered in court to be paid to the plaintiff in case the trade was rescinded, it was held error for the court to order a judgment for the difference between the sum in court and the amount of the damages awarded plaintiff for the taking and detention of his mule.[3] Where money which is brought into an equity court for a party is ordered to be paid out to him on his executing a refunding bond, and he executes the bond and takes the money out, he will not be estopped from showing that a larger sum is due to him.[4] So, if money is taken out of court in pursuance of a stipulation that it will be accounted for and paid over to the other party if adjudged his, the same as if it actually remained in court; such withdrawal will not work an admission against the party withdrawing the money; nor divest the court of the power, by an order in the same suit, to direct the fund to a new ownership.[5] If the suit is dismissed the plaintiff may withdraw the money deposited by him.[6] And it has been held that a withdrawal of the money by the plaintiff pending an appeal by him was not a waiver of his claim.[7] The court observed, however, that if the money was not forthcoming

[2] Caesar v Capel 83 Fed Rep 403 Foster v Mayer, 21 N Y Supp 16, Mayor v Patton, 1 Cranch C Ct 201 See Goslin v Hodson 24 Vt 140 also Haenssler v Duross 14 Mo App 103

[3] Sanders v Britten 45 S W Rep 200

[4] Byrd v Odem 9 Ala 755

[5] Re Application of Rochester, 40 N R A 161

[6] Cummins v Raphey 17 Ark 84

[7] Vail v McMillIn 17 O St 617

38

on a second trial on an election of the defendant to take it, some question might perhaps arise. Where, after a decree *pro confesso* and money deposited in court in pursuance of the decree, the trial court, on an application of the defendant to be let in to defend, set aside the decree, and at the same time permitted the plaintiff to withdraw his money from court, it was held that such withdrawal, the defendant avail ing himself of the benefits of the order, did not affect the validity of the plaintiff's tender, the court having the power to impose equitable conditions for the granting of the order [8] After a decree has been made for the conveyance of title upon payment of a certain sum, the plaintiff will not be allowed to withdraw money deposited by him without the decree being changed as to the conveyance.[9]

§ 510. Appeal after withdrawal of money—Withdrawal no admission of a tender—Waiver of objection to kind of money.— Where a statute provides that a party after obtaining judg ment shall not take an appeal after receiving any money paid or collected thereon, a withdrawal of money in court by a judgment creditor destroys his right to an appeal.[1] In ab sence of a statute, such withdrawal would not have this effect. Taking money out of court is no admission of the alleged tender.[2] Withdrawing money in court is a waiver of all objections to the kind of money.[3]

§ 511. The judgment awarded a plaintiff or defendant after money has been brought into court upon the common rule. —The practice at common law where the plaintiff elects to accept as the full amount due money brought into court upon the common rule, is to take it out in full satisfaction and stay proceedings or enter a discontinuance The costs incurred by the plaintiff up to the time of the application for leave to bring the money into court, together with the costs necessary to dispose of the action of record, under the modern practice, must necessarily be brought in at the time of bringing in the

---

[8] Wright v Young, 6 Wis 127, s c 70 Am Dec 453

[9] Hopkins v Stephenson, 1 J J Marsh, 341

[1] Martin v Bott 46 N E Rep (Ind ) 151

[2] Le Grew v Cooke, 1 B. & P 332

[3] Wells v Robb, 9 Bush (Ky )

amount admitted to be due upon the demand.[1] So, that, now, the plaintiff, after interposing his reply accepting the sum paid in in full satisfaction, has but to enter the stay or discontinuance and withdraw the money under the rule or order of the court. After the defendant has brought into court upon the common rule the sum of the money he thinks sufficient, and the plaintiff has refused to accept it in full satisfaction, the defendant is entitled to have it considered as a payment made on the date on which it was brought in. It is in the effect and under the term of the rule stricken from the declaration, and the defendant is answerable only for such further sum as the plaintiff may be able to prove to be due him.[2] He stands precisely on the same ground as if he had pleaded a tender before suit, together with *profert in curia*, as far as the effect upon subsequent costs are concerned.[3]

Although the above rule, heretofore, has uniformly been stated in the general terms, as above, without qualification, it is now in many of the states subject to a very material qualification. It is considered as a payment, and stricken from the declaration only in the event of a failure of the plaintiff upon proceeding further with his action, to recover no more than the sum so paid in; for if the defendant pays into court the sum actually due, the plaintiff ought in justice, at the time it is paid, take it out and end the litigation; but in the event of the sum so paid in being proven to be insufficient, and the plaintiff is entitled to recover a sum ultra the sum paid, it is in its effect upon the costs, neither considered a payment as of the date it was brought in, nor is it stricken from the declaration. Such ought in justice to be the rule in its effect upon the interest, if the money be left in court until

---

[1] Berkheimer v Geise, 82 Pa St 64, Levan v Sternfeld, 55 N J L 41 See Fishburn v Sanders, 1 N & M 242 Formerly, the practice was for the plaintiff, after interposing his reply accepting the money as sufficient, to proceed with the taxation of his costs and in the event of the costs not being paid forthwith or within a certain time, to sign formal judgment for them, but the rule was changed so that the costs are required to be brought in with the amount paid in upon the demand.

[2] Coglan v South Car R Co, 32 Fed 316, Bank of Columbia v Sotherland, 3 Cow 336 See Black v. Rose, 14 S C 279, where it is said that the sum brought in is stricken from the record whether the plaintiff take out the money or not.

[3] Borden v Moore, 5 Mass 366

after judgment, for a plaintiff ought not to be required to receive his demand in parcels. Formerly, the strict rule everywhere, was to strike it from the declaration, and to take judgment for the sum found due above the amount paid into court,[4] and such rule may yet obtain in some jurisdictions; and it is without injustice to the plaintiff when he is entitled to all his costs regardless of the amount of the recovery: but in those commonwealths where, under the statute, in actions at law the costs follow the judgment and the amount of the recovery controls the costs which may be taxed against the defendant, the plaintiff, in the event of a verdict for a sum in excess of the sum paid in, in order to preserve his right to costs is entitled to a judgment for the full amount paid in and the excess, and the defendant is entitled to have the amount of the deposit credited upon the judgment.[5] If the plaintiff refuses to receive the money so brought into court in full satisfaction of his demand, he may deny that it is sufficient, and go to trial. On the trial if no more is found due than the sum paid into court, the defendant is entitled to a non suit, or verdict,[6] and the plaintiff if he has not already done so, on an application to the court, may have the money in court paid out to him.

§ 512. **Costs when money has been brought into court upon the common rule.**—If the plaintiff proves that there is any sum due him above the amount brought into court the defendant

---

[4] Menger v Smith, 4 B. & A. 673, Cox v Perry, 1 T R. 464, Cox v. Robinson, Stra 1027, Bank of Columbia v Sutherland, 3 Cow 336, Slack v Brown, 13 Wend 390; Tidd's Pr 677, Boyden v Moore, 5 Mass 366, Phelphs v Town, 14 Mich 374  See Murray v. Windley, 7 Iredell's Law, 201

[5] See Goldstein v Stern, 9 N Y. S 274, and Dakin v Dunning, 7 Hill, 30, Bennett v Odom, 30 Ga. 940.

[6] Wilson v Doran, 39 Hon 88; Hart v Mills, 15 M & W 85, Logue v Gellick, 1 E D Smith, 398  Where $160 was paid into court under a statute which provided that in case issue thereon being found for defendant he shall be entitled to costs, on a verdict for plaintiff for $160 without stating whether it was for the sum paid in or for damages ultra, it was held that the verdict, being for the precise sum, the lower court should, after directing the money to be paid to the plaintiff, order judgment with costs for the defendant  Gamble v Seutman, 11 Atl Rep (Md) 584

pays all the costs.[1] The authorities bearing upon the question of the effect of bringing money into court upon the common rule, upon the right of the plaintiff or of the defendant to costs, when the plaintiff proceeds to the trial after the payment into court, and fails to recover a greater sum, are somewhat conflicting. The subject now appears all the more difficult to harmonize with the old authorities on account of the modern practice of requiring the defendant to bring into court, with the amount admitted to be due, all accrued costs, and those necessary to a proper disposition of the action of record. A plaintiff being entitled to withdraw the amount paid in at any time, and does so before a verdict for the defendant, or he does not withdraw the money, how is the matter of cost already paid by the defendant to be adjusted under a statute regulating the cost of the successful party? If the inflexible rule, that a person paying money into court does so at his peril, applies to costs paid in, then the subject is free from doubt, for under it the plaintiff may have the sum paid in, and the defendant, if successful, must be satisfied with the taxable cost allowed him as a prevailing party in resisting the claim of plaintiff to a sum above the amount paid in. If this be not the rule, then the court in actions at law must assume equitable powers, and require the plaintiff to leave the cost in court to await the final determination of the action, and if the defendant is successful order them paid out to him, or allow the cost to be withdrawn by plaintiff, and in case the defendant is successful, award a judgment in his favor for the cost previously paid, and leave him to add thereto by taxation his costs as a prevailing party. The former view appears to be the most equitable, since the defendant is required to pay no more than the plaintiff's just dues, and costs to which he would be entitled in the event of his recovery of the amount due (assuming the amount paid in is the amount due) in absence of a deposit in court, while he may have reasonable and probable cause for believing that more is due, and ought not by reason of a confession of a part of his claim, be required to proceed with his cause for the residue at the peril of losing his cost incurred previous to the deposit in court. Under such rule the defendant pays all

[1] See Murray v Windely, 7 Dec 324, Levan v Sternfeld, 55 Iredell's Law, 201, s c 47 Am N. J Law, 41

costs to the time of the application for leave to bring the money into court and the cost necessary to dispose of the case of record, and the plaintiff pays all costs of the defendant necessarily incurred subsequent to that time.[2]

Where money is brought into court to a part of a plaintiff's claim, and the residue is met by other defences, such as payment, &c., the plaintiff cannot avoid paying the costs of those pleas to the defendant by taking the money out of court in satisfaction of the whole demand.[3] The plaintiff, by claiming more than is due, thus occasions the necessity for such further pleas, and he will not be allowed to pass over them unnoticed.[4] But the rule is said to be otherwise if the money

---

[2] Atkin v Colton, 3 Wend 326 Here, after the evidence was in, the plaintiff submitted to a non suit. The appeal went upon the question whether the defendant was entitled to cost incurred before the payment of the money into court—Held he was not. See Murray v Windely, 7 Iredell's Law, 201 s c 47 Am. Dec 324, Logue v Gelleh, 1 E D Smith, 398 It has been held that where the plaintiff does not at once accept the money brought in, but proceeds further without going to trial, he is entitled to the costs prior to the time the money was brought in, and the defendant to his costs subsequently incurred. 1 Tidd's Pr 677, citing Hartley v. Bateson, 1 D & E 629, Willes, 191, Savage v Franklyn, Barnes, 280, Pr Reg 254, 3 S C See Say, Rep 196, contra. And again it has been held that the plaintiff is entitled to the costs incurred previous to the time of bringing the money into court, though he has given notice of trial, and neglects to withdraw it, and the defendant is entitled to enter judgment as in case of non suit 1 Tidd's Pr 677, citing 2 Taunt. 361. So, where the plaintiff entered the cause for trial and withdrew it

Id. 677 So, it has been held contrary to the text, that after the defendant has obtained judgment as in case of non suit, or judgment upon plaintiff's failure to prosecute the action, the plaintiff is not entitled to the costs incurred previous to the time of obtaining the rule. Id. 677, citing 2 M & S. 335, Postle v. Beckington, 6 Taunt. 158, s c. 1 Marsh. 510 So, where a juror was withdrawn by consent, it was held that the plaintiff was not entitled to the costs previous to the time of bringing the money into court Id 678, citing 3 D & E. 657; and again, that in case of a verdict against the plaintiff he neither receives or pays costs incurred prior to the time the money was brought into court Williams v. Ingersoll, 12 Pick 345 See Rev. St Mass C 121, Sec 14

[3] 1 Chitty's Precedents 367, n, citing Topham v Kidmore, 5 Dowl 676 Emmett v Stanton, Evch. T T 1838, Goodee v Goldsmith, 2 M & W 202, s. c 5 Dowl 288 See Hatch v. Thompson, 67 Conn. 74 and see, also, James v Raggett, 2 B & A. 776, and Skarratt v Vaughan, 2 Taunt 266

[4] See Bailhe v Cazelet, 4 T. R. 579.

be paid in upon the whole declaration, where the defence to the recovery of any further sum is not by way of confession and avoidance of such further sum, but in effect that no more than the sum paid in was ever due.[5] So, if the money be paid in upon the whole declaration and the defendant improperly pleads other pleas to all except the sum paid in, he is not entitled to the costs of the other pleas.[6]

§ 513. **The judgment awarded the plaintiff or defendant after money has been brought into court on a plea of tender with profert in curia—Costs.**—Where, on a plea of tender with *profert in curia* made good by a deposit in court of the sum tendered, the plaintiff elects to take, in full satisfaction of his claim, the amount alleged to have been tendered, the money will be ordered paid over to him and a judgment rendered against him for the cost.[1] So, if the plaintiff fails to prove any more to be due than the sum tendered and brought into court, such tender bars the right to a judgment for the amount tendered and costs,[2] and he must pay the defendant costs.[3] If the tender is made after action brought, under a statute authorizing it, the plaintiff, if no more is found due than the sum tendered, is liable only for the costs accruing after the tender.[4] In such cases the verdict must be for the defendant.[5] In England, formerly, and at present in the United States in those commonwealths where a judgment for merely nominal damages carries the cost, a successful plaintiff, where money has been deposited in court on a plea of tender, is entitled to a judgment for the balance found due over and above the amount brought into court.[6] So,

[5] See Coats v Stevens, 2 C M. & R 118, s c. 3 Dowl 784

[6] See Coats v Stevens, 1 Gale, 75

[1] Monroe v Chelleck, 78 Ill 429, Griffiths v. School Board, 24 L R (Q B. D.) 307 See Gardner v. Black 98 Ala 638

[2] Foote v. Palmer, Wright 336; Wetherbee v. Krusterer, 2 N. W. Rep. 45; Cornell v Green, 10 S. & R (Pa ) 17

[3] Elder v Elder, 43 Kan 514, Pollock v. Warwick, 104 N Car. 638, Foote v Palmer, Wright 366, Reed v Armstrong 18 Ind 446, Dakin v Dunning, 7 Hill, 30.

[4] Grafeman v St Louis Dairy Co, 70 S W Rep (Mo App.) 390

[5] Syson v Hieronymus, 20 So. Rep (Ala ) 967; Pennepacker v. Umberger, 22 Pa St 492

[6] Supply Ditch Co v. Elliott, 10 Colo 327; Drew v Towle, 30 N. H 531, Call v Lathrop, 39 Me 434, Boyden v. Moore, 5 Mass. 365; Dickinson v Boyd, 82 Ill. App 251

under those statutes where the amount sued for, and not the amount of the recovery, governs the right to costs,[7] a tender and payment into court does not affect plaintiff's right to costs, though the amount recovered, by reason of the tender, is below the amount for which costs are allowed.[8]  Under such rules the practice is well enough, and works no injustice to either party; but in those states where, under the statute, the costs follow the judgment and are made to depend upon the amount of the judgment, the plaintiff, where more is found to be due him than the amount deposited in court, in order to preserve his right to costs, is entitled to the judgment for the full amount found due,[9] and the amount brought into court must be credited upon the judgment.[10]  So, if the whole amount of the demand is brought into court on an alleged tender, and issue is joined thereon, or issue is joined upon a plea of a subsequent demand and refusal, which is found for the plaintiff, he is entitled to a judgment for the whole amount tendered and costs, and the amount paid in must likewise be credited on the judgment and execution issued for the residue.[11]  If the defendant fails to bring the money into court a judgment will be rendered against him for the amount tendered and costs;[12] for bringing money into court, is what saves the defendant harmless, in case the tender be otherwise sufficient.[13]

The rule heretofore considered in reference to the amount of the judgment which a plaintiff is entitled to have where he proceeds with his actions after a deposit of money in

[7] Haley v Newport, 6 R. I. 582

[8] Thompson v Townsend, 41 Mich 346

[9] Goldstein v Stern, 9 N Y Supp. 274; Dahin v Dunning, 7 Hill, 30, Lewis v. Larson, 45 Wis 263, State Bank v Holcomb, 7 N J L 193, Reed v Armstrong, 18 Ind 446, Martin v. Bott, 46 N E. Rep (Ind) 151, Dresser v Witherle, 7 Me 111.  See Meeker v Hurd, 31 Vt 639, Haley v. Newport, 6 R I. 582, and Reed v. Wilson 11 Gray 486

[10] Reed v. Armstrong, 18 Ind 416; Murphy v. Gold, 3 N Y.

Supp 304, Martin v Bott, 46 N E Rep (Ind.) 151; Erie v. Grimes, 82 Tex 89, Bennet v. Odom, 30 Ga 940.

[11] Schnur v. Hickcox, 45 Wis. 200.  A finding in favor of the plaintiff for a less sum than the amount paid in imports in finding against the tender  Berkheimer v. Geise, 82 Pa St. 64

[12] Monroe v. Cheldeck, 78 Ill 429; Rverson v Kitchell, 2 N J. L 168; Alexander v. Oneida Co., 54 N W. Rep 21.

[13] Warrington v Pollard, 24 Iowa, 231

court, and disproves the tender, or proves a subsequent demand and refusal, or shows himself to be entitled to more than the sum paid in either on a plea of tender or upon the common rule, unquestionably apply where the money which has been brought in is allowed to remain in court until after a verdict; but where the plaintiff before a verdict in his favor withdraws the money, for what amount must the judgment be? In a case before the Supreme Court of Indiana, the court said: "If the money is accepted—taken out of court—by the plaintiff before verdict, and the pleadings shaped to continue litigation for a balance still due, the judgment should only be for the amount found due over and above that so taken out of court." [14] Lord Mansfield, according to Mr. Tidd, in a case where the issue upon a plea of a subsequent demand and refusal was found for the plaintiff, said· "The money having been taken out of court, the plaintiff shall recover only *nominal* damages, but otherwise the verdict would have been for the sum tendered." [15] The question recurs, in those states where under the statute the amount of the judgment determines the plaintiff's right to costs, what effect will such a withdrawal have upon the plaintiff's right to cost? Upon this point there appears to be a total lack of precedents. That would appear a just rule which would permit a plaintiff to withdraw the money, and at the same time reserve his right to costs, and right to have a judgment for the full amount found due, in case he is entitled to a judgment, and credit the amount withdrawn upon such judgment, as a party may do on an acceptance of a payment after an action brought, made between the parties out of court. Such a rule would not violate the statute, nor deprive the plaintiff of the use of the money which is his absolutely and which the defendant cannot use  Care, however, should be taken to adjust by the verdict the question of interest, so that the plaintiff may not have interest on the amount withdrawn after the withdrawal as well as the use of the money.

§ 514. **What may be brought into court—Money.**—Where a plea is of a tender of legal-tender money, or of money generally, with *profert in curia*, and where a defendant seeks to

---

14 Reed v Armstrong, 18 Ind.  446  See Martin v. Bott, 46 N E
Rep (Ind) 151            15 Tidd's Pr 672

bring money into court upon the common rule, and in equity
where money as such is allowed to be deposited in court, the
money brought in must be a legal tender,[1] because all debts
and contracts to pay money generally are payable in legal
tender money, and a court has no power to compel the acceptance of anything else, and discharge the debtor or the obligor.
But money which is not a legal tender may be brought into
court, where a tender of the kind brought in is pleaded to
gether with the proper allegations showing a waiver by the
defendant as to the medium of payment.  The plea must state
specifically the kind of money which was offered and make a
*profert* of that very money, if the defendant desires to take
advantage of any subsequent depreciation of the money
which was offered.[2]  If the plea is of a tender of uncurrent
money which was current when the tender was made, the
identical money which had been tendered must be brought
in.[3]  If the identical money has been used by the tenderor or
otherwise disposed of, then he must bring into court the same
nominal sum in legal tender.  The reason that the identical
notes are required to be brought into court where, at the time
of interposing the defence of tender, they are uncurrent or
valueless, is that the tenderor may have used the notes tendered when they were of a value, and obtained and deposited
in court the same nominal amounts of such notes when they
were uncurrent or valueless[4]  But, if the money which was
tendered has continued current at par from the time of the
tender, it is unnecessary to bring into court the identical
money but other money of like kind may be brought in, as
one dollar of the issue of any particular bank is the equiva-

[1] Shelby v Boyd, 3 Yates, 321
[2] Downman v. Downman, 1
Wash 26  Jeter v Littlejohn, 3
Murp 386, was a suit in equity to
be relieved from the payment of
interest  A tender of the amount
due upon a bond was made during
the Revolutionary War in paper
money, then a legal tender and at
par, but afterwards (1798) when a
demand was made, and an action
commenced upon the bond, money
of the kind offered was worthless
The relief was granted, because,
as the court thought, when the
money became worthless the rule
requiring it to be brought into
court failed, and that a debtor
ought not to be expected to preserve the identical money throughout so long a period of civil con-
vulsions as that which occurred
after the tender
[3] Pong v Lindsay, 1 Dyer, 82 a;
Downman v. Downman, 1 Wash.
26
[4] See Gilkeson v Smith, 15 W.
Va 44

lent of any other dollar of the same bank. So, the same may be said of any form of money issued by the government. Although a tender of a bank check is good if objection be not made at the time of the tender that it is not money, yet the tender must be kept good in money, and the money, not the check, brought into court.[5] Nor can the money which was tendered be deposited in a bank and a certificate of deposit for the same, payable either to the order of the clerk or to the creditor, be brought into court.[6]

**§ 515. Same subject—Specific articles—Exceptions—Trover for money or note.**—It is a general rule that specific articles which have been tendered need not be brought into court. One reason advanced why it is unnecessary is that they are usually ponderous, and it would be inconvenient, and in some cases impossible, to bring them in[1] While this reason, usually, given, is good, yet the better reason seems to be that the title to the articles tendered having passed to the tenderee, the tenderor is under no obligation to keep them in his possession, and produce them anywhere, but the tenderee must take his goods where they have been deposited and kept for him. Where notes, bonds, or mortgages are offered in satisfaction of a debt, the tender must be kept good, and the tender pleaded with *profert in curia* and the securities brought into court. Owing to the peculiar nature of the property the tender is held not to be governed by the rules applicable to specific chattels, but is like a tender of money.[2] So, the same is true where a note is drawn payable in bank bills; though the contrary has been held, and bank notes placed in the same class as ponderous articles.[3] Where a tenderor seeks to enforce an executory contract for the conveyance of land, if he pleads a tender of a deed he must also allege that he has kept the tender good, plead a *profert in curia* and bring the

[5] Lewis v Larson, 15 Wis 353 See Bradford v Foster, 87 Tenn. 1 and Wright v Robinson, 84 Hun 172.

[6] Smith v Merchants' & F. Bank, 14 Ohio, C C. 199 *Contra* Steckle v Standly, 107 Iowa, 694, 77 N W Rep 189

[1] 9 Bac Abr Tit Tender (II), Mitchell v Merrill, 2 Blackf. 89; Spann v Baltzell, 1 Flo 301, Patton v Hunt, 64 N Car 163.

[2] Brooklyn Bank v DeGraew, 23 Wend 342 s c. 35 Am. Dec 569

[3] Patton v Hunt, 64 N C 163

deed into court.[4] A replication setting up a subsequent de
mand and refusal to deliver a deed has been held not to cure
the want of such *profert*.[5] In trover for money, the court will
grant the defendant leave for bringing the money into court.[6]
And the court might, perhaps, in trover grant leave to bring
a note or other document into court where there was no
tort which would go to enhance the damages above the real
value. But in none of these cases can the common rule be
had. The order goes more by favor and only in those cases
where as a matter of law, the plaintiff is not damaged beyond
the real value of the thing itself. Those cases where a court,
on a proper showing, will stay proceedings on the defendant
returning the article and paying costs, are not within the
scope of this treatise, the article passing between the parties
out of court.

§ 516. **With whom money brought into court is deposited.**—
In England, under the old practice, the money was delivered
to the signer of the writs if the action was in the King's
Bench, and to the Prothonotarie if in the Common Pleas.[1]
In the United States it is delivered to the clerk of the court,[2]
or the officer, by whatever name, performing the functions
of that office.[3] If the statute directs that the money must be

---

[4] Goodwin v Morey, 111 Ind 68.
See Taylor v Browder, 1 Oh St
225 This was an action for damages It was held the deed should
have been set out in the pleading
or a profert made so that the
court can see if it is sufficient.

[5] Sook v Knowles, 1 Bibb. 383
In Indiana under a statute (Rev
St 1881, Sec 5850) authorizing
the clerks of the several courts to
receive money in payment of all
judgments, dues and demands of
records in their respective offices,
and all such funds as may be
ordered to be paid into the respective courts by the judges, &c,
it was held that a county order
paid into court under the order of
the proper judge was "funds"
See Ch. 320, Gen Laws Minn
1895, which permits a bailee and

the like where there are two or
more claimants, to deposit property with the clerk of court.

[6] Tidd's Pr 541, citing 1 Sti
142

[1] Tidd's Pr 672

[2] Mahan v Waters, 60 Mo 167;
Phelps v Town, 11 Mich 374;
Walters v Wilkinson, 92 Iowa,
120 s c 60 N W Rep 514, Dirks
v Tuel, 80 N W Rep 1045 See
Morgan v Long 29 Iowa, 434,
McDonald v Atkins, 13 Neb 568,
s c 14 N W Rep 532, Moore v
Boyer 52 Neb 446 s c 72 N. W.
Rep 586

[3] In Kansas under a section of
the Code (Sec 131) which prescribes the time when money must
be deposited in court in support
of a plea of tender, it was held,
in case where the money was paid

deposited in a bank or trust company, or with a constable,[4] or other officer, it must be deposited with the person designated. The possession of the money by the clerk, or the officer or depositary, where properly paid in, is that of the court; as much so as is the possession by the clerk of the records and files of the court. In a justice court, when a tender is pleaded, the money is paid directly to the justice in open court.[5] A deposit of money with an auditor on a trial before him,[6] or with a referee, is not a payment into court.[7]

The clerk of the court or other subordinate officer authorized to receive and hold money brought into court, as of the custody of the court, can receive the money officially only upon a tender pleaded and where the party has obtained leave of the court allowing him to make the deposit.[8] In other cases, if money be delivered to the clerk, he receives it as the agent of the depositor,[9] and it may at any time be withdrawn by him.[10]

§ 517. **Liability for the safe keeping of money in court—Duty of retiring clerk—Kind of money to be returned—Investment.**—The clerk having money in his possession as of the

to the judge instead of the clerk, that, as the statute did not provide that the money shall be paid to the clerk, there was no good reason why the judge of the court might not receive and hold possession of the money  Authur v. Authur, 38 Kan. 691, s c 17 Pac. 187  This is in direct conflict with the practice in court of record at common law, a practice in which the code in no way affected, as it merely changed the rule at common law as to the time when the money should be brought in  The practice ought to have been condemned  However, the money having been paid in under an order, the observation of the court that because one officer is in possession of the money and not another ought not to prejudice the one paying it in, was em-

mently a proper view of the question in that respect.  See Wright v Harris, 31 Iowa, 272, where the money was deposited with the county judge.

[4] Kansas City Ti. v. Neiswanger, 27 Mo 356; Vose v McGuire, 26 Mo. App 452  It must be paid to a constable of the township when the action is commenced.

[5] Phelps v. Town, 14 Mich 374

[6] Wing v. Hurlburt, 15 Vt 607

[7] Becker v. Boon, 61 N. Y. 317.

[8] Baker v. Hunt, 1 Wend 103.

[9] Mazyck v McEwen, 2 Bailey (S. C ), 28; Sowle v. Holdridge, 25 Ind. 119, Commercial Inv. Co. v. Peck. 73 N. W Rep 452

[10] Hamner v Kaufman, 39 Ill. 87.  In this case the court seems to go to the extent of holding that the court, before the depositor

custody of the court is responsible for its safe keeping, and the clerk and his bondsmen are liable to the person entitled to the money, in case of refusal or neglect of the clerk to account for and deliver it over.[1] An administrator of an estate to which money in court belongs, cannot by agreement with the clerk relieve him from his liability.[2] A person entitled to money which has been brought into court, in absence of a general rule, should apply to the court on notice to all parties interested for an order directing the clerk to pay the money to him, and until the party shows himself entitled to the fund, by obtaining on such application an order for the payment of the money to him, he cannot maintain an action against the clerk and his bondsmen for the money,[3] for although he may have good reasons to believe the clerk has converted the funds, yet he cannot know for certain that the clerk will not respond to a demand for the fund until the court by its order decides that the money belongs to the applicant, and such order has been served upon the clerk. Before a rule on the clerk will be granted it must appear that he holds the money in an official capacity.[4] It is the duty of a clerk, on retiring from office, to pay over money which he holds as of the custody of the court to his successor,[5] and a failure to do so is a breach of one of the conditions of his bond, for which an action may be maintained by the proper party. The statute of limitation does not commence to run until an order is made directing the clerk to pay over the money; and a failure to respond is a breach of the clerk's bond in force at that time and is not a breach of the bond in force at the time the money was deposited.[6] The fact that the clerk has retired from office without turning over the

withdraws the money may recognize it as a fund in its control

[1] Jewett v State, 94 Ind 549, Walters v Wilkinson, 60 N W Rep (Iowa) 514, Mott v Pettit, 1 N J L (1 Coxe) 298 See Northern Pac Ry Co v Owens, 90 N W Rep (Minn) 371, and see, also, Thompson v St Joseph, 23 Kan 209 and Morgan v Penick, 62 S W Rep (Ky) 479

[2] Sullivan v The State, 121 Ind 342.

[3] Schnur v. Hickcox, 45 Wis 200, Walters v Wilkinson, 60 N W Rep (Iowa) 514

[4] Lewis v Cockrell, 31 Ill. App 476

[5] Walters v Wilkinson, 60 N. W. Rep (Iowa) 514

[6] Walters v Wilkinson, 60 N. W Rep (Iowa) 514; Dirks v Juel, 80 N W (Neb) 1045

money does not affect the jurisdiction of the court to make an order directing its payment.[7]

The clerk must keep the identical money brought in separate from his private or other funds, as a party paying it in or the opposite party, upon an order allowing it to be withdrawn, is entitled to the identical money. The clerk has no right to employ for his own purposes money deposited in his office,[8] or to mingle it with other moneys so that it cannot be distinguished from the other moneys. If allowed to handle the fund indiscriminately with other funds, the clerk might pay away gold and have only paper money to deliver over when ordered. He must not deposit it to his credit or that of any other person in a bank or other depositary, as that would be to substitute the credit of the depositary for the money.[9] Such a deposit would amount to a conversion of the fund.[10] He may, however, place it in a safety deposit vault or other place for safe keeping, taking care to keep it always under his immediate control. The clerk cannot invest the money for the party entitled to it; but cases are to be found in the books where the court has directed the money to be invested [11] But such cases are rare, and perhaps the practice is not strictly proper, except possibly in suits when the money has been brought in to abide the final determination of the action, and then only upon the joint application or mutual consent of the parties When money is brought in upon a plea of tender where the action is to recover a debt, or it is brought in upon the common rule, the money belongs to the plaintiff absolutely, and he is at liberty to withdraw it at any time, and an order directing the investment of the fund

7 Schnur v Hickcox, 15 Wis 200

8 Mott v Pettit, 1 N J. L. (Cox 2) 298

9 See Northern Pac Ry Co. v. Owens, 90 N W Rep (Minn) 371, where the clerk and his bondsmen were held liable for the loss of money deposited by the clerk in a bank which afterwards failed

10 Dirks v Juel, 80 N W Rep (Neb) 1045, citing Greenfield v Bank, 102 Mass 174, Pine Co. v.

Willard, 39 N. W Rep (Minn) 71, 1 L R A 118, Williams v Williams, 55 Wis 300, 12 N W. Rep 465, and 13 N W. Rep. 271; Hammon v Cottle, 6 Serg & R 290, Cartmell v Allard 7 Bush. 182, Bartlett v Hamilton, 46 Me 435, Com v McAllister, 28 Pa St. 480 and Naltun v Dolan, 108 Ind 500 8 N E Rep 289

11 Taylor v Lancaster 33 Gratt (Va) 1, De Peyster v Clarkson, 2 Wend 77.

will not be made upon the application of the party paying it
in, as he has no further control over it, and there is no good
reason why the court should undertake to direct the investment of the funds concerning the ownership of which there
can be no question, either upon the mutual consent of the
parties or upon the application of the plaintiff.

§ 518. **The risk of loss of money in court on whom.**—Money
which has been brought into court in a case where it may be
properly brought in, is thereafter at the risk of the party
for whom it is brought in.[1] But the rule is subject to the
limitation that it must be paid in unconditionally, so that
the plaintiff may take it out and go for more, as where it
is brought in in satisfaction of that part of plaintiff's claim
conceded to be due by the defendant. Its acceptance must
not necessitate an abandonment of the action by the party
accepting it,[2] as where it is brought in, in a suit to be allowed
to pay a mortgage debt and have a discharge of record, in
actions for specific performance and the like   In all such
cases it is either unnecessary to bring it in or is required as
evidence of good faith in connection with the plaintiff's offer
to do equity, and it is always brought in conditionally, and
the risk of loss is legitimately a part of the hazard of the
litigation, and the loss, if any, must be borne by the party
bringing it in, for manifestly the other party cannot take the
money out without admitting that his opponent's contention
is well founded, and abandoning his side of the case.  Where
money is brought into court in an action where it cannot

[1] Taylor v. Lancaster, 33 Gratt (Va ) 1   Here the money in court, was in 1860 lent out under an order of the court, and in 1863 under another order authorizing it, it was repaid in Confederate money then almost exclusively the circulating medium of Virginia. Held, a sufficient payment though Confederate money was worth only one fourth as much as gold.

[2] See De Peyster v Clarkson, 2 Wend 77  In this case the money was paid in generally and not in satisfaction of so much of plain-tiff's demand  The money was invested under an order of the court  A loss having occurred, it was held that it must be borne by the defendant inasmuch as it was merely a deposit to abide such disposition as the court might determine to be equitable on the final determination of the action   An offer of plaintiff to accept the money as a payment *pro tanto* was rejected by the defendant, as was also his suggestion as to an investment

properly be brought in, the loss, if any, must fall upon the party depositing it.³ In an action to recover the possession of certain real estate where the defendant interposed the defence that the plaintiff's deed was executed as a mortgage, and deposited the amount admitted to be due thereon with the clerk who afterwards went out of office and converted the money, it was held that the plea was good in itself, and was in no way aided by the deposit of the money, and that the defendant must bear the loss occasioned by the clerk's conversion of the money.⁴ It remains to be observed that in all cases where money may properly be brought into court in an action, but it does not really become a fund of the court, as where the money is deposited with the clerk without obtaining a rule or order in cases where a rule or order of the court is necessary, any loss or depreciation of the money must be borne by the party making the deposit.⁵

§ 519. How action proceeds after money has been brought in—Nonsuit.—After money has been brought into court either in support of a plea of tender, or upon the common rule, the plaintiff may be nonsuited.¹ Where money has been brought

---

³ See Commercial Ins. Co. v. Peck, 53 Neb. 204, s. c 73 N. W Rep 452.

⁴ Sowle v. Holdridge, 25 Ind 119 In this case it does not appear that any order was obtained authorizing the deposit, but that does not affect the question further than to furnish an additional reason why the loss should be borne by the party depositing the money. See Commercial Ins Co v Peck, 53 Neb. 204, s c 73 N. W. Rep 452, where no order was obtained

⁵ Hammer v Kaufman, 39 Ill. 87, Sowle v Holdridge, 25 Ind. 119 See Blake v Enslow, 41 W. Va. 744, s. c. 24 S E Rep 679, citing Mazych v McEwen, 2 Bailey, 28, Niolon v Drakeford (Id ), Keith v Smith, 1 Swan. 92, Currie v Thomas, 8 Port (Ala )

293, Re Ficks, 11 Fed. Rep 383, Jenkins v Lemonds, 29 Ind 294. Money deposited pursuant to a statute with a sheriff or a county judge, in proceedings under eminent domain, is paid to such officer as the agent of the one instituting the proceedings and is at the risk of the one making the deposit Brown v. Chicago R I. & P R, 89 N W. Rep (Neb.) 405, citing White v Railway Co, 64 Iowa, 281, s c 20 N W Rep 436, and Blackshire v. Railway Co., 13 Kan 514

¹ Jenkins v Cutchens, 2 Miles (Pa.), 65; McCredy v Fey, 7 Watt (Pa ) 496; Supply Ditch Co v Elliott, 10 Colo 327. See Tidd's Pr. 674, citing Elliot v. Callow, 2 Salk 597 Pr Reg 250, Cas Pr C P 36, s c Cas *Temp.* Hardw 206, 2 Str 1027, s c Stevenson v

into court and the plaintiff does not choose to accept it, the cause proceeds much in the same manner as if the money had not been paid in at all.[2] The money being conceded by the defendant, by the deposit to belong to the plaintiff, the latter may withdraw it upon an application to the court for that purpose, and he needs no judgment therefor; and in so far as his right to the sum brought in is concerned, it is immaterial whether a judgment goes in his favor or against him.

§ 520. **In custodia legis.**—Money which has been brought into court in an action, and deposited with the clerk, or deposited under a statute in a bank or trust company, or with a constable or other officer upon a plea of tender or upon an order of the court, is in *custodia legis*, and is exempt from process. A clerk of court or other person having in his possession, as of the custody of the court, money which he holds subject to the order of the court in an action, cannot be made a party in an independent proceeding in that court or another to affect the control of such funds.[1] A court of equity cannot make an order affecting the control or disposition of the money in custody of a court of law.[2] A party desiring to reach such fund must first, by an application to the court in which the money was brought into court, obtain leave of the court to proceed against the fund in a collateral proceeding. In a case in which leave of the court having custody of a fund was not obtained the court said: "The futility of such a bill is sufficient to defeat them, because, notwithstanding the pendency of one of them, the court having control of the fund may order the entire disposition of it summarily, thus

---

Yorke 1 Durnf & East 10. 7 Durnf & East 372. 2 Esp Rep 181. 607. 2 H Blac 374, and 1 Campl 127, 8 in note. See also 1 Arch Pr 188. and Burstall v Horner 7 T R 372

2 Tidd's Pr 675

1 Tuck v Manning, 150 Mass 211, s c 22 N E Rep 1001 5 L R A 666, citing Columbian Book Co v De Golyer, 115 Mass 67, Jones v Jones 1 Bland Ch 443,

and Wilder v Bailey 3 Mass 289, Voss v McGuire, 26 Mo App 452, Drake on Attachment, Sec 257. Bowden v Schatzell 1 Bailey 360, Jones v Merchants' Nat Bank, 35 L R A 698, Pace v Smith 57 Tex 555, Curtis v Ford 78 Tex 262, Kansas City Ti Co v Neiswanger, 27 Mo App 356, Voss v McGuire, 26 Mo App 452

2 Bowden v Schatzell, 1 Bailey, 360

leaving nothing for the bill to act on."[3]   It is absolutely
necessary that every court have plenary and absolute control
over the subject-matter involved in an action pending before
it, and any unauthorized interference in such cases with the
full exercise of judicial functions is to subvert the fundamental principles upon which judicial authority rests.  Leave
being granted, the money is in effect impounded to await the
determination of the collateral proceedings.  All persons who
have been decreed to have an interest in the fund must be
made parties both in the application for leave of court to
proceed against the fund, and in the collateral proceedings.
A clerk of court, master in chancery, or other person having
custody of money as of the custody of the court, is not a
necessary or even a proper party to either proceeding, as he
could not legally dispose of it until the order impounding it
was superseded by some subsequent order of the court made
therein.  The application for leave to attach or otherwise
hold the fund cannot be entertained until the court, having
the custody of the fund, determines by its judgment to whom
it belongs, otherwise it might turn out that the money did
not belong to the party against whom the collateral proceedings were instituted.  Parties claiming a direct interest in the
fund, as that of an owner, &c., must proceed by a complaint
of intervention in the action in which the fund is deposited.

§ **521. Impounding money in court for costs.**—Where money
has been brought into court, and the party for whom it was
brought in allows it to remain until a verdict passes for the
other party, the court will impound so much of it as may be
necessary to satisfy the costs of the prevailing party.[1]  The
cases supporting such a rule are not numerous, but this undoubtedly is due to the fact that few litigants have neglected
to withdraw money in court which they were at liberty to
take at any time—and fewer still, having neglected to withdraw it, cared to risk an appeal from the order directing the
payment of costs out of such fund   In Pennsylvania, it has

[3] Jones   v   Merchants' Nat
Bank, 35 L R A 698
[1] Le Grew \ Cook, 1 B & P
332, Birks v Trippet. 1 Saund

Rep  33  a  note; Anonymous,
Barns, 280  3 Bl Com 304  Shais-
wood Ed N 19  Dillenback v
The Rossend Castle, 30 Fed Rep
462

been held that where money has been brought into court by
the defendant, and the plaintiff dies and his administrator is
substituted, who does not appear and is nonsuited, the money
will be impounded to answer the defendant's costs.[2] So, it
has been held that where the money had been brought into
court upon the common rule and a verdict for the defendant,
the latter will be allowed to take it out in payment of his
costs.[3] So, when a plaintiff in support of a plea of tender in
an action to redeem brought money into court and the defendant prevailed, it was held that the latter might impound
sufficient of the money on deposit to pay the costs.[4]

It may be impounded by the order of the court either in
an independent application therefore, or by a counter motion
at the time the defeated party seeks to withdraw the money
from court. It can only be impounded after a verdict. But
ler, J., said: "It is perfectly certain, that whatever may become of this action, the Plaintiff will be entitled to the money
tendered; and if that be the case, by what right can the Court
retain it, as a security for the Defendant's costs, on the
chances of a verdict being given in his favor? I agree that
if the plaintiff be negligent and does not take the money out
of Court until after the verdict has passed for the defendant,
the Court will lay hold of it to secure the Defendant's
costs; and if it could be shown that Plaintiff was now in that
situation, the Court would not let him take out the money
without doing justice to the Defendant. It being once admitted that the Plaintiff would be entitled to the money tendered in all events, the application must fall to the ground."[5]

[2] Jenkins v Cutchens, 2 Miles,
65, citing 2 Arch Pr 184

[3] Rathbone v. Stedman, Cooke's
Cas Prac C P 82 Maddox v
Paston, Id 177. See Tidd's Pr. p
679, citing Cas P C P 54 Pr
Reg 251, s. c. Barnes, 280; 9 Bac
Al Title Tender (N)

[4] Dunn v. Hunt, 78 N. W. Rep.
(Minn) 1110

[5] Le Grew v Cooke, 1 Bos &
Pul. 332

## CHAPTER XVI.

### OFFER OF JUDGMENT.

**§ 522. In general—A statutory right.**—At common law the general rule is, that after an action has been commenced, the defendant cannot escape paying costs without prevailing in his entire defence [1] Under the New York code, and similar statutes in other states, two courses may be pursued by the defendant after an action has been commenced. He may make a tender of a certain sum with accrued costs, and if it is refused, he may deposit the money in court; or he may offer to allow judgment to be taken against him for a certain sum with costs. Such statutes afford a defendant an opportunity to escape the payment of damages and costs accruing subsequent to the tender, where, in cases where a tender can be made, he has neglected to make one before suit; and, in those cases covered by the statute, whether a tender can or cannot be made, an offer of judgment solely confers the same benefits. Provided, however, in either case, he is successful in resisting plaintiff's demand beyond the sum offered. The right extends to justice and police courts, as well as courts of record. By making an offer the defendant does not waive

[1] See Rand v Wiley, 70 Iowa, 110, s c 29 N. W. Rep 814

his right to costs allowed him as a successful party upon other issues.[2]

**§ 523. Cases in which an offer of judgment may be made.—** In Kansas, an offer of judgment may be made in actions founded upon tort as well as in actions upon contract;[1] and in proceedings under the right of eminent domain.[2] And in New York, in equitable actions as well as actions at law;[3] and whether there is one or several defendants.[4] It may be made in foreclosure suits, where a personal judgment against the mortgagor for a deficiency is asked.[5] A defendant who seeks to save himself costs by making an offer of judgment under one section of a statute, applicable to certain actions, cannot, on being defeated, avail himself of the benefits of a general provision.[6] The statute of each state determines the kind of actions in which an offer of judgment may be made, and should be examined before making an offer in any given case.[7]

**§ 524. How made—Unconditional—Service.—** In New York, where an offer of judgment is subscribed by the attorney, it must be accompanied by the affidavit of the attorney, to the effect that he is duly authorized to make the offer in

[2] McClatchey v. Finley, 62 Iowa 200, s c 17 N W Rep 169

[1] Kaw v. Valley Fair Ass'n v. Miller, 42 Kan 20, Chippenger v. Ingram, 17 Kan 586 See Boyd v. Cronan 71 Me 286, where the Maine statute is held applicable to an action of trespass

[2] Chicago Ry Co v. Townsdin, 45 Kan 771, Harrison v. Iowa Ry 36 Iowa 323 See Cherokee v. Sioux City 52 Iowa 279, where a municipal corporation in proceedings to assess damages after a street had been opened sought to affect the proceedings by making an offer Held that the statute (Sec 3819) was not applicable

[3] Singleton v. Home Ins Co, 121 N Y 644, Bridenbecker v. Mason, 16 How Pr 203

[4] Pomeroy v. Hulin, 7 How 161. See La Forge v. Chilson, 3 Sandf 752

[5] Bathgate v. Hoskin, 63 N Y 26 See People's Bank v. Collins, 27 Conn 142

[6] Smith v. Morgan, 73 Wis 375

[7] In Nebraska the statute is not applicable to proceedings in ad quod damnum Johnson v. Sutliff 17 Neb 123, s c 21 N W Rep 9 In Maine to a writ of entry Carson v. Walton 51 Me 382 In Wisconsin to actions for damages for cutting timber where not done by mistake Smith v. Morgan 73 Wis 375 In California to actions for a recovery of delinquent taxes Sacramento v. Central Pac R 61 Cal 250 See Cherokee v. Sioux City, ante

behalf of the party. Such an offer, which is not accompanied by the affidavit of the attorney, is a nullity. Plaintiff does not waive any right by retaining it without objection.[1] Even where the plaintiff served notice declining to accept an offer, which was not accompanied by the affidavit showing the attorney's authority to make it, the plaintiff was held not to be estopped to insist that the offer was a nullity. The court said "There is no such thing as creating an offer by *waiver*; either there was an *effective offer* or there was not." That if the defendant desired the benefit of the statute he was bound to do just what the statute pointed out, and having failed, the case proceeded without a statutory offer.[2] Where a statute provides that after an action is brought, the defendant may offer in court to confess judgment for a part of the plaintiff's claim, such offer may be made orally, the statute not otherwise providing.[3] In case of a dispute, the amount of such offer may be proven by oral testimony.[4] Where the offer may be made in open court it is not sufficient to place a written offer on file.[5] In a case considered in the Federal Court, it was held that an offer to submit to a certain judgment should be made in open court, and the court asked to act thereon after due notice to the other party.[6] The statute, in nearly every state, provides that an offer of judgment shall be in writing, and signed by the defendant or his attorney, and served upon the plaintiff,[7] or his attorney.[8] If not properly served upon all the persons named in the statute, the offer is of no effect.[9] Service by copy is sufficient.[10] It should be made by a separate writing,[11] and entitled in the cause,

[1] McFarren v St John 14 Hun 387

[2] Riggs v Waydell, 17 Hun 515  See Citizens Bank v Shaw 46 Hun 589

[3] Barlow v Buckingham, 68 Iowa 169 s c 26 N W Rep 58 See Armstrong v Spears 18 Oh St 373

[4] Barlow v Buckingham, *ante*

[5] Fisk v France 12 Oh St 624

[6] New Providence v Halsey, 117 U S 336

[7] Enos v St Louis Ry 41 Mo App 269. Liemance v McComas, 59 Mo App 118

[8] Holland v Pugh 16 Ind 21

[9] Smith v Hinds 30 How Pr 187. Purvis v Gray 39 How Pr 1

[10] Smith v Kerr 49 Hun 29 See Marks v Epstein 13 Civ Proc Rep 203, and see also Norman v Smith 12 Abb N C 337 aff'm'd. 84 N Y 672 where it is held that if a service by copy is not sufficient retaining the copy is a waiver

[11] Armstrong v Spears 18 Oh St 373

but it need not be sworn to.[12] In Nebraska an offer of judgment which is not signed is insufficient.[13] So, filing an offer without serving it on the plaintiff or his attorney is insufficient when not made in open court.[14] In Indiana, filing an offer of judgment in open court and orally calling the attention of the counsel thereto, was held a sufficient notice.[15] In Wisconsin and Kansas, where the statutes require the offer to be in writing, it has been held that an entry in writing by a justice, in his docket, on an oral offer, was a compliance with the statute,[16] though not signed by the defendant.[17] A tender in open court is not equivalent to an offer of judgment.[18] An offer to pay $50 if plaintiff would dismiss the action and not prosecute it further, was held to be neither an offer to allow judgment to be entered, nor a tender.[19] An offer must not be made conditional upon the plaintiff doing anything,[20] or contingent upon the happening of any event.[21] It has been held, however, that an offer need not be unconditional, if the condition attached is no more than the legal effect of acceptance, as, in such case, its acceptance and entry of judgment thereon is a full and complete settlement of the action.[22] The object of the law, providing for such an offer, is to put an end to the litigation, by the acceptance by the plaintiff of a judgment for the amount offered by the defendant. It is always made on condition that its acceptance will be a final settlement of the action.

§ 525. Difference between an offer of judgment in the answer and statutory offer.—An offer of judgment for a certain amount may be made in the answer, and a defence interposed to the residue of the demand. When made in this way it is nothing more or less than an admission of a part of plain-

---

[12] Pfister v Stumne 7 N. Y Misc 525

[13] Ossenlop v Akeson, 15 Neb. 622

[14] Rose v Peck 18 Neb 529

[15] Keller v Allen 87 Ind 252

[16] Williams v Ready. 72 Wis 108, s c 39 N W Rep 779

[17] Masterson v Homberg, 29 Kan 106

[18] M'Dowell v Glass, 4 Watts 389

[19] Quinton v Van Tuyl. 30 Iowa, 554

[20] Pinckney v Childs 7 Bosw 660, Quinton v Van Tuyl, 30 Iowa, 554

[21] Pinckney v Childs, 7 Bosw. 660

[22] De Long v Wilson. 80 Iowa, 216, s c 45 N W Rep 764

tiff's claim, and cannot be withdrawn without an amendment of the pleadings. And, after an amendment, the offer may still be offered in evidence by the plaintiff, as an admission made by the defendant. An admission of a part of the plaintiff's claim in this way, in no way affects the plaintiff's right to recover his entire costs.[1] An admission or offer of judgment in an answer must not be confounded with the statutory offer. The latter is an offer which may be made regardless of the answer or the allegations contained therein. However, where the same matters embraced in an offer are admitted in the answer, the offer amounts to nothing and plaintiff is entitled to costs.[2]

§ 526. **When an offer may be made.**—An offer of judgment being purely a statutory right, the statute of the state where the action is pending must be consulted to determine the time when the offer may be made. In New York it may be made at any time before trial.[1] And, after an appeal from a judgment of a justice's court, the defeated party may offer to allow a judgment for a certain sum.[2] So, the prevailing party may offer to reduce the judgment to a certain amount,[3] or offer to allow judgment for a certain amount in favor of the appellant. The offer to reduce the judgment must be made in the appellate court and not in the justice's court.[4] An offer to remit a part, may be made after verdict but not after entry of judgment,[5] the justice not having authority to modify the judgment by reversing or entering a new one.[6] In Minnesota an offer may be made at any time before trial or judgment.[7] In general it can only be made after an action is brought.[8] A second offer may be made if time enough re

[1] Gans v Woodfork, 2 Mont. 458, Armstrong v. Spears, 18 Oh. St 373, Davenport v Chicago Ry, 38 Iowa, 633

[2] Bradbury v. Winterbottom, 13 Hun 536

[1] New York Code Civ Pro Sec 738, Warner v Babcock, 9 N. Y App 398

[2] McKuskie v Hendrickson, 128 N Y 555

[3] Pike v Johnson, 47 N Y. 1

[4] Birdsall v Keyes, 66 Hun 233

[5] Allen v Swan, 32 Hun 363

[6] Loomis v Higbie, 29 How. Pr 232

[7] 1894 G St Minn Sec, 5405

[8] Crane v Hirshfelder, 17 Cal 582; Horner v Pilkington, 11 Ind 110 See Kitts v Seeber, 10 How Pr 270 Adolph v. De Ceu, 45 Hun 130

mains in which to do so pursuant to the statute.[0] Making an offer of judgment before answering will not extend the time to answer. The answer must be served within the prescribed time, and its service does not affect the plaintiff's right to accept the offer.

§ 527. **Amendment of offer.**—If the plaintiff amends his complaint after an offer of judgment has been made, the court may allow an amendment of the offer to meet the amendment in the complaint;[1] and, unless the offer be amended it is of no effect.[2] But where the amendment is one of form merely, not changing the issues, the defendant is entitled to the benefit of his offer.[3] Before acceptance, on a proper showing, as in case of a mistake, the court may allow an amendment, or allow the offer to be withdrawn.[4] In New York after a judgment has been awarded the plaintiff for an amount less than the offer, the court will not allow the offer to be amended, by annexing thereto the affidavit of the attorney showing his authority to make the offer, for such an amendment would make it, for the first time, a good offer, and deprive the plaintiff of his statutory right to accept within the ten days.[5] The failure to attach this affidavit is a defect in substance.[6] Such an amendment may be allowed before trial, if the full statutory time in which to accept would elapse before the case would be reached for trial in its regular order on the calendar.[7]

§ 528. **When available on appeal—Renewal.**—An offer of judgment when not withdrawn is a part of the record, and is

[0] Hibbard v Randolph, 72 Hun. 626. In Kansas, it has been held that the defendant by making a second offer is not without any offer and if the first offer be not withdrawn the plaintiff must recover at least more than the first or lesser offer. Chicago Ry. Co v Townsdin, 45 Kan 770

[1] Brooks v Mortimer, 42 N Y Supp 229, s c 10 App Div 581

[2] See Woeltle v Schmenger, 12 Civ Proc Rep 312

[1] Kilts v Seeber, 10 How Pr 270, Woeltle v. Schmenger, 12 Civ Pro Rep 24

[4] See McVicar v Keating, 19 App Div 581, s c 46 N Y. Supp 298

[5] Riggs v Wardell 17 Hun. 515.

[6] Werbolowsky v. Greenwich 14 Abb N C 96

[7] See Hibbard v Randolph, 72 Hun 626, and Chicago Ry Co v Townsdin, 45 Kan 771 as to making a second offer. See Sec 526

available in the appellate court,[1] without a renewal of the
offer.[2] In New York, under the statute, on an appeal from a
judgment of a justice's court, an original offer may be made
in the appellate court, and unless made in that court the
offer has no effect upon the question of costs.[3] But it appears
that a different rule was applied, where a case was sent up
because the title to real estate was involved.[4] A transcript
of the record of a case tried before a justice of the peace
imports verity, and a transcript which shows an offer by the
defendant, made in writing, to confess judgment in favor of
plaintiff for a certain amount, cannot be supported nor con
tradicted by affidavits.[5]

§ 529. By whom made.—An offer of judgment may be made
by the defendant or his attorney, but the latter must be au
thorized to make the offer. The general rule is that when
a defendant appears by attorney, the offer should be subscribed by the attorney. If made by the party after such
appearance, the plaintiff should apply to the court for leave
to enter judgment upon it.[1] In New York under the code,
the offer must be accompanied by the affidavit of the attorney, to the effect that he is duly authorized to make the
offer in behalf of the defendant. One joint debtor or partner
cannot make an offer of judgment in behalf of the other.[2] It

[1] Underhill v Shea, 21 Neb 154,
s. c. 31 N W Rep 510, Kliftel v
Bullock, 8 Neb 336, s c 1 N W
250, Kellogg v Pierce, 60 Wis.
342; Erd v Chicago Ry, 41 Wis
65, Lewis v Morrison 10 Ind
411, Cohoon v Kincon, 46 Oh St
570.

[2] Underhill v Shea, 21 Neb.
154

[3] Mock v Salle, 52 Hun 198.
This was an appeal from the
municipal court of Rochester, to
the county court. It was insisted
by the appellant that the offer of
judgment in the lower court had
the same effect on the question of
costs as if made after an appeal.
See Birdsall v Keyes, 66 Hun
233, where it is held that as far

as the costs are concerned it becomes an original action.

[4] Niagara v Buchanan, 4 Lans.
523

[5] Sloss v Bailey, 74 N W Rep
(Iowa) 17 See Underhill v Shea,
21 Neb 151, where it is held that
there was no presumption that the
offer was not in writing.

[1] Webb v Dill, 18 Abb. N S
264

[2] Garrison v. Garrison, 67 How.
Pr 271, Bridenbecker v. Mason,
16 How 203, Binney v Le Gal 1
Abb. Pr 283; Eversen v Gehr-
man, 1 Abb. Pr 167. In Bridenbecker v Mason, it appears that
in absence of fraud, one partner
may employ an attorney for all,
who may do what the individual
partner could not do.

must be made by all the defendants who have been served, and whose time to answer has not expired, or by their common attorney, and must be in such form that will enable the plaintiff, if he accepts, to enter judgment against all the defendants.[1] If the attorney was not authorized to appear for all the defendants, the court will allow the defendant not represented by the attorney to plead, if he has a defence, allowing the judgment to stand as security[1]. In New York, if there are two or more defendants, and the action can be severed, an offer may be made by one or more of those against whom a separate judgment may be taken.[5] It has been held that where only one of several joint debtors has been served, he may make an offer which will bind the joint property and the separate property of the one served.[6]

**§ 530. Amount offered—Relief offered—Costs—Counterclaim —Offer conditional upon recovery by plaintiff.**—A statutory offer of a judgment must be for a specific sum independent of costs, and the costs accrued at the date of the offer;[1] unless the statute provides that the offer shall carry costs, in which case the costs need not be mentioned.[2] An offer of a judgment for a certain sum without mentioning any costs, if not accepted, will not avail the defendant as a statutory offer.[3] A recovery by plaintiff, in absence of an offer, entitles him to recover all his costs, and the defendant cannot deprive the plaintiff of the costs accrued to a certain date, by conceding that he is entitled to recover a sum less than his claim, and offering a judgment for that amount. An offer of judgment for $48 and interest and costs, is a tender of a judgment for $48 and costs only, where the record does not disclose any fact indicating the time from which interest is to be com-

[3] Williamson v. Lock's Creek Canal Co, 84 N C 629; Griffith v De Forest, 16 Abb Pr. 292

[4] Blodget v. Conklin, 9 How 412, Yates v Horanson, 7 Rob 12

[5] Garrison v. Garrison, 67 How Pr 271 See New York Ry v Clark, 54 Oh St 509

[6] Bridenbecker v Mason, 16 How 203; Emery v Emery, 9 How 130

[1] Adams v Phifer, 25 Oh St. 301, DeLong v Wilson, 80 Iowa, 216.

[2] See Hammond v. Northern Pac. Ry., 23 Or 157

[3] Brown v Bosworth, 58 Wis. 379, s c 17 N W Rep 241, Ranney v. Russell, 3 Duer 680

puted.[4] The sum offered need not be specifically set out in the offer. Reference may be made to the amount set forth in any particular cause of action, or the amount claimed in the complaint. But it must be so definite that the clerk can, by mere computation, ascertain the amount of the judgment.[5] The offer may be to allow judgment for the whole of plaintiff's claim,[6] or for a part, or for the whole amount claimed in any particular cause set forth and an answer interposed to the other claim.[7] In the latter case the question of subsequent costs depends upon the result of the action in regard to the litigated claim.[8] In North Carolina, it is held that an offer in writing to allow judgment to be taken for the amount therein stated and costs, must be a proposition to pay a specific sum, in discharge of plaintiff's claim, and not a sum in excess of a counterclaim.[9] The statute contemplates solely an offer of judgment for the plaintiff's claim, and in full satisfaction of the full claim, and the defendant cannot throw the costs on the plaintiff by bringing in a counterclaim to be litigated. If it were otherwise the plaintiff would have to accept the defendant's counterclaim at the amount stated or refuse the difference at his peril, besides being deprived of the benefit of an offer to allow the defendant's claim at a certain amount. Again, in such case, a plaintiff, if he recovers anything over and above the counterclaim, practically recovers of the defendant the amount of the counterclaim, as his claim goes to satisfy it, which ought not to throw the costs upon the plaintiff.[10] The statutes of the various states, however, must be examined to ascertain the right of a defendant to include a counterclaim in his offer of judgment.[11] In

[4] Slattington Bangor State Syndicate v Sener, 12 Mont C L Rep 162, s. p. Smith v. Bowes, 11 Daly, 320.

[5] Burnett v Westfall, 15 How 420, 425; Marble v Lewis, 36 How. 337.

[6] Ross v Bridge, 24 How 163, Boyd v Ward, 38 Mo. App. 210.

[7] Bradbury v. Winterbottom, 13 Hun 536.

[8] Bradbury v. Winterbottom, 13 Hun. 536; Budd v Jackson 26 How Pr 398.

[9] Rand v. Harris, 83 N. Car 486

[10] Tompkins v Ives, 36 N Y 75, citing Fieldings v. Mills, 2 Bosw. 489, Ruggles v. Fogg, 7 How 324, Budd v Jackson, 26 How. 401, Schneider v. Jacobie, 1 Duer, 694

[11] In New York, by statute, where a defendant sets up a counterclaim greater than the plaintiff's claim, or which is sufficient to reduce the plaintiff's recovery below fifty dollars, the

Maine, a plaintiff who had rejected an offer of the defendant to be defaulted for the difference between a set off and plaintiff's claim, when the amount due, by reason of being reduced by the set off was found to be less than the amount offered, was required to pay the defendant's full costs accruing since the date of the offer.[12] But this was because the set off, by reason of the status of the case at the time of the offer, was included in the offer. It should be stated distinctly what judgment the plaintiff may have, so that there may be no doubt or misunderstanding about it.[13] If made in an equitable action, the relief offered should be clearly indicated, and, either in equity or at law, where the title to property is involved, the offer should include everything necessary to vest the title to the property in the plaintiff. Thus in replevin, where the plaintiff has a right to have the title to the property determined by the judgment, an offer of judgment for the return of the property, which does not offer to allow judgment determining the title, is of no avail.[14] The offer must relate to the cause of action set out.[15] It must be something the plaintiff is entitled to have under the pleadings. Thus, in conversion, an offer of the property is insufficient.[16] This would be so were it a cash offer, when the court would allow a return of the property and assess nominal damages. In an action to recover interest, an offer of judgment for the principal not due, is insufficient.[17] The defendant in his offer need not state a definite sum as costs. "Accrued Costs,"[18] or "all costs to date,"[19] or "costs accrued to

plaintiff may serve upon the defendant a written offer to allow judgment to be taken against him, for a specific sum with costs, or against the defendant for a specific sum, and against the plaintiff for costs. The effect of an acceptance or rejection of an offer under this statute and the rules of practice, are the same as under a statute allowing defendant to make an offer of judgment. See 385 Code of Civil Pro.

[12] Higgins v Raines, 72 Me 110

[13] Post v New York Cent R R

Co, 12 How 552, Upton v Foster, 118 Mass 592, Bettis v Goodwill 32 How 187

[14] Oleson v Newell, 12 Minn 186

[15] Phillipps v Sheaver, 56 Iowa, 261

[16] Stephens v Koonee, 103 N Car 266

[17] Howard v Fales, 29 How, Pr 4

[18] Petrosky v Flanagan, 38 Minn 26, s c 35 N W Rep 665

[19] Keller v Allen, 87 Ind 252.

the present time," [20] is sufficient. An offer of a judgment for a specific sum and costs, carries with it the costs necessary in entering the judgment,[21] and the statutory attorney fee to which the plaintiff would have been entitled, had he, in absence of an offer, gone on and recovered only the amount of the offer. Under those statutes,[22] which provide that, in action for the recovery of money only, where a justice of the peace has jurisdiction, the plaintiff cannot recover any costs and disbursements, and must pay the defendant's costs and disbursements, if he brings the action in a court of record and recover no more than a specified sum, it is the amount claimed in the complaint, and not the amount of the recovery, which determines the question of jurisdiction. Hence, where the amount claimed in the complaint is not within the juris diction of the justice, the defendant in offering a judgment for a sum within the jurisdiction of the justice must include the costs in his offer. If an action commenced in a court of record is one within the jurisdiction of a justice of the peace, and the amount of the offer is within the limit, which, if recovered by the plaintiff in absence of an offer, would pre vent him from recovering his costs and disbursements, or the amount is within the limit, which, if recovered, would subject him to a liability for the costs of the defendant, the offer need not include the plaintiff's costs, or it may be for a sum less the defendant's costs, as the case may be. But where the amount received governs costs and not the amount claimed in the complaint, an offer of a judgment for a sum less than that for the recovery of which costs are allowed. neither party is entitled to costs.[23] The term "cost" as used in these statutes includes disbursements.[24] The statutes in no way interfere with the discretion of the court in awarding costs to either party on motions and interlocutory proceedings [25] In some states an offer may be made to allow the

[20] Rose v Grimstead, 55 Ind 202

[21] Petrosky v Flanigan, 38 Minn 26 Holland v Pugh 16 Ind 21 Keller v Allen, 87 Ind 252

[22] See Gen St Minn Sec 5500

[23] Moffett v Deom s Civ Pro Rep 85 See Lee v Stearn 22 Mo 575

[24] Woolsey v O'Brien, 23 Minn 71 See Commissioners v Spofford 19 How Pr 28 s c 3 Hun 52

[25] See Commissioners v Spofford, 3 Hun 52 s c 5 N Y Sup Ct 353 and 19 How Pr 48

damages to be assessed at a certain sum in case the defendant fails in his defence. In such cases, if the offer is accepted, and plaintiff proves a right to recover any thing, the damages must be assessed at the amount offered.[20] If the offer is rejected, the plaintiff must not only establish his cause of action, but the amount of his damages, which, if short of the amount offered, subjects him to the expense of the defendant incurred in preparing for trial of the question of damages. Such an offer may be made whether the defence goes to the whole action, or some part or item.[27]

§ 531. **Effect of rejecting an offer.**—The effect of an offer of judgment, properly made, if rejected, and the plaintiff fails to obtain a more favorable judgment, under the New York Code, is to deprive the plaintiff of all costs subsequent to the offer, and render him liable for the costs of the defendant from that time.[1] The Nebraska and other statutes are to the same effect.[2] In most states the plaintiff is entitled to the costs incurred prior to the offer, notwithstanding the recovery may be less favorable than the offer.[3] In Minnesota, a rejection of an offer of judgment and a failure to obtain more favorable judgment, deprive the plaintiff of his right to recover any costs, and subject him to a liability for all defendant's costs and disbursements.[4] If the offer is insufficient it has no effect upon the costs[5] It has been held that "defendant's costs" are such as are legally allowable, either by stat-

---

[20] See N Y Code, Sec 736. Civ Code Ky. Sec 635.

[27] Maxwell v Dudley, 13 Bush 403

[1] Schulte v Lestershire, 88 Hun 226, Lumbard v. Syracuse Ry, 62 N Y 290, London v. Van Etten, 57 Hun 22, Sturgis v. Spofford, 58 N Y 103

[2] Wachsmuth v Orient Ins Co, 49 Neb 590, s c 68 N W Rep 935

[3] Magin v Densemore, 47 How. 11, s c 15 Abb. Pr N S 331, Douthill v Finch, 84 Cal 214; Russ v. Brown, 113 N Car 227, DeLong v Wilson, 80 Iowa, 216,

Rand v Wiley, 70 Iowa, 110; Manning v Irish, 47 Iowa, 650; Higgins v Rines, 72 Me 440; Gilman v Pearson 47 Me 352, Petsinger v Bever, 44 Ark 562; Wichita Ry v Beebe, 38 Kan 427, Kaw Valley v. Miller, 42 Kan 20, Rose v. Grinstead, 53 Ind 202, Bull v Harragan, 17 B Mon 349; Chicago Ry v Groh, 85 Wis 641

[4] 1894 Gen. St Minn Sec 5405, Woolsey v O'Brien, 23 Minn 71. See Upton v Foster, 148 Mass 592, s c 20 N E. 198

[5] McClatchey v Finley, 62 Iowa, 200.

ute or in the discretion of the Court.[6]  If the defendant does
not accept the offer by serving a written notice of such acceptance, the offer is deemed to be withdrawn, and cannot be
given in evidence on the trial,[7] nor alluded to in any way.[8]  In
replevin, or an action for trespass to personalty, an offer of
a judgment for damages, or to return the property, if refused,
cannot be envoked by plaintiff as an estoppel on the part of
the defendant, to deny plaintiff's title.[9]  An unaccepted offer
is no waiver of objection to the process.[10]  When an offer of
judgment is rejected, as far as the plaintiff is concerned, it is
the same in legal effect as if it had never been made, and
thereafter it is in the case only for the purpose of determining whether the judgment obtained by plaintiff is more favorable than the offer, and its bearing then is merely upon
the question of costs  An offer for judgment in reality admits nothing.[11]  It is an offer to allow a judgment for a certain amount regardless of what is due.  It is nothing more
than an offer to buy peace in its effect upon the right of plaintiff to recover anything.

§ 532.  What is a more favorable judgment—Reduction on
appeal.—If the plaintiff recovers all that the defendant offers,
and something else besides, his judgment is more favorable
than the offer.  In determining whether the judgment obtained is more favorable than that offered, interest cannot
be added by defendant to the amount offered.[1]  But it is said
that this rule is only applicable to actions where the damages
are unliquidated.[2]  If the verdict is made up of principal and

[6] Commissioners v Spofford, 3
Hun 52, s. c. 5 N. Y. Sup Ct. 353.
See Coats v Goddard, 34 N Y
Sup Ct 118.

[7] Murray v Cunningham, 10
Neb 167, s c. 4 N W Rep. 953;
Finney v Veeder, 1 Abb Pr N
S 366.

[8] See Riech v Bolch, 68 Iowa,
526, where by a divided court, it
was held that when the plaintiff's
attorney referred to the offer, but
the defendant did not ask to have
the jury discharged, but proceeded to trial, he waived the objection.

[9] Auley v Ostermann, 65 Wis
118, s c 25 N. W. Rep. 657.

[10] Tibbetts v. Shaw, 19 Me 204

[11] Wentworth v. Lord, 39 Me.
71

[1] Johnston v. Catlin, 57 N. Y.
652; Wordin v. Bemis, 33 Conn
216  See Erd v. Chicago Ry, 41
Wis. 65

[2] Bathgate v. Hoskin, 63 N. Y.
261; Hirschspiing v Boe, 20 Abb
N Cas 402, Kellogg v Pierce, 60
Wis 342; Schultz v Lestershire,
88 Hun. 226

interest, interest which has accrued since the offer must be rejected in determining whether the judgment is more favorable than the offer.[3]  Costs of the plaintiff or of an intervenor cannot be added to the amount recovered, for the purpose of determining whether the judgment obtained was more favorable than the one offered[4]  In New York, where an offer is made after an answer containing a counterclaim is interposed, such counterclaim is embraced in the offer and its extinguishment cannot be considered as increasing the amount of plaintiff's recovery so as to make the amount recovered more favorable than the offer.[5]  But where an answer is served after an offer, and a counterclaim is pleaded, proved and allowed, its extinguishment by the verdict is beneficial to the plaintiff, and the amount of such counterclaim is properly added to the amount recovered by the plaintiff, for the purpose of determining whether the judgment is more favorable to the plaintiff.[6]  Where after an offer is rejected, a counterclaim is pleaded and the plaintiff under the statute compells satisfaction of his claim as admitted by the answer, it was held that the prevailing party, upon the issues as to the counterclaim, was entitled to costs[7]  But where the defendant's offer is for a money judgment, and he afterwards asks in his answer for some equitable relief, which is denied him, in whole or in part, and the plaintiff recovers a money judgment for less than the amount of the offer, it is difficult to determine whether the recovery is more favorable than the offer.  In such cases, it would seem that the just rule would be to disregard the offer, unless it had been renewed after the

[3] Budd v Jackman, 26 How 398, Pike v Johnson, 47 N Y., 1; Smith v. Bower, 11 Daily, 320, Schneider v Jacobi, 1 Duer 694, Ruggles v Fogg, 7 Hun 324; Kellogg v Pierce, 60 Wis 342

[4] Singleton v Home Ins. Co, 121 N Y 644  See Atchison Ry v Ireland, 39 Kan 405, where an attorney fee was added, it appearing that some fees were earned before the offer

[5] Bathgate v. Hoskin, 63 N Y 261, Schneider v Jacobi, 1 Duer 694

[6] Tompkins v Ives, 36 N Y 75, s c 3 Abb N. S 269, Ruggles v. Fogg, 7 How 327, Fielding v. Mills, 2 Bosw 489, Tipton v. Tipton, 19 Ohio, St 364: Kautz v. Vandenberg, 77 Hun 591, Adolph v DeCeu. 45 Hun, 130, Turner v Housinger, 31 How. Pr 66  See Dowd v Smith, 8 Misc Rep. 619, which appears to hold to the contrary

[7] Scoville v Kent, 8 Abb Pr N S 17

answer was served. A judgment for the exact amount of the offer is not more favorable.[8] A more favorable judgment does not necessarily mean more favorable in point of amount. Where one of two persons sued jointly offers judgment against himself, and plaintiff recovers judgment against both, it is more favorable than the one offered.[9] So, if plaintiff recovers a judgment giving him all the defendant offered, and obtains any equitable relief, or anything not mentioned in the defendant's offer, the judgment is more favorable, and plaintiff will be entitled to all his costs. So, when the plaintiff recovers a less sum than that offered, but obtains an adjudication of a sum not due,[10] or, a less sum and security for a deficiency judgment,[11] the recovery is more favorable than the offer. Where a judgment of the trial court, which entitles a plaintiff to costs by reason of being more favorable than the offer, is, on an appeal, reduced so that it is less favorable than the offer, the defendant is entitled to the benefit of his offer and entitled to costs subsequent to the offer.[12] And, this was held to be the rule though the offer was not returned with the appeal papers, the trial court, on coming down of the remittitur, having power to award cost on the correction of the judgment.[13] So, where the appeal was from the judgment of a justice of the peace, and the amount recovered was on the appeal reduced below the amount of the offer in the justice's court, it was held that the defendant was entitled to his costs accruing subsequent to the offer.[14] In New York, where

[8] Schultz v. Lestershire, 88 Hun 226, Hammond v Northern Pac Ry, 23 Or 157, Walls v Lumbertson, 39 Iowa, 272

[9] Bannerman v Quackenbush 13 Daly (N Y) 160, Griffiths v De Forrest, 25 How 396, s c 16 Abb 921 See New York Ry v. Clark, 54 Ohio, St. 599 where a judgment against two defendants, where one only made an offer, does not appear to have been considered more favorable At least the point was not raised

[10] Bettis v Goodwill, 32 How Pr. 137

[11] Kennedy v McKone, 10 N Y App Div 88.

[12] Bathgate v Hoskin, 63 N Y 261; Sturgis v. Spofferd, 58 N Y 103, Cockerell v. Moll, 18 Kan 154, Williford v Gadson, 27 S Car. 87; Watts v Lumbertson, 39 Iowa, 272

[13] Lumbard v Syracuse, 62 N Y 290

[14] Watts v Lumbertson, 39 Iowa 272 See Williford v Gadsen, 27 S Car 87

[15] Wallace v Patterson, 29 How Pr 170

an appeal is for a reversal merely,[15] or, the ground of
the appeal is that the judgment should have been against
the plaintiff with costs,[16] an offer cannot be made in compliance with the notice of appeal, and if the judgment is
affirmed, or revised, or modified, as the case may be, the successful party is entitled to costs. In such cases the plaintiff
is entitled to costs though he recovers less than the amount
of the judgment in the lower court.[17] Provided, however,
that the sum is large enough to carry costs in the appellate
court. But where the ground of appeal is, that the judgment
should have been for a less sum, and no offer to reduce the
judgment is made by the plaintiff, a reduction of the judg
ment in any sum, though not reduced as low as the sum
stated in the notice of appeal, will entitle the defendant to
costs, he being the successful party.[18] The provision of the
statute is to the effect that if neither party make an offer,
the party in whose favor the judgment in the appellate court
is given, shall be entitled to his costs upon the appeal.[19] Under this statute, if the recovery in the lower court is for a
sum less than that for which costs are allowed in the
appellate court, and the plaintiff made no offer to take judgment for a certain amount, he is not entitled to costs on
the appeal, if the sum recovered is below the statutory
amount for the recovery of which costs are allowed in that
court, even though he recovers a greater sum than he did
in the lower court  A plaintiff, in such case, to be entitled to
costs, must make an offer.[20] When a recovery is more favorable than an offer, the offer has no effect upon the costs.[21]
It is the judgment which is entered, and not the verdict,
which determines the right to costs [22] If the judgment which
the plaintiff recovers is not more favorable than the one
offered, the defendant's costs, where he is entitled to them,

[16] Loomis v. Higbie, 29 How.
Pr 232

[17] Loomis v Higbie, 29 How
Pr. 232, overruling Barnard v
Pierce, 28 How. Pr. 232

[18] Fox v. Nellis, 25 How. Pr.
114; Younghouse v. Fingar. 47 N.
Y 99

[19] N Y Code Civ Pr. Sec. 307

[20] McKushie v Hendrickson,
128 N. Y 555, s. c. 28 N E. Rep
650

[21] Birdsall v Keyes, 66 Hun
233; Wallace v. Patton, 29 How
Pr 170, Baldwin v Brown, 37
How Pr 385

[22] Wallace v American Linen
Thread Co, 16 Hun, 404. See Budd
v. Jackson, 26 How Pr. 398

should be deducted from the amount recovered by plaintiff, and one judgment entered for the residue.[23]

**§ 533. Giving a defendant preference.**—A debtor, against whom several actions have been commenced, may offer judgment in any one of them, and thus enable the plaintiff therein to obtain a preference by securing the first judgment.[1] The right to give a preference in this way is the same as in the case of a confession of judgment.[2] In either case the statutory requirements must be strictly complied with

**§ 534. Acceptance—Manner—Time for consideration—Amounts to a contract—Withdrawal—Costs.**—Where an offer is made, the plaintiff, according to most statutes, has ten days in which to accept or reject the offer, and the defendant cannot, as a matter of right, withdraw the offer within the time given the plaintiff to consider and act upon it.[1] The plaintiff, if he desires to take advantage of the offer, must serve a written notice of acceptance.[2] But where an offer of judgment may be made orally in open court, it would seem that an oral acceptance might be made in the same way. The offer and acceptance, entered in the minutes of the court, is a sufficient record upon which to enter judgment. Plaintiff has ten full days (or the statutory time whatever it is), excluding the day of service, in which to reject the offer or give notice of his acceptance.[3] By proceeding to trial before the time to accept has expired, without taking action upon the offer, the plaintiff in effect elects not to accept the offer.[4] If the offer

---

[23] Stone v Waitt. 31 Me 409; Dingiee v. Shears 9 Hun. 210, Hibbard v. Randolph, 72 Hun, 626

[1] Breads v. Wheeler 76 N Y 213, Hill v Northrup, 9 How. Pr 525

[2] Trier v. Herman, 115 N Y 163

[1] McVicker v Keating, 46 N Y Sup 298

[2] See White v Bogart, 73 N Y 256 where it was held that an entry of judgment without filing a formal acceptance was an irregularity merely. And see also, Beecher v. Kendall, 14 Hun, 327, where a judgment was entered in a justice's court on an oral acceptance

[3] Mansfield v Fleck, 23 Minn. 61, Pomeroy v. Hulin, 7 How Pr 161 If the offer is served by mail plaintiff has double the time in which to accept Van Allen v. Glass, 60 Hun 546

[4] Gottloff v. Wallace, 22 N. Y. Sup. 715; Mansfield v. Fleck, 23 Minn 61

is made by the defendant within the ten days before the case
is reached in its regular order on the calendar, the plaintiff
may treat it as a nullity, and proceed with the action as if
no offer had been made.[5] If the case is reached on the calendar within the ten days (or the statutory time allowed plaintiff to accept), the defendant cannot proceed and obtain judgment by default.[6] As to the defendant, the offer amounts
to a stay of proceedings, and he cannot force the plaintiff
to trial within the time. An offer and an acceptance, under
these statutes, constitute a contract between the parties, and
cannot be changed without their consent.[7] An acceptance of
an offer is not equivalent to obtaining a judgment.[8] On an
acceptance of an offer the right to enter judgment accrues.[9]
Where an offer may be made in a justice court, on return of
process and before answer, an offer may be made immediately
after the service and the actual return, though before the
regular return day, and if at once accepted, the judgment
entered thereupon is valid.[10] An acceptance and entry of
judgment upon a general offer, concludes the plaintiff from
bringing a new action for any part of the claim embraced in
the complaint, and which might have been litigated.[11] If the
plaintiff, after accepting an offer, was permitted to show that
the amount offered was due on one of several causes of action
embraced in the original action, or that the whole claim
originally was recoverable, it would destroy the only consideration upon which the defendant acted in making the offer.
Such offers are made with the intention that its acceptance
will extinguish the entire claim,[12] and end the litigations It
has been held that where an offer is rejected, and the plaintiff recovers a verdict for the amount which the defendant
pays into court, the plaintiff may accept the amount ad

[5] Mansfield v Fleck 23 Minn
61, Pomeroy v Huhn, 7 How 161,
Herman v Lyons, 2 Abb N. S
90, Walker v Johnson, 8 How
Pr 240

[6] Walker v. Johnson, 8 How.
240

[7] Stillwell v Stillwell, 30 N Y
Supp 961, 81 Hun, 392

[8] Lippman v Petersberger, 18
How 270

[9] Petrosky v Flanagan, 38
Minn 26, s c 35 N. W Rep 665

[10] Fowler v Haynes, 91 N. Y.
346

[11] Manning v Irish, 17 Iowa,
650; Robertson v Railway Co, 57
Iowa, 376

[12] Davis v Mayor, 93 N Y 250,
Stillwell v Stillwell, 30 N. Y.
Sup Ct 961 See Shepherd v.
Moodhe, 150 N. Y. 183, s c 44 N.
E 963

mitted to be due, without waiving his right to appeal from that portion of the judgment which is adverse to him.[13] Where an offer is made after the answer is served, its acceptance will extinguish all the claims set forth in the answer. If made before answering, and the defendant intends to set up a counterclaim or any thing which he desires to litigate, he must refer to it in his offer, so that it will be extinguished upon the acceptance of the offer. Or he should renew the offer after the answer is served. The effect of the offer is to be determined by the pleadings as they are at the time of the offer.[14] If no action is taken on an offer of judgment within the time limited, it is deemed to be withdrawn.[15]

The plaintiff is only entitled to the costs accrued before the offer and any costs made by him between the date of the offer and its acceptance must be borne by him[16] Unless the offer is made after an appeal has been taken and before it is perfected, in which case the perfection of the appeal is necessary before entering a judgment upon the offer.[17]

**§ 535. Entering judgment**—The judgment may be entered without the direction of the court.[1] Upon serving the notice of acceptance, the plaintiff may file the offer, together with an affidavit of notice of acceptance, and the clerk must enter judgment according to the offer. However, where the offer of judgment is in equity an application to the court is, ordinarily, required to perfect the judgment.[2]

[13] Union Mnfg Co v Hulsh, 29 N W. Rep (Iowa) 62

[14] Tompkins v. Ives, 36 N Y 75

[15] Auley v Ostermann, 25 N W Rep (Wis) 657, Rose v Peck, 18 Neb 529, Holmes v Hamberg, 47 Iowa 348, Wentworth v Lord, 39 Me 71, Mazanec v. Manhatten, 2 N Y App Div 489

[16] Douglas v Macduimid. 2 How Pr N. S 289, Woodcock v McCormick, 55 Me 532

[17] Hollenback v Knapp, 42 Hun, 207

[1] Hill v Northrup, 9 How 525

[2] Bathgate v. Hoskin 63 N Y 261

# INDEX.

## A.

41

*See Accord*

43

45

Section

CPSIA information can be obtained
at www.ICGtesting.com
Printed in the USA
LVHW060613240920
666980LV00008B/1187

9 781240 194216